ELEVENTH EDITION

HUMAN RELATIONS
INTERPERSONAL JOB-ORIENTED SKILLS

Andrew J. DuBrin

College of Business
Rochester Institute of Technology

Prentice Hall

Boston   Columbus   Indianapolis   New York   San Francisco   Upper Saddle River
Amsterdam   Cape Town   Dubai   London   Madrid   Milan   Munich   Paris   Montreal   Toronto
Delhi   Mexico City   Sao Paulo   Sydney   Hong Kong   Seoul   Singapore   Taipei   Tokyo

To Melanie, once again

Editor in Chief: Vernon Anthony
Acquisitions Editor: Gary Bauer
Editorial Assistant: Tanika Henderson
Development Editor: Linda Cupp
Director of Marketing: David Gessel
Senior Marketing Manager: Leigh Ann Sims
Senior Marketing Assistant: Les Roberts
Project Manager: Holly Shufeldt
Senior Art Director: Diane Ernsberger
Manager, Rights and Permissions: Karen Sanatar
Full-Service Project Management and Composition: Jogender Taneja, Aptara®, Inc.
Printer/Binder: R. R. Donnelley & Sons
Cover Printer: Lehigh-Phoenix Color
Text Font: 10/12 Sabon

Photo Credits: iStockphoto.com, pp. 2, 20, 75, 261; Photodisc/Getty Images, pp. 8, 213; Photolibrary.com, p. 13; Getty Images-Stockbyte, Royalty Free, p. 23, 321; Image Source/Corbis RF p. 34; Granger Wootz/ Getty Images Royalty Free, p. 46; Photos.com, p. 52; Stockbyte/Thinkstock, p. 61, 257; Blend Images/ Getty Images/Jose Luis Pelaez Inc., p. 68; Goodshoot/Fotosearch.Com, LLC/Royalty Free p. 94; PBNJ Productions/Getty Images Royalty Free, p. 105; Yuri Arcurs/Shutterstock pp. 116, 138; Getty Images-Stockbyte, p. 120; John Rowley/Thinkstock, p. 131; © Keith Dannemiller/CORBIS SABA, p. 141; OJO images/Fotosearch.Com, LLC/Royalty Free, p. 146; Image Source-Royalty Free, p. 158; Jacobs Stock Photography/Getty Images, Inc.-PhotoDisc, p. 164; Digital Vision/Thinkstock, p. 165; Pixland/Jupiter Images-Pixland Royalty Free, p. 180, Photodisc/Getty Images, p. 188; Creatas Images/Thinkstock, p. 198; Laflor/ iStockphoto/Vetta Collection, p. 206; Greg Miller/Greg Miller Photography, p. 215; Vetta Collection/ iStockphoto.com, p. 232; © Colin Hawkins/Getty Images, p. 241; Eugene Gebhardt, p. 244; Blend Images/ Getty Images/ JGI, p. 254; Neustockimages/iStockphoto.com, p. 278; Getty Images-Stockbyte, p. 282; Image Source/Corbis RF, p. 299; BananaStock/Thinkstock, pp. 308, 332; AP Wide World Photos, p. 336; Alamy/Stockbroker/MBI, p. 356; Tetra Images/Alamy Images Royalty Free, p. 362; Aidon/Thinkstock, p. 373.

Library of Congress Cataloging-in-Publication Data

DuBrin, Andrew J.
   Human relations : interpersonal job-oriented skills / Andrew J. DuBrin.—11th ed.
      p. cm.
   ISBN-13: 978-0-13-510941-0
   ISBN-10: 0-13-510941-8
   1. Industrial sociology.   2. Personnel management.   3. Organizational behavior.   I. Title.
   HD6955.D82 2012
   658.3—dc22   2010043768

10 9 8 7 6 5 4 3 2

Prentice Hall
is an imprint of

www.pearsonhighered.com

ISBN 10:   0-13-510941-8
ISBN 13: 978-0-13-510941-0

BRIEF CONTENTS

Go to www.mybizskillskit.com for Chapter 17 content.

CONTENTS

Chapter 9   Resolving Conflicts with Others 180

Chapter 10   Becoming an Effective Leader 206

Chapter 12   Helping Others Develop and Grow 254

Chapter 13   Positive Political Skills 278

Chapter 17 Job Search and Career Management Skills

Go to www.pearsonhighered.com/dubrin for Chapter 17 content.

PREFACE

Welcome to the 11th edition of *Human Relations: Interpersonal Job-Oriented Skills.* Success in any position involving interaction with people requires two broad sets of competencies: functional skills and generic skills. *Functional skills* refer to knowledge of one's discipline (or organizational function), technical skills, specialty skills, or simply details of the job. *Generic skills* refer to competencies important in a variety of jobs. Among these generic skills are good work habits and time management, information technology skills, high ethics, and interpersonal skills.

My purpose in writing this book is to help readers enhance their interpersonal skills, including ethical behavior, in the workplace. By enhancing interpersonal skills, a person has a better chance of capitalizing upon his or her other skills. Two primary approaches are used in this text to achieve the lofty goal of improving interpersonal skills. First, basic concepts are introduced to enhance understanding of key topics in interpersonal relations in organizations.

Second, skill-building suggestions, exercises, and cases are presented that are designed to improve interpersonal skills related to the topic. Chapter 6, for example, presents general information about the nature of teamwork, followed by suggestions for improving teamwork. The chapter also includes several exercises or experiential activities and two case problems—all designed to improve teamwork skills.

Third, examples and box inserts provide insight into how a particular skill is applied on the job. For example, in Chapter 8 I describe how call center operators learn another culture, so they can relate effectively to their customers.

AUDIENCE FOR THE BOOK

The primary audience for this book is people taking courses that emphasize the development of interpersonal skills. Such courses typically include the term *human relations.* Because interpersonal relations contribute so heavily to effective leadership, the text is suited for participants in leadership and supervisory training courses that emphasize interpersonal skills rather than leadership theory and research.

FRAMEWORK FOR THE BOOK

The book is a blend of current and traditional topics dealing with interpersonal relations in organizations with a heavy component of skill development and self-assessment. The information is organized into chapters, all emphasizing interpersonal relations between two or more people. Chapter 1, "A Framework for Interpersonal Skill Development," sets the stage for improving one's interpersonal skills on the job. Chapter 2, "Understanding Individual Differences," presents information that is the foundation of effective interpersonal relations. Chapter 3, "Building Self-Esteem and Self-Confidence," describes how to develop self-esteem and self-confidence both for oneself and to improve relationships with others. Chapter 4, "Interpersonal Communication," deals with skills in sending and receiving messages.

Chapter 5, "Interpersonal Skills for the Digital World," describes how interpersonal skills can enhance the use of digital devices, as well as how these devices lend themselves to poor interpersonal skills, such as cell phone abuse. Chapter 6, "Developing Teamwork

Skills," sensitizes the reader to a vital set of skills in the workplace. Chapter 7, "Group Problem Solving and Decision Making," provides additional skill in collaborative effort. Chapter 8, "Cross-Cultural Relations and Diversity," is about developing cross-cultural skills in a diverse workforce. Chapter 9, "Resolving Conflicts with Others," helps the reader develop skills in finding constructive solutions to differences of opinion and disputes with others.

Four consecutive chapters deal with exerting influence over others: Chapter 10, "Becoming an Effective Leader," presents information relevant to exercising leadership in the workplace; Chapter 11, "Motivating Others," emphasizes skills in getting others to work hard to achieve goals; Chapter 12, "Helping Others Develop and Grow," is about coaching, counseling, and teaching others; and Chapter 13, "Positive Political Skills," describes how to use power and influence for constructive purposes.

Chapter 14, "Customer Satisfaction Skills," describes several approaches to enhancing skills in satisfying customers, and thus lies at the heart of the importance placed on pleasing customers. Chapter 15, "Enhancing Ethical Behavior," translates ethical principles into usable skills. The rationale is that an ethical base is important for achieving career-long effectiveness in interpersonal relations. Chapter 16, "Stress Management and Personal Productivity," supports development of interpersonal skills by showing that productive people who have stress under control can relate more effectively to others. Chapter 17, "Job Search and Career Management Skills," includes information about the application of interpersonal skills (such as networking) to enhance one's career.

CHANGES IN THE NEW EDITION

The new edition of *Human Relations* adds a chapter about interpersonal skills for the digital age (Chapter 5). In many places throughout the text, we add a third level of heading to better organize the information for the student. We have added six new skill-building exercises, two new self-quizzes, and five new role-playing exercises. New questions or statements are added to several of the self-quizzes. New information, research findings, and examples appear throughout the text. Fifteen of the case openers and 20 of the cases are new. Material that may have lost some of its relevance has been selectively pruned. The new topics in the text are as follows:

- Description of personality types and cognitive styles as measured by Golden Personality Type Profiler (Chapter 2)
- New system of classifying values and associated goals (Chapter 3)
- How a manager builds the self-esteem of group members (Chapter 4)
- More information about active listening (Chapter 4)
- New chapter that includes information from previous edition about etiquette in relation to the use of electronic devices in the workplace (Chapter 5)
- New section on face-to-face versus virtual teams, replacing the section, "Types of Teams"
- More information about the advantages of group work and teamwork (Chapter 6)
- The importance of collective efficacy for group problem solving (Chapter 7)
- Cultural factors and group decision making (Chapter 7)
- New dimension of differences in cultural values, social support seeking (Chapter 8)
- Work-to-family conflict and family-to-work conflict (Chapter 9)
- The issue of work-life choices (Chapter 9)
- More about bullies in the workplace (Chapter 9)
- More about workplace violence (Chapter 9)
- Cross-generational conflict (Chapter 9)
- Workplace violence (Chapter 9)
- Conflict resolution technique of allowing for face saving (Chapter 9)
- A type of self-confidence specifically for leaders—leadership efficacy (Chapter 10)

- Group of personality traits associated with leadership effectiveness—positive core evaluation (Chapter 10)
- Making critical assessments as a leadership skill (Chapter 10)
- Self-sacrificing personality and leadership effectiveness (Chapter 10)
- Techniques for self-motivation (Chapter 11)
- Expansion of discussion of types of difficult people (Chapter 12)
- New section on political skills and other human relations skills (Chapter 13)
- Organizational citizenship behavior as part of impression management (Chapter 13)
- New job-oriented skills in action about a training and sales development manager (Chapter 13)
- Customer-centric sales process (Chapter 14)
- New survey on the extent of ethical problems (Chapter 15)
- Wasting company time as an ethical dilemma (Chapter 15)
- Figure listing representative suggestions for helping a company contribute to a sustainable environment (Chapter 15)
- Adverse interaction with customers and emotional labor in relation to stress (Chapter 16)
- Job loss as a source of stress (Chapter 16)
- Cognitive behavioral approach to stress management (Chapter 16)
- Salary discussion during a job interview (Chapter 17)
- Career-advancement strategy of pursuing fields and industries many others overlook (Chapter 17)

EXPERIENCE THE DUBRIN TOTAL LEARNING SYSTEM

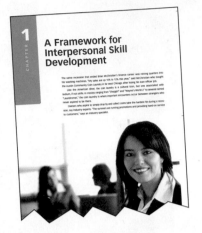

Human Relations: Job-Oriented Skills 11e is not just a textbook. The eleventh edition includes a wealth of experiential exercises, including new cases and self-assessment quizzes that can be completed in class or as homework.

CHAPTER OPENING CASES SETS THE STAGE

Following a listing of the chapter objectives and chapter outline, all chapters begin with a case scenario that deals with the chapter topic sets the stage for the chapter narrative.

PEDAGOGICAL FEATURES RELATE CONCEPTS TO WHAT'S HAPPENING TODAY, PERSONALLY AND IN THE WORKPLACE

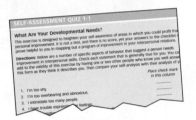

- **Back to the Opening Case** boxes within the chapter provide further insight into the situation posed in the chapter opening case related to chapter content.

- **Self-Assessment Exercises** give students the opportunity to explore their own opinions, feelings, and behaviors patterns related to chapter topics. All chapters include one or more self-assessment quizzes with a summary overview of assessment outcomes included at the end of the chapter.

- **Job-Oriented Interpersonal Skills in Action** in all chapters illustrate a real human relations business practice in today's business world.

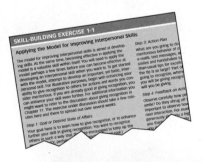

- **Skill Building Exercises** provide students with opportunities to apply concepts at the point at which they are being discussed in the textbook.

ASSIGNMENT MATERIAL REINFORCES CONCEPTS AND BUILDS SKILLS

End of chapter assignment material has been reorganized and expanded into two sections: **Concept Review and Reinforcement** featuring exercises that focus on concept retention and developing critical thinking skills and **Developing Your Human Relations Skills** focusing on developing skills that can be used immediately in life and on the job.

Concept Review and Reinforcement	Key Terms
	Summary of Key Concepts provides an excellent detailed review of key chapter concepts
	Check Your Understanding objective questions review key chapter topics
	The **Web Corner** provides informational Web sites and asks students to use the power of the Web in researching outside resources

Developing Your Human Relation Skills	**Two Human Relations Case Studies** put students into a realistic scenario so that they can practice making decisions in tough situations
	Interpersonal Skills Role-Play exercises provide students with the opportunity to develop personal insight through interactive exercises.

SUPPLEMENTAL MATERIALS

RESOURCES FOR STUDENTS:

mybizskillskit NEW! MYBIZSKILLSKIT for Human Relations

MyBizSkillsKit contains a wealth of study aids, illustrated case simulations, and access to the Golden Personality Type Profiler Assessment. An access code to MybBizSkillsKit can be value packaged with the textbook or purchased online at www.pearsonhighered.com <http://www.pearsonhighered.com/>. It includes:

BizSkills Illustrated Business Simulation Cases present students with workplace situations where they have to make the call. These illustrated case applications contain built-in feedback and scoring and can feed a gradebook, if desired.

The Golden Personality Type Profiler. This popular personality assessment, similar to the full Myers-Briggs assessment program, but oriented toward workplace behavioral assessment, provides students with information about fundamental personality dimensions. It takes about 15–20 minutes to complete and students receive an easy to use and practical feedback report based on their results. This tool helps students improve their self knowledge and ability to work effectively with others by providing students with feedback on their leadership and organizational strengths, communication and teamwork preferences, motivation and learning style, and opportunities for personal growth.

Professionalism Videos. These videos written by Lydia Anderson and Sandy Bolt focus on key challenges students face getting a job and maintaining and prospering on the job. Topics include making ethical choices, workplace etiquette, proper dress and deportment, customer service orientation, conflict management, sexual harassment, meeting management, preparing for the job search, writing effective resumes and cover letters, interviewing technique, and how to behave in a performance evaluation.

Test-prep Quizzes for each chapter, including true/false, multiple choice, and short essay questions; all questions include immediate feedback.
Web exercises for each chapter
Web Links to useful online resources

mysearchlab MySearchlab gives students access to EBSCO's ContentSelect Research Database. MySearchLab also includes a plagiarism tutorial, citation tutorial, and tools to help improve student writing including Longman Online Handbook of Writing. Preview at www.mysearchlab.com.

Also available separately:

Prentice Hall's Self-Assessment Library (SAL)

SAL is a print with CD-ROM product developed by Steve Robbins that contains 51 research-based self-assessments that provide students with insights into their skills, abilities, and interests. It is easy to use, self-scoring, and can be packaged with this text at a discounted price. Please contact your Prentice Hall representative to obtain a review copy.

RESOURCES FOR INSTRUCTORS:

To access supplementary materials online, instructors need to request an instructor access code. Go to **www.pearsonhighered.com/irc,** where you can register for an instructor access code. Within 48 hours of registering you will receive a confirming e-mail including an instructor access code. Once you have received your code, locate your text in the online catalog and click on the Instructor Resources button on the left side of the catalog product page. Select a supplement and a log in page will appear. Once you have logged in, you can access instructor material for all Prentice Hall textbooks.

Instructor's Manual with Test Item File

The Instructor's Manual for this text is available as a downloadable Word document at http://www.prenhall.com under instructor resources. It contains multiple-choice and true/false test questions, chapter outlines and lecture notes, answers to case problems, and comments about the exercises.

Pearson Mytest Electronic Testing Program

Pearson MyTest is a powerful assessment generation program that helps instructors easily create and print quizzes and exams. Questions and tests can be authored online, allowing instructors ultimate flexibility and the ability to efficiently manage assessments anytime, anywhere. Educator access to MyTest is already included in Pearson's Instructor Resource Center (IRC) Educator suite. Simply go to www.pearsonmytest.com <http://www.pearsonmytest.com/> and log in with your existing IRC login name and password.

Powerpoint Lecture Presentation Package

The package contains lecture Presentation screens for each chapter.

ACKNOWLEDGMENTS

My appreciation goes to the many people who contributed to the development and production of this book. Special thanks to Robert A. Herring III at Winston–Salem State University and Nancy Kriscenski at Manchester Community College for their insightful comments on this revision. Appreciation is also expressed to the outside reviewers who made suggestions for shaping this and previous editions of the text: Abhirjun Dutta, Bainbridge College; Robert G. DelCampo, University of New Mexico; David W. Robinson, Malaspina University College; Tim Blood, Lane Community College; and Jane Bowerman, University of Oklahoma. John Adamski II, Ivy Tech State College; Patricia Lynn Anderson, Valdosta State University; Judy Bowie, DeVry Institute of Technology; Robert A. Herring III, Winston–Salem State University; H. Frederick Holmes, Ogeechee Technical Institute; Ruth V. Kellar, Ivy Tech State College; Diane Paul, TVI Community College; Lou Jean Peace, Valdosta Technical Institute; Gary W. Piggrem, Ph.D., DeVry Institute of Technology; Dean Weeden, Utah Career College; and James F. Wetz, Central Florida Community College.

My family members give me an additional reason for writing, so I extend my appreciation to Drew, Douglas, Melanie, Gizella, Will, Rosie, Clare, Camila, Sofia, Eliana, Julian, and Carson. I thank Stefanie, the woman in my life, for her contribution to my well-being.

Andrew J. DuBrin
Rochester, New York

HUMAN RELATIONS
INTERPERSONAL JOB-ORIENTED SKILLS

A Framework for Interpersonal Skill Development

The same recession that ended Brian McChristian's finance career was raining quarters into his washing machines. "My sales are up 10% to 12% this year," said McChristian who bought the Austin Community Coin Laundry in far west Chicago after losing his loan officer job.

Like the American diner, the coin laundry is a cultural icon, but one associated with tedium, if not strife. In movies ranging from "Shopgirl" and "Wayne's World 2" to several named "Laundromat," the coin laundry is where important encounters occur between strangers who never aspired to be there.

Owners who aspire to simply drop by and collect coins take the hardest hit during a recession, say industry experts. "The survivors are running promotions and providing hand-on service to customers," says an industry specialist.

After reading and studying this chapter and doing the exercises, you should be able to

1. Explain how interpersonal skills are learned.
2. Explain the model for interpersonal skill improvement, including how to set goals effectively.
3. Pinpoint your needs for improvement in interpersonal relations.
4. Describe potential opportunities for developing interpersonal skills on the job.

After decades in a coat and tie, McChristian now wears jeans and sweatshirts 40 hours a week in the Austin Community Coin Laundry. To some extent, his double-digit sales increase in one year came because of the recession. One Monday morning, the crowd inside his store included several newcomers whose home equipment had broken down or who had moved back into this low-income neighborhood following job loss.

The most difficult challenge facing McChristian, a 54-year-old college graduate from the suburbs, involved confronting the loiterers who had hung out in his store under its previous owner. In this stretch of inner-city Chicago, drug dealers reign among economic desolation, and their presence in the laundry had scared off business.

"I didn't like coming here before he bought it," says Muriel Moore, a nurse who now visits the laundry each Monday morning. "There were just too many guys hanging out doing things they shouldn't."

After employing locals to help him run the store, McChristian issued a plea though them: Anyone without clothes to clean please stay away from the laundry and its parking lot. Its customers—largely mothers, grandmothers, and children—deserve a crime-free place to clean clothes, he told them. It worked. "We don't allow any hanging around," says Jimmie Burnett, the assistant manager at the laundry. [1]

One of the several themes emerging from the story about the coin laundry is that you need good skill in human relations to be successful. The owner worked with his team to gain the cooperation of neighborhood members who were frightening away customers. As the Dale Carnegie organization states, "To achieve success in today's work world—with its emphasis on collaboration, teamwork, motivation, and leadership—you need to perfect your interpersonal skills."[2]

Effective interpersonal relations must be combined with technical knowledge and good work habits to achieve success in any job involving interaction with people. Workers at all levels are expected not only to solve problems and improve processes (how work is performed), but also to interact effectively with other employees.[3] Many employers, including Southwest Airlines, emphasize hiring people with positive attitudes rather than focusing strictly on technical skills. And another airline JetBlue refuses to hire pilots who are arrogant or nasty despite their piloting skills.

Furthermore, the lack of good interpersonal skills can adversely affect a person's career. A study found that 90 percent of firings result from poor attitudes, inappropriate behavior, and problems in interpersonal relationships rather than substandard interpersonal skill.[4] An example of poor interpersonal relations that led to job loss was a receptionist at a boat dealer who told several potential customers something to the effect: "Are you just here to look. You don't look like you could afford one of our speed boats."

Another way of looking at the importance of interpersonal skills is that they enable you to connect with others, thereby being more successful in business. Author Susan Scott observes that the next frontier for growth in business lies in the area of human connectivity.[5]

This chapter explains how people develop interpersonal skills and presents a model that can serve as a foundation for improving your interpersonal skills. In addition, the chapter explains how the workplace can be a natural setting for developing interpersonal skills.

PLAN OF THE BOOK

LEARNING OBJECTIVE 1

This entire book is devoted to many different ways of improving interpersonal relations in organizations. A three-part strategy is presented for achieving the high level of effectiveness in interpersonal relations required in today's workplace. First, each chapter presents key concepts required for understanding a particular aspect of interpersonal relations, such as resolving conflict. Second, the chapter provides specific suggestions or behavioral guidelines for improvement in the aspect of interpersonal relations under consideration.

Third, a variety of exercises give you the opportunity to work on and improve your skills. Among these exercises are self-assessment quizzes, skill-building exercises, and cases for analysis. In addition, the questions at the end of each chapter give you an opportunity to think through and apply the key ideas in the chapter. Figure 1-1 illustrates the plan of the book.

interpersonal skill training

The teaching of skills in dealing with others so they can be put into practice.

Much of this book is concerned with **interpersonal skill training,** the teaching of skills in dealing with others so they can be put into practice. Interpersonal skills training is referred to as *soft-skills* training to differentiate it from technical training. (Technical skill training is referred to as *hard-skills* training.) Soft-skills training builds interpersonal skills, including communication, listening, group problem solving, cross-cultural relations, and customer service. Several specific competencies related to soft skills are as follows:

- Effectively translating and conveying information
- Being able to accurately interpret other people's emotions
- Being sensitive to other people's feelings
- Calmly arriving at resolutions to conflicts
- Avoiding negative gossip
- Being polite [6]
- Being able to cooperate with others to meet objectives (teamwork)

Soft-skills training is more important than ever as organizations realize that a combination of human effort and technology is needed to produce results. Multiple studies have shown that soft skills can compensate for more traditional cognitive (or analytical) intelligence. For example, a supervisor with good interpersonal skills might perform well even if he or she is not outstandingly intelligent. The statement does not mean, however, outstanding soft skills will compensate for high cognitive intelligence when doing highly analytical work such as analyzing the value of an investment or a company.

FIGURE 1-1   Plan for Achieving Effectiveness in Interpersonal Relations

Executive Learns About the Importance of Interpersonal Skills

Several years ago, while visiting a regional branch of Lee Hecht Harrison, a global management services company, then-president Stephen Harrison was stopped short by Ray, his chief operating officer. "You didn't greet the receptionist," said Ray, who proceeded to show Harrison how to do what he called the "two minute schmooze." Introducing himself, Ray inquired about the receptionist's commute and impressions of the company.

Ray explained to Harrison: "A receptionist is a corporate concierge. He or she will talk to more important people in a day—suppliers, customers, even CEOs—than you will talk to all year."

"Decency is not just about being nice," noted Harrison, author of *The Manager's Book of Decencies*. Rather, it is about creating a "bubble wrap" of good deeds that will protect a company in hard times. "Our willingness to be decent at work cannot depend on whether business is up or whether we're in a bad mood or whether it's raining. Decencies don't amount to anything unless we take the trouble to make them come alive through concrete acts in all kinds of weather."

Questions

1. What might an executive chatting with a receptionist be considered an interpersonal skill?
2. In what way might be *decent* to employees help make a company more profitable?

Source: "Talking with the Receptionist, Pausing When You Speak, and Other Secrets of Leadership Success," *Knowledge@Wharton* (http://knowledge. wharton.upenn.edu/article.cfm?articleid=1792), p. 1.

Soft skills are often the differentiating factor between adequate and outstanding performance because dealing with people is part of so many jobs.[7] Assume that a company establishes an elaborate intranet system to enable employees to exchange work-related information with each other. The system will not achieve its potential unless employees are motivated to use it properly and they develop a spirit of cooperation. The employees must also be willing to share some of their best ideas with each other. Consider this example also:

Sara, a newly hired intake receptionist in a cardiac clinic, notices that too often the patients present incomplete or inaccurate information, such as omitting data about the next of kin. Sara spends considerable amounts of time reworking forms with the patients, until she begins using soft skills more effectively. With coaching from her supervisor, Sara learns that if she attempts to calm down a patient first, the patient is more likely to complete the intake form accurately. The accompanying box illustrates the importance of interpersonal skills for a business executive.

Well-known executive coach Marshall Goldsmith reminds us that building relationships with people is important for workers at every level in the organization, including the CEO. An example of an interpersonal skill that would help build relationships would be demanding good results from others yet showing them respect at the same time.[8]

A MODEL FOR IMPROVING INTERPERSONAL SKILLS

Acquiring and improving interpersonal skills is facilitated by following a basic model of learning as it applies to changing your behavior. Learning is a complex subject, yet its fundamentals follow a five-part sequence, as shown in Figure 1-2. To change your behavior, and therefore improve, you need a goal and a way to measure your current reality against this goal. You also need a way to assess that reality, and a way to obtain feedback on the impact of your new actions.[9]

LEARNING OBJECTIVE 2

FIGURE 1-2 A Model for Improving Interpersonal Skills

Goal or Desired State of Affairs

Changing your behavior, including enhancing your interpersonal relations, requires a clear goal or desired state of affairs. Your goal can also be regarded as what you want to accomplish as a result of your effort. A major reason that a goal is important is that having a specific goal improves performance. With a goal in mind, a person will usually not be satisfied until the goal is attained. So he or she keeps plugging away until the goal is attained, thereby increasing both personal satisfaction and performance on the task. Goals are also important because where people perceive that they have not attained their goal they typically increase their effort or modify their strategy for reaching the goal.[10]

As a concrete example, let us take the common problem of a person who nibbles his fingernails during tense situations, such as being called on in a meeting. The nibbler might say, "My hopes [a goal] are to be able to sit in a meeting and not nibble my nails even though I know I might be called on." This man's desired state of affairs (his goal) is to avoid putting his nails in his mouth in order to appear calm and professional. Having a goal helps provide motivation and makes it possible to exercise the self-discipline necessary to follow through on your plans. In short, the goal focuses your effort on acquiring the improvements in behavior you seek.

Here we turn to Sean, a credit analyst who is being blocked from promotion because his manager perceives him as having poor interpersonal skills. After a discussion with his manager, Sean recognizes that he must improve his interpersonal relations if he wants to become a team leader.

Sean's goal is to be considered worthy of promotion to a leadership position. To achieve his goal, he will have to achieve the general goal of improving his interpersonal relations. By conferring with the human resources director, Sean learns that his broad goal of "improving my interpersonal relations" will have to be supported by more specific goals. Having poor interpersonal relations or "rubbing people the wrong way" includes many different behaviors. To begin, Sean selects one counterproductive behavior to improve: He is exceptionally intolerant of others and does not hide his intolerance. Sean's goal is to become less intolerant and more patient in his dealings with others on the job.

Fine Points about Goal Setting.   So far we have made goal setting seem easy. A truer description of goal setting is that it involves several fine points to increase the probability that the goal will be achieved. Key points about setting effective goals are outlined in Figure 1-3, and described next.

1. State Each Goal as a Positive Statement To express your goals in positive statements is likely to be more energizing than focusing on the negative.[11] An example of a positive statement would be, "During the next year when I am attending networking events, I will create a positive, professional impression on everybody I meet." The negative counterpart would be, "During the next year, I will avoid making a fool of myself when I am attending networking events." Despite this suggestion, there are times when a negative goal is useful, such as in reducing errors.

2. Formulate Specific Goals A goal such as "attain success" is too vague to serve as a guide to daily action. A more useful goal would be to state specifically what you mean by success and when you expect to achieve it. For example, "I want to be the manager of patient services at a large medical clinic by January 1, 2015, and receive above-average performance reviews."

FIGURE 1-3   Guidelines for Goal Setting

> 1. State each goal as a positive statement.
> 2. Formulate specific goals.
> 3. Formulate concise goals.
> 4. Set realistic goals as well as stretch goals.
> 5. Set goals for different time periods.

3. Formulate Concise Goals A useful goal can usually be expressed in a short, punchy statement, for example, "Decrease input errors in bank statements so that customer complaints are decreased by 25 percent by September 30 of this year." People new to goal setting typically commit the error of formulating lengthy, rambling goal statements. These lengthy goals involve so many different activities that they fail to serve as specific guides to action.

4. Set Realistic as Well as Stretch Goals A realistic goal is one that represents the right amount of challenge for the person pursuing the goal. On the one hand, easy goals are not very motivational—they may not spring you into action. On the other hand, goals that are too far beyond your capabilities may lead to frustration and despair because there is a good chance you will fail to reach them. The extent to which a goal is realistic depends on a person's capabilities.

An easy goal for an experienced person might be a realistic goal for a beginner. **Self-efficacy** is also a factor in deciding whether a goal is realistic. (The term refers to the confidence in your ability to carry out a specific task.) The higher your self-efficacy, the more likely you are to think that a particular goal is realistic. A person with high self-efficacy for learning Chinese might say, "I think learning two new Chinese words a day is realistic."

Several goals that stretch your capability might be included in your list of goals. An extreme stretch goal might be for a store manager trainee to become the vice president of merchandising for Target within four years. Another type of stretch goal is striving for a noble cause. A Home Depot supervisor might not get excited about having the store associates load lumber onto the steel shelves. However, she might get excited about the lumber being used to build homes, schools, and hospitals.

5. Set Goals for Different Time Periods Goals are best set for different time periods, such as daily, short range, medium range, and long range. Daily goals are essentially a to-do list. Short-range goals cover the period from approximately one week to one year into the future. Finding a new job, for example, is typically a short-range goal. Medium-range goals relate to events that will take place within approximately two to five years. They concern such things as the type of education or training you plan to undertake and the next step in your career.

Long-range goals refer to events taking place five years into the future and beyond. As such, they relate to the overall lifestyle you wish to achieve, including the type of work and family situation you hope to have. Although every person should have a general idea of a desirable lifestyle, long-range goals should be flexible. You might, for example, plan to stay single until age 40. But while on vacation next summer, you might just happen to meet the right partner for you.

Short-range goals make an important contribution to attaining goals of longer duration. If a 1-year career goal is to add 25 worthwhile contacts to your social network, a good way to motivate yourself is to search for two contacts per month for 11 months, and three for 1 month. Progress toward a larger goal is self-rewarding.

Assessing Reality

The second major requirement for a method of changing behavior is to assess reality. Sean needs a way to assess how far he is from his goal of being eligible for promotion and how intolerant he is perceived to be. Sean has already heard from his manager, Alison, that he is not eligible for promotion right now. Sean might want to dig for more information by finding answers to the following questions:

"If I were more tolerant, would I be promoted now?"

"How bad are my interpersonal relations in the office?"

"How many people in the office think I rub them the wrong way?"

"How many deficiencies do my manager and coworkers perceive me to have?"

A starting point in answering these questions might be for Sean to confer with Alison about his behavior. To be more thorough, however, Sean might ask a friend in the office to help him answer the questions. A coworker is sometimes in an excellent position to provide feedback on how one is perceived by others in the office. Sean could also ask a confidant outside the office about his intolerance. Sean could ask a parent, a significant other, or both about the extent of his intolerance.

self-efficacy
The confidence in your ability to carry out a specific task.

An Action Plan

action plan

A series of steps to achieve a goal.

The learning model needs some mechanism to change the relationship between the person and the environment. An **action plan** is a series of steps to achieve a goal. Without an action plan, a personal goal will be elusive. The person who sets the goal may not initiate steps to make his or her dream (a high-level goal) come true. If your goal is to someday become a self-employed business owner, your action plan should include saving money, establishing a good credit rating, and developing dozens of contacts.

Sean has to take some actions to improve his interpersonal relations, especially his intolerance. The change should ultimately lead to the promotion he desires. Sean's action plan for becoming more tolerant includes the following:

- Pausing to attempt to understand why a person is acting the way he or she does. An example would be attempting to understand why a sales representative wants to extend credit to a customer with a poor credit rating.
- Learning to control his own behavior so that he does not make intolerant statements just because he is experiencing pressure.
- Taking a course in interpersonal skills or human relations.
- Asking Alison to give him a quick reminder whenever she directly observes or hears of him being intolerant toward customers or workmates.

In addition to formulating these action plans, Sean must have the self-discipline to implement them. For example, he should keep a log of situations in which he was intolerant and those in which he was tolerant. He might also make a mental note to attempt to be cooperative and flexible in most of his dealings at work. When a customer does not provide all the information Sean needs to assess his or her creditworthiness; Sean should remind himself to say, "I want to process your credit application as quickly as possible. To do this, I need some important additional information." Sean's reflex in the same situation had been to snap, "I can't read your mind. If you want to do business with us, you've got to stop hiding the truth."

Feedback on Actions

The fourth step in the learning model is to measure the effects of one's actions against reality. You obtain feedback on the consequences of your actions. When your skill-improvement goal is complex, such as becoming more effective at resolving conflict, you will usually have to measure your progress in several ways. You will also need both short- and long-term measures of the effectiveness of your actions. Long-term measures are important because skill-development activities of major consequence have long-range implications.

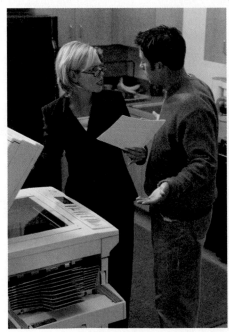

To obtain short-range feedback, Sean can consult with Alison to see whether she has observed any changes in his tolerance. Alison can also collect any feedback she hears from others in the office. Furthermore, Sean will profit from feedback over a prolonged period of time, perhaps one or two years. He will be looking to see whether his image has changed from an intolerant person who rubs people the wrong way to a tolerant person who has cordial interactions with others.

Frequent Practice

The final step in the learning model makes true skill development possible. Implementing the new behavior and using feedback for fine-tuning is an excellent start in acquiring a new interpersonal skill. For the skill to be long lasting, however, it must be integrated into your usual way of conducting yourself. In Sean's case, he will have to practice being tolerant regularly until it becomes a positive habit.

After a skill is programmed into your repertoire, it becomes a habit. This is important because a skill involves many habits. For example, good customer service skills include the habits of smiling and listening carefully. After you attempt the new interpersonal skills described in this book, you will need to practice them frequently to make a noticeable difference in your behavior.

A sports analogy is appropriate here. Assume that Marisa, a tennis player, takes a lesson to learn how to hit the ball with greater force. The instructor points out that the reason Marisa is not hitting with much force is that she is relying too much on her arm and not enough on her leg and body strength. To hit the ball with more force, Marisa is told that she must put one foot out in front of her when she strikes the ball (she must "step into" the ball).

Under the watchful eye of the coach, Marisa does put a foot out in front when she strikes the ball. Marisa is excited about the good results. But if Marisa fails to make the same maneuver with her feet during her tennis matches, she will persist in hitting weakly. If Marisa makes the effort to use her legs more effectively on almost every shot, she will soon integrate the new movement into her game.

In summary, the basics of a model for learning skills comprise five steps: goal or desired state of affairs → assessing reality → an action plan → feedback on actions → frequent practice. You must exercise self-discipline to complete each step. If you skip a step, you will be disappointed with the results of your interpersonal skill-development program.

BACK TO THE OPENING CASE

If Brian McChristian wants his business to survive, he must continue to practice his skills in developing good relationships with his assistant manager and community members. Gaining the cooperation of non-customers to stay away from the store will be a continuing challenge. McChristian must continue to work closely with neighborhood people he hired, so they can help him continue to maintain a peaceful and nonthreatening environment for customers and potential customers of his coin laundry.

SKILL-BUILDING EXERCISE 1-1

Applying the Model for Improving Interpersonal Skills

The model for improving interpersonal skills is aimed at developing skills. At the same time, becoming effective in applying the model is a valuable skill within itself. You will need to apply the model perhaps a few times before you can become effective at developing an interpersonal skill when you want to. To get started with the model, attempt to develop an important, yet basic, interpersonal skill. For illustrative purposes, begin with enhancing your ability to give recognition to others for actions and words you consider meritorious. If you are already good at giving recognition, you can enhance your skill even further. For additional information you might want to refer to the discussion about giving recognition in Chapter 11. The exercise under discussion should take a few minutes here and there to spread out over several weeks.

Step 1: Goal or Desired State of Affairs

Your goal here is to learn how to give recognition, or to enhance further your skill in giving recognition. You want to recognize others in such a way that they are encouraged to keep up the good work. (Or, perhaps you have another related goal.)

Step 2: Assessing Reality

Ask a few confidants how good you already are in giving recognition. Ask questions such as, "How good have I been in saying thank you?" "When you have done something nice for me, how did I react to you?" "How many thank-you notes have I sent you since you've known me?" Also, reflect on your own behavior in such matters as giving a server a big tip for exceptional service, or explaining to a tech specialist how much he or she has helped you. Ask yourself whether you have ever thanked a teacher for an outstanding course, or explained to a coach how much his or her advice helped you.

Step 3: Action Plan

What are you going to do in the next few weeks to recognize the meritorious behavior of others? Will you be sending thank-you e mails, text messages, and warmly-worded postal cards; offering smiles and handshakes to people who help you; or giving larger-than-usual tips for excellent service with an explanation of why the tip is so large? Part of the action plan will be *who* are you going to recognize, *where* you are going to recognize them, *when* you will be giving recognition, and *how* (what form) of recognition will you be giving.

Step 4: Feedback on Actions

Observe carefully how people react to your recognition. Do they smile? Do they shrug off your form of recognition? It is especially important to observe how the person reacts to you during your next interaction. For example, does the server who you tipped so generously give you a big welcome? Does the bank teller who you thanked so sincerely seem eager to cash your next check? If you do not get the intended result from your recognition efforts, you might need to fine-tune your sincerity. Maybe when you sent a recognition e-mail or text message, you did not mention the person's name, and just wrote "Hey." Maybe you did not combine a thank you with a smile. Analyze carefully the feedback you receive.

Step 5: Frequent Practice

For this exercise, perhaps you can only practice giving recognition in one or two settings. Yet if this exercise appears promising, you might continue to practice in the future. Should you continue to practice, you will be taking personal step to make the world a better place.

IDENTIFICATION OF DEVELOPMENTAL NEEDS

LEARNING OBJECTIVE 3

An important concept in skill development is that people are most likely to develop new skills when they feel the need for change. The importance of the perceived need for change is reflected in a variation of an old joke:

> **Question:** How many psychologists does it take to change a light bulb?
>
> **Answer:** None, if the light bulb wants to change.

As you read this book and do the experiential exercises, you will probably be more highly motivated to follow through with skill development in areas in which you think you need development. A specific area in which a person needs to change is referred to as a **developmental need.** For instance, some people may be too shy, too abrasive, or too intolerant, and some may not give others the encouragement they need.

developmental need

A specific area in which a person needs to change or improve.

To improve interpersonal skills, we must first be aware of how we are perceived by people who interact with us.[12] Developmental needs related to interpersonal skills can be identified in several ways. First, if you are candid with yourself you can probably point to areas in which you recognize that change is needed. You might reflect on your experiences and realize that you have had repeated difficulty in resolving conflict. Second, a related approach is to think of feedback you have received. If there has been consistency in asking you to improve in a particular area, you could hypothesize that the feedback has merit. Perhaps five different people have told you that you are not a good team player. "Becoming a better team player" might therefore be one of your developmental needs.

A third approach to assessing developmental needs is to solicit feedback. Ask the opinion of people who know you well to help you identify needs for improvement with respect to interpersonal skills. Present and previous managers are a valuable source of this type of feedback. A fourth approach to pinpointing developmental needs is closely related to the previous three: feedback from performance evaluations. If you have worked for a firm that uses performance evaluations to help people develop, you may have received constructive suggestions during the evaluation. For example, one manager told his assistant: "You need to project more self-confidence when you answer the phone. You sound so unsure and vague when you talk on the telephone. I have noticed this, and several customers have joked about it." The recipient of this feedback was prompted to participate in assertiveness training where she learned how to express herself more positively.

Self-Assessment Quiz 1-1 gives you the opportunity to identify your developmental needs. The same exercise is a first step in improving your interpersonal relations on the job because identification of a problem is the first—and most important—step toward change. For example, if you cite improving your relationships with people from cultures different from your own, you have planted the seeds for change. You are then more likely to seek out people from other cultures in the workplace or at school and cultivate their friendship.

Now that you (and perhaps another person) have identified specific behaviors that may require change, you need to draw up an action plan. Proceed with your action plan even though you have just begun studying this text, but peek ahead to relevant chapters if you wish. Describe briefly a plan of attack for bringing about the change you hope to achieve for each statement that is checked. Ideas for your action plan can come from information presented anywhere in this text, from outside reading, or from talking to a person experienced in dealing with people. A basic example would be to study materials about customer service and observe an effective model if you checked "I feel awkward dealing with a customer."

UNIVERSAL NEEDS FOR IMPROVING INTERPERSONAL RELATIONS

LEARNING OBJECTIVE 4

universal training need

An area for improvement common to most people.

I have just described how understanding your unique developmental needs facilitates improving your interpersonal skills. There are also areas for skill improvement in interpersonal relations that are shared by most managerial, professional, technical, and sales personnel. These common areas for improvement are referred to as **universal training needs.**

What Are Your Developmental Needs?

This exercise is designed to heighten your self-awareness of areas in which you could profit from personal improvement. It is not a test, and there is no score, yet your answers to the checklist may prove helpful to you in mapping out a program of improvement in your interpersonal relations.

Directions: Below are a number of specific aspects of behavior that suggest a person needs improvement in interpersonal skills. Check each statement that is generally true for you. You can add to the validity of this exercise by having one or two other people who know you well answer this form as they think it describes you. Then compare your self-analysis with their analysis of you.

Place check mark in this column

1. I'm too shy. _____
2. I'm too overbearing and obnoxious. _____
3. I intimidate too many people. _____
4. I have trouble expressing my feelings. _____
5. I make negative comments about people too readily. _____
6. I have a difficult time solving problems when working in a group. _____
7. I'm a poor team player. _____
8. Very few people listen to me. _____
9. It is difficult for me to relate well to people from different cultures. _____
10. When I'm in conflict with another person, I usually lose. _____
11. I hog too much time in meetings or in class. _____
12. I'm very poor at office politics. _____
13. People find me boring. _____
14. It is difficult for me to criticize others. _____
15. I'm too serious most of the time. _____
16. My temper is too often out of control. _____
17. I avoid controversy in dealing with others. _____
18. It is difficult for me to find things to talk about with others. _____
19. I don't get my point across well. _____
20. I feel awkward dealing with a customer. _____
21. I am a poor listener. _____
22. I don't get the point of the importance of ethics in business. _____
23. My attempts to lead others have failed. _____
24. I rarely smile when I am with other people. _____
25. I multitask when people are talking to me. _____
26. I insult too many people on social networking sites. _____
27. _____ (Fill in your own statement.) _____

Almost any professional person, for example, could profit from enhancing his or her negotiation and listening skills.

This book provides the opportunity for skill development in a number of universal training needs. In working through these universal training needs, be aware that many of them will also fit your specific developmental needs. A given universal training need can be an individual's developmental need at the same time. It is reasonable to expect that you will be more strongly motivated to improve skills that relate closely to your developmental needs.

The major universal training needs covered in this text are as follows:

1. **Understanding individual differences.** To deal effectively with others in the workplace, it is necessary to recognize that people have different capabilities, needs, and interests.

2. **Self-esteem and self-confidence.** To function effectively with people in most work and personal situations, people need to feel good about themselves and believe that they can accomplish important tasks. Although self-esteem and self-confidence are essentially attitudes about the self, they also involve skills such as attaining legitimate accomplishments and using positive self-talk.

3. **Interpersonal communication.** Effective communication with people is essential for carrying out more than 50 percent of the work conducted by most professional and managerial workers.

4. **Behaving appropriately when using digital devices.** Digital devices are integrated into most facets of our work and personal lives. Knowing how to use various electronic devices including e-mail, cell phones, and smart phones in a positive, constructive way instead of being uncivil and unproductive can be a major contributor to your interpersonal relationships.

5. **Developing teamwork skills.** The most sweeping change in the organization of work in the last 35 years has been a shift to teams and away from traditional departments. Knowing how to be an effective team player therefore enhances your chances for success in the modern organization.

6. **Group problem solving and decision making.** As part of the same movement that emphasizes work teams, organizations now rely heavily on group problem solving. As a consequence, being an above-average contributor to group problem solving is a key part of effective interpersonal relations on the job. In addition to solving the problem, a decision must be made.

7. **Cross-cultural relations.** The modern workplace has greater cultural diversity than ever before. Being able to deal effectively with people from different cultures, from within and outside your own country, is therefore an important requirement for success.

8. **Resolving conflicts with others.** Conflict in the workplace is almost inevitable as people compete for limited resources. Effective interpersonal relations are therefore dependent upon knowing how to resolve conflict successfully.

9. **Becoming an effective leader.** In today's organizations, a large number of people have the opportunity to practice leadership, even if on temporary assignment. Enhancing one's leadership skills is therefore almost a universal requirement.

10. **Motivating others.** Whether you have the title of manager or leader or are working alone, you have to know how to motivate the people whom you depend on to get your work accomplished. Given that few people are gifted motivators, most people can profit from skill development in motivation.

11. **Helping others develop and grow.** As power is shared in organizations among managers and individual contributors (non-managers) alike, more people are required to help each other develop and grow. To carry out this role, most of us need skill development in coaching and mentoring.

12. **Positive political skills.** Whether you work in a small or large firm, part of having effective interpersonal relations is being able to influence others so that your interests are satisfied. Positive political skills help you satisfy your interests without being unethical or devious.

13. **Customer service skills.** The current emphasis on customer satisfaction dictates that every worker should know how to provide good service to customers. Most people can benefit from strengthening their skills in serving both external and internal customers. (Internal customers are the people with whom you interact on the job.)

14. **Enhancing ethical behavior.** Although most workers in their heart know right from wrong, we can all sharpen our ability to make ethical decisions. By consistently making highly ethical decisions, people can improve their interpersonal relations.

15. **Stress management and personal productivity.** Having your stress under control and having good work habits and time-management skills contributes to relating

well to others even though they are not interpersonal skills themselves. By having your stress under control and being efficient and productive, you are in a better position to relate comfortably to others. Coworkers enjoy relating to a person who is not visibly stressed and who does not procrastinate.

16. **Job search and career-management skills.** Finding an outstanding job for yourself, holding onto the job, and moving ahead are not specifically interpersonal skills. However, both finding the right job for yourself and managing your career rely heavily on good interpersonal skills. Two basic examples are conducting yourself well in an interview and developing a network of contacts that can help you advance.

DEVELOPING INTERPERSONAL SKILLS ON THE JOB

The primary thrust of this book is to teach interpersonal skills that can be applied to the job. As part of enhancing your skills, it is essential to recognize that opportunities also exist in the workplace for developing interpersonal skills. This dual opportunity for learning soft skills is similar to the way hard skills are learned both inside and outside the classroom. Studying a text and doing laboratory exercises, for example, will help you learn useful information technology skills. On the job, one day you might be asked to establish your company's presence on Facebook. Having never performed this task before, you may search a computer manual, ask questions of coworkers, telephone a help desk, and use trial and error. Within an hour, you have acquired a valuable new skill. The information technology skills you learned in the course facilitated learning new computer tasks, yet the actual learning of how to set up a Facebook presence for your company was done on the job.

Here, we look at two related aspects of learning interpersonal skills on the job—informal learning and specific developmental experiences.

Informal Learning

Business firms, as well as nonprofit organizations, invest an enormous amount of money and time in teaching interpersonal skills. Teaching methods include paying for employees to take outside courses, conducting training on company premises, using videoconferencing or Web-based courses, and reimbursing for distance learning courses on the Internet. Workers also develop interpersonal skills by interacting with work associates and observing how other people deal with interpersonal challenges. Figure 1-4 presents a summary of how people learn on the job. Observe that the learning experiences are a mixture of formal learning such as company-provided training and informal learning such as interaction with coworkers. Much of the learning shown in Figure 1-4 refers to technical skills and knowledge, but learning about interpersonal skills is also included.

Informal learning is the acquisition of knowledge and skills that takes place naturally outside a structured learning environment. In the context of the workplace, informal learning takes place without being designed by the organization. Learning can take place informally in such ways as speaking to the person in the next cubicle, asking a question of a coworker while in the hall, or calling the tech support center. A study of more than 1,000 employees at seven companies in seven states found that up to 70 percent of learning takes place informally. Another researcher reported about the same figure.[13] The director of the first study emphasizes that formal training includes both a goal stated by the organization and a defined method or process. Informal learning can occur whether or not a goal is stated or the method is defined.

A more recent study conducted by the American Society for Training Directors also found that informal learning is part of how employees learn. Nearly one-half of the 1,104 respondents said that informal learning is occurring to a high or very-high extent in their

informal learning

The acquisition of knowledge and skills that takes place naturally outside a structured learning environment.

FIGURE 1-4   Sources of Learning on the Job

Capital Works reported that we learn at work through the following means:

Source: Reprinted with permission. Capital Works, LLC, *http://aglesslearner.com/intros/informal.html.*

organizations. E-mail emerged as the top-ranked informal learning tool, with accessing information from an Intranet being a close second.[14]

Learning interpersonal skills informally can take place through such means as observing a coworker, manager, or team leader deal with a situation. A newly hired assistant store manager couldn't help seeing and overhearing a customer screaming at the store manager about a defective space heater. The manager said calmly, "It appears you are pretty upset about your heater that caused a short circuit in your house. What can I do to help you?" The customer calmed down as quickly as air being released from a balloon. The assistant store manager thought to herself, "Now I know how to handle a customer who has gone ballistic. I'll state what the customer is probably feeling, and then offer to help."

Informal learning can also occur when another person coaches you about how to handle a situation. The store manager might have said to the new assistant manager, "Let me tell you what to do in case you encounter a customer who goes ballistic. Summarize in a few words what he or she is probably feeling, and then offer to help. The effect can be remarkable." (This incident is classified as informal learning because it takes place outside a classroom.)

Formal and informal learning of interpersonal skills are useful supplements to each other. If you are formally learning interpersonal skills your level of awareness for enhancing your interpersonal skills will increase. By formally studying interpersonal skills, you are likely to develop the attitude "What hints about dealing more effectively with people can I pick up on the job?" You may have noticed that if you are taking lessons in a sport, you become much more observant about watching the techniques of outstanding athletes in person or on television.

Specific Developmental Experiences

Another perspective on developing interpersonal skills in the workplace is that certain experiences are particularly suited to such development. Coping with a difficult customer, as previously suggested, would be one such scenario. Morgan W. McCall, Jr., for many years has studied ways in which leaders develop on the job. Contending with certain challenges is at the heart of these key learning experiences. Several of the powerful learning experiences McCall has identified are particularly geared toward developing better interpersonal skills.[15]

- **Unfamiliar responsibilities.** The person has to handle responsibilities that are new, very different, or much broader than previous ones. Dealing with these unfamiliar responsibilities necessitates asking others for help and gaining their cooperation.

For example, being assigned to supervise a group doing work unfamiliar to you would put you in a position of gaining the cooperation of group members who knew more about the work than you.

- **Proving yourself.** If you feel added pressure to show others that you can deal effectively with responsibilities, you are likely to develop skills in projecting self-confidence and persuading others.

- **Problems with employees.** If you supervise employees, or have coworkers, who lack adequate experience, are incompetent, or are poorly motivated, you need to practice such skills as effective listening and conflict resolution in order to work smoothly with them.

- **Influencing without authority.** An excellent opportunity for practicing influence skills is being forced to influence coworkers, higher management, company outsiders, and other key people over whom you have no formal control. Team leaders typically face the challenge of needing to influence workers whom they lack the authority to discipline or grant raises. (The reason is that a team leader usually does not have as much formal authority as a traditional manager.)

- **Difficult manager.** If you and your manager have different opinions on how to approach problems, or if your manager has serious shortcomings, you will have to use your best human relations skills to survive. You will need to develop such subtle skills as using diplomacy to explain to your manager that his or her suggestion is completely unworkable.

The general point to be derived from these scenarios is that certain on-the-job challenges require a high level of interpersonal skill. Faced with such challenges, you will be prompted to use the best interpersonal skills you have. Formal training can be a big help because you might remember a skill that should be effective in a particular situation. Assume that you are faced with an overbearing manager who belittles you in front of others. You might be prompted to try a conflict-resolution technique you acquired in class.

SELF-ASSESSMENT QUIZ IN OVERVIEW

Self-Assessment Quiz 1-1, "What Are My Developmental Needs," if answered accurately then acted upon will help you considerably in your job performance and your career. However, capitalizing on your strengths is even more important for your personal growth, and these topics will discussed in Chapter 3 about building self-esteem, and Chapter 17 about advancing your career.

Concept Review and Reinforcement

Key Terms

interpersonal skill training 4
self-efficacy 7

action plan 8
developmental need 10

universal training need 10
informal learning 13

Summary

Effective interpersonal relations must be combined with technical knowledge to achieve success in any job involving interactions with people. This book presents a three-part strategy for achieving a high level of interpersonal skill. Each chapter presents concepts related to an area of interpersonal skill, behavioral guidelines, and experiential exercises. Interpersonal skill training is also referred to as soft-skills training to differentiate it from technical training.

A five-part model of learning can be applied to improving interpersonal skills. First, state a goal or desired state of affairs. Second, assess the reality of how far you are from your goal. Third, develop an action plan to change the relationship between the person and the environment. Self-discipline is required to implement the action plan. Fourth, solicit feedback on actions to measure the effects of your actions against reality. Fifth, continue to practice your newly learned skill.

To use the learning model effectively, it is useful to understand the goal-setting process. The guidelines offered here for goal setting are to (1) state each goal as a positive statement, (2) formulate specific goals, (3) formulate concise goals, (4) set realistic as well as stretch goals, and (5) set goals for different time periods.

People are most likely to develop new skills when they feel the need for change. A developmental need is the specific area in which a person needs to change. Identifying your developmental needs in relation to interpersonal relations can be achieved through self-analysis and feedback from others. You can also solicit feedback and make use of the feedback you have received in performance appraisals.

Universal training needs are those areas for improvement that are common to most people. The major topics in this text reflect universal training needs because they are necessary for success in most positions involving interaction with people.

Opportunities exist in the workplace to develop interpersonal skill. A general approach to developing these skills is informal learning, whereby you acquire skills naturally outside a structured work environment. Informal learning of interpersonal skills often takes place through such means as observing a coworker, manager, or team leader cope with a situation. Certain workplace experiences are particularly well suited to developing interpersonal skills. These include unfamiliar responsibilities, proving yourself, having problems with employees, influencing without authority, and having a difficult manager.

Questions for Discussion and Review

1. Several of the most prestigious business schools, such as those of Wharton, MIT, and the University of Virginia, now give much more emphasis on teaching soft skills. Why do you think this change might have come about?

2. In your opinion, do supervisors of entry-level workers rely more on soft skills or hard skills to accomplish their work?

3. Why do people need soft skills in an era of high technology?

4. Why are soft skills quite important for job seekers when there is a shortage of good jobs open in their field?

5. How does a person know whether or not the feedback he or she receives from another person is accurate?

6. How could doing a thorough job with Self-Assessment Quiz 1-1 have a major impact on a person's career?

7. A statement frequently made in business is, "If you are obnoxious, you need to be very talented to succeed." How does this conclusion relate to the learning of interpersonal skills?

8. Based on what you have learned so far in this book, and your own intuition, how would you respond to the statement, "You can't learn how to get along with people from reading a book"?

9. Give an example of a skill you might have learned informally at any point in your life.

10. The coin laundry operator described at the outset of this chapter salvaged his business by applying soft skills. Can you give another example of how a small-business owner needs good soft skills to survive?

The Web Corner

www.internettime.com/Learning
(Informal learning)

www.impactfactory.com
(Interpersonal skill development)

www.winsportcanada.ca/cop
(Developing interpersonal skills through a challenge course)

Internet Skill Builder: The Importance of Interpersonal Skills

One of the themes of this chapter and the entire book is that interpersonal skills are important for success in business. But what do employers really think? To find out, visit the Web sites of five of your favorite companies, such as www.Starbucks.com or www.Apple.com. Go to the employment section and search for a job that you might qualify for now or in the future. Investigate which interpersonal or human relations skills the employer mentions as a requirement, such as "Must have superior spoken communication skills." Make up a list of the interpersonal skills you find mentioned. What conclusion or conclusions do you reach from this exercise?

Developing Your Human Relations Skills

Interpersonal Relations Case 1.1

Nobody Likes Me

Marge Caitlin, the supervisor of inventory control, was walking down the isle with BlackBerry in hand thinking about the major inventory-reduction program taking place at the company. She thought to herself, "The CEO is putting a lot of pressure on us to trim inventory to the bone. Yet the manufacturing and sales groups want enough inventory available so they can do their job. We really have to get focused and creative to satisfy everybody."

As Caitlin hurried down the isle thinking about the inventory challenge, she still kept a watchful eye on her staff working in their cubicles. She noticed that Phil Baxter, one of the inventory control analysts, was looking even more discouraged than usual. Caitlin put aside her BlackBerry, and tapped on the entrance to Baxter's cubicle. "Can we talk?" said Caitlin with a reassuring smile on her face.

"Sure," said Baxter. "Did I screw up again?"

"Phil, there you go putting yourself down again," said Caitlin. "I just noticed that you look a little glum today. I want to know if you are having a problem that I could help with."

"Thanks, Marge, for being interested in my problems. It's really nothing new—just the same old problem that I have had in school and on the job. Nobody likes me. Nobody wants me. It gets sickening after awhile."

"What makes you so sure that nobody likes you and that nobody wants you?" asked Caitlin.

Baxter responded, "First of all, almost nobody asks me to go out to lunch with him or her. Second, when you asked us to form our own teams, no team invited me to join them. I was finally chosen to be on one of the three teams because I was the last person not assigned."

"What do you think is your problem?" asked Caitlin.

"Maybe you could tell me. I think people see me as kind of a nerd. Maybe I'm just not likeable. I don't think I'm special in any way."

"Just hang in there for awhile," said Caitlin. "After this big inventory overhaul is completed, I will get back to you with some suggestions."

"I'll be waiting for your magic bullet," said Baxter with a dejected look.

Case Questions

1. What developmental needs does Phil Baxter appear to have?
2. If you were Marge Caitlin, what would you recommend that Baxter do?
3. From the little evidence that you have, what is your opinion of Caitlin's interpersonal skills?

Interpersonal Relations Case 1.2

Betty Lou Sets Some Goals

Betty Lou is a marketing specialist at Pasta Mucho, the biggest pasta maker in her region. Two years in the position, she contributed to the success of the Pasta Mucho product line. Although Betty Lou admits that a recession has contributed to the upswing in pasta sales nationwide, she believes that more than luck is involved. "After all," she says," "I contributed to the marketing campaign that preparing pasta at home makes you cool."

Betty Lou's boss, Garth, is pleased with her job performance; but as part of the performance evaluation process, he has encouraged Betty Lou to prepare a goal sheet, mapping out her plans for the upcoming year. "Make it impressive," said Garth, "because my boss will be reviewing your goals also." Three days later, Betty Lou sent Garth an e-mail laying out her goals as follows:

1. Help make Pasta Mucho one of the great brands on the planet, much like Coca-Cola, Mercedes, and Microsoft.
2. Become the best marketing executive I can be.
3. Help the company develop some other wildly successful brands.

4. Get in good with more buyers at supermarket chains.
5. Get Pasta Mucho all over Facebook and Twitter.

After reading the set of goals, Garth thought to himself, "What can I tell Betty Lou without hurting her feelings?"

Case Questions

1. If you were Garth, what would you tell Betty Lou about her goals without hurting her feelings?

2. What suggestions can you offer Betty Lou to improve her goal statement?

3. How might interpersonal skills contribute to Betty Lou attaining her goals?

Interpersonal Skills Role-Play

Selling at the office

One student plays the role of Kristina, who sells wellness products such as vitamins and food supplements for a direct sales company. (Direct sales are from person to person, and not distributed through stores.) Kristina is working hard to reach her goal for the month, and she just needs to sell $100 more of products to attain her goal. Another student plays the role of Ricardo who enjoys working with Kristina but thinks that wellness products are overrated. During lunch in the company cafeteria, Kristina approaches Ricardo and begins her sales pitch about her wonderful life-enhancing products.

Run the role-play for about six minutes, while other class members observe the interactions and later provide feedback about the interpersonal skills displayed by Kristina and Ricardo. Observers rate the role players on two dimensions, using a 1-to-5 scale from very poor to very good. One dimension is "effective use of human relations techniques." The second dimension is "acting ability." A few observers might voluntarily provide feedback to the role players in terms of sharing their ratings and observations. The course instructor might also provide feedback.

Understanding Individual Differences

U.S. Airways Captain Chesley "Sully" Sullenberger III, the hero of the January 2009 airline ditching in the Hudson River, told investigators he determined in a matter of seconds that only the river was "long enough, wide enough and smooth enough" to put down the crippled jetliner. Testifying before the National Transformation Safety Board, Sullenberger said that when both engines of his Airbus 320 lost power at about 2,700 feet after sucking in birds, he quickly decided that the plane was losing speed and altitude and that returning to New York's LaGuardia Airport was "problematic." After spotting a flock of birds that were very large and filled the entire windscreen of the jet, Sullenberger noticed a dramatic drop in thrust. Disregarding air traffic controller suggestions to return to LaGuardia or try to swoop into another nearby airport, he set his sights on the surface of the Hudson. With the plane's flaps out, speed dwindling fast, and splashdown barely seconds away, Sullenberger asked his first officer: "Got any ideas?" Copilot Jeff Skiles instantly replied, "Actually not."

Once the plane settled in the water and the crew realized the fuselage remained intact, Sullenberger turned to his first officer and both instinctively blurted out at the same instant, "That wasn't as bad as I thought." Responding to questions about the lessons to be learned from the landing, Capt. Sullenberger mentioned training to help pilots work together as a team and additional efforts to improve emergency evacuations. His comments repeatedly swung back to the notion of an airline culture that stresses safety and respects the judgment of experienced pilots. "The captain's authority is a precious commodity that cannot be denigrated," he said. The captain's testimony also highlighted the importance of relying on experience and memory, rather than rigidly using checklists to deal with unexpected emergencies. With both pilots in the cockpit boasting about 20,000 hours of total flight time, Captain Sullenberger said, "Teamwork and experience allowed us to focus on the high priorities without referring to written checklists."[1]

The story about the hero pilot "Sully" illustrates several of the key topics about differences among people to be described in

Objectives

After reading and studying this chapter and doing the exercises, you should be able to

1. Make adjustments for the individual differences among people in dealing with them on the job.
2. Develop insight into how your personality, mental ability, emotional intelligence, and values differ from others.
3. Respond to personality differences among people.
4. Respond to mental ability differences among people.
5. Respond to differences in values among people.

this chapter. Native intelligence including the capacity to memorize details, practical intelligence (wisdom and common sense), and emotional control all play an important role in job performance. The major theme of this chapter deals with how people vary in a wide range of personal factors. **Individual differences** exert a profound effect on job performance and behavior. Such differences refer to variations in how people respond to the same situation based on personal characteristics. One of hundreds of possible examples is that some people can concentrate longer and harder on their work, thereby producing more and higher quality work, than others.

This chapter describes several of the major sources of individual differences on the job. It also gives you the chance to measure your standing on several key dimensions of behavior and helps you develop skill in responding to individual differences. Knowing how to respond to such differences is the cornerstone of effective interpersonal relations. To be effective in human relations, you cannot treat everybody the same.

individual differences
Variations in how people respond to the same situation based on personal characteristics.

PERSONALITY

"We're not going to promote you to department head," said the manager to the analyst. "Although you are a great troubleshooter, you've alienated too many people in the company. You're too blunt and insensitive." As just implied, most successes and failures in people-contact jobs are attributed largely to interpersonal skills. And personality traits are major contributors to interpersonal, or human relations, skills.

Personality refers to those persistent and enduring behavior patterns and tend to be expressed in a wide variety of situations. A person who is brash and insensitive in one situation is likely to behave similarly in many other situations. Your personality is what makes you unique. Your walk, your talk, your appearance, your speech, and your inner values and conflicts all contribute to your personality.

Here, we illustrate the importance of personality to interpersonal relations in organizations by describing eight key personality traits and personality types related to cognitive styles. In addition, you will be given guidelines for dealing effectively with different personality types.

LEARNING OBJECTIVE 1

LEARNING OBJECTIVE 2

personality
Persistent and enduring behavior patterns that tend to be expressed in a wide variety of situations.

Eight Major Personality Factors and Traits

Many psychologists believe that the basic structure of human personality is represented by five broad factors, known as the Big Five: neuroticism, extraversion (the scientific spelling of *extroversion*), openness, agreeableness, and conscientiousness. Three more key personality factors—self-monitoring of behavior, risk taking and thrill seeking, and optimism—are so important for human relations that they are considered here.

All eight factors have a substantial impact on interpersonal relations and job performance. The interpretations and meanings of these factors provide useful information because they help you pinpoint important areas for personal development. Although these

FIGURE 2-1 Eight Personality Factors Related to Interpersonal Skills

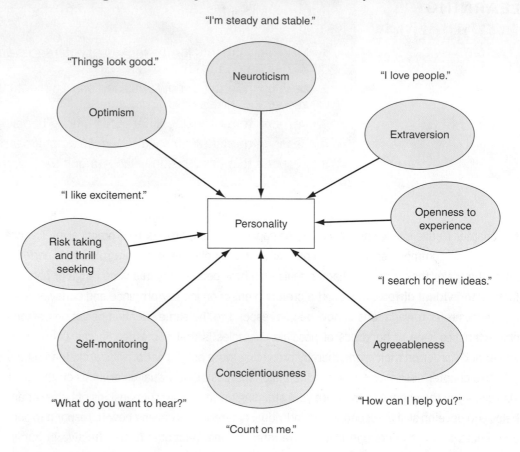

factors are partially inherited, most people can improve them providing they exert much conscious effort over a period of time. For example, it usually takes a minimum of three months of effort before a person is perceived to be more agreeable. The eight factors, shown in Figure 2-1, are described in the following list.

1. *Neuroticism* reflects emotional instability and identifies people prone to psychological distress and coping with problems in unproductive ways. Traits associated with this personality factor include being anxious, insecure, angry, embarrassed, emotional, and worried. A person of low neuroticism—or high emotional stability—is calm and confident, and usually in control.

2. *Extraversion* reflects the quantity or intensity of social interactions, the need for social stimulation, self-confidence, and competition. Traits associated with extraversion include being sociable, gregarious, assertive, talkative, and active. An outgoing person is often described as extraverted, whereas introverted persons are described as reserved, timid, and quiet.

3. *Openness* reflects the proactive seeking of experience for its own sake. Traits associated with openness include being creative, cultured, intellectually curious, broadminded, and artistically sensitive. People who score low on this personality factor are practical, with narrow interests.

4. *Agreeableness* reflects the quality of one's interpersonal orientation. Traits associated with the agreeableness factor include being courteous, flexible, trusting, good-natured, cooperative, forgiving, softhearted, and tolerant. The other end of the continuum includes disagreeable, cold, and antagonistic people.

5. *Conscientiousness* reflects organization, self-restraint, persistence, and motivation toward attaining goals. Traits associated with conscientiousness include being hardworking, dependable, well-organized, and thorough. The person low in conscientiousness is lazy, disorganized, and unreliable.

6. *Self-monitoring* of behavior refers to the process of observing and controlling how we are perceived by others. Self-monitoring involves three major and somewhat distinct tendencies: (1) the willingness to be the *center of attention*, (2) *sensitivity* to the reactions of others, and (3) ability and willingness to *adjust* behavior to induce positive reactions in others. High self-monitors are pragmatic and even chameleonlike actors in social groups. They often say what others want to hear. Low self-monitors avoid situations that require them to adapt to outer images. In this way, their outer behavior adheres to their inner values. Low self-monitoring can often lead to inflexibility. Take Self-Assessment Quiz 2-1 to measure your self-monitoring tendencies.

7. *Risk taking and thrill seeking* refers to the propensity to take risks and pursue thrills. Persons with high standing on this personality trait are sensation-seekers who pursue novel, intense, and complex sensations. They are willing to take risks for the sake of such experiences. The search for giant payoffs and daily thrills motivates people with an intense need for risk taking and thrill seeking.[2] Take Self-Assessment Quiz 2-2 to measure your propensity for risk taking and thrill seeking.

8. *Optimism* refers to a tendency to experience positive emotional states, and to typically believe that positive outcomes will be forthcoming from most activities. The other end of the scale is *pessimism*—a tendency to experience negative emotional states and to typically believe that negative outcomes will be forthcoming from most activities. Optimism versus pessimism is also referred to in more technical terms as positive affectivity versus negative affectivity, and is considered a major personality trait. A person's tendency toward having positive affectivity (optimism) versus negative affectivity (pessimism) also influences job satisfaction. Being optimistic, as you would suspect, tends to enhance job satisfaction.[3]

   A potential downside of optimism is that it can lead a person to not fear risks, such as the possibility of being fired for poor performance. Also, Martin Seligman, director of the Positive Psychology Center at the University of Pennsylvania, notes that bad things, such as getting lung cancer from smoking, do happen to optimists.[4]

Evidence for the relevance of the Big Five model (traits one through five of the previous list) of personality in understanding human behavior comes from a cross-cultural study involving 7,134 individuals. The five-factor structure of the American personality was also found to hold true for German, Portuguese, Hebrew, Chinese, Korean, and Japanese samples when the personality test questions were translated into each of these languages. Based on this extensive study, it was concluded that personality structure is universal, much like the structure of the brain or the body.[5]

Another reason the Big Five model is useful in understanding individual differences is that the five traits included contribute heavily to what is being measured by most personality tests. The evidence of the contribution of the Big Five traits stems from the self-ratings of the people taking the test as well as rating by persons who know the test take well.[6]

As already suggested, a high standing on a given trait is not always an advantage, and that having a low standing is not always a disadvantage.[7] For example, a person who is highly extraverted might spend so much time interacting with coworkers that he or she does not spend enough time on analytical work. Also, a person who is a low self-monitor might give people such honest feedback—rather than telling them what they want to hear—that he or she helps others grow and develop.

The Eight Factors and Traits and Job Performance

Depending on the job, any one of the preceding personality factors can be important for success. One explanation for personality being tied to performance is that a particular personality trait gives us a bias or positive spin to certain actions.[8] A person high in conscientiousness, for example, believes that if people are diligent they will accomplish more

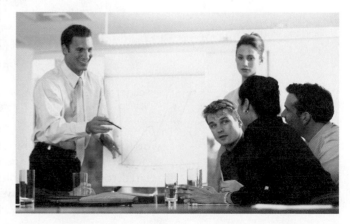

The Self-Monitoring Scale

Directions: The statements below concern your personal reactions to a number of different situations. No two statements are exactly alike, so consider each statement carefully before answering. IF a statement is TRUE or MOSTLY TRUE as applied to you, **circle the "T"** next to the question. If a statement is FALSE or NOT USUALLY TRUE as applied to you, **circle the "F"** next to the question.

(T) (F) 1. I find it hard to imitate the behavior of other people.

(T) (F) 2. My behavior is usually an expression of my true inner feelings, attitudes, and beliefs.

(T) (F) 3. At parties and social gatherings, I do not attempt to do or say things that others will like.

(T) (F) 4. I can only argue for ideas that I already believe.

(T) (F) 5. I can make impromptu speeches even on topics about which I have almost no information.

(T) (F) 6. I guess I put on a show to impress or entertain people.

(T) (F) 7. When I am uncertain how to act in a social situation, I look to the behavior of others for cues.

(T) (F) 8. I would probably make a good actor.

(T) (F) 9. I rarely seek the advice of my friends to choose movies, books, or music.

(T) (F) 10. I sometimes appear to others to be experiencing deeper emotions than I actually am.

(T) (F) 11. I laugh more when I watch a comedy with others than when alone.

(T) (F) 12. In groups of people, I am rarely the center of attention.

(T) (F) 13. In different situations and with different people, I often act like very different persons.

(T) (F) 14. I am not particularly good at making other people like me.

(T) (F) 15. Even if I am not enjoying myself, I often pretend to be having a good time.

(T) (F) 16. I'm not always the person I appear to be.

(T) (F) 17. I would not change my opinions (or the way I do things) in order to please someone else or win their favor.

(T) (F) 18. I have considered being an entertainer.

(T) (F) 19. In order to get along and be liked, I tend to be what people expect me to be rather than anything else.

(T) (F) 20. I have never been good at games like charades or improvisational acting.

(T) (F) 21. I have trouble changing my behavior to suit different people and different situations.

(T) (F) 22. At a party, I let others keep the jokes and stories going.

(T) (F) 23. I feel a bit awkward in company and do not show up quite as well as I should.

(T) (F) 24. I can look anyone in the eye and tell a lie with a straight face (if for a right end).

(T) (F) 25. I may deceive people by being friendly when I really dislike them.

Scoring and Interpretation: Give yourself one point each time your answer agrees with the key. A score that is between 0–12 would indicate that you are a relatively low self-monitor; a score that is between 13–25 would indicate that you are relatively high self-monitor.

1. F	10. T	19. T
2. F	11. T	20. F
3. F	12. F	21. F
4. F	13. T	22. F
5. T	14. F	23. F
6. T	15. T	24. T
7. T	16. T	25. T
8. T	17. F	
9. F	18. T	

Source: Mark Snyder, "Self-Monitoring of Expressive Behavior, *Journal of Personality and Social Psychology,* Number 4, October 1974, pp. 528–537.

work and receive just rewards. Conscientiousness relates to job performance for many different occupations, and has proven to be the personality factor most consistently related to success. As explained in the discussion above, each of the Big Five factors is composed of more narrow or specific traits. With respect to conscientiousness, the specific trait of *dependability* may be the most important contributor to job performance.[9]

The Risk-Taking Scale

Directions: Answer true or false to the following questions to obtain an approximate idea of your tendency to take risks, or your desire to do so:

	True	False
1. I eat sushi or other raw fish.	☐	☐
2. I think that amusement park roller coasters should be abolished.	☐	☐
3. I don't like trying foods from other cultures.	☐	☐
4. I would choose bonds over growth stocks.	☐	☐
5. I like to challenge people in positions of power.	☐	☐
6. I don't always wear a seat belt while driving.	☐	☐
7. I sometimes talk on my cell phone or send text messages while driving at highway speeds.	☐	☐
8. I would love to be an entrepreneur (or I love being one).	☐	☐
9. I would like helping out in a crisis such as a product recall.	☐	☐
10. I would like to go cave exploring (or already have done so).	☐	☐
11. I would be willing to have at least one-third of my compensation based on a bonus for good performance.	☐	☐
12. I would be willing to visit a maximum security prison on a job assignment.	☐	☐

Scoring and Interpretation: Give yourself one point each time your answer agrees with the key. If you score 10–12, you are probably a high risk taker; 6–9, you are a moderate risk taker; 3–5, you are cautious; 0–2, you are a very low risk taker.

1. T	5. T	9. T
2. F	6. T	10. T
3. F	7. T	11. T
4. F	8. T	12. T

Source: The idea of a test about risk-taking comfort, as well as several of the statements on the quiz, comes from psychologist Frank Farley.

Extraversion and Self-Monitoring. Another important research finding is that extraversion is associated with success for managers and sales representatives. The explanation is that managers and salespeople are required to interact extensively with other people.[10] For people who want to advance in their careers, being a high self-monitor is important. An analysis was made of the self-monitoring personality by combining 136 studies involving 23,101 people. A major finding was that high self-monitors tend to receive better performance ratings than low self-monitors. High self-monitors were also more likely to emerge as leaders and work their way into top management positions.[11] Another advantage to being a high self-monitor is that the individual is more likely to help out other workers, even when not required. An example would be helping a worker outside your department with a currency exchange problem even though this was not your responsibility. Self-monitors are also much more likely to *click* with other workers and to succeed in the workplace. The "clicking" may lead to good relationships which facilitate performing well.[12]

Organizational Citizenship Behavior. The willingness to go beyond one's job description without a specific reward apparent is referred to as **organizational citizenship behavior.** (We mention organizational citizenship behavior here because it is linked to other traits, particularly agreeableness and conscientiousness.) Good organizational citizens are highly valued by employers. An analysis of studies based on a total of more than 50,000 employees highlights the importance of organizational citizenship behavior in understanding how a willingness to help others contributes to both individual and organizational success.

organizational citizenship behavior

The willingness to go beyond one's job description without a specific reward apparent.

Among the findings were that being a good organizational citizen leads to better performance ratings by supervisors, higher salary increases, and less turnover and absenteeism. Organizational citizenship behavior also contributes to higher productivity, reduced costs, and better customer satisfaction.[13]

Another perspective on organizational citizenship behavior is that an employee will make a short-term sacrifice that leads to long-term benefits to the organization.[14] An example would be an employee voluntarily working from home to deal with customer confusion about a product recall, which would lead to more loyal and appreciative customers.

Turnover and Personality. A recent synthesis of studies suggests that personality can be linked to turnover. Employees who are emotionally stable are less likely to plan to quit, or to actually quit. Employees who score higher on the traits of conscientiousness and agreeableness are less likely to leave voluntarily. Another finding of note is that workers who are low on agreeableness and high on openness to experience are likely to quit spontaneously.[15] (Maybe the grouchy, intellectually curious employee may jump on a sudden opportunity for another job.)

Optimism and Pessimism. Optimism and pessimism also can be linked to job performance. Optimism can be quite helpful when attempting such tasks as selling a product or service or motivating a group of people. Yet psychologist Julie Normen has gathered considerable evidence that pessimism can sometimes enhance job performance. Pessimists usually assume that something will go wrong, and will carefully prepare to prevent botches and bad luck. A pessimist, for example, will carefully back up computer files or plan for emergencies that might shut down operations.[16]

Combination of Standing on Several Personality Traits. A combination of personality factors will sometimes be more closely associated with job success than one factor alone. A study about personality and job performance ratings was conducted with diverse occupations including clerical workers and wholesale appliance sales representatives. A key finding was that conscientious workers who also scored high on agreeableness performed better than conscientious workers who were less agreeable.[17] (Being agreeable toward your manager helps elevate performance evaluations!) A study with experienced pharmaceutical sales representatives found that the combination of extraversion and conscientiousness was associated with higher sales. However, being conscientious was the personality factor most closely associated with growth in sales over several years for the experienced sales representatives.[18]

Personality Types and Cognitive Styles

People go about solving problems in various ways. You may have observed, for example, that some people are more analytical and systematic while others are more intuitive. Modes of problem solving are referred to as **cognitive styles**. According to this method of understanding problem-solving styles, your personality traits influence strongly how you approach problems, such as being introverted pointing you toward dealing with ideas. Knowledge of these cognitive styles can help you relate better to people because you can better appreciate how they make decisions.

cognitive styles

Mental processes used to perceive and make judgments from situations.

One of the best-known methods of measuring personality types is the Myers-Briggs Type Indicator (MBTI®), a self-report questionnaire designed to make the theory of psychological types developed by psychoanalyst Carl Jung applicable to everyday life.[19] Another leading method of measuring types is the Golden Personality Type Profiler.[20] Jung developed the theory of psychological types, but did not develop the two measuring instruments just developed.

As measured by the Golden instrument, four separate dichotomies direct the typical use of perception and judgment by an individual. The four dichotomies can also be considered a person's cognitive style.[21]

1. **Energy flow: Extraversion versus introversion.** Extraverts direct their energy primarily toward the outer world of people and objects. In contrast, introverts direct their energy primarily toward the inner world of experiences and ideas.

2. **Information gathering: Sensation versus intuition.** People who rely on sensing focus primarily on what can be perceived by the five primary senses of touch, sight, sound, smell, and taste. People who rely on intuition focus primarily on perceiving patterns and interrelationships.

3. **Decision making: Thinking versus feeling.** People who rely primarily on thinking base conclusions on logical analysis and emphasize objectivity and detachment. People who rely on feelings base conclusions on personal or social values, and focus on understanding and harmony.

4. **Lifestyle orientation: Judging versus perceiving.** Individuals high on Judging tend to orient their lives in a deliberate and planned manner. Individuals high on perceiving tend to orient their lives in a spontaneous and open-ended manner.

Combining the four types with each other results in 16 personality types, such as the ESFP, or "The Entertainer." ESFP refers to extraverted/sensing/feeling/perceiving. It is believed that approximately 13 percent of the population can be classified as the ESFP type. People of this type are optimistic, and are skilled at living joyfully and entertaining others. ESFPs are effective at communicating their good-natured realism to others.

You might want to take the Golden Personality Type Profiler (see the Appendix to this book). Here our concern is with how your personality influences your learning style. Figure 2-2 presents 4 of the 16 personality types along with the implications for each one with respect to cognitive style.

FIGURE 2-2 Four Cognitive Styles of the Golden Personality Types

Personality Type	Highlights of Type
ENFP (The Proponent) Extraverted/ iNtuitive/Feeling/Perceiving	Lives continually in the realm of the possible. When absorbed in their latest project, they think of little else. Filled with energy, they are tireless in their pursuit of goals. Have an almost magnetic quality that enables them to have fun in almost any setting. The combination of Extraversion, Intuition, and Perceiving is well suited for leadership.
ENFJ (The Communicator) Extraverted/ iNtuitive/Feeling/Judging	Chief concern is fostering harmony and cooperation between self and others. Has strong ideals and a potent sense of loyalty, whether to a mate, a school, a hometown, or a favorite cause. Usually good at organizing people to get things done while keeping everyone happy. At work, well armed to deal with both variety and action. Typically patient and conscientious, make a concerted effort of sticking with a job until finished.
INFP (The Advocate) Introverted/ iNtuitive/Feeling/Perceiving	Capable of immense sensitivity and has an enormous emotional capacity that is guarded closely. Has to know people well before displaying warmth, letting down the guard, and displaying warmth. Interpersonal relationships are a crucial focus. Has powerful sense of faithfulness, duty, and commitment to the people and causes he or she is attracted to. Able to express emotion and move people through his or her communication. A perfectionist on the job. Prefers a quiet working environment and, despite attraction for human companionship, will often work best alone. Will work at best only in job he or she truly believes in.
INFJ (The Foreseer) Introverted/ iNtuitive/Feeling/Judging	Imaginative, inspired, tenacious, creative, and inward looking. Also stubborn, easily bored by routine work, and often pays little attention to obstacles. Makes decisions easily. Lives in a world of ideas, and will have a unique vision. Pours all own energy into achieving his or her goal. Trusts own intuition. Can express emotion and move people through written communication. Although cherishes the companionship of people, prefers a quiet working environment, and working alone. Perfectionist about quality. Creativity is his or her hallmark.

Code: E = Extraverted, N = iNtuitive, F = Feeling, P = Perceiving, I = Introverted, J = Judging

Source: Karen A. Deitz and John P. Golden, *Boundless Diversity: An Introduction to the Golden Personality Type Profiler* (San Antonio, Texas: Pearson TalentLens, 2004).

Far too many people perceive personality types as being definitive indicators of an individual's personality and therefore think they know exactly how to classify that person in terms of personality. The developers of the Golden point out that the instrument is an accurate and dependable measure of the aspects of personality measured. However, it is up to the person taking the Golden to determine if the report's description of him or her is accurate.[22] If the results are completely out of line with what you believe to be true about yourself, or what others have told you about your personality type, the results of the Golden (or other type indicator) should not be a cause for concern.

An interpersonal skills application of understanding the Golden personality types is to help people get along better within a work group. All the group or team members would have their types assessed using the Golden instrument, and all members would be made aware of each other's type or working style. Knowing your type among the 16 types and the type of the other group members would give you some clues for working smoothly together.

To illustrate, I will use a couple of the types shown in Figure 2-2. Visualize yourself as a member of a work group. You know that Nick is a forseer (INFJ). The group has an assignment that calls for creating something new, so you consult with Nick to capitalize on his imaginative thinking, determination to attain goals, and fine written communication skills. Yet you know that you and Margot are proponents (ENFP), so you two will play a heavy role in helping translate Nick's plan into action. And, you, Nick, and Margot know that Jason is an advocate (INFP), so you will have to work slowly with him to get him to believe in the new project so that he can make good use of his tendencies toward perfectionism. You will also not discourage Jason from spending some time working alone, so he can be at his best.

Guidelines for Dealing with Different Personality Types

LEARNING OBJECTIVE 3

A key purpose in presenting information about a sampling of various personality types is to provide guidelines for individualizing your approach to people. As a basic example, if you wanted to score points with an introvert, you would approach that person in a restrained, laid-back fashion. In contrast, a more gregarious, lighthearted approach might be more effective with an extravert. The purpose of individualizing your approach is to build a better working relationship or to establish rapport with the other person. To match your approach to dealing with a given personality type, you must first arrive at an approximate diagnosis of the individual's personality. The following suggestions are therefore restricted to readily observable aspects of personality:

1. When relating to a person who appears to be neurotic based on symptoms of worry and tension, be laid back and reassuring. Attempt not to project your own anxiety and fears. Be a good listener. If possible, minimize the emphasis on deadlines and the dire consequences of a project's failing. Show concern and interest in the person's welfare.

2. When relating to an extraverted individual, emphasize friendliness, warmth, and a stream of chatter. Talk about people more than ideas, things, or data. Express an interest in a continuing working relationship.

3. When relating to an introverted individual, move slowly in forming a working relationship. Do not confuse quietness with a lack of interest. Tolerate moments of silence. Emphasize ideas, things, and data more heavily than people.

4. When relating to a person who is open to experience, emphasize information sharing, idea generation, and creative approaches to problems. Appeal to his or her intellect by discussing topics of substance rather than ordinary chatter and gossip.

5. When relating to a person who is closed to experience, stick closely to the facts of the situation at hand. Recognize that the person prefers to think small and deal with the here and now.

6. When relating to an agreeable person, just relax and be yourself. Reciprocate with kindness to sustain a potentially excellent working relationship.

7. When relating to a disagreeable person, be patient and tolerant. At the same time, set limits on how much mistreatment you will take. Disagreeable people sometimes secretly want others to put brakes on their antisocial behavior.

8. When relating to a conscientious person, give him or her freedom and do not nag. The person will probably honor commitments without prompting. Conscientious people are often taken for granted, so remember to acknowledge the person's dependability.

9. When relating to a person of low conscientiousness, keep close tabs on him or her especially if you need the person's output to do your job. Do not assume that because the person has an honest face and a pleasing smile he or she will deliver as promised. Frequently follow up on your requests, and impose deadlines if you have the authority. Express deep appreciation when the person does follow through.

10. When dealing with a person whom you suspect is a high self-monitor, be cautious in thinking that the person is really in support of your position. The person could just be following his or her natural tendency to appear to please others, but not really feel that way.

11. When relating to a person with a high propensity for risk taking and thrill seeking, emphasize the risky and daring aspects of activities familiar to you. Talk about a new product introduction in a highly competitive market, stock options, investment in high-technology startup firms, skydiving, and race car driving.

12. When relating to a person with a low propensity for risk taking and thrill seeking, emphasize the safe and secure aspects of activities familiar to you. Talk about the success of an established product in a stable market (like pencils and paperclips), investment in U.S. Treasury bonds, life insurance, camping, and gardening.

13. When dealing with a sensation type of information gatherer, emphasize facts, figures, and conventional thinking without sacrificing your own values. To convince the sensation type, emphasize logic more than emotional appeal. Focus on details more than the big picture.

14. When dealing with an intuition type of information gatherer, emphasize feelings, judgments, playing with ideas, imagination, and creativity. Focus more on the big picture than details.

To start putting these guidelines into practice, do the role plays in Skill-Building Exercise 2-1. Remember that a role-player is an extemporaneous actor. Put yourself in the shoes of the character you play and visualize how he or she would act. Because you are given only the general idea of a script, use your imagination to fill in the details.

SKILL-BUILDING EXERCISE 2-1

Personality Role-Plays

The Extravert: One student assumes the role of a successful outside sales representative who has just signed a $3 million order for the company. The sales rep comes back to the office elated. The other student assumes the role of a member of the office support staff. He or she decides this is a splendid opportunity to build a good relationship with the triumphant sales rep. Run the role-play for about seven minutes. The people not involved in the role-play will observe and then provide feedback when the role-play is completed. (These directions regarding time, observation, and feedback also apply to the two other role-plays in this exercise and throughout the book.)

Openness: One student plays the role of an experienced worker in the department who is told to spend some time orienting a new co-op student or intern. It appears that this new person is open to experience. Another student plays the role of the co-op student who is open to experience and eager to be successful in this new position.

Organizational Citizenship Behavior: One student plays the role of a strong organizational citizen who wants to help other people, going beyond what is found in his or her job description. The strong organizational citizen is thinking, "What can I do today to help somebody?" As the student walks down the row of cubicles, he or she spots a person who is staring at the computer with an agonized, perplexed look. The good organizational citizen thinks, "Maybe here is a good opening to be useful today." The other student plays the role of the perplexed worker who might need help with a specific problem facing him or her at the moment.

For the three scenarios, observers rate the role players on two dimensions, using a 1-to-5 scale from very poor to very good. One dimension is "effective use of human relations techniques." The second dimension is "acting ability." A few observers might voluntarily provide feedback to the role players in terms of sharing their ratings and observations. The course instructor might also provide feedback.

COGNITIVE ABILITY

Cognitive ability (also referred to as mental ability or intelligence) is one of the major sources of individual differences that affects job performance and behavior. **Intelligence** is the capacity to acquire and apply knowledge, including solving problems. Intelligent workers can best solve abstract problems. In an exceedingly simple job, such as packing shoes into boxes, having below-average intelligence can be an advantage because the employee is not likely to become bored.

Understanding the nature of intelligence contributes to effective interpersonal relations in the workplace. Your evaluation of a person's intelligence can influence how you relate to that person. For example, if you think a person is intelligent, you will tend to seek his or her input on a difficult problem. If you realize that different types of intelligence exist, you are more likely to appreciate people's strengths. You are thus less likely to judge others as being either good or poor problem solvers.

Four important aspects of cognitive ability include (1) the components of traditional intelligence, (2) practical intelligence, (3) multiple intelligences, and (4) emotional intelligence. (This fourth type of intelligence can also be regarded as personality, not cognitive ability.) Knowledge of the four aspects will enrich your understanding of other workers and yourself.

Components of Traditional Intelligence

Intelligence consists of more than one component. A component of intelligence is much like a separate mental aptitude. Evidence suggests that intelligence consists of a *g* (general) factor and *s* (special) factors that contribute to problem-solving ability. Scores of tests of almost any type (such as math, aptitude for spatial relations, or reading skill) are somewhat influenced by the *g* factor. The *g* factor helps explain why some people perform well in so many different mental tasks. Substantial evidence has accumulated over the years that workers with high intelligence tend to perform better. The relationship between *g* and job performance is likely to be strongest for those aspects of jobs involving thinking and knowledge, such as problem solving and technical expertise.[23]

Over the years, various investigators have arrived at different special factors contributing to overall mental aptitude. The following seven factors have been identified consistently:

1. **Verbal comprehension.** The ability to understand the meaning of words and their relationship to each other and to comprehend written and spoken information.
2. **Word fluency.** The ability to use words quickly and easily, without an emphasis on verbal comprehension.
3. **Numerical acuity.** The ability to handle numbers, engage in mathematical analysis, and to do arithmetic calculations.
4. **Spatial perception.** The ability to visualize forms in space and manipulate objects mentally, particularly in three dimensions.
5. **Memory.** Having a good rote memory for symbols, words, and lists of numbers, along with other associations.
6. **Perceptual speed.** The ability to perceive visual details, to pick out similarities and differences, and to perform tasks requiring visual perception.
7. **Inductive reasoning.** The ability to discover a rule or principle and apply it in solving a problem and to make judgments and decisions that are logically sound.

Being strong in any of the preceding mental aptitudes often leads to an enjoyment of work associated with that aptitude. The reverse can also be true: enjoying a type of mental activity might lead to the development of an aptitude for the activity.

Attempts to improve cognitive skills, or intelligence, have become an entire industry, including both brain-stimulating exercises and food supplements. Common wisdom suggests that staying in shape mentally by such activities as doing crossword puzzles, surfing the Internet, or studying a foreign language can slow the decline of an aging brain. Brain-imaging studies support the idea that mental workouts help preserve **cognitive fitness,** a state of optimized ability to remember, learn, plan, and adapt to changing circumstances. Acquiring expertise in such diverse areas as playing a cello, juggling, speaking a foreign language, and playing video games and computer games expands your neural systems and helps them communicate with one another. This means that by learning new skills you can alter the physical makeup of the brain even in later life. Engaging in play also enhances brain functioning that helps explain the link between creativity and play.[24]

The contribution of food supplements to enhancing or maintain in cognitive ability is debatable. For example, a study published in the *Journal of the American Medical Association* found that ginko biloba, a widely used supplement for improving memory, does not appear to delay or prevent the onset of demential in elderly adults.[25] Nevertheless, a balanced, healthy diet contributes to the propering functioning of the brain as well as any other organ of the body.

Practical Intelligence

Many people, including psychologists, are concerned that the traditional way of understanding intelligence inadequately describes mental ability. An unfortunate implication of intelligence testing is that intelligence as traditionally calculated is largely the ability to perform tasks related to scholastic work. Thus, a person who scored very high on an intelligence test could follow a complicated instruction manual, but might not be street smart.

To overcome the limited idea that intelligence mostly involves the ability to solve abstract problems, the **triarchic theory of intelligence** has been proposed.[26] See Figure 2-3. The theory holds that intelligence is composed of three different subtypes: analytical, creative, and practical. The *analytical* subtype is the traditional intelligence needed for solving difficult problems. Analytical intelligence is required to perform well in most school subjects. The *creative* subtype is the type of intelligence required for imagination and combining things in novel ways. The *practical* subtype is the type of intelligence required for adapting your environment to suit your needs. The idea of practical intelligence helps explain why a person who has a difficult time getting through school can still be a successful businessperson, politician, or athlete. Practical intelligence incorporates the ideas of common sense, wisdom, and street smarts.

A person with high practical intelligence would also have good **intuition**, an experience based way of knowing or reasoning in which the weighing and balancing of evidence are

triarchic theory of intelligence

An explanation of mental ability holding that intelligence is composed of three different subtypes: analytical, creative, and practical.

intuition

An experience-based way of knowing or reasoning in which the weighing and balancing of evidence are done automatically.

FIGURE 2-3   The Triarchic Theory of Intelligence

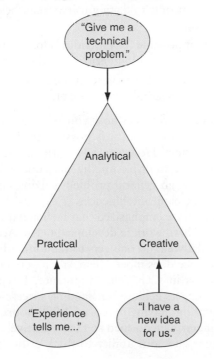

done automatically. Examples of good intuition include a merchandiser who develops a hunch that a particular style will be hot next season, a basketball coach who sees the possibilities in a gangly youngster, and a supervisor who has a hunch that a neighbor would be a great fit for her department. Intuition is also required for creative intelligence.

An important implication of practical intelligence is that experience is helpful in developing intellectual skills and judgment. At younger ages, raw intellectual ability such as required for learning information technology skills may be strongest. However, judgment and wisdom are likely to be stronger with accumulated experience. This is why people in the forties and older are more likely to be chosen for position such as the CEO of a large business or a commercial airline pilot. Poor judgment is *sometimes* associated with inexperience and youth, and the frequent impulsiveness of young people is often referred to as the *teenage brain*.

One major reservation some have about practical intelligence is the implication that people who are highly intelligent in the traditional sense are not practical thinkers. In truth, most executives and other high-level workers score quite well on tests of mental ability. These tests usually measure analytical intelligence.

Multiple Intelligences

Another approach to understanding the diverse nature of mental ability is the theory of **multiple intelligences**. According to Howard Gardner, people know and understand the world in distinctly different ways and learn in different ways. Individuals possess the following eight intelligences, or faculties, in varying degrees:

1. **Linguistic.** Enables people to communicate through language, including reading, writing, and speaking.
2. **Logical-mathematical.** Enables individuals to see relationships between objects and solve problems, as in calculus and statistics.
3. **Musical.** Gives people the capacity to create and understand meanings made out of sounds and to enjoy different types of music.
4. **Spatial.** Enables people to perceive and manipulate images in the brain and to recreate them from memory, as is required in making graphic designs.
5. **Bodily kinesthetic.** Enables people to use their body and perceptual and motor systems in skilled ways such as dancing, playing sports, and expressing emotion through facial expressions.
6. **Intrapersonal.** Enables people to distinguish among their own feelings and acquire accurate self-knowledge.
7. **Interpersonal.** Makes it possible for individuals to recognize and make distinctions among the feelings, motives, and intentions of others as in managing or parenting.
8. **Naturalist.** Enables individuals to differentiate among, classify, and utilize various features of the physical external environment.

Your profile of intelligences influences how you best learn and to which types of jobs you are best suited. Gardner believes that it is possible to develop these separate intelligences through concentrated effort. However, any of these intelligences might fade if not put to use.[27] The components of multiple intelligences might also be perceived as different talents or abilities. Having high general problem-solving ability (*g*) would contribute to high standing on each of the eight intelligences.

Two books in recent years have emphasized that having natural abilities of the type just described is not as important as hard work in developing talent. According to the 10,000-hour rule proposed by Malcolm Gladwell, no one gets to the top without 10,000 hours of practice in a field.[28] Guided practice does indeed help, but a person still needs some basic talent to attain high-level success in such fields as finance, foreign languages, and sports. Recognize also that many teenagers achieve outstanding success in information technology, science, sports, and music without having practiced 1,000 hours per year for 10 years.

The three types of intelligence mentioned so far (cognitive, practical, and multiple) all contribute to but do not guarantee our ability to think critically. Critical thinking is the process of evaluating evidence, and then based on this evaluation, making judgments and decisions. Through critical thinking, we find reasons to support or reject an argument.[29] Personality factors contribute heavily to whether we choose to use the various types of intelligence. For example, the personality factor of openness facilitates critical thinking because the individual enjoys gathering evidence to support or refute an idea. Also, conscientiousness also facilitates critical thinking because the individual feels compelled to gather more facts and think harder.[30]

Emotional Intelligence

How effectively people use their emotions has a major impact on their success. **Emotional intelligence** refers to qualities such as understanding one's own feelings, having empathy for others, and regulating one's emotion to enhance living. The intelligence aspect focuses on the ability to engage in complex information processing about your own emotions and those of others. At the same time you use this information as a guide to thinking and behavior.[31] A person with high emotional intelligence would be able to engage in such behaviors as sizing up people, pleasing others, and influencing them. Four key factors included in emotional intelligence are as follows:[32]

emotional intelligence

Qualities such as understanding one's own feelings, empathy for others, and the regulation of emotion to enhance living.

1. **Self-awareness.** The ability to understand your moods, emotions, and needs as well as their impact on others. Self-awareness also includes using intuition to make decisions you can live with happily. A person with good self-awareness knows whether he or she is pushing other people too far. Imagine that Amanda is an assistant to the food service manager at a financial services company. Amanda believes strongly that the cafeteria should ensure that no food served on company premises contains trans-fats. However, the food services manager seems lukewarm to the idea. So instead of badgering the manager, Amanda decides to fight her battle bit by bit by presenting facts and reminders in a friendly way. Eventually, the manager agrees to have a meeting on the subject with a nutritionist invited. So Amanda's self-awareness has paid off.

2. **Self-management.** The ability to control one's emotions and act with honesty and integrity in a consistent and acceptable manner. The right degree of self-management helps prevent a person from throwing temper tantrums when activities do not go as planned. Effective workers do not let their occasional bad moods ruin their day. If they cannot overcome the bad mood, they let coworkers know of their problem and how long it might last. A person with low self-management would suddenly decide to drop a project because the work was frustrating.

   Imagine that Jack is an assistant to the export sales manager, and today is a big day because a company in Russia appears ready to make a giant purchase. The export sales manager says, "Today we need peak performance from everybody. If we nail down this sale, we will exceed our sales quota for the year." Unfortunately, Jack is in a grim mood. His favorite NFL team was eliminated from the playoffs the night before, and his dog has been diagnosed as having a torn abdominal muscle. Jack would like to lash out in anger against everybody he meets today, but instead he focuses his energy on getting the job done, and does not let his personal problems show through.

3. **Social awareness.** Includes having empathy for others and having intuition about work problems. A team leader with social awareness, or empathy, would be able to assess whether a team member has enough enthusiasm for a project to assign him to that project. Another facet of social skill is the ability to interpret nonverbal communication, such as frowns and types of smiles.[33] A supervisor with social awareness, or empathy, would take into account the most likely reaction of group members before making a decision affecting them.

   Imagine that Cindy has been working as an assistant purchasing manager for six months. Company policy prohibits accepting "lavish" gifts from vendors or potential vendors attempting to sell the company goods or services. Cindy has been placed in charge of purchasing all paper toweling for the company. Although most of the purchasing is made over the Internet, sales representatives still make the occasional call. The rep from the paper towel company asks Cindy if she would like an iPhone as a token gift for even considering his company. Cindy badly wants an iPhone, and it is not yet in her budget. After thinking through the potential gift for five minutes, Cindy decides to refuse. Perhaps an iPhone is not really a lavish gift, but her intuition tells her it would look to be a conflict of interest if she accepted the iPhone.

4. **Relationship management.** Includes the interpersonal skills of being able to communicate clearly and convincingly, disarm conflicts, and build strong personal bonds. Effective workers use relationship management skills to spread their enthusiasm and solve disagreements, often with kindness and humor. A worker with relationship management skill would use a method of persuasion that is likely to work well with a particular group or individual. A study showed that emotional intelligence is closely related to the evaluation by a superior of a manager's interpersonal behaviors. The specific skills noted were "guides, mentors, and develops people," and "someone who communicates clearly."[34]

Much of this book is about relationship management, but here is yet another example. Donte is an information technology specialist. His assignment for the first six months is to visit users at their workplace to help then with any IT problems they might be experiencing. In discussing his role with his supervisor, Donte begins to realize that helping with technical problems is not his only job. He is an ambassador of good will for the IT department. He and his manager want to build a network of support for the efforts of the department. So when Donte visits the various departments, he is courteous and friendly, and asks about how an IT rep could make work easier for the person in question.

Emotional intelligence thus incorporates many of the skills and attitudes necessary to achieve effective interpersonal relations in organizations. Most of the topics in this book, such as resolving conflict, helping others develop, and possessing positive political skills, would be included in emotional intelligence. It is therefore reasonable to regard emotional intelligence as being a mixture of cognitive skills and personality.

BACK TO THE OPENING CASE

The heroics of Captain Sullenberger have been reported in thousands of places. As he viewed the situation, he and his crew were just doing their job of responding well to a high-pressure, life-or-death situation. Here we want to emphasize one of "Sully's" traits that has not received much attention. Sullenberger, the copilot Skiles, and the flight attendants all displayed high emotional stability, enabling them to prevent a total airline disaster. In addition to personality factors, Sullenberger's lengthy experience was an enormous asset when he faced an extraordinarily high-pressure situation. Sullenberger had logged 19,000 hours of flight time spread out over 40 years.

Guidelines for Relating to People of Different Levels and Types of Intelligence

LEARNING OBJECTIVE 4 Certainly you cannot expect to administer mental ability and emotional intelligence tests to all your work associates, gather their scores, and then relate to associates differently based on their scores. Yet it is possible to intuitively develop a sense for the mental quickness of people and the types of mental tasks they perform best. For example, managers must make judgments about mental ability in selecting people for jobs and assigning them to tasks. Following are several guidelines worth considering for enhancing your working relationships with others.

1. If you perceive another worker (your manager included) to have high cognitive skill, present your ideas in technical depth. Incorporate difficult words into your conversation and reports. Ask the person challenging questions.

2. If you perceive another worker to have low cognitive skill, present your ideas with a minimum of technical depth. Use a basic vocabulary, without going so far as to be patronizing. Ask for frequent feedback about having been clear. If you have supervisory responsibility for a person who appears to be below average in intelligence, give the person the opportunity to repeat the same type of task rather than switching assignments frequently.

3. If you perceive a work associate to relish crunching numbers, use quantitative information when attempting to persuade that person. Instead of using phrases such as "most people," say "about 65 percent of people."

4. If you perceive a work associate to have high creative intelligence, solicit his or her input on problems requiring a creative solution. Use statements such as "Here's a problem that requires a sharp, creative mind, so I've come to you."

5. If you perceive a work associate to have low emotional intelligence, explain your feelings and attitudes clearly. Make an occasional statement such as "How I feel about his situation is quite important" to emphasize the emotional aspect. The person may not get the point of hints and indirect expressions.

To start putting these guidelines into practice, do the role-plays in Skill-Building Exercises 2-2 and 2-3.

VALUES AS A SOURCE OF INDIVIDUAL DIFFERENCES

Another group of factors influencing how a person behaves on the job is that person's values and beliefs. A **value** refers to the importance a person attaches to something. Values are also tied to the enduring belief that one's mode of conduct is better than another mode of conduct. If you believe that good interpersonal relations are the most important part of your life, your humanistic values are strong. Similarly, you may think that people who are not highly concerned about interpersonal relations have poor values.

Values are closely tied in with **ethics,** or the moral choices a person makes. A person's values influence which kinds of behaviors he or she believes are ethical. Ethics convert

value

The importance a person attaches to something.

ethics

The moral choices a person makes. Also, what is good and bad, right and wrong, just and unjust, and what people should do.

values into action. An executive who strongly values profits might not find it unethical to raise prices higher than needed to cover additional costs. Another executive who strongly values family life might suggest that the company invest money in an on-site childcare center. Ethics is such an important part of interpersonal relations in organizations that the topic receives separate mention in Chapter 15.

Classification of Values

An almost automatic response to classifying values is that people have either good or bad values, with bad values meaning those that are quite different than yours. To the person with a strong work ethic, an individual who took a casual approach to work might have "bad values." To the person with a weak work ethic, the person who was work obsessed might have "bad values." Shalom H. Schwartz, a professor from the Hebrew University of Jerusalem, has developed a particularly useful method of classifying values because it points to how we establish goals to fit our values.[35] For example, as shown in Table 2-1, people who value power are likely to set the goals of attaining power, strength, and control. And those who value benevolence are likely to establish the goals of being kind, charitable, and showing respect for others. The link between values and goals has extensive research support.

Generational Differences in Values

Differences in values among people often stem from age, or generational, differences. Workers above 50 years of age, in general, may have different values than people who are much younger. These age differences in values have often been seen as a clash between Baby Boomers and members of Generation X and Generation Y. The category of Baby Boomers is so broad that part of the Baby Boomer generation is said to include Generation Jones, the younger boomers born between 1954 and 1964. This group comprises one-fourth of the U.S. population. Members of Generation Jones are typically entering the peak of their careers, and are not yet thinking much about retirement.[36]

According to the stereotype, Boomers see Generation Xers and Yers as disrespectful of rules, not willing to pay their dues, and being disloyal to employers. Generation Xers and Yers see Boomers as worshipping hierarchy (layers of authority), being overcautious, and wanting to preserve the status quo.

Table 2-2 summarizes these stereotypes with the understanding that massive group stereotypes like this are only partially accurate because there are literally millions of

TABLE 2-1 A Classification of Values and Associated Goals

Value	Goals Associated with Each Value
Power	power, strength, control
Achievement	achievement, ambition, success
Hedonism	luxury, pleasure, delight
Stimulation	excitement, novelty, thrill
Self-direction	independence, freedom, liberty
Universalism	unity, justice, equality
Benevolence	kindness, charity, mercy
Tradition	tradition, custom, respect
Conformity	restraint, regard, consideration
Security	security, safety, protection

Source: Anat Bardi, Rachel M. Calogero, and Brian Mullen, "A New Archival Approach to the Study of Values and Value-Behavior Relations: Validation of the Value Lexicon," *Journal of Applied Psychology*, May 2008, pp. 483–497. Based on Shalom. H. Schwartz, "Universals in the Content and Structure of Values: Theoretical Advances and Empirical Tests in 20 Countries," in Mark P. Zanna, ed., *Advances in Experimental and Social Psychology* (New York: Academic Press, Vol. 25, 1992), pp. 1–65.

TABLE 2-2   Value Stereotypes for Several Generations of Workers

Baby Boomers (1946–1964) including Generation Jones (1954–1965)	Generation X (1961–1980)	Generation Y (1981–2002) Millenials
Uses technology as a necessary tool, but not obsessed with technology for its own sake	Techno-savvy	Techno-savvy, and even questions the value of standard IT techniques such as e-mail, with a preference for communications on a Web site
Appreciates hierarchy	Teamwork very important	Teamwork very important, highly team focused
Tolerates teams but values independent work	Dislikes hierarchy	Dislikes hierarchy, prefers participation
Strong career orientation	Strives for work-life balance but will work long hours for now; prefers flexible work schedule	Strives for work-life balance, and may object to work interfering with personal life; expects flexible work schedule
More loyalty to organization	Loyalty to own career and profession	Loyalty to own career and profession and feels entitled to career goals
Favors diplomacy and tact	Candid in conversation	Quite direct in conversation
Seeks long-term employment	Will accept long-term employment if situation is right	Looks toward each company as a stepping stone to better job in another company
Believes that issues should be formally discussed	Believes that feedback can be administered informally, and welcomes feedback	Believes that feedback can be given informally, even on the fly, and craves feedback
Somewhat willing to accept orders and suggestions	Often questions why things should be done in certain way	Frequently asks why things should be done in a certain way, and asks loads of questions
Willing to take initiative to establish starting and completion dates for projects	Slight preference for a manager to provide structure about project dates	Prefer structure on dates and other activities based on childhood of structured activities
Regards rewards as a positive consequence of good performance and seniority	Expects frequent rewards	Feels strong sense of entitlement to rewards, including promotions
Will multitask in front of work associates when it seems necessary	Feels comfortable in multitasking while interacting with work associates	Assumes that multitasking, including listening to music on earphones while dealing with work associates, is acceptable behavior

Note: Disagreement exists about which age bracket fit Baby Boomers, Generation X, and Generation Y with both professional publications and dictionaries showing slight differences.

Source: The majority of ideas in this table are from Sommer Kehrli and Trudy Sopp, "Managing Generation Y: Stop Resisting and Start Embracing the Challenges Generation Y Brings to the Workplace," *HR Magazine*, May 2006, pp. 113–119; Ron Alsop, *The Trophy Kids Grow Up: How the Millenial Generation is Shaking Up the Workforce* (San Francisco: Jossey-Bass/Wiley, 2008); Alsop, "Schools, Recruiters Try to Define Traits for Future Students," *The Wall Street Journal*, February 14, 2006, p. B6; Kathryn Tyler, "Generation Gaps: Millennials May Be Out of Touch with the Basics of Workplace Behavior," *HR Magazine*, January 2008, pp. 69–72; Lindsay Holloway, "Stick Together," *Entrepreneur*, March 2008, p. 30; Martha Irvine, "Recession Intensifies Gen X Discontent at Work," *The Detroit News* (www.detnews.com), November 16, 2009; Chris Penttila, "Talking about My Generation," *Entrepreneur*, March 2009, pp. 53–55.

exceptions. For example, many Baby Boomers are fascinated with technology, and many Generation Yers like hierarchy.

How Values Are Learned

People acquire values in the process of growing up, and many values are learned by the age of four. Whereas in the past the family was the most important environment for shaping values, attitudes, and beliefs, today children are exposed via television and the Internet to many more role models, values, ways of thinking, and choices than ever before.[37] Models can be teachers, friends, brothers, sisters, and even public figures. If we identify with a particular person, the probability is high that we will develop some of his or her major values. For example, if a parent valued helping less fortunate people, the child might place a high value on helping people in need later in life.

Another major way values are learned is through the communication of attitudes. The attitudes that we hear expressed directly or indirectly help shape our values. Assume that using credit to purchase goods and services was considered an evil practice among your family and friends. You might therefore hold negative values about installment purchases. Unstated but implied attitudes may also shape your values. If key people in your life showed no enthusiasm when you talked about work accomplishments, you might not place such a high value on achieving outstanding results. If, however, your family and friends centered their lives on their careers, you might develop similar values. (Or you might rebel against such a value because it interfered with a more relaxed lifestyle.) Many key values are also learned through religion and thus become the basis for society's morals. For example, most religions emphasize treating other people fairly and kindly. To "knife somebody in the back" is considered immoral both on and off the job.

Although many core values are learned early in life, our values continue to be shaped by events later in life. The media, including the dissemination of information about popular culture, influence the values of many people throughout their lives. The aftermath of Hurricane Katrina intensified a belief in the value of helping less fortunate people. Volunteers from throughout the United States and several other countries invested time, money, and energy into helping rebuild New Orleans and several other Gulf Coast cities. Influential people, such as NBA players, were seen on television building houses for Katrina victims. Such publicity sent a message that helping people in need is a value worth considering.

The media, particularly advertisements, can also encourage the development of values that are harmful to a person intent on developing a professional career. People featured in advertisements for consumer products, including snack food, beer, and vehicles, often flaunt rudeness and flagrantly incorrect grammar. The message comes across to many people that such behavior is associated with success.

Changes in technology can also change our values. As the world has become increasingly digitized, more and more people come to value a *digital lifestyle* as the normal way of life. Many people would not think of spending time away from the house, even while participating in sports, or watching sports to leave their electronic gadgets behind. Being part of the digital lifestyle is therefore an important value for many people of all ages.

Clarifying Your Values

The values that you develop early in life are directly related to the kind of person you are and to the quality of the relationships you form.[38] Recognition of this fact has led to exercises designed to help people clarify and understand some of their own values. Self-Assessment Quiz 2-3 gives you an opportunity to clarify your values.

The Mesh between Individual and Job Values

Under the best of circumstances, the values of employees mesh with those required by the job. When this state of congruence exists, job performance is likely to be higher. Suppose that Jacquelyn strongly values giving people with limited formal education an opportunity to work and avoid being placed on welfare. So she takes a job as a manager of a dollar store that employs many people who would ordinarily have limited opportunity for employment. Jacquelyn is satisfied because her employer and she share a similar value.

A group of researchers attempted to discover why congruence between individual and organizational values leads to positive outcomes such as low turnover and high performance. The major factor creating positive outcomes appears to be employees trusting managers based on the congruence. Communication also plays a role because when communication is regular, open, and consistent, trust is enhanced. For example, trust is enhanced when management explains the reasons behind major decisions. Good communication also enhanced interpersonal attraction between managers and employees. Goal congruence also came about to a lesser extent because employees liked the managers. Liking, in turn, was enhanced by managers communicating well with employees.[39]

When the demands made by the organization or a superior clash with the basic values of the individual, he or she suffers from **person–role conflict**. The individual wants to obey orders, but does not want to perform an act that seems inconsistent with his or her values. A situation such as this might occur when an employee is asked to produce a product that he or she feels is unsafe or of no value to society.

person–role conflict

The situation that occurs when the demands made by the organization clash with the basic values of the individual.

Clarifying Your Values

Directions: Rank from 1 to 20 the importance of the following values to you as a person. The most important value on the list receives a rank of 1; the least important a rank of 20. Use the space next to "Other" if the list has left out an important value in your life.

_____ Having my own place to live

_____ Having one or more children

_____ Having an interesting job and career

_____ Owning a car

_____ Having a good relationship with coworkers

_____ Having good health

_____ Spending considerable time on social networking Websites

_____ Being able to stay in frequent contact with friends by cell phone and text messaging

_____ Watching my favorite television shows

_____ Participating in sports or other pastimes

_____ Following a sports team, athlete, music group, or other entertainer

_____ Being a religious person

_____ Helping people less fortunate than myself

_____ Loving and being loved by another person

_____ Having physical intimacy with another person

_____ Making an above-average income

_____ Being in good physical condition

_____ Being a knowledgeable, informed person

_____ Completing my formal education

_____ Other

1. Discuss and compare your ranking of these values with the person next to you.

2. Perhaps your class, assisted by your instructor, can arrive at a class average on each of these values. How does your ranking compare to the class ranking?

3. Look back at your own ranking. Does it surprise you?

4. Are there any surprises in the class ranking? Which values did you think would be highest and lowest?

A manager of a commercial weight-reduction center resigned after two years of service. The owners pleaded with her to stay, based on her excellent performance. The manager replied, "Sorry, I think my job is immoral. We sign up all these people with great expectations of losing weight permanently. Most of them do achieve short-term weight reduction. My conflict is that over 90 percent of our clientele regain the weight they lost once they go back to eating standard food. I think we are deceiving them by not telling them up front that they will most likely gain back the weight they lose."

Guidelines for Using Values to Enhance Interpersonal Relations

Values are intangible and abstract, and thus not easy to manipulate to help improve your interpersonal relations on the job. Despite their vagueness, values are an important driver of interpersonal effectiveness. Ponder the following guidelines:

LEARNING OBJECTIVE 5

1. Establish the values you will use in your relationships with others on the job, and then use those values as firm guidelines in working with others. For example, following the Golden Rule, you might establish the value of treating other people as you want to be treated. You would then not lie to others to gain personal advantage, and you would not backstab your rivals.

2. Establish the values that will guide you as an employee. When you believe that your values are being compromised, express your concern to your manager in a

tactful and constructive manner. You might say to your manager, "Sorry, I choose not to tell our customers that our competitor's product is inferior just to make a sale. I choose not to say this because our competitor makes a fine product. But what I will say is that our service is exceptional."

3. Remember that many values are a question of opinion, not a statement of being right versus wrong. If you believe that your values are right, and anybody who disagrees is wrong, you will have frequent conflict. For example, you may believe that the most important value top managers should have is to bring shareholders a high return on their investment. Another worker believes that profits are important, but providing jobs for as many people as possible is an equally important value. Both of you have a good point, but neither is right or wrong. So it is better to discuss these differences rather than hold grudges because of them.

4. Respect differences in values and make appropriate adjustment when the value clash is reasonable. If you are an older person recognize that you may have to win the respect of a younger coworker rather than assume that because you are more experienced, or a manager, that respect will come automatically.[40] If you are a younger person, recognize that an older person might be looking for respect, so search for something you can respect right away, such as his or her many valuable contacts in the company.

5. Recognize that many people today are idealistic about their jobs, and want to have an impact on the lives of others.[41] In the mean time, you might feel that you need that person's cooperation to get an important task done right now, such as fulfilling a larger order. Invest a couple of minutes in helping that person understand how an ordinary task might be having an impact on the lives of others—such as earning money to feed a hungry baby at home!

To help you put these guidelines into practice, do Skill-Building Exercise 2-4. Remember, however, that being skilled at using your values requires day-by-day monitoring.

SKILL-BUILDING EXERCISE 2-4

The Value-Conflict Role-Play

One student plays the role of a company CEO who makes an announcement to the group that the company must soon lay off 10 percent of the workforce in order to remain profitable. The CEO also points out that the company has a policy against laying off good performers. He or she then asks four of the company managers to purposely give below-average performance ratings to 10 percent of employees. In this way, laying them off will fit company policy.

Four other students play the role of the company managers who receive this directive. If such manipulation of performance

evaluations clashes with your values, engage in a dialogue with your manager expressing your conflict. Remember, however, that you may not want to jeopardize your job.

Conduct this role-play for about seven minutes. Observers rate the role players on two dimensions, using a 1-to-5 scale from very poor to very good. One dimension is "effective use of human relations techniques." The second dimension is "acting ability." A few observers might voluntarily provide feedback to the role players in terms of sharing their ratings and observations. The course instructor might also provide feedback.

SELF-ASSESSMENT QUIZZES IN OVERVIEW

The several self-assessment quizzes presented in this chapter taken collectively will help you paint a verbal portrait of your personality. Self-Assessment Quiz 2-1, the self-monitoring scale, gives you insight into how much you go out of your way to please others, often by telling them what they want to hear. Self-Assessment Quiz 2-2, the risk-taking scale, looks at a dimension of personality that could lead you toward being adventuresome and innovative. Quite often people who are high risk takers are low self-monitors because they risk telling people what they do not want to hear, such as pointing out flaws in a company product.

Self-Assessment Quiz 2-3 gives you a chance to reflect on what is important to you. Your values are linked to the first two scales in that some people want to please others, and therefore would place a high premium on values like "helping people less fortunate than myself" and "loving and being loved by another person." Examples of strong values for a high risk taker would be "having an interesting job and career" and "making an above-average income."

Concept Review and Reinforcement

Key Terms

individual differences 21
personality 21
organizational citizenship behavior 25
cognitive styles 26
intelligence 30

g (general) factor 30
s (special) factors 30
triarchic theory of intelligence 31
intuition 31
multiple intelligences 32

emotional intelligence 33
value 35
ethics 35
person–role conflict 38

Summary

Individual differences are among the most important factors influencing the behavior of people in the workplace. Knowing how to respond to such differences is the cornerstone of effective interpersonal relations.

Personality is one of the major sources of individual differences. The eight major personality factors described in this chapter are neuroticism, extraversion, openness, agreeableness, conscientiousness, self-monitoring of behavior, risk taking and thrill seeking, and optimism. Depending on the job, any one of these personality factors can be important for success, and they also affect interpersonal relations. Conscientiousness relates to job performance for many different occupations, and has proven to be the personality factor most consistently related to success.

Personality also influences a person's cognitive style, or modes of problem solving. According to the Golden Personality Profiler, four separate dichotomies direct the typical use of perception and judgment by the individual as follows: (a) energy flow: extraversion vs. introversion, (b) information gathering: sensing vs. intuition, (c) decision making: thinking vs. feeling, and (d) lifestyle orientation: judging vs. perceiving. Combining the four types with each other results in 16 personality types, such as being a proponent, communicator, advocate, or enforcer. For example, the proponent (ENFP) scores high on extraversion, intuition, feeling, and perceiving.

Mental ability, or intelligence, is one of the major sources of individual differences that affects job performance and behavior. Understanding the nature of intelligence contributes to effective interpersonal relations in organizations. For example, understanding that different types of intelligence exist will help a person appreciate the strengths of individuals.

Intelligence consists of many components. The traditional perspective is that intelligence includes a general factor (*g*) along with special factors (*s*) that contribute to problem-solving ability. A related perspective is that intelligence consists of seven components: verbal comprehension, word fluency, numerical acuity, spatial perception, memory, perceptual speed, and inductive reasoning.

To overcome the idea that intelligence involves mostly the ability to solve abstract problems, the triarchic theory of intelligence has been proposed. According to this theory, intelligence has three subtypes: analytical, creative, and practical (street smarts included). Another approach to understanding mental ability contends that people have multiple intelligences, or faculties, including linguistic, logical-mathematical, musical, spatial, bodily kinesthetic, intrapersonal, interpersonal, and naturalist.

Emotional intelligence refers to factors other than traditional mental ability that influence a person's success. The four components of emotional intelligence are (1) self-awareness, (2) self-management, (3) social awareness, and (4) relationship management. Emotional intelligence is a skill through which employees treat emotions as valuable information in navigating a situation.

Values and beliefs are another set of factors that influence behavior on the job, including interpersonal relations. Values are closely tied in with ethics. A useful way of classifying values points to how we establish goals to fit our values, as shown in Table 2-1. Differences in values among people often stem from age, or generational, differences.

People acquire values in the process of growing up and modeling others, and the communication of attitudes. Later life influences such as the media also shape values. The values a person develops early in life are directly related to the kind of adult he or she becomes and to the quality of relationships formed. Values-clarification exercises help people identify their values.

When the values of employees mesh with those required by the job, job performance is likely to be higher. **Person–role conflict** occurs when the demands made by an organization or a superior clash with the basic values of an individual.

Questions for Discussion and Review

1. Why is responding to individual differences considered to be the cornerstone of effective interpersonal relations?
2. How can knowledge of major personality factors help a person form better interpersonal relations on the job?
3. Identify three job situations (or entire jobs) in which being optimistic might be an asset.
4. Suppose a high self-monitoring person is attending a company-sponsored social event and that person dislikes such events. How is he or she likely to behave?
5. Identify two business occupations for which a high propensity for risk taking and thrill seeking would be an asset. Also, identify two business occupations for which risk taking and thrill seeking might be a liability.
6. Imagine yourself going about your job in your field, or intended field. Give an example of how you might use the five primary senses of touch, sight, sound, smell, and taste to gather information.
7. Which of the seven components of traditional intelligence represents your best mental aptitude? What is your evidence?
8. How could you use the concept of multiple intelligences to raise the self-esteem of people who did not consider themselves to be very smart?
9. Suppose a person is quite low in emotional and social intelligence. In what type of job is he or she most likely to be successful?
10. How can you use information about a person's values to help you relate more effectively to him or her?

The Web Corner

http://myskillprofile.com
(This site provides many self-quizzes, including emotional intelligence, sports mental skills, and spiritual intelligence. Several of the tests are free.)

http://www.queendom.com
(This site provides many tests and quizzes related to cognitive factors, personality, and emotional I.Q.)

Internet Skills Builder: Boosting Your Mental Ability

Do you want to be smarter? Thousands of specialists think they have developed intelligent ways of making people more intelligent. You will find at least two million

Websites that provide information about improving brain functioning through such methods as practice in problem solving and taking food supplements. Try out one of these sights. Evaluate the suggestions for plausibility. You might even try the exercises for a couple of weeks and observe if you become smarter. Ask somebody close to you if have become smarter. You might also see if you do better on tests with the same amount of study and classroom attentiveness.

Developing Your Human Relations Skills

Interpersonal Relations Case 2.1

Capitalizing on Hidden Talent at Westmont Center

Ginette Gagnon is the director of Westmont Center, a residential center for older persons who require assisted living, such as being served meals, help with taking baths, and supervision for taking daily medication. Many of the residents also need readily available professional health care provided by physicians or nurses. Westmont takes care of an average of 125 guests on a given month.

At a recent meeting with the Westmont board of directors, Gagnon addressed the Center's most critical problem. She explained, "We are in good shape financially. Because of the aging population in the area we serve, there is a never-ending supply of people who want entrance to Westmont. I say with pride that the good reputation of our staff, and our comfortable physical facilities have enhanced our reputation."

"Our biggest need is for to attract staff who will stick around long enough after they are trained and experienced. You will recall that we used to emphasize hiring young people. We still hire young people, but they tend not to stay very long. Many of them see taking care of older people as a stepping stone to other work. Our program of recruiting young retirees has worked somewhat. The older folks usually have developed nurturing skills, and that is exactly what our residents need. The big problem is that we cannot find enough retirees who want to take care of people not much older than themselves."

"Ginette, please get to the point," said Karl Adams, one of the board members.

"Okay, here is what I am proposing. I would like to start a pilot program of hiring about five workers with developmental disabilities to work on our staff. Our local university has a program of preparing people with light intellectual deficiencies for the workforce. The people in the program are not college students, but individuals whose parents or guardians have enrolled them in this cooperative program between the psychology department and a community agency.

"We would assign these workers to basic jobs like baking bread and muffins, folding laundry, and bring meals to residents. Running the dishwashing machine would be another possibility, as would be trimming bushes. We would make sure that the workers in the pilot program perform the same task everyday. McDonald's has had a program like this for years, and both the workers and the restaurants have benefited quite well."

"Hold on," said Jean Weiss. "When the word gets out that we are staffing our Center with mentally unstable people, we will be in big trouble. I can imagine headlines in the newspapers and the blogs."

Ginette responded with a tone of anger, "I must say Jean, you do not understand the meaning of an intellectual deficiency, or I am not making myself clear. A developmental disability such as having difficulty learning has nothing to do with mental instability which refers to emotional problems. Emotional stability and I.Q. are not particularly related."

The discussion with the board lasted another hour. Ralph Goodwin, the chairperson of the board, concluded the meeting in these words: "I think we see advantages and disadvantages in hiring about five people with intellectual deficiencies to work at Westmont. We would be doing a social good, we would have a new source of dependable workers. Yet, we have some concerns about hiring people who might not be able to think well in emergencies. Also, maybe some of our constituents would think that we are hiring mentally unstable people."

"I am disappointed that we could not reach an approval of my plan today," said Gagnon. "However, with more study, I think the board will see the merit in my plan of hiring a group of workers who have mild intellectual deficiencies."

Case Questions

1. What do you recommend that the board should do in terms of approving Gagnon's plan for hiring about five people with intellectual deficiencies to work at Westmont?

2. Assuming that the workers with mild intellectual deficiencies are hired, what recommendations can you make to the supervisors for their training and supervision?

3. Gagnon mentioned a few potential jobs at the Center for workers with light intellectual deficiencies. What other tasks would you recommend?

Interpersonal Relations Case 2.2

Values Are Big at Zappos

At the Las Vegas headquarters of Zappo.com, an online retail company best known for its array of shoes and free shipping, employees can get goal-setting tips from the on-site life coach Dr. Vik, who is a chiropractor by trade. In front of the human resources department, anyone who stops by is welcome to have his or her picture taken wearing a "mullet" wig—the 1980s hairstyle that recruiting manager Christa Foley says represents her group's motto: "Business in the front, party in the back."

On a typical day, Jamie Naughton, whose title is "Cruise Ship Captain," is planning events for employees. More than 50 percent of the 774 people in the headquarters (another 721 work in a Kentucky warehouse) are on the company-wide Twitter feed, which enables them to meet up easily after work and get to know coworkers in other departments. Those on break can head to the company library, which houses hundreds of self-help and positive psychology books.

Cultivating happiness is the ultimate goal of Tony Hsieh, the CEO of Zappos. Back when he started and sold a tech firm in the '90s, he formed a theory: If you create a work culture that fosters well-being, good practices and good profits will naturally flow out of the operation. "In the first company, we made the right hires in terms of skill sets and experience, but we didn't look for a culture fit. I remember dreading going to the office," he says, because that vital sense of a shared purpose among employees was missing. When Hsieh was put in charge of the fledging Zappos in 1999, he vowed to organize the business around 10 "core values"—by which every single employee would be hired and fired. (See Exhibit 1 for a list of these values.)

Ten years later, Zappos was raking in $1 billion work of annual gross sales, and employees widely report that their work is exciting and challenging. "We know our employees are happy based on our very low turnover rate and high employee satisfaction scores on surveys," says Rebecca Ratner, director of human resources. The success of Zappos caught the attention of Amason.com, which purchased the company for $900 million in 2009.

Hsieh believes that his entire business revolves around happiness. As part of this attitude, managers are encouraged to goof off with the people they manage. Every day he sends a steady stream of playful messages to 350,000 people on Twitter. Hsieh also takes employees out to restaurants frequently because he wants a company where employee can hang out together.

Prospective employees undergo a "culture interview" to help figure out whether they would fit in to the slightly wacky, drama club atmosphere. Augusta Scott, a representative on the customer loyalty team, recalls that in her culture interview she was asked to draw a pig. "I was quite surprised. I made him rainbow colored. "I still have him on my cubicle wall." Scott says Zappos is by far the best company she's worked for because it allows her to express her individuality.

If not caught in the interview, a values mismatch is easily revealed during the company's four-week training session, where even new managers must learn how to work the customer service phones. "It's a pretty good screening metric for determining how humble someone is," Foley says. One highly specialized techie was paid to go back to San Francisco after he showed up late to training and claimed it was something he just "had to get through." New hires are offered $2,000 to refuse the job and go away. According to company representatives, those who stay (about 96%) are more committed and engaged thereafter.

Employees share values, but they don't share styles and personalities. A quiet employee is encouraged to connect with customers in his own low-key way, while loudmouths are free to be as chatty as they wish—as long as they are going above and beyond to make sure that the client will come back.

"We're not just motivated. We're inspired," Scott says. "We jump on calls—we don't want customers to be on hold." That empowering sense of fulfilling a higher purpose at her work has spilled into Scott's after-hours life. "It's built my self-confidence. And I notice I hold doors open for strangers, I smile at them, I try to help them with anything I can. I'm just a much happier person."

Case Questions

1. In what way does the case about Zappos.com illustrate the role of values in the workplace?

2. In what way does management at Zappos.com take into account individual differences?

3. Suppose you were applying for a position in your field at Zappos.com, and that you were asked one of their culture-fit questions, "How weird are you?" What would be your answer?

4. To what extent do you think a Zappos.com employee would need good interpersonal skills?

5. Explain why you would or would not want to work for a company that espoused the Zappos.com values.

Source: Excerpted from Carline Flora, "Paid to Smile," *Psychology Today*, September/October 2009, pp. 58–59. A few additional facts are from Max Chafkin, "The Zappos Way of Managing," *Inc.com*, May 1, 2009, pp. 1–8.

EXHIBIT 1   Zappos Core Values

As we grow as a company, it has become more and more important to explicitly define the Zappos core values from which we develop our culture, our brand, and our business strategies. These are the 10 core values that we live by:

1. Deliver the WOW through service.
2. Embrace and drive change.
3. Create fun and a little weirdness.
4. Be adventuresome, creative, and open-minded.
5. Pursue growth and learning.
6. Build open and honest relationships with communication.
7. Build a positive team and family spirit.
8. Do more with less.
9. Be passionate and determined.
10. Be humble.

Source: "Zappos.com Powered by Service," *about.zappos.Com.*

CHAPTER 3

Building Self-Esteem and Self-Confidence

Scott Gould went from trader to waiter—by choice. Growing up in Florida, Gould enjoyed working in restaurants as a waiter and bartender. But he also liked working with numbers; and after graduating from the University of Florida, he went into finance. He got a job as a fixed income trader in 2000, and later raised money to invest in new markets and helped develop avenues for investors. He learned to do research and listen to customers. Every client wanted something a little different with respect to risk.

After studying the information and doing the exercises in this chapter, you should be able to

1. Describe the nature, development, and consequences of self-esteem.
2. Explain how to enhance self-esteem.
3. Describe the importance of self-confidence and self-efficacy.
4. Pinpoint methods of enhancing and developing your self-confidence.

On the morning of September 11, 2001, Gould was working in his office near the World Trade Center. He evacuated after the first plane hit. As he walked down 36 flights of stairs, he saw the second plane flying into the tower. It made him reevaluate his career. "I had to think, 'Do I love what I'm doing?' and I couldn't answer yes," he says. "It's not like I hated going to work, but we spend so much time working and it wasn't exciting and I wasn't running to the office on Monday morning."

Gould kept thinking back to how he had liked working at restaurants. As a trader, he had taken clients regularly to Del Frisco's, a steakhouse in Midtown Manhattan. On a whim, he called a manager he knew and asked for a job. And, he was told that there was an opening as a server. He handed in his notice the next day, and started at Del Frisco's in August 2002. Three months later, he moved behind the bar for another three months.

"Obviously coming here as a guest two months earlier and then becoming a waiter—it wasn't insulting but it messes with your pride a little," he says. "I think if you can get over the pride factor of taking a step down and understand that sometimes you take a step backwards to eventually take three steps forward, it is more than worth it."

In February 2003, Gould got a big break. A sommelier (wine specialist) was leaving, and he was offered the chance to step in by David O'Day, the director of wine for Del Frisco's Restaurant Group. O'Day says Gould's financial background helped him work with customers. Some of them wanted to talk about a $40 bottle of wine and others asked about a $4,000 bottle. Gould was comfortable working with both. In November 2007, he was promoted to general manager of the restaurant, a big popular place with 475 seats. He now oversees 17 managers and 250 employees.

Gould says he has brought the listening skills he learned during his finance days onto the restaurant floor, and the hectic pace of trading helps him stay calm during crises now. One Sunday night in fall 2007, the ventilation system stopped working, causing the room to overheat and the kitchen sprinklers to go off.

There were inches of water on the kitchen floor, a fire department on the way and 300 diners waiting to eat. "I went from table to table with my cell phone in one hand and a Zagat's in the other, asking people what their second choice was," Gould said. (Zagat is an online restaurant directory.) He tried to stay calm, thinking that if he panicked, so would his staff.

"Instead," he says, "For months people came back and said, 'I was here on that Sunday night. That was so crazy.'"[1]

The story about the career-switching Wall Street trader illustrates many human relations topics covered in this book. Our focus, however, is how high self-esteem and self-confidence enabled Scott Gould to do the type of work he really loved. For example, his strong self-esteem enabled him to shift down to a server's job temporarily without worrying about status. Gould's self-confidence helped him recognize that he could move upward in the restaurant, and also help him stay cool under pressure.

Many other people you will meet in this book score high in self-esteem and self-confidence—otherwise they would never have been so successful. In this chapter, we focus on two of the biggest building blocks for more effective human relations: the nature and development of self-esteem and self-confidence. The development of both self-esteem and self-confidence includes refining certain skills.

THE MEANING OF SELF-ESTEEM, ITS DEVELOPMENT AND CONSEQUENCES

LEARNING OBJECTIVE 1
Understanding the self from various perspectives is important because who you are and what you think of you influence many different facets of your life both on and off the job. A particularly important role is played by **self-esteem,** the overall evaluation people make about themselves whether positive or negative.[2] A useful distinction is that our self-concept is what we *think* about ourselves whereas self-esteem is what we *feel* about ourselves.[3] People with positive self-esteem have a deep-down, inside-the-self feeling of their own worth. Consequently, they develop a positive self-concept. Before reading further, you are invited to measure your current level of self-esteem by doing Human Relations Self-Assessment Quiz 3-1. We look next at the development of self-esteem and many of its consequences.

HUMAN RELATIONS SELF-ASSESSMENT QUIZ 3-1

The Self-Esteem Checklist

Indicate whether each of the following statements is Mostly True or Mostly False as it applies to you.

	Mostly True	Mostly False
1. I am excited about starting each day.	_____	_____
2. Most of any progress I have made in my work or school can be attributed to luck.	_____	_____
3. I often ask myself, "Why can't I be more successful?"	_____	_____
4. When my manager or team leader gives me a challenging assignment, I usually dive in with confidence.	_____	_____
5. I believe that I am working up to my potential.	_____	_____
6. I am able to set limits to what I will do for others without feeling anxious.	_____	_____
7. I regularly make excuses for my mistakes.	_____	_____
8. Negative feedback crushes me.	_____	_____
9. I care very much how much money other people make, especially when they are working in my field.	_____	_____
10. I feel like a failure when I do not achieve my goals.	_____	_____
11. Hard work gives me an emotional lift.	_____	_____
12. When others compliment me, I doubt their sincerity.	_____	_____
13. Complimenting others makes me feel uncomfortable.	_____	_____
14. I find it comfortable to say, "I'm sorry."	_____	_____
15. It is difficult for me to face up to my mistakes.	_____	_____
16. My coworkers think I am not worthy of promotion.	_____	_____
17. People who want to become my friends usually do not have much to offer.	_____	_____
18. If my manager praised me, I would have a difficult time believing it was deserved.	_____	_____

(Continued)

19. I'm just an ordinary person. _____ _____
20. Having to face change really disturbs me. _____ _____
21. When I make a mistake, I have no fear owning up to it in public. _____ _____
22. When I look in the mirror, I typically see someone who is attractive and confident. _____ _____
23. When I think about the greater purpose in my life, I feel like I am drifting. _____ _____
24. When I make a mistake, I tend to feel ashamed and embarrassed. _____ _____
25. When I make a commitment to myself, I usually stick to it with conviction and await the rewards that I believe will come from it. _____ _____

Scoring and Interpretation: The answers in the high self-esteem direction are as follows:

1. Mostly True	8. Mostly False	15. Mostly False	22. Mostly True
2. Mostly False	9. Mostly False	16. Mostly False	23. Mostly False
3. Mostly False	10. Mostly False	17. Mostly False	24. Mostly False
4. Mostly True	11. Mostly True	18. Mostly False	25. Mostly True
5. Mostly True	12. Mostly False	19. Mostly False	
6. Mostly True	13. Mostly False	20. Mostly False	
7. Mostly False	14. Mostly True	21. Mostly True	

20–25 You have very high self-esteem. Yet if your score is 25, it could be that you are denying any self-doubts.

14–19 Your self-esteem is in the average range. It would probably be worthwhile for you to implement strategies to boost your self-esteem (described in this chapter) so that you can develop a greater feeling of well-being.

0–13 Your self-esteem needs bolstering. Talk over your feelings about yourself with a trusted friend or with a mental health professional. At the same time, attempt to implement several tactics for boosting self-esteem described in this chapter.

Questions:

1. How does your score on this quiz match your evaluation of your self-esteem?
2. What would it be like being married to somebody who scored 0 on this quiz?

Source: Statements 21–25 are based on information in the National Association for Self-Esteem, "Self-Esteem Self-Guided Tour – Rate Your Self-Esteem," http://www.self-esteem-nase.org/jssurvey.shtml, accessed May 6, 2005, pp. 1–4.

How Self-Esteem Develops

Part of understanding the nature of self-esteem is to know how it develops. Self-esteem develops and evolves throughout our lives based on interactions with people, events, and things.[4] As an adolescent or adult, your self-esteem might be boosted by a key accomplishment. A 44-year-old woman who was studying to become licensed practical nurse (LPN) said that her self-esteem increased when she received an A in a pharmacology course. Self-esteem can also go down in adulthood by means of a negative event such as being laid off, and not being able to find new employment.

Early life experiences have a major impact on self-esteem. People who were encouraged to feel good about themselves and their accomplishments by family members, friends, and teachers are more likely to enjoy high self-esteem. Early life experiences play a key role in the development of both healthy self-esteem and low self-esteem, according to research synthesized at the Counseling and Mental Health Center of the University of Texas.[5] Childhood experiences that lead to healthy self-esteem include

- being praised
- being listened to
- being spoken to respectfully
- getting attention and hugs
- experiencing success in sports or school

In contrast, childhood experiences that lead to low self-esteem include

- being harshly criticized
- being yelled at or beaten
- being ignored, ridiculed, or teased
- being expected to be "perfect" all the time
- experience failures in sports or school
- often being given messages that failed experiences (losing a game, getting a poor grade, and so forth) were failures of their whole self.

A widespread explanation of self-esteem development is that compliments, praise, and hugs alone build self-esteem. Yet many developmental psychologists seriously question this perspective. Instead, they believe that self-esteem results from accomplishing worthwhile activities and then feeling proud of these accomplishments. Receiving encouragement, however, can help the person accomplish activities that build self-esteem.

Leading psychologist Martin Seligman argues that self-esteem is caused by a variety of successes and failures. To develop self-esteem, people need to improve their skills for dealing with the world.[6] Self-esteem therefore comes about by genuine accomplishments, followed by praise and recognition. Heaping undeserved praise and recognition on people may lead to a temporary high, but it does not produce genuine self-esteem. The child develops self-esteem not from being told he or she can score a goal in soccer but from scoring that goal.

In attempting to build the self-esteem of children and students, many parents and teachers give children too many undeserved compliments. Researchers suggest that inappropriate compliments are turning too many adults into narcissistic praise-junkies. As a result, many young adults feel insecure if they do not receive compliments regularly.[7]

As mentioned above, experiences in adult life can influence the development of self-esteem. David De Cremer of the Tilburg University (Netherlands) and his associates conducted two studies with Dutch college students about how the behavior of leaders and fair procedures influence self-esteem. The focus of the leaders' behavior was whether he or she motivated the workers/students to reward *themselves* for a job well done, such as a self-compliment. Procedural fairness was measured in terms of whether the study participants were given a voice in making decisions. Self-esteem was measured by a questionnaire somewhat similar to Self-Assessment 3-1 in this chapter. The study questionnaire reflected the self-perceived value that individuals have of themselves as organizational members.

The study found that self-esteem was related to procedural fairness and leadership that encourages self-rewards. When leadership that encouraged rewards was high, procedural fairness was more strongly related to self-esteem. The interpretation given of the findings is that a leader/supervisor can facilitate self-esteem when he or she encourages self-rewards, and uses fair procedures. Furthermore, fair procedures have a stronger impact on self-esteem when the leader encourages self-rewards.[8] A takeaway from this study would that rewarding yourself for a job well done, even in adult life, can boost your self-esteem a little.

The Consequences of High Self-Esteem

High self-esteem has many positive consequences for people, as well as a few potential negative ones. Table 3-1 outlines these consequences, and they are described in the following

TABLE 3-1   Several Consequences of High Self-Esteem

1. Career success, including a high income
2. Good mental health
3. Profiting from feedback
4. Organizational success
5. Trying too hard to preserve one's status (negative consequence)

paragraphs. Low-self esteem would typically have a negative impact on the first three factors. People with low self-esteem are likely to have less career success, poorer mental health, and profitless from feedback. Also, an organization populated with low self-esteem workers would be less successful. Yet on the positive side of low self-esteem, it would not lead to trying too hard to preserve one's status.

Career Success.   No single factor is as important to career success as self-esteem, as observed by psychologist Eugene Raudsepp. People with positive self-esteem understand their own competence and worth, and have a positive perception of their ability to cope with problems and adversity.[9]

As part of a larger study of personal characteristics and career success, the University of Florida psychology professors Timothy A. Judge, Chalice Hurst, and Lauren S. Simon studied the impact of *core self-evaluation*. Core self-evaluation is a personality trait representing the favorability of a person's overall self-concept. The self-evaluation includes self-esteem, belief in self-control of events in one's life, self-confidence, and emotional stability. Three hundred participants were studied over a 10-year period. One of the many findings in the study was that people with a higher core self-evaluation tended to have higher incomes. Two other factors studied, general mental ability and physical attractiveness, were also found to have a positive relationship with income from employment. A partial explanation of these findings was that being smart and physically attractive contributed to having high self-esteem.[10]

Good Mental Health.   One of the major consequences of high self-esteem is good mental health. People with high self-esteem feel good about themselves and have a positive outlook on life. One of the links between good mental health and self-esteem is that high self-esteem helps prevent many situations from being stressful. Few negative comments from others are likely to bother you when your self-esteem is high. A person with low self-esteem might crumble if somebody insulted his or her appearance. A person with high self-esteem might shrug off the insult as simply being the other person's point of view. If faced with an everyday setback, such as losing keys, the high self-esteem person might think, "I have so much going for me, why fall apart over this incident?"

Positive self-esteem also contributes to good mental health because it helps us ward off being troubled by feelings of jealousy, and acting aggressively toward others because of our jealousy. Particularly with adolescents, lower self-worth leads to jealousy about friends liking other people better.[11]

Profiting from Feedback.   Although people with high self-esteem can readily shrug off undeserved insults, they still profit well from negative feedback. Because they are secure, they can profit from the developmental opportunities suggested by negative feedback.

Organizational Success.   Workers with high self-esteem develop and maintain favorable work attitudes and perform at a high level. These positive consequences take place because such attitudes and behavior are consistent with the personal belief that they are competent individuals. Mary Kay Ash, the legendary founder of a beauty products company, put it this way: "It never occurred to me I couldn't do it. I always knew that if I worked hard enough, I could." Furthermore, research has shown that high self-esteem individuals value reaching work goals more than do low-self-esteem individuals.[12]

The combined effect of workers having high self-esteem helps a company prosper. Long-term research by Nathaniel Branden, as well as more recent studies, suggests that self-esteem is a critical source of competitive advantage in an information society. Companies gain the edge when, in addition to having an educated workforce, employees have high self-esteem, as shown by such behaviors as the following:

- Being creative and innovative
- Taking personal responsibility for problems
- A feeling of independence (yet still wanting to work cooperatively with others)
- Trusting one's own capabilities
- Taking the initiative to solve problems[13]

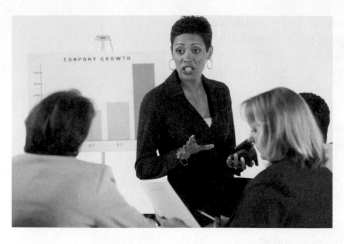

Behaviors such as these help workers cope with the challenge of a rapidly changing workplace where products and ideas become obsolete quickly. Workers with high self-esteem are more likely to be able to cope with new challenges regularly because they are confident that they can master their environment.

Potential Negative Consequences. High self-esteem can sometimes have negative consequences, particularly because individuals with high self-esteem work hard to preserve their high status relative to others. When people with high self-esteem are placed in a situation where undermining others helps them maintain their status, they will engage in behaviors that diminish others. In one study, it was shown that high self-esteem individuals who are also a little neurotic (somewhat emotionally unstable) will often engage the following undermining behaviors: criticizing group members in front of others, intentionally ignoring others, talking down to other group members, going back on their word, giving others the silent treatment, belittling others, and not listening to people.[14]

According to economist Robert H. Frank of Cornell University, our own reference group has the biggest impact on self-esteem. He writes: "When you see Bill Gates' mansion, you don't actually aspire to have one like it. It's who is local, who is near you physically and who is most like you—your family members, coworkers and hold high school classmates—with whom you compare yourself. If someone in your reference group has a little more, you get a little anxious."[15]

ENHANCING SELF-ESTEEM

Improving self-esteem is a lifelong process because self-esteem is related to the success of your activities and interactions with people. Following are approaches to enhancing self-esteem that are related to how self-esteem develops. (See Figure 3-1.) Each of these approaches

FIGURE 3-1 Methods of Enhancing Self-Esteem

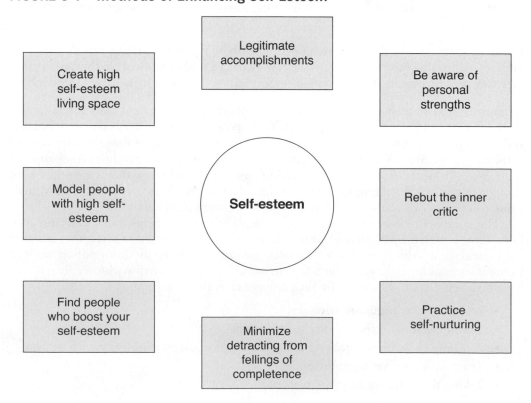

has a skill component, such as learning to avoid situations that make you feel incompetent. In addition to working on skills to enhance self-esteem, it is helpful to maintain a constructive attitude. A representative statement to keep in mind as you work on self-esteem enhancement is as follows:[16]

"I am a very special, unique and valuable person. I deserve to feel good about myself."

Attain Legitimate Accomplishments

To emphasize again, accomplishing worthwhile activities is a major contributor to self-esteem (as well as self-confidence) in both children and adults. Social science research suggests this sequence of events: Person establishes a goal; person pursues the goal; person achieves the goal; person develops esteem-like feelings.[17] The opposite point of view is this sequence: Person develops esteem-like feelings; person establishes a goal; person pursues the goal; person achieves the goal. Similarly, giving people large trophies for mundane accomplishments is unlikely to raise self-esteem. More likely, the person will see through the transparent attempt to build his or her self-esteem and develop negative feelings about the self. What about you? Would your self-esteem receive a bigger boost by (1) receiving an A in a course in which 10 percent of the class received an A or by (2) receiving an A in a class in which everybody received the same grade?

Be Aware of Personal Strengths

Another method of improving your self-esteem is to develop an appreciation of your strengths and accomplishments. A good starting point is to list your strengths and accomplishments on a word processing document or paper. This list is likely to be more impressive than you expected.

You can sometimes develop an appreciation of your strengths by participating in a group exercise designed for such purposes. A group of about seven people meet to form a support group. All group members first spend about 10 minutes answering the question, "What are my three strongest points, attributes, or skills?" After each group member records his or her three strengths, the person discusses them with the other group members.

Each group member then comments on the list. Other group members sometimes add to your list of strengths or reinforce what you have to say. Sometimes you may find disagreement. One member told the group, "I'm handsome, intelligent, reliable, athletic, self-confident, and very moral. I also have a good sense of humor." Another group member retorted, "And I might add that you're unbearably conceited."

Skill-Building Exercises 3-1 and 3-2 provide additional ways of developing self-esteem, both of which focus on appreciation of strengths.

SKILL-BUILDING EXERCISE 3-1

Reinforcing a Positive Self-Image

To do this exercise, you will need a piece of paper and a pencil or pen or a word processor, and a timer or clock. Set a timer for 10 minutes or note the time on your watch, cell phone, or a clock. Write your name across the top of the document. Then write everything positive and good you can think of about yourself. Include special attributes, talents, and achievements. You can use single words or sentences. You can write the same things over and over if you want to emphasize them. Your ideas do not have to be well organized. Write down whatever comes to mind. You are the only one who will see this document. Avoid using any negative words. Use only positive ones.

When the 10 minutes are up, read the document over to yourself. You may feel sad when you read it over because it is a new,

different, and positive way of thinking about yourself. Your document will contradict some of the negative thoughts you have had about yourself. Those feelings will diminish as you reread this document. Read the document over again several times. Print the document if written by computer, and put it in a convenient place, such as in your pocket, purse, wallet, or your bedside table. Read it over at least once a day to keep reminding yourself of how great you are! Find a private space and read it aloud. If you have a good friend or family member who is supportive, read it to that person. Maybe your confidant can think of a positive attribute that you have missed.

Source: Adapted from "Building Self-esteem: A Self-Help Guide," *http://mentalhealth.samhsa.gov/*, accessed September 7, 2007.

The Self-Esteem Building Club

You and your classmates are invited to participate in one of the most humane and productive possible human-relations skill-building exercises, membership in the "self-esteem building club." Your assignment is for three consecutive weeks to help build the self-esteem of one person. Before embarking upon the exercise, review the information about self-esteem development in the chapter. One of the most effective tactics would be to find somebody who had a legitimate accomplishment, and give that person a reward or thank you. Record carefully what the person did, what you did, and any behavioral reactions of the person whose self-esteem you attempted to build. An example follows, written by a 46-year-old student of human relations:

> Thursday night two weeks ago, I went to the athletic club to play racquetball. Different than usual, I had a date after the club. I wanted to look good, so I decided to wear my high school class ring. The ring doesn't have much resale value, but I was emotionally attached to it, having worn it for special occasions for 28 years. I stuffed the ring along with my watch and wallet in my athletic bag.
>
> When I was through with racquetball, I showered, and got dressed. My ring was missing from my bag even though my wallet and watch were there. I kind of freaked out because I hate to lose a prized possession. I shook

the bag out three times, but no luck. Very discouraged, I left my name, telephone number, and e-mail address at the front desk just in case somebody turned in the ring. I kept thinking that I must have lost the ring when I stopped at the desk to check in.

> The next morning before going to class, I got a phone call from a front-desk clerk at the club. The clerk told me that Karl, from the housekeeping staff, heard a strange noise while he was vacuuming near the front desk. He shut off the vacuum cleaner immediately, and pulled out my ring. To me Karl was a hero. I made a special trip to the club that night to meet with Karl. I shook his hand, and gave him a ten-dollar bill as a reward. I also explained to Karl what a difference he had made in my mood. I told him that honest, hardworking people like him who take pride in their work make this world a better place. It made my day when Karl smiled and told me it was a pleasure to be helpful.

Your instructor might organize a sharing of self-esteem building episodes in the class. If the sharing does take place, look for patterns in terms of what seemed to work in terms of self-esteem building. Also, listen for any patterns in failed attempts at self-esteem building.

Rebut the Inner Critic

Another early step in attaining better self-esteem is to rebut your inner critic—the voice inside you that sends negative messages about your capabilities. Rebutting critical statements about you might also be considered another way of appreciating your strengths. Two examples of rebutting your inner critic follow:[18]

> **Your unfairly harsh inner critic says:** "People said they liked my presentation, but it was nowhere as good as it should have been. I can't believe no one noticed all the places I messed up. I'm such an imposter."

> **Your reassuring rebuttal:** "Wow, they really liked it. Maybe it wasn't perfect, but I worked hard on that presentation and did a good job. I'm proud of myself. This was a great success."

> **Your harsh inner critic makes leaps of illogic:** "He is frowning. He didn't say anything, but I know it means that he doesn't like me!"

> **Your rebuttal that challenges the illogic:** "Okay, he's frowning, but I don't know why. It could have nothing to do with me. Maybe I should ask."

The above are but two examples of the type of putdowns we often hear from our inner critic. To boost your self-esteem in spite of such criticism, you need to develop the skill of rebuttal by rebutting your inner critic frequently.

Practice Self-Nurturing

Although you may be successful at pointing to your strengths and rebutting the inner voice that puts you down, it is also helpful to treat yourself as a worthwhile person. Start to challenge negative experiences and messages from the past by nurturing and caring for yourself in ways that show how valuable, competent, deserving, and lovable you really are. Self-nurturing is often referred to as treating yourself well or spoiling yourself. Here are two suggestions for self-nurturing, both of which involve a modest amount of skill development.

- **Administer self-rewards for a job well done.** When you have carried out an activity especially well in relation to your typical performance, reward yourself in a small, constructive way. You might dine at a favorite restaurant, take an afternoon off to go for a nature walk, or spend an hour at a Website you usually do not have the time to visit.

- **Take good care of yourself mentally and physically.** Make sure that you get enough sleep and rest, eat nutritious foods, avoid high-bacteria environments such as a public keyboard unless you use a bacteria spray, and participate in moderate physical exercise. Even taking an extra shower or bath can give you a physical and mental boost. The suggestions just mentioned are also part of stress management.

Real estate agent Laura provides a helpful example of how self-nurturing can help bolster self-esteem. While watching her son play soccer at 4 in the afternoon, she was asked by another soccer parent, "How's business?" Laura replied, "I haven't made a deal in two weeks, but I know times will get better. So for now, I'm enjoying myself watching Todd [her son] play his little heart out. Afterwards we are going for pizza, and a few video games. My soul will be energized again."

Minimize Settings and Interactions That Detract from Your Feelings of Competence

Most of us have situations in work and personal life that make us feel less than our best. If you can minimize exposure to those situations, you will have fewer feelings of incompetence. The problem with feeling incompetent is that it lowers your self-esteem. Suppose, for example, Sally is a very poor golf player, and intensely dislikes the sport. She is better off excusing herself from a small group of people at the office who invite her to a golf outing. A problem with avoiding all situations in which you feel lowly competent is that it might prevent you from acquiring needed skills. Also, it boosts your self-confidence and self-esteem to become comfortable in a previously uncomfortable situation. In Sally's case perhaps she can eventually learn to play golf better, and then she will be mentally prepared to participate in golf outings.

Get Help from Others

Self-esteem is strongly shaped by how others perceive us, so getting help from other is major step a person can take to improve his or her self-esteem. However, getting help from others can also be difficult. People with low self-esteem often do not ask for help because they may not think they are worthy of receiving help. Yet help from others is effective in overcoming the negative messages received from others in the past.

Asking for support from friends can include such basic steps as these: (1) Ask friends to tell you what they like about you or think that you do well. (2) Ask someone who cares about you to listen to your complain about something without offering a solution to your problem. (3) Ask for a hug. (4) Ask someone who loves you to remind you that he or she does.

Getting help from teachers and other helps can include these steps: (1) Ask professors or tutors for help with work you find challenging. (2) If you lack self-confidence in certain areas, take classes or attempt new activities to increase your competence. An increasing number of retired people today are taking classes in such subjects as computer utilization and digital photography to help catch up with younger people whose skills have challenged their self-esteem.[19]

Another way of getting help from others is to talk and socialize frequently with people who can boost your self-esteem. Psychologist Barbara Ilardie says that the people who can raise your self-esteem are usually those with high self-esteem themselves. They are the people who give honest feedback because they respect others and themselves. Such high self-esteem individuals should not be confused with yes-people who agree with others just to be liked. The point is that you typically receive more from strong people than weak ones. Weak people will flatter you but will not give you the honest feedback you need to build self-esteem.[20]

For many people with low self-esteem, casual help with others will not increase self-esteem. In these situations, discussing low self-esteem with a mental health specialist might be the most effective measure.

Model the Behavior of People with High Self-Esteem

Observe the way people who believe to have high self-esteem stand, walk, speak, and act. Even if you are not feeling so secure inside, you will project a high self-esteem image if you act assured. Raudsepp recommends, "Stand tall, speak clearly and with confidence, shake hands firmly, look people in the eye and smile frequently. Your self-esteem will increase as you notice encouraging reactions from others."[21] (Notice here that self-esteem is considered to be about the same idea as self-confidence.)

Choose your models of high self-esteem from people you know personally, as well as celebrities you might watch on television news and interview shows. Observing actors on the large or small screen is a little less useful because they are guaranteed to be playing a role. Identifying a teacher or professor as a self-esteem model is widely practiced, as is observing successful family members and friends.

Create a High Self-Esteem Living Space

A panel of mental health specialists recommends that to enhance your self-esteem you should make your living space that honors the person you are.[22] Whether you live in a single room, a small apartment, or a large house, make that space comfortable and attractive for you. If you have a clean, inviting living space, others are likely to treat you with more respect, which will contribute to your self-esteem. If you share your living space with others, dedicate some space just for you—a place where you can keep your things and know that they will not be disturbed and that you can decorate any way you choose.

Your living space is part of your self-image, so you may want to ask yourself if your living space projects the right self-image. Also, you arrange your living space to fit your preferences you will feel better about yourself.

How a Manager Helps Build the Self-Esteem of Group Members

Above we mentioned that leaders who are fair and who encourage self-rewards contribute to the self-esteem of subordinates. There are many other actions and attitudes of managers that help group members enhance their self-esteem. Many of these approaches are related to suggestions for enhancing self-esteem just mentioned. For example, a manager who provides subordinates with an opportunity to accomplish challenging tasks, and then rewards them appropriately will help bolster their self-esteem. Also, if the manager has high self-esteem, he or she can be your person to model in terms of developing high self-esteem.

Giving subordinates positive feedback about legitimate accomplishments is a powerful approach to enhancing their self-esteem. When accomplishments are out of the ordinary, they can be celebrated through such means as public recognition electronically or during a face-to-face meeting. Accurately assessing the strengths and skill sets of subordinates will often point them in the direction of accomplishing tasks that will boost self-esteem. Helping subordinates develop new skills by coaching can be quite useful in developing their self-esteem. (See Chapter 12.)

Skill-Building Exercise 3-3 presents an easy, non-time-consuming activity for enhancing your self-esteem. Should the exercise not have a remarkable impact on your self-esteem, at least it will have no damaging emotional consequences.

SKILL-BUILDING EXERCISE 3-3

The Self-Esteem Calendar

Find a calendar or daily planner on paper or on the computer, with large blank spaces for each day. Schedule into each day a small activity that you enjoy doing such as "watching YouTube to look for videos about people I know personally," "jogging through my neighborhood," "texting a few people I care about," "reading the classified ads in *The Wall Street Journal*," or "hugging somebody I love." Now make a commitment to check your enjoy-life calendar every day, and follow through to make sure that you engaged in the activity you entered into the calendar. The accumulation of small, enjoyable activities should boost your self-esteem a little because you will feel better about yourself.

Source: Adapted from "Building Self-Esteem: A Self-Help Guide," *Health* (athealth.com/Consumer/disorder/self-esteem.html, p. 7).

THE IMPORTANCE OF SELF-CONFIDENCE AND SELF-EFFICACY

LEARNING OBJECTIVE 3

Although self-confidence can be considered part of self-esteem (or almost its equivalent), it is important enough to study separately. Self-efficacy is confidence in your ability to carry out a specific task in contrast to generalized self-confidence. Various studies have shown that people with a high sense of self-efficacy tend to have good job performance, so being self-confident is important for your career. They also set relatively high goals for themselves.[23] Self-confidence has also long been recognized as a trait of effective leaders. A straightforward implication of self-efficacy is that people who think they can perform well on a task do better than those who think they will do poorly.

Research by college professors and psychological consultants George P. Hollenbeck and Douglas T. Hall suggests that our feelings of self-confidence stem from five sources of information.[24] The first source is the *actual experience, or things we have done.* Having done something before and succeeded is the most powerful way to build self-confidence. If you successfully inserted a replacement battery into your watch without destroying the watch, you will be confident to make another replacement.

The second source of self-confidence is the *experiences of others, or modeling.* You can gain some self-confidence if you have carefully observed others perform a task, such as resolving conflict with a customer. You might say to yourself, "I've seen Tracy calm down the customer by listening and showing sympathy, and I'm confident I could do the same thing." The third source of self-confidence is *social comparison, or comparing yourself to others.* If you see other people with capabilities similar to your own perform a task well, your will gain in confidence. A person might say to himself or herself, "If that person can learn how to work with enterprise software, I can do it also. I'm just as smart."

The fourth source of self-confidence is *social persuasion, the process of convincing another person.* If a credible person convinces you that you can accomplish a particular task, you will often receive a large enough boost in self-confidence large enough to give the task a try. If the encouragement is coupled with guidance on how to perform the task, your self-confidence gain will be higher. So the boss or teacher who says, "I know you can do it, and I'm here to help you," knows how to build self-confidence.

The fifth source of information for making a self-confidence judgment is *emotional arousal, or how we feel about events around us and manage our emotions.* We rely somewhat on our inner feelings to know if we are self-confident enough to perform the task. Imagine a person standing on top of a high mountain ready to ski down. However, he or she is trembling and nauseous with fear. Contrast this beginner to another person who simply feels mildly excited and challenged. Skier number one has a self-confidence problem, whereas skier number two has enough confidence to start the descent. (Have your emotional sensations ever influenced your self-confidence?)

The more of these five sources of self-confidence are positive for you, the more likely your self-confidence will be positive. A subtle point about self-confidence is that being too low in self-confidence is a problem yet being too high is also a problem. The overly self-confident person may not listen carefully to the suggestions of others, and may be blind to criticism.

Human Relations Self-Assessment Quiz 3-2 provides some insight into your level of self-confidence.

TECHNIQUES FOR DEVELOPING AND ENHANCING YOUR SELF-CONFIDENCE

LEARNING OBJECTIVE 4

Self-confidence is generally achieved by succeeding in a variety of situations. A confident civil engineering technician may not be generally self-confident unless he or she also achieves success in activities such as forming good personal relationships, navigating complex software, writing a letter, learning a second language, and displaying athletic skills.

Although this general approach to self-confidence building makes sense, it does not work for everyone. Some people who seem to succeed at everything still have lingering self-doubt.

How Self-Confident Are You?

Indicate the extent to which you agree with each of the following statements. Use a 1-to-5 scale: (1) disagree strongly; (2) disagree; (3) neutral; (4) agree; (5) agree strongly.

	DS	D	N	A	AS
1. I frequently say to people, "I'm not sure."	5	4	3	2	1
2. I perform well in most situations in life.	1	2	3	4	5
3. I willingly offer advice to others.	1	2	3	4	5
4. Before making even a minor decision, I usually consult with several people.	5	4	3	2	1
5. I am generally willing to attempt new activities for which I have very little related skill or experience.	1	2	3	4	5
6. Speaking in front of the class or other group is a frightening experience for me.	5	4	3	2	1
7. I experience stress when people challenge me or put me on the spot.	5	4	3	2	1
8. I feel comfortable attending a social event by myself.	1	2	3	4	5
9. I'm much more of a winner than a loser.	1	2	3	4	5
10. I am cautious about making any substantial change in my life.	5	4	3	2	1

Total score: _____

Scoring and Interpretation: Calculate your total score by adding the numbers circled. A tentative interpretation of the scoring is as follows:

45–50 Very high self-confidence with perhaps a tendency toward arrogance

38–44 A high, desirable level of self-confidence

30–37 Moderate, or average, self-confidence

10–29 Self-confidence needs strengthening

Questions:

1. How does your score on this test fit with your evaluation of your self-confidence?
2. What would it be like working for a manager who scored 10 on this quiz?

Low self-confidence is so deeply ingrained in this type of personality that success in later life is not sufficient to change things. Following are seven specific strategies and tactics for building and elevating self-confidence, as outlined in Figure 3-2. They will generally work unless the person has deep-rooted feelings of inferiority. The tactics and strategies are arranged approximately in the order in which they should be tried to achieve best results.

Develop a Solid Knowledge Base

A bedrock strategy for projecting self-confidence is to develop a knowledge base that enables you to provide sensible alternative solutions to problems. Intuition is very important, but working from a base of facts helps you project a confident image. Formal education is an obvious and important source of information for your knowledge base. Day-by-day absorption of information directly and indirectly related to your career is equally important. A major purpose of formal education is to get you in the right frame of mind to continue your quest for knowledge. In your quest for developing a solid knowledge base to project self-confidence, be sensitive to abusing this technique. If you bombard people with quotes, facts, and figures, you are likely to be perceived as an annoying know-it-all.

A solid knowledge base contributes to self-confidence also because the knowledge facilitates engaging in conversation with intelligent people. A weak counterargument is that having information stored in your brain is no longer important because information is so accessible online. When in a gathering of people, you could then use a smart phone to access some facts to talk about. Such behavior is unlikely to help a person project a confident, intelligent image.

FIGURE 3-2   Boosting Your Self-Confidence

Develop solid
knowledge base

Bounce back
from setbacks
and embarrassments

Use positive
self-talk

Strive for peak
performance

Self-confidence

Avoid negative
self-talk

Develop
explanatory style
of optimists

Use positive
visual imagery

Set high self-
expectations
(Galeta effect)

BACK TO THE OPENING CASE

Scott Gould, the fixed-income trader turned manager of a luxury restaurant, used his self-confidence to help propel him toward an ideal position for himself. He needed self-confidence to move from server to bartender in a New York restaurant with the most demanding clientele. Gould then needed even more self-confidence to think that his knowledge and love for wines would enable him to work as a sommelier in the same restaurant. He was then self-confident enough to tackle the job of being the manager of a Del Frisco restaurant, only seven years after beginning as a server. Furthermore, Gould's high self-confidence facilitated his being able to cope with the pressures of managing an upscale restaurant.

Use Positive Self-Talk

A basic method of building self-confidence is to engage in **positive self-talk,** saying positive things about yourself. The first step in using positive self-talk is to objectively state the incident that is casting doubt about self-worth.[25] The key word here is *objectively.* Terry, who is fearful of poorly executing a report-writing assignment, might say, "I've been asked to write a report for the company, and I'm not a good writer."

The next step is to objectively interpret what the incident *does not* mean. Terry might say, "Not being a skilled writer doesn't mean that I can't figure out a way to write a good report or that I'm an ineffective employee."

Next, the person should objectively state what the incident *does* mean. In doing this, the person should avoid put-down labels, such as "incompetent," "stupid," "dumb," "jerk," or "airhead." All these terms are forms of negative self-talk. Terry should state what the incident does mean: "I have a problem with one small aspect of this job."

The fourth step is to objectively account for the cause of the incident. Terry would say, "I'm really worried about writing a good report because I have very little experience in writing along these lines."

The fifth step is to identify some positive ways to prevent the incident from happening again. Terry might say, "I'll get out my textbook on business communications and review the chapter on report writing" or "I'll enroll in a course or seminar on business report writing."

The final step is to use positive self-talk. Terry imagines his boss saying, "This report is really good. I'm proud of my decision to select you to prepare this important report."

Positive self-talk builds self-confidence and self-esteem because it programs the mind with positive messages. Making frequent positive statements or affirmations about the self creates a more confident person. An example would be, "I know I can learn this new equipment rapidly enough to increase my productivity within five days."

Business coach Gary Lockwood emphasizes that positive self-talk is also useful for getting people past difficult times. "It's all in your head," he said. "Remember you are in charge of your feelings. You are in control of your attitude." Instead of berating yourself after making a mistake, learn from the experience and move on. Say to yourself, "Everyone makes mistakes," "Tomorrow is another day," or "What can I learn from this?"[26]

Despite the many advantages of positive self-talk, as with optimism, there can be times when thinking too positively can create problems. Negative thoughts are often useful in alerting us to potential problems, and prompting us to develop a plan of correction. Imagine that Lisa is job hunting, and that she has urgent need of employment. She has a promising interview, and her positive thinking prompts her to think, "There is no doubt that I will receive an offer real soon." Her positive thinking blocks her from continuing her job search. When the offer in question does not come through, Lisa has lost momentum in her job search. In the words of author John Derbyshire, we must be "vigilantly realistic" toward against the potential dangers of positive thinking.[27]

Avoid Negative Self-Talk

As implied, you should minimize negative statements about yourself to bolster self-confidence. A lack of self-confidence is reflected in statements, such as "I may be stupid but . . .," "Nobody asked my opinion," "I know I'm usually wrong, but . . .," and "I know I don't have as much education as some people, but. . . ." Self-effacing statements like these serve to reinforce low self-confidence.

It is also important not to attribute to yourself negative, irreversible traits, such as "idiotic," "ugly," "dull," "loser," and "hopeless." Instead, look on your weak points as areas for possible self-improvement. Negative self-labeling can do long-term damage to your self-confidence. If a person stops that practice today, his or her self-confidence may begin to increase.

Use Positive Visual Imagery

Assume you have a situation in mind in which you would like to appear confident and in control. An example would be a meeting with a major customer who has told you by e-mail that he is considering switching suppliers. Your intuitive reaction is that if you cannot handle his concerns without fumbling or appearing desperate, you will lose the account. An important technique in this situation is **positive visual imagery**, or picturing a positive outcome in your mind. To apply this technique in this situation, imagine yourself engaging in a convincing argument about why your customer should retain your company as the primary supplier. Imagine yourself talking in positive terms about the good service your company offers and how you can rectify any problems.

Visualize yourself listening patiently to your customer's concerns and then talking confidently about how your company can handle these concerns. As you rehearse this moment of truth, create a mental picture of you and the customer shaking hands over the fact that the account is still yours.

Positive visual imagery helps you appear self-confident because your mental rehearsal of the situation has helped you prepare for battle. If imagery works for you once, you will be even more effective in subsequent uses of the technique.

Set High Expectations for Yourself (the Galatea Effect)

If you set high expectations for yourself and you succeed, you are likely to experience a temporary or permanent boost in self-confidence. The **Galatea effect** is a type of self-fulfilling prophecy in which high expectations lead to high performance. Similar to positive self-talk, if you believe in yourself you are more likely to succeed. You expect to win, so you do. The Galatea effect may not work all the time, but it does work some of the time for many people.

Workplace behavior researchers D. Brian McNatt and Timothy A. Judge studied the Galatea effect with 72 auditors within three offices of a major accounting firm over a three-month period. The auditors were given letters of encouragement to strengthen their feelings of self-efficacy. Information in the letters was based on facts about the auditors, such as information derived from their résumés and company records. The results of the experiment showed that creating a Galatea effect bolstered self-efficacy, motivation, and performance. However, the performance improvement was temporary, suggesting that self-expectations need to be boosted regularly.[28]

Develop the Explanatory Style of Optimists

According to the research and observations of consultant and trainer Price Pritchett, optimism is linked to self-confidence. Explaining events in an optimistic way can help preserve self-confidence and self-esteem. When experiencing trouble, optimists tend to explain the problems to themselves as temporary. Bad events are expected to be short-lived, and optimists look to the future when times will be better. Another aspect of optimists' explanatory style protects their self-confidence. Rather than condemn themselves for failures, they look for how other factors or circumstances have contributed to the problem. Optimists then do not take all the blame for a problem, but look to external factors to help explain what went wrong.

Interpreting difficulties in this way gives the optimists a sense of control. Instead of looking at the unfortunate situation as hopeless, they have faith in their ability to deal with the problem.[29] Suppose an optimist purchases a computer workstation that comes packed in a box with many parts along with directions. A problem arises is that some of the screws and dowels do not fit, and the directions are unclear. A pessimist might suffer a drop in self-confidence and self-esteem, saying "What a fool I am. I can't even assemble a piece of office furniture." In contrast, the optimist might say, "I'm doing something wrong here, and I will get a buddy to help show me my mistake. But the manufacturer can also be blamed. The instructions are terrible, and all the parts may not fit together." In this way, the optimist does not take such a big hit to self-confidence and self-esteem.

Strive for Peak Performance

A key strategy for projecting self-confidence is to display **peak performance,** or exceptional accomplishment in a given task. The experience is transient but exceptionally meaningful. Peak performance refers to much more than attempting to do your best. Experiencing peak performance in various tasks over a long period of time would move a person toward self-actualization.[30] To achieve peak performance, you must be totally focused on what you are doing. When you are in the state of peak performance, you are mentally calm and physically at ease. Intense concentration is required to achieve this state. You are so focused on the task at hand that you are not distracted by extraneous events or thoughts. To use an athletic analogy, you are *in the zone* while you are performing the task. In fact, many sports psychologists and other sports trainers work with athletes to help them attain peak performance.

The mental state achieved during peak performance is akin to a person's sense of deep concentration when immersed in a sport or hobby. On days when tennis players perform way above their usual game, they typically comment, "The ball looked so large, I could read the label as I hit it." On the job, focus and concentration allow the person to sense and respond to relevant information coming both from within the mind and from outside stimuli. When you are at your peak, you impress others by responding intelligently to their input. While turning in peak performance, you are experiencing a mental state referred to as *flow*.

Building Your Self-Confidence and Self-Efficacy

Most people can use a boost to their self-confidence. Even if you are a highly confident individual, perhaps there is room for building your feelings of self-efficacy in a particular area, such as a proud and successful business owner learning a new skill such as editing digital photos or speaking a foreign language. For this, skill-building exercise enhances your self-confidence or self-efficacy in the next two weeks by trying out one of the many suggestions for self-confidence building described in the text.

As part of planning the implementation of this exercise, think about any area in which your self-confidence could use a boost. A candid human relations student, who was also a confident cheerleader, said, "Face it. I'm terrible at PowerPoint presentations. I put up so many details on my slides that the audience is trying to read my slides instead of looking at me. I have to admit that my PowerPoint presentation consists mostly of my reading my slides to the audience. I'm much better at cheerleading." So this student studied information in her human relations text about making better graphic presentations. She revamped her approach to using her slides as headlines and talking points. She tried out one presentation in class, and one for at her church. She received so many compliments about her presentations that now she has much higher self-efficacy with respect to PowerPoint presentations.

Your instructor might organize a sharing of self-confidence building episodes in the class. If the sharing does take place, look for patterns in terms of what seemed to work in terms of self-confidence or self-efficacy building. Also, listen for any patterns in failed attempts at self-confidence building.

Although you are concentrating on an object or sometimes on another person during peak performance, you still have an awareness of the self. You develop a strong sense of the self, similar to self-confidence and self-efficacy, while you are concentrating the task. Peak performance is related to self-confidence in another important way. Achieving peak performance in many situations helps you develop self-confidence.

Skill-Building Exercise 3-4 gives you the opportunity to work on enhancing your self-confidence.

Bounce Back from Setbacks and Embarrassments

Resilience is a major contributor to personal effectiveness. Overcoming setbacks also builds self-confidence, as implied from the description of the explanatory style of optimists. An effective self-confidence builder is to convince yourself that you can conquer adversity such as setbacks and embarrassments, thus being resilient. The vast majority of successful leaders have dealt successfully with at least one significant setback in their careers, such as being fired or demoted. In contrast, crumbling after a setback or series of setbacks will usually lower self-confidence. Two major suggestions for bouncing back from setbacks and embarrassments are presented next.

Get Past the Emotional Turmoil. Adversity has enormous emotional consequences. The emotional impact of severe job adversity can rival the loss of a personal relationship. The stress from adversity leads to a cycle of adversity followed by stress, followed by more adversity. A starting point in dealing with the emotional aspects of adversity is to *accept the reality of your problem*. Admit that your problems are real and that you are hurting inside.

A second step is *not to take the setback personally*. Remember that setbacks are inevitable so long as you are taking some risks in your career. Not personalizing setbacks helps reduce some of the emotional sting. If possible, *do not panic*. Recognize that you are in difficult circumstances under which many others panic. Convince yourself to remain calm enough to deal with the severe problem or crisis. Also, *get help from your support network*. Getting emotional support from family members and friends helps overcome the emotional turmoil associated with adversity.

Find a Creative Solution to Your Problem. An inescapable part of planning a comeback is to solve your problem. You often need to search for creative solutions. Suppose a person faced the adversity of not having enough money for educational expenses. The person might search through standard alternatives, such as applying for financial aid, looking for more lucrative part-time work, and borrowing from family members. Several students have solved their problem more creatively by asking strangers to lend them money as intermediate-term investments. An option the investors have is to receive a payback based on the future earnings of the students.

A useful approach to finding a creative solution to your problem is to use response-oriented thinking that focuses on finding answers. A resilience program developed by Joshua D. Margolis of the Harvard Business School and Paul G. Stoltz, the founder of a global research and consulting firm, includes finding answers to then four following questions:

1. What features can I improve or potentially improve?
2. What sort of positive impact can I personally have on what happens next?
3. How can I contain the negatives of the situation and generate currently unseen positives?
4. What can I do to begin addressing the problem now?[31]

It is highly recommended that you write down answers to these questions rather than merely thinking about them. Writing offers people more command over an adverse situation than does mere reflection. A plausible reason is that writing down something is an early step in developing an action plan. Getting back to the person concerned about educational expenses, he or she might write down in response to question 4, "What do I or my family members own that I might be able to sell over eBay that would raise a little cash to get me started?"

SELF-ASSESSMENT QUIZZES IN OVERVIEW

The two self-assessment quizzes presented in this chapter support each other well. Self-Assessment Quiz 3-1 is a self-esteem checklist. People who score high on the Self-Esteem Checklist should theoretically score high on Self-Assessment Quiz 3-2, How Self-Confident Are You? The reason is that self-esteem and self-confidence are closely related and may be part of the same concept. An exception is that some people might like themselves even though they are not particularly self-confident in many situations. Perhaps their attitude is, "So who cares if I am not self-confident? I like me anyway."

Concept Review and Reinforcement

Key Terms

self-esteem 48   positive visual imagery 60   peak performance 61

Summary

Self-esteem refers to the overall evaluation people make about themselves. People with high self-esteem develop a positive self-concept. Self-esteem develops from a variety of early-life experiences. People who were encouraged to feel good about themselves and their accomplishments by key people in their lives are more likely to enjoy high self-esteem. Of major significance, self-esteem also results from accomplishing worthwhile activities, and then feeling proud of these accomplishments. Praise and recognition for accomplishments also help develop self-esteem.

Self-esteem has many important consequences, as follows: career success, including a high income; good mental health; profiting from feedback, and organizational success. One of the links between good mental health and self-esteem is that high self-esteem helps prevent many situations from being stressful. Workers with high self-esteem develop and maintain favorable work attitudes and perform at a high level. A company with high self-esteem workers has a competitive advantage.

High self-esteem can sometimes have negative consequences such as undermining others to preserve one's own status. Our own reference group has the biggest impact on self-esteem. Self-esteem can be enhanced in many ways: (a) attain legitimate accomplishments, (b) be aware of your personal strengths, (c) rebut the inner critic, (d) practice self-nurturing, (e) minimize settings and interactions that detract from your feelings of competence, (f) get help from others including talking and socializing frequently with people who boost your self-esteem, (g) model the behavior of people with high self-esteem, and (h) create a high self-esteem living space. The manager can play an important role in helping build the self-esteem of group members, such as giving positive feedback for legitimate accomplishments.

Various studies have shown that people with a high sense of self-efficacy tend to have good job performance, so self-confidence is important for your career. Our feelings of self-confidence stem from five sources of information: actual experiences, or things that we have done; experiences of others, or modeling; social comparison, or comparing yourself to others; social persuasion, the process of convincing another person; and emotional arousal, or how we feel about events around us and manage our emotions.

A general principle of boosting your self-confidence is to experience success (goal accomplishment) in a variety of situations. The specific strategies for building self-confidence described here are: (a) develop a solid knowledge base, (b) use positive self-talk, (c) avoid negative self-talk, (d) use positive visual imagery, (e) set high expectations for yourself (the Galatea effect), (f) develop the explanatory style of optimists, (e) strive for peak performance, and (f) bounce back from setbacks and embarrassments.

Questions for Discussion and Review

1. Why does holding an important job contribute to a person's self-esteem?

2. A study by economists indicated that workers with higher levels of self-esteem tended to be more productive. What would be an explanation for this finding?

3. Exercises to boost self-esteem and self-confidence often emphasize focusing on your positive qualities.

Why might it also be important to be aware of your weak points to develop self-esteem?

4. The criticism is often heard that the American emphasis on building the self-esteem of children has resulted in a generation of young adults who expect to be strongly praised by their bosses, no matter what they accomplish. What is your opinion of this criticism?

5. When you meet another person, on what basis do you conclude that he or she is self-confident?

6. What positive self-talk can you use after you have failed on a major assignment?

7. In what way does your program of studies contribute to building your self-esteem and self-confidence?

8. Many pharmaceutical firms actively recruit cheerleaders as sales representatives to call on doctors to recommend their brand of prescription drugs. The firms in question say that cheerleaders make good sales reps because they are so self-confident. What is your opinion on this controversial issue?

9. For what type of job might a worker having low self-esteem and self-confidence actually be an asset?

10. Interview a person whom you perceive to have a successful career. Ask that person to describe how he or she developed high self-esteem. Be prepared to discuss your findings in class.

The Web Corner

www.athealth.com/Consumer/disorders/self-esteem.html
(Measuring and building your self-esteem)

www.self-confidence.co.uk
(Developing your self-confidence)

www.mindtools.com/selfconf.html
(The difference between self-confidence and low self-confidence)

Internet Skills Builder: Learning More about Your Self-Esteem

The Self-Esteem Checklist in this chapter gave you one opportunity to assess you self-esteem. To gain additional insights into your self-esteem, visit www.more-selfesteem.com. Go to "quizzes" under Free Resources, and take the self-esteem test. How does your score on this quiz compare to your score on *The Self-Esteem Checklist*? If your level of self-esteem as measured by the two quizzes is quite different (such as high versus low), explain why this discrepancy might occur.

Developing Your Human Relations Skills

The Confetti Man

Nick Jablonski works for a manufacturer of property maintenance and recreational vehicles such as lawnmowers, snow blowers, and all-terrain vehicles. The company prospers even during downturns in the economy. This is true because when economic conditions are worrisome many people invest more money in taking care of their property and enjoying themselves close to home instead of traveling. Nick holds the job title, "celebrations assistant." The more traditional part of his job is to organize company events like picnics, sales meetings, and shareholder meetings.

When asked to explain the celebrations assistant part of his job in more detail, Nick replied with a smile:

My job is to help workers throughout the company celebrate accomplishments that help the company reach its goals. I'll give you a couple of examples. Suppose I learn that a production technician has exceeded quota on inserting dashboards on riding mowers, I will visit the factory floor and help the technician celebrate. Sometimes I will attach a smiley face to his or her work area. I might shake his or her hand or pat the person on the back. Yet to be dramatic, I will shower the person with confetti.

Just last week I was told by her supervisor that one of our customer service reps was working on the phone with a woman suffering from arthritis. The customer was having a difficult time starting one of our lawnmowers. The rep stayed on the phone twenty minutes with the lady until she could pull the start cord correctly. The customer was so pleased that she wrote a letter to the CEO praising the helpfulness of the rep.

My response was to visit the customer service rep's area and have a little celebration. Not only did I throw two bags of confetti, I blew a fog horn. I could tell the rep became a little embarrassed because she blushed. Yet I knew that I really boosted her self-esteem.

When Jablonski was asked why his work as a celebrations assistant boosted worker self-esteem, he answered as follows: "My job is to make our employees feel good about themselves. My smiley faces, my encouraging message, and especially my confetti throwing make people feel great. If people feel great about themselves and their accomplishments, their self-esteem heads north. It's that simple."

Case Questions

1. To what extent do you think that the celebrations assistant is really boosting the self-esteem of workers?
2. Assume that Nick is successful in boosting worker self-esteem. How might this help the company?
3. Advise the CEO of the company in question as to whether having a celebrations assistant on the payroll is a good investment of company money.

Source: Several facts in this case are based on Jeffrey Zaslow, "The Most-Praised Generation Goes to Work," *The Wall Street Journal,* April 20, 2007, pp. W1, W7.

Homeboy Industries Helps Ex-Cons Go Green

When Albert Ortega was released from prison, he was determined to turn his life around. So he went green. Ortega sports tattoos of an Aztec warrior on his back, a dragon on his chest, and the name of his former gang rings his biceps. Drug trafficking kept him locked up for most of the past seven years, he says. But after serving his last term, he heard about a solar installation course. "I wanted a new way of life," says the tall, brawny 34-year old. "Solar puts me on the cutting edge."

In the race to train America's "green collar" workforce, a group composed mostly of former Los Angeles gang members on parole is an early participant. Their training is funded by Homeboy Industries, a Los Angeles nonprofit that helps people with criminal pasts find employment.

For years, Homeboy Industries put former felons to work at a bakery and café it runs in East Los Angeles. A few summers ago, founder Greg Boyles, a Jesuit priest, was approached by a supporter about the idea of preparing them for the green economy. "I leapt at the opportunity," says Father Boyle.

Homeboy joined forces with the East Los Angeles Skills Center, a public vocational school that offers a hands-on program to teach the design, construction, and installation of solar panels. The center created an intensive course for Homeboy. "I loved the idea of doing something for these guys," says Brian Hurd, the senior instructor who designed it. "My best student ever in a construction course was a Homeboy referral who needed a second chance." Homeboy participants are paid an hourly wage of $8. The class meets for two months, weekdays from 9 A.M. to 3 P.M.

"I was so motivated, I would fall asleep with the books on my bed," says Ortega. Determined to get into the course, he phoned or visited Father Boyle for two weeks, until he was asked to take a drug test. Ortega passed and was offered a spot in the class. "I knew I was good at wiring," says Ortega, who once installed car-stereo systems. "I was always good at math."

Manuel Delgado, 42, who dropped out of high school, said he struggled at first. But four weeks into the class, he's doing "real good," he says. "I got 76% on my last math test." Another student, Jessica Espinoza, 23, says she couldn't find a job after being locked up for two years because she helped a felon escape from a courthouse. "The minute they saw I went to jail, employers didn't give me the time of day," she says. "Hopefully I can take what this school gave me and make a career in this new industry."

Doug Lincoln, 61, who once managed luxury car dealerships, was offered admission in the Homeboy course after he inquired about a faster-paced class. On hearing it was mainly for ex-cons, he said, "I thought it was a joke." Now, Lincoln is about to graduate. He plans to start a solar-panel installation firm and hire some of his former classmates. "These guys are more motivated than hundreds of employees I've managed in the car business," he says.

Ortega recently passed an examination that qualifies him to install solar panels nationwide. He says he has already been approached by employers. But he says he is waiting until when he is off parole before starting work, because until then he can't travel out of Los Angeles County. When that happens, he says, "I'll be just another citizen."

Several of his classmates who completed the course are already working, earning about $15 an hour. Experienced installers can make about $30 an hour. Phillip Hartley, general manager of Phat Energy, a Los Angeles solar company, has hired several Homeboy graduates. The Los Angeles Unified School District plans to start hiring some graduates of the program to install 50 megawatts of solar power units on its campuses. "Being former gang members doesn't preclude them from building a career in solar technology," says Veronica Soto, a school district director.

Case Questions

1. Why might an ex con enrolled in the Homeboy solar-panel building program have a self-esteem problem?
2. In what way might the Homeboy solar-panel training program be building the self-esteem and self-confidence of its students?
3. What suggestions can you offer for the staff at Homeboy to do an even better job of building the self-esteem and self-confidence of its students?
4. Should the instructor for the solar-panel installation class give high grades in math to all the students, just to raise their self-esteem? Explain your reasoning.

Source: Miriam Jordan, "A New Gang Comes to Los Angeles: Solar-Panel Installers," *The Wall Street Journal*, February 14–15, 2009, pp. A1, A9.

4

Interpersonal Communication

Maria is the director of e-commerce for a company in Brooklyn, New York, that was a re-seller of a variety of specialty machines used in manufacturing. Many of the machines the company sells are new, and many are refurbished. Competition from overseas manufacturers, particularly in China, is making the sales of machines more difficult. Almost all of Maria's contacts with customers and prospective customers are over the Internet, including e-mail as well as Facebook.

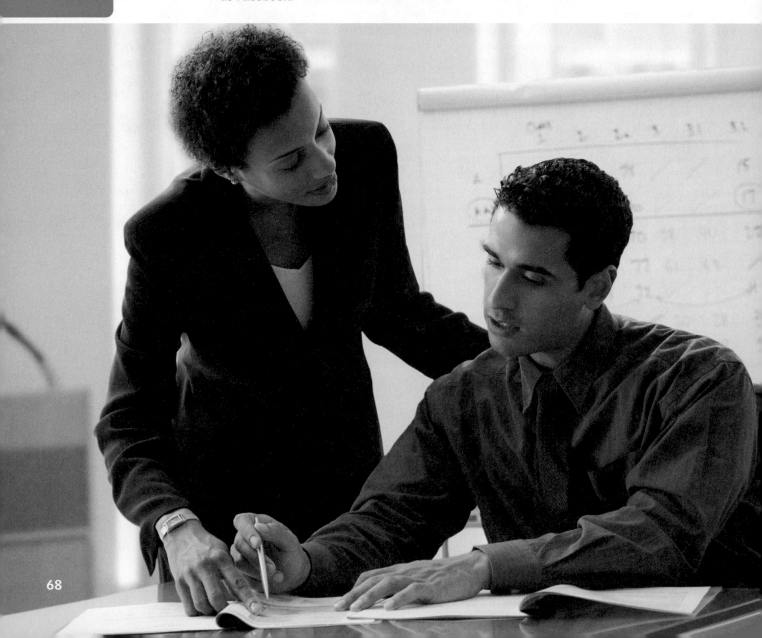

After reading and studying this chapter and doing the exercises, you should be able to:

1. Explain the basic steps in the communication process.
2. Explain the relationship-building aspect of interpersonal communication.
3. Understand nonverbal communication and improve your nonverbal communication skills.
4. Understand barriers to communication, including gender differences, and know how to overcome them.
5. Enhance your listening skills.

Maria noticed one year ago that she had not received an order from one of the company's largest customers, a successful machine tool company in Detroit, Michigan. Maria wrote a few e-mails to her contact at the company, Larry, the chief operating officer, asking if there was any way her company could help his company. Larry basically ignored the e-mail messages, except for one response that his company was in good shape with respect to machinery.

Maria decided to telephone Larry and ask if she could visit him at his office. Larry responded, "We've done everything over the Internet so far. I had never thought of seeing you in person. But if you think the trip is worth your time and money, let's schedule a date." Maria did visit her customer in Detroit, and her visit lasted two hours. Larry proudly showed Maria how his company was expanding, and how her company's machines were being deployed. Larry also went into detail what he liked and did not like about the machines he had bought from Maria's company.

Within three months after the visit, Maria's company received two orders for machines that would help the Detroit company expand on a new product line. Larry also wrote Maria explaining that it was refreshing to see an e-commerce manager in person.

The story about the e-commerce manager actually making an in-person visit to a customer illustrates that in this era of high technology, face-to-face communication still plays an important role in business. **Communication** is the sending, receiving, and understanding of messages. It is also the basic process by which managers, customer-contact workers, and professionals accomplish their work. For example, a customer service representative cannot resolve a thorny customer problem without carefully receiving and sending information. Communication is also important because communication skills are a success factor for workers in a wide variety of jobs.

communication
The sending, receiving, and understanding of messages.

The subject of this chapter is interpersonal, or face-to-face, communication rather than electronic communication, such as e-mail, instant messaging, text messaging, and videoconferencing. However, almost all principles of interpersonal communication also apply to electronic communication. Chapter 5 deals with the interpersonal aspects of communication in the digital world. Chapter 8 includes a section about coping with cross-cultural communication barriers.

The importance of face-to-face communication has increased in the age of electronic communication. Many companies have discovered that the subtle aspects of communication possible in face-to-face communication can help productivity. A key example would be talking to a person to help build a good working relationship. As illustrated in the case opener, there is yet no good substitute for face-to-face contact in building relationships. Entrepreneurship consultant Jim Blasingame reports, "There is a comfort level that is achieved when you've met the person you're doing business with."[1]

The information in this chapter is aimed at reducing communication problems among people and helping you enhance your communication effectiveness. The chapter approaches these ends in two ways. First, it explains the nature of a few key facets of interpersonal communication. Second, it presents guidelines for improving your effectiveness, along with skill-building exercises. We place particular emphasis on listening as part of achieving good communication. Keep in mind that communication underlies almost every human relations activity, as much as running supports almost every sport. You need good communication skills to get through job interviews, perform well on the job, and get promoted.

STEPS IN THE COMMUNICATION PROCESS

LEARNING OBJECTIVE 1

One way to understand how people communicate is to examine the steps involved in transmitting and receiving a message, as shown in Figure 4-1. For effective communication to take place, six components must be present: a sender, a message, a channel, a receiver, feedback, and the environment. In addition, a seventh component, noise, affects the entire communication process. To help understand the communication process, assume that a production manager in a bicycle factory wants to inform a team leader that productivity in her department slipped last month.

message

A purpose or idea to be conveyed.

1. **Sender (or source).** The sender in a communication event is usually a person (in this case the production manager) attempting to send a spoken, written, sign language, or nonverbal message to another person or persons. The perceived authority and credibility of the sender are important factors in influencing how much attention the message will receive.

2. **Message.** The heart of the communication event is the **message,** a purpose or idea to be conveyed. Many factors influence how a message is received. Among them are clarity, the alertness of the receiver, the complexity and length of the message, and how the information is organized. The production manager's message will most likely get across if he says directly, "I need to talk to you about last month's below-average productivity figures."

3. **Channel (medium).** Several communication channels, or media, are usually available for sending messages in organizations. Typically, messages are written (usually electronically), spoken, or a combination of the two. Some kind of nonverbal signal such as a smile or hand gesture accompanies most spoken messages. In the production manager's case, he has chosen to drop by the team leader's office and deliver his message in a serious tone.

4. **Receiver.** A communication event can be complete only when another party receives the message and understands it properly. In the example here, the team

FIGURE 4-1   A Basic Model of the Communication Process

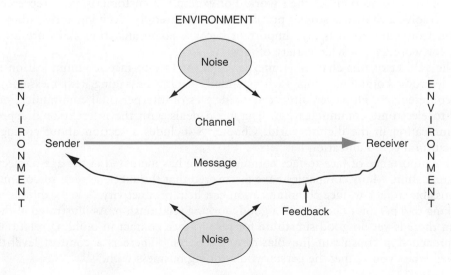

leader is the receiver. Perceptual distortions of various types act as filters that can prevent a message from being received as intended by the sender. If the team leader is worried that her job is at stake, she might get defensive when she hears the production manager's message.

5. **Feedback.** Messages sent back from the receiver to the sender are referred to as **feedback.** Without feedback it is difficult to know whether a message has been received and understood. The feedback step also includes the reactions of the receiver. If the receiver takes action as intended by the sender, the message has been received satisfactorily. The production manager will know his message got across if the team leader says, "Okay, when would you like to review last month's productivity reports?" Effective interpersonal communication therefore involves an exchange of messages between two people. The two communicators take turns being receivers and senders.

6. **Environment.** A full understanding of communication requires knowledge of the environment in which messages are transmitted and received. The organizational culture (attitudes and atmosphere) is a key environmental factor that influences communication. It is easier to transmit controversial messages when trust and respect are high than when they are low.

7. **Noise.** Distractions such as noise have a pervasive influence on the components of the communication process. In this context, **noise** is anything that disrupts communication, including the attitudes and emotions of the receiver. Noise includes such factors as stress, fear, negative attitudes, and low motivation.

feedback

In communication, messages sent back from the receiver to the sender.

noise

Anything that disrupts communication, including the attitudes and emotions of the receiver.

RELATIONSHIP BUILDING AND INTERPERSONAL COMMUNICATION

Another way of understanding the process of interpersonal communication is to examine how communication is a vehicle for building relationships. According to Ritch Sorenson, Grace DeBord, and Ida Ramirez, we establish relationships along two primary dimensions: dominate–subordinate, and cold–warm. In the process of communicating, we attempt to dominate or subordinate. When we dominate, we attempt to control communication. When we subordinate, we attempt to yield control, or think first of the wishes and needs of the other person. Dominators expect the receiver of messages to submit to them; subordinate people send a signal that they expect the other person to dominate.[2]

LEARNING OBJECTIVE 2

We indicate whether we want to dominate or subordinate by the way we speak and write, or by the nonverbal signals we send. The dominator might speak loudly or enthusiastically, write forceful messages filled with exclamation points, or gesture with exaggerated, rapid hand movements. He or she might write a harsh e-mail message such as, "It's about time you started taking your job seriously, and put in some real effort."

In the subordinate mode, we might speak quietly and hesitantly, in a meek tone, and being apologetic. A subordinate person might ask, "I know you have better things on your mind than to worry about me, but I was wondering when can I expect my reimbursement for travel expenses?" In a work setting we ordinarily expect people with more formal authority to have the dominant role in conversations. However, in more democratic, informal companies, workers with more authority are less likely to feel the need to dominate conversations.

The *cold–warm dimension* also shapes communication because we invite the same behavior that we send. Cold, impersonal, negative messages evoke similar messages from others. In contrast, warm verbal and nonverbal messages evoke similar behavior from others. Getting back to the inquiry about the travel-expense check, here is a colder versus warmer response by the manager:

Colder: Travel vouchers really aren't my responsibility. You'll just have to wait like everybody else.

Warmer: I understand your problem. Not getting reimbursed on time is a bummer. I'll follow up on the status of your expense; check sometime today or tomorrow.

FIGURE 4-2 Communication Dimensions of Establishing a Relationship

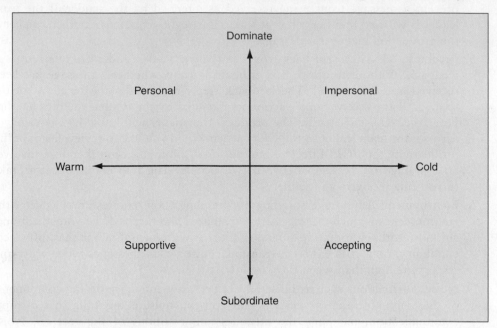

Source: Sorenson, Ritch; Debord, Grace; Ramirez, Ida, *Business and Management Communication: A Guide Book*, 4th Edition, © 2001. Adapted by permission of Pearson Education, Inc. Upper Saddle River, NJ.

The combination of dominate and cold communication sends the signal that the sender of the message wants to control and limit or even withdraw from a personal relationship. A team leader might say that she cannot attend a Saturday morning meeting because she has to go out of town for her brother's wedding. A dominant and cold manager might say, "I don't want to hear about your personal life. Everyone in this department has to attend our Saturday meeting."

Subordinate actions combined with warm communication signal a desire to maintain or build the relationship while yielding to the other person. A manager communicating in a warm and subordinate manner in relation to the wedding request might say, "We'll miss you on Saturday morning because you are a key player in our department. However, I recognize that major events in personal life sometimes take priority over a business meeting."

Figure 4-2 summarizes how the dual dimensions of dominate–subordinate and cold–warm influence the relationship-building aspects of communication. Rather than regarding these four quadrants of relationships as good or bad, think of your purposes. In some situations, you might want to dominant and be cold, yet in most situations you might want to submit a little and be warm in order to build a relationship. For example, being dominant and cold might be necessary for a security officer who is trying to control an unruly crowd at a sporting event.

Observe that the person in the quadrant *dominate–cold* has an impersonal relationship with the receiver, and the person in the *warm–subordinate* quadrant has a supportive relationship with the receiver. Being *dominant and warm* leads to a personal relationship, whereas being *subordinate and cold* leads to an accepting relationship. The combinations of *dominate–cold* and *warm–subordinate* are more likely to produce the results indicated.

Harvard psychologist Steven Pinker adds additional insight into how warm acquaintances communicate. They go out of their way not to look as if they are presuming a dominate–subordinate–relationship but instead a relationship of equals.[3] Your friend who values your relationship might say, "If you are going to the recycling center today, is there any chance you might be able to take along my old cell phone and laptop with you?"

An acquaintance not interested in maintaining a relationship with you might communicate in a cold, dominate–subordinate fashion by saying, "When you visit the recycling center today, take along my old cell phone and laptop with you."

NONVERBAL COMMUNICATION IN ORGANIZATIONS

A substantial amount of communication between people takes place at the nonverbal level. **Nonverbal communication** refers to the transmission of messages through means other than words. These messages accompany verbal messages or sometimes stand-alone. The general purpose of nonverbal communication is to communicate the feeling behind a message. For instance, you can say no with either a clenched fist or a smile to communicate the intensity of your negative or positive feelings. Workers who rely solely on verbal messages to communicate with employees miss what the majority of what work associates are saying.[4]

The following paragraphs **summarize** the major modes of transmission of nonverbal communication and provide guidelines for improving nonverbal communication. Chapter 8, about cross-cultural relations, describes cultural differences in nonverbal communication.

Modes of Transmission of Nonverbal Communication

Nonverbal communication can be transmitted in many modes. You may be surprised that certain factors, such as dress and appearance, are considered as part of nonverbal communication.

Environment.   The setting or environment in which you send a message can influence how that message is received. Assume that your manager invites you out to lunch at an upscale restaurant to discuss a problem. You will think it is a more important topic under these circumstances than you would if the manager had lunch with you in the company cafeteria.

Other important environmental silent messages include room color, temperature, lighting, and furniture arrangement. A person who sits behind a large, uncluttered desk, for example, appears more powerful than a person who sits behind a small, messy desk.

Interpersonal Distance.   The placement of one's body in relation to someone else is widely used to transmit messages (see Figure 4-3). In general, getting physically close to another person conveys a positive attitude toward that person. Putting your arm around someone is generally interpreted as a friendly act. (Some people, however, recoil when touched by someone other than a close friend. Touching others on the job can also be

nonverbal communication

The transmission of messages through means other than words.

summarization

The process of summarizing, pulling together, condensing, and thereby clarifying the main points communicated by another person.

FIGURE 4-3   Four Circles of Intimacy

Intimate Distance
Close - 0″ to 6″

Far - 6″ to 18″

Personal Distance
Close - 1-1/2′ to 2′

Far - 2′ to 4′

Social Distance
Close - 4′ to 7′

Far - 7′ to 12′

Public Distance
12′ to 25′ and Beyond

interpreted as sexual harassment.) Watch out for cultural differences in preferences for interpersonal distance, such as French people standing much closer to each other while conversing than do Americans.

Closely related to interpersonal distance is where and how you sit in relation to another person during a meeting. Sitting across the table from a person during a negotiation session creates a defensive, competitive atmosphere, often leading to each party taking a firm stand on his or her point of view. The table becomes a tangible and psychological barrier between both parties. Recognition of this observation leads many managers and salespeople to sit down with another person with either no table or a coffee table between the two. Even when seated on separate chairs instead of a sofa, removal of a large table or desk separating the two parties leads to a friendlier, more open negotiation or sales discussion.

Posture.   Posture communicates a variety of messages. Standing erect usually conveys the message that the person is self-confident and experiencing positive emotion. Slumping makes a person appear to be lacking in self-confidence or down in the dumps. Another interpersonal message conveyed by posture involves the direction of leaning. Leaning toward the sender suggests that you are favorably disposed toward his or her message; leaning backward communicates the opposite. Openness of the arms or legs serves as an indicator of liking or caring. In general, people establish closed postures (arms folded and legs crossed) when speaking to people they dislike.

Can you think of an aspect of your posture that conveys a specific message?

Hand Gestures.   Frequent hand movements show positive attitudes toward another person. In contrast, dislike or disinterest usually produces few gestures. An important exception is that some people wave their hands furiously while arguing. Gestures are also said to provide clues to a person's levels of dominance and submission. The gestures of dominant people are typically directed outward toward the other person. Examples include a steady, unwavering gaze and touching one's partner. Submissive gestures are usually protective, such as touching oneself or shrugging one's shoulders. A person who tucks his or her thumbs under his arms so that only the fingers are exposed is resisting what is being said.[5]

Facial Expressions and Eye Contact.   Using your head, face, and eyes in combination provides the clearest indications of interpersonal attitudes. Looking at the ceiling (without tilting your head), combined with a serious expression, almost always communicates the message "I doubt what you're saying is true." Maintaining eye contact with another person improves communication. To maintain eye contact, it is usually necessary to move your face and eyes with the other person. Moving your face and eyes away from the other person is often interpreted as defensiveness or a lack of self-confidence.

The face is often used as a primary source of information about how we feel. We look for facial clues when we want to determine another person's attitude. You can often judge someone's current state of happiness by looking at his or her face. The term "sourpuss" attests to this observation. Happiness, apprehension, anger, resentment, sadness, contempt, enthusiasm, and embarrassment are but a few of the emotions that can be expressed through the face.

Voice Quality.   Often more significance is attached to the *way* something is said than to *what* is said. A forceful voice, which includes a consistent tone without vocalized pauses, connotes power and control. Closely related to voice tone are volume, pitch, and rate of speaking. Anger, boredom, and joy often can be interpreted from voice quality. Anger is noted when the person speaks loudly, with a high pitch and at a fast rate. Boredom is indicated by a monotone. Joy is indicated by loud volume. Avoiding an annoying voice quality can make a positive impact on others. The research of voice coach Jeffrey Jacobi provides some useful suggestions. He surveyed a nationwide sample of 1,000 men and women and asked, "Which irritating or unpleasant voice annoys you the most?" The most irritating was a whining, complaining, or nagging tone.

Jacobi notes that we are judged by the way we sound. He also notes that careers can be damaged by voice problems such as those indicated in the survey. "We think about

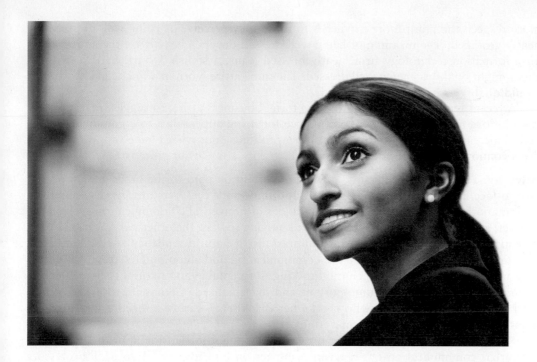

how we look and dress," says Jacobi, "and that gets most of the attention. But people judge our intelligence much more by how we sound than how we dress."[6] Do Self-Assessment Quiz 4-1 to apply Jacobi's findings to your development.

Voice quality can be even more important over the phone because you cannot rely on facial expressions and eye contact to improve your message. Ed Barks who trains public speakers says that small-business owners need to make effective use of their vocal pitch, articulation, volume, and rate of speech. Furthermore, "Paying attention to all of these factors is essential if a small-business owner has any hope of capturing the fancy of his or her attendant at the other end of the line."[7] The same suggestions would apply to anyone trying to create a favorable impression in other work environments.

Personal Appearance. Your external image plays an important role in communicating messages to others. Job seekers show recognition of the personal appearance aspect of nonverbal communication when they carefully groom for a job interview. People pay

---

SELF-ASSESSMENT QUIZ 4-1

Voice Quality Checkup

The voice quality study cited in the text ranked voice quality in decreasing order of annoyance, as follows:

- Whining, complaining, or nagging tone—44.0 percent
- High-pitched, squeaky voice—15.9 percent
- Mumbling—11.1 percent
- Very fast talking—4.9 percent
- Weak and wimpy voice—3.6 percent
- Flat, monotonous tone—3.5 percent
- Thick accent—2.4 percent

Directions: Ask yourself and two other people familiar with your voice whether you have one or more of the preceding voice-quality problems. If your self-analysis and feedback from others does indicate a serious problem, get started on self-improvement. Record your voice on tape and attempt to modify the biggest problem. Another avenue of improvement is to consult with a speech coach or therapist.

more respect and grant more privileges to those they perceive as being well dressed and neatly groomed. The meaning of being well dressed depends heavily on the situation. In an information technology firm, neatly pressed jeans, a stylish T-shirt, and clean sport shoes might qualify as being well dressed. The same attire worn in a financial service firm would qualify as being poorly dressed.

A recent tendency is a return to more formal business attire, to suggest that a person is ambitious and successful. The best advice for using appearance to communicate nonverbal messages is to size up the environment to figure out what type of appearance and dress connotes the image you want to project.

Attention Paid to Other Person.   The more attention paid to the other person during face-to-face interaction, the more valued and important that person feels. Paying attention to another individual includes other modes of nonverbal communication such as eye contact, an interested facial expression, and moving toward the other person. In a society that increasingly accepts and values multitasking, a natural tendency is to divide your attention between the person you are communicating and a computer screen, cell phone message, or a text message. Such multitasking is acceptable and natural to some people, yet makes many others feel unimportant and marginalized. Communication consultant Erick Krell writes, "A CEO who checks her BlackBerry during a meeting can give the impression that the session is unimportant."[8]

Recent research using electronic data supports the idea that the appropriate type of nonverbal communication has a positive impact on effectiveness. Two MIT professors Sandy Pentland and Daniel Olguín outfitted executives as a party with electronic devices that recorded data on their nonverbal signals, including tone of voice, gesticulation, and proximity to others. Five days later the same executives presented business plans to a panel of judges in a contest related to business plans. Without reading or hearing the presentations made to the judges, Pentland correctly predicted the winners, using only data collected at the party. The presence of a larger number of positive nonverbal signals was used to predict success in presenting a business plan.[9]

Guidelines for Improving Nonverbal Communication

Nonverbal communication, like verbal communication, can be improved. Here are six suggestions to consider.

1. **Obtain feedback on your body language by asking others to comment upon the gestures and facial expressions you use in conversations.** Be videotaped conferring with another individual. After studying your body language, attempt to eliminate those mannerisms and gestures that you think detract from your effectiveness. Common examples include nervous gestures such as moving knees from side to side, cracking knuckles, rubbing the eyes or nose, head scratching, and jingling coins.

2. **Learn to relax when communicating with others.** Take a deep breath and consciously allow your body muscles to loosen. Tension-reducing techniques should be helpful here. A relaxed person makes it easier for other people to relax. You are likely to elicit more useful information from other people when you are relaxed. Also, you will appear more confident and credible when you are relaxed to an appropriate degree.

3. **Use facial, hand, and body gestures to supplement your speech, but don't overdo it.** A good starting point is to use hand gestures to express enthusiasm. You can increase the potency of enthusiastic comments by shaking the other person's hand, nodding approval, or smiling.

4. **Avoid using the same nonverbal gesture indiscriminately.** If you want to use nodding to convey approval, do not nod with approval when you dislike what somebody else is saying. Also, do not pat everybody on the back. Nonverbal gestures that are used indiscriminately lose their communication effectiveness.

5. **Use role-playing to practice various forms of nonverbal communication.** A good starting point would be to practice selling your ideas about an important project

The Mirroring Technique

To practice mirroring, during the next 10 days each class member schedules one mirroring session with an unsuspecting subject. An ideal opportunity would be an upcoming meeting on the job. Another possibility would be to ask a friend if you could practice your interviewing techniques with him or her—but do not mention the mirroring technique. A third possibility would be to sit down with a friend and conduct a social conversation.

While holding an interview or discussion with the other party, use the mirroring technique. Imitate the person's breathing pattern, rate of speech, hand movements, eye movements, leg movements, or any other noticeable aspect of behavior.

After the mirroring sessions have been conducted, hold a class discussion about the results. Questions include the following:

1. Did the other person notice the mirroring and comment on the behavior of the person doing the mirroring?
2. Was the rapport enhanced (or hindered) by the mirroring?
3. How many of the students intend to repeat the mirroring technique in the future?

or concept to another person. During your interchange, supplement your spoken messages with appropriate nonverbal cues, such as posture, voice intonation, gestures, and so forth. Later, obtain the other person's perception of the effectiveness of your nonverbal communication.

6. **Use mirroring to establish rapport.** Nonverbal communication can be improved through **mirroring,** or subtly imitating someone. The most successful mirroring technique is to imitate the breathing pattern of another person. If you adjust your own breathing rate to match someone else's, you will soon establish rapport with that individual. Another effective mirroring technique is to adopt the voice speed of the person with whom you are communicating. If the other person speaks more slowly than you typically do, slow down to mirror him or her.

mirroring

Subtly imitating someone

You can also use mirroring by imitating a manager to win favor. Many subordinates have a relentless tendency to copy the boss's mannerisms, gestures, way of speaking, and dress. As a consequence, without realizing why, your manager may think more favorably of you.

Caution: Do not use mirroring to the extent that you appear to be mocking another person, thereby adversely affecting rapport. Do Skill-Building Exercise 4-1 to get started developing your mirroring skills.

GUIDELINES FOR OVERCOMING COMMUNICATION PROBLEMS AND BARRIERS

Communication problems in organizations are ever-present. Some interference usually takes place between ideation and action, as suggested earlier by the noise factor in Figure 4-1. The type of message influences the amount of interference. Routine or neutral messages are the easiest to communicate. Interference is most likely to occur when a message is complex, emotionally arousing, or clashes with a receiver's mental set.

LEARNING OBJECTIVE 4

An emotionally arousing message deals with topics such as money or a relationship between two people. A message that clashes with a receiver's mental set requires the person to change his or her typical pattern of receiving messages. Try this experiment. The next time you visit a restaurant, order dessert first and the main meal second. The server probably will not receive your dessert order because it deviates from the normal sequence.

Here we will describe strategies and tactics for overcoming some of the more frequently observed communication problems in the workplace, as outlined in Figure 4-4. A useful guideline is that the communicator should take the initiative to increase the probability that his or her message will get across as intended. In the words of Jess Thomas, the chairman, president, and CEO of Molina Healthcare of Michigan, "A sobering reality in communication is that the greater burden and basis for breakdown in effective communication rests with the communicator. The communicator has to be very articulate in communicating what he or she wants."[10]

FIGURE 4-4   Overcoming Communication Problems and Barriers

1. Understand the receiver.
2. Minimize defensive communication.
3. Repeat your message using multiple channels.
4. Check comprehension and feelings via verbal and nonverbal feedback.
5. Display a positive attitude.
6. Communicate persuasively.
7. Engage in active listening.
8. Prepare for stressful conversations.
9. Engage in metacommunication.
10. Recognize gender differences in communication style.

Understand the Receiver

Understanding the person you are trying to reach is a fundamental principle of overcoming communication barriers. The more you know about your receiver, the better you are able to deliver your message effectively. Three important aspects of understanding the receiver are (1) developing empathy, (2) recognizing his or her motivational state, and (3) understanding the other person's frame of reference.

empathy

In communication, imagining oneself in the receiver's role, and assuming the viewpoints and emotions of that individual.

Developing **empathy** requires placing yourself in the receiver's shoes. To accomplish this, you have to imagine yourself in the other person's role and assume the viewpoints and emotions of that individual. You have to imagine how you would feel if placed in that situation.[11] For example, if a supervisor were trying to communicate the importance of customer service to sales associates, the supervisor might ask himself or herself, "If I were a part-time employee being paid close to the minimum wage, how receptive would I be to messages about superior customer service?" To empathize you have to understand another person. *Sympathy* means that you understand and agree.

Research suggests that subtle patterns of brain cells, called mirror neurons, help us empathize with others. These brain circuits reflect the actions and intentions of others as if they were our own. Neuroscientist Marco Iacoboni explains that the mirror system gives us an open-mindedness and a propensity to understand others and cultures. The cells work in this manner: When another person smiles or wrinkles his or her nose in distaste, motor cells in your own brain linked to those expressions resonate in response like a tuning fork. As a result, you get a hint of the feeling itself. The more empathy you have, the stronger the motor neuron response.[12]

The biological component to empathy should not lead you to conclude that empathy is not a skill that can be acquired. It is conceivable that as you develop empathy, your mirror neurons grow in number or become better developed, just as your calf muscles become better defined if you run frequently.

motivational state

Any active needs and interests operating at a given time.

The receiver's **motivational state** could include any active needs and interests operating at the time. People tend to listen attentively to messages that show promise of satisfying an active need or interest. Management usually listens attentively to a suggestion framed in terms of cost savings or increased profits. A coworker is likely to be attentive to your message if you explain how your idea can lead to a better year-end financial bonus for the group.

frame of reference

The fact that people perceive words and concepts differently because their vantage points and perspectives differ.

People perceive words and concepts differently because their vantage points and perspectives differ. Such differences in **frame of reference** create barriers to communication. A frame of reference can also be considered a lens through which we view the world. A manager attempted to chastise a team member by saying, "If you keep up your present level of performance, you'll be a repair technician all your life." The technician replied, "That's good news," because he was proud of being the first person in his family to hold a skilled job. Understanding another person's frame of reference requires empathy.

On a day-by-day basis, understanding another person's frame of reference often translates into figuring out his or her mindset. A woman telephoned a tech support center located in India with a sense of frustration in her voice. She said she was instructed by her computer to "press any key to continue," and was upset that her keyboard didn't have an "any" key. The caller's mindset was that she had to search for the "any" key.[13] Of course, a more perceptive person might have noticed that the instructions did not say, press *the* any key to continue, but *any key*.

Minimize Defensive Communication

An important general communication barrier is **defensive communication**—the tendency to receive messages in such a way that our self-esteem is protected. Defensive communication is also responsible for people sending messages to make them look good. For example, when being criticized for low production, a financial sales consultant might blame high interest rates that are drawing customers away from stock and mutual funds.

Overcoming the barrier of defensive communication requires two steps. First, people have to recognize the existence of defensive communication. Second, they have to try not to be defensive when questioned or criticized. Such behavior is not easy because of the unconscious or semiconscious process of **denial**—the suppression of information we find uncomfortable. For example, the sales consultant just cited would find it uncomfortable to think of himself or herself as being responsible for below-average performance.

defensive communication

The tendency to receive messages in such a way that our self-esteem is protected.

denial

The suppression of information we find uncomfortable.

Repeat Your Message Using Multiple Channels (in Moderation)

Repetition enhances communication, particularly when different channels are used to convey the same message. Effective communicators at many job levels follow spoken agreements with written documentation. Since most communication is subject to at least some distortion, the chances of a message being received as intended increase when two or more channels are used. Many firms have a policy of using a multiple-channel approach to communicate the results of a performance evaluation. The worker receives an oral explanation from the manager of the results of the review. The worker is also required to read the form and indicate by signature that he or she has read and understands the meaning of the review. Another useful way of using multiple channels is to follow up a telephone call or in-person conversation with an e-mail or text message summarizing key facts or agreements.

When repeating your message or using multiple channels, use moderation to avoid contributing to the problem of **information overload**—a phenomenon that occurs when people are so overloaded with information that they cannot respond effectively to messages. Current research suggests that the expanding volume of information can affect not only create stress but also decision making, innovation, and productivity.[14]

Check Comprehension and Feelings through Verbal and Nonverbal Feedback

Ask for feedback to determine whether your message has been received as intended. A frequent managerial practice is to conclude a meeting with a question such as, "Okay, what have we agreed upon?" Unless feedback of this nature is obtained, you will not know whether your message has been received until the receiver carries out your request. If the request is carried out improperly, or if no action is taken, you will know that the message was received poorly.

Obtaining feedback is important because it results in two-way communication in which people take turns being sender and receiver, thereby having a dialogue. Dialogues take time because they require people to speak more slowly and listen more carefully. The results of having employees engage in dialogue are said to include a deeper sense of community (a feeling of belongingness) and greater trust among employees.[15] Relate this finding to your own experiences. Do you trust people more when you both exchange ideas and listen to each other?

Feedback is also important because it provides reinforcement to the sender, and few people will continue to communicate without any reinforcement. The sender is reinforced when the receiver indicates understanding of the message. When the original receiver indicates that he or she understands the message, that person becomes the sender. A nod of approval would be an appropriate type of nonverbal reinforcement for the sender to receive.

In addition to looking for verbal comprehension and emotions when you have delivered a message, check for feelings after you have received a message. When a person speaks, we too often listen to the facts and ignore the feelings. If feelings are ignored, the true meaning and intent of the message is likely to be missed, thus creating a communication barrier. Your boss might say to you, "You never seem to take work home." To clarify what your boss means by this statement, you might ask, "Is that good or bad?" Your boss's response will give you feedback on his or her feelings about getting all your work done during regular working hours.

When you send a message, it is also helpful to express your feelings in addition to conveying the facts. For example, "Our defects are up by 12 percent (fact), and I'm quite disappointed about those results (feelings)." Because feelings contribute strongly to comprehension, you will help overcome a potential communication barrier.

Display a Positive Attitude

Being perceived as having a positive attitude helps melt communication barriers. This is true because most people prefer to communicate with a positive person. According to Sharon Lund O'Neil, you must establish credibility and trustworthiness if you expect others to listen, let alone get them to react positively to your communication.[16] Being positive helps make you appear more credible and trustworthy, whereas being consistently negative makes you less credible and trustworthy. As one coworker said about a chronic complainer in his office, "Why take Margot seriously? She finds something wrong with everybody and everything."

Communicate Persuasively

A powerful tactic for overcoming communication barriers is to communicate so persuasively that obstacles disappear. Persuasiveness refers to the sender convincing the receiver to accept his or her message. Persuasion thus involves selling to others. Hundreds of articles, books, audiotapes, and videos have been developed to help people become more persuasive. Following are some representative suggestions for becoming a more persuasive communicator, both in speaking and in writing.[17]

1. **Know exactly what you want.** Your chances of selling an idea increase to the extent that you have clarified the idea in your own mind. The clearer and more committed you are at the outset of a selling or negotiating session, the stronger you are as a persuader.

2. **Never suggest an action without telling its end benefit.** In asking for a raise, you might say, "If I get this raise, I'll be able to afford to stay with this job as long as the company likes. I will also increase my productivity because I won't be distracted by thinking about meeting my expenses."

3. **Get a yes response early on.** It is helpful to give the persuading session a positive tone by establishing a "yes pattern" at the outset. Assume that an employee wanted to convince the boss to allow the employee to perform some work at home during normal working hours. The employee might begin the idea-selling questions with "Is it important for the company to obtain maximum productivity from all its employees?"

4. **Use power words.** An expert tactic for being persuasive is to sprinkle your speech with power (meaning powerful) words. Power words stir emotion and bring forth images of exciting events. Examples of power words include consequences, impact, commitment, bonding with customers, surpassing previous profits, sustaining customer loyalty, and sustainability. Using power words is part of having a broad vocabulary.

> " If you want to get to a certain level, especially in a professional environment like most businesses, you have to project the right image. You have to speak the way people you aspire to be speak. Your speech is related to status. "
>
> —Dian DiResta, speech pathologist who runs her own consulting firm in New York, Quoted in Alyssa Danigelis, "Like, Um, You Know," *Fast Company*, May 2006, p. 99.

5. **Minimize raising your pitch at the end of sentences.** Part of being persuasive is not to sound unsure and apologetic. In English and several other languages, a convenient way to ask a question or to express doubt is to raise the pitch of your voice at the end of a sentence or phrase. As a test, use the sentence "You like my ideas." First say *ideas* using approximately the same pitch and tone as with every other word. Then say the same sentence by pronouncing *ideas* with a higher pitch and louder tone. By saying *ideas* loudly, you sound much less certain and are less persuasive.

6. **Talk to your audience, not the screen.** Computer graphic presentations have become standard practice even in small-group meetings. Many presenters rely so heavily on computer-generated slides and transparencies that they basically read the slides and transparencies to the audience. In an oral presentation, the predominant means of connection between sender and receiver should be eye contact. When your audience is frequently distracted by movement on the screen, computer sounds, garish colors, or you looking at the screen, eye contact suffers. As a result, the message is weakened, and you are less persuasive.[18]

7. **Back up conclusions with data.** You will be more persuasive if you support your spoken and written presentations with solid data. You can collect the data yourself or quote from a printed or electronic source. Relying too much on research has a potential disadvantage, however. Being too dependent on data could suggest that you have little faith in your intuition. For example, you might convey a weak impression if, when asked your opinion, you respond, "I can't answer until I collect some data."

8. **Minimize "wimp" phrases and words.** Persuasive communicators minimize statements that make them appear weak and indecisive. Such phrases convey the impression that they are not in control of their actions. Wimp phrases include: "It's one of those days," "I'm not sure about that," "Don't quote me on that," and "I'll try my best to get it done." (It is better to commit yourself forcibly by saying, "I'll get it done.") Wimpy words include "sort of," "hopefully," and "maybe." Although wimp phrases and words should be minimized, there are times when they reflect honest communication, such as a team leader saying to the manager, "Maybe we can get this crash project completed by the end of the month."

    Another problem with wimp words and phrases is that they can mark your image, or make you appear not in control of your work. Three examples follow:

    - "I'm too busy/I don't have time/I'm just swamped."
    - "I'm having one of those days/Things are crazy here/You have caught me at a bad time."
    - "We'll see how it goes/I'll try my best."[19]

9. **Avoid or minimize common language errors.** You will enhance your persuasiveness if you minimize common language errors because you will appear more articulate and informed. Here are several common language errors:

    a. "Just between you and I" is wrong. "Just between you and me" is correct.
    b. *Irregardless* is not a word; *regardless* is correct.
    c. Avoid double negatives when you want to express the negative, despite the increasing popularity of double negatives. Common examples of double negatives are "I got no nothing from my best customer this week" and "We don't have no money in the budget for travel." If expressed with the right inflection, a double negative can be correct. For example, to say "We don't have no money" with an emphasis on *no money* means that the budget is not completely depleted. Yet in general, double negatives make the sender appear so ill-informed that they fail to persuade.
    d. "We are customer-oriented" is correct. "We are customer-orientated" is wrong. Here is an example of an error so widely committed that it would be fair to wonder if dictionaries will soon include *orientated*.
    e. "Ask you guest what *they* want for lunch" is incorrect despite the widespread use of using a plural pronoun instead of the singular. "Ask your guest what *he*

(or *she*) wants" is correct. A caution here is that it appears about 90 percent of Americans including the well-educated confuse the singular and plural today, so using "they" instead of "he" or "she" is not a dreadful error in grammar. However, using "themselves" instead of "him" or "her" is a dreadful error. An example of this misuse is, "I prefer a coworker who can speak up for *themselves*."

10. **Avoid overuse of jargon and clichés.** To feel "in" and hip many workers rely heavily on jargon and clichés, such as referring to their "fave" (for *favorite*) product, or that "At the end of the day" something counts, or that software is "scalable" (meaning it can get bigger). Add to the list "a seamless company" to mean the various departments cooperate with one another. The caution is that if a person uses jargon and hip phrases too frequently the person appears to be too contrived, and lacking in imagination.[20]

If you can learn to implement most of the preceding 10 suggestions, you are on your way toward becoming a persuasive communicator. In addition, you will need solid facts behind you, and you will need to make skillful use of nonverbal communication. If you are looking for an example of a persuasive communicator in business, check out David A. Brandon, the former CEO of Domino's Pizza. Brandon is such a great motivator and communicator that many people have encouraged him to run for public office. He is now the director of intercollegiate athletics at the University of Michigan. See if you can find a video of Brandon on the Internet.

Skill-Building Exercise 4-2 provides you an opportunity to practice persuasive communication.

Engage in Active Listening

LEARNING OBJECTIVE 5

Persuasion deals primarily with sending messages. Improving one's receiving of messages is another part of developing better communication skills. Unless you receive messages as they are intended, you cannot perform your job properly or be a good companion. A major challenge in developing good listening skills is that we process information much more quickly than most people speak. The average speaking rate is about 130 words per minute. In contrast, the average rate of processing information is about 300 words per minute.[21] So, you have to slow down mentally to listen well. A related problem is that many people like to dominate conversations, making it difficult to listen. As expressed by investment banker Herb Allen, "It's tough to listen when you're talking."[22]

Listening can be even more essential than talking when engaged in face-to-face communication. Listening is a particularly important skill for anybody whose job involves troubleshooting, because one needs to gather information in order to solve problems. Another reason that improving the listening skills of employees is important is that insufficient listening is extraordinarily costly. Listening mistakes lead to reprocessing letters,

SKILL-BUILDING EXERCISE 4-2

I Want a Raise

The purpose of this exercise is to practice your persuasive skills using a topic of interest to many people—obtaining a salary increase. One by one, students make a presentation in front of the class, presenting a persuasive argument why they merit a salary increase. The instructor will decide whether to use a handful of volunteers or the entire class. The audience represents the boss. The student will first explain his or her job title and key responsibilities. (Use your imagination here.) Next, make a three-minute convincing argument as to why you merit a salary increase, and perhaps indicate how much you want. You will probably have to spend about 15 minutes into preparation, inside or outside of class.

After the presentations, volunteers will offer feedback on the effectiveness of selected presentations. During the presentations

of the other students, make a few notes about the presenter's effectiveness. You may need a couple of minutes between presenters to make your notes. Consider these factors:

- Overall, how convincing was the presenter? If you were the boss, would you give him or her the requested salary increase?
- Which techniques of persuasion did he or she use?
- What aspect of the presentation was unconvincing or negative?

What lessons did you take away from this exercise about persuasive communication?

rescheduling appointments, reshipping orders, and recalling defective products. Effective listening also improves interpersonal relations because the people listened to feel understood and respected.

A major component of effective listening is to be an **active listener**. The active listener listens intensely, with the goal of empathizing with the speaker. Several important skills and behaviors associated with active listening are presented next.

Accept the Sender's Figure of Speech.   A useful way of showing empathy is to accept the sender's figure of speech. By so doing, the sender feels understood and accepted. Also, if you reject the person's figure of speech by rewording it, the sender may become defensive. Many people use the figure of speech "I'm stuck" when they cannot accomplish a task. You can facilitate smooth communication by a response such as, "What can I do to help you get unstuck?" If you respond with something like, "What can I do to help you think more clearly?" the person is forced to change mental channels and may become defensive.[23]

Paraphrase and Listen Reflectively.   As a result of listening actively, the listener can give feedback to the speaker what he or she thinks the speaker meant. Feedback of this type relies on both verbal and nonverbal communication. Feedback is also important because it facilitates two-way communication. To be an active listener, it is also important to **paraphrase**, or repeat in your own words what the sender says, feels, and means. Paraphrasing is also referred to as reflective listening, because the listener reflects back what the sender said. You might feel awkward the first several times you paraphrase. Therefore, try it with a person with whom you feel comfortable. With some practice, it will become a natural part of your communication skill kit. Here is an example of how you might use paraphrasing:

> **Other Person:** I'm getting ticked off at working so hard around here. I wish somebody else would pitch in and do a fair day's work.
>
> **You:** You're saying that you do more than your fair share of the tough work in our department.
>
> **Other Person:** You bet. Here's what I think we should be doing about it. . . .

Life coach Sophronia Scott advises that, after you have paraphrased, it is sometimes helpful to ask the person you listened to whether your impression of what he or she said is correct. Your goal is not to make others repeat themselves but to extend the conversation so that you can obtain more useful details.[24]

Minimize Distractions.   If feasible, keep papers and your computer screen out of sight when listening to somebody else. Having distractions in sight creates the temptation to glance away from the message sender. Avoid answering a cell telephone call unless you are anticipating an emergency call. At the start of your conversation, notice the other person's eye color to help you establish eye contact. (But don't keep staring at his or her eyes!)

Ask Questions.   A major technique of active listening is to ask questions rather than making conclusive statements. Asking questions provides more useful information. Suppose a teammate is late with data you need to complete your analysis. Instead of saying, "I must have your input by Thursday afternoon," try, "When will I get your input?"

Allow Sender to Finish His or Her Sentence.   Be sure to let others speak until they have finished. Do not interrupt by talking about you, jumping in with advice, or offering solutions unless requested. Equally bad for careful listening is to finish the sentence of a receiver. Almost all people prefer to complete their own thoughts, even though there are two curious traditions that run counter to this idea. One is that business partners who have been working together for many years, and understand each other well, have a tendency to finish the other partner's sentence. Couples in personal life behave similarly. Also, have you noticed how when you start to enter a phrase into a major search engine, suddenly you are given about 10 choices that are not necessarily what you are planning to write? (Of course, this is responding to writing and not really listening, but the overtaking of your thinking is the same.)

Use Nonverbal Communication. Another component to active listening is to indicate by your body language that you are listening intently. When a coworker comes to you with a question or concern, focus on that person and exclude all else. If you tap your fingers on the desk or glance around the room, you send the message that the other person and his or her concerns do not warrant your full attention. Listening intently through nonverbal communication also facilitates active listening because it demonstrates respect for the receiver.

Observing nonverbal communication is another important part of active listening. Look to see if the speaker's verbal communication matches his or her nonverbal communication. Suppose you ask another person if he or she would like to join your committee. If the person says "yes," but looks bored and defensive, he or she is probably not really interested in joining your committee. Quite often a person's nonverbal communication is more indicative of the truth than is verbal communication.

Minimize Words That Shut Down Discussion. A key part of listening is to keep the conversation flowing. According to executive coach Marshall Goldsmith, an especially useful approach to keep conversation going in most work situations is for the listener to minimize certain negatively tone words that frequently shut down conversation. When you say "no," "but," or "however," you effectively shut down or limit the conversation. No matter what words follow, the sender receives a message to the effect, "You are wrong and I am right." Even if you say "I agree, but . . ." the shutdown message still comes through. The other person is likely to get into the defensive mode.[25] Another way of shutting down conversation is to say, "I already know that."

After the person has finished talking, there are times it will be appropriate to say "no," "but," or "however." Assume, for example, that a worker says to the business owner that the company should donate one-third its profits to charity each year. The owner might then reply, "I hear you, but if we give away all that money our profits will be too slim to grow the business."

Avoid the Need to Lie or Fake When You Have Not Been Paying Attention. A consequence of active listening is that you will avoid the need to pretend that you have been paying attention. Performance management coach Joe Takash suggests that you

> remind yourself that other people can sense if you're not listening. Force yourself to be honest and admit that you didn't catch everything that was said. That means asking the other person to repeat or requesting clarification. In this way you're being honest rather than deceitful—and deceit kills results-producing relationships fast.[26]

Specific suggestions for improving active listening skills are summarized in Figure 4-5. These suggestions relate to good listening in general, as well as active listening. Many suggestions reinforce what has already been described. As with any other suggestions for developing a new skill, considerable practice (with some supervision) is needed to bring about actual changes in behavior. One of the problems a poor listener would encounter is the difficulty of breaking old habits in order to acquire new ones. Self-Assessment Quiz 4-2 gives

BACK TO THE OPENING CASE

Much of Maria's success in expanding her business with the Detroit business firm can be attributed to the relationship building that took place based on face-to-face communication. Notice also that Maria engaged in active listening as she provided Larry an opportunity to describe what he liked and disliked about the machines he bought from her company. Maria listened carefully instead of becoming defensive when Larry described his concerns.

FIGURE 4-5   Suggestions for Active Listening

- *While your target is talking, look at him or her intently.* At the same time, maintain steady eye contact.

- *Be patient about your turn to speak.* A common barrier to effective listening is to mentally prepare an answer while another person is speaking.

- *Nod your head in agreement from time to time.*

- *Mutter "mmh" or "uh-huh" periodically but not incessantly.*

- *Ask open-ended questions to encourage the other person to talk.* For example, you encourage more conversation by saying "What do you think of . . . ?" rather than asking "Do you agree that . . . ?"

- *Reflect your target's content or meaning.* Rephrase and summarize concisely what the other person is saying.

- *Reflect the other person's feelings.* Reflection-of-feeling responses typically begin with "You feel that . . . "

- *Keep your ratio of talking to listening down to about one to five.* In other words, spend 20 percent of your time talking, and 80 percent listening to be perceived as a great listener.

- *Ask yourself whether anything the other person is saying could benefit you.* Maintaining this perspective will enable you to benefit from most listening episodes and will motivate you to listen intently.

you an opportunity to think about bad listening habits you may have acquired. To practice your listening skills, do Skill-Building Exercise 4-3.

Prepare for Stressful Conversations

Communication barriers will frequently surface when two or more people are engaged in conversation fraught with emotion, such as giving highly negative performance feedback, rejecting a person for membership in your team, or firing an employee. Giving praise is another exchange that can make both or either parties uncomfortable. The sender might feel that he or she is patronizing the receiver, and the receiver might feel unworthy of the praise. One technique for reducing the stress in potentially stressful conversations is to prepare for them in advance.

A starting point in preparing for a stressful conversation is self-awareness about how you react to certain uncomfortable exchanges. For example, how do you feel when the receiver of the negative feedback reacts with hostility? Do you clam up, or do you become counterhostile? If you anticipate a hostile reception to an upcoming conversation, rehearse the scenario with a neutral friend. Deliver the controversial content that you will be delivering during the real event. Practice the body language you will use when you deliver a phrase such as, "As team leader, I must tell you that you have contributed almost nothing of value to our current project." Another part of the rehearsal is to practice delivering clear content—be explicit about what you mean. "Almost nothing of value to our current project" is much more explicit than "Your contribution has much room for improvement."

Also, practice *temperate phrasing*, or being tactful while delivering negative feedback. Communications specialist Holly Weeks suggests the following: Instead of snapping at someone, "Stop interrupting me"—try this: "Can you hold on a minute? I want to finish before I lose my train of thought." Temperate phrasing will take some of the sting out of a stressful conversation.[27]

Listening Traps

Communication specialists at Purdue University have identified certain behavior patterns that interfere with effective hearing and listening. After thinking carefully about each trap, check how well the trap applies to you: *not a problem,* or *need improvement.* To respond to the statements accurately, visualize how you acted when you recently were in a situation calling for listening.

	Not a problem	Need improvement
• **Mind reader.** You will receive limited information if you constantly think "What is this person really thinking or feeling?"	❏	❏
• **Rehearser.** Your mental rehearsals for "Here's what I'll say next" tune out the sender.	❏	❏
• **Filterer.** You engage in selective listening by hearing only what you want to hear. (Could be difficult to judge because the process is often unconscious.)	❏	❏
• **Dreamer.** You drift off during a face-to-face conversation, which often leads you to an embarrassing "What did you say?" or "Could you repeat that?"	❏	❏
• **Identifier.** If you refer everything you hear to your experience, you probably did not really listen to what was said.	❏	❏
• **Comparer.** When you get sidetracked sizing up the sender, you are sure to miss the message.	❏	❏
• **Derailer.** You change the subject too quickly, giving the impression that you are not interested in anything the sender has to say.	❏	❏
• **Sparrer.** You hear what is said, but quickly belittle or discount it, putting you in the same class as the derailer.	❏	❏
• **Placater.** You agree with everything you hear just to be nice or to avoid conflict. By behaving this way, you miss out on the opportunity for authentic dialogue.	❏	❏

Interpretation: If you checked *need improvement* for five or more of the above statements, you are correct—your listening needs improvement! If you checked only two or fewer of the above traps, you are probably an effective listener and a supportive person.

Source: Listening Traps Quiz from *Messages: The Communication Skills Handbook* (Oakland, CA: New Harbinger Publications, 1983).

Listening to a Coworker

Before conducting the following role-plays, review the suggestions for effective listening presented in the text and Figure 4-5. Restating what you hear (summarization) is particularly important when listening to a person who is talking about an emotional topic.

The Elated Coworker: One student plays the role of a coworker who has just been offered a six-month assignment to the Rome, Italy, unit of the company. She will be receiving a 30 percent pay increase during the assignment plus a supplementary living allowance. She is eager to describe full details of her good fortune to a coworker. Another student plays the role of the coworker to whom the first worker wants to describe her good fortune. The second worker decides to listen intently to the first worker. Other class members will rate the second student on his or her listening ability.

The Discouraged Coworker: One student plays the role of a coworker who has just been placed on probation for poor job performance. His boss thinks that his performance is below standard and that his attendance and punctuality are poor. He is afraid that if he tells his girlfriend, she will leave him. He is eager to tell his tale of woe to a coworker. Another student plays the role of a coworker he corners to discuss his problems. The second worker decides to listen intently to his problems but is pressed for time. Other class members will rate the second student on his or her listening ability.

When evaluating the active listening skills of the role players, consider using the following evaluating factors, on a scale of 1 (low) to 5 (high):

Evaluation Factor	Rating 1 2 3 4 5
1. Maintained eye contact	
2. Showed empathy	
3. Summarize what the other person said	
4. Focused on other person instead of being distracted	
5. Asked questions	
6. Let other person speak until he or she was finished	

Engage in Metacommunication

Sometimes the best way to overcome a communication barrier with another person is to describe the nature of the relationship between you two at the moment. Metacommunication is to communicate about your communication to help overcome barriers or resolve a problem. If you, as a team leader, are facing heavy deadline pressures, you may say to a team member, "I might appear brusque today and tomorrow. Please don't take it personally. It's just that I have to make heavy demands on you because the team is facing a gruesome deadline." A more common situation is when the person with whom you are attempting to communicate appears angry or indifferent. Instead of wasting the communication event, it would be better to say, "You do not seem receptive to listening to me now. Are we having a problem? Should I try again later?"

metacommunication
To communicate about your communication to help overcome barriers or resolve a problem.

Recognize Gender Differences in Communication Style

A trend in organizations for many years has been to move toward gender equality. Despite this trend, substantial interest has arisen in identifying differences in communication styles between men and women. People who are aware of these differences face fewer communication barriers between themselves and members of the opposite sex. As we discuss these differences, recognize that they are group stereotypes. Please do not be offended by these stereotypes; they are exaggerations noticed by some researchers and observers. To cite one example that runs counter to the stereotype, some women dominate meetings whereas some men focus on listening to and supporting others during a meeting. Individual differences in communication style usually are more important than group (men vs. women) differences. Here we will discuss the major findings of gender differences in communication patterns.[28]

1. **Women prefer to use conversation for rapport building.** For most women, the intent of conversation is to build rapport and connections with people. Women are therefore more likely to emphasize similarities, to listen intently, and to be supportive.

2. **Men prefer to use talk primarily as a means to preserve independence and status by displaying knowledge and skill.** When most men talk, they want to receive positive evaluation from others and maintain their hierarchical status within the group. Men are therefore more oriented to giving a *report* while women are more interested in establishing *rapport*.

3. **Women want empathy, not solutions.** When women share feelings of being stressed out, they seek empathy and understanding. If they feel they have been listened to carefully, they begin to relax. When listening to the woman, the man may feel blamed for her problems or that he has failed the woman in some way. To feel useful, the man might offer solutions to the woman's problems.

4. **Men prefer to work out their problems by themselves, whereas women prefer to talk out solutions with another person.** Women look upon having and sharing problems as an opportunity to build and deepen relationships. Men are more likely to look upon problems as challenges they must meet on their own. The

communication consequence of these differences is that men may become uncommunicative when they have a problem.

5. **Women are more likely to compliment the work of a coworker, whereas men are more likely to be critical.** A communication problem may occur when a woman compliments the work of a male coworker and expects reciprocal praise.

6. **Men tend to be more directive in their conversation, whereas women emphasize politeness.** Women are therefore more likely to frequently use the phrases "I'm sorry" and "Thank you," even when there is no need to express apology or gratitude. For example, a supermarket manager notices that the store has suddenly become busy. She would therefore say to a store associate unpacking boxes, "I'm sorry Pedro, but we've become busy all of a sudden. Could you please open up a new lane up front? Thank you." A manager who is a stereotyped male might say, "Pedro, we need you to open a line up front, pronto. Put down the boxes and get up there."

7. **Women tend to be more conciliatory when facing differences, whereas men become more intimidating.** Again, women are more interested in building relationships, whereas men are more concerned about coming out ahead.

8. **Men are more interested than women in calling attention to their accomplishments or hogging recognition.** In one instance, a sales representative who had already made her sales quota for the month turned over an excellent prospect to a coworker. She reasoned, "It's somebody else's turn. I've received more than my fair share of bonuses for the month."

9. **Men tend to dominate discussions during meetings.** One study of college faculty meetings found that women's longest turns at speaking were, on the average, of shorter duration than men's shortest turns. A possible explanation here is that women are still less assertive than men in the workplace.

How can the information just presented help overcome communication problems on the job? As a starting point, remember that these gender differences often exist. Understanding these differences will help you interpret the communication behavior of people. For example, if a male coworker is not as effusive with praise as you would like, remember that he is simply engaging in gender-typical behavior. Do not take it personally.

A woman can remind herself to speak up more in meetings because her natural tendency might be toward diffidence. She might say to herself, "I must watch out to avoid gender-typical behavior in this situation." A man might remind himself to be more complimentary and supportive toward coworkers. The problem is that although such behavior is important, his natural tendency might be to skip the praise.

A woman should not take it personally when a male coworker or subordinate is tight-lipped when faced with a problem. She should recognize that he needs more encouragement to talk about his problems than would a woman. If the man persists in not wanting to talk about the problem, the woman might say, "It looks like you want to work out this problem on your own. Go ahead. I'm available if you want to talk about the problem."

Men and women should recognize that when women talk over problems, they might not be seeking hard-hitting advice. Instead, they might simply be searching for a sympathetic ear so that they can deal with the emotional aspect of the problem.

A general suggestion for overcoming gender-related communication barriers is for men to improve communication by becoming more empathic (showing more empathy) listeners. Women can improve communication by becoming more direct.

SELF-ASSESSMENT QUIZZES IN OVERVIEW

Self-Assessment Quiz 4-1 might be easy to overlook as dealing with a superficial part of behavior. Yet, if a person aspires toward a high-level professional or managerial job, voice quality is quite important. Even more so than clothing, people judge by your voice quality. From time to time, it is valuable to listen to a recording of your voice and reflect on whether the quality projects the image you want. For example, are you mumbling or talking way too fast? Self-assessment Quiz 4-2 encourages you to take a careful look at another major component of communication, listening. The truly effective worker who deals with other people listens carefully. Even if you work mostly with equipment, listening can be valuable. Unusual pings coming from a motor, for example, could indicate that a breakdown is on the way.

Concept Review and Reinforcement

Key Terms

communication 69
message 70
feedback 71
noise 71
nonverbal communication 73

summarization 73
mirroring 77
empathy 78
motivational state 78
frame of reference 78

defensive communication 79
denial 79
active listener 83
metacommunication 87

Summary

Communication is the basic process by which managers, customer-contact workers, and professionals accomplish their work, yet many communication problems exist in organizations. Communication among people is a complex process that can be divided into six components: sender or source, message, channel (or medium), receiver, feedback, and environment. Noise, or interference, can disrupt communication within any component.

Nonverbal communication plays an important part in sending and receiving messages and is especially important for imparting the emotional aspects of a message. The modes of nonverbal communication include the environment in which the message is sent, interpersonal distance, posture, gestures, facial expressions, voice quality, and personal appearance.

Nonverbal communication can be improved through such means as obtaining feedback, learning to relax, using gestures more discriminately, role-playing, and mirroring. The latter refers to subtly imitating someone.

Methods of overcoming communication barriers include the following: (1) understand the receiver, (2) minimize defensive communication, (3) repeat your message using multiple channels, (4) check comprehension and feelings via verbal and nonverbal feedback, (5) display a positive attitude, (6) use persuasive communication, (7) engage in active listening, (8) prepare for stressful conversation, (9) engage in metacommunication (communicating about your communication), and (10) recognize gender differences in communication styles.

Skills and behaviors associated with active listening include the following: (1) accept the sender's figure of speech, (2) paraphrase and listen reflectively, (3) minimize distractions, (4) allow the sender to finish his or her sentence, (5) use nonverbal communication, (6) minimize words that shut down discussion, and (7) avoid the need to lie or fake when you have not been paying attention.

Questions for Discussion and Review

1. Why are communication skills important in the field you are in or intend to enter?

2. What is your opinion on the importance of face-to-face communication in the business world of the future? For example, with all the new communication technology tools, will we still have face-to-face meetings, and sales representatives calling on customers?

3. How can knowing the steps in the communication process help a person become a more effective communicator?

4. What type of voice quality do you think would be effective in most work situations?

5. In what way might you have ever experienced information overload? What did you do, or what are you doing, to cope with the situation?

6. Should a person use power words when he or she is not in a powerful job? Explain.

7. Why does giving employees training in listening often lead to increased productivity and profits?

8. Based on your personal experience, are bartenders the great listeners that their stereotype suggests they are? (If you have not observed many bartenders in person, ask a friend to help you answer this question.)

9. Identify three scenarios in the workplace that are likely to result in stressful conversations.

10. Suppose your manager does not listen to your suggestions for job improvements. How would you metacommunicate to deal with this problem?

The Web Corner

http://www.optimalthinking.com/quiz-communication-skills.asp
(Rate your level of communication.)

http://www.queendom.com
(Look for the Communication Skills Test.)

http://nonverbal.ucsc.edu
(Explore nonverbal communications, and test your ability to read nonverbal communication.)

http://center-for-nonverbal-studies.org
(Nonverbal dictionary of gestures, signs, & body language cues.)

Internet Skill Builder: Practicing Listening Skills

Infoplease offers some practical suggestions for improving your listening skills that both support and supplement the ideas offered in this chapter. Infoplease divides listening into three basic steps: hearing, understanding, and judging. Visit the site at www.infoplease.com/homework/listeningskills1.html.

Developing Your Human Relations Skills

Interpersonal Relations Case 4.1

Why Am I Not Getting Through to These People?

A few years ago, Laura left her position as a supervisor in a health insurance company to start a lawn care, landscaping, and snow removal business. She started the business by taking care of the lawns and snow removal for a few relatives and friends. Laura charged them approximately half price just so that she could establish the legitimacy of her business, and get started seeking customers. Her first employees were a 16-year-old nephew, an 18-year-old niece, and an uncle.

After passing out hundreds of flyers in her neighborhood, and three adjoining neighborhoods, Laura finally developed a big enough customer base to start obtaining referral business. After two years into running her firm, "Laura's Property Service," Laura was breaking even, including paying herself a modest salary. Her firm had grown to taking care of more than 100 customers, with 3 full-time and 6 part-time employees.

When asked about her biggest challenge in operating her business, Laura replied,

Getting through to my workers is my biggest headache, no doubt. A big money drain in my business is repairing the damage we do to people's lawn and driveway in the process of removing snow. Also, the fellows and gals sometimes bang into garages and drain pipes with our lawnmowers when they are cutting grass.

I keep telling the gang to be careful, but I am not making much of a dent in terms of reducing customer complaints about damage. The typical response I get when I deliver my message about being careful is "Yeah, yeah, I'll be careful."

Case Questions

1. What kind of communication problem does Laura appear to be facing?
2. What do you recommend Laura do so that her employees act positively in response to her message?

Interpersonal Skills Role-Play

Getting through to a Property Specialist

One person plays the role of Laura who is somewhat frustrated. It is early spring, and five different customers have called to complain about the damage the snow removal team did to their driveways and lawn during the winter. Laura has gathered three of her workers (Tammy, Jud, and Ben) to explain once again the need for doing less damage to customer lawns and driveways while snow plowing. Three other students play the roles of Tammy, Jud, and Ben are wondering why Laura is complaining because they think such damage is inevitable.

Conduct this role-play for about seven minutes. Observers rate the role players on two dimensions, using a 1-to-5 scale from very poor to very good. One dimension is "effective use of human relations techniques." Focus on the communication skill that Laura demonstrates. The second dimension is "acting ability." A few observers might voluntarily provide feedback to the role players in terms of sharing their ratings and observations. The course instructor might also provide feedback.

Karl Walks Around

Karl Bennett, a supervisor in a call center located in Iowa, was urged by his manager to walk around the center from time to time to chat informally with the call center workers. His boss said to Karl, "It's always good to know what the call center specialists are feeling and thinking. You might pick up some good ideas." Bennett had studied the technique of *management by walking around* in a human relations course, so he was enthused about the idea.

Karl chose a Tuesday evening to conduct his walk around, and decided to stop by the cubicles of four call center operators to test the technique. If it worked well, he would walk around again in another week.

Karl first stopped by the cubicle of Mandi, making sure first that she was not on the telephone with a customer. "I just dropped by the say hello, and see how things are going" said Karl. "I take it everything is going fine, and that you have no problems," he continued. "Am I right?"

Mandi answered, "Yes, no real problems. Thanks for stopping by."

Next, Karl stopped by the cubicle of Pete, a relatively new operator. "How's it going Pete?" asked Karl. "What kind of problems might you be facing?"

Pete answered, "I'm having trouble understanding the accent of some of my customers. And some of the customers say I talk too fast. Other than that, the job is going well."

"That's interesting," said Karl. "But I see I have a couple of e-mails waiting for me on my BlackBerry. Maybe you do talk to fast. I'll get back to you later."

Karl thought to himself that the walk around was going fine so far. He then dropped by the Brittany's cubicle. "What's happening, Brittany?" asked Karl as Brittany was completing a customer inquiry about a defective piece of equipment. Brittany raised the palm of her right hand to signal that she was not quite finished with the call.

Karl then asked, "Are your wedding plans going along okay?"

Brittany replied, "Yes, Karl. Everything is fine; thanks for stopping by."

A few minutes later, Karl completed his walk around by stopping to visit Derek, a rabid Chicago Bear's fan. "Hey Derek, how goes it?" said Karl. "I think the Bears are headed to the league championship this year. What do you think?"

Derek answered, "Oh yes, the Bears are strong this season, and I'm optimistic. But so long as you have dropped by, I wanted to mention that our instruction manuals seem to be too complicated. People are calling in again and again with the most basic question, like how to find the serial number."

"Don't worry too much about that. A lot of our customers can hardly read these days. I think the term is functional illiterate," said Karl with a smile.

Case Questions

1. How successful is Karl is using his walk around to uncover useful information?
2. What can Karl do to increase his questioning effectiveness?
3. What can Karl do to increase his listening effectiveness?

Interpersonal Skills for the Digital World

Trevor worked as a product designer for Sensor Products, based in Portland, Oregon. The company designs and manufactures electronic controls used in automobiles, trucks, and related vehicles. His wife, Rita, an executive assistant, had to relocate back to Boston because her mother and father were in poor health. So, Trevor and Rita made the decision to move to an apartment in Boston.

Rita felt confident she could find employment in Boston, but Trevor did not want to leave his position as a senior product designer. With his reputation as a talented and dedicated worker, top-level manager at Sensor agreed to let Trevor work from home, yet spend about three days per month in Portland.

Objectives

After reading and studying this chapter and doing the exercises, you should be able to

1. Describe interpersonal skills related to one-on-one interactions in the digital world.
2. Describe interpersonal skills related to social networking.
3. Describe interpersonal skills related to working with small audiences with respect to digital devices.

After several weeks of working from home in their cramped Boston apartment, Trevor began to feel uncomfortable. "I was going stir crazy," he said. "I enjoy my technical work, but I'm also a people person. Much of my career success stems from my enjoyment of interacting with people. Doing my designs on a computer, and interacting with colleagues through e-mail, is not enough for me."

After some careful thought, Trevor modified his idea of working from home. He found a place called Galaxy Towers just 15 minutes from his apartment in Boston, where he was able to share office space, have his own desk, free Internet, a conference room, and free coffee and tea for $325 per month. Trevor would become what is now called a *co*-worker. His company agreed to pay the bill to keep Trevor happy and productive.

Trevor was now able to interact with other workers on occasion, even if they were working for different companies. As Trevor puts it, "Just shooting the breeze with intelligent, working adults stimulates by thinking. Our dog Lila is wonderful, but she doesn't provide the kind of warm, human presence that I need to be at my professional best. Also, I can even brainstorm a bit with a few of the other tenants at Galaxy."[1]

The story about the senior product designer illustrates one of the ways in which interpersonal skills figure into the digital age. Trevor's ability to interact positively with others stimulates his own thinking—making him productive—and also contributes to his job satisfaction. In this chapter, we examine the interpersonal skill aspects of working in the digital age, an often-neglected aspect of making good use of the communication and information technology surrounding us in the workplace. We organize this information into two broad categories. First, we describe interpersonal skills for using digital devices in one-on-one interaction. Second, we examine the interpersonal skill aspects of using communication technology for social networking and small audiences.

To begin thinking through interpersonal skills in relation to the digital world, you are invited to take Self-Assessment Quiz 5-1. The statements in the quiz cover many of the behaviors relevant to digitally based interactions.

INTERPERSONAL SKILLS FOR ONE-ON-ONE INTERACTIONS

As with interpersonal skills in general, interactions with people one at a time create the majority of opportunities for displaying interpersonal skills related to the digital age. In this section, we describe four such settings or scenarios in which the communication is typically (not always) directed toward one person: cell phones and text messaging; e-mail messages and instant messaging; webcam job interviews; and the interpersonal aspect of multitasking.

The Interpersonal Skills for the Digital World Checklist

Indicate whether each of the following statements is Mostly True or Mostly False as it applies to you (or would apply to you if you were in the situation indicated by the statement). Even if your reaction to a particular statement is "duh," remember that all the statements reflect incidents of real behavior.

Statement	Mostly True	Mostly False
1. I get really upset if I send a coworker an instant message (IM), and I do not receive an answer within five minutes.	_____	_____
2. While being interviewed for a job, I receive and send text messages to a work associate or friend.	_____	_____
3. While working in a group, I regularly check my e-mail and text messages.	_____	_____
4. I often check Web sites such as ESPN, Facebook, Twitter, or home shopping channels on my laptop while at a meeting.	_____	_____
5. I often eat while talking on my cell phone.	_____	_____
6. I typically check my e-mail, text messages, or a Web site while talking on my cell phone.	_____	_____
7. If I made a webcam presentation for work purposes, I would make sure that my grooming was at its best.	_____	_____
8. I would bring a pet such as a cat, dog, or parrot along to a webcam conference for business purposes.	_____	_____
9. If I were giving a presentation at a business banquet, I would keep my personal digital assistant in my hand.	_____	_____
10. I keep my bottle of water in my hand at all times where making a PowerPoint presentation.	_____	_____
11. When making a PowerPoint presentation, I use the information on the slide as headlines for talking points rather than reading the slides to the audience.	_____	_____
12. If I attended a two-hour videoconference, I would see no problem in leaving the room from time to time just for a break.	_____	_____
13. I have posted, or would be willing to post, some outrageous videos of myself on Facebook, such as driving a vehicle with a bottle of beer in my hand.	_____	_____
14. I use, or would use, a social networking site to really blast a company whose product proved to be faulty.	_____	_____
15. For me, social networking sites are a useful place to post nasty things about people I do not like.	_____	_____
16. Older workers who are not savvy about information technology deserve nicknames like "Mr. Depends," or "Ms. Dinosaur."	_____	_____
17. I laugh when I see somebody doing something as old-fashioned as reading a newspaper.	_____	_____
18. I have received compliments about my ability to explain how to use technology to another worker.	_____	_____
19. I am patient and polite when a tech support person cannot resolve my technology problem right away.	_____	_____
20. I have sent hand-written thank-you notes to people even if they use e-mail and text messaging.	_____	_____

Scoring and interpretation: Give yourself one point (+1) for each statement you gave in agreement with the keyed answer. The keyed answer indicates a positive interpersonal skill for the digital world.

1. Mostly false	4. Mostly false	7. Mostly true	10. Mostly false
2. Mostly false	5. Mostly false	8. Mostly false	11. Mostly true
3. Mostly false	6. Mostly false	9. Mostly false	12. Mostly false

Cell Phones and Text Messaging

Cell phones have become such an integrated part of life both on and off the job that many photographs in magazines and newspapers of business people show them using their phone. Television advertisements also often depict workers using a cell phone even when the advertisement is not for phones. In the business section of most cities, it appears that approximately two-thirds of the people in business attire are using a cell phone, smart phones, and personal digital assistants included. Cell phones, including using them to send text messages, therefore represent an enormous opportunity for displaying good, as well as poor, interpersonal skills.

Positive Interpersonal Skills While Using Cell Phones. The many positive behaviors possible when using cell phones for one-on-one interaction usually are a question of doing the opposite of negative behaviors. The behaviors in the following list illustrate how positive interpersonal skills can be demonstrated while using cell phones and text messaging during one-on-one interactions.[2]

1. **Use a standard ringtone instead of a loud, unusual tone.** In this way if your phone rings in the presence of a work associate, your behavior will not provoke surprise or laughter.

2. **Inform the caller that you are receiving his or her call on a cell phone.** If you let the caller know that you are on a cell phone, the call will not be surprised when the reception fades in and out, or when you are interrupted by honking horn, or other background noises including conversations of people walking by.

3. **Inform work associates ahead of time if you are waiting for a call from a medical professional or in reference to an urgent home situation.** Assume, for example, that you and a coworker are discussing a customer problem. Let your coworker know that your conversation might be interrupted by the type of urgent call just described. In this way, accepting a call will not be interpreted as rudeness.

4. **Ask your work associate if he or she would like you to access an item of work-related information using your smart phone.** Assume that sales rep Ashley is talking with customer Todd, and Todd wants to know if her company would have a large quantity of a specific product in stock. Ashley would be displaying good interpersonal skills by saying, "Todd, would you like me to access this information on my iPhone? It will take just a minute." Todd will inevitably agree, and he will also understand why Ashley is using her iPhone in the middle of their conversation.

5. **Inform your coworker that you are shutting off your cell phone or smart phone during your conversation.** Because so many people do not think to, or refuse to, turn off their cell phone or smart phone, you can gain some psychological capital by mentioning your courteous behavior. You tell your work associate, "Our meeting is important, so just one second. I want to turn off my cell phone and put it out of view."

6. **For business purposes, use a fully functioning phone and stay current with your cell phone bill.** You will appear much more professional to work associates when your cell phone call is not interrupted by a disappearing voice or reception much

like you are in heavy traffic or a shower. Keeping current with your bill avoids the unprofessional image created by a message that your phone number is "temporarily out of service" or your inability to send an outgoing message.

7. **When making calls from outside the office, search for a relatively quiet environment so that your message will be clearer, and you will not have to ask the receiver to repeat information.** Even in a busy environment like an airport, it is possible to find a relatively quiet alcove from which to make a call. The interpersonal skill link here is that you appear more professional when your communication is relatively free of environmental noise.

8. **If absolutely necessary to take a cell phone call while interacting with a work associate, excuse yourself and move at least 15 feet away to process the call.** Work associates who are themselves polite will appreciate your display of polite behavior.

9. **When you are the driver of the vehicle, explain to your work associate that for safety's sake you are putting your cell phone away.** Point out that just as you would not be the driver when you are drunk, you will not use your cell phone for voice communication or text messaging while you are driving. Although many coworkers might think you are eccentric, the data are convincing about the dangers of cell phone use while driving. On balance, your concern for the safety of your passenger will be interpreted as a positive interpersonal skill.

10. **When at work, make any cell phone calls on break, and away for your assigned physical location, such as outside the building or in an employee lounge (but not in the restroom!)** Blocking your personal calls and making them outside your assigned work area shows you have enough interpersonal skill to care about the need of other workers for a tranquil work environment.

Negative Interpersonal Skills While Using Cell Phones. The dissatisfaction with, and anger toward, people who abuse cell phones in the workplace continues to appear in articles, books, blogs, and letters to the editor. All this negativity, however, must be placed in the proper context. If the person with whom you are interacting does not perceive a particular use of the cell phone as rudeness, then it is not rude. For example, if your coworker smiles at you while you receive a phone call in his or her presence, you are probably not being perceived as displaying negative interpersonal behavior. Following is a list of frequent cell phone and text messaging behaviors that many (not all) people will interpret as rudeness and insensitivity. As a result, the person engaging in the act will be perceived as showing negative interpersonal skill.[3]

1. **Accepting a call during a work conversation.** You communicate the fact that your coworker or other work associate is less important than the caller when you allow a call to interrupt your conversation. Some people interpret making a call as even more insensitive than receiving a call, but both behaviors are dismissive of the importance of the work associate with whom you are interacting. Customers are likely to be irritated even more so than coworkers if you interrupt your conversation to accept or make a phone call. CEOs who use their cell phones while talking to other workers are likely to be perceived as power abusers, and therefore as arrogant. In short, by accepting a cell phone call in the presence of others, you diminish the status of the person who is physically present—hardly an impressive interpersonal skill.

2. **Wearing a cell phone earpiece in the presence of a coworker when not on the phone.** Wearing an earpiece while interacting with a coworker suggests that you do not intend to remain fully engaged in your conversation. Also, when wearing a phone earpiece, the person in your physical presence is never sure if you are listening to another call at the same time. Building rapport with a work associate includes making him or her feel important. The fact that you appear to be ready to connect to the outside world trivializes that person.

3. **Making frequent personal calls on your phone in earshot of coworkers.** A major complaint of people who work in cubicles is that someone in an adjoining cubicle

spends much on the day making calls loudly on a cell hone. The same practice would be possible on a landline phone, but many people perceive using their cell phone for personal calls as more justified than using the office phone. Loud, personal calls made throughout the day suggest lack of consideration for others, as well as a low work ethic and an unwillingness to contribute a fair share of work.

4. **Talking loudly and shouting on the cell phone.** Whether in one-on-one interactions, or in the middle of a group of work associates, talking loudly and shouting on the cell phone is widely disliked. Particularly annoying for many people is the compulsion many cell phone shouters have to repeatedly say "Okay" in a especially loud voice. Talking so loudly on the cell phone suggests insensitivity to the feelings of others as well as being egocentric.

5. **Eating while making a phone call.** Eating with the mouth open in a restaurant is a major violation of etiquette. Equally annoying and disgusting to many receivers of these messages is the sender eating while talking. Although the practice of eating while talking on the phone is widespread, its vulgarity to many people is not diminished, and will not be tolerated by many customers. On display is the negative interpersonal skill of poor etiquette.

6. **Constant handling or looking at the cell phone even when not in use.** Many workers have become so dependent on their cell phones and personal digital assistants that they handle them during conversations, as well as keeping the phone in constant view. Workers have also been observed placing their cell phones on their laps while speaking with others. One manager frequently polishes his chrome covered smart phone while talking to subordinates.

   The physical attachments just mentioned all suggest the negative trait of being so dependent on a physical device that it interferes with concentrating on others. The constant physical or visual contact with the cell phone also has the negative impact of making the worker appear immature. An explanation offered for the physical attachment so many people have to their cell phones is that the phones have become "electronic pets." A technology reporter observed, "You constantly see people taking their little pets out and stroking the scroll wheel, coddling them basically petting them."[4]

7. **Driving a work associate while under the influence of a cell phone including text messaging.** A positive interpersonal skill is not using your cell phone while driving a vehicle in which a work associate is present. A negative interpersonal skill is doing the opposite, even if you live in a state, province, or country where cell phone use is permitted for drivers. A study published in a British medical journal reported that talking on the cell phone while driving quadruples your risk of being in an accident. Using a hands-free device does little to reduce the risk of an accident.[5] Many work associates will accept driving while using a cell phone, including sending text messages, as typical and appropriate behavior. Yet, others will interpret your behavior as a propensity to engage in senseless risks.

8. **Accepting and sending phone messages from rest rooms.** A widely reported form of cell phone rudeness is sending and receiving cell phone calls from public rest rooms. Many receivers of these calls who hear the water running from the faucets or toilets flushing will be appalled and disgusted. The restroom cell phone user therefore be perceived as insensitive and lacking in social graces—both quite negative interpersonal skills.

Skill-Building Exercise 5-1 gives you an opportunity to practice a core skill with the use of a cell phone and text messaging in the office.

E-Mail Messages and Instant Messaging

E-mail messages and instant messages (IMs) provide another opportunity for displaying positive as well as negative interpersonal skills linked to the digital age. Many people believe that formality and careful use of language can be neglected when sending messages by e-mail, instant messaging, and when sending text messages. Remember, however, that

Two coworkers are discussing a joint assignment about preparing a spreadsheet related to product returns. The analysis needs to be completed by 5 p.m. One student plays the role of the worker who is intently focusing on the task. Another student plays the role of the worker who feels the cell phone attached to his or her belt vibrate. The worker notices a text message from the bank indicat-ing that five checks have bounced, which appears to be a bank mistake. The worker with the text message does not want to be totally rude, yet this is an urgent problem. Run the role-play for about four minutes. Observers might provide feedback on the quality of the interpersonal skills displayed in dealing with this text message challenge.

the way in which any message is sent tells something about the sender. E-mail messages should be proofread, should be sent only when necessary, and generally should be no longer than one screen—not including attachments. Although many e-mail users rely on a strikingly informal and casual writing style, such informality for business correspondence is poor etiquette. For example, avoid confirming a meeting with your CEO in these words: "C U LTR, 4 sure."☺ Overloading the company system with attachments containing space-consuming graphics is often considered rude. Text messaging, because of its limited space, can be more casual than other electronic messages.

An e-mail etiquette problem with legal implications is that company e-mail messages are the property of the company, not the sender. So avoid sending through e-mail insulting, vulgar, or inflammatory comments because even deleted e-mail messages can be retrieved. Be careful not to forward an e-mail message that has negative comments about the recipient. For example, a customer service representative sent an e-mail to a customer attempting to resolve a complaint. However, instead of beginning with a fresh e-mail, the representative included an e-mail from her boss that said, "Give this idiot what she wants to get her off our back." The customer later sued the company, and then agreed to a small financial settlement.

Instant messaging has created new challenges for e-mail etiquette. Because instant messaging allows you to intrude on coworkers anytime—and them to drop in on you—the opportunities to be rude multiply. Managers should not intrude upon workers through instant messaging unless it is urgent. Think before you send, and make sure the message has real value to the recipient. Suggest politely to "buddies" who are taking up too much of your time with messages that they contact you after work.

Many companies are shifting from extensive use of e-mail to having some of the written communication among people placed on intranets, and internal Web sites similar to Facebook. For example, you can inform all your work associates at once that you are going on a business trip for three days and will not be able to respond to their messages. (Of course, this is a good way to invite criminals to burglarize your home.) All of the comments about the polite use of language apply to these replacement technologies for e-mail.

Figure 5-1 summarizes a large amount of information about etiquette related to e-mails and instant messaging. Following this accumulated wisdom will enhance your interpersonal skills linked to the digital age.

Webcam Job Interviews

Yet another interpersonal skill useful in the digital age is to perform well during a webcam interview. Performing well in such an interview combines interpersonal skills with those related to communication technology. On occasion, a hiring manager or human resource representative will request that an interview be conducted by webcam. The job candidate might have a webcam, or use one owned by a friend or the college placement office. (Skype is the leading webcam system.) A challenge in being interviewed via a webcam is that some job candidates do not come across as strongly as they believe.

As webcam technology continues to improve, and more managers are familiar with the technique, the number of these computer-based interviews is likely to increase. Some companies use webcam interviews to reduce travel costs, and this type of interview provides more data than a phone call. Christa Foley, recruiting manager at Zappos.com, says,

FIGURE 5-1 E-Mail and Messaging Etiquette

Observing the following tips will enhance your e-mail etiquette and electronic communication effectiveness, as well as enhancing your interpersonal skills.

Address and sign your e-mail messages. Many people neglect to mention a person's name in an e-mail, or sign their own name. Giving your e-mail a personal touch is a useful interpersonal micro-skill.

Keep it simple. Each message should have only one piece of information or request for action so that it's easier for the receiver to respond. However, avoid sending an e-mail with an attachment without some type of greeting or explanation. Do not allow e-mail threads longer than a couple of pages. E-mail messages longer than one screen often are filed instead of read. Brief e-mails messages show compassion for the recipient's workload.

Include an action step. Clearly outline what type of reply you're looking for as well as any applicable deadlines.

Use the subject line to your advantage. Generic terms such as "details" or "reminder" do not describe the contents of your message or whether it's time sensitive. So the receiver may delay opening it. "Came in Under Budget" illustrates a specific (and joyful) title. Do not forward a long chain of e-mails without changing the subject; otherwise, you might have a confusing subject line, such as "RE: FW: RE: FW: RE: FW."

Take care in writing e-mails. Clearly organize your thoughts to avoid sending e-mails with confusing, incomplete, or missing information. Use business writing style and check carefully for grammatical and typographical errors. (Also, generally avoid the trend to refer to spell "I" in lowercase.) When in doubt use traditional formatting rather than bright colors and unusual fonts because many people prefer standard formatting.

Inform receivers when sending e-mails from a mobile device. If you use a BlackBerry or comparable device, include a tagline informing people that you are using such a device that will help explain your terseness. Without explanation, you might project an image of rudeness or limited writing skill.

Be considerate. Use "please" and "thank you" even in brief messages. Part of being considerate, or at least polite, is to begin your e-mail with a warm salutation, such "Hello Gina," rather than jumping into the subject with no greeting. Avoid profane or harsh language. Another way of being considerate is to send e-mails only when necessary, to help combat information overload. Sending copies to only recipients who need or want the information is part of being considerate. (Note that some people use that notation "cc" for copies, which really refers to carbon copy. "Copy" is more precise because you are sending an electronic copy.)

Don't include confidential information. The problem is that e-mail is occasionally forwarded to unintended recipients. If your message is in any way sensitive or confidential, set up a meeting or leave a voice mail in which you request confidentially. Also, avoid including gossip including negative rumors on e-mail messages because the subject of the gossip could voice a major complaint.

Do not use e-mail to blast a coworker, and send copies to others. Criticizing another person with e-mail is equivalent to blasting him or her during a large meeting.

Ask before sending huge attachments. Do not clog e-mail systems without permission.

Encourage questions and demands for clarification. E-mail functions best when it is interactive, so ask receivers to send along questions they might have about your message, including any requests for clarification.

Consider the timing of e-mail messages. An e-mail that makes a major request should be sent earlier in the day so that the person has time to process the request. Good news can be sent almost anytime. For some recipients, bad news is best sent early in the day so that they can ask for your support in dealing with the problem. However, very bad news (such as being laid off) is best delivered in person. Some people prefer to receive bad news later in the day so that it will not interrupt their entire workday.

Avoid keeing a personal e-mail account on the job unless welcomed by management. An estimated one-quarter of e-mails received at work are for personal purposes.

(Continued)

FIGURE 5-1 **Continued**

To resist the temptation of spending too much time with personal e-mails, it is best not to have a personal e-mail account, such as Gmail, on the office computer. You will appear more professional if you avoid the temptation to spend a lot of work time sending and receiving personal e-mail and instant messages.

Minimize "BIF" messages on evening and weekends. In today's demanding workplace, it is easy to send "before I forget" messages in the evening, on weekends, and during holidays. Some people will regard you as insensitive to their lifestyle if you badger them outside of regular working hours with e-mail messages. Save your urgent messages for the next workday—unless an immediate exchange of information is essential.

Instant messaging requires a few additional considerations for practicing good electronic etiquette:

Use instant messaging sparingly because it is interruptive. An instant messaging is likely to interrupt a person's concentration on an important task, so it should be sent infrequently. Be careful not to send an instant message to a coworker who you know is working on an analytical task. However, if the company culture encourages the use of instant messaging, you display good interpersonal skill by going with the flow.

Don't be Big Brother. Some bosses use instant messaging to check up on others, to make sure that they are seated at their computer. Never intrude on workers unless it is urgent.

Lay down the instant messaging law. Make sure that your message has some real value to the recipient before jumping right in front of someone's face. Instant messaging is much like walking into someone's office or cubicle without an appointment or without knocking.

Take it offline. When someone on your buddy list becomes too chatty, don't vent your frustration. By phone, in-person, or through regular e-mail, explain tactfully that you do not have time for processing so many instant messages. Suggest that the two of you might get together for lunch or coffee soon.

Set limits to avoid frustration. To avoid constant interruptions, use a polite custom status message, such as "I will be dealing with customers today until 4:40."

Source: "Communicating Electronically: What Every Manager Needs to Know," *Communication Solutions,* Sample Issue, 2008, p. 2; Heinz Tschabitscher, "The Ten Most Important Rules of Email Etiquette," http://email.about.com/cs/netiquettetips/tp/core_netiquette.htm, accessed September 9, 2003; Monte Enbysk, "Bosses: 10 Tips for Better E-mails," *Microsoft Small Business Center,* www.microsoft.com/smallbusiness/resources/technology/communications/bossess_10, 2006; Nancy Flynn, "50% of Bosses Ban Personal E-mail Accounts," *Workplace Communication Examiner* (www.examiner.com), July 28, 2009; "5 Tactics to Curb E-Mail Overload," *Manager's Edge,* June 2008, p. 6.

"If you see facial expressions and body language, you have a different sense of what a person is saying."[6] After candidates are interviewed by webcam, the strongest ones are typically invited for an in-person visit to the company.

Above all, a webcam interview is still an interview; so review the interview suggestions in Chapter 17 to appear at your best. In addition, keep in mind the following positive suggestions, all of which imply mistakes to avoid at the same time.[7]

1. **Use even lighting.** As with all forms of photography, lighting is a big part of making a successful webcam appearance. A bright light behind you is particularly poor because your face will be in shadow. Lighting bounced off the ceiling works the best for a soft, even image, yet side-lighting will often suffice. Do not place a bright light on the computer in front of you to avoid too much glare on your face, particularly if you are light skinned.

2. **Wear appropriate clothing.** Dress as if you were having an in-person interview, and minimize the color white because it comes across poorly on computer screens. Loud patterns are also distracting. Unless otherwise directed, it is best to wear a

business suit or dress. Investigate what type of clothing job applicants typically wear. For example, if you were applying for a management training position at Home Depot, business casual dress might be appropriate.

3. **Do your best to appear relaxed and not overly stressed.** Light exercise and a shower about 30 minutes before the interview will help give you a refreshed look. Use you favorite stress reduction technique shortly before the webcam interview. Familiarity with the webcam technology will help you feel relaxed.

4. **Use or create an uncluttered area free of personal belongings, pets, and television sets.** Although your living quarters may be the locale of your interview, you still want to simulate the appearance of a professional office. Tidy up the interview area, and move away as much clutter as possible. Background noise, including a ringing telephone or a television set turned on, would detract from a professional image.

5. **Sit tall with good posture, and stay at approximately the same distance from the computer screen that you do for most of you computer work.** The worst mistake posture error webcam interviewees typically make is to move the head within a few inches of the screen. A close-up shot of this nature distorts the face and looks a little bizarre to most interviewers.

6. **Rehearse so that you will be better able to implement the previous five suggestions.** Collaborate with someone in your network of contacts to interview each other on webcam. The rehearsal will familiarize you with the technology, and you can also get feedback on the adequacy of the lighting, and how natural and positive you appeared. As was often said in the early days of photography, "Smile, you're on camera."

A fundamental reason that rehearsal for a webcam interview is important is that people have a tendency to overrate the image they project on video. A webcam image is, of course, a variation of a video image. Karen Friedman, a video presentation trainer, has this to say about the importance of getting an accurate feedback on the video image you project:

> People will tell you that they're perceived as dynamic, engaging, and interesting, with full command of the material. And when they see themselves on videotape or DVD and it's a rude awakening, because they see how other people really see them. You can pick up odd mannerisms you're not aware of. You may have the words down and the verbal techniques, but your body language might give away that you're nervous or unsure of yourself.[8]

Interpersonal Aspects of Multitasking

Multitasking has two meanings, and the difference is of major significance for interpersonal relationships. One meaning of multitasking is that you have two or more projects that you are working on, but you do not work on these projects at the same time. For example, today a person might be responsible for investigating customer complaints as well as purchasing new furniture for the office. In the morning she works on the complaints, and in the afternoon she negotiates a furniture purchase. The other type of multitasking creates more potential interpersonal problems. With this type of multitasking, the person does two or more things simultaneously, such as visiting an office-furniture Web site while talking on the phone with a dissatisfied customer.

Chapter 16 deals with the productivity problems often associated with multitasking. Also, the discussion of cell phone use described the insensitivity of accepting and sending calls while talking to another person (a frequent type of multitasking). Here we explain how multitasking might have (a) a positive influence on interpersonal relationships and (b) a negative influence on interpersonal skills.

Multitasking and Positive Interpersonal Skills. In some situations, performing two tasks at once can enhance interpersonal skills because you are helping another person. Imagine that Sally asks Fernando for help in inserting accents into Spanish words, such

Multitasking

(a) Having two or more projects that you are working on, but you do not work on these projects at the same time. (b) Doing two or more tasks simultaneously.

as wanting to convert "carino" into "cariño" (with caring). Fernando sits down next to Sally at her computer, and says, "Watch me Sally. I'm moving my hand over to the Num Lock keyboard. With a finger on my left hand, I press Alt. Then with a finger on my right hand, I press 0241 in sequence. See, we have an ñ. Next, I will show you how to use the character map that will get you all the Spanish accents you will ever need."

Fernando is indeed doing two tasks at once—manipulating the keyboard and talking to Sally. If he had not multitasked, he would not have been a good tutor. Fernando is also not being rude because he has Sally's implicit permission to multitask. A lot of coaching and tutoring requires multitasking of the nature just described.

The scenario of Sally and Fernando illustrates another key principle of using multitasking to enhance interpersonal skills. When two people are holding a conversation for purposes of joint problem solving, multitasking will sometimes enhance the problem solving, thereby creating a stronger interpersonal relationship. Visualize Mike and Tammy driving together on a business trip. Mike is driving, and his vehicle is not equipped with a GPS. Mike says to Tammy, "I think we may have missed the Liberty Road exit on this highway. It would be a nightmare to exit and find the way back. What should we do?"

"Hold on Mike," says Tammy. I'll access the GPS app on my BlackBerry and get us centered in a minute." Fifty seconds later, Tammy says to Mike while still looking at the screen on her BlackBerry "We're good. The Liberty Road exit is 5.6 miles down the road. We'll make a right turn off the exit ramp."

Multitasking and Negative Interpersonal Skills. The major negative interpersonal skill aspect of multitasking is that it trivializes the person with whom you are interacting, as described with cell phone abuse. Imagine you are listening to a coworker who is describing a proposed solution to a problem. You shift your gaze to your computer so that you can seek who just "poked" you on Facebook. This immediately sends the message that your "poker" is more important at the moment than your coworker who wanted to discuss a legitimate work problem.

Another negative interpersonal skill associated with multitasking is more subtle. When you respond to an electronic interruption, such as an instant message or an e-mail alert, your attention is sapped for more time than it takes to read the message. You have to recover from the interruption and refocus your attention on your work associate. While you are in the recovery mode, perhaps even 30 seconds, you are paying less than full attention to the other person.[10] And this inattentiveness is obvious by the blank stare on your face, or recovery murmurs such as "yeah, yeah."

BACK TO THE OPENING CASE

Trevor, the senior product designer, appears to have found the right balance between engaging in highly analytical tasks using his computer and interacting with other people. You will recall that he felt isolated working alone in a small apartment. By renting communal office space, he had enough interaction with people to help him feel attached to the workforce. Although Trevor does not spend loads of time with his co-renters, he finds the interaction with a mix of people to be intellectually stimulating.

Harassment of Others

A negative consequence of communication technology in the workplace is that it is easier to harass coworkers than in the analog age. To harass coworkers in the past, it was necessary to say nasty things to them in person, telephone them in a menacing way, write them threatening notes, or send them upsetting words on paper or photographs. The Internet including e-mail and the Web has made it much easier to harass people.

Creating a hostile environment by displaying pornography to coworkers who do not want to see it has become one of the most frequent forms of harassment. Aside from being rude, sexual harassment through pornography has frequently been ruled as illegal.

A representative example is that the 2nd Circuit Court of Appeals in New York State consistently has ruled that "the mere presence of pornography in a workplace can alter the 'status' of women and may be objective proof of a hostile environment."[11] (A hostile environment is one of the two forms of sexual harassment as described in Chapter 9.)

An employee can be accused of hostile environment harassment by simply leaving open a porn site on his or her desktop. Sending coworkers sexually oriented jokes by e-mail can result in similar accusations. If you work for a company that distributes adult films, pornography would be part of your job, and you therefore might be excluded from the harassment accusation.

Harassment can also deal with a person's race or ethnicity, such as making insulting comments, or jokes about a person's race. Age is another demographic factor that could possibly lead to a person being harassed, such as continuous joking by e-mail that a senior worker was suffering from Alzheimer's disease.

Harassing others through communication technology is a negative interpersonal skill. A possible positive twist would be that the person who abstains 100 percent from any computer-related actions that could be interpreted as harassment is demonstrating a positive interpersonal skill. A behavioral specific would be to delete without opening an advertisement for adult videos that made its way past the company spam filter.

INTERPERSONAL SKILLS FOR SOCIAL NETWORKING AND SMALL AUDIENCES

Interpersonal skills related to the digital age are also demonstrated while interacting with large numbers of people, as well as groups. Among these settings are social networking by Internet; using laptop and netbook computers, and smart phones during a meeting; making electronic presentations; videoconferencing; telecommuting; and preserving your online reputation. You will notice that a couple of these settings could be focused more on an individual than a large number of people or a group. For example, you might be sending a message on a social networking site to one person, and while telecommuting you might be interacting with one person.

Social Networking by Internet

Almost infinite knowledge exists about social networking, including its technology, application for building a personal network, and marketing.[12] Included in this abundance of

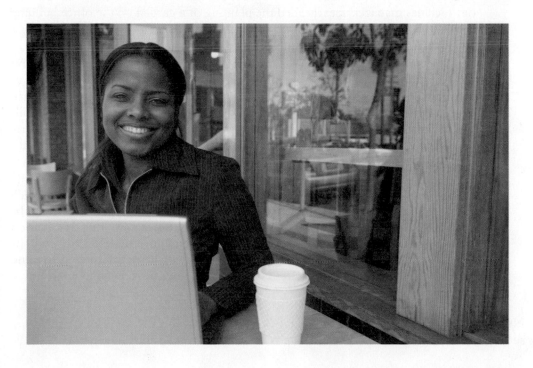

information is how Twitter and Facebook have completely transformed the way we live, and how e-mail has now become obsolete because of social networking sites. Our aim here is to simply list a few of the positive and negative interpersonal skills associated with the use of social networking sites.

Positive Interpersonal Skills and Social Networking. The use of Twitter, Facebook, and the like provides the serious worker with several opportunities for displaying positive interpersonal skills, as follows:

1. **Demonstrate your loyalty by posting gracious comments about your employer.** Social networking sites include a heavy component of being mini-blogs, and therefore present an open forum for your ideas about the company. You can demonstrate empathy and compassion for the mission of your company by commenting on an action taken by the company that you perceive as positive. An example: "I'm proud to work for the Jeep division of Fiat/Chrysler. My wife and our three children were caught in a snow storm. I put my Cherokee into four-wheel drive and made it through the storm until we could find a motel. There were dozens of overturned vehicles, but we made it to safety. The vehicle stabilization feature is really functional."

2. **Display your compassion for people in need.** Post on the company social networking site, and also a public site, that you want to help people in need in some specific way. For example, you might state that you have bunch of clothing that you want to give to a needy family in any way associated with the company. Or, explain that you have developed your language tutoring skills and that you are willing to help for free any person who needs help in learning to read. Compassion might be considered a value, but it also translates into a skill in terms of helping people.

3. **Demonstrate professional-level communication skills.** When making entries on Twitter in particular, many people feel compelled to write carelessly, foolishly, and viciously. Demonstrate your professionalism by writing in a style suited for a printed newspaper or a term paper. Remember that many influential people regard written communication skills as a subset of interpersonal skills.

4. **Pay deserved compliments to company personnel.** The ability to compliment others in a sensible way is an advanced interpersonal skill. Complimenting a person in private may be useful, but public compliments are welcome also. An example of a Facebook post of this nature: "I want everybody to know that Tom Barnes, our facilities manager, spearheaded the planting of a garden on the office building roof. We are saving the planet, one petunia at a time."

5. **Establish meaningful contact with workers far and wide.** The major purpose of social networking is to develop valuable contacts with many people with whom it would be difficult to maintain person-to-person or phone contact. Selective use of the social networking sites enables you to relate, at least on a written level, to a variety of people in your fields. You might be able to enhance your cross-cultural skills by interacting with professionals in different countries. (LinkedIn is particularly good for this purpose because so many of its members have a professional intent.)

6. **Display a desire to help others grow and develop.** Social networking sites afford an easy opportunity to point others toward helpful information, such as referring friends to useful Web sites and books. You can also alert people to dangers, such as a new scam related to the sale of gold. Although the same type of alerts can be accomplished by e-mail, social networking sites do not require long distribution lists. By pointing people in the direction of useful information, you will be demonstrating part of a useful interpersonal skill of helping others grow and develop. Instead of just writing about yourself on your post, include information that will help others.

Negative Interpersonal Skills and Social Networking. Social networking provides a setting for displaying negative as well as positive interpersonal skills. In general, all of the positive opportunities mentioned above could be reversed to become negative. For example, instead of helping others grow and develop with postings on your site or their site, you slam and demean these people. Several adolescent suicides have been reported that appeared to have been triggered by being insulted on a teen-oriented social networking site. The following list presents a few ways in which negative interpersonal skills are sometimes displayed on social networking sites.

1. **Using social networking sites to eliminate face-to-face interactions with work associates.** As with e-mail, social networking sites provide an opportunity to avoid face-to-face interaction with coworkers, managers, and customers. However, the temptation is even greater with social networking sites because they tout the concept of being "friends" with people on your list of electronic contacts. A person might think consciously or subconsciously, "If my customer is already my friend, why should I have to talk to or personally visit him? Our relationship is already good." If all relationships could be built and maintained electronically, you would not need to be studying human relations.

2. **Posting confidential or derogatory information about your employer.** In the words of technology writer Bridget Carey, "Employees need to realize some conversations are privileged. Just because you're in a meeting about a new product, or worse, layoffs, doesn't mean you should be broadcasting to the world."[13] Posting negative information and insults about your employer demonstrates even lower emotional intelligence. Nasty comments about the employer, even if deserved, are often made out of uncontrolled anger. Hundreds of employees have been fired because of making inflammatory comments on social networking sites about their employers. Poor interpersonal skill is also displayed by joining a social networking group dedicated to destroying the reputation of your employer.

3. **Posting derogatory information and photos about a coworker.** Social networking site administrators generally do not edit posts, so anybody registered on the site can post dreadful comments about another person as a mean prank or a deliberate effort to ruin the target's reputation. YouTube can serve a similar evil purpose. Some of these negative posts reflect backstabbing because another person encourages you to engage in embarrassing behavior. He or she may quote you, or posts a photo or video of you engaged in outrageous behavior.

4. **Engaging in social networking at inappropriate times.** Many "Tweeters" in particular are so habituated to visiting their favorite social networking site that they do so at inappropriate times, such as during work. Several NFL teams, including the Miami Dolphins, had to clamp down on players tweeting during practice. Many office workers access their social networking sites during meetings. The interpersonal skill deficiency of accessing a social network site for nonbusiness purposes during working hours is that it reflects insensitivity and immaturity. (Print-related distractions would also be unwelcome, such as doing crossword puzzles during a football practice or in a meeting.)

Laptop and Personal Digital Assistant Use during Meetings

Whether the use of laptop and netbook computers as well as personal digital assistants (smart phones) during meetings enhances your interpersonal skills depends on company custom and why you are using your computer. Some companies welcome computer use during meetings; while in other companies, such practice is considered distracting and inconsiderate. Laptops are widely used during meetings at the business process consulting company, Accenture.

At Ford Motor Company, CEO Alan Mulally is adamant about meetings not being interrupted by people using their BlackBerry or laptop computer—as well as the interruption of side conversations.[14] Another example of a company intent on boosting the productivity of meetings by banning digital devices is Adaptive Path, a design firm in San Francisco. Meeting participants must leave their laptops on their desks, and they must place mobile phones on a counter or in a box.[15]

Justifying Laptop Use during a Meeting

Five students play the role of a group of workers who are developing a marketing campaign for a new energy drink, Vitalize27. Ideas are flying around the meeting room. One student plays the role of a member of the group, who suddenly opens a laptop computer, and begins watching the screen. By mistake the audio is turned on, and the other members of the group can easily hear that the laptop user has accessed a sports channel, ESPN.com. The laptop user gets a few frowns, also with some stern questioning from the team leader. The student playing the role of the laptop user must present a sensible and diplomatic excuse as to why he or she was tuned into ESPN during the meeting. Another student plays the role of the team leader who is disappointed with the behavior he or she has observed. The other three role players might make any comments they deem to be appropriate.

Observers rate the role players on two dimensions, using a 1-to-5 scale from very poor to very good. One dimension is "effective use of human relations techniques." The second dimension is "acting ability." A few observers might voluntarily provide feedback to the role players in terms of sharing their ratings and observations. The course instructor might also provide feedback.

The practice of consulting a smart phone during a meeting has the potential to annoy, therefore detracting from the image of the smart phone user. An example is Joel L. Klein, the New York City schools chancellor. He has gained such a negative reputation for checking his BlackBerry during meetings that some parents joke that they might be better off sending him an e-mail message.[16]

As with cell phones, when laptop computers and smart phones are used at meetings to facilitate information gathering, and with permission, they can enhance interpersonal skills. If you contribute to the purpose of the meeting, and are not being rude or interruptive, you are displaying good interpersonal skill. Imagine you are present at a marketing meeting of a swimsuit designer and manufacturer. The head of marketing says, "We have been thinking of finding a distributor in Alaska, but I wonder what percentage of Alaskans own a swim suit." You say, "If you would like, give me five minutes to search the Internet for a factual answer to your question." Particularly if you find a plausible answer, you will be perceived as constructive.

The etiquette aspect of laptops, netbooks, and smart phones at meetings has created a spirited debate. People with traditional attitudes about etiquette say the use of smart phones at meetings is as gauche as ordering out for pizza. In contrast, techno-evangelists insist that to ignore real-time text messages invites peril because so many people demand an immediate response to their e-mail messages.[17] Again, to avoid being perceived as gauche (rude), follow the corporate culture. Skill-Building Exercise 5-2 deals with this issue.

Interpersonal Aspects of Presentation Technology

Presentation technology has become almost synonymous with PowerPoint and other computer graphics. However, presentation technology also includes laptops, data projectors, remote controls, and presentation software. The use of presentation technology provides an exceptional opportunity to display interpersonal skills—good or poor.

The biggest challenge in using presentation technology is to maintain a human presence while still making effective use of the technology. Among the obvious indicators of good interpersonal skill during an electronic presentation are to maintain eye contact with the audience, smile, show a sense of humor, and interact with the audience. Among the potential displays of negative interpersonal skills would be reading detailed slides to the audience, not maintaining eye contact, and continuous fiddling with your equipment thereby ignoring participants at the meeting.

All you have learned about making presentations (or public speaking) applies even though you might be tapping a key on your laptop computer while making a presentation. Self-assessment Quiz 5-2 presents a checklist of behaviors that summarizes major points of demonstrating effective interpersonal skills during a presentation. Many people who are watching you make a presentation will be making judgments about your interpersonal and cognitive skills. One reason is that the digitized workplace has decreased other opportunities, such as visits to your work area, to form judgments about you.

The Presentation Technology Checklist of Interpersonal Behaviors

Directions: Indicate whether each of the following statements is Mostly True or Mostly False as it applies to you (or would apply to you if you were in the situation indicated by the statement).

Statement Number	Mostly True	Mostly False
1. I make frequent eye contact with as many members of the audience as feasible.	_____	_____
2. I like to present a large number of slides in rapid sequence just to dazzle the audience.	_____	_____
3. I tend to get irritated if a member of the audience disagrees with one of my points.	_____	_____
4. I will often attempt to loosen up the audience by telling a joke related to nationality, age, or hair color.	_____	_____
5. I attempt to pack as much information onto a slide as possible even it requires using a 10 font.	_____	_____
6. If somebody in the audience complains about not being able to hear me, I like to retort with a negative comment like, "Have you had your hearing checked lately?"	_____	_____
7. I smile frequently during my presentation.	_____	_____
8. I explain to the members of the audience that they can revisit my presentation on a specific Web site, or that I am willing to send them an e-mail attachment of the presentation.	_____	_____
9. At the end of the presentation, I will typically thank the audience for having watched.	_____	_____
10. I will ask the audience an open-ended question such as "What questions do you have?" rather than a close-ended question like, "Any questions?"	_____	_____

Scoring and interpretation: Give yourself one point (+1) for each statement you gave in agreement with the keyed answer. The keyed answer indicates a positive interpersonal skill for presentation technology.

1. Mostly true	5. Mostly false	9. Mostly true
2. Mostly false	6. Mostly false	10. Mostly true
3. Mostly false	7. Mostly true	
4. Mostly false	8. Mostly true	

9–10 You have good skills related to the interpersonal aspects of presentation technology.

1–8 You have much room for improvement in terms of your skills related to the interpersonal aspects of presentation technology.

Videoconferencing

Videoconferencing places extra demands on making a good first impression, as well as demonstrating good interpersonal skills. Keep the following considerations in mind for creating a good impression and demonstrating sensitivity to the situation at a videoconference:[18]

1. **Choose your clothing carefully.** Some participants expect the screen to display only their upper torso, and therefore wear business attire above the waste, and perhaps shorts and sports shoes below. Busy patterns do not look good on camera. Clothing may be more superficial than interpersonal skill, but your choice of clothing reflects on your judgment and how seriously you take the conference.

2. **Speak in crisp, conversational tones, and pay close attention.** Maintain eye contact with live participants and remote viewers because this is an important interpersonal skill as it is with presentation technologies. Getting up to leave the room looks particularly bad on camera.

3. **Never forget the powerful reach of the video camera.** Behavior such as falling asleep or rolling the eyes in response to an executive's suggestions are readily seen by associates in the same and other locations. Such behavior is likely to be interpreted as indicative of immaturity.

4. **Avoid culturally insensitive gestures.** For example, large hand and body motions make many Asians uncomfortable. Also, extreme behaviors sometimes appear magnified on video camera although they might be less distracting in person.

5. **Decrease nervousness about video interviews by rehearsing.** Use a camcorder to see how you appear and sound during a practice interview, engaging the help of a friend. Solicit his or her feedback about your performance. Appearing relaxed during a videoconference helps you project the important interpersonal skill of being self-confident.

Interpersonal Skills Linked to Telecommuting

As illustrated in the case introduction, people who work from home face challenges to their interpersonal skills related to communication. Telecommuters can communicate abundantly via electronic devices, but they miss out on the face-to-face interactions so vital for dealing with complex problems. Another communication problem telecommuters face is feeling isolated from activities at the main office and missing out on the encouragement and recognition that take place in face-to-face encounters. (Of course, many telecommuters prefer to avoid such contact.) Many telecommuters have another communications problem: Because they have very little face-to-face communication with key people in the organization, they believe that they are passed over for promotion. Most telecommuters spend some time in the traditional office, yet they miss the day-by-day contact.

Another communication problem with telecommuting is that it lacks a solid human connection. As one telecommuting marketing consultant put it, face time is critical for building empathy. "It's a human connection. It takes time, and human beings need visual cues, the symbols of being together and caring for one another."[19] To combat the problem of isolation, most companies schedule some face time with remote workers perhaps every few months. At a minimum, a supervisor might phone the teleworkers at least once a week, or hold a monthly videoconference.[20]

To display positive interpersonal skills as a worker from home or other remote location, the individual should make good use of the limited face-to-face contact he or she has with other workers. Display warmth toward and interest in work associates. Staying in touch online with a human relations twist is also important. Occasionally asking how the other person is doing is helpful, as is an occasional question about the person's interests or family life. Many telecommuters are asked to attend an occasional company meeting. On these occasions, it is important to display high enthusiasm. To keep interpersonal skills sharp, it is good to interact with store associates, and service workers such as the postal service and package delivery workers. The designer described at the chapter outset, kept his interpersonal skills in use by interacting with other workers sharing the same office space.

Successful telecommuters also need the interpersonal skill of being able to work well without supervision. You also need to be able to work well in isolation, and not be dependent on frequent interaction with coworkers or a supervisor.[21] High maintenance employees who need frequent praise and attention are much better suited for working in a traditional office than working from home.[22]

Avoiding Damage to Your Online Reputation

Postings on the Internet, including newspaper articles, blogs, and video Web sites, can rapidly broadcast favorable or unfavorable data about your interpersonal skills and judgment. Based largely on the Internet, the much more information about a person's private life has become public. Some aspects of your personal life therefore affect your professional reputation. If an Internet blog contends that a given individual was an accessory to an armed robbery, that person's job might become in jeopardy.[23]

Matt Zimmerman, senior staff attorney for the Electronic Frontier Foundation, explains the importance of having a squeaky clean reputation in these terms: "Now we have this giant megaphone of the Internet, where every little whisper about someone shows up in Google."[24]

A positive interpersonal and cognitive skill is therefore to avoid having embarrassing information or photographs linked to you accessible through search engines. Your reputation can also be damaged by posting extreme viewpoints on Web because these extreme viewpoints might be unwelcome by employers who want to void offending customers or potential customers. Two examples of extreme viewpoints are stating that (a) all people who wear fur coats should be physically attacked, and (b) all investment bankers who earn more than $2 million in an annual bonus should be sent to jail.

Another aspect of your online reputation is that you might need to distance yourself from others who share your name. If you have a LinkedIn or Facebook profile, insert a clear photo of yourself. During a job search when you send your résumé either by a hard copy or by online, provide a link to your profile.[25] Also, alert the present or prospective employers if someone with the same name as yours has a negative online presence. A challenge in terms of job hunting is that an Internet search has become part of the employer's background investigation. Negative information about oneself on the Web can sometimes be removed by asking or hiring a service for such purposes.

SELF-ASSESSMENT QUIZZES IN OVERVIEW

Self-Assessment Quiz 5-1 gave you an opportunity to take an overview of how politely and sensibly you use information and communication technology with respect to dealing with others. Self-Assessment Quiz 5-2 focuses your digitally related interpersonal skills on making presentations with technology. The two quizzes supplement each other, with the second quiz being a special case of the other. In general, your standing on both quizzes should be close.

Concept Review and Reinforcement

Key Term

multitasking 103

Summary

Effective interpersonal skills help make good use of the communication and information technology surrounding us in the workplace. Interactions with people one at a time create the majority of opportunities for displaying interpersonal skills related to the digital age. Cell phones and text messaging represent an enormous opportunity for displaying good, as well as poor, interpersonal skills. An example of positive skill would be to ask your work associate if he or she would like you to access an item of work-related information using your cell phone. An example of a negative skill would be work-related driving under the influence of a cell phone including text messaging.

E-mail messages and instant messaging (IM) provide another opportunity for displaying positive as well as negative interpersonal skills related to the digital age. The way in which a message is sent, positive or negative, tells something about the sender. Figure 5-1 summarizes a large amount of information about etiquette related to e-mail and instant messaging.

Another interpersonal skill useful in the digital age is to perform well during a webcam interview. Performing well in such an interview combines interpersonal skills with those related to communication technology. In some situations, performing two tasks at once can enhance interpersonal skills because you are helping another person, as is often done in coaching and tutoring. The major negative interpersonal skill aspect of multitasking is that it trivializes the person with whom you are interacting.

A negative consequence of communication technology in the workplace is that it is easier to harass coworkers than in the analog age. Creating a hostile environment by displaying pornography to workers who do not want to see it has become one of the most frequent forms of harassment.

Positive interpersonal skills associated with social networking include (1) demonstrating your loyalty by posting gracious comments about your employer, (2) displaying your compassion for people in need, and (3) demonstrating professional-level communication skills.

Negative interpersonal skills associated with social networking include (a) using social networking sites to eliminate face-to-face interactions with work associates, (2) posting confident or derogatory information about your employer, and (3) engaging in social networking at inappropriate times.

Whether the use of laptop and notebook computers, as well as smart phones, during meetings enhances your interpersonal skills depends on company custom and why you are using your computer. When laptop computers and smart phones are used at meetings to facilitate information gathering, and with permission, they can enhance interpersonal skills.

The biggest challenge in using presentation technology is to maintain a human presence while still making effective use of the technology. An example of a positive interpersonal skill is maintaining eye contact with the audience; a negative skill would be continuous fiddling with the equipment, thereby ignoring the audience.

Videoconferencing places extra demands on creating a good first impression, as well as demonstrating good interpersonal skill. A positive skill would be to speak in crisp, conversational tones, and paying close attention. People who work from home face challenges to their interpersonal skills related to communication. To display positive interpersonal skills, the worker from home should make good use of the limited face-to-face contact he or she has with other workers.

Protecting your online reputation is a skill. A positive interpersonal and cognitive skill is therefore to avoid having embarrassing information and photographs linked to you accessible through search engines.

Questions for Discussion and Review

1. You and a coworker are having a work-related conversation, seated on a bench outside the office building during lunch break. Your friend's cell phone rings; he notices from the number that the boss is calling, so he answers the call immediately. Explain whether or not your friend's answering the call is appropriate.

2. Assume that you send an instant message to the company CEO stating that you enjoy working for the company. Explain whether you think the CEO is obliged to respond immediately, or at all, to your message.

3. What should a person who is invited for a webcam job interview do if he or she does not feel telegenic (photogenic on TV) to perform well in such an interview?

4. Suppose you are interacting with an executive in your company who interrupts the conversation several times to make and receive calls on his or her smart phone. Explain whether you would reciprocate by making your own calls during your interaction with the executive.

5. What might you be able to do in the next several days to demonstrate on Facebook or Twitter a positive aspect of your interpersonal skills?

6. Imagine that you are attending an in-person meeting as your favorite sports team is playing a championship game in a different time zone. Explain whether you would take a quick peak at the score from time to time on your smart phone during the meeting.

7. Give an example of a one of the best displays of interpersonal skills you have seen in a PowerPoint presentation by one of your professors.

8. Explain why when a politician such as the president of the United States, the prime minister of Canada, or a U. S. senator makes an address to the public, he or she never uses PowerPoint.

9. How might a person who telecommutes four days a week demonstrate to management that he or she has good interpersonal skills?

10. What could you possibly do to use YouTube to demonstrate to others that you have good interpersonal skills?

The Web Corner

www.akdrt.com/cell.html
(Avoiding cell phone rudeness.)

aol.com/video-detail
(Presenting yourself well during a videoconference.)

www.onlinereputationmanager.com
(Developing a good online reputation.)

Internet Skill Builder: Interpersonal Skills of a Technology Executive

Think of a well-known information technology executive, such Steve Jobs at Apple Corp or Marissa Mayer at

Google, Inc. Arrive at a judgment about his or her interpersonal skills through video research on the Internet. For example, you might find a brief video of your target executive on YouTube, Hulu, or Facebook. Based on this small sample of behavior, reach any conclusion you can about the technology executive's interpersonal skills. Two traits to judge would be rudeness and insensitivity to people because some well-known technology executives have the reputation of treating others poorly. Forget about the opinion of others—you are the judge in this assignment.

Developing Your Human Relations Skills

Interpersonal Relations Case 5.1

Unveiled on Facebook

Lisa works as tech support field representative in the digital printer division of a telecommunications company. The digital printers manufactured and sold by the company are designed for large, commercial printing companies. The starting price for these sophisticated and complex machines is $400,000. In addition to the machines, the company sells service contracts that include field visits by a tech support representative. These visits are necessary when there is a problem with the machine that cannot be resolved by telephone or computer to computer.

Lisa's company is located in Cleveland, Ohio. During a February cold spell in Cleveland, a major customer located in Miami was having trouble with a new digital printer. The problem could not be resolved by phone or through computer diagnostics, so Lisa was sent down to Miami. After Lisa arrived, she estimated that the job would take three days to accomplish.

At the end of the second day, Lisa received an urgent call from Barry, her boss, who told her to return home as quickly as possible because a customer in Chicago needed her expertise to solve a problem with its giant printing press. Lisa thought that because she had done such a great job in fixing the Miami printing press, she deserved a day of vacation in Florida. So she explained to Barry that the customer needed one more day of hands-on support. As a result, she would be back to the office one day later than planned.

The next morning Lisa headed to South Beach in Miami along with two contacts she had made at the cus-tomer. One of the customer employees, Jessica, brought along a camcorder because in her words, "I love to have souvenirs of good times." Without Lisa granting permission, Jessica then posted a video of her frolicking in the water at South Beach. She also sent a message to the Facebook account of Lisa's boss, alerting him to "check out my new video."

When Lisa arrived back in the office, Barry confronted her about the video and asked, "Explain to me clearly how you were helping our customer with their problem while you were in the water at South Beach. Our company cannot tolerate liars."

Lisa replied, "I was thinking about the customer's problem while I was at South Beach. Besides, after all that hard work I needed a little rest and relaxation."

Case Questions

1. What does this case have to do with interpersonal skills?
2. What would you advise Lisa to do so that she can resolve her problem with her employer? (You might want to glance at Chapter 9, which includes a discussion of conflict resolution.)
3. What advice would you offer Jessica, Lisa's work associate who posted a video of her on Facebook?
4. If you were Barry, how would you handle this situation of Lisa having taken a day off to visit South Beach?

Interpersonal Relations Role-Play

Dealing with the Surprise Video on Facebook

The case just presented provides the storyline and the scenario for this role-play. One student plays the role of Lisa who wants to defend herself with respect to the extra day off she took. She might also want to defend herself with respect to the Facebook video. Another student plays the role of Barry who is angry with Lisa, yet he is an ardent Facebook fan. Barry also recognizes that the company badly needs Lisa because of her technical expertise. Run the role-play for about seven minutes. Observers might provide feedback as to how well the issue of the Facebook unveiling has been resolved.

Kevin, the Twitter Guy

Kevin, a real estate agent, specializing in low-priced homes in Detroit, Michigan, is an avid Twitter user. He spends approximately two hours per day checking out his followers and the people he is following. Kevin posts about six tweets a day with the hope of building his reputation as an intelligent professional, as well as obtaining referrals of potential homebuyers. The contents of 10 tweets Kevin posted last month are presented next.

1. The Detroit Lions might be good this season. Owing a home in downtown is a good investment. http://www.kevin@MetroRealty.com.
2. My buddies love my barbeques. Get in touch to buy a house. http://www.kevin@MetroRealty.com.
3. Looks like I have pink eye today. Send along your home-hunting friends. http://www.kevin@MetroRealty.com.
4. I tried one of those electronic cigarettes. No thanks. Home ownership is a great investment. http://www.kevin@MetroRealty.com.
5. My niece sent me a Valentine's Day card saying she loves me. http://www.kevin@MetroRealty.com.
6. Just advised my folks to get a reverse mortgage. I told them home ownership is good. http://www.kevin@MetroRealty.com.
7. Keep an eye on your BMI (body mass index). Did you know that I sell houses? http://www.kevin@MetroRealty.com.
8. I may need a new transmission on my SUV. I'm waiting for a referral from you guys. http://www.kevin@MetroRealty.com.
9. It's hot and my AC in the SUV is down. Home ownership is the American Dream. http://www.kevin@MetroRealty.com.
10. Did you know that Domino's has made its pizzas spicier and tastier? Pizza goes great with a house. http://www.kevin@MetroRealty.com.

Case Questions

1. How well is Kevin doing in terms of projecting the image of an intelligent professional?
2. What advice might you give to Kevin so that his tweeting might lead to more referrals?
3. To what extent is Kevin just wasting time with his Twitter activity?

Developing Teamwork Skills

Ann Livermore, head of Hewlett-Packard's storage and servers, software and services businesses, has faced decisions at her company that might have sent some executives heading for the door. But despite deals that cut into her territory, she keeps her focus on the big picture, on the challenges at hand, and on new opportunities for growth. It's all part of knowing that "business is a team sport," she says.

That sentiment isn't common among business leaders these days. Many senior executives are more focused on their individual well-being than on furthering their company goals. They're quick to jump to new employers when they don't feel appreciated.

Some outside H-P had speculated that Livermore was unhappy about relinquishing part of her portfolio after the company announced plans to acquire Electronic Data Systems, an IT

After reading and studying this chapter and doing the exercises, you should be able to

1. Explain the difference between a traditional team and a virtual team.
2. Understand the advantages and disadvantages of teams.
3. Identify various team member roles.
4. Apply interpersonal-related tactics for effective team play.
5. Apply task-related tactics for effective team play.

outsourcing company. She says that she's staying put. "This isn't about me," she said in an interview. "It's about what is best for H-P. It makes sense to combine all outsourcing businesses—and with a merger this big for EDS to report directly to Mark (Mark Hurd, former CEO of H-P)."[1]

The attitude of the executive just described illustrates a spirit of teamwork that can help a company prosper. The modern organization depends on teamwork throughout the company. Many firms rely more on teamwork than on individuals acting alone to accomplish work. To be successful in the modern organization, it is therefore necessary to be an effective team player. You have to work smoothly with other members of the team to accomplish your goals. Teamwork is more important as people work their way up through the organization. Executives, such as CEOs, preach teamwork but tend to dominate meetings and make more decisions by themselves.[2] (Ann Livermore might be an exception.)

The challenges a team member faces come to light when the true nature of a team is recognized. A **team** is a special type of group. Team members have complementary skills and are committed to a common purpose, a set of performance goals, and an approach to the task. In other words, the members of a team work together smoothly, and all pull in the same direction. A workplace team should be more like an effective athletic team than a group of individuals out for individual glory.[3]

This chapter gives you the information, insights, and preliminary practice necessary to develop effective teamwork skills. Self-Assessment Quiz 6-1 will help you assess your current mental readiness to be a contributing team member.

team

A small number of people with complementary skills who are committed to a common purpose, set of performance goals, and approach for which they hold themselves mutually accountable.

FACE-TO-FACE VERSUS VIRTUAL TEAMS

All teams in the workplace have the common element of people working together cooperatively and members possessing a mix of skills. No matter what label the team carries, its broad purpose is to contribute to a *collaborative workplace* in which people help each other achieve constructive goals. The idea is for workers to collaborate (a high level of cooperation) rather than to compete with or prevent others from getting their work done.

As teams have become more common in the workplace, effort has been directed toward specifying the skills and knowledge a person needs to function effectively on a team. Self-Assessment Quiz 6-2 presents a representative listing of team skills as perceived by employers.

Although many different types of teams exist, a useful distinction is between the traditional teams in which workers share the same physical space and virtual teams whereby the team members rarely see each other in person.

LEARNING OBJECTIVE 1

Face-to-Face (Traditional) Teams

The best-known workplace team is a group of workers who take some of the responsibility for managing their own work. Face-to-face teams are used in a wide variety of activities,

Team Player Attitudes

Directions: Describe how well you agree with each of the following statements, using the following scale: disagree strongly (DS); disagree (D); neutral (N); agree (A); agree strongly (AS). Circle the number in the appropriate column.

		DS	D	N	A	AS
1.	I am at my best when working alone.	5	4	3	2	1
2.	I have belonged to clubs and teams ever since I was a child.	1	2	3	4	5
3.	It takes far too long to get work accomplished with a group.	5	4	3	2	1
4.	I like the friendship of working in a group.	1	2	3	4	5
5.	I would prefer to run a one-person business than to be a member of a large firm.	5	4	3	2	1
6.	It's difficult to trust others in the group on key assignments.	5	4	3	2	1
7.	Encouraging others comes to me naturally.	1	2	3	4	5
8.	I like the give-and-take of ideas that is possible in a group.	1	2	3	4	5
9.	It is fun for me to share responsibility with other group members.	1	2	3	4	5
10.	Much more can be accomplished by a team than by the same number of people working alone.	1	2	3	4	5

Total Score _____

Scoring and Interpretation: Add the numbers you circled to obtain your total score.

41–50 You have strong positive attitudes toward being a team member and working cooperatively with other members.

30–40 You have moderately favorable attitudes toward being a team member and working cooperatively with other members.

10–29 You prefer working by yourself to being a team member. To work effectively in a company that emphasizes teamwork, you may need to develop more positive attitudes toward working jointly with others.

including producing motorcycles, telephone directories, a major component for a large computer, or launching a new product. Team members interact with other frequently rather than doing their work in isolation from one another.

Members of a traditional team typically work together on an ongoing, day-by-day basis, thus differentiating it from a task force or a committee. The team is often given total responsibility for or "ownership" of an entire product or service, such as producing a telephone directory. At other times, the team is given responsibility for a major chunk of a job, such as building an airplane engine (but not the entire airplane).

A major hurdle in forming a true team is to help employees overcome the attitude reflected in the statement "I'm not paid to think." Teams often rely less on supervisors and more on the workers assuming more responsibilities for managing their own activities.

As with all teams, mutual trust among members contributes to team effectiveness. A study conducted with business students, however, showed that if the members trust each other too much, they may not monitor (check up on) each other's work enough. As a result, group performance will suffer. This problem of too much trust surfaces primarily when the team members have individual assignments that do not bring them into frequent contact with each other.[4] An example of an individual, or autonomous, project would be preparing a statistical report that would later be given to the group.

Virtual Teams

virtual team

A small group of people who conduct almost all of their collaborative work by electronic communication rather than face-to-face meetings.

Some teams conduct most of their work by sending electronic messages to each other rather than conducting face-to-face meetings. A **virtual team** is a small group of people who conduct almost all of their collaborative work by electronic communication rather than by face-to-face meetings. E-mail, including IM (instant messaging), is the usual medium

Team Skills

A variety of skills are required to be an effective member of various types of teams. Several business firms use the skill inventory here to help guide team members toward the competencies they need to become high-performing team members.

Directions: Review each team skill listed, and rate your skill level for each one using the following classifications:

S = strong (capable and comfortable with effectively implementing the skill)

M = moderate (demonstrated skill in the past)

B = basic (minimum ability in this area)

N = not applicable (not relevant to the type of work I do)

Communication skills	*Skill level (S, M, B, or N)*
Speak effectively	_____
Foster open communications	_____
Listen to others	_____
Deliver presentations	_____
Prepare written communication	_____
Self-management skills	
Act with integrity	
Demonstrate adaptability	
Engage in personal development	_____
Strive for results	_____
Display a commitment to work	_____
Thought process skills	
Innovate solutions to problems	_____
Use sound judgment	_____
Analyze issues	_____
Think "outside the box"	
Organizational skills	
Know the business	_____
Use technical/functional expertise	_____
Use financial/quantitative data	_____
Strategic (broad business perspective) skills	
Recognize "big picture" impact	____
Promote corporate citizenship	_____
Focus on customer needs	_____
Commit to quality	_____
Manage profitability	_____

Interpretation: There is no scoring key for this questionnaire. Its purpose is to raise your awareness of the types of skills that are required to be a successful team member in business.

for sharing information and conducting meetings. *Groupware* is another widely used approach to conducting an electronic meeting. Using groupware, several people can edit a document at the same time, or in sequence. Desktop videoconferencing, such as a webcam, is another technological advance that facilitates the virtual team.

Most high-tech companies make some use of virtual teams and electronic meetings. Strategic alliances in which geographically dispersed companies work with each other are ideally suited for virtual teams. It is less expensive for the field technician in Iceland to hold an electronic meeting with her counterparts in South Africa, Mexico, and California than it is to bring them all together in one physical location. Virtual teams are sometimes the answer to the challenge of hiring workers with essential skills who do not want to relocate. Because the members of a virtual team might be working in different countries, they are often considered to be multicultural teams.

With team members geographically dispersed, precise communications are all the more important for virtual teams. The virtual team members usually need a formal document outlining the objectives, job responsibilities, and team goals. Another communication problem takes place when the virtual team is composed of both in-house workers and those in remote locations. The office-bound members become jealous of the seemingly cushy setup enjoyed by the telecommuters. One solution to this problem is for every member of the team to be given a chance to prove that he or she can work off-site.[5] Another consideration is that the work should be distributed fairly among office-bound workers and virtual team members. Last-minute assignments are often handed to the first in-house worker the manager sees.[6]

Establishing trust is a major challenge in a virtual team because the team members have to rely on people they never see to carry out their fair share of the workload, and to exchange reliable information. Trust is also needed in terms of what information should be shared outside of the team. For example, if the team is behind schedule on a project, can each member be trusted not to inform outsiders about the problem? For example, one virtual team had an external communication norm that prohibited team members from conveying negative information to anyone outside the team.[7]

Despite the efficiency of virtual teams, there are times when face-to-face (or at least telephone) interaction is necessary to deal with complex and emotional issues. Negotiating a new contract between management and a labor union, for example, is not well suited to an electronic meeting.

> "Virtual teams need to know that their coworkers are 'real people.' It's the personal information they learn from one another that will foster the social ties that allow collaboration to occur naturally."
> —Tammy Burch, CEO of Virtual Concepts International in Milford, Michigan.

THE ADVANTAGES AND DISADVANTAGES OF TEAMS AND TEAMWORK

LEARNING OBJECTIVE 2

synergy

A situation in which the group's total output exceeds the sum of each individual's contribution.

Groups have always been the building blocks of organizations. Yet groups and teams have recently grown in importance as the basic unit for organizing work. In an attempt to cope with numerous changes in the outside world, many organizations have granted teams increased independence and flexibility. Furthermore, teams are often required to work more closely with customers and suppliers.

The increased acceptance of teams suggests that group work offers many advantages. Nevertheless, it is useful to specify several of these advantages and also examine the potential problems of groups. Being aware of these potential pitfalls can often help a person avoid them. These same advantages and disadvantages also apply to group decision making, to be described in Chapter 7.

Advantages of Group Work and Teamwork

Group work and group decision making offer several advantages over individual effort. Because so much of what is accomplished in organizations is done by groups, it may appear that groups and teams have many advantages. However, the importance of this topic warrants mentioning a few of the advantages of groups, teams, and group decision making.

Synergy. If several knowledgeable people are brought into the decision-making process, a number of worthwhile possibilities may be uncovered. It is also possible to gain **synergy**, whereby the group's total output exceeds the sum of each individual's contribution. For example, it would be a rare person working alone who could build a racing car. At the same time, groups and teams are the building block of the larger organization.

Work Accomplishment and High Productivity.   Without groups, including teams, an organization could not get its work accomplished. Clarence Otis, Jr., the CEO of Darden Restaurants (which includes the Olive Garden, Red Lobster, and Bahama Breeze), says that the thrust of his leadership is to build the team because the team accomplishes so much of the work.[8]

A major justification for relying on teams in the workplace is that under the right circumstances, they can enhance productivity and profitability. The right circumstances include an atmosphere that promotes teamwork and financial bonuses for high-performing teams. A classic example is American steel maker Nucor Corp. The company is committed to the spirit of teamwork, and bonuses for teams of steelworkers average 170 percent to 180 percent. Since Nucor had implemented its team incentive plan in 1966, the company has been profitable each quarter through 2009 despite foreign competition. Also, the company has increased the dividend to shareholders for 37 consecutive years.[9]

A broad perspective about the advantages of groups is that because of groups and teams, large organizations can be built that provide useful goods and services to the world. For example, a company such as Apple, Inc., or Johnson & Johnson is only possible because of group effort. Furthermore, the existence of large organizations, including business firms, colleges, universities, and hospitals, helps advance civilization.

Acceptance and Commitment.   Group decision making is also helpful in gaining acceptance and commitment. The argument is that people who contribute to making a decision will feel some ownership about implementing the decision. Under these conditions, it becomes more difficult to object to a decision because your contribution is included in the decision. At times, managers will deliberately ask for input into a decision they have already made as a manipulative way of gaining acceptance for and commitment to the decision.

Avoidance of Major Errors.   Team members often evaluate each other's thinking, so the team is likely to avoid major errors. An advertising specialist was developing an advertising campaign to attract seniors to live in a retirement community. The proposed ads had photographs of senior citizens engaged in playing shuffleboard, visiting the pharmacy, and sleeping in a hammock. Another team member on the project pointed out that many seniors perceive themselves to be energetic and youthful. Ads emphasizing advanced age might therefore backfire. A successful advertising campaign was then developed that featured seniors in more youthful activities, such as jogging and dancing.

Increased Job Satisfaction.   Working in teams and groups also enhances the job satisfaction of members. Being a member of a work group makes it possible to satisfy more needs than working alone. Among these needs are affiliation, security, self-esteem, and self-fulfillment. (Chapter 11 provides more details about psychological needs.)

A major reason that groups and teams contribute to worker satisfaction is that many people find working in groups to be a natural way of life. In school, sports, and the community, they have been accustomed to working collaboratively and therefore feel more comfortable in group than in individual effort.

Disadvantages of Group Work and Teamwork

Group activity has some potential disadvantages for both individuals and the organization, as described in the following paragraphs. Some of these disadvantages serve as alerts for preventing problems.

Time Wasting.   Teams and other groups often waste time because they talk too much and act too little. Committees appear to suffer from more inaction than teams. Abigail Johnson, president of Fidelity Employer Services Division, says that committees are not effective decision makers. "They have tended to be slow and overly risk averse. Even worse, I believe, they can drain an organization of talent, because the group can only be as good as the average."[10]

Pressures toward Conformity.   A major problem is that members face pressures to conform to group standards of performance and conduct, as just implied. Some teams might shun a person who is much more productive than his or her coworkers. Also, to be liked by coworkers, as well as avoiding conflict, a group member will sometimes agree with the opinion of other group or team members. Group members will often use the same jargon, whether or not it is precise. For example, workers at Microsoft refer to e-mail as "mail," thereby snubbing postal mail.

Conformity in dress and appearance is also apparent in many work groups. You might want to examine a photo of Google, Microsoft, or Apple employees and observe how much conformity in dress you find. Conformity in dress, however, is not much of a disadvantage except when a group member is dissatisfied because of the pressure to dress in the same manner as coworkers.

Self-Assessment Quiz 6-3 gives you an opportunity to think about your tendencies toward conformity.

Shirking of Individual Responsibility (Social Loafing).   Shirking of individual responsibility is another problem frequently noted in groups. Unless work is assigned carefully to each team member, an undermotivated person can often squeeze by without contributing his or her fair share to a group effort. **Social loafing** is the psychological term for shirking individual responsibility in a group setting. The social loafer risks being ostracized (shunned) by the group but may be willing to pay the price rather than to work hard. Loafing of this type is sometimes found in groups such as committees and project teams. Have you ever encountered a social loafer on a group project at school?

Fostering of Conflict.   At their worst, teams and other groups foster conflict on the job. People within the work group often bicker about such matters as doing a fair share of the undesirable tasks within the department. Cohesive work groups can also become xenophobic (fearful of outsiders). As a consequence, they may grow to dislike other groups and enter into conflict with them. A customer service group might put considerable effort into showing up a sales group because the latter makes promises to customers that the customer service group cannot keep. For example, a sales representative might promise that a customer can get a loaner if his or her equipment needs repair, although customer service has no such policy.

Groupthink.   A well-publicized disadvantage of group decision making is **groupthink**, a deterioration of mental efficiency, reality testing, and moral judgment in the interest of group solidarity. Simply put, groupthink is an extreme form of consensus. The group atmosphere values getting along more than getting things done. The group thinks as a unit, believes it is impervious to outside criticism, and begins to have illusions about its own invincibility. As a consequence, the group loses its powers of critical analysis.[11] Groupthink appears to have contributed to several of the major financial scandals of the previous decade. Members of top management got together to vote themselves huge bonuses just before filing bankruptcy for their company. Several of the executives, including a few from Enron Corporation, were later sent to prison for their outrageous decisions.

Two conditions are important for overcoming the potential disadvantages of teams and groups.[12] First, the members must strive to act like a team following some of the suggestions given in the upcoming pages. Second, the task given to the group should require collective effort instead of being a task that could better be performed by individuals. For example, an international business specialist would probably learn to conjugate verbs in a foreign language better by working alone than on a team. What is your opinion on this issue? Figure 6-1 presents more information about key factors associated with effective work teams and groups. The more of these factors that are present, the more likely it is that a given team or group will be productive.

LEARNING OBJECTIVE 3

TEAM MEMBER ROLES

A major challenge in learning to become an effective team member is to choose the right roles to occupy. A **role** is a tendency to behave, contribute, and relate to others in a particular way. If you carry out positive roles, you will be perceived as a contributor to team effort. If you neglect carrying out these roles, you will be perceived as a poor contributor.

social loafing

The psychological term for shirking individual responsibility in a group setting.

groupthink

A deterioration of mental efficiency, reality testing, and moral judgment in the interest of group solidarity.

role

A tendency to behave, contribute, and relate to others in a particular way.

The Conformity Quiz

Directions: Circle the extent to which each of the following statements describes your behavior or attitude: agree strongly (AS); agree (A); neutral (N); disagree (D); disagree strongly (DS). You may have to respond in terms of any team or group experience you have had if you are not currently a member of a work team, a class project team, or a sports team. Consider that having someone who is familiar with your behavior and attitudes helps you respond accurately.

		AS	A	N	D	DS
1.	I rarely question the decision reached by the team.	5	4	3	2	1
2.	Whatever the group wants is fine with me.	5	4	3	2	1
3.	My clothing distinguishes me from the other members of the team.	1	2	3	4	5
4.	I consider myself to be one of the gang.	5	4	3	2	1
5.	I rarely express disagreement during a group discussion.	5	4	3	2	1
6.	I routinely have lunch with other members of the team.	5	4	3	2	1
7.	My teammates sometimes complain that I think too independently.	1	2	3	4	5
8.	My preference is to piggyback on the ideas of others rather than contributing the ideas of my own.	5	4	3	2	1
9.	When I notice that the other members of the team make the same error in speech, I will copy them rather than sound different.	5	4	3	2	1
10.	I am often the first person to get up at the scheduled ending of the meeting.	1	2	3	4	5
11.	I do almost all of my creative thinking for the team task when I'm with the team.	5	4	3	2	1
12.	I'm particularly careful not to criticize an idea submitted by the team leader.	5	4	3	2	1
13.	The number of hours I work per week corresponds closely to the number worked by my teammates.	5	4	3	2	1
14.	When I think it is necessary, I bring information to the group conflicting with the path we are following.	1	2	3	4	5
15.	I would rather keep my mouth closed than point out weaknesses in a teammate's ideas.	5	4	3	2	1
16.	I've been called a maverick on more than one occasion by teammates.	1	2	3	4	5
17.	I encourage team members to express doubts about proposed solutions to problems.	1	2	3	4	5
18.	I invite criticism of my ideas.	1	2	3	4	5
19.	When the team laughs at a comment, I laugh too even if I don't think the comment was funny.	5	4	3	2	1
20.	Most of my social life centers on activities with my teammates.	5	4	3	2	1

Interpretation: Calculate your score by adding the numbers you have circled, and use the following guide:

80–100 You are a high-conforming individual who readily goes along with the team without preserving your individuality. In an effort to be liked, you might be overcompromising your thinking.

40–79 You have probably achieved the right balance between following group norms (standards of conduct) and expressing your individuality. With actions and attitudes like this, you are on your way to becoming a good team player, yet also in a position to attain individual recognition.

20–29 You are highly individualistic, perhaps to the point of not working smoothly in a team setting. Be careful that you are not going out of your way to be a nonconformist, thereby interfering with your ability to be an effective team player.

Skill development: Examine your responses to the 20 questions because the response might give you a clue to needed development, often just by making a subtle change within your control. Here are two examples: If you answered agree strongly or agree to question 8, you might work toward contributing ideas of your own. If you answered disagree or disagree strongly to question 14, you might work toward helping the team think more critically about the path it is following.

FIGURE 6-1 Key Characteristics of Effective Teams and Work Groups

- The group has collective efficacy, or a belief that it can handle the assigned task.
- The team has clear-cut goals linked to organizational goals so that group members feel connected to the entire organization. However, the group does not have so many goals that confusion results. Goals include having a mission that helps explain what the group is attempting to accomplish.
- Group members are empowered so that they learn to think for themselves rather than expecting a supervisor to solve all the difficult problems. At the same time, the group believes it has the authority to solve a variety of problems without first obtaining approval from management.
- Group members are assigned work they perceive to be challenging, exciting, and rewarding. As a consequence, the work is self-rewarding.
- Members depend on one another to accomplish tasks, and work toward a common goal. At the same time, the group believes in itself and that it can accomplish an independent task.
- Diversity exists within the group, including differences in education, experience, and cultural background. Different backgrounds lead to more creative problem solving. Also, the differences prompt more discussion and analysis.
- Members receive extensive training in technical knowledge, problem-solving skills, and interpersonal skills.
- Members receive part of their pay related to team or group incentives rather than strictly based on individual performance.
- Group size is generally about 6 people, rather than 10 or more.
- Team members have good intelligence and personality factors, such as conscientiousness and pride that contribute to good performance.
- There is honest and open communication among group members and with other groups in the organization.
- Members have the philosophy of working as a team—6 brains, not just 12 hands.
- Members are familiar with their jobs, coworkers, and the work environment. This experience adds to their expertise. The beneficial effects of experience may diminish after awhile because the team needs fresh ideas and approaches.
- The team has emotional intelligence in the sense that it builds relationships both inside and outside the team. Included in emotional intelligence are norms that establish mutual trust among members, a feeling of group identity, and group efficacy.
- Stronger performing group members assist weaker performing group members accomplish their task, particularly when the performance of the "weakest link" in the group is key for group performance.

Sources: Alexander D. Stajkovic, Dongseop Lee, and Anthony J. Nyberg, "Collective Efficacy, Group Potency, and Group Performance: Meta-Analysis of their Relationships, and Test of a Mediation Model," *Journal of Applied Psychology*, May 2009, p. 815; Stanley M. Gulley, Kara A. Incalcaterra, Aparna Joshi, and J. Matthew Beaublien, "A Meta-Analysis of Team Efficacy, Potency, and Performance: Interdependence and Level of Analysis as Moderators of Observed Relationships," *Journal of Applied Psychology,* October 2002, pp. 819–832; Stephen R. Covey, "Secrets Behind Great Teams," *USA Weekend,* July 11–13, 2008, p. 7; Katherine W. Phillips, Katie A. Liljenquist, and Margaret A. Neale, "Is the Pain Work the Gain? The Advantages and Liabilities of Agreeing With Socially Distinct Newcomers," *Personality and Social Psychology Bulletin*, March 2009, pp. 336–350; Shawn L. Berman, Vanessa Urch Druskat, and Steven B. Wolff, "Building the Emotional Intelligence of Groups," *Harvard Business Review*, March 2001, pp. 80–90; Claus W. Langred, "Too Much of a Good Thing? Negative Effects of High Trust and Individual Autonomy in Self-Managing Work Teams," *Academy of Management Journal,* June 2004, pp. 385–389; Bernhard Weber and Guido Hertel, "Motivation Gains of Inferior Group Members: A Meta-Analytical Review," *Journal of Personality and Social Psychology*, No. 6, 2007, pp. 973–993.

Self-Assessment Quiz 6-4 will help you evaluate your present inclinations toward occupying effective roles as a team member. In this section, we describe a number of the most frequently observed positive roles played by team members.[13] We will also mention a group of negative roles. The description will be followed by an activity in which the roles can be practiced.

Team Player Roles

Directions: For each of the following statements about team activity, check *mostly agree* or *mostly disagree*. If you have not experienced such a situation, imagine how you would act or think if placed in that situation. In responding to the statements, assume that you are taking the questionnaire with the intent of learning something about yourself.

	Mostly agree	*Mostly disagree*
1. It is rare that I ever miss a team meeting.	_____	_____
2. I regularly compliment team members when they do something exceptional.	_____	_____
3. Whenever I can, I avoid being the note taker at a team meeting.	_____	_____
4. From time to time, other team members come to me for advice on technical matters.	_____	_____
5. I like to hide some information from other team members so that I can be in control.	_____	_____
6. I welcome new team members coming to me for advice and learning the ropes.	_____	_____
7. My priorities come first, which leaves me with very little time to help other team members.	_____	_____
8. During a team meeting, it is not unusual for several other people at a time to look toward me for my opinion.	_____	_____
9. If I think the team is moving in an unethical direction, I will say so explicitly.	_____	_____
10. Rarely will I criticize the progress of the team even if I think such criticism is deserved.	_____	_____
11. It is typical for me to summarize the progress in a team meeting, even if not asked.	_____	_____
12. To conserve time, I attempt to minimize contact with my teammates outside our meetings.	_____	_____
13. I intensely dislike going along with a consensus decision if the decision runs contrary to my thoughts on the issue.	_____	_____
14. I rarely remind teammates of our mission statement as we go about our work.	_____	_____
15. Once I have made up my mind on an issue facing the team, I am unlikely to be persuaded in another direction.	_____	_____
16. I am willing to accept negative feedback from team members.	_____	_____
17. Just to get a new member of the team involved, I will ask his or her opinion.	_____	_____
18. Even if the team has decided on a course of action, I am not hesitant to bring in new information that supports another position.	_____	_____
19. Quite often I talk negatively about one team member to another.	_____	_____
20. My teammates are almost a family to me because I am truly concerned about their welfare.	_____	_____
21. When it seems appropriate, I joke and kid with teammates.	_____	_____
22. My contribution to team tasks is as important to me as my individual work.	_____	_____
23. From time to time, I have pointed out to the team how we can all improve in reaching our goals.	_____	_____
24. I will fight to the last when the team does not support my viewpoint and wants to move toward consensus.	_____	_____
25. I will confront the team if I believe that the members are thinking too much alike.	_____	_____

Total Score _____

(Continued)

DEVELOPING TEAMWORK SKILLS   **125**

Scoring and Interpretation: Give yourself one point (+1) for each statement you gave in agreement with the keyed answer. The keyed answer indicates carrying out a positive, as opposed to a negative, role.

Question number	Positive role answer	Question number	Positive role answer	Question number	Positive role answer
1.	Mostly agree	10.	Mostly disagree	19.	Mostly disagree
2.	Mostly agree	11.	Mostly agree	20.	Mostly agree
3.	Mostly disagree	12.	Mostly disagree	21.	Mostly agree
4.	Mostly agree	13.	Mostly disagree	22.	Mostly agree
5.	Mostly disagree	14.	Mostly disagree	23.	Mostly agree
6.	Mostly agree	15.	Mostly disagree	24.	Mostly disagree
7.	Mostly disagree	16.	Mostly agree	25.	Mostly agree
8.	Mostly agree	17.	Mostly agree		
9.	Mostly agree	18.	Mostly agree		

20–25 You carry out a well-above-average number of positive team roles. Behavior of this type contributes substantially to being an effective team player. Study the information in this chapter to build upon your already laudable sensitivity to occupying various positive roles within the team.

10–19 You carry out an average number of positive team roles. Study carefully the roles described in this chapter to search for ways to carry out a greater number of positive roles.

0–9 You carry out a substantially above average number of negative team roles. If becoming an effective team player is important to you, you will have to diligently search for ways to play positive team roles. Study the information in this chapter carefully.

According to the role theory developed by R. Meredith Belbin and his group of researchers, there are nine frequent roles occupied by team members. All of these roles are influenced to some extent by an individual's personality.

1. **Creative problem solver.** The creative problem solver is imaginative, and unorthodox. Such a person solves difficult problems. A potential weakness of this role is that the person tends to ignore fine details and becomes too immersed in the problem to communicate effectively.

2. **Resource investigator.** The resource investigator is extraverted, enthusiastic, and communicates freely with other team members. He or she will explore opportunities and develop valuable contacts. A potential weakness of this role is that the person can be overly optimistic and may lose interest after the initial enthusiasm wanes.

3. **Coordinator.** The coordinator is mature, confident, and a natural team leader. He or she clarifies goals, promotes decision making, and delegates effectively. A downside to occupying this role is that the person might be seen as manipulative and controlling. Some coordinators delegate too much by asking others to do some of the work they (the coordinators) should be doing.

4. **Shaper.** The shaper is challenging, dynamic, and thrives under pressure. He or she will use determination and courage to overcome obstacles. A potential weakness of the shaper is that he or she can be easily provoked and may ignore the feelings of others.

5. **Monitor-evaluator.** The monitor-evaluator is even tempered, engages in strategic (big picture and long-term) thinking, and makes accurate judgments. He or she sees all the options and judges accurately. A potential weakness of this role occupant is that he or she might lack the drive and the ability to inspire others.

6. **Team worker.** The team worker is cooperative, focuses on relationships, and is sensitive and diplomatic. He or she is a good listener who builds relationships, dislikes confrontation, and averts friction. A potential weakness is that the team worker can be indecisive in a crunch situation or crisis.

7. **Implementer.** The implementer is disciplined, reliable, conservative, and efficient. He or she will act quickly on ideas, and convert them into practical actions. A potential weakness is that the implementer can be inflexible and slow to see new opportunities.

8. **Completer-Finisher.** The completer-finisher is conscientious and eager to get the job done. He or she has a good eye for detail, and is effective at searching out errors. He or she can be counted on for finishing a project and delivering on time. A potential weakness is that the completer-finisher can be a worrier and reluctant to delegate.

9. **Specialist.** The specialist is a single-minded self-starter. He or she is dedicated and provides knowledge and skill in rare supply. A potential weakness of the specialist is that he or she can be stuck in a niche with little interest in other knowledge and may dwell on technicalities.

The weaknesses in the first nine roles point to problems the team leader or manager can expect to emerge, and therefore an allowance should be made. Belbin refers to these potential problems as *allowable weaknesses* because an allowance should be made for them. To illustrate, if a team worker has a tendency to be indecisive in a crisis, the team should not have high expectations of the team worker when faced with a crisis. Team workers will be the most satisfied if the crisis is predicted and decisions involving them are made before the pressure mounts.[14]

Another perspective on team roles is that team members will sometimes engage in *self-oriented roles*. Members will sometimes focus on their own needs rather than those of the group. The individual might be overly aggressive because of a personal need, such as wanting a bigger budget for his or her project. The individual might hunger for recognition or power. Similarly the person might attempt to dominate the meeting, block others from contributing, or serve as a distraction. One of the ploys used by distracters recently is to engage in cell phone conversations during a meeting, blaming it on "those people who keep calling me."

The many roles just presented overlap somewhat. For example, the implementer might engage in specialist activities. Do not be concerned about the overlap. Instead, pick and choose from the many roles as the situation dictates—whether or not overlap exists. Skill-Building Exercise 6-1 gives you an opportunity to observe these roles in action. The behavior associated with the roles just described is more important than remembering the labels. For example, remembering to be creative and imaginative is more important than remembering the specific label "creative problem solver."

GUIDELINES FOR THE INTERPERSONAL ASPECTS OF TEAM PLAY

LEARNING OBJECTIVE 4

The purpose of this and the following section is to help you enhance your effectiveness as a team player by describing the skills, actions, and attitudes required to be an effective team player. You can regard these behaviors (the collective term for skills, actions, and attitudes) as goals for personal improvement. Identify the actions and attitudes for which you need the most improvement, and proceed accordingly with self-development. Apply the model for skill development presented in Chapter 1.

One convenient method for classifying team activities in the pursuit of goals is to categorize them as people-related or task-related. Remember, however, that the categorization of people- versus task-related activities is not entirely accurate. For example, if you are challenging your teammates with a difficult goal, are you focusing more on the people (offering them a motivational challenge) or the task (achieving the goal)? We begin first with people-related actions and attitudes, (see also Figure 6-2) followed in the next section by task-related actions and attitudes.

BACK TO THE OPENING CASE

A key aspect of Ann Livermore being a good team player was to not care about experiencing a decrease in her power and authority because her company acquired a large outsourcing firm. She said that her main concern was the prosperity of her employer, H-P. In crediting Livermore for her team spirit, recognize that Livermore already has had an outstanding career and was once a candidate to become CEO of H-P. She still has enough responsibility left to satisfy her needs for power and influence. A person still pursuing loftier positions might not have such a strong team spirit.

Team Member Roles

A team of approximately six people is formed to conduct a 20-minute meeting on a significant topic of their choosing. The possible scenarios follow:

Scenario A: Management Team. A group of managers are pondering whether to lay off one-third of the workforce in order to increase profits. The company has had a tradition of caring for employees and regarding them as the company's most precious asset. However, the CEO has said privately that times have changed in our competitive world, and the company must do whatever possible to enhance profits. The group wants to think through the advisability of laying off one-third of the workforce, as well as explore other alternatives.

Scenario B: Group of Sports Fans. A group of fans have volunteered to find a new team name to replace "Redskins" for the local basketball team. One person among the group of volunteers believes that the name "Redskins" should be retained because it is a compliment, rather than an insult to Native Americans. The other members of the group believe that a name change is in order, but they lack any good ideas for replacing a mascot team name that has endured for over 50 years.

Scenario C: Community Group. A community group is attempting to launch an initiative to help battered adults and children. Opinions differ strongly as to what initiative would be truly helpful to battered adults and children. Among the alternatives are establishing a shelter for battered people, giving workshops on preventing violence, and providing self-defense training. Each group member with an idea strongly believes that he or she has come up with a workable possibility for helping with the problem of battered people.

While the team members are conducting their heated discussion, other class members make notes on which team members carry out which roles. Students should watch for the different roles as developed by Belbin and his associates, as well as the self-oriented roles. For example, students in the first row might look for

examples of the plant. Use the role worksheet that follows to help make your observations. Summarize the comment that is indicative of the role. An example would be noting in the shaper category: "Linda said naming the team the 'Washington Rainbows' seems like too much of an attempt to be politically correct."

Creative Problem Solver _____

Resource Investigator _____

Coordinator _____

Shaper _____

Monitor-Evaluator _____

Team Worker _____

Implementer _____

Completer-Finisher _____

Specialist _____

Self-Oriented Roles _____

Understanding team member roles will contribute to working effectively as a member of a team. However, a foundation contributor to effective team play is recognizing individual differences and having good communication skills. The same two factors are fundamental for effectiveness in any setting involving interaction between and among people. Here is an example of how recognizing individual differences and having effective communication skills can help in a team setting: Max and Beth are teammates, and Max notices that Beth is shy and somewhat sullen. (He observes individual differences.) Max gives Beth a playful fist in the air, and says, "Come on Beth, we need your contribution in the 10 o'clock meeting. You have one of the sharpest minds on the team, and you're hiding it from us." With such warm encouragement, Beth then has the courage to contribute more to the morning meeting.

Trust Team Members

The cornerstone attitude of an outstanding team player is to trust team members, including the leader. Working on a team is akin to a small-business partnership. If you do not believe that the other team members have your best interests at heart, it will be difficult for you to share opinions and ideas. You will fear that others will make negative statements behind your back.

Trusting team members also includes believing that their ideas are technically sound and rational until proven otherwise. Another manifestation of trust is taking risks with others. You can take a risk by trying out one of their unproved ideas. You can also take a risk by submitting an unproved idea and not worrying about being ridiculed.

FIGURE 6-2   Interpersonal Aspects of Team Play

1. Trust team members.
2. Display a high level of cooperation and collaboration.
3. Recognize the interests and achievements of others.
4. Give and receive helpful criticism.
5. Share the glory.
6. Take care not to rain on another person's parade.

One of the goals of offsite training is to help team members trust each other. As is familiar to most readers, such trust builders include falling into each other's arms, rappelling up a wall, racing down rapids in a raft, and dangling from cables over gorges.[15]

Display a High Level of Cooperation and Collaboration

Cooperation and collaboration are synonymous with teamwork. If you display a willingness to help others by working cooperatively with them, you will be regarded as a team player. If you do not cooperate with other team members, the team structure breaks down. Collaboration at a team level refers to working jointly with others to solve mutual problems. Although working with another person on a given problem may take longer than working through a problem alone, the long-term payoff is important. You have established a climate favorable to working on joint problems where collective action is necessary. Sharing success stories with each other about what worked in the past is another useful approach to collaboration.[16]

Achieving a cooperative team spirit is often a question of making the first move. Instead of grumbling about poor teamwork, take the initiative and launch a cooperative spirit in your group. Target the most individualistic, least cooperative member of the group. Ask the person for his or her input on an idea you are formulating. Thank the person, and then state that you would be privileged to return the favor.

Another way of attaining good cooperation is to minimize confrontations. If you disagree with the opinion of another team member, patiently explain the reasons for your differences and look for a workable way to integrate both your ideas. A teammate might suggest, for example, that the team stay until midnight to get a project completed today. You have plans for the evening and are angered by the suggestion. Instead of lashing out at your teammate, you might say, "I agree we need to put in extra time and effort to get the job done. But why can't we spread out this extra effort over a few days? In this way those of us who cannot work until midnight this evening can still contribute."

A side advantage of cooperation within the group is that the part of the brain associated with pleasure is activated when people cooperate. According to team building specialist Anna Maravelas, "It is intrinsically rewarding for human beings to pull together."[17]

Skill-Building Exercise 6-2 is a widely used technique for demonstrating the importance of cooperation and collaboration.

Recognize the Interests and Achievements of Others

A fundamental tactic for establishing yourself as a solid team player is to actively recognize the interests and achievements of others. Let others know you care about their interests. After you make a suggestion during a team meeting, ask: "Would my suggestion create any problems for anybody else?" or "How do my ideas fit into what you have planned?"

Recognizing the achievements of others is more straightforward than recognizing interests. Be prepared to compliment any tangible achievement. Give realistic compliments by making the compliment commensurate with the achievement. To do otherwise is to

---

SKILL-BUILDING EXERCISE 6-2

The Scavenger Hunt

The purpose of this teamwork exercise is to demonstrate the importance of cooperation and collaboration in accomplishing a task under pressure. The class is divided into teams of about five students. How much time you can devote to the task depends upon your particular class schedule. The instructor will supply each team with a list of items to find within a prescribed period of time—usually about 35 minutes. Given the time constraints, the group will usually have to conduct the hunt on campus. Following is a representative list of items to find in an on-campus scavenger hunt:

- A piece of chalk
- A tie
- A brick
- A cap from a beer bottle
- A pocket knife
- A flash drive

When the group returns within 30 minutes, hold a public discussion about what you learned about teamwork and what insights you acquired.

compromise your sincerity. For example, do not call someone a genius just because he or she showed you how to compute an exchange rate from one currency to another. Instead, you might say, "Thank you. I am very impressed by your knowledge of exchange rates."

A technique has been developed to enable the entire team to recognize the interests and achievements of others. Playing the anonymous praise game, each team member lists what he or she admires about a specific coworker. The team leader collects the responses and sends each team member the comments made about him or her. Using this technique, team members see a compilation of praise based on how coworkers perceive them. The anonymous praise game helps overcome the hesitancy some people have to praise another person face-to-face.[18]

Give and Receive Helpful Criticism

The outstanding team player offers constructive criticism when needed, but does so diplomatically. To do otherwise is to let down the team. A high-performance team demands sincere and tactful criticism among members. No matter how diplomatic you are, keep your ratio of criticism to praise small. Keep two time-tested principles in mind. First, attempt to criticize the person's work, not the person. It is better to say, "The conclusion is missing from your analysis" than "You left out the conclusion." (The latter statement hurts because it sounds like your teammate did something wrong.)

Another key guideline for criticism is to ask a question rather than to make a declarative statement. By answering a question, the person being criticized is involved in improving his or her work. In the example at hand, it would be effective to ask, "Do you think your report would have a greater impact if it contained a conclusion?" In this way, the person being criticized contributes a judgment about the conclusion. The person has a chance to say, "Yes, I will prepare a conclusion."

Criticism works both ways, so the effective team player is willing to accept helpful criticism, such as "You are speaking too fast for several of our team members for whom English is their second language." Becky Blalock, the vice president and chief information officer (CIO) of the electric utility the Southern Company, regards being open to feedback as one of the core principles of teamwork.[19]

Share the Glory

An effective team player shares praise and other rewards for accomplishment even if he or she is the most deserving. Shared praise is usually merited to some extent because teammates have probably made at least some contribution to the achievement that received praise. For example, if a team member comes up with a powerful suggestion for cutting costs, it is likely that somebody else in the group sparked his or her thinking. Effective examples of sharing glory are easy to find. Think back to watching athletes and other entertainers who win a title or an award. Many of them are gracious enough to share the glory. It has become almost standard practice for an award-winning coach or player to say, "I never would have accomplished what I did if I hadn't played with such a great group of people."

Take Care Not to Rain on Another Person's Parade

As teamwork specialist Pamela Lovell observes, we all have achievements and accomplishments that are sources of pride. Belittling the achievements of others for no legitimate reason brings about tension and anger. Suppress your feelings of petty jealousy.[20] An example would be saying to someone who is proudly describing an accomplishment, "Don't take too much credit. It looks to me like you were at the right place at the right time." If you support teammates by acknowledging their accomplishments, you are more likely to receive their support when needed.

GUIDELINES FOR THE TASK ASPECTS OF TEAM PLAY

LEARNING OBJECTIVE 5

The task aspects of team play also make a key contribution to becoming an effective team player. Here we describe seven major task-related tactics (see Figure 6-3). As mentioned earlier, a task aspect usually has interpersonal consequences.

FIGURE 6-3   Task Aspects of Team Play

1. Provide technical expertise (or knowledge of the task).
2. Assume responsibility for problems.
3. See the big picture.
4. Believe in consensus.
5. Focus on deadlines.
6. Help team members do their jobs better.
7. Be a good organizational citizen.

Provide Technical Expertise (Or Knowledge of the Task)

Most people are selected for a work team primarily because of their technical expertise. *Technical* refers to the intimate details of any task, not just tasks in engineering, physical science, and information technology. The sales promotion specialist on a product development team has technical expertise about sales promotion, whether or not sales promotion requires knowledge of engineering or computers.

As team consultant Glenn Parker observes, to use your technical expertise to outstanding advantage you must have the willingness to share that expertise.[21] Some experts perceive their esoteric knowledge as a source of power. As a consequence, they are hesitant to let others share their knowledge for fear of relinquishing power. It is also necessary for the technical expert to be able to communicate with team members in other disciplines who lack the same technical background. The technical person who cannot explain the potential value of his or her contribution may fail to receive much attention.

An analysis of 72 studies based on more than 17,000 individuals in a variety of work settings lends credibility to the belief that information sharing is beneficial to teams. A major finding of the analysis is that team performance is enhanced when team members share information not commonly shared by all team members. A somewhat distressing side finding of the study is that many teams do not share information when the sharing is most needed. An example of information being most needed is when the other team members are not aware of the useful information possessed by the other members.[22]

Assume Responsibility for Problems

The outstanding team player assumes responsibilities for problems. If a problem is not yet assigned to anybody, he or she says, "I'll do it." One team member might note that the true progress on the team's effort is blocked until the team benchmarks (compares itself) with other successful teams. The effective team player might say, "You are right, we need to benchmark. If it's okay with everybody else, I'll get started on the benchmarking project tomorrow. It will be my responsibility." Taking responsibility must be combined with dependability. The person who takes responsibility for a task must produce, time after time.

See the Big Picture

Effective team players need to think conceptually, or see the big picture. A trap in team effort is that discussion can get bogged down in small details and the team might lose sight of what it is trying to accomplish. The team player (including the team leader) who can help the group focus on its broader purpose plays a vital role. The following case history illustrates what it means to see the big picture.

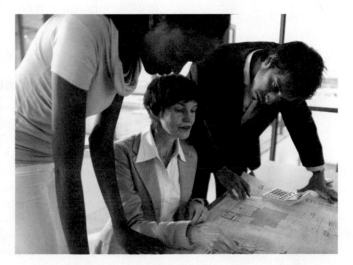

A group of retail sales associates and customer service representatives were sent to a one-day seminar about customer service training. The group was sent to training because customer service ratings at their store were

below the level store executives thought was acceptable. During the lunch breaks, the conversation quickly turned to the fact that the coffee was not as hot as desired, the snacks were mediocre, the restrooms were too far from the meeting room, and the presenter had a phony smile and told goofy jokes. Next came a few complaints about a couple of the PowerPoint slides having too much detail.

Alyssa, an experienced sales associate, stepped in with a comment. She noted, "I think all of you have valid complaints, but your points are minor. We are here to learn how to improve customer service. If we want our store to survive, and earn bigger bonuses, we have to learn what we can to help us do our jobs better. Whether or not you like our trainer's smile or jokes, he is trying to be helpful." The group returned after lunch with a more determined effort to focus on the purpose of the seminar—picking up ideas to improve customer service.

Believe in Consensus

consensus

General acceptance by the group of a decision.

A major task-related attitude for outstanding team play is to believe that consensus has merit. **Consensus** is general acceptance of a decision by the group. Every member may not be thrilled about the decision, yet they are unopposed and are willing to support the decision. Believing that consensus is valuable enables you to participate fully in team decisions without thinking that you have sacrificed your beliefs or the right to think independently. To believe in consensus is to believe that the democratic process has relevance for organizations and that ideal solutions are not always possible.

Focus on Deadlines

A notable source of individual differences among work group members is how much importance they attach to deadlines. Some work group members may regard deadlines as a moral contract, to be missed only in case of emergency. Others may view deadlines as an arbitrary date imposed by someone external to the group. Other work group members may perceive deadlines as moderately important. Differences in perception about the importance of deadlines influence the group's ability to meet deadlines.[23]

Keeping the group focused on the deadline is a valuable task behavior because meeting deadlines is vital to team success. Discussing the importance of the deadlines is helpful because of the varying attitudes about deadlines that are likely to be found among group members.

Help Team Members Do Their Jobs Better

Your stature as a team player will increase if you take the initiative to help coworkers make needed work improvements. Helping other team members with their work assignments is a high-level form of cooperation. Make the suggestions in a constructive spirit rather than displaying an air of superiority. Identify a problem that a coworker is having, and then suggest alternatives he or she might be interested in exploring. Avoid saying to team members that they "should" do something, because many people become defensive when told what they should do. The term *should* is usually perceived as a moral judgment given to one person by another, such as being told that you should save money, should learn a second language, or should improve your math skills.

Be a Good Organizational Citizen

A comprehensive way of carrying out the task aspects of team play (as well as relationship aspects) is to help out beyond the requirements of your job description. As discussed in Chapter 2, such extra-role activity is referred to as organizational citizenship behavior— working for the good of the organization even without the promise of a specific reward. As a result of many workers being good organizational citizens, the organization functions more effectively in such ways as improved product quantity and quality.[24] Good citizenship on the job encompasses many specific behaviors, including helping a coworker with a job task and refraining from complaints or petty grievances. A good organizational citizen would carry out such specific acts as picking up litter in the company parking lot, and turning out lights when they are not in use. He or she would also bring a reference to the office that could help a coworker solve a job problem. Most of the other team player tactics described here are related to organizational citizenship behavior.

Two experiments, one with business students and one with managers, suggested that organizational citizenship behavior is even more important when people depend on each other to accomplish a task.[25] An example is filling an order with components from different departments. Given that most tasks on a team are interdependent, organizational citizenship behavior is quite important for effective teamwork.

A recent synthesis of studies about the type of team processes described in this chapter supports the relevance of such actions by team members. (A team process is essentially an action taken by one or more team members.) A group of researchers examined the results of a variety of team member processes in 147 different samples of workers. The major conclusion reached was that teamwork processes are positively associated with both team member performance and satisfaction.[26] You can therefore have some assurance that if you engage in the activities described in this chapter, your efforts will help increase performance and satisfaction.

Skill-Building Exercise 6-3 will help you integrate the many suggestions presented here for developing teamwork skills.

SELF-ASSESSMENT QUIZZES IN OVERVIEW

Self-Assessment Quiz 6-1 gave you an opportunity to think through the extent to which you really enjoy, or are interested, in teamwork. Being part of a close-knit team is important for many types of work, but there is always room for some people who prefer to work alone doing analytical or creative work. For example, at Microsoft Corp. the office layout gives space to people who want to work alone and not be distracted by other people. Self-Assessment Quiz 6-2 follows up your interests and attitudes about teamwork with an opportunity to review your skills. Interest and skills are not the same. A given individual who likes the idea of skydiving might lack the eye-hand coordination to pull the cord under pressure, and therefore would be a disaster as a skydiver.

If you have the attitudes for teamwork, another subtle factor about teamwork can influence your effectiveness. As measured in Self-Assessment Quiz 6-3, your level of conformity can influence your effectiveness. Too much or too little conformity can detract from your effectiveness. Self-Assessment Quiz 6-4 takes you even further into the intricacies of teamwork by measuring your tendency to play positive team roles. With few exceptions, a person needs to focus on positive team roles to be a successful team member.

Concept Review and Reinforcement

Key Terms

team 117

virtual team 118

synergy 120

social loafing 122

groupthink 122

role 122

consensus 132

Summary

To be successful in the modern organization, it is necessary to be an effective team player. Team members have complementary skills and are committed to a common purpose. All teams have some elements in common. Teams can be broadly classified into face-to-face versus virtual types. A virtual team does most of its work electronically instead of in face-to-face meetings.

Groups and teams offer such advantages as (1) gaining synergy, (2) work accomplishment and high productivity, (3) gaining increased acceptance of and commitment to decisions, (4) avoidance of major errors, and (5) increased job satisfaction.

Groups and teams also have disadvantages, such as (1) time wasting, (2) pressures toward conformity, (3) shirking of individual responsibility, (4) fostering of conflict, and (5) groupthink. The latter refers to making bad decisions as a by-product of strong consensus. Key characteristics of effective work groups are outlined in Figure 6-1.

An important part of being an effective team player is to choose effective roles. The roles studied here are: creative problem solver, resource investigator, coordinator, shaper, monitor-evaluator, team worker, implementer, completer-finisher, and specialist. Self-oriented roles are less effective and detract from group productivity. Understanding roles does not supplant the need for recognizing individual differences and communicating well.

Guidelines for effectively contributing to the interpersonal aspects of team play include (1) trusting team members, (2) displaying a high level of cooperation and collaboration, (3) recognizing the interests and achievements of others, (4) giving and receiving helpful criticism, (5) sharing the glory, and (6) taking care not to rain on another person's parade.

Guidelines for effectively contributing to the task aspects of team play include (1) providing technical expertise, (2) assuming responsibility for problems, (3) seeing the big picture, (4) believing in consensus, (5) focusing on deadlines, and (6) helping team members do their jobs better.

A synthesis of research studies demonstrates that the types of teamwork processes described here are positively associated with both team member performance and satisfaction.

Questions for Discussion and Review

1. What do executives really mean when they say that "business is a team sport"?

2. From your perspective, what would be the satisfactions and frustrations of being a member of a virtual team?

3. How do team members know when they have achieved synergy?

4. What should the other team members do when they uncover a social loafer?

5. How can the *monitor-evaluator* role backfire for a person?

6. Assume that you are a team member. What percentage of your pay would you be willing to have based on a group reward? Explain your reasoning.

7. Many retail companies, banks, and medical offices require customer-contact employees to wear the same uniform. In what ways might these uniforms enhance teamwork?

8. A number of companies have sent employees to a team-building exercise in which they prepare a gourmet meal. Why would preparing a gourmet meal help build teamwork?

9. The "little picture" in studying this chapter is learning details about teamwork skills. What is the "big picture"?

10. How can a person achieve individual recognition yet still be a team player?

The Web Corner

http://www.timeanalyzer.com/lib/teamroles.htm
(Belbin's team roles to improve team performance.)

http:/www.quintcareers.com/team_player_quiz.html
(Take the quiz, "Are You a Team Player: A Quintessential Careers Quiz.")

Internet Skill Builder: Becoming a Better Team Player

The purpose of this exercise duplicates the major purpose of the chapter—finding practical suggestions for improving your teamwork skills. Visit several Web sites that deal with enhancing teamwork skills from the standpoint of the individual, not the manager. An example of such a Web site is www.confidencecenter.com. Write down at least three concrete suggestions you find, and compare these suggestions to those made in this chapter. If the opportunity arises, practice one of these skills in the next 10 days and observe the results.

Developing Your Human Relations Skills

Interpersonal Relations Case 6.1

Leah Puts on Her Team Player Face

Leah was happy to find a position as a scanning technician at a business process outsourcing company, Expert Resource, Inc. A major part of the Expert's business was converting paperwork related to human resource management into digital form. Clients would mail their forms, such as medical claims, to Expert. Scanning technicians would then insert the claim forms into large scanning machines to make the conversion to digital. Clients would then have digital instead of paper documents for health claims and other human resource records.

The scanning technicians had to interact with other employees in several ways. Many of the claims received contained illegible identifying information, so they had to be sent to a security department that attempted to obtain the proper identification for the forms. The scanning technicians were expected to help level the workload among the technicians. For example, if one of the technicians was overwhelmed, and another was caught up, the latter was supposed to help out the former. Also, the company frequently held small celebrations in the office. A typical celebration would be to hold a brunch in honor of a new employee joining the company.

Leah believed that if she performed well in her position as scanning technician, she would be eligible for promotion to the information technology department. Eventually being promoted to a supervisor position was also within the realm of possibility. Leah also recognized that having good skills and speed in scanning documents were not sufficient to be promoted to a supervisory position. Her size-up of the situation was that being a good team player would be required to be considered for promotion. Leah then set out to develop the reputation of being a good team player.

The next Monday morning, Leah arrived at the office with a box of donuts that she placed in the break room, with a note attached that said, "Enjoy your coffee or tea this morning with a treat from your coworker Leah." Several of the other scanning technicians thanked Leah; however, one technician said to her, "Why did you bring us donuts? You're not our supervisor."

A week later, Leah implemented another tactic designed to boost her reputation as a team player. She sent an e-mail to the other technicians informing them that they were free to send her an e-mail or an IM anytime they were overloaded with documents to scan. Leah said that she would help the overloaded coworker so long as she was caught up on her own work.

A week later Lean reflected, "I think I am developing a reputation as a good team player, but I can't give up yet. I think I know a way to really cement being regarded as a strong team player." Leah then wrote an e-mail to the other scanning technicians, as well as her supervisor. The e-mail read in part.

"We all know that it takes a village to raise a child. But did you also know that it takes a group of friendly and cooperative coworkers to get a scanning technician up to speed? I want to thank you all for your cooperation and friendliness. You have been very helpful to me."

Case Questions

1. How effective do you think Leah's initiatives are in helping her develop a reputation as a strong team player?
2. If you were Leah's supervisor, how would you react to the e-mails she sent to the group?
3. What advice might you offer Leah to help her advance her reputation as a team player?

Interpersonal Relations Case 6.2

Ruth Waves a Red Flag

Carlos is the team leader of a cost-reduction team within a well-established baked-goods company that produces bakery products under its own label, as well as private labels for grocery-store chains such as Giant and Win-Dixie. Top-level management formed the team to arrive at suggestions for reducing costs throughout the organization. A transcript of one of the meetings is presented next.

Carlos: We've been gathering information for a month now. It's about time we heard some specific suggestions.

Jack: At the top of my list is cutting pension benefits. Our pension payments are higher than the minimum required by law. Our medical benefits are way above average. If we cut back on pension benefits, no current employees would be adversely affected.

Melissa: I like your analysis, Jack. No sense risking laying off employees just to keep retirees happy.

Jordan: We should make absolutely certain there are no legal complications here. Then we can sharpen our cost-cutting knives and dig right in.

Gunther: I'd support cutting pension benefits. It would probably reduce expenses more dramatically than the ways I have uncovered.

Carlos: There seems to be consensus so far that we should consider making recommendations about cutting pension benefits. Ruth, what do you think?

Ruth: I think it is much too early to reach consensus on such a sensitive issue. Cutting pension benefits would create panic among our retirees. Out older employees would be screaming as well. We'll have an avalanche of negative publicity in the media.

Jordan: Hold on, Ruth. I said the team should first check out this idea with the legal department.

Ruth: Just because cutting pension benefits could squeeze by legally doesn't mean that it's a good idea. We haven't examined the negative ramifications of cutting pension benefits. Let's study this issue further before word leaks out that we're taking away the golden egg.

Carlos: Maybe Ruth has a point. Let's investigate this issue further before making a recommendation.

Case Questions

1. What role, or roles, is Ruth occupying on the cost-reduction team?
2. How effective does she appear to be in her role?
3. What role, or roles, is Jack occupying on the cost-reduction team?
4. How effective does he appear to be in his role?
5. How effective is Carlos in his role as a team leader?

Group Problem Solving and Decision Making

Jim Graf has his sights set on a target 100 million miles away. Sometimes it's closer. Sometimes it's farther. Mars. The target is moving. So is he. Each morning he leads a team of several managers in a standup meeting in his office at NASA's Jet Propulsion Laboratory on the top floor of a sprawling, four-story building tucked into the foothills above Pasadena, California. Sitting is not allowed. All the meeting's participants are constantly in motion, changing positions with respect to one another, even as their target changes position with respect to earth.

"We have a daily standup so we can talk about things," said Graf. "We physically stand up here. I want everybody a little uncomfortable so they get right to the point." Usually these meetings last about 15 minutes. Some mornings, they go longer.

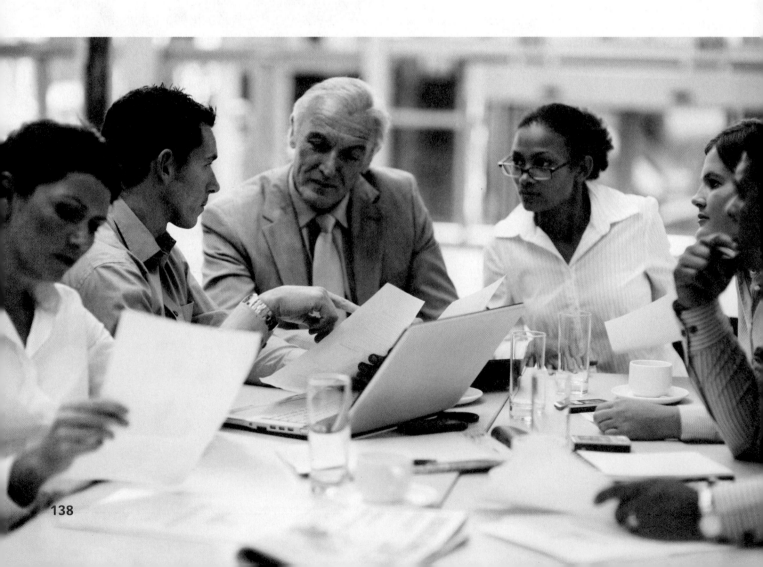

LEARNING
Objectives

1. Understand the difference between rational and political decision making.
2. Use the general approach to problem-solving groups.
3. Use brainstorming effectively.
4. Use of the nominal group technique effectively.
5. Understand how to increase the efficiency of group problem solving through e-mail and groupware.
6. Pinpoint several suggestions for being an effective meeting participant.
7. Explain how national culture and organizational culture might influence the acceptance of group decision making.

"It's important to communicate," said Graf. "You wouldn't think a team member working on one thing would need to know about another team working on another thing, until suddenly you hear someone say, 'Wow, that impacts me!' The standup meetings are essential to our success."[1]

Standup meetings are but one way in which groups solve many key problems. Part of having high-level interpersonal skills is the ability to work closely with others in solving problems and making decisions. This chapter will enhance your group problem-solving and decision-making skills. You will receive guidelines for applying several major group problem-solving methods, along with suggestions for being an effective contributor at meetings. As a starting point in studying these techniques, first think through your present level of receptiveness toward group problem solving by doing Self-Assessment Quiz 7-1.

RATIONAL VERSUS POLITICAL DECISION MAKING IN GROUPS

Group decision making is the process of reaching a judgment based on feedback from more than one individual. Most people involved in group problem solving may share the same purpose in agreeing on a solution and making a decision. Nevertheless, they may have different agendas and use different methods. Two such different approaches to group decision making are the rational model and the political model.

The **rational decision-making model** is the traditional, logical approach to decision making, based on the scientific method. It is grounded in establishing goals, establishing alternatives, examining consequences, and hoping for optimum results. The search for optimum results is based on an economic view of decision making—the idea that people hope to maximize gain and minimize loss when making a decision. For example, a team would choose the lowest cost, highest quality supplier even though the team leader may be a good friend of the sales representative of a competitor.

The rational model also assumes that each alternative is evaluated in terms of how well it contributes to reaching the goals involved in making the decision. For example, if one of the goals in relocating a factory was to reduce energy costs and taxes, each alternative would be carefully examined in terms of its tax and energy consequences. A team member might say, "Setting up a factory in the Phoenix area sounds great. It's true that taxes are low, the labor market is wonderful, and we won't lose any days to snow emergencies. But did you know that the energy costs are very high because of the amount of air conditioning required?"

LEARNING OBJECTIVE 1

group decision making

The process of reaching a judgment based on feedback from more than one individual.

rational decision-making model

The traditional, logical approach to decision making based on the scientific method.

My Problem-Solving Tendencies

Directions: Describe how well you agree with the following statements, using the following scale: disagree strongly (DS); disagree (D); neutral (N); agree (A); agree strongly (AS). Circle the number in the appropriate column.

	DS	D	N	A	AS
1. Before reaching a final decision on a matter of significance, I like to discuss it with one or more other people.	1	2	3	4	5
2. If I'm facing a major decision, I like to get away from others to think it through.	5	4	3	2	1
3. I get lonely working by myself.	1	2	3	4	5
4. Two heads are better than one.	1	2	3	4	5
5. A wide range of people should be consulted before an executive makes a major decision.	1	2	3	4	5
6. To arrive at a creative solution to a problem, it is best to rely on a group.	1	2	3	4	5
7. From what I've seen so far, group decision making is a waste of time.	5	4	3	2	1
8. Most great ideas stem from the solitary effort of great thinkers.	5	4	3	2	1
9. Important legal cases should be decided by a jury rather than by a judge.	1	2	3	4	5
10. Individuals are better suited than groups to solve technical problems.	5	4	3	2	1

Total Score _____

Scoring and Interpretation: Add the numbers you circled to obtain your total score.

46–50 You have strong positive attitudes toward group problem solving and decision making. You will therefore adapt well to the decision-making techniques widely used in organizations. Be careful, however, not to neglect your individual problem-solving skills.

30–45 You have neutral attitudes toward group problem solving and decision making. You may need to remind yourself that group problem solving is well accepted in business.

10–29 You refer individual to group decision making. Retain your pride in your ability to think independently, but do not overlook the contribution of group problem solving and decision making. You may need to develop more patience for group problem solving and decision making.

---

political decision-making model

The assumption about decision making that people bring preconceived notions and biases into the decision-making situation.

The **political decision-making model** assumes that people bring preconceived notions and biases into the decision-making situation. Because the decision makers are politically motivated (a focus on satisfying one's own interests), the individuals often do not make the most rational choice. The growing field of behavioral economics is based on the idea that many decisions are irrational or politically based. Revenge and cheating are among the irrational behaviors that underlie the behavior of many employees and customers.[2] Most computer hackers make their decision to create a virus or destroy computer records based on revenge, cheating, or a sadistic delight in creating misfortune for others.

People who use the political model may operate on the basis of incomplete information. Facts and figures that conflict with personal biases and preferences might get blocked out of memory or rationalized away. A team member might say, "Those air conditioning costs are exaggerated. I have heard that if you use thermal pumps in a factory, the cooling costs go way down."

blind spots

Areas of unawareness about our attitudes, thinking, and behaviors that contribute to poor decisions.

Another unintentional contributor to political decision making is **blind spots**—areas of unawareness about our attitudes, thinking, and behaviors that contribute to poor decisions. Shawn O. Utsey, a psychology professor at Virginia Commonwealth University, says that blind spots prevent us from making sound decisions by distorting vision, impairing judgment, and impairing personal and professional growth. An example of a frequent blind spot would be not stopping to think, particularly when under pressure.[3] For example, a person might purchase a luxury SUV on the spot that will wind up creating a monthly negative cash flow.

Greed and gluttony are major contributors to irrational (or political) decision making. During the mid-2000s, an astounding number of financial managers decided to invest in subprime mortgage loans and then convert these loans into equity investments. Eventually, many holders of these high-risk mortgages were unable or unwilling to make their payments.[4] As the securities collapsed in value, an enormous stock market crisis took place. The securities were based on complex mathematic models, yet were believed in because the investment bankers were looking for ways to capture millions of dollars in bonuses for themselves.

In the relocation example at hand, two of the members may say "Thumbs up to Phoenix" for reasons that satisfy their own needs. One team member might be fascinated with the American Indian culture so prevalent in Arizona and therefore want to move to Phoenix. Another member might have retired parents living in Phoenix and be interested in living near them.

In practice, it is sometimes difficult to determine whether a decision maker is being rational or political. Have you ever noticed that hotels almost never have a 13th floor? The reason is both rational and political. The hotel manager might say rationally, "Many people are superstitious about the number 13, so they will refuse to take a room on the 13th floor. So if we want to maximize room use, the rational decision for us is to label the 13th floor as 14. In this way we will avoid the irrational [political] thinking of guests."

Although the examples about political and irrational decision making have been related mostly to individuals, the same problems may surface in group decision making. This is true because a group decision is still based on what takes place in the brains of its members.

GUIDELINES FOR USING GENERAL PROBLEM-SOLVING GROUPS

LEARNING OBJECTIVE 2

Solving problems effectively in groups requires skill. The effort is often worthwhile because participation in group decision making frequently leads to better acceptance of the decision, and stronger commitment to the implications of the decision. For example, a group involved in making decisions about cost cutting might be more willing to carry through with the suggestions than if participants had not made the decision. Group decision making can also lead to higher quality decisions and innovations because the group collectively has more information than might individuals.[5] Similarly, the group might come up with better suggestions for cost cutting because of group members sharing information.

Here we examine three aspects of group problem solving useful in making more effective decisions: working through the group problem-solving steps, managing disagreement about the decision, and aiming for inquiry rather than advocacy.

Working through the Group Problem-Solving Steps

When team members get together to solve a problem, they typically hold a discussion rather than rely on formal problem-solving techniques. Several team members might attempt to clarify the true nature of the problem, and a search then begins for an acceptable solution. Although this technique can be effective, the probability of solving the problem well (and therefore making the right decision) increases when the team follows a systematic procedure.

The Problem-Solving Steps. The following guidelines represent a time-tested way of solving problems and making decisions within a group.[6] You may recognize these steps as having much in common with the scientific method. The same steps are therefore ideal for following the rational decision-making model. Two other aspects of group decision making will be described here: managing disagreement and inquiry versus advocacy.

Assume that you are a team member of a small business that distributes food supplies to hospitals, nursing homes, and schools. Your business volume is adequate, but you have a cash-flow problem because some of your customers take over 30 days to pay their bills. Here is how problem solving would proceed following the steps for effective group problem solving and decision making:

Step One. *Identify the problem.* Describe specifically what the problem is and how it manifests itself. The surface problem is that some customers are paying their bills late. Your company's ultimate problem is that it does not have enough cash on hand to pay expenses.

Step Two. *Clarify the problem.* If group members do not see the problem the same way, they will offer divergent solutions to their own individual perceptions of the problem. To some team members, late payments may simply mean the company has less cash in the bank. As a result, the company earns a few dollars less in interest. Someone else on the team might perceive the problem as mostly an annoyance and inconvenience. Another person may perceive late payers as being immoral and therefore want to penalize them. The various perceptions of the problem solvers contribute to their exercising a political model of decision making. It is important for the group to reach consensus that the ultimate problem is not enough cash on hand to run the business, as explained in Step 1.

Step Three. *Analyze the cause.* To convert what exists into what they want, the group must understand the cause of the specific problems and find ways to overcome the causes. Late payment of bills (over 30 days) can be caused by several factors. The customers may have cash-flow problems of their own, they may have slow-moving bureaucratic procedures, or they may be understaffed. Another possibility is that the slow-paying customers are dissatisfied with the service and are holding back on payments in retaliation. Research, including interviewing customers, may be needed to analyze the cause or causes.

Step Four. *Search for alternative solutions.* Remember that multiple alternative solutions can be found to most problems. The alternative solutions you choose will depend on your analysis of the causes. Assume that you did not find customers to be dissatisfied with your service, but that they were slow in paying bills for a variety of reasons. Your team then gets into a creative mode by developing a number of alternatives. Among them are offering bigger discounts for quick payment, dropping slow-paying customers, sending out your own bills more promptly, and using follow-up e-mail messages and phone calls to bring in money. For regular customers, you might try for automatic withdrawals from their checking account. Another possibility would be to set up a line of credit that would enable your firm to make short-term loans to cover expenses until your bills were paid.

Step Five. *Select alternatives.* Identify the criteria that solutions should meet; then, discuss the pros and cons of the proposed alternatives. No solution should be laughed at or scorned. Specifying the criteria that proposed solutions should meet requires you to think deeply about your goals. For example, your team might establish the following criteria for solutions: that they (a) improve cash flow, (b) do not lose customers, (c) do not cost much to implement, and (d) do not make the company appear desperate. The pros and cons of each proposed alternative can be placed on a flip chart, board, or computer screen.

For many complex problems, it is best to select an alternative solution that is based on a variety of options. The blended options solutions will often be stronger because it contains several useful ideas.[7] At the same time, several group members will be satisfied that at least part of their suggestion was incorporated in the final solution. For example, if the problem under group discussion was choosing a theme for decorating a new office, several ideas might be selected. An advertising agency used group decision making to arrive at a dual theme for decorating the office—cool, yet affluent at the same time.

Step Six. *Plan for implementation.* Decide what actions are necessary to carry out the chosen solution to the problem. Suppose your group decides that establishing a bank line of credit is the most feasible alternative. The company president or the chief financial officer might then meet with a couple of local banks to apply for a line of credit at the most favorable rate. Your group also chooses to initiate a program of friendly follow-up telephone calls to encourage more rapid payment.

Step Seven. *Clarify the contract.* The contract is a restatement of what group members have agreed to do and deadlines for accomplishment. In your situation, several team members are involved in establishing a line of credit and initiating a system of follow-up phone calls.

Step Eight. *Develop an action plan.* Specify who does what and when to carry out the contract. Each person involved in implementing alternatives develops an action plan in detail that stems logically from the previous steps.

Step Nine. *Provide for evaluation and accountability.* After the plan is implemented, reconvene to discuss progress and to hold people accountable for results that have not been achieved. In the situation at hand, progress will be measured in at least two objective ways. You can evaluate by accounting measures whether the cash-flow problem has improved and whether the average cycle time on accounts receivable has decreased.

When to Apply the Problem-Solving Steps. The steps for effective group problem solving are best applied to complex problems. Straightforward problems of minor consequence (such as deciding on holiday decorations for the office) do not require all the steps. Nevertheless, remember that virtually every problem has more than one feasible alternative. A classic example of searching for the best alternative to a problem is as follows:

> At one time complaints of late room service were plaguing a Ritz-Carlton hotel, a chain known for its superior service. To solve the problem, president Horst Schulze dispatched a team composed of a room-service order taker, a waiter, and a cook. Everything seemed fine except that the service elevator took a long time. Next, the group consulted with the engineers in charge of the elevator. Neither the engineers nor the elevator company representative could find a technical problem with the elevator.
>
> Next, team members took turns riding the elevators at all hours for a week. Finally, one of them observed that every time the elevator made its trip from the first floor to the twenty-fourth, it stopped four or five times. At each step, housemen (who assisted the housekeepers) got on the elevators to different floors. The housemen were taking towels from other floors to bring them to housekeepers on their own floors who were short of towels. Foraging for towels was slowing down the elevators.
>
> The team discovered that the Ritz-Carlton didn't really have a room-service problem or an elevator problem; it had a towel shortage. As the hotel bought more towels, room-service complaints dropped 50 percent.[8]

The Importance of Collective Efficacy. How well a given group solves a problem depends on many of the characteristics of an effective work group outlined in Figure 6-1 (the previous chapter). Of particular relevance is the group's level of confidence that it can solve the problem at hand. **Collective efficacy** is a group's belief that it can handle certain tasks. Collective efficacy influences a group to initiate action, how much effort it will apply to the task, and how long the group's effort will be sustained.[9] If the group members say spontaneously, "We can do it, let's go," they will usually be successful in solving the problem, assuming they have the necessary knowledge and talent.

For practice in using the problem steps described above, do Skill-Building Exercise 7-1. Skill-Building Exercise 7-2 gives you an opportunity to solve a few more of the perplexing type of problems that the Ritz-Carlton faced.

Managing Disagreement about Group Decision Making

A major reason that group decision making does not proceed mechanically is that disagreement may surface. Such disagreement is not necessarily harmful to the final outcome of the decision because those who disagree may have valid points and help prevent groupthink. For committees and other groups to work well, they should be composed of people with different perspectives and experiences who are not hesitant to speak their minds, says psychologist Richard Larrick at the Fuqua School of Business, Duke University.[10]

The idea is to manage disagreement so that the decision-making process does not break down, and the dissenters are not squelched. Conflicts about decisions were studied among 43 cross-functional teams engaged in new product development. Disagreeing about major issues led to positive outcomes for team performance (as measured by ratings made by managers) under two conditions.[11]

First, the dissenters have to feel they have the freedom to express doubt. To measure such freedom, participants in the study responded to such statements as "I sometimes get the feeling that others are not speaking up although they harbor serious doubts about the direction being taken." (Strongly disagreeing with this statement would suggest that group members had the freedom to express doubt.)

Second, doubts must be expressed collaboratively (trying to work together) rather than contentiously (in a quarrelsome way). An example of collaborative communication would be having used the following statement during decision making: "We will be working together for a while. It's important that we both [all] feel comfortable with a solution to this problem." An example of contentious communication would be high agreement with the statement, "You're being difficult and rigid."

More recent research lends strength to the idea that teams are more likely to make optimal decisions when they take the time to debate the issues and thoughtfully discuss alternative solutions. A study about hiring pilots for long-distance flights found that when groups disagreed over who to hire, there was more information sharing. Also, the strong disagreement led to more intense discussions that prompted participants to repeat their reasoning in front of other group members. A debate over which candidate to hire encourages team members to focus on information that may be inconsistent with how they formed their original opinion.[12]

Conflict-resolution techniques, as described in Chapter 9, are another potentially useful approach to managing disagreement about decision making.

Aiming for Inquiry versus Advocacy in Group Decision Making

Another useful perspective on group decision making is to compare the difference between group members involved in *inquiry* (looking for the best alternative) versus *advocacy* (or fighting for one position). Inquiry is an open process designed to generate multiple alternatives, encourage the exchange of ideas, and produce a well-reasoned solution. Decision makers who care more about the good of the firm than personal gain are the most likely to engage in inquiry. According to David A. Garvin and Michael A. Roberto, this open-minded approach doesn't come easily to most people.[13]

Instead, most groups charged with making a decision tend to slip into the opposite mode, called advocacy. The two approaches look similar because under either mode the group members are busily immersed in work and appear to be searching for the best alternative. Yet, the results from the two modes are quite different. Using an advocacy approach, participants approach decision making as a contest with the intent of selecting the winning alternative. One member of the group might be trying to gain the largest share of the budget, and become so passionate about winning budget share that he loses objectivity. Advocates might even withhold important information from the group, such as not revealing that their budget is big enough considering their decreased activity.

With an advocacy approach, the disagreements that arise tend to separate the group, and are antagonistic. Personality conflicts come into play, and one person might accuse the other side of not being able to see the big picture. In contrast, an inquiry-focused group carefully considers a variety of alternatives and collaborates to discover the best solution.

Conflict resolution methods can be useful in helping the decision makers overcome the advocacy approach. As part of resolving the conflict, the group leader must make sure that everyone knows that his or her viewpoint is being carefully considered.

GUIDELINES FOR BRAINSTORMING

In many work situations, groups are expected to produce creative and imaginative solutions to problems. When the organization is seeking a large number of alternatives for solving the problems, **brainstorming** is often the technique of choice. Brainstorming is a group problem-solving technique that promotes creativity by encouraging idea generation through noncritical discussion. Alex Osborn, who developed the practice of brainstorming, believed that one of the main blocks to organizational creativity was the premature evaluation of ideas.[14] The basic technique is to encourage unrestrained and spontaneous participation by group members. The term *brainstorm* has become so widely known that it is often used as a synonym for a clever idea.

Brainstorming is used both as a method of finding alternatives to real-life problems and as a creativity-training program. In the usual form of brainstorming, group members spontaneously call out alternative solutions to a problem facing them. Any member is free to enhance or "hitchhike" upon the contribution of another person. At the end of the session, somebody sorts out the ideas and edits the more unrefined ones.

Brainstorming is widely used to develop new ideas for products, find names for products, develop advertising slogans, and solve customer problems. For instance, the design firm Ideo uses brainstorming as standard practice, such as thinking of new high-tech gadgets for children. Brainstorming has also been used to develop a new organizational structure in a government agency, and it is now widely used in developing software.

Adhering to a few simple rules or guidelines helps ensure that creative alternative solutions to problems will be forthcoming. The brainstorming process usually falls into

LEARNING OBJECTIVE 3

brainstorming

A group problem-solving technique that promotes creativity by encouraging idea generation through noncritical discussion.

place without frequent reminders about guidelines. Nevertheless, here are nine rules to improve the chances of having a good session. Unless many of these rules are followed, brainstorming becomes a free-for-all, and is not brainstorming in its original intent.

1. **Group size should be about five to seven people.** If there are too few people, not enough suggestions are generated; if there are too many people, the session becomes uncontrolled. However, brainstorming can be conducted with as few as three people.

2. **Everybody is given the chance to suggest alternative solutions.** Members spontaneously call out alternatives to the problem facing the group. (Another approach is for people to speak in sequence.)

3. **No criticism is allowed.** All suggestions should be welcome; it is particularly important not to use derisive laughter.

4. **Freewheeling is encouraged.** Outlandish ideas often prove quite useful. It's easier to tame a wild idea than to originate one.

5. **Quantity and variety are very important.** The greater the number of ideas put forth, the greater the likelihood of a breakthrough idea.

6. **Combinations and improvements are encouraged.** Building upon the ideas of others, including combining them, is very productive. Hitchhiking or piggybacking is an essential part of brainstorming.

7. **Notes must be taken during the session by a person who serves as the recording secretary.** The session can also be taped, but this requires substantial time to retrieve ideas.

8. **Invite outsiders to the brainstorming session.** Inviting an outsider to the brainstorming session can add a new perspective the "insiders" might not think of themselves. (Such is the argument for having a diverse problem-solving group.)

9. **Do not overstructure by following any of the above eight ideas too rigidly.** Brainstorming is a spontaneous group process.

A widely accepted suggestion for brainstorming effectiveness is to have diverse group members. Diversity includes differences in age, sex, race, experience levels, and educational background, as well as functional background (e.g., marketing and information technology).[15] The diversity contributes to different perspectives that facilitate a variety of ideas surfacing during the brainstorming session.

According to one observer, the most productive brainstorming sessions take place in physically stimulating environments as opposed to a drab conference room. Natural light may stimulate thinking, so work in a room with windows or outside if weather permits. Changing from a seated position to walking around from time to time can be mentally stimulating. Food and drink also contribute to an enhanced environment for brainstorming.[16]

Another useful perspective on brainstorming is that the process really involves establishing and attaining a series of goals. The rules for brainstorming can be interpreted as goals, as with the following examples:

- Establish the quantity goal of establishing as many ideas as possible.
- Establish the goal of avoiding criticism.
- Establish the goal of attempting to combine ideas and build on them.[17]

Brainstorming is an effective technique for finding a large number of alternatives to problems, particularly when the list of alternatives is subsequently refined and edited. Brainstorming in groups is also valuable because it contributes to job satisfaction for many people. Skill-Building Exercise 7-3 gives you an opportunity to practice a commercially useful application of brainstorming.

A curious feature of brainstorming is that individuals working alone typically produce more useful ideas than those placed in a group. Brainstorming by individuals working alone is referred to as **brainwriting**. Skill-Building Exercise 7-4 gives you a chance to compare brainstorming with brainwriting.

brainwriting

Brainstorming by individuals working alone.

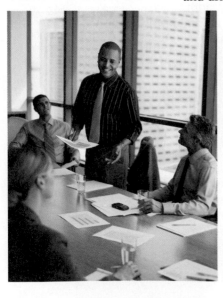

Stretch Your Imagination

A global contest was organized by Stanford University through its Technology Ventures Program. Anyone in the world was permitted to enter. The assignment was to take ordinary rubber bands and "add value" to them. Entries were submitted by video, posting them on YouTube. Entrants included people from many different occupations, including computer scientist. The winner received the Genius Award.

Here is where you fit in. Through brainstorming, come up with at least six ways of adding value (making more useful) a rubber band, or a bunch of rubber bands. You must stretch your imagination to

be successful. After the brainstorming sessions have been completed, perhaps taking 10 minutes of class time, a representative of each group might share results with the class. Students might then assign a Genius Award to the entry that seems the most useful. Or, the instructor might be the judge.

Source: The facts about the contest stem from Lee Gomes, "Our Columnist Judges a Brainstorming Bee, and Meets a Genius," *The Wall Street Journal*, March 5, 2008, p. B1.

Brainstorming versus Brainwriting

Half the class is organized into brainstorming groups of about six people. The rest of the class works by themselves. Groups and individuals then work on the same problems for 10 minutes. The brainstorming groups follow the aforementioned guidelines. Individuals jot down as many alternatives as come to mind without interacting with other people. After the problem-solving sessions are completed, compare the alternatives developed by the groups and individuals. Groups and individuals choose one of the following problems so that solutions can be compared to the same problems:

1. How might we reduce the carbon dioxide emissions in our community?

2. How can we earn extra money, aside from holding a regular job?

3. How can we find new people to date?

4. How can we save money on food costs?

5. How can we use Twitter and Facebook to make money?

GUIDELINES FOR THE NOMINAL GROUP TECHNIQUE

LEARNING OBJECTIVE 4

A team leader or other manager who must make a decision about an important issue sometimes needs to know what alternatives are available and how people will react to them. In such cases, group input may be helpful. Spoken brainstorming is not advisable because the problem is still in the exploration phase and requires more than a list of alternative solutions.

A problem-solving technique called the **nominal group technique (NGT)** was developed to fit the situation. The NGT is a group problem-solving technique that calls people together in a structured meeting with limited interaction. The group is called nominal (in name only) because people first present their ideas without interacting with each other, as they would in a real group. However, group discussion does take place at a later stage in the process. Figure 7-1 outlines the nominal group technique.

nominal group technique (NGT)

A group problem solving technique that calls people together in a structured meeting with limited interaction.

A problem that is an appropriate candidate for NGT is a decision about which suppliers or vendors should be eliminated. Many companies are shrinking their number of suppliers because they believe that working with a smaller number of suppliers can lead to higher quality components. It is easier to train a small number of suppliers, and it is also possible to build better working relationships when fewer people are involved. Also, with fewer suppliers there are fewer transactions to bother with.

A decision of this type can lead to hurt feelings and breaking up of old friendships. Suppose Pedro, the team leader, is empowered to make this decision about reducing the number of suppliers. The NGT involves a six-step decision process:

1. Work-team members are assembled because they will all participate in the decision to reduce the number of companies that serve as suppliers to the team. All team members are told in advance of the meeting and the agenda. The meeting is called, and an office assistant is invited to help take care of the administrative details of the meeting.

FIGURE 7-1 The Nominal Group Technique

2. The team leader presents a specific question. Pedro tells the group, "Top management says we have to reduce our number of suppliers by two-thirds. It's too difficult to keep track of all these different suppliers and train them to meet our quality specs. I dislike terminating a supplier as much as anybody, but I can understand the logic of top management. Right now our team is doing business with 12 suppliers, and we should shrink that number to 4. Your assignment is to develop criteria for choosing which suppliers to eliminate. I also need to know how you feel about the decision you make on supplier reduction and how it might affect the operations of our team."

3. Individual team members write down their ideas independently, without speaking to other members. Using notepads, e-mail, or word processors, the five team members write down their ideas about reducing the number of suppliers by two-thirds.

4. Each team member in turn presents one idea to the group. Sometimes these ideas are presented to the group by the team leader without identifying which person contributed the idea. In this way, ideas are submitted anonymously. The group does not discuss the ideas. The office assistant summarizes each idea by writing it on a flip chart. Here are the ideas submitted by each team member:

Alternative A. We'll carefully study the prices offered by all 12 suppliers. The eight suppliers with the highest average prices for comparable goods are given the boot. I like this idea because our team will save the company a bundle of money.

Alternative B. Let's keep the four suppliers who have the best quality record. We'll ask each supplier if it has won a quality award. If a supplier has won a quality award, the company is put on the retained list. We'll include awards from their customers or outside standards such as ISO 9000. If we find more than four suppliers have won awards, we'll retain those with the most impressive awards.

Alternative C. I say we reward good service. We keep the 4 suppliers among the 12 who have been the most prompt with deliveries. We'll also take into account how good the suppliers have been about accepting returns of damaged or defective merchandise.

Alternative D. Here's an opportunity to get in good with top management. Stop kidding each other. We know that the plant's general manager [Jake] has his favorite suppliers. Some of them are his fishing and golfing buddies. The suppliers who are friends with Jake get our vote. In this way, Jake will think our team shows really good judgment.

Alternative E. Let's reward the suppliers who have served us best. We'll rate each supplier on a 1 to 10 scale on three dimensions: the quality of goods they have provided us, price, and service in terms of prompt delivery and returns policy. We could do the ratings in less than one hour.

5. After each team member has presented his or her idea, the group clarifies and evaluates the suggestions. The length of the discussion for each of the ideas varies

The Nominal Group Technique

With a clear understanding of the mechanics of the NGT as described in the text, the technique can be demonstrated in about 30 minutes. The class is divided into groups of about seven. One person plays the role of the team leader, who can also assume the responsibility of the office assistant (recording information on flip charts or a computer).

You are the key member of a motion picture and television film production company. You have a contract to produce a series of four films. The problem you face is which North American (United States, Canadian, or Mexican) city to choose as the film site. The president has ruled out Hollywood because expenses are too high. Solve this problem using the NGT, and make a decision about which city to choose for your film site.

substantially. For example, the idea about rating suppliers on three criteria might precipitate a 30-minute discussion. The discussion about retaining the plant manager's political connections might last only five minutes.

6. The meeting ends with a silent, independent rating of the alternatives. The final group decision is the pooled outcome of the individual votes. The team members are instructed to rate each alternative on a 1 to 10 scale, with 10 being the most favorable rating. The ratings that follow are the pooled ratings (the sum of the individual ratings) received for each alternative. The maximum score is 50 (10 points × 5 raters).

Alternative A, price alone: 35

Alternative B, quality-award record: 30

Alternative C, good service: 39

Alternative D, plant manager's favorites: 14

Alternative E, combination of quality, price, and service: 44

Team leader Pedro agrees with the group's preference for choosing the four suppliers with the best combination of quality, price, and service. He schedules a meeting to decide which suppliers meet these standards. Pedro brings the team's recommendations to the plant manager, and they are accepted. Although the team is empowered to make the decision, it is still brought to management for final approval. To practice the nominal group technique, do Skill-Building Exercise 7-5.

USING STANDUP MEETINGS TO FACILITATE PROBLEM SOLVING

LEARNING OBJECTIVE 5

Problem solving and decision making can sometimes be improved by conducting meetings while standing up instead of sitting down. The general idea is that participants standing up in the problem-solving group are likely to be more alert and will come to a decision more quickly. Some people solve problems better when standing because they literally "think well on their feet." Few people would be willing to stand for several hours, so they reach a decision quickly.

Many meeting leaders who use standup meetings are pleased with the results in terms of reaching high-quality decisions rapidly. At United Parcel Service (UPS), every morning and several times a day, managers assemble workers for a required standup meeting that lasts precisely three minutes. Among the topics covered are local information, traffic conditions, or customer complaints. Each meeting ends with a safety tip. The 180-second limit helps enforce punctuality throughout UPS.[18] Many problem-solving meetings at Google are held standing up. For example, details about a recent version of the Google results page were hammered out at a meeting of 10 people.[19]

A team of researchers investigated the effectiveness of standup meetings.[20] Study participants were 555 students in an introduction to management course who were offered extra credit for participating in the study. The students were randomly assigned to five-person groups, producing 111 groups. They were divided almost equally into standup and sit-down groups.

All groups were assigned the Lost on the Moon exercise, which presents a scenario involving a crash on the moon. Participants were asked to rank 15 pieces of equipment that survived the crash in terms of their importance for survival. Correct answers to the problem were the ranking of the equipment given by NASA astronauts and scientists. The major results of the experiment were as follows:

1. Sit-down meetings lasted about 34 percent longer than the standup meetings (788 seconds versus 589 seconds).
2. Sit-down and standup meetings made decisions of equal quality.
3. More suggestions about task accomplishment were used by groups in the sit-down meetings than in the standup meetings.
4. Participants in the sit-down meetings were more satisfied than participants in the standup meetings.

One implication for this study is that people make decisions more quickly when standing up, without sacrificing decision quality. However, people prefer to sit down. In general, if you think that a task can be performed in 30 minutes or less, a standup meeting is likely to be effective.

BACK TO THE OPENING CASE

Indeed, the rocket scientists and other workers at the Jet Propulsion Lab use standup meetings to make major decisions. At one standup meeting, Graf challenged the group to come up with an alternative method for covering the spacecraft deck so that they could avoid potential heat loss while operating the radar antenna. The current plan could cost the orbiter to lose 15 watts of power as wasted heat, and every watt of power and every ounce of heat counts in space. So the group thrashed out a complicated solution to the problem of a minor heat loss.

USING E-MAIL AND GROUPWARE TO FACILITATE GROUP DECISION MAKING

The presence of so many teams in the workplace means that people must work collectively and that they must make decisions together. Collective effort usually translates into meetings. Without any meetings, people are working primarily alone and thus are not benefiting from working in teams. Yet with too many meetings, it is difficult to accomplish individual work, such as dealing with e-mail, making telephone calls, analyzing information, and preparing reports.

Appropriate use of e-mail and groupware can facilitate interaction among team members and group decision making, while at the same time minimizing the number of physical meetings. Such use of e-mail and other electronic tools makes possible the virtual teams described in the previous chapter.

Using E-Mail to Facilitate Meetings

By using e-mail, team members can feed important information to all other members of the team without the ritual of entering a meeting and passing around handouts.[21] Using e-mail, many small details can be taken care of in advance of the meeting. During the meeting, major items can be tackled. The typical use of e-mail is to send brief memos to people on a distribution list. A more advanced use of e-mail is to distribute word processing documents as well as spreadsheets and graphics, including photographs, as attachments. If the subject of the meeting deals with uncomplicated issues, text messaging can be used instead of e-mail.

Think back to the decision reached by the team using the nominal group technique. As a follow-up to the meeting, the team was to get together to rate all 12 suppliers on quality, price, and service. Using e-mail, the group could cut down substantially on the amount of time they would have to spend in a group meeting. They might even be able to eliminate a group meeting. Pedro might instruct the team members to send their ratings and explanations to each other within 10 working days.

Each team member would then rate all 12 suppliers on quality, service, and price. The ratings would then be sent to all other team members by e-mail. Pedro could tally the results and report the final tally to each team member by e-mail. Since all team members could have performed the same calculation themselves, there would be no claims of a biased decision. A team meeting could be called to discuss the final results if Pedro or the other team members thought it was necessary.

Pushing the use of e-mail too far can inhibit rather than enhance group decision making and teamwork. If people communicate with each other almost exclusively by e-mail, the warmth of human interaction and facial expressions is lost. Piggybacking of ideas is possible by reading each other's ideas on a computer monitor. Nevertheless, the wink of an eye, the shared laughter, and the encouraging smiles that take place in a traditional meeting make an important contribution to team effort, including group problem solving. Also, face-to-face interaction facilitates creativity as people exchange ideas.

Using Groupware to Facilitate Group Problem Solving

The application of e-mail just described can be considered part of groupware because e-mail was used to facilitate work in groups. Electronic brainstorming also relies on groupware because software is applied to facilitate group decision making. Using electronic brainstorming, as well as the other electronic approaches to group problem solving, participants are free to comment on, or suggest a modification of, the ideas of other contributors. Assume that Sara, a marketing assistant at a bicycle company, enters the following comment on her e-mail: "I say, let's push for selling more adult tricycles in Florida because of the many seniors down there." Engineering technician, Jason, then adds to Sara's comment, "I love Sara's idea. But why limit the marketing push to Florida? Let's follow the senior crowd right into Arizona and the Carolinas."

At its best, groupware offers certain advantages over single-user systems. Some of the most common reasons people use groupware are as follows:[22]

- To facilitate communication by making it faster, clearer, and more persuasive
- To communicate when it would not otherwise be possible
- To enable telecommuting (working from home)
- To reduce travel costs
- To bring together multiple perspectives and expertise
- To assemble groups with common interests where it would not be possible to gather a sufficient number of people face-to-face
- To facilitate group problem solving

Another example of groupware is a *shared whiteboard* that allows two or more people to view and draw on a common drawing surface even when they are at a distance. The link to group decision making is that drawing sketches and diagrams might be an important part of the decision making. An example would be a sales team suggesting ways of dividing a geographic territory for selling. Yet another electronic approach to meetings is for all participants to post comments on a social networking site such as Facebook. In this way, all participants see the comments made by the other participants. Many companies have developed Web sites of their own modeled after Facebook.

An advantage of virtual problem solving is that it avoids the problem of a couple of people dominating the meeting, and some people making no contribution because they are timid. The extreme view is expressed by Ajay Finze, information systems professor of Arizona State University, who says: "The key to effective meetings is the ability to make them anonymous—an idea that runs against the conventional wisdom that it's better to meet face to face than via computer linkup."[23] A more human relations oriented perspective is that in-person meetings are useful for a final discussion or vote because of the exchange of ideas possible.[24] Another problem with anonymity in problem solving is that many workers want to receive credit for their good ideas.

Despite all these potential applications and benefits of groupware, the system will break down unless almost all the parties involved use the software successfully. For example, all members of the virtual team must be willing to get online at the same time to have a productive meeting.

SUGGESTIONS FOR BEING AN EFFECTIVE MEETING PARTICIPANT

Except for virtual meetings such as those made possible by groupware, group problem solving takes place within the context of a face-to-face meeting. A major problem with most meetings is that they frustrate the participants, particularly those who are accomplishment-oriented. Steven G. Rogelberg and his associates conducted an online survey of 980 participants from the United States, Australia, and the United Kingdom. The more meetings the accomplishment-oriented workers attended, the worse they felt about their job and the lower their feelings of well-being. The meetings appeared to have been perceived as an interruption to the tasks these ambitious people set out to accomplish.[25] However, many workers do enjoy the social interaction involved in meetings, as well as a change of pace from individual work.

Meetings are not likely to be eliminated despite their unpopularity with accomplishment-oriented workers. A possible solution is for meeting participants to conduct themselves in a professional, task-oriented manner. In this way, meetings will most likely be shorter and more productive. A few key suggestions follow for being an effective meeting participant.[26]

- Arrive at the meeting prepared, such as having studied the support material and agenda, thought through your potential contribution, and taken care of some details by e-mail beforehand.
- Arrive on time, and stay until the meeting is completed. The meeting leader will often wait for the last participant before getting down to business. Leaving early distracts other participants.
- Do not hog the meeting or sit silently. Meetings are much more effective when the participants make balanced contributions.
- Use constructive nonverbal communication rather than slouching, yawning, looking bored and frustrated, leaving the room frequently, chewing gum, checking your cell phone or laptop computer, or engaging in similar negative behaviors.
- Converse only with others in the meeting when someone else is not speaking. Some executives will oust from a meeting if they engage in *sidebar conversations*.
- Be prepared to offer compromise solutions when other meeting participants and the meeting leader are haggling about a conflict of opinion.
- When possible, have data ready to support your position, such as estimating from industry data how much money your suggestion will save the company.

From studying these suggestions, you will observe that conducting yourself productively and professionally in a meeting is yet another job-oriented, interpersonal skill.

CULTURAL FACTORS AND GROUP DECISION MAKING

Most aspects of human relations and interpersonal skills are affected by cultural factors, including both national and organizational cultures. Chapter 8 focuses on developing cross-cultural skills, and describes many national differences in culture. Here we present a couple of example of how cultural factors can influence the acceptance of group problem solving and decision making.

Whenever differences attributed to national cultures are mentioned, it must be recognized that these are sweeping generalizations that apply to average, or typical, behaviors. The same is true for generational and gender differences. Craig L. Pearce and his associates studied three sets of cultural differences in workplace attitudes and behaviors related to how well workers are willing to share decision making. Highlights of the findings are as follows:[27]

1. **Acceptance of unequal distribution of power in institutions and organizations.** Workers in societies where worker expect managers to have more power—and who accept this reality —are more hesitant to participate in group decision making. The same workers might be hesitant to contribute radical ideas to brainstorming because they think the manager is responsible for producing innovative ideas. Countries where workers believe in managers holding most of the power are Arab countries and France. Positive attitudes toward power sharing are more common in the United States and Canada.

2. **The degree to which a country is aggressive versus nurturing.** Aggressive societies are less prone to group decision making because aggressive people prefer to dominate. People in an aggressive society are oriented toward the achievement of goals at the expense of others. Managers from a nurturing society are more likely to believe in group decision making because the process helps workers to develop. On the list of aggressive societies are Ireland and the United States.

3. **The degree to which a society is individualistic or collectivistic.** Members of an individualistic society tend to be self-reliant and value independence, whereas members of a collectivistic society are oriented toward groups. Workers from an individualistic society might not enjoy working in teams and would not be so enthusiastic about group decision making. Workers from a collectivistic society take naturally to group decision making. People from Germany and the United States tend to value individualism. This stereotype exists despite the emphasis on teamwork in the United States.

The organizational culture, or values and behaviors of most members of the organization, exerts a strong influence on the preference for group decision making. When the organizational culture emphasizes collaboration, group problem solving and decision-making is prevalent and welcome. Procter & Gamble and Xerox are two examples of successful corporations that emphasize group decision making. The General Motors of old emphasized individual decision making.

SELF-ASSESSMENT QUIZ IN OVERVIEW

Self-Assessment Quiz 7-1 provided an indication of your tendencies toward being interested in group problem solving, and is much like the quiz you took in the previous chapter in terms of attitude toward teamwork. You will most likely perform better in group decision making if you enjoy the activity. Learning about techniques of group problem solving will most likely be of more interest to you if you have a positive attitude toward the process.

Concept Review
and Reinforcement

Key Terms

Summary

An important aspect of interpersonal relations in organizations is that groups solve many key problems. Group problem solvers and decision makers often use the rational model or the political model. The rational decision-making model is the traditional, logical approach to decision making based on the scientific method. The model assumes that each alternative is evaluated in terms of how well it contributes to reaching the goals involved in making the decision.

The political decision-making model assumes that people bring preconceived notions and biases into the decision-making situation. Because the decision makers are politically motivated, the individuals often do not make the most rational choice. Instead, the decision makers attempt to satisfy their own needs. Blind spots are an unintended contributor to political decision making, and so are greed and gluttony.

General problem-solving groups are likely to arrive at better decisions when they follow standard steps or guidelines for group problem solving. The steps are as follows: (1) Identify the problem, (2) clarify the problem, (3) analyze the cause, (4) search for alternative solutions, (5) select alternatives, (6) plan for implementation, (7) clarify the contract, (8) develop an action plan, and (9) provide for evaluation and accountability. The group's collective efficacy influences its ability to solve problems.

Disagreements about group decisions can be managed by giving dissenters the freedom to express doubt and by expressing doubts collaboratively rather than contentiously. Group decision making is more productive when group members are involved in inquiry, or looking for the best alternative. Advocacy, or fighting for one position, leads to poorer decisions. Research indicates that teams are more likely to make optimal decisions when they take the time to debate the issues and thoughtfully discuss alternative solutions.

When the organization is seeking a large number of alternatives to problems, brainstorming is often the technique of choice. Brainstorming is used as a method of finding alternatives to real-life problems and as a creativity-training program. Using the technique, group members spontaneously call out alternative solutions to the problem. Members build on the ideas of each other, and ideas are not screened or evaluated until a later stage. Diversity within the group facilitates brainstorming, as does the right physical environment, such as sunlight. Brainstorming by working alone, or brainwriting, is also effective in generating alternative solutions.

The nominal group technique (NGT) is recommended for a situation in which a leader needs to know what alternatives are available and how people will react to them. In the NGT, a small group of people contributes written solutions to the problem. Other members respond to their ideas later. Members rate each other's ideas numerically, and the final group decision is the sum of the pooled individual votes.

Problem solving and decision making can sometimes be improved by conducting meetings while standing up instead of sitting down. The general idea is that participants who are standing up are more likely to be alert and come to a decision quickly. An experiment with management students indicated that standup groups made decisions more quickly, but that decision makers who sat down were more satisfied.

Electronic mail can be used to facilitate group decision making because members can feed information to each other without having to meet as a group. Memos, spreadsheet analyses, and graphics can be distributed through the network. Too much emphasis on e-mail, however, results in losing the value of face-to-face human interaction.

Various types of groupware, including e-mail and electronic brainstorming, can facilitate group decision making. Also, a shared whiteboard allows two or more people to view and draw on a common drawing surface even when they are at a distance. Facebook, or a company Web site of the same type, can also be used for group decision making. Virtual problem solving helps avoid individual domination of decision making, but face-to-face discussion is important in making a final decision.

To help avoid the frustration of many accomplishment-oriented people in meetings, participants should conduct themselves in a professional, task-oriented manner. The suggestions presented here include: arrive prepared, arrive on time and stay for the full meeting, do not hog the meeting or sit silently, use constructive non-verbal communication, avoid sidebar conversations, offer compromise solutions to conflicts, and use data to support your position.

Questions for Discussion and Review

1. In this age of advanced communication technology, why bother having face-to-face problem-solving groups?
2. Which personality characteristics described in Chapter 2 do you think would help a person be naturally effective in group problem solving?
3. Give an example of how knowledge of the team member roles presented in Chapter 6 could help you be a better contributor to group problem solving.
4. Identify several problems on or off the job for which you think brainstorming would be effective.
5. What is your opinion of the importance of the physical setting (such as sunlight and refreshments) for stimulating creative thinking during brainstorming?
6. Identify two work-related problems for which the nominal group technique is particularly well suited.
7. In what way do athletic teams, such as those for football and basketball, make use of standup meetings?
8. How can a team leader apply groupware to help the group become more productive?
9. What annoys you the most about how some people conduct themselves in problem-solving meetings of any type? What changes in their behavior would you recommend?
10. Which group decision-making technique described in this chapter do you think members of a professional sports team are the most likely to use? Why?

The Web Corner

http://www.mindtools.com/
(Techniques for group and individual problem solving, and creativity.)

http://www.nova-mind.com/
(Mind mapping for group and individual problem solving. See the demonstration.)

Internet Skill Builder: Where Did I Put that Great Idea I Had?

Many people involved in group brainstorming hit upon useful ideas when away from the brainstorming session, then forget the idea by the time they get to the session. So during the session, the person fails to make an outstanding contribution. Search the Internet for some cool ideas for recording your ideas. An example would be sending yourself an e-mail or voicemail message if you come upon a useful idea while hiking. You are encouraged to look widely for a couple of concrete suggestions for filing your creative ideas right on the spot. Remember that fresh ideas are the building block for all types of group, as well as individual problem solving.

Developing Your Human Relations Skills

Pet Groomers on Wheels Get into a Huddle

Ted and Erin, a married couple, both loved pets and both craved becoming small-business owners. So several years ago while still holding down corporate positions, they launched a new business, Pet Groomers on Wheels. The basic model of the business is to make house calls to groom pets at the pet owner's home.

The key services for dogs are shampoos, haircuts, nail clips, teeth polishing, and ear cleaning. Except for the shampoos, the services are similar for cats. Ted and Erin travel in a van fully equipped with their supplies, and the pet grooming is conducted in the van rather than bringing all the equipment into the customer's home. Ted and Erin started the operation part-time by making their calls at night and on weekends. Soon it appeared the business was ready to become a full-time business, so the couple both quit their corporate positions.

Operating in the prosperous North Virginia geographic area, Pet Groomers on Wheels has far exceeded the sales volume and profits projected by Ted and Erin. To successfully manage all the client demands, the couple hired two close relatives, Tanya and Nick, to make some of the calls. To help keep Tanya and Nick motivated—as well as not going into competition with Pet Care on Wheels—Ted and Erin made them part owners of the business.

After three years of operation, Pet Groomers on Wheels has generated $85,000 in profits beyond paying Ted, Erin, Tanya, and Nick salaries of an average of $65,000 each. In the process of preparing the income tax for Pet Groomers, Erin decided that the company was not managing its money effectively by leaving the profits in a checking account. After chatting about the situation with Ted, they both agreed that the company should manage its money more professionally. Ted said jokingly, "I guess we could run to Vegas and parlay the money into a fortune. Or, we could take a comparable risk and invest in the stock market."

Erin replied, "I have a better idea. Let's get together with Tanya and Nick, and really thrash out what to do with Pet Groomers profits. We can all have dinner together, followed by a no-holds-barred problem-solving session."

Case Questions

1. Does the problem facing the owners of Pet Groomer on Wheels seem suited for going through the steps for group problem solving? Or, what other problem-solving technique would you recommend?
2. Take the problem of what to do with Pet Groomer profits through the group problem-solving steps, even if you have to make assumptions about some of the data for the steps.
3. Compare the conclusion you reach in response to question 2 with the conclusion reached by other individuals or groups within the class.

The Torpedoed Submarine Rolls

Chad is the sales manager at Guarino's Bakery, a supplier of bread products, cakes, and pastries to local restaurants and stores. He enjoys the challenge of his job and welcomes the opportunity to practice the skills and techniques of a professional manager. Chad has acquired some of these techniques through experience and many others through reading business books and through course work.

During the last three months, five accounts have stopped ordering the Italian bread from Guarino's that they use for submarine sandwiches. The president and owner, Angelo Guarino, told Chad, "Our submarine bread sales are being torpedoed. Our reputation is getting so bad that we'll soon be out of business. Find out by next week what has gone wrong with our line of bread. Max (the head baker) swears the bread hasn't changed."

"Angelo, I've been trying hard to find the answer," responded Chad. "So far, the only clue I have is that our submarine rolls just don't taste right. Something is wrong, but our customers don't know what it is. Several of them have complained that their customers say the bread is just not as good as in the past."

Angelo retorted, "Then go back and investigate some more. We've got to know what's wrong."

Chad said to himself, "Now is the time for action. But I'm not sure which action. Should I take a survey of dissatisfied customers? Should I increase the advertising budget?"

Case Questions

1. How might the problem facing Guarino's bakery be resolved through group decision making?
2. Which technique should Chad use to solve the problem of customer resistance to the submarine rolls?
3. What is the underlying, or true, problem facing Guarino's Bakery?

CHAPTER

Cross-Cultural Relations and Diversity

In 2009, Walgreens opened a distribution center in Windsor, Connecticut, where close to one-third of the workforce consists of people with disabilities. Employees with disabilities work alongside other team members, having the same productivity goals, and earning the same pay. Disabilities include autism and mental retardation, as well as hearing and physical impairments. An on-site training facility assists those with special needs become prepared for employment so that everyone can work productively and effectively.

"We've worked technology and creativity into every inch of this place, but the people here will amaze you," said Walgreen's senior vice president of supply chain and logistics Randy Lewis. "We originally went into this project wanting to change the work environment but soon discovered we were the ones who changed in dramatic and wonderful ways." Lewis, whose son Austin has autism, developed the idea of the outreach program for people with disabilities.

This giant 700,000 square foot facility can fit 12 football fields inside its walls, and serves hundreds of Walgreens stores throughout the Northeast. The center was planned to be 20 percent more efficient than the company's previous generation of distribution centers and has some of the most innovative logistics systems in the distribution industry.

The Windsor location and the facility in Anderson, South Carolina, that opened in 2007 are now the models for all future Walgreens distribution centers. The company's goal is to fill 10 percent of its distribution center production jobs with people with disabilities. Walgreens is more than halfway there.

For Julia Turner, a person with Down syndrome, a full-time job seemed unat-

After reading and studying this chapter and doing the exercises, you should be able to

1. Recognize who fits under the diversity umbrella.
2. Describe the major values accounting for cultural differences.
3. Overcome many cross-cultural communication barriers.
4. Improve your cross-cultural relations.

tainable, yet at the Southeastern distribution center in Anderson, it was possible. "I have found what I want, and I'm satisfied," Turner said as she scanned boxes at the center. Fully one-third of the workforce at the distribution center is disabled.

"For many, (working in the distribution center) is their first full-time job," said Lewis. "For a parent to finally see their (his or her) son or daughter experience what it's like to hold a job, be responsible and actually look forward, can fulfill a lifelong dream."[1]

The story about the giant drugstore company illustrates how some business firms and not-for-profit organizations value diversity in the workforce by reaching out to potential workers who may have been overlooked or discriminated against by many other employers.

Top management at business firms continues to recognize the importance of a diverse workforce as well as diverse customers. Not only is the workforce becoming more diverse, but business has also become increasingly international. Approximately 15 percent of the U.S. workforce is composed of people born in another country. Small- and medium-size firms, as well as corporate giants, are increasingly dependent on trade with other countries. An estimated 10 to 15 percent of jobs in the United States depend on imports or exports. Also, more and more work, such as call centers and manufacturing, is subcontracted to companies in other countries.

All this workplace diversity has an important implication for the career-minded individual. To succeed in today's workplace, a person must be able to relate effectively to people from different cultural groups from within and outside his or her country. Being able to relate to a culturally diverse customer base is also necessary for success. Being skilled at cross-cultural relations is also an asset in personal life because of the diversity within the society.

This chapter presents concepts and techniques you can use to sharpen your ability to work effectively with people from diverse backgrounds. To get you started thinking about your readiness to work in a culturally diverse environment, take Self-Assessment Quiz 8-1.

THE DIVERSITY UMBRELLA

Improving cross-cultural relations includes understanding the true meaning of appreciating diversity. To appreciate diversity, a person must go beyond tolerating and treating people from different racial and ethnic groups fairly. The true meaning of valuing diversity is to respect and enjoy a wide range of cultural and individual differences. Appreciating these differences is often referred to as *inclusion* to emphasize unity rather than diversity. To be diverse is to be different in some measurable way, even if what is measurable is not visible (such as religion or sexual orientation).

LEARNING OBJECTIVE 1

To be highly skilled in interpersonal relations, one must recognize and appreciate individual and demographic (group or category) differences, as well as cultural differences. People from the same demographic group often come from many different cultures. For example, the Latino demographic group is composed of many different cultures. Some people are more visibly diverse than others because of physical features or disabilities. Yet the diversity umbrella is supposed to include everybody in an organization. To value diversity is therefore to appreciate individual differences among people.

Appreciating cultural diversity in organizations was originally aimed at assisting women and minorities. The diversity umbrella continues to include more people as the

Cross-Cultural Skills and Attitudes

Directions: Listed below are skills and attitudes that various employers and cross-cultural experts think are important for relating effectively to coworkers in a culturally diverse environment. For each of the statements, check *applies to me now* or *not there yet.*

	Applies to me now	Not there yet
1. I have spent some time in another country.	_____	_____
2. At least one of my friends is deaf, blind, or uses a wheelchair.	_____	_____
3. Currency from other countries is as real as the currency from my own country.	_____	_____
4. I can read in a language other than my own.	_____	_____
5. I can speak in a language other than my own.	_____	_____
6. I can write in a language other than my own.	_____	_____
7. I can understand people speaking in a language other than my own.	_____	_____
8. I use my second language regularly.	_____	_____
9. My friends include people of races different from my own.	_____	_____
10. My friends include people of different ages.	_____	_____
11. I feel (or would feel) comfortable having a friend with a sexual orientation different from mine.	_____	_____
12. My attitude is that although another culture may be very different from mine, that culture is equally good.	_____	_____
13. I am willing to eat (or have eaten) food from other countries that is not served in my own country.	_____	_____
14. I would accept (or have already accepted) a work assignment of more than several months in another country.	_____	_____
15. I have a passport.	_____	_____
16. I know the approximate difference in value between the U.S. dollar and the euro.	_____	_____
17. I know how many hours difference there is between my time zone and at least two other overseas time zones.	_____	_____

Interpretation: If you answered *applies to me now* to 11 or more of the preceding questions, you most likely function well in a multicultural work environment. If you answered *not there yet* to 11 or more of the questions, you need to develop more cross-cultural awareness and skills to work effectively in a multicultural work environment. You will notice that being bilingual gives you at least five points on this quiz.

Sources: Several ideas for statements on this quiz are derived from Ruthann Dirks and Janet Buzzard, "What CEOs Expect of Employees Hired for International Work," *Business Education Forum,* April 1997, pp. 3–7; and Gunnar Beeth, "Multicultural Managers Wanted," *Management Review,* May 1997, pp. 17–21.

workforce encompasses a greater variety of people. For example, in recent years much attention has been paid to the rights of employees included in the group GLBT (gay, lesbian, bisexual, and transsexual). Janis Walworth, co-founder of the Center for Gender Sanity, says, "The country is on a path of increasing respect for gays and lesbians as well, and transgender people are riding the coattails."[2] The rights of members of diverse religious groups are also receiving attention. At times, some of the religious groups may oppose the advances of the GLBT group.

The goal of a diverse organization is for persons of all cultural backgrounds to achieve their full potential, not restrained by group identities such as gender, nationality, or race. Another important goal is for these groups to work together harmoniously.

Figure 8-1 presents a broad sampling of the ways in which workplace associates can differ from one another. Studying this list can help you anticipate the types of differences to understand and appreciate in a diverse workplace. The differences include cultural as well as individual factors. Individual factors are also important because people can be discriminated

FIGURE 8-1 The Diversity Umbrella

- Race
- Sex (or gender)
- Religion
- Age (young, middle-age, and old)
- Ethnicity (country of origin)
- Education
- Abilities
- Mental disabilities (including attention deficit disorder)
- Physical disabilities (including hearing status, visual status, able-bodied, wheelchair user)
- Values and motivation
- Sexual orientation (heterosexual, homosexual, bisexual, transsexual)
- Marital status (married, single, cohabitating, widow, widower)
- Family status (children, no children, two-parent family, single parent, grandparent)
- Personality traits
- Functional background (area of specialization)
- Technology interest (high-tech, low-tech, technophobe)
- Weight status (average, obese, underweight, anorexic)
- Hair status (full head of hair, bald, wild hair, tame hair, long hair, short hair)
- Tobacco status (smoker versus nonsmoker, chewer versus nonchewer)
- Styles of clothing and appearance (dress up, dress down, professional appearance, casual appearance)
- Socioeconomic status, such as some groups having low income and formal education, whereas others have high income and high formal education

against for personal characteristics as well as group factors. Many people, for example, believe they are held back from promotion because of their weight-to-height ratio.

A diverse workforce is noted to have many consequences to the organization, mostly positive, but some negative. A sampling of these consequences is as follows:

- Multicultural experiences are strongly associated with creative thinking, and creative outcomes such as ideas for new products.[3] If you work with people from different cultures on the job or association with them in personal life, your creativity is likely to be enhanced.

- A diverse workforce helps generate more profits through such means as having employees onboard who look similar to and share the same customs as their customers.[4] Allstate and Wal-Mart exemplify companies whose culturally diverse workforce helps them attract more customers.

- When employees and managers working for a large retailer perceive that a positive climate (atmosphere) for diversity exists, the store is likely to prosper. A one-year study of more than 650 store units at J. C. Penney found that the largest sales growth occurred in stores wherein subordinates and managers perceived highly pro-diversity climates. In contrast, the lowest sales growth was found in stores where both managers and subordinates reported a less hospitable climate for diversity.[5]

- Cultural diversity within groups can sometimes lead to so much conflict and disagreement that productivity suffers. Diversity in educational background and age

> "In this extreme war for talent, we need to create a culture of inclusion."
> —Lynn Weaver, vice president of human resources at Yazaki of North America

can also lead to conflict. However, a study in Germany found that in teams where the need for intellectual stimulation was relatively high, team performance increased in the presence of diversity in educational experience and age.[6]

- The setting of the diverse workgroup can sometimes influence whether or not cultural diversity leads to enhanced performance. A compilation of many studies found that relations-oriented diversity led to high performance in service industry settings. (Relations-oriented includes race, ethnicity, gender, and age.) In contrast, this type of diversity had slightly negative effects in manufacturing settings.[7]

UNDERSTANDING CULTURAL DIFFERENCES

LEARNING OBJECTIVE 2

The groundwork for developing effective cross-cultural relations is to understand cultural differences. The information about different communication patterns between men and women presented in Chapter 4 is relevant here. Here we discuss six aspects of understanding cultural differences: (1) cultural sensitivity including political correctness, (2) cultural intelligence, (3) respect for all workers, (4) cultural fluency, (5) dimensions of differences in cultural dimensions, and (6) avoidance of cultural bloopers. To work smoothly with people from other cultures, it is important to become competent in all six areas.

Cultural Sensitivity and Political Correctness

In order to relate well to someone from a foreign country, a person must be alert to possible cultural differences. When working in another country, a person must be willing to acquire knowledge about local customs and learn how to speak the native language at least passably. When working or socializing with people from different cultures, even from his or her own country, the person must be patient, adaptable, flexible, and willing to listen and learn. The characteristics just mentioned are part of **cultural sensitivity**, an awareness of and willingness to investigate the reasons why individuals of another culture act as they do.[8] A person with cultural sensitivity will recognize certain nuances in customs that will help build better relationships from cultural backgrounds other than his or her own.

cultural sensitivity

An awareness of and willingness to investigate the reasons why people of another culture act as they do.

Another aspect of cultural sensitivity is **political correctness**—being careful not to offend or slight anyone, and being extra civil and respectful.[9] An effective use of political correctness would be to say, "We need a ladder in our department because we have workers of different heights who need access to the top shelves." It would be politically incorrect to say, "We need ladders because we have some short workers who cannot reach the top shelves." Carried too far, political correctness can push a person in the direction of being too bland and imprecise in language. The ultra-politically person for example will almost never mention a person's race, sex, ethnicity, or health status when referring to another worker. For example, the ultra-politically person would not make a statement like, "Sadie is German, so she was a natural to be our liaison with the manufacturing group." (The cultural stereotype here is that Germans are quite interested in manufacturing technology and think precisely.)

Ultra-political correctness also involves using supposedly correct terms to describe people even if a given individual rejects the label. For example, many black people are correctly referred to as "black" rather than "African American" because they might be citizens of Africa, Haiti, England, etc. Also, the same people do not consider themselves to be African American.

Empathy is a major trait and skill that facilitates cultural sensitivity and political correctness. You have to place yourself in the other person's perspective, and ask yourself questions like, "How would I like it if somebody snarled and said an ugly word when he or she looked at my favorite food." Kim Oliver and Sylvester Baugh offer this insight into developing the type of empathy helpful in building cross-cultural relations in the workplace, "We want to try to develop an understanding for the majority about what it might be like to be the minority, and help the minority understand what it's like to be the majority."[10]

cultural intelligence (CQ)

An outsider's ability to interpret someone's unfamiliar and ambiguous behavior the same way that person's compatriots would.

Cultural Intelligence

An advanced aspect of cultural sensitivity is to be able to fit in comfortably with people of another culture by observing the subtle cues they give about how a person should act in their presence. **Cultural intelligence (CQ)** is an outsider's ability to interpret someone's unfamiliar and ambiguous behavior the same way that person's compatriots would.[11] With high cultural intelligence, a person would be able to figure out what behavior would be true of all people and all groups, such as rapid shaking of a clenched fist to communicate anger. Also, the person with high cultural intelligence could figure out what is peculiar to this group, and those aspects of behavior that are neither universal nor peculiar to the group. These ideas are so abstract that an example will help clarify.

An American expatriate manager served on a design team that included two German engineers. As other team members floated their ideas, the engineers condemned them as incomplete or underdeveloped. The manager concluded that the Germans in general are rude and aggressive.

With average cultural intelligence, the American would have realized he was mistakenly equating the merit of an idea with the merit of the person presenting it. The Germans, however, were able to make a sharp distinction between the two. A manager with more advanced cultural intelligence might have tried to figure out how much of the two Germans' behavior was typically German and how much was explained by the fact that they were engineers.

Similar to emotional intelligence, cultural intelligence encompasses several aspects of behavior. The three sources of cultural intelligence relate to the cognitive, emotional/motivational, and the physical, shown in Figure 8-2, and explained as follows:[12]

1. **Cognitive (the Head).** The cognitive part of CQ refers to what a person knows and how he or she can acquire new knowledge. Here you acquire facts about people from another culture such as their passion for football (soccer in North America), their business practices, and their promptness in paying bills. Another aspect of this source of cultural intelligence is figuring out how you can learn more about the other culture.

2. **Emotional/Motivational (the Heart).** The emotional/motivational aspect of CQ refers to energizing one's actions and building personal confidence. You need both confidence and motivation to adapt to another culture. A man on a business trip to Africa might say to himself, "When I greet a work associate in a restaurant, can I really pull off kissing him on both cheeks. What if he thinks I'm weird?" With strong motivation, the same person might say, "I'll give it a try. I kind of greet my grandfather the same way back in the United States."

3. **The Body (Physical).** The body aspect of CQ is the action component. The body is the element for translating intentions into actions and desires. Kissing the same-sex African work associates on both cheeks is the *physical* aspect just mentioned. We often have an idea of what we should do, but implementation is not so easy. You might know, for example, that when entering an Asian person's home you should

FIGURE 8-2   The Components of Cultural Intelligence

take off your shoes, yet you might not actually remove them—thereby offending your Asian work (or personal life) associate.

To practice high cultural intelligence, the mind, heart, and body have to work together. You need to figure out how to act with people from another culture, you need motivation and confidence to change, and you have to translate your knowledge and motivation into action. So when you are on a business trip to London, go ahead and hold your fork in your left hand!

Respect for All Workers and Cultures

An effective strategy for achieving cross-cultural understanding is to simply respect all others in the workplace, including their cultures. Respecting people from other cultures works equally well in personal life. An example would be not joking at the fact that an acquaintance of yours puts his head on the floor to pray.

An important component of respect is to believe that although another person's culture is different from yours, it is equally good. Respect comes from valuing differences. Respecting other people's customs can translate into specific attitudes, such as respecting one coworker for wearing a yarmulke on Friday or another for wearing African clothing to celebrate Kwanzaa. Another way of being respectful would be to listen carefully to the opinion of a senior worker who says the company should never have converted to voicemail and a voice recognition system in place of assistants answering the phone (even though you disagree).

An aspect of respecting all workers that achieves current attention is the importance of respecting the rights of majorities, particularly white males. Many of these men want to be involved in—not excluded from—bringing about cultural diversity in organizations. For example, they might want to mentor minority group members.

Company policies that encourage respect for the rights of others are likely to create a positive influence on tolerance throughout the firm. An example is that many employers have taken steps to recognize and affirm the existence of gay and lesbian workers. Among these steps are publishing formal statements of nondiscrimination, and the inclusion of issues about sexual orientation in diversity training programs. A major policy change has been to grant same-sex couples the same benefits granted to opposite-sex couples.

Another formal (official) way of demonstrating respect for all workers is to provide for the presence of **employee network** (or **affinity**) **groups**. Such a group is composed of employees throughout the company who affiliate on the basis of group characteristics, such as race, ethnicity, gender, sexual orientation, or physical ability status. The network group provides members of the same demographic or cultural group and avenue for sharing ideas with management. Employee network groups at McDonald's, for example, include the African-American Council, the Hispanic Employee Network, the Asian Employee Network, and the Gays, Lesbians and Allies at McDonald's.[13]

A study of 537 gay and lesbian employees working for a variety of organizations demonstrated that the more prevalent policies dealing with respect, the more equitably sexual minorities are likely to be treated at work. More equitable treatment, in turn, was associated with gays and lesbians being more satisfied, and less likely to leave the firm.[14]

BACK TO THE OPENING CASE

Management at Walgreens continues to be successful in building a culturally diverse workforce that includes persons with physical disabilities, as well as those with developmental (intellectual) disabilities. Management's most important approach to accomplishing this end is to show respect for all workers by treating them equally. Employees with good ideas are listened too, and both majority group members and minority group members who appear to have leadership skill have an equal shot at being part of the management training program. Should you visit a neighborhood Walgreens, you might notice that the store associates as well as the pharmacists are culturally diverse.

Developing Cultural Sensitivity

Carefully observe products and services such as tennis shoes, notebooks, bicycles, and banking services, and attempt to find out how they are marketed and sold in other countries. For a convenient reference source, interview foreign students and foreigners outside class about these products and services. Your digging for information might uncover such nuggets as the following:

- In India, cricket champions are celebrities comparable to U.S. basketball stars who endorse soft drinks like Coca-Cola and Pepsi.

- In Hungary, peanut butter is considered a luxury food item.
- In some countries in warm climates, meat is freshly killed and hung on hooks for sale—without refrigeration or freezing.

After conducting these product and service interviews, arrive at some kind of interpretation or conclusion. Share your insights with other class members.

Source: "Teaching International Business," *Keying In,* January 1999, p. 1. National Business Education Association. Reprinted with permission.

Cultural Fluency

A high-level goal in understanding cultural differences is to achieve **cultural fluency,** the ability to conduct business in a diverse, international environment.[15] Achieving cultural fluency includes a variety of skills, such as relating well to people from different cultures and knowing a second language. Cultural fluency also includes knowledge of the international business environment, such as how the exchange rate can affect profits. Having high cultural intelligence would contribute to cultural fluency because such intelligence makes it easier to work well with people from other cultures. If you are culturally fluent, you will also find it easier to make friends (real and virtual) from other cultures.

Skill-Building Exercise 8-1 is a warm-up activity for achieving cultural sensitivity, and perhaps respect for all workers.

cultural fluency

The ability to conduct business in a diverse, international environment.

Dimensions of Differences in Cultural Values

One way to understand how national cultures differ is to examine their values or cultural dimensions. The formulation presented here is based on the worldwide research in 62 societal cultures and builds on previous analyses of cultural dimensions.[16] The cultural dimensions presented here are those most directly related to interpersonal skills. Keep in mind that these cultural dimensions are stereotypes that apply to a representative person from a particular culture, and are not meant to insult anybody. These cultural dimensions are differences between national societies and may not be representative of a given individual. As with gender stereotypes in communication, individual differences are substantial. For example, any Americans are not assertive, and many French are willing to work 70 hours per week.

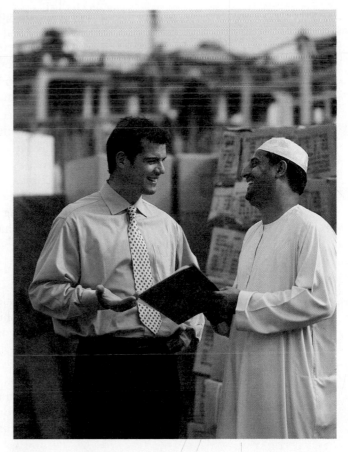

1. **Performance orientation** is the degree to which a society encourages, or should encourage, and rewards group members for performance improvement and excellence. Countries high on this dimension are the United States and Singapore, whereas those low on this dimension are Russia and Greece.
2. **Assertiveness** is the degree to which individuals are (and should be) assertive, confrontational, and aggressive in their relationships with one another. Countries scoring high on this dimension are the United States and Austria, whereas those low on this dimension are Sweden and New Zealand. Assertive people enjoy competition in business, in contrast to less assertive cultural groups who prefer harmony, loyalty, and solidarity.

3. **Time orientation** is the importance nations and individuals attach to time. People with an urgent time orientation perceive time as a scarce resource and tend to be impatient. People with a casual time orientation view time as an unlimited and unending resource and tend to be patient. Americans are noted for their urgent time orientation. They frequently impose deadlines and are eager to get started doing business. Asians, Mexicans, and Middle Easterners, in contrast, are patient negotiators.

4. **Humane orientation** is the degree to which a society encourages and rewards, and should encourage and reward, individuals for being fair, altruistic, caring, and kind toward others. Egypt and Malaysia rank high on this cultural dimension, and France and Germany rank low.

5. **In-group collectivism** is the degree to which individuals express, and should express, pride, loyalty, and cohesiveness in their organizations and families. Asian societies emphasize collectivism, as do Egypt and Russia. One consequence of collectivism is taking pride in family members and the organizations that employ them.

6. **Gender egalitarianism** is the degree to which a culture minimizes, and should minimize, gender inequality. European countries emphasize gender egalitarianism, and so do the United States and Canada. South Korea is an example of a country that is low on gender egalitarianism, and is male dominated.

7. **Acceptance of power and authority** is the degree to which members of a society expect, and should expect, power to be distributed unequally. Individuals who accept power and authority expect the boss to make the major decisions. These same individuals are more formal; however, being formal toward people in positions of authority has decreased substantially throughout the world in recent years. Examples of societies that score high on acceptance of power and authority are Thailand, Brazil, France, and Japan.

8. **Work orientation** is the number of hours per week and weeks per year people expect to invest in work versus leisure, or other nonwork activities. American corporate professionals typically work about 55 hours per week, take 45-minute lunch breaks, and two weeks of vacation. Americans tend to have a stronger work orientation than Europeans but a weaker one than Asians. U.S. employees average 1,804 hours of work per year, compared with 1,407 for Norwegian workers and 1,564 for the French. Workers in seven Asian countries including South Korea, Bangladesh, and China worked 2,200 hours per year.[17]

9. **Social support seeking** is the degree to which people seek out others to help them with difficult problems through such means as listening, offering sympathy, and giving advice. Asians and Asian Americans are more reluctant to explicitly request support from close others than are European Americans. The hesitancy comes about because the Asians and Asian Americans are more concerned about negative relationship consequences, such as disrupting group harmony or receiving criticism from the other person. Another possible reason for the hesitancy is that Asians and Asian Americans expect social support without having to ask.[18]

How might someone use information about cultural differences to improve his or her interpersonal relations on the job? A starting point would be to recognize that a person's national values might influence his or her behavior. Assume that you wanted to establish a good working relationship with a person from a high humane orientation culture. An effective starting point would be to emphasize care and concern when communicating with the individual.

Attitudes toward acceptance of power and authority can make a difference in establishing working relationships. A worker who values deference to age, gender, or title might shy away from offering suggestions to an elder or manager to avoid appearing disrespectful. This worker would need considerable encouragement to collaborate in decision making.[19] *Time-orientation* may create a conflict if you are committed to

Charting Your Cultural Dimension Profile

Directions: For each of the nine cultural dimensions, circle the number that most accurately fits your standing on the dimension. For example, if you perceive yourself to be "highly humane," circle 6 on the fourth dimension (item 4).

1. High performance orientation   Low performance orientation
   1   2   3   4   5   6   7

2. Low assertiveness   High assertiveness
   1   2   3   4   5   6   7

3. Urgent time orientation   Casual time orientation
   1   2   3   4   5   6   7

4. High humane orientation   Low humane orientation
   1   2   3   4   5   6   7

5. In-group collectivism   In-group individualism
   1   2   3   4   5   6   7

6. High gender egalitarianism   Low gender egalitarianism
   1   2   3   4   5   6   7

7. High acceptance of power and authority   Low acceptance of power and authority
   1   2   3   4   5   6   7

8. Work orientation   Leisure orientation
   1   2   3   4   5   6   7

9. Social support seeking   Social support avoidance
   1   2   3   4   5   6   7

Scoring and Interpretation: After circling one number for each dimension, use a pen or pencil to connect the circles, thereby giving yourself a profile of cultural values. Do not be concerned if your line cuts through the names of the dimensions. Compare your profile to others in the class. Should time allow, develop a class profile by computing the class average for each of the nine points and then connecting the points.

making deadlines and a team member has a laid-back attitude toward time. You might explain that although you respect his attitudes toward time, the company insists on getting the project completed on time.

Self-Assessment Quiz 8-2 will help you think about how cultural dimensions might be influencing your interpersonal relations in the workplace.

Cultural Bloopers

An effective way of being culturally sensitive is to minimize actions that are likely to offend people from another culture based on their values. Cultural bloopers are most likely to take place when you are visiting another country. The same bloopers, however, can also be committed with people from a different culture within your own country. To avoid these bloopers, you must carefully observe persons from another culture. Studying another culture through reading is also helpful.

E-commerce and other forms of Internet communication have created new opportunities for creating cultural bloopers. The Web site developers and workers responsible for adding content must have good cross-cultural literacy, including an awareness of how the information might be misinterpreted.

- Numerical date formats can be readily misinterpreted. To an American, 4/9/13 would be interpreted as April 9, 2013 (or 1913!). However, many Europeans would interpret the same numerical expression as September 4, 2013.

- Colors on Web sites must be chosen carefully. For example, in some cultures purple is the color of royalty, whereas in Brazil purple is associated with death.

- Be careful of metaphors that may not make sense to a person for whom your language is a second language. Examples include "We've encountered an ethical meltdown" and "Our biggest competitor is over the hill."

English has become the language of business and science throughout the world, yet communicating in a customer's native tongue has its advantages. Being able to communicate your message directly in your customer's mother tongue provides a competitive advantage. Bilingualism also has career implications. Some telemarketing, banking, engineering, and financial service companies are searching for workers with bilingual skills. The two major contributing factors are the growing immigrant population in the United States, and because companies are engaged more in international business.[20]

Furthermore, according to the research firm International Data Corporation (IDC), consumers are four times more likely to purchase a product online if the Web site is in their preferred language.[21] The translator, of course, must have good knowledge of the subtleties of the language to avoid a blooper. An English-to-French translator used the verb *baiser* instead of *baisser* to describe a program of lowering prices. *Baisser* is the French verb "to lower," whereas *baiser* is the verb "to kiss." Worse, in slang *baiser* is a verb that refers to having intimate physical relationships!

Keep two key facts in mind when attempting to avoid cultural mistakes. One is that members of any cultural group show individual differences. What one member of the group might regard as an insensitive act, another might welcome. Recognize also that one or two cultural mistakes will not peg you permanently as a boor. Skill-Building Exercise 8-2 will help you minimize certain cultural bloopers.

OVERCOMING CROSS-CULTURAL COMMUNICATION BARRIERS

LEARNING OBJECTIVE 3

We have already discussed the importance of overcoming communication barriers in Chapter 4. Cultural differences create additional barriers. Here are some guidelines for overcoming cross-cultural communication barriers.

1. **Be sensitive to the fact that cross-cultural communication barriers exist.** If you are aware of these potential barriers, you will be ready to deal with them. When you are dealing with a person in the workplace with a different cultural background than yours, solicit feedback in order to minimize cross-cultural barriers to communication. Being aware of these potential barriers will help you develop cultural sensitivity.

2. **Show respect for all workers.** The same behavior that promotes good cross-cultural relations in general helps overcome communication barriers. A widely used comment that implies disrespect is to say to another person from another culture, "You have a funny accent." Should you be transposed to that person's culture, you, too, might have a "funny accent."

3. **Use straightforward language and speak slowly and clearly.** When working with people who do not speak your language fluently, speak in an easy-to-understand manner. Minimize the use of idioms and analogies specific to your language. A computer analyst from Greece left confused after a discussion about a software problem with her manager. The manager said, "Let's talk about this another time because *I can't seem to get to first base with you.*" (The manager was referring to the fact that the conversation was headed nowhere because he couldn't come to an agreement with the analyst.) The computer analyst did not ask for clarification because she did not want to appear uninformed.

4. **Observe cultural differences in etiquette.** Violating rules of etiquette without explanation can erect immediate communication barriers. A major rule of etiquette in many countries is that people address superiors by their last name unless they have worked together for a long time. Or, the superior might encourage being on a first-name basis with him or her. Be aware that an increasing number of cultures are moving toward addressing each other and customers by using the first name only. Yet, it is best to error on the side of formality.

Cultural Mistakes to Avoid with Selected Cultural Groups

EUROPE

Great Britain
- Asking personal questions. The British protect their privacy.
- Thinking that a businessperson from England is unenthusiastic when he or she says, "Not bad at all." English people understate their positive emotion.
- Gossiping about royalty.

France
- Expecting to complete work during the French two-hour lunch.
- Attempting to conduct significant business during August—*les vacances* (vacation time).
- Greeting a French person for the first time and not using a title such as "sir," or "madam," or "miss" (*monsieur, madame,* or *mademoiselle*).

Italy
- Eating too much pasta, as it is not the main course.
- Handing out business cards freely. Italians use them infrequently.

Spain
- Expecting punctuality. Your appointments will usually arrive 20 to 30 minutes late.
- Making the American sign for "okay" with your thumb and forefinger. In Spain (and many other countries) this is vulgar.

Scandinavia (Denmark, Sweden, Norway)
- Being overly rank conscious. Scandinavians pay relatively little attention to a person's rank in the hierarchy.

ASIA

All Asian countries
- Pressuring an Asian job applicant or employee to brag about his or her accomplishments. Asians feel self-conscious when boasting about individual accomplishments; they prefer to let the record speak for itself. In addition, they prefer to talk about group rather than individual accomplishment.

Japan
- Shaking hands or hugging Japanese (as well as other Asians) in public. Japanese consider these practices to be offensive.
- Not interpreting "We'll consider it" as a "no" when spoken by a Japanese businessperson. Japanese negotiators mean "no" when they say "We'll consider it."
- Not giving small gifts to Japanese when conducting business. Japanese are offended by not receiving these gifts.
- Giving your business card to a Japanese businessperson more than once. Japanese prefer to give and receive business cards only once.

China
- Using black borders on stationery and business cards, because black is associated with death.
- Giving small gifts to Chinese when conducting business. Chinese are offended by these gifts.
- Making cold calls on Chinese business executives. An appropriate introduction is required for a first-time meeting with a Chinese official.

Korea
- Saying no. Koreans feel it is important to have visitors leave with good feelings.

India
- Telling Indians you prefer not to eat with your hands. If the Indians are not using cutlery when eating, they expect you to do likewise.

Thailand
- It is considered extremely rude to point the soles of your shoes at anyone. (It's not too cool in other countries also.)

MEXICO AND LATIN AMERICA

Mexico
- Flying into a Mexican city in the morning and expecting to close a deal by lunch. Mexicans build business relationships slowly.

Brazil
- Attempting to impress Brazilians by speaking a few words of Spanish. Portuguese is the official language of Brazil.

Most Latin American countries
- Wearing elegant and expensive jewelry during a business meeting. Latin Americans think people should appear more conservative during a business meeting.

Note: A cultural mistake for Americans to avoid when conducting business in most countries outside the United States and Canada is to insist on getting down to business quickly. North Americans in small towns also like to build a relationship before getting down to business. The preceding suggestions will lead to cross-cultural skill development if practiced in the right setting. During the next 30 days, look for an opportunity to relate to a person from another culture in the way described in these suggestions. Observe the reaction of the other person for feedback on your cross-cultural effectiveness.

5. **Be sensitive to differences in nonverbal communication.** Stay alert to the possibility that a person from another culture may misinterpret your nonverbal signal. Hand signals of various types, such as a thumb up or the okay sign to indicate acceptance, are the most liable to misinterpretation. Another key area of cross-cultural differences in nonverbal communication is the handshake. In some cultures, a woman is expected to extend her hand first to shake with a man. In other cultures, people, hug, embrace, or bow instead of shaking hands.[23] (With good cultural sensitivity and cultural intelligence, you can figure out what to do when meeting another person.)

Behavioral mirroring, as described in Chapter 4, is another example of how the effectiveness of nonverbal behavior might be influenced the other person's culture. Three experiments with bank managers required Anglos and Latinos to interact with an interviewer who was trained to mirror the behavior of the interviewee. It was found that Latino interviewees rated interviewers higher who used behavioral mirroring. Also, the Latinos experienced more anxiety when the interviewer did not mirror their behavior. [24] The intercultural explanation for these findings is that Lations, as a group, value nonverbal behavior more than do Anglos. The implication of the experiment for cross-cultural communication is to attempt to determine if you are making appropriate use of nonverbal communication techniques when interacting with a person from another culture.

6. **Do not be diverted by style, accent, grammar, or personal appearance.** Although these superficial factors are all related to business success, they are difficult to interpret when judging a person from another culture. It is therefore better to judge the merits of the statement or behavior.[25] A brilliant individual from another culture may still be learning your language and thus make basic mistakes in speaking your language. Also, he or she might not yet have developed a sensitivity to dress style in your culture.

7. **Be attentive to individual differences in appearance.** A major intercultural insult is to confuse the identity of people because they are members of the same race or ethnic group. An older economics professor reared in China and teaching in the United States had difficulty communicating with students because he was unable to learn their names. The professor's defense was "So many of these Americans look alike to me." Research suggests that people have difficulty seeing individual differences among people of another race because they code race first, such as thinking "He has the nose of an African American." However, people can learn to search for more distinguishing features, such as a dimple or eye color.[26] In this way, individual differences are recognized.

8. **Pronounce correctly the names of people you interact with from other countries.** Communication is much smoother when you correctly pronounce the name of another person. For many Americans, this is a challenging task because they are accustomed to names with one or two syllables that are easy to pronounce, such as Bob or Ann. A trouble spot for many people whose only language is English is that "H" and "J" might be silent in another language.[27] Suppose one of your work or personal associates has the first name "Hyuntak." After listening to his name for the first time, develop a phonetic spelling that will help you pronounce the name in the future. (How about "High-oon-tack"?)

TECHNIQUES FOR IMPROVING CROSS-CULTURAL RELATIONS

LEARNING OBJECTIVE 4

Many training programs have been developed to improve cross-cultural relations and to help workers value diversity. All of the information presented so far in this chapter is likely to be included in such programs. In this section, we describe programs for improving cross-cultural relations, including cultural training, cultural intelligence training, language training, diversity training, and cross-cultural mentoring.

Cultural Training

cultural training

A set of learning experiences designed to help employees understand the customs, traditions, and beliefs of another culture.

For many years, companies and government agencies have prepared their workers for overseas assignments. The method most frequently chosen is **cultural training,** a set of learning experiences designed to help employees understand the customs, traditions, and beliefs of another culture. In today's diverse business environment and international marketplace, learning about individuals raised in different cultural backgrounds has become more important. Many industries therefore train employees in cross-cultural relations.

Mexican Call Center Workers Learn to Deal Effectively with Americans

In a high-rise office building, one dozen young Mexicans are studying the customs of a country most of them have never visited. One by one, the students present their conclusions about the United States. "Americans think Mexicans eat mostly tacos and drink Margaritas everyday. They give big tips if they like you. Unless they are Latino-Americans, they probably speak only one language." says Maria. "People are self-centered. The average American uses a credit card even to pay for lunch in a restaurant," says Hugo.

The Mexicans, who range in age from 20 to 29, have been hired to take calls from confused or angry Americans who are having a functioning problem with their prepaid cell phone. The problem could be technical, or relating to customer service problem such as their prepaid minutes not being accurately recorded or their phone being shut down. The cell phone company works on a slim profit margin, so it cannot afford to maintain a tech support and customer service center in the United States. The company offers a Web site for providing technical support and customer service, yet many customers feel the need to interact with a live person.

To communicate with the Americans, the Mexican workers must communicate in their second language but a culture that is foreign. "We're not saying that Mexico is better or the United States is better," says their trainer, Tanya. "We just want our tech support staff to develop cultural awareness so there is better rapport when someone calls in for help."

Call centers for inexpensive cell phone service took root in Mexico when the demand for mobile phones skyrocketed in the mid-2000s, yet many people did not have good enough credit to purchase traditional cell phone service. Large prepaid cell phone providers like Tracfone wanted to provide the best tech support they could yet still remain profitable.

At first, training at the tech support centers and customer service centers was simple. The centers gave employees names that were easy for Americans to understand such as Pedro, Suzie, Maria, and Bob in cases where they had names difficult for Americans to pronounce. The new hires were instructed to watch American television shows to get an idea of American pop culture. In this way, if there was a waiting period during the help session, they could make a few minutes of small talk.

Shortly after the support center was established, problems in dealing with the Americans began to surface. Although the customers were paying the minimum price possible for cell phone service, they were often quite demanding and aggressive. One man swore at the customer service rep because he couldn't figure out how to use his phone to make a call to Ontario, Canada. Roberta, the recipient of the outrage, attempted to explain that instructions on how to telephone Canada from the United States are presented on page 8 of the manual that comes with the phone. A woman kept calling another rep a "stupid fool" because the rep couldn't understand her problem having to do with not being credited for enough minutes.

The Mexican support staff felt uncomfortable in being too firm with belligerent customers. Instead of being assertive about the company's position on a particular problem, the reps tended to be too conciliatory, often blaming the company for the problem. However, being conciliatory did not result in customers being totally satisfied. Problems were often left unresolved. As a result, the prepaid cell phone service company noticed that renewal rates were slipping. A renewal in this sense is a customer purchasing more minutes at a store or through the company Web site.

The cell phone company hired a firm that offers cultural training to help the Mexican call center workers deal more effectively with upset American customers. (Tanya was the trainer assigned to the account.) The workers were given careful instructions on how to express sympathy, using phrases such as "I am sorry that you are having this problem. I know that your phone is important to you." When a customer is explosively angry, the call center workers were coached on how to let the customer finish the outburst, and then say, "I hear that you are upset. But let us see how we can get this problem solved."

New hires as well as experienced employees were also taught to defend the company when the company is right. For example, to fix a technical problem such as the voicemail feature not working, the caller usually has to key in a long series of numbers. A frustrated customer often has difficulty with such a task. To deal with the frustration, the call center worker is taught to say something like, "Please try entering the numbers again slowly and carefully." If the customer enters the sequence of numbers incorrectly again, the worker is coached on how to be assertive, such as "This method does work. If you want to fix your phone, you have to do it carefully."

Many customer complaints that get back to the company deal with not being able to understand the English spoken by the call center workers. So the Mexican workers are coached on how to speak key English words with a general American accent. For example, instead of saying "She-ca-go" for "Chicago," the worker is taught to say "Sha-ca-go." And the workers are coached to pronounce "nine" as "nyne" instead of "neen."

Questions

1. What do you see as a major cultural difference between Mexicans and Americans that make the call center job so challenging for Mexicans?
2. Some of the call center representatives in Mexico are instructed to identify themselves as students in Kansas City, in addition to giving them American first names. What is your take on the ethics of these disguises?

Source: Case history collected from human resource specialist at the mobile phone company in question.

Cultural training is also important for helping people of one culture understand their customers from another culture in particular, such as Chinese people learning to deal more effectively with their American customers. For example, in one training program Chinese businesspeople are taught how to sprinkle their e-mail with English phrases like "How are you?" "It was great to hear from you," and "Can we work together?"[28]

The Job-Oriented Interpersonal Skills in Action Box describes how cultural training can improve the effectiveness of establishing call centers overseas.

To practice improving your cross-cultural relations, do Skill-Building Exercise 8-3.

Cross-Cultural Relations Role-Play

One student plays the role of Ritu, a call center representative in New Delhi, India. Her specialty is helping customers with cell phone problems. Another student plays the role of Todd, an irate American. His problem is that he cannot get his camera-equipped cell phone to transmit his photos over e-mail. He is scheduled to attend a party in two hours, and wants to take loads of photos with his cell phone. Todd is impatient, and in the eyes of Ritu,

somewhat overbearing. Ritu is good natured and pleasant, but feels she must help Todd solve his problem without being bullied by him. Because Ritu is instructed to spend the minimum time necessary to resolve the problem, she spends about five minutes on this problem.

The observers should make note of how well Ritu has made the necessary cross-cultural adaptations.

Cultural Intelligence Training

A new development in assisting people work more effectively with workers in other cultures is *cultural intelligence training*, a program based on the principles of cultural intelligence described earlier in this chapter. A key part of the training is to learn the three contributors to CQ—head, heart, and body. Instead of learning a few simple guidelines for working effectively with people from another culture, the trainee is taught strategies for sizing up the environment to determine which course of action is best. The culturally intelligent overseas worker would learn how to determine how much humor to interject into meetings, what kind of handshake is most appropriate, and so forth. The following excerpt will give you a feel for what is involved in cultural intelligence training:

> *A Canadian manager is attempting to interpret a "Thai smile." First, she needs to observe the various cues provided in addition to the smile gesture itself (e.g., other facial or bodily gestures, significance of others who may be in proximity, the source of the original smile gesture) and to assemble them into a meaningful whole and make sense of what is really experienced by the Thai employee. Second, she must have the requisite motivation (directed effort and self-confidence) to persist in the face of confusion, challenge, or apparently mixed signals. Third, she must choose, generate, and execute the right actions to respond appropriately.*
>
> *If any of these elements is deficient, she is likely to be ineffective in dealing with the Thai employee. A high CQ manager has the capability with all three facets as they action in unison.*[29]

As the example illustrates, to be culturally intelligent you need to apply cognitive skills, have the right motivation, and then put your knowledge and confidence into action. Armed with such skills you would know, for example, whether to greet a Mexican worker on a business trip to Texas with a handshake, a hug, or a kiss on both cheeks.

Language Training

Learning a foreign language is often part of cultural training, yet it can also be a separate activity. Knowledge of a second language is important because it builds better connections with people from other cultures than does relying on a translator. Building connections with people is still important even if English has become the international language of business. Many workers, aside from international business specialists, also choose to develop skills in a target language. Speaking another language can help build rapport with customers and employees who speak that language. As mentioned earlier, it is easier to sell to customers when using their native language.

Almost all language training has elements similar to taking a course in another language or self-study. Companies invest heavily in helping employees learn a target language because it facilitates conducting business in other countries. For this reason, companies

Using the Internet to Help Develop Foreign Language Skills

A useful way of developing skills in another language, and learning more about another culture, is to create a computer "bookmark," "favorite," or front page written in your target language. In this way, each time you go to the Internet on your own computer, your cover page will contain fresh information in the language you want to develop.

Enter a search word such as "Italian newspaper" or "Spanish language newspaper" in the search probe. After you find a suitable choice, enter the edit function for "Favorites" or "Bookmarks" and insert that newspaper as your front page. For example, imagine that French is your target language and culture. The search engine

might have brought you to the site http://www.france2.fr. This Web site keeps you abreast of French and international news, sports, and cultural events—written in French. Every time you access the Internet, you can spend five minutes on your second language, thereby becoming multicultural. Another advantage is that your foreign-language site is likely to present brief videos, giving you an opportunity to hear your target language. You can save a lot of travel costs and time using the Internet to help you become multi-cultural, including developing proficiency in another language. You might be able to find an app for your smart phone for learning another language by linking to an appropriate Web site.

that offer language training and translation services are currently experiencing a boom. Medical specialists, police officers, and firefighters also find second language skills to be quite helpful because clients under stress, such as an injured person, are likely to revert to their native tongue. Learning a second language is particularly important when many of your customers and employees do not speak your country's official language. For example, Casa Rio, in San Antonio, Texas, found that its English speaking managers were unable to communicate with Spanish-speaking employees regarding benefits and other issues.[30]

Skill-Building Exercise 8-4 presents a low-cost, pleasant method of enhancing your foreign language and cross-cultural skills.

As with any other skill training, investments in language training can pay off only if the trainee is willing to work hard at developing the new skill outside the training sessions. Allowing even 10 days to pass without practicing your target language will result in a sharp decline in your ability to use that language.

Diversity Training

The general purpose of cultural training is to help workers understand people from other cultures. Understanding can lead to dealing more effectively with them as work associates or customers. **Diversity training** has a slightly different purpose. It attempts to bring about workplace harmony by teaching people how to get along better with diverse work associates. Quite often the program is aimed at minimizing open expressions of racism and sexism. In recent years, diversity training has acquired the additional goal of accepting all dimensions of diversity based on the belief that enhanced business performance will result. For example, learning how to relate effectively to diverse customers can increase sales.[31]

diversity training

Training that attempts to bring about workplace harmony by teaching people how to get along better with diverse work associates.

Forms of Diversity Training.   Diversity training takes a number of forms. Nevertheless, all center on increasing awareness of and empathy for people who are different in some noticeable way from oneself. Training sessions in appreciating cultural diversity focus on the ways that men and women or people of different races reflect different values, attitudes, and cultural backgrounds. These sessions can vary from several hours to several days. Training sessions can also be held over a long period of time. Sometimes the program is confrontational, sometimes not.

An essential part of relating more effectively to diverse groups is to empathize with their points of view. To help training participants develop empathy, representatives of various groups explain their feelings related to workplace issues, including how they have felt different in a way that made them feel uncomfortable. A representative segment of a training program designed to enhance empathy took the following format. A minority group member was seated at the middle of a circle. First, the coworkers listened to a Vietnamese woman explaining how she felt excluded from the in-group composed of whites and

Class members come up to the front of the room one by one and give a brief presentation (perhaps even three minutes) of any way in which they have been perceived as different, and how they felt about this perception. Sometimes this exercise is referred to as "When I Felt Different." The difference refers to feeling different from the majority. The difference can be of any kind, relating to characteristics such as ethnicity, race, choice of major, physical appearance, height, weight, hair color, or body piercing. After each member of the class (perhaps even the instructor) has presented, class members discuss what they learned from the exercise. It is also important to discuss how this exercise can improve relationships on the job.

African Americans in her department. "I feel like you just tolerate me. You do not make me feel that I am somebody important." The next person to sit in the middle of the circle was a Muslim. He complained about people wishing him Merry Christmas. "I would much prefer that my coworkers stop to think that I do not celebrate Christian holidays. I respect your religion, but it is not my religion."

Another form of diversity training is cross-generational diversity, or relating effectively to workers much older or younger than you. Cross-generational awareness training is one component in the corporate training program. The premise behind the program is that after acquiring cognitive knowledge, engaging in dialogue, and role-playing, employees will learn to accept people's differences, some of which are age driven. For example, younger employees might feel less guilty than would seniors when calling in sick just to have a day's vacation. Another part of cross-generational training would be to help older and younger generations appreciate their different preferences in communication. An example would be sending e-mails versus text messages for disseminating brief bits of information.

Concerns about Diversity Training. Diversity training has frequently improved cross-cultural relationships in the workplace. Yet such programs can also create ill will and waste time. One problem is that participants are sometimes encouraged to be too confrontational and express too much hostility. Companies have found that when employees are too blunt during these sessions, it may be difficult to patch up interpersonal relations in the work group later on.

Another potential negative consequence of diversity training is that it sometimes results in perpetuating stereotypes about groups, such as people from Latin America not placing much value on promptness for meetings. A related problem is that diversity training might focus too much on differences instead of similarities.[32] For example, even if people are raised with different cultural values, they must all work harmoniously together to accomplish work. Although a worker believes that relationships are more important than profits, he or she must still produce enough to be a good investment for the company.

Skill-Building Exercise 8-5 provides you an opportunity to simulate an empathy-building experience in a diversity training program.

Cross-Cultural and Cross-Gender Mentoring Programs

An advanced method of improving cross-cultural relations is mentoring members of targeted minority groups. The mentoring demonstrates the company's interest in enhancing cross-cultural relations, and simultaneously enhances the minority group member's opportunities for advancement. To achieve cross-culture and cross-gender mentoring, companies often assign the member of the minority group a mentor who is typically an experienced manager. For example, a 24-year-old African-American woman might be mentored by a 45-year-old Caucasian middle manager. Or, a minority group member could be the mentor, such as a 45-year-old African-American woman mentoring a 24-year-old Indian man.

As described in Chapter 12, mentors might help the person being mentored in such ways as making the right contacts, and learning useful professional skills. A challenge noted with cross-cultural and cross-gender mentoring is a shortage of mentors with the right knowledge and interpersonal skills.

Sprint started a trial mentoring program with 50 employees at company headquarters. Although open to all employees, the program targeted minority groups. Soon the program had 500 participants. "The demand was overwhelming," says Tammy Edwards, director of inclusion and diversity," who became a mentor to several employees. She adds that the mentee (person who is mentored) became so large that each mentor is paired with up to five mentees.[33]

SELF-ASSESSMENT QUIZZES IN OVERVIEW

Self-Assessment Quiz 8-1 provides a reminder of your cross-cultural skills and attitudes mostly based on previous experiences. As you develop more exposure to cross-cultural relations, your score is likely to increase. The weight given to knowing a second language is an alert to its importance in the modern world even though English has become the official language of business and science. Self-Assessment Quiz 8-2 asks you to assess a finer point about cross-cultural relations—where you stand on nine key cross-cultural dimensions. A subtle point here is that people from the same culture often vary widely on these dimensions despite stereotypes of the average person from that culture. For example, many Mexicans have an urgent time orientation, and many Americans have a casual time orientation.

Concept Review and Reinforcement

Key Terms

cultural sensitivity 162
cultural intelligence (CQ) 162

cultural fluency 165
cultural training 170

diversity training 173

Summary

Today's workplace has become more culturally diverse, and business has become increasingly international. As a result, to succeed one must be able to relate effectively to people from different cultural groups from within and outside one's country. The true meaning of valuing diversity is to respect and enjoy a wide range of cultural and individual differences. The diversity umbrella continues to include more people as the workforce encompasses a greater variety of people.

A diverse workforce brings potential advantages to the organization, including higher creativity, more profits because of a demographic match with customers, and overall business prosperity. Cultural diversity within groups can lead to conflict. Results suggest that relations-oriented diversity leads to high performance in service industry settings.

The groundwork for developing effective cross-cultural relations is to understand cultural differences. Six key aspects of understanding cultural differences are (1) cultural sensitivity including political correctness, (2) cultural intelligence, (3) respect for all workers and all cultures, (4) cultural fluency—the ability to conduct business in a diverse and international environment, (5) differences in cultural dimensions, and (6) avoidance of cultural bloopers. Cultural intelligence is based on cognitive, emotional/motivational, and physical (taking action) factors.

Countries differ in their national values or cultural dimensions, leading to differences in how most people from a given country will react to situations. The dimensions studied here are (1) performance orientation, (2) assertiveness, (3) time orientation, (4) human orientation, (5) in-group collectivism, (6) gender egalitarianism, (7) acceptance of power and authority, (8) work orientation, and (9) social support seeking.

An effective way of being culturally sensitive is to minimize actions that are likely to offend people from another culture based on their values. These cultural bloopers can take place when working in another country or when dealing with foreigners in one's own country. Studying potential cultural bloopers is helpful, but recognize also that individual differences may be of significance.

Communication barriers created by cultural differences can often be overcome by the following: (1) Be sensitive to the fact that these barriers exist; (2) show respect for all workers; (3) use straightforward language and speak slowly and clearly; (4) observe cultural differences in etiquette; (5) be sensitive to differences in nonverbal communication; (6) do not be diverted by style, accent, grammar, or personal appearance; (7) be attentive to individual differences in appearance, and (8) pronounce correctly the names of people you interact with from other countries.

Cultural training is a set of learning experiences designed to help employees understand the customs, traditions, and beliefs of another culture. In today's diverse business environment and international marketplace, learning about individuals raised in different cultural backgrounds has become more important. Cultural intelligence training includes developing strategies for sizing up the environment to determine which course of action is best. Learning a foreign language is often part of cultural training, yet it can also be a separate activity.

Diversity training attempts to bring about workplace harmony by teaching people how to get along better with diverse work associates. Another goal of diversity training is to improve business performance. Most forms of diversity training center on increasing awareness of and empathy for people who are different in some noticeable way from you. Cross-cultural and cross-gender mentoring are advanced methods of improving cross-cultural relations. The minority group member or woman is assigned a mentor who helps the person advance in his or her career.

Questions for Discussion and Review

1. What is your evaluation of the fairness of Walgreens expecting workers with physical disabilities to attain the same productivity goals as those of able-bodied workers?

2. What can you do this week to sharpen your cross-cultural skills?

3. Some companies, such as Singapore Airlines, make a deliberate effort for all customer-contact personnel to be of the same ethnic group (Singapore natives). How is this practice justified in an era of cultural diversity and valuing differences?

4. Provide an example of cultural insensitivity of any kind that you have seen, read about, or could imagine.

5. What have you personally observed about Asians and Asian Americans being less likely to ask for social support when they are facing a difficult problem?

6. Many workers in the United States who were born in other countries assign themselves short names, easy-to-pronounce by Americans, such as "Joe" and "Sue." What do you see as the pros and cons of this practice of shortening a foreign name?

7. How useful is the adage "When in Rome, do as the Romans do" for someone who wants to work in another country for a while?

8. If you were a supervisor, how would you deal with a group member who had a very low acceptance of power and authority?

9. The cultural bloopers presented in Skill-Building Exercise 8-2 all dealt with errors people make in regard to people who are not American. Give an example of a cultural blooper a person from another country might make in the United States.

10. Many people speak loudly to other people who are deaf, blind, and those who speak a different language. Based on the information presented in this chapter, what mistakes are these people making?

The Web Corner

http://www.DiversityInc.com
(Extensive information including videos about cultural diversity in organizations.)

http://www.berlitz.com
(Information about language training and cultural training in countries throughout the world. Investigate in your second language to enhance the cross-cultural experience.)

Internet Skill Builder: Avoiding Cultural Insensitivity

One of the most effective ways of hampering relationships with people of another culture is to be grossly insensitive. If you can avoid these gross errors, you will be on your way toward at least acceptable relationships with people from another domestic or foreign culture. Two examples of cultural insensitivity uncovered on the Internet are: In Alberta, Canada, a sign in the window of a large chain restaurant read, "No drunken Indians allowed." Wal-Mart performed poorly in Germany because it did not recognize the cultural fact that Germans do not like to spend a lot of time shopping by walking through a giant store and waiting on line. Search the Internet for examples of cultural insensitivity. You may have to dig hard to find these nuggets of insensitivity, but the activity will help you become more culturally sensitive and aware.

Developing Your Human Relations Skills

Interpersonal Relations Case 8.1

What to Do with Shabana?

Shabana was raised in Pakistan and graduated from the University of Punjab with a major in commerce. She then moved to Chicago, Illinois, to live with her married aunt, as well as to begin a career in business in the United States. Shabana is fluent in her native Punjabi, but also has spoken and written English since the beginning of her primary education.

Having a sponsor in the United States made it possible for Shabana to enter the job market in Chicago. In addition to having a good formal education, Shabana makes a positive physical appearance that includes a warm smile, and a comfortable, relaxed manner. After a two-month long job search, Shabana found employment as a store associate in a cell-phone store of one of the major mobile phone providers. She was content with this position because she thought it would be a stepping stone to store management in the field of consumer electronics.

Shabana enjoyed interacting with the other store associates, as well as the customers. An important part of her role was explaining some of the intricacies of cell phones, as well as the contracts, to customers. She willingly worked Saturday nights and Sunday afternoons, store hours unpopular with other associates.

From time to time, Shabana was perplexed as to why some customers did not understand her. With a few of the older customers, Shabana attributed their lack of understanding to limited knowledge of technology, or hearing impairments. One customer looked straight at Shabana and said, "I do understand a word you are saying."

One day Trevor, the store manager, took Shabana aside and told her, "You are a wonderful sales associate in many ways. The other associates enjoy working with you, and you get along well with many of our customers. Yet we are getting too many complaints by e-mail and phone that many of our customers cannot understand you. It seems like some of these Chicago people just can't understand English with a Pakistani accent."

"Maybe some of our customers aren't the most sophisticated, but they are still customers. And we need every dollar we can take it to meet our sales goals. You need to become better understood by all our customers, or we can't keep you as a sales associate."

A little perplexed, Shabana replied, "I am so sorry to know that I have disappointed you and some of our valued customers. Please give me several weeks to correct this situation of my not being so well understood by all our customers."

Trevor replied, "Okay, but I am going to keep close watch on your progress."

Case Questions

1. What should Shabana do to improve her ability to be understood by more customers?
2. Is the problem of language comprehension in this case really a problem of customers not being too sharp mentally?
3. What actions do you recommend that Trevor take to help Shabana improve her ability to be understood by her customers? Or, should he just fire her?
4. To what extent do you think Trevor is practicing job discrimination by even hinting that he might fire Shabana if she is not better understood by a wider variety of customers?

Interpersonal Relations Case 8.2

Akiak Wants to Fit In

Akiak Nori was raised in Noorvik, Alaska, and then attended a career school in Juneau, Alaska, majoring in electronic technology. Approaching graduation, he sorted out dozens of job offers he had obtained, several of which did not even require an in-person interview.

Akiak accepted a position with a construction company in International Falls, Minnesota, because of the job opportunities and the long brisk winters that would be natural and comfortable for him. He was assigned to a construction team for new buildings, and was also assigned maintenance work for existing electronic systems in office buildings, factories, and mills.

Akiak's goal from the first day on the job was to perform well and fit in with his coworkers. He recognized that fitting in with a non-Eskimo group would require some patience on his part. Akiak had been counseled by several teachers that patience was not one of his strong points.

During employee orientation, two other new employees asked Akiak if his name meant kayak in Eskimo language. With a smile, Akiak replied, "No, it means brave. I guess my parents thought I would have to be brave to grow up in Noorvik, where you have to be tough to survive."

Later that morning, Akiak was asked if ice fishing and seal hunting were his two favorite sports. "Not at all," said Akiak, "We had a first-rate hockey rink in town, so I got to love hockey. And, I'm a Minnesota Viking (professional football team) fan. That's why I took a job in Minnesota." (Said with a smile.)

During lunch, Mary, another new employee, asked Akiak, "Tell me Akiak, are you an Eskimo? Or are you an Inuit? I don't want to make a mistake."

Akiak responded, "It's no mistake to call me an Eskimo. It's no mistake to call me an Inuit. Some people think that the term Eskimo is wrong, and that we should be called Inuit. It doesn't matter to me or to my friends and family. We like both terms."

"Yet, Mary, the mistake you are making is not thinking of me as just another American. Alaska is one of the 50 states. We vote. We pay and receive Social Security. And, we learn English in school, and we eat at McDonalds."

"I'm sorry," said Mary. "I was just trying to be friendly."

Ned, the supervisor of the orientation program, said to the group. "I think we have asked Akiak enough about his cultural heritage for now. Yet, I have just one favor to ask Akiak. I wish he would show us how he positions his arm, head, and body to spear a big fish."

Akiak said with a sarcastic tone, "Time out. I'm taking a break from this orientation right now. I have to go back to my igloo and chew on some frozen fish."

Case Questions

1. What does this case tell us about cultural sensitivity?
2. How might have Akiak's coworkers related better to him during the orientation?
3. How might have Akiak done a better job of relating to his new coworkers so far?
4. Does Akiak have an *attitude* (meaning negative attitude problem)?

Interpersonal Skills Role-Play

Building a Relationship with an Eskimo Electronic Technician

Several class members play the role of new workers at the company in International Falls, Minnesota, as described in the case presented above. One of the other new workers is Akiak Nori. You want to welcome him, and help him feel part of the group. At the same time, you believe that recognizing his Eskimo heritage would be part of showing respect for his culture. Yet, you do not want to be patronizing or make Akiak feel that he is unusual. Another student plays the role of Akiak who regards himself as an American, yet is also proud of his Eskimo heritage.

Conduct this role-play for about seven minutes. Observers rate the role players on two dimensions, using a 1-to-5 scale from very poor to very good. One dimension is "effective use of human relations techniques." Focus on the cross-cultural sensitivity of the workers attempting to build a relationship with Akiak. Also provide feedback about Akiak's interpersonal skills. The second dimension is "acting ability." A few observers might voluntarily provide feedback to the role players in terms of sharing their ratings and observations. The course instructor might also provide feedback.

Resolving Conflicts with Others

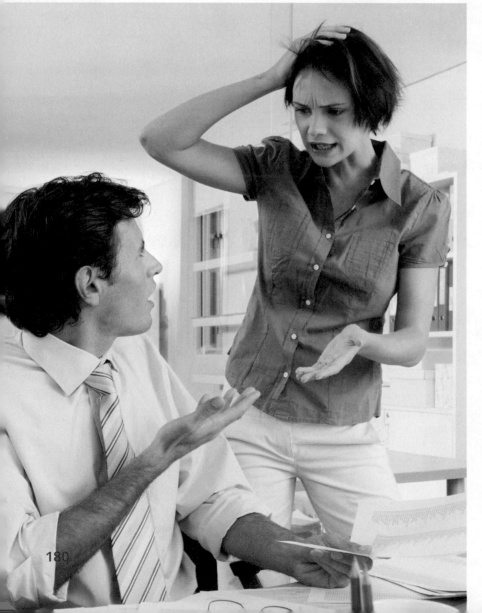

Karen was one of five members of a group of workers who repaired and installed desktop and laptop computers for individuals and small businesses. Her company, Elite Computers, also installed new software and repaired virus damage. Karen enjoyed the technical challenges in her work, as well as the opportunity to work directly with a variety of clients and provide them valuable assistance.

A major challenge facing Karen and her teammates was that some of the on-site repair work had to be done on Saturdays and Sundays to accommodate clients who worked on weekends as well as weekdays. When their computer is down, some clients could not wait until Monday for an Elite technician to begin the repairs.

One of Karen's teammates, Charlie, seemed to often have an excuse for not making a weekend client visit when it was his turn. Several times Charlie sent Karen an urgent text message saying that he or a family member was sick, and that he needed Karen to take the service call for him. Each time, Charlie ended his message with "Please help. I'll return the favor later."

One Friday at 8 a.m. Karen received a voice message from Charlie that read, "One of our biggest clients, Silver Motor Sales, has a system breakdown, and needs help this morning. It could be a virus attack. I have to take my brother to the emergency room. Please go to Silver Motors for me, ASAP."

Karen thought, "This dependency of Charlie on me has gotten out of hand. I don't know if he is lying. But if our team screws up with Silver Motors, we will all look bad. Maybe I should call Fred (the team leader). I think Charlie is taking advantage of me. I've got to work on my problem with him."

After reading and studying this chapter and doing the exercises, you should be able to

1. Specify why so much interpersonal conflict exists in organizations.
2. Recognize your typical method of resolving conflict.
3. Identify the five styles of handling conflict.
4. Acquire effective techniques for resolving conflict and negotiating.
5. Understand how to combat sexual harassment in the workplace.

The situation of computer repair technicians Karen and Charlie illustrates how so often it becomes imperative to resolve conflicts with a coworker to fix an intolerable problem. This chapter will help you improve your ability to resolve conflicts with people at work. The same techniques are also useful in personal life. To improve your understanding of how to resolve conflict, this chapter will present specific techniques and also explain why so much conflict exists. To get you started relating the topic of conflict to you, take Self-Assessment Quiz 9-1.

SOURCES OF INTERPERSONAL CONFLICT IN ORGANIZATIONS

A **conflict** is a situation in which two or more goals, values, or events are incompatible or mutually exclusive. A conflict is also a strife, quarrel, or battle, such as would be the case if computer repair technician Karen told Charlie he was a lazy jerk, and he replied that she was callous and unfeeling about his problems.

Conflict between and among people has many sources, or causes. In this section, I describe six of the leading sources. A seventh category, workplace violence, is both a cause and a consequence of conflict. If you understand the cause of a conflict, it can help you resolve the conflict and help prevent a similar recurrence. For example, if you learn that much conflict on the job is caused by people being uncivil toward each other, you might remind yourself to behave civilly. You can also learn how to deal with uncivil coworkers so that they treat you less rudely. Although specific sources of conflict can be identified, keep in mind an important fact—all conflict includes the underlying theme of incompatibility between your goals, values, or events and those of another person.

Competition for Limited Resources

An underlying source of job conflict is that few people can get all the resources they want. These resources include money, material, and human resources. Conflicts arise when two or more people squabble over who should get the resources. Even in a prosperous organization, resources have to be divided in such a manner that not everybody gets what he or she wants.

Assume that you believe you need to have a document scanner immediately accessible the full workday. Yet the company has decided that 10 people must share one scanner. As a result, you are likely to enter into conflict with the coworkers sharing the scanner. The conflict will be intense if several of your coworkers also think they need full-time access to a scanner.

In recent years, news magazines have been able to resolve the competition for limited resources that had taken place among reporters. In the past, reporters would squabble about getting their share of space for their stories in the magazines. *Newsweek* writer Jonathan Alter said, "The old fight over space is different than it was. If there's no room in the magazine for something, you can just do it online."[1]

Role Conflict

A major source of conflict (and stress) on the job relates to being placed in a predicament. **Role conflict** stems from having to choose between two competing demands or expectations.

LEARNING OBJECTIVE 1

conflict

A situation in which two or more goals, values, or events are incompatible or mutually exclusive.

role conflict

The situation that occurs when a person has to choose between two competing demands or expectations.

SELF-ASSESSMENT QUIZ 9-1

Collaborative versus Competitive Styles of Conflict Management

Answer on a 1-to-5 scale how well you agree with each of the following statements: Disagree strongly; disagree; neutral; agree; agree strongly.

		Disagree Strongly	Disagree	Neutral	Agree	Agree Strongly
1.	I like to see the other side squirm when I resolve a dispute.	5	4	3	2	1
2.	Winning is everything when it comes to settling conflict.	5	4	3	2	1
3.	After I have successfully negotiated a price, I like to see the seller smile.	1	2	3	4	5
4.	I have a "smash-mouth" attitude toward resolving conflict.	5	4	3	2	1
5.	In most conflict situations, one side is clearly right, and the other side is clearly wrong.	1	2	3	4	5
6.	I think there are effective alternatives to strikes for settling union versus management disputes.	1	2	3	4	5
7.	The winner should take all.	5	4	3	2	1
8.	Conflict on the job is like a prize fight: The idea is to knock out the opponent.	5	4	3	2	1
9.	I like the idea of tournaments in which first-round losers receive another opportunity to play.	1	2	3	4	5
10.	Nice guys and gals usually finish first.	1	2	3	4	5

Scoring and Interpretation: Add the point value of your scores to obtain your total. Scores of 40 and higher suggest that you prefer a *collaborative*, or *win–win*, approach to resolving conflict. You tend to be concerned about finding long-term solutions to conflict that will provide benefits to both sides. Scores of 39 and lower suggest that you prefer a *competitive* approach to resolving conflict. You want to maximize gain for yourself, with little concern about the welfare of the other side.

If you comply with one aspect of a role, compliance with the other is difficult or impossible. An important example would be receiving contradictory orders from two people above you in your company. If you comply with the wishes of one person, you will antagonize the other. A higher-ranking manager might encourage as many employees as possible to work from home a few days per week. In contrast, your own manager demands that you be on the work premises full time.

Role conflict can take various forms. You might be asked to accomplish two objectives that are in apparent conflict. If your boss asks you to hurry up and finish your work but also decrease your mistakes, you would experience the conflict of incompatible demands (plus perhaps a headache!). Another problem is when two or more people give you incompatible directions. Your immediate supervisor may want you to complete a crash project on time, but company policy temporarily prohibits authorizing overtime payments to clerical help or hiring office temporaries.

Role conflict also results when two different roles that you play are in conflict. Your company may expect you to travel 50 percent of the time, whereas your spouse threatens a divorce if you travel over 25 percent of the time. To complete the picture, *role–person conflict* takes place when the role(s) your organization expects you to occupy is in conflict with your basic values. Your company may ask you to fire the bottom 10 percent of performers, but this could be in conflict with your humanistic values.

Competing Work and Family Demands

Balancing the demands of career and family life has become a major role conflict facing today's workforce. Caring about work and family responsibilities is more likely to intensify work-family conflict. The challenge is particularly intense for employees who are part of a two-wage-earner family. **Work-family conflict** occurs when an individual's roles of worker and active participant in social and family life compete with one another. This type of conflict is frequent because the multiple roles are often incompatible. Imagine having planned to attend your child's solo recital and then being ordered at the last minute to be present at an after-hours meeting. Work-family conflict can lead to interpersonal conflict because your boss or coworkers might think that you are asking them to cover for you while you attend to personal matters.

Work-to-Family and Family-to-Work Conflict. Work-family conflict can be viewed from two perspectives, with both leading to conflict and stress. A person's work can interfere with family responsibilities, or family responsibilities can interfere with work. In the above example, the person might say, "This is terrible. The meeting called for at the last minute will block me from attending my child's solo recital." Or, the same person might say, "This is terrible. My child's solo recital is going to block me from attending an important last-minute meeting."

An analysis of many scientific studies on the subject found that work demands can create some stress and low satisfaction at home, and that personal demands can create some stress and low satisfaction on the job.[2] Have you ever noticed that problems at work or school can negatively influence personal life? Have you also noticed that problems in personal life can negatively influence work or school?

Another study investigated the effect of work-family conflict on the emotions of guilt and hostility among employed adults. The study also explored how work-family conflict, guilt, and hostility affected job satisfaction and marital satisfaction. It was found that work-to-family conflict and family-to-work conflict led to guilt and hostility at work and at home, respectively. A sidelight finding of interest to the study of human relations is that hostile people suffer even more conflict at home and on the job.[3]

The Issue of Work-Life Choices. A continuing debate exists over whether a person can give equal balance between work and family life, and still advance far in his or her career. If getting far in your field requires 60 hours per week of hardwork, you might not be able to meet that demand and still be a full contributor to family life. Jack Welch, former GE chief executive and now business writer and educator, told participants at a human resources conference, "There are work-life choices, and you make them, and they have consequences."[4]

Another issue related to work-life choices is that when managers perceive subordinates to be experiencing family-work conflict, there is a tendency for the bosses to think that the subordinate is not a good candidate for promotion. A study with supervisors in a large transportation company found that managers tended to categorize women as experiencing greater family-work conflict even when the women did not perceive themselves to have much family-work conflict. As a result, the managers downgraded their perception of the women supervisors fit for the job, as well as their promotability.[5] Even if the managers' perceptions were biased, the supervisors still had to deal with these misperceptions.

Making a work-life (or work-family) choice can sometimes reduce conflict. It is helpful to develop a general guideline about how much time a person wants to invest in both work and family life, and then be satisfied with the compromise. Certain types of careers have to be excluded in order to spend most evenings and weekend in family and other personal activities. For example, to be a successful small business owner or a Wall Street financial analyst typically requires working between 60 and 70 hours per week. From the opposite standpoint, certain types of social activities have to be controlled to attain career success. An adult who wants to play video games and visit social networking sites for a combined nine hours per day will not succeed in most careers. After choices are made about type of work and type of personal life activities, work-family conflict will be minimized.

Company Initiatives to Reduce Work-Family Conflict. Companies can often avoid or minimize serious work-family conflict among employees by implementing equitable time-off policies. The underlying company attitude is that all employees need a work-life balance. Encouraging such an atmosphere of good will among coworkers can help prevent conflicts and resentments when one employee leaves early to take care of family responsibility.[6]

Many companies offer flexible working hours to a majority of their employees. In this way, a worker might be able to meet family demands that take place during typical working hours. An example would be taking off the morning to care for an ill parent, and working later that same evening to make up the time. People who are exceptionally good at organizing their time and efforts will often experience less work-family conflict, by such behaviors as staying on top of work to minimize periods of time when they are completely work-centered.[7]

During the Great Recession of 2008–2010, many companies reduced programs designed to reduce work-family conflict. A 2008 survey of human resource professionals found that only 20 percent of their organizations planned to implement policies aimed at encouraging a better work-family balance.[8] Furthermore, many employees hesitated to make such demands as flexible working hours or working from home because they worried about being fired for being not committed enough to the job. Long vacations were also avoided out of fear that if the company can get by without you during your vacation, why keep you on the payroll?

Personality Clashes

Many workplace disagreements arise because people simply dislike each other. A **personality clash** is thus an antagonistic relationship between two people based on differences in personal attributes, preferences, interests, values, and styles. A personality clash reflects negative chemistry between two people, whereas personal differences are based more specifically on a value clash. According to the research of psychologist Judith Sills, the most commonly reported office problem is the personality conflict. One of the most frequent conflicts is between the sweeping big picture person and the cautious detail-oriented person.[9] The big-picture concern manager might say, "Give me a general idea of ticket sales for the Dixie Chicks," expecting a response like "Might even have a full house with luck." Instead, the detail-oriented person says, "Last time I checked we had 37,431 tickets sold."

People involved in a personality clash often have difficulty specifying why they dislike each other. The end result, however, is that they cannot maintain an amiable work relationship. A peculiarity about personality clashes is that people who get along well may begin to clash after working together for a number of years. A contributing factor is that as both people change and as the situation changes, the two people may no longer be compatible. An example of a personality clash in the executive suite took place a few years ago at Motorola Corp, as follows:

> Paul Liska, the chief financial officer, came into a board meeting and heavily criticized the company's ailing mobile phone unit. Liska's pointed criticisms were seen as a stab against Sanjay Jha, the head of the mobile division who had been recently hired by Motorola. Liska had objected to his appointment. Shortly after his tirade, Liska was fired. The company claimed in a filing, "Mr. Liska developed what now appears to be a vendetta against Dr. Jha and the Mobile Devices business." An attorney who has litigated similar cases said that Motorola would have a difficult time getting the jury to accept that Liska's firing was for a legitimate cause. "Nine times out of 10, these terminations are for personality clashes," said the attorney.[10]

Bullies in the Workplace

Coworkers naturally disagree about topics, issues, and ideas. Yet some people convert disagreement into an attack that puts down other people and damages their self-esteem. As a result, conflict surfaces. **Bullies** are people who verbally, and sometimes physically, attack others frequently. Among the typical behaviors of bullies are interrupting others, ranting in a loud voice, and making threats. A typical attitude of a bullying boss is "My way or the highway," sending the message that the employee's suggestions are unwelcome. Bullied workers complain of a range of psychological and physical ailments, such as anxiety, sleeplessness, panic attacks, and low self-esteem. Recent research suggests that the most likely victims of supervisory bullying are those workers with less power, especially those working in personal service roles, such as housekeepers, nannies, and personal service roles.[11]

Online interviews with 7,740 adults conducted by the Workplace Bullying Institute found that 60 percent of bullies are male, and 40 percent are female. An estimated 37 percent of American workers have been bullied on the job. Male bullies appear to choose men and women as targets in equal number. In contrast, women choose their targets as women 71 percent of the time.[12] Gary Namie, research director at the Bullying Institute, says that one reason women often choose other women as targets "is probably some idea that they can find a less confrontational person or someone less likely to respond to aggression with aggression."[13] Bullying women sometimes sabotage their competition through intimidation or by limiting access to important meetings and committees; withholding information, assignments, and promotions; or blocking the way to mentors and higher management.

Methods of dealing with bullies are described in the section in Chapter 12 about dealing with difficult people.

Incivility and Rudeness

A milder form of aggressiveness than bullying in the workplace is being rude or uncivil toward work associates. **Incivility** (or employees' lack of regard for one another) has gained attention as a cause of workplace conflict. What constitutes being uncivil or rude depends upon a person's perceptions and values.

incivility

In human relations, employees' lack of regard for each other.

> Imagine two people having a business lunch together. One of them answers his cell phone during lunch, and while still eating engages the caller in conversation. To some people this everyday incident would be interpreted as double rudeness—interrupting lunch with a cell phone call and eating while talking. Another person might perceive the cell phone incident to be standard behavior in a multitasking world.

Rudeness also includes swearing at coworkers, a cubicle dweller shouting loudly on the phone while making a personal call, and performing other work at a meeting. Typical forms of "other work" are sorting through paper mail or surfing the Internet on a notebook computer.

A study conducted by Lisa Penney found that 69 percent of 300 workers she surveyed reported experiencing condescending behavior and put-downs in the workplace. Also, those who reported incivility on the job were more likely to engage in counterproductive behaviors, including bad-mouthing their company, missing deadlines, and being rude to customers or clients. "Even though civility may not seem like a very serious thing," says Penney, "it is related to behaviors that have more serious consequences that can affect profits."[14]

A survey of workplace incivility was conducted with three different workplace groups, including university employees, attorneys, and federal court employees. Overall, employees subjected to incivility tended to feel frustrated, annoyed, and a little bit offended. Also, when employees are subjected to coworkers or managers who yell and swear, make them the object of mean jokes, or intentionally exclude them from friendship-building activities, their morale and performance often suffers.[15] (Does this finding surprise you?)

To place rudeness and incivility in perspective, it may simply be part of modern life where self-expression counts for everything and manners nothing. Rudeness in the workplace is therefore just a natural extension of rudeness occurring in everyday life.[16] Yet, a person who has good manners and behaves civilly can capitalize on these behaviors in his or her career.

Cross-Generational Conflict

As explained in Chapter 2, differences in values across generations lead to differences in behavior. And these value-based differences in behavior can lead to conflict, such as disputes about Gen Y workers wanting members of Gen X and baby boomers to be continuously logged on to instant messaging (IM). The following list presents three examples of potential work-related conflict across generations. The illustrations presented are stereotypes that apply to a *typical* member of each generation.

- **Preferred approach to communication.** Gen X members prefer to send text messages, use cell phones, and IM. Gen Y members prefer e-mail, IM, and cell phones. Some Gen Y members prefer abbreviated conversation rather than fully explaining what they mean. Baby boomers prefer e-mail, cell phones, and face-to-face communication.
- **Approach to problem solving.** Gen X members prefer to form a team to brainstorm a solution, as well as use the Web and social networking for research. Gen Y members prefer to think up a list of solutions on their own, then call a meeting to discuss the alternative solutions. Baby boomers like to think about what has worked in the past and how it can be replicated. Then they call a meeting to discuss possible alternatives. Traditionalists (born 1922–1945) tend to be thorough and detail oriented. Gen Y (millenials) will often multitask while solving a problem. Often they want to move quickly to another problem because of a short attention span, whereas traditionalists and baby boomers may want to drag out a problem.
- **Requirement for being respected.** Gen X members want to have their ideas valued by coworkers. Gen Y members want to have their professionalism and growing knowledge valued. Baby boomers want to have their decades of work experience and input still valued.[17]

Although cross-generational conflict is mild in nature, it can still lead to miscommunication and hard feelings that disrupt work.

Workplace Violence (A Cause and Effect of Conflict)

Aggressiveness in the workplace can take extreme forms, such as the shooting or knifing of a former boss or colleague by a mentally unstable worker recently dismissed from the company. Workplace violence is a cause of conflict in the sense that being the subject of violence, witnessing violence, or worrying about violence creates two opposing needs—the worker wants a peaceful environment yet is forced to experience chaos. Conflict is also created by any physical altercation between the perpetrator and the victim. Workplace violence is an effect of conflict because as an extreme response to conflict, such as being fired, some workers strike back at their employer through physical aggression directed at the former boss and coworkers.

Violence has become so widespread that homicide is the fourth leading cause of workplace deaths, with about 600 workers murdered each year in the United States. According to the Bureau of Labor Statistics Census of Fatal Occupations, homicides account for about 10 percent of all fatal workplace injuries.[18] Most workplace deaths result from a robbery or commercial crime. Many of these killings, however, are perpetrated by a disgruntled worker or fired employee harboring an unresolved conflict. As companies have continued to reduce their workforce despite being profitable, these incidents have increased in frequency.

Workplace violence is often predictable, with the worker who may erupt into violence, showing early signals, according to Lynne McClure, a specialist in managing high-risk employees.[19] Predictors of workplace violence include the following employee behaviors and verbal expressions: talk about weaponry, paranoid (highly suspicious) or antisocial behavior, reference to not being heard by management, expression of extreme desperation, history of violence, and being a loner who does not fit into the group. Multiple behaviors such as those just described might be reported to the manager or human resource professional. Yet, you need to be careful about not referring a coworker who displays just one predictor of violent behavior.

CONFLICT-MANAGEMENT STYLES

LEARNING OBJECTIVE 3

The information presented so far is designed to help you understand the nature of conflict. Such background information is useful for resolving conflict because it helps you understand what is happening in a conflict situation. The next two sections offer more specific information about managing and resolving conflict. Before describing specific methods of resolving conflict, it is useful to present more details about five general styles, or modes, of handling conflict. You received preliminary information on two of these five styles when you completed Self-Assessment Quiz 9-1.

As shown in Figure 9-1, Kenneth Thomas identified five major styles of conflict management. Each style is based on a combination of satisfying one's own concerns (assertiveness) and satisfying the concerns of others (cooperativeness).[20]

Competitive Style

The competitive style is a desire to win one's own concerns at the expense of the other party, or to dominate. A person with a competitive orientation is likely to engage in power struggles in which one side wins and the other loses (an approach referred to as win–lose). "My way or the highway" is a win–lose strategy. Workplace bullies prefer the competitive style of conflict management. The competitive style works best when quick, decisive action is essential, such as in an emergency.

Accommodative Style

The accommodative style favors appeasement, or satisfying the other's concerns without taking care of one's own. People with this orientation may be generous or self-sacrificing just to maintain a relationship. An irate customer might be accommodated with a full refund, just to calm down the person. The intent of such accommodation might also be to retain the customer's loyalty. Accommodation sounds harmless; but according to Sidney Simon, when it runs unchecked at the expense of what somebody really wants, it can lead to debilitating resentment, sickness, or even violence.[21] The problem is that the suppressed feelings create inner conflict and stress.

Accommodation works best when you are wrong, or when the issues are more important to the other side. For example, an automobile sales associate might say "yes" to a last-minute demand for another $50 concession, rather than continuing to haggle.

Sharing Style

The sharing style is halfway between domination and appeasement. Sharers prefer moderate but incomplete satisfaction for both parties, which results in a compromise. The phrase "splitting the difference" reflects this orientation and is commonly used in such activities as purchasing a house or car. The sharing (or compromising) style is well suited to a situation in which both sides have equal power, yet are committed to mutually exclusive goals such as the buyer and the seller of the house wanting to maximize financial gain.

Collaborative Style (Win–Win)

In contrast to the other styles, the collaborative style reflects a desire to fully satisfy the desires of both parties. It is based on an underlying philosophy of **win–win,** the belief that after conflict has been resolved, both sides should gain something of value. The use of a win–win approach is aimed at arriving at a settlement that meets the needs of both parties, or at least does not badly damage the welfare of the other side. The option chosen results in a mutual gain. When collaborative approaches to resolving conflict are used, the relationships among the parties are built on and improved. The following example uses a win–win approach to resolve conflict.

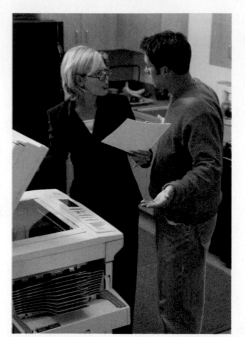

win–win

The belief that after conflict has been resolved both sides should gain something of value.

> *Bruce is an office assistant in a company that supplies food to restaurants, hospitals, and nursing homes. According to his budget analysis, Bruce needed a 5 percent salary increase to meet his monthly expenses. The company owner explained that there was no money in the budget for a salary increase. A cordial discussion about the issue led to an option for mutual gain. Bruce would receive the 5 percent salary increase as long as he increased his productivity enough to cover the increase. His target was to increase his productivity to the point that the company could decrease the hours worked by an office temporary. The amount of the decrease covered the 5 percent salary increase.*

Mobile phone companies in search of antenna sites have led to win–win conflict resolution between companies and communities. Many of these companies have integrated antennas into church steeples, high-rise buildings, and other tall structures without defacing them. A mobile telephone company has sometimes constructed a new church steeple that harbors a giant antenna. The company wins by having an antenna to provide cell telephone service, and community groups do not object to the sight of a freestanding antenna. At the same time, the church wins by having a new steeple.

Collaborating is particularly important when both sides must be committed to the solution, such as the situation with the hidden cell antennae. Divorcing parents also need collaboration in their division of assets because they need to work together long term for the good of the children.

Finding win–win solutions to problems (or options for mutual gain) is one of the most important conflict-resolution skills. To obtain practice in this skill, do Skill-Building Exercise 9-1.

SKILL-BUILDING EXERCISE 9-1

Win–Win Conflict Resolution

The class organizes into small problem-solving groups. Each group spends about 10 minutes finding a win–win solution to one of the following conflict situations.

1. Two coworkers want you to work with them after hours in establishing an online marketing firm. You do not want to take time away from your primary career to get involved in a side business. However, you want to maintain cordial relations with these two coworkers.

2. William, an accountant, wants workmates to call him "William." Yet, several people in the office persist in calling him "Bill" or "Will."

3. You are offered a transfer within your company to an exciting job that you want strongly. Your manager says he cannot let you go because you are too valuable.

4. A group of workers at a small business would like a giant-screen, high-definition television set placed in the employee lounge to enhance their enjoyment of breaks. The business owner wants to keep employees satisfied but concludes that investing about $4,000 in a television set for the lounge is too big an investment.

After the groups have found their solutions for mutual gains, specify carefully what gain each side attained. Share your solutions with other class members to obtain their feedback about the effectiveness of the mutual gains.

Avoidant Style

The avoider is a combination of a person who is uncooperative and unassertive. He or she is indifferent to the concerns of either party. The person may actually be withdrawing from the conflict to rely upon fate. Avoiding works well when an issue is trivial, or there are more pressing issues to worry about. For example, a supervisor might not bother reprimanding workers who are a few minutes late because the supervisor is flooded with other work.

In the following description of specific techniques for resolving conflict, attempt to relate most of them to these five key styles. For example, you will observe that the confrontation and problem-solving technique reflects the collaborative (win–win) style.

GUIDELINES AND TECHNIQUES FOR RESOLVING CONFLICTS

LEARNING OBJECTIVE 4

Interpersonal conflict in organizations is inevitable. A career-minded person must therefore learn effective ways of resolving conflict. This section describes methods of conflict resolution that you can use on your own. All are based somewhat on the underlying model of win–win, or integrating the interests of both parties. Integrating both interests focuses on resolving the underlying concerns of the parties in conflict. By dealing with these concerns, it is more worthwhile for both sides to resolve the conflict than it is to have no agreement.

> Suppose a woman named Molly Coors wanted to open a beer brewery and name her beer Coors. The company lawyers from Coors-Molson, which own the rights to the brand name Coors, would attempt to block her from using the same brand name—even if her family name is Coors. Molly Coors would hire her own lawyer to fight back. Two key concerns must be addressed. Molly Coors' underlying concern is that she feels her civil liberties have been violated because she cannot name a business after herself. And Molly must deal with Coors-Molson's concern about a smaller company capitalizing on its well-known name (brand equity).

Later in the chapter, you will be asked to resolve the beer company conflict. The following paragraphs describe four methods of conflict resolution.

Confrontation and Problem Solving

The ideal approach to resolving any conflict is to confront the real issue and then solve the problem. **Confrontation** means taking a problem-solving approach to differences and identifying the underlying facts, logic, or emotions that account for them. When conflicts are resolved through confronting and understanding their causes, people feel responsible for finding the soundest answer.

Confrontation can proceed gently, in a way that preserves a good working relationship, as shown by this example. Assume that Mary, the person working at the desk next to you, loudly cracks chewing gum while she works. You find the gum chewing both distracting and nauseating. If you don't bring the problem to Mary's attention, it will probably grow in proportion with time. Yet, you are hesitant to enter into an argument about something that a person might regard as a civil liberty (the right to chew gum in public places).

A psychologically sound alternative is for you to approach her directly in this manner:

You: Mary, there is something bothering me that I would like to discuss with you.

She: Go ahead, I don't mind listening to other people's problems.

You: My problem concerns something you are doing that makes it difficult for me to concentrate on my work. When you chew gum, you make loud cracking noises that grate on my nerves. It may be my problem, but the noise does bother me.

She: I guess I could stop chewing gum when you're working next to me. It's probably just a nervous habit.

When resolving conflict through confrontation and problem solving, as well as other method of conflict resolution, it is helpful to bring closure by shaking hands, repeating your individual commitments, and then saying "thank you." Following through on your commitments is also essential for effective conflict resolution.[22]

Karen needs to resolve her conflict with Charlie in a way that will still preserve their working relationship. Perhaps informing their boss of the problem is not the most effective approach from the standpoint of preserving the relationship. Instead, it would be constructive for Karen to meet with Charlie to use the technique of confrontation and problem solving. Karen should let Charlie know clearly how difficult it is to cover for him so frequently. A slightly more aggressive approach would be for Karen to bring along a coworker who also has been inconvenienced by Charlie. The two-on-one approach can be powerful, so long as Charlie does feel "ganged-up" on. Karen acting alone, or accompanied by coworkers, should use a gentle, constructive approach.

Constructive Handling of Criticism

Learning to profit from criticism is an effective way of benefiting from conflict. People who benefit from criticism are able to stand outside themselves while being criticized. It is as if they are watching the criticism from a distance and looking for its possible merits. People who take criticism personally anguish when receiving negative feedback. Following are several specific suggestions for dealing with criticism, including two methods that will often get the other party on your side.[23]

1. **See yourself at a distance.** Place an imaginary Plexiglas shield between you and the person giving the criticism. Attempt to be a detached observer looking for useful information.

2. **Ask for clarification and specifics.** Ask politely for more details about the negative behavior in question so that you can change if change is warranted. If your boss is criticizing you for being rude to customers, you might respond: "I certainly do not want to be rude. Can you give me a couple of examples of how I was rude? I need your help in working on this problem." After asking questions, you can better determine whether the criticism is valid.

3. **Decide on a response.** An important part of learning from criticism is to respond appropriately to the critic. Let the criticizer know what you agree with. Apologize for the undesirable behavior, such as saying, "I apologize for being rude to customers. I know what I can do differently now. I'll be more patient so as not to appear rude." Apology is a highly effective method of getting the criticizer on your side. Without an apology, the attack is likely to continue.

4. **Look for a pattern in terms of other criticism.** Is the criticism you are receiving something you have heard several times before from different people? The more times you have heard the same criticism, the more likely it is to be valid. If three different supervisors have told you that you do not follow through with your promises to get work done, the criticism is most likely valid.

5. **Disarm the opposition.** As an extension of point 3 is that you will often decide to agree with the criticizer because the person has a legitimate complaint about you. If you deny the reality of that person's complaint, he or she will continue to harp on that point and the issue will remain unresolved. By agreeing with the criticism of you, you may set the stage for a true resolution of the problem.

Agreeing with criticism made by a person with formal authority over you is effective because by doing so you are then in a position to ask for his or her help in improving the situation. Rational managers realize that it is their responsibility to help group members overcome problems, not merely to criticize them. Imagine that you have been chronically late with reports during the last six months. It is time for a performance evaluation, and you know that you will be reprimanded for your tardiness. You also hope that your manager will not downgrade all other aspects of your performance because of your tardy reports. Here is how disarming the opposition would work in this situation:

Your manager: Have a seat. It's time for your performance evaluation, and we have a lot to talk about. I'm concerned about some things.

You: So am I. It appears that I'm having a difficult time getting my reports in on time. I wonder if I'm being a perfectionist. Do you have any suggestions?

Disarming the Opposition

In each of these two scenarios, one person plays the role of the person with more power in the situation. The other person plays the role of the individual attempting to disarm the criticizer.

1. A representative from a credit agency telephones you at work to inform you that you are 60 days behind schedule on your car payment. The agent wants a settlement as soon as possible. Unfortunately, the credit agent is correct. Run this happy scenario for about five minutes.

2. Your manager calls you into the office to discuss the 10-page report you just submitted. The boss says in a harsh tone, "Your report is a piece of trash. I counted 25 word-use mistakes such as writing *whether* for *weather* and *seen* for *scene*. (Your spell checker couldn't catch these errors.) Besides that I can't follow many of your sentences, and you left out the table of statistics. I'm wondering if you are qualified for this job."

Observers of the role-play will judge how effective the person being criticized was in reducing some of the anger directed against him or her. Look also for any changes in attitude on the part of the criticizer.

Your manager: Well, I like your attitude. Maybe you are trying to make your reports too perfect before you turn them in. I think you can improve in getting your reports in on time. Try not to figure out everything to three decimal places. We need thoroughness around here, but we can't overdo it.

Disarming is effective because it takes the wind out of the other person's sails and has a calming effect. The other person is often waiting to clobber you if you deny guilt. If you admit guilt, you are more difficult to clobber. Skill-Building Exercise 9-2 gives you an opportunity to practice disarming the opposition.

Reframing

Another useful approach to resolving conflict is to reexamine or *reframe* the conflict situation by looking at in a different light. Following are two practical approaches to reframing, one by searching for the positives in the situation, and the other by asking questions.

Reframing through Cognitive Restructuring.   An indirect way of resolving interpersonal conflict is to lessen the conflicting elements in a situation by viewing them more positively. According to the technique of **cognitive restructuring,** you mentally convert negative aspects into positive ones by looking for the positive elements in a situation. How you frame or choose your thoughts can determine the outcome of a conflict situation. Your thoughts influence your actions. If you search for the beneficial elements in the situation, there will be less area for dispute. Although this technique might sound like a mind game to you, it can work effectively.

cognitive restructuring

Mentally converting negative aspects into positive ones by looking for the positive elements in a situation.

Imagine that a coworker of yours, Jeff, has been asking you repeated questions about how to carry out a work procedure. You are about ready to tell Jeff, "Go bother somebody else; I'm not paid to be a trainer." Instead, you look for the positive elements in the situation. You say to yourself, "Jeff has been asking me a lot of questions. This does take time, but answering these questions is valuable experience. If I want to become a manager, I will have to help group members with problems."

After having completed this cognitive restructuring, you can then deal with the conflict situation more positively. You might say to Jeff, "I welcome the opportunity to help you, but we need to find a mutually convenient time. In that way, I can better concentrate on my own work." To get started with cognitive restructuring, do Skill-Building Exercise 9-3.

Reframing by Asking Questions.   Another way to use reframing is to ask step back, take a deep breath, and then ask the following questions about the conflict situation that arises within the work group:

- Do I fully understand the situation?
- Am I sure what my coworker is really saying?
- Is the person really angry with me or just worried and anxious?
- Have I missed something important?

Reframing through Cognitive Restructuring

The following are examples of negative statements about others in the workplace. In the space provided, cognitively restructure (reframe) each comment in a positive way.

Negative: Nancy is getting on my nerves. It takes her two weeks longer than anyone else in the team to complete her input.

Positive:

Negative: Rob is so obsessed with sports that he is hurting my productivity. Where does it say in the employee handbook that I have to spend 30 minutes on Monday listening to Rob's comments on his team's weekend performance? Doesn't he know that I have a job to do and that I just don't care about his team?

Positive:

Negative: My boss is driving me crazy. He is forever telling me what I did wrong and making suggestions for improvement. He makes me feel like I'm in elementary school.

Positive:

- Do I have all the facts?
- What is the real issue here?
- How do I want to react in this situation?
- How would I want to be treated if the situation were reversed?

By taking such a approach, you are more likely to communicate more effectively and constructively with each your coworkers when conflict situations arise. You carefully talk through the issues rather than becoming explosive, defensive, and arguing. A useful scenario for reframing through questioning would be when a coworker accuses you of not carrying your fair share of the workload.[24]

Negotiating and Bargaining

negotiating

Conferring with another person to resolve a problem.

Conflicts can be considered situations calling for **negotiating,** or conferring with another person to resolve a problem. When you are negotiating a fair salary for yourself, you are trying to resolve a conflict. At first the demands of the two parties may seem incompatible, but through negotiation, a salary figure may emerge that satisfies both.

Another perspective on negotiation is that people are not just negotiating for the economic value of the negotiation. They are also negotiating for intangibles, such as feeling good about the negotiation process, the other party, and themselves.[25] For example, after the negotiation is complete, the individual might want to be perceived as an honest, sincere, professional, rather than as a dishonest person out to maximize gain.

Managers and staff specialists must negotiate both internally (e.g., with subordinates, managers, and team leaders) and externally (e.g., with customers, suppliers, and government agencies). Considerable negotiation also takes place among coworkers. Team members, for example, sometimes negotiate among themselves about work assignments. One might say to the other, "I'm willing to be notetaker this year if there is some way I can cut back on the amount of plant visits I make this year." Six useful negotiating tactics are presented here. Before studying them, do Self-Assessment Quiz 9-2.

The Negotiator Quiz

Directions: The following quiz is designed to give you tentative insight into your tendencies toward being an effective negotiator. Check whether each statement is mostly true or mostly false as it applies to you.

	Mostly true	Mostly false
1. Settling differences of opinion is a lot of fun.	_____	_____
2. I try to avoid conflict and confrontation with others as much as possible.	_____	_____

(Continued)

3. I am self-conscious asking people for favors they have not offered me spontaneously. _____ _____
4. I am generally unwilling to compromise. _____ _____
5. How the other side feels about the results of our negotiation is of little consequence to me. _____ _____
6. I think very well under pressure. _____ _____
7. People say that I am tactful and diplomatic. _____ _____
8. I have heard that I express my viewpoint clearly. _____ _____
9. Very few things in life are not negotiable. _____ _____
10. I always (or would always) accept whatever salary increase is offered to me. _____ _____
11. A person's facial expression often reveals as much as what the person actually says. _____ _____
12. I wouldn't mind taking a few short-term losses to win a long-term battle. _____ _____
13. I'm willing to work long and hard to win a small advantage. _____ _____
14. I'm usually too busy talking to do much listening. _____ _____
15. It's fun to haggle over price when buying a car. _____ _____
16. I almost always prepare in advance for a negotiating session. _____ _____
17. When there is something I need from another person, I usually get It. _____ _____
18. It would make me feel cheap if I offered somebody only two-thirds of his or her asking price. _____ _____
19. People are usually paid what they are worth, so there's no use haggling over starting salaries. _____ _____
20. I rarely take what people say at face value. _____ _____
21. It's easy for me to smile when involved in a serious discussion. _____ _____
22. For one side to win in negotiation, the other side has to lose. _____ _____
23. Once you start making concessions, the other side is bound to get more than you. _____ _____
24. A good negotiating session gets my competitive urges flowing. _____ _____
25. When negotiations are completed, both sides should walk away with something valuable. _____ _____

Total Score _____ _____

Scoring and Interpretation: Score yourself 1 for each of your answers that agrees with the scoring key. The higher your score, the more likely it is that you currently have good negotiating skills, providing your self-assessment is accurate. It might prove useful to also have somebody who has observed you negotiate on several occasions to answer the Negotiator Quiz for you. Scores of 7 or lower and 20 or higher are probably the most indicative of weak or strong negotiating potential. Here is the scoring key:

1. Mostly true	8. Mostly true	15. Mostly true	22. Mostly false
2. Mostly false	9. Mostly true	16. Mostly true	23. Mostly false
3. Mostly false	10. Mostly false	17. Mostly true	24. Mostly true
4. Mostly false	11. Mostly true	18. Mostly false	25. Mostly true
5. Mostly false	12. Mostly true	19. Mostly false	
6. Mostly true	13. Mostly true	20. Mostly true	
7. Mostly true	14. Mostly false	21. Mostly true	

Understand the Other Party's Perspective

As in being a good listener, empathy can be an important part of negotiation. Deepak Malhotra and Max H. Bazerman observe that negotiators often channel too much effort into pushing their own position and too little into understanding the other side's perspective.[26] To obtain a good deal, or sometimes any deal at all, negotiators have to dig for information about *why* the other side wants what it demands. Inaccurate assumptions about the other side's motives can lead negotiators to propose solutions to the wrong problems, waste money, or kill a deal. How about a personal life example for dog lovers?

> *You have wanted a Great Dane puppy for a long time. You enter into negotiations with the owner of the puppy and his mother. The owner is asking $900, and is adamant about her demands. If you are low on empathy, you will raise such negotiating points as how much the little Great Dane is costing the owner in food; that you will pay cash; and that the little fellow is ugly and therefore is only worth $500. (You might get invited off the premises in a hurry.) In contrast, with high empathy and a detective-like mind, you recognize that the owner wants the puppy to go to a wonderful home. So, if she asks for a lot of money, the potential owner is likely to be really interested in finding someone who truly wants the dog, and would therefore probably take good care of the puppy.*
>
> *With this negotiating point in mind, you point out what great care you will give the Great Dane, what a spacious yard you have, how you would take him jogging every day, and how he would be your dream dog. The owner is happy because one of her key motives is for the pup to have a wonderful home. She is touched and agrees to your offer of $600.*

Another key part of understanding the other party's perspective is that you look for common ground. Your talk of care and concern about the dog's health indicates that both you and the owner share a humanitarian attitude toward dogs.

To understand the other party's perspective, you often have to prepare in advance. Obtain as much information as you can about the other party's side before the negotiation session. A basic example is that many prospective car buyers first research the fair value of a vehicle before making an offer. Knowing how long the vehicle has been sitting on the lot or in the showroom is also useful advance information because dealers often borrow money to build inventory.

Focus on Interests, Not Positions. Rather than clinging to specific negotiating points, keep your overall interests in mind and try to satisfy them. Remember that the true object of negotiation is to satisfy the underlying interests on both sides, as in the case of Molly Coors. Part of focusing on interests is to carefully study the other side's comments for clues to the type of agreement that will satisfy both of you.

Careful listening will help you uncover the negotiating partner's specific interests and motivations. (This is another application of understanding the other party's perspective.) Here is how this strategy works:

> *You are considering accepting a job offer that will enable you to work on the type of problems you prefer and also develop your professional skills. You have a starting salary in mind that would make you very happy—10 percent higher than you are currently making. Your negotiating position is thus your present salary plus 10 percent. However, your true interests are probably to have more discretionary income than at present. (You want to make more purchases and invest more.) You will therefore be better off negotiating for a work situation that spreads your money further. You can now accept the offer by negotiating other points in addition to a 10 percent higher salary, including (1) working in a geographic area with a lower cost of living, (2) having a better opportunity for earning a bonus, or (3) receiving a generous expense account. During the negotiations, you may discover that the other party is looking for a talented employee at a salary and benefits the company can afford.*

compromise

Settlement of differences by mutual concessions.

Compromise. The most widely used negotiating tactic is **compromise**, settlement of differences by mutual concessions. One party agrees to do something if the other party agrees to do something else. Compromise is a realistic approach to resolving conflict. Most labor–management disputes are settled by compromise. For instance, labor may agree to accept a smaller salary increase if management will subcontract less work to other countries.

Some people argue that compromise is not a win–win tactic. The problem is that the two parties may wind up with a solution that pacifies both but does not solve the problem.

One example would be purchasing for two team leaders half the new equipment each one needs. As a result, neither department really shows a productivity gain. Nevertheless, compromise is both inevitable and useful.

Begin with a Plausible Demand or Offer, Yet Allow Room for Negotiation. The commonsense approach to negotiation suggests that you begin with an extreme, almost fanciful demand or offer. The final compromise will therefore be closer to your true demand or offer than if you opened the negotiations more realistically. However, a plausible demand is useful because it shows you are bargaining in good faith. Also, if a third party has to resolve a conflict, a plausible demand or offer will receive more sympathy than an implausible one will. An example would be an arbitrator giving only a minimum settlement to an investor who wanted $10 million in damages for having received bad advice from an investment broker. (The arbitrator thinks that a $10 million settlement would be ridiculous.)

Although it is advisable to begin with a plausible demand, one must still allow room for negotiation. A basic strategy of negotiation is to begin with a demand that allows room for compromise and concession. If you think you need $5,000 in new software for your department, you might begin negotiations by asking for a $7,000 package. Your boss offers you $4,000 as a starting point. After negotiation, you may wind up with the $5,000 you need.

Make Small Concessions Gradually. Making steady concessions leads to more mutually satisfactory agreements in most situations. Gradually, you concede little things to the other side. The hard-line approach to bargaining is to make your concession early in the negotiation and then grant no further concession. The tactic of making small concessions is well-suited to purchasing a new car. In order to reach a price you consider acceptable, you might grant concessions such as agreeing to finance the car through the dealer or purchasing a service contract.

Know Your Best Alternative to a Negotiated Agreement. The reason you would probably negotiate would be to produce something better than the result obtainable without negotiating. The goal of negotiating is thus not just to agree, but to obtain more valuable results than would otherwise have occurred. When you are aware of your best alternative to a negotiated agreement (BATNA), it sets a floor to the agreement you are willing to accept. Your BATNA becomes the standard that can protect both parties from accepting terms that are too unfavorable. It also keeps you from walking away from terms that would be beneficial for you to accept.

What might a BATNA look like in practice? Suppose you are negotiating a starting salary for a full-time, professional position. The figure you have in mind is $42,000 per year. Your BATNA is $36,500 because this is the salary your future in-laws will pay you to enter the family business. You will therefore walk away from any offer of less than $37,000—just taking salary into account.

Knowing the other side's BATNA is also important because it helps define the other participant's bargaining zone. Understanding each other's bargaining zones makes it possible to arrive at mutually profitable trade-offs. In the preceding salary negotiations, the company's BATNA might be to hire a less well-educated job candidate at $30,500 and then upgrade his or her knowledge on the job.

An underlying advantage of knowing your BATNA is that it capitalizes on the power of a positive "no." Famous negotiator William Ury reasons that being able to say "no" to a demand places you in a strong position.[27] During negotiations, a statement such as "I am not willing to make that big a concession" can bring you respect because you are standing up for your principles. For best effect "no" should be expressed in a friendly and firm manner.

Use Anger to Your Advantage. Master negotiators make selective use of anger a negotiating and bargaining tool. When a person becomes genuinely angry, the anger can energize him or her to be more resourceful and creative while bargaining. If you are angry about an issue or a negotiating point, the other side may be willing to submit to your demand rather than receive more of your anger. The director of a company wellness program might say with an angry look toward top management, "Why is there money in the budget for all kinds of frills like corporate jets, when a program that is preventing millions of dollars in lost productivity has to grovel for a decent budget?"

The downside of anger is that it can degenerate into incivility and personal insults. A touch of anger can be effective, but overdone it becomes self-defeating. You have to size up how far you can push people before damaging a work relationship—or being fired. To make effective use of anger during negotiation, it has to be used at the right time, with the right tone, and in the right amount.[28] A person who is always angry will often not be taken seriously.

Allow for Face-Saving.   We have saved one of the most important negotiating and conflict resolution strategies for last. Negotiating does not mean that you should try to squash the other side. You should try to create circumstances that will enable you to continue working with that person if it is necessary. People prefer to avoid looking weak, foolish, or incompetent during negotiation or when the process is completed. If you do not give your opponent an opportunity to save face, you will probably create a long-term enemy.

Face-saving could work in this way. A small-business owner winds up paying a higher starting salary for director of manufacturing than she wanted. The employment agency who placed the director of manufacturing says to the business owner, "I know that Derek costs more than you have budgeted. But don't worry about it, you have made a great investment. Derek will increase your manufacturing productivity so much that his salary and benefits will be a bargain for you."

Effective negotiation, as with any other form of conflict resolution, requires extensive practice and knowledge of basic principles and techniques. As a starting point, you might take one of the negotiating tactics just described and practice it where the stakes are not so high. You might attempt to negotiate the price of a consumer electronics device, or negotiate for getting a particular Friday afternoon off from work.

A major theme running through the various approaches to conflict resolution, including negotiating and bargaining, is that cooperating with the other side is usually preferable to competing. A study with 61 self-managing teams with 489 employees supports this idea of the superiority of cooperation over competition in successful conflict resolution. The style of conflict resolution was measured through questionnaires. For example, a statement geared toward cooperative behavior was "We seek a solution that will be good for the whole team." Conflict efficacy was measured by a questionnaire indicating that the extent to which team members believed that they could successfully manage different conflict situations. Group effectiveness was measured by the ratings of supervisor and team leaders on productivity, quality, and cost savings—central reasons why self-directed teams are formed.

The study found that the cooperative approach to conflict was positively related to conflict efficacy. In contrast, the competitive approach to conflict was negatively related to conflict efficacy. Equally important, conflict efficacy was strongly associated with supervisory and team leader ratings of team effectiveness.[29]

Skill-Building Exercise 9-4 provides you the opportunity to practice negotiating in a scenario that most people encounter at least once in their career.

COMBATING SEXUAL HARASSMENT: A SPECIAL TYPE OF CONFLICT

LEARNING OBJECTIVE 5

sexual harassment

Unwanted sexually oriented behavior in the workplace that results in discomfort or interference with the job.

Many employees face conflict because a supervisor, coworker, or customer sexually harasses them. **Sexual harassment** is generally defined as unwanted sexually oriented behavior in the workplace that results in discomfort or interference with the job. It can include an action as violent as rape or as subtle as a sexually oriented comment about a person's body or appearance. Harassment creates conflict because the harassed person has to make a choice between two incompatible motives. One motive is to get ahead, keep the job, or have an unthreatening work environment. But to satisfy this motive, the person is forced to sacrifice the motive of holding on to his or her moral value or preferences. Here we will focus on the types and frequency of sexual harassment, the effects of harassment, and guidelines for dealing with the problem.

Types of Harassment

The courts recognize two types of sexual harassment. In *quid pro quo* sexual harassment, the individual suffers job loss, or threatened loss of a job benefit, as a result of his or her responses to a request for sexual favors. The demands of a harasser can be explicit or implied. An example of quid pro quo harassment would be a manager promising an employee a promotion in exchange for sexual favors and then not promoting the employee because the employee refused.

The other form of sexual harassment is *hostile environment*. It occurs when someone in the workplace creates an intimidating, hostile, or offensive working environment. An employee who is subjected to sexually suggestive comments, lewd jokes, or advances is a victim of hostile environment harassment. No tangible loss has to be suffered in this form of sexual harassment.

Different Perceptions of Sexual Harassment. An analysis of many studies indicated that women perceive a broader range of social-sexual behaviors as harassing. The analysis also found that the female–male difference was larger for behaviors associated with hostile work environment harassment, derogatory attitudes toward women, dating pressure, or physical sexual contact. Men and women, however, agree closely that various types of sexual coercion, such as encounters that are made a condition of promotion, can be classified as quid pro quo harassment.[30]

In attempting to understand what constitutes sexual harassment, research and common sense suggest that not all sexually oriented behaviors such as jokes about sex and a mild flirting are offensive or unwanted. Many workers perceived such behavior as enjoyable. Especially with e-mail, many men and women send each other sexually oriented jokes. Sexual behavior has to be *unwanted* to be classified as sexual harassment. A surprising aspect of the research in question is that even when employees enjoyed sexually oriented behavior at work, they still experienced negative effects. The negative effects were thinking about quitting and lower psychological well-being.[31] More about the negative effects of sexual harassment is presented below.

Sexual Harassment as Power. Sexual harassment is also regarded as an expression of power by one individual over another because the harasser often has more formal power than the harassed. The coworker who harasses another coworker may be attempting to use personal rather than formal power. Similarly, customers and clients who sexually harass a worker may be attempting to exert power. The harasser, following this logic, is a power abuser as well as a legal offender.

Frequency and Setting of Sexual Harassment

Sexual harassment is widespread in the U.S. workplace and in other countries as well. According to one large-scale study when conclusions are based on more scientific studies, 58 percent of women report having experienced potential harassment behaviors, and 24 percent report having experienced sexual harassment on the job.[32] More recent data suggest that sexual harassment directed at professional women by clients and customers is more frequent than harassment within the company. Sexist hostility, such as putting a person down because of his or her sex, was the most frequently noted type of harassment.[33]

Women in nontraditional jobs (such as welder or pressroom supervisor) are especially likely to be harassed. Similarly, a study found that women in male-dominated manufacturing plants are harassed more than women in female-dominated community service centers.[34] A possible reason is that in a male-dominated organization men may feel that they have more power over women. An earlier study in the same organizations just mentioned indicated that minority women are the most likely to be harassed, perhaps because of sex and race discrimination.[35]

Although women in nontraditional jobs run a high risk of being sexually harassed, harassment takes place in many other settings as well, and at all levels in an organization. An example of a seemingly unusual setting for sexual harassment is the United Nations (UN). The organization aspires to protect human rights, yet has struggled to deal with an embarrassing series of complaints within its own ranks. Many UN workers who have been harassed say that the system for dealing with complaints is arbitrary, unfair, and bogged down in complicated rules.

The UN is now working to decrease the amount of sexual harassment, as well as to improve the process for dealing with legitimate complaints. UN Secretary-General Ban Ki-Moon wrote to a women rights group that had complained to him, "I fully share your concerns regarding sexual harassment and sex discrimination. This scourge remains a high priority for me."[36]

The Adverse Effects of Sexual Harassment

Aside from being unethical, immoral, and illegal, sexual harassment is widely thought to have adverse consequences. The harassed person may experience job stress, lowered

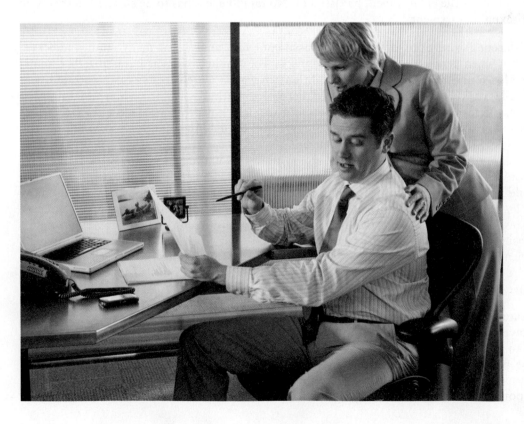

TABLE 9-1   Consequences of Sexual Harassment

Job-Related Outcomes	Number of Responses to the Question about the Problem	Direction of Change
Coworker satisfaction	34,221	Decreased
Supervisor satisfaction	34,450	Decreased
Work satisfaction	33, 486	Decreased
Global job satisfaction	14,455	Decreased
Organizational commitment	31,194	Decreased
Job withdrawal	6,201	Increased
Work withdrawal	4,940	Increased
Workgroup productivity	27,425	Decreased
Health and Well-Being Outcomes	**Number of Responses to the Question about the Problem**	**Direction of Change**
Mental health	45,880	Decreased
Physical health	32,121	Decreased
PTSD (posttraumatic stress disorder)	4,076	Increased number of cases
Life satisfaction	4,545	Decreased

Source: Portion of a table adapted from Chelsea R. Willness, Piers Steel, and Kibeom Lee, "A Meta-Analysis of the Antecedents and Consequences of Workplace Sexual Harassment," *Personnel Psychology*, Spring 2007, p. 141.

morale, severe conflict, and lowered productivity. Table 9-1 summarizes the results of a synthesis of many studies about the adverse effects of sexual harassment. The studies indicate that harassment negatively affects job performance, loyalty to the firm, and personal well-being. Note also that some women suffered posttraumatic stress disorder, almost as if they had been involved in a serious accident.[37]

Guidelines for Preventing and Dealing with Sexual Harassment

A starting point in dealing with sexual harassment is to develop an awareness of the types of behaviors that are considered sexual harassment. Often the difference is subtle. Suppose, for example, you placed copies of two nudes painted by Renoir, the French painter, on a coworker's desk. Your coworker might call that harassment. Yet if you took that coworker to a museum to see the originals of the same nude prints, your behavior usually would not be classified as harassment. Following is a sampling of behaviors that will often be interpreted as environmental harassment.[38] Awareness of these behaviors is important because many harassers have no desire to offend, or knowledge that they are offending others. Such individuals are insensitive, and often ill informed.[39] If people refrain from doing these acts, many instances of sexual harassment will be avoided.

1. **Inappropriate remarks and sexual implications.** Coworkers, subordinates, customers, and suppliers should not be referred to as sexual beings, and their appearance should not be referred to in a sexual manner. Telling a coworker she has gorgeous feet, or he has fabulous biceps, is out of place at work.

2. **Terms of endearment.** Refrain from calling others in the workplace by names such as "cutie," "sweetie pie," "honey," "dear," or "hunk." One might argue that these terms are simply sexist (different roles for men and women) and not sexual harassment. However, this argument is losing ground because any behavior that puts people down based on their gender can be interpreted as harassment from a legal perspective. Keep in mind also that some people find terms of endearment

to have a sexual connotation. If you felt no physical attraction toward another adult, would you call that person "beauty" or "hunk"?

3. **Suggestive compliments.** It is acceptable to tell another person that he or she looks nice, but avoid sexually tinged comments, such as mentioning that the person's clothing shows off his or her body to advantage.

4. **Physical touching.** To avoid any appearance of sexual harassment, it is best to restrict physical touching to handshakes and an occasional sideways hug. High-five handshakes are favored by many because they are less intimate than the traditional type. Hugging a long-term work associate is much more acceptable than hugging a new hire. Minimize such behaviors as adjusting a coworker's earring, touching hair, and tweaking a person's chin.

5. **Work-related kissing.** It is best to avoid all kissing in a work context—except, perhaps, a light kiss at an office party or picnic. It is much more professional to greet a work associate with a warm, sincere handshake, including the high-five type. Cultural differences must be taken into account here, such as many Europeans and Africans greet work associates with a peck on both sides of the face.

Company management also plays a major role in preventing and dealing with sexual harassment. Based on the observations of dozens of human resource specialists and employment law attorneys, several actions by management are critical.[40] The cornerstone of control of sexual harassment is creating and widely disseminating a policy about harassment. The policy should carefully define harassment and state that the company has zero tolerance for such behavior. Company officials designated for hearing complaints should be specified. In addition, the company should have an *open-door policy* about harassment. Such a policy means that any employee with a concern about being harassed is able to go directly to a senior manager without worrying about his or her supervisor taking revenge.

Brief company training programs covering the type of information presented in this chapter are also part of a serious program to prevent and deal with sexual harassment. However, a one-time presentation of a 15-minute videotape about sexual harassment is not sufficient. Periodic discussion about the topic is recommended.

After sexual harassment has taken place, the victim will usually want to resolve the conflict. Two key strategies are either to use a formal complaint procedure or to resolve the conflict on your own. If you choose the latter course, you will save yourself the time of going through a lengthy investigation procedure. Figure 9-2 presents details about the two key strategies for dealing with sexual harassment. Skill-Building Exercise 9-5 offers you an opportunity to simulate the control of sexual harassment.

FIGURE 9-2   How to Deal with Sexual Harassment

The potential or actual victim of sexual harassment is advised to use the following methods and tactics to deal with the problem.

Formal Complaint Procedure. Whenever an employee believes that he or she has encountered sexual harassment, or if an employee is suspected to be the perpetrator of sexual harassment, the complainant should report the incident to his or her immediate supervisor (if that person is not the harasser) or to the next higher level of management if the supervisor is the harasser. The supervisor contacted is responsible for contacting a designated company official immediately regarding each complaint. The officer will explain the investigative procedures to the complainant and any supervisor involved. All matters will be kept strictly confidential, including private conversations with all parties.

Dealing with the Problem on Your Own. The easiest way to deal with sexual harassment is to speak up before it becomes serious. The first time it happens, respond with a statement such as: "I won't tolerate this kind of talk," "I dislike sexually oriented jokes," or "Keep your hands off me."

Combating Sexual Harassment

The two role-plays in this exercise provide practice in applying the recommended techniques for combating sexual harassment. The activities have an implied sexual content, and they are for educational purposes only. Any students offended by these role-plays should exclude themselves from participating.

Scenario 1: The Offensive Jester. One student plays the role of Max, a man who delights in telling sexually oriented jokes and anecdotes in the office. He often brings a tabloid newspaper to the office to read sexually oriented passages to coworkers, both male and female. Another student assumes the role of Maxine, a woman in the office who takes offense to Max's humor. She wants to convince Max that he is committing sexual harassment with his sexually oriented humor. Max does not see himself as committing sexual harassment.

Scenario 2: The Flirtatious Office Manager. One student assumes the role of Bertha, an office manager who is single. Another student plays the role of Bert, a married man who recently joined the company as an office assistant. Bert reports to Bertha, and she finds him physically attractive. Bertha visits Bert at his desk and makes such comments as "It looks like you have great quadriceps. I wonder what you look like in running shorts." Bert wants to be on good terms with Bertha, but he feels uncomfortable with her advances. He also wants to behave professionally in the office.

Run both role-plays in front of the class for about eight minutes. Other students in the class will observe the role-plays and then provide feedback about how well Maxine and Bert were able to prevent or stop sexual harassment. Observe if Maxine and Bert used any of the recommended techniques for dealing with harassment.

A major recommendation for documenting acts of sexual harassment is to keep a running diary of incidents against you. A log of the incidents is impressive to company officials, lawyers, and judges (should a lawsuit ultimately be involved). Examples of log entries from a woman and a man are given below:

- January 17, 2012: Jim Quattrone, the manager of accounts payable, asked me to have dinner with him for the sixth time, and I turned him down again. I said "no," "no," "no."

- March 13, 2011: Meg Evans, my supervisor, said that I would receive a much better performance evaluation if I could come over to her house for dinner. She said her husband would be out of town, so I could stay overnight if I wanted to. I felt so uncomfortable and pressured. I made up an excuse about having an exclusive relationship.

SELF-ASSESSMENT QUIZZES IN OVERVIEW

Self-Assessment Quiz 9-1, Styles of Conflict Management, provides some tentative insights into your style of managing conflict. A possible clue to personal development stemming from this quiz is whether you are able to use different style of conflict resolution to adapt to a situation. Sue might be the assistant manager at a fashion boutique. A customer might be raising a big fuss about wanting to return shoes that she says are uncomfortable. Although the customer has passed the limit for returns, Sue accommodates the customer by giving her a complete merchandise exchange just to "shut her up." At other times, Sue might be more collaborative in resolving conflict.

Self-Assessment Quiz 9-2 measures your negotiating skills as reflected in your attitudes toward negotiating. These attitudes must be backed up with good communication skills to translate into effective negotiating. The two quizzes are related because negotiation is a major part of resolving conflict, such as attaining a compromise or collaborating with the other side.

Concept Review and Reinforcement

Key Terms

conflict 181
role conflict 181
work-family conflict 183
personality clash 184

incivility 185
win–win 188
cognitive restructuring 191
negotiating 192

compromise 194
sexual harassment 196

Summary

A conflict is a situation in which two or more goals, values, or events are incompatible or mutually exclusive. Interpersonal conflicts have many sources or causes. An underlying source of job conflict is that people compete for limited resources. Another leading cause of incompatibility is role conflict, having to choose between two competing demands or expectations. Competing work and family demands represent a major role conflict. Other key sources of conflict are personality clashes, aggressive personalities including bullies, incivility and rudeness, and cross-generational conflict. Workplace violence is both a cause and an effect of job conflict.

Five major styles of conflict management have been identified: competitive, accommodative, sharing, collaborative (win–win), and avoidant. Each style is based on a combination of satisfying one's own concerns (assertiveness) and satisfying the concerns of others (cooperativeness).

Confrontation and problem solving is the ideal method for resolving conflict. Learning to benefit from criticism is an effective way of benefiting from conflict. People who benefit from criticism are able to stand outside themselves while being criticized. Another way to deal with criticism is to disarm the opposition by agreeing with his or her criticism. Reframing a situation can be helpful in resolving conflict. Reframing through cognitive restructuring lessens conflict by the person looking for the positive elements in a situation. Asking questions such as "How would I want to be treated if the situation were reversed" is another type or reframing.

Negotiating and bargaining is a major approach to resolving conflict. People negotiate for economic value and also for intangibles such as feeling good. Negotiation tactics include understanding the other party's perspective, focusing on interests rather than positions, compromising, beginning with a plausible demand or offer yet allowing room for negotiation, and making small concessions gradually. It is also important to know your BATNA (best alternative to a negotiated agreement). Using anger to your advantage can sometimes work. Allowing for face saving is also recommended.

Sexual harassment is a form of interpersonal conflict with legal implications. The two forms of sexual harassment are (1) demanding sex in exchange for favors and (2) creating a hostile environment. People have differing perceptions of what constitutes sexual harassment, and some workers enjoy sexually oriented behavior on the job. Sexual harassment is often an expression of power. Sexual harassment is widespread in the workplace. Research has pinpointed adverse mental and physical consequences of sexual harassment.

A starting point in dealing with sexual harassment is to develop an awareness of the types of behaviors it encompasses. Company policies and complaint procedures about harassment are a major part of dealing with the problem. To deal directly with harassment, the harassed person can file a formal complaint or confront the harasser when the behavior first begins. Keeping a diary of harassing events is strongly recommended.

Questions for Discussion and Review

1. Several large companies dismiss each year the 5 percent of their workforce receiving the lowest performance evaluations. What kind of conflicts do you think this practice leads to?

2. During the recent recession, many workers were hesitant to take more than a three-day vacation from the office. Their reasoning was that if the company could get by without them for a week or more, it might be concluded that they were not really needed. To what extent do you think that not taking a vacation was a useful way of holding on to a job?

3. Suppose someone finds out that a coworker raises dogs for dog-fighting, leading the first person to conclude that the coworker is potentially violent. Describe whether you think the first worker should tell the supervisor that the coworker is potentially violent on the job.

4. What are the disadvantages of having an accommodative style of handling conflict?

5. Several school systems in recent years have requested that teachers correct student work with a purple marker rather than a red one because the color red is associated with harsh criticism. What is your opinion of the merits of a shift from red markers to purple?

6. Have you ever attempted to disarm the opposition? How effective was the tactic?

7. How might a student use cognitive restructuring to get over the anger of having received a low grade in a course?

8. Visualize yourself buying a vehicle of your choice. Which negotiating technique (or techniques) would you be most likely to use?

9. Sexual harassment involves an unwanted sexual advance, and people at work have many different interpretations of an "unwanted sexual advance," including asking a coworker to join you for lunch. So how can a career-minded person completely avoid any behavior that might be interpreted as an "unwanted sexual advance"?

10. Imagine yourself as a human resources professional who wants to alert top-level management to the importance of developing a policy against sexual harassment. What interpretations could you make of Table 9-1 to help you emphasize the importance of developing such a policy?

The Web Corner

http://www.ehow.com
(Resolving workplace conflict)

http://www.karass.com
(Resolving workplace conflict)

Internet Skill Builder: Finding Suggestions for Resolving Conflict on YouTube

YouTube.com often has a generous sampling of brief videos about resolving conflict that apply mostly to personal life, but some are about the workplace. Visit YouTube.com, and watch a handful of videos about conflict resolution, and look for a few serious messages. Look for any similarities between the information presented in YouTube videos and in this chapter. Also, does it appear that any of the videos you find present a humorous aspect to conflict resolution?

Developing Your Human Relations Skills

The Apprehensive Sales Trainee

Maria was ecstatic about the position she just landed as a sales representative for a company that provides payroll and human resources services for small companies throughout the country. She was to be assigned a sales territory in Madison, Wisconsin, where she lived with her husband and three young children. Before working her territory, Maria had to attend 10 days of training and orientation at the company headquarters in Boston, Massachusetts.

One of the key trainers in the program was the national sales manager, Todd, an energetic and successful-looking man in his early forties. During a beverage break at the first morning of the training program, Todd approached Maria and complimented her on her "great tan" and "fabulous appearance." Maria was not particularly comfortable with the comments, but she let them pass.

Before the dinner meeting at the second night of the program, Todd came over to Maria and engaged her in a brief conversation about how she was enjoying the sales training. He then handed her a business card and said, "I imagine you might get lonely being away from home for so long, so here is my business card. Please get in touch if you would just like to hang out a little with me." Maria thought that Todd was stepping over the line of good business judgment, but she just smiled politely and said, "Thanks anyway, but I am so overwhelmed with all this great information I am receiving, I have no spare time."

The following morning, Maria received a text message from Todd on her BlackBerry that said, "Your beauty is devastating. Get back."

Maria later phoned her best friend in Madison, and said, "Todd carries a lot of weight being the national sales manager. But I think his behavior toward me borders on sexual harassment. Yet five days into my job, I guess I shouldn't attempt to rat on a company executive."

Maria's friend replied, "You have got to do something. That sales manager is a predator."

Questions

1. To what extent is Todd engaging in sexual harassment toward Maria?
2. If Todd is guilty, what type of sexual harassment is he committing?
3. What steps should Maria take so that she can stop the harassment, yet still maintain a good working relationship with Todd?
4. What would be the positives and negatives of Maria filing a complaint about Todd with the company?

Interpersonal Skills Role-Play

Maria Tries to Fend Off Todd

The case about Maria, the sales trainee, provides the background information and storyline for this role-play. One person plays the role of serious-minded Maria who wants to receive high ratings in her sales training. She does not want to create problems at the company, yet she recognizes she has the right to a harassment-free environment. Another student plays the role of Todd, who is infatuated with Maria, and also believes that he is powerful, and somewhat irresistible to women. Todd corners Maria during a cocktail hour prior to dinner on the third night of the sales training program. He once again starts to hit on her, and Maria wants to avoid being hit on. At the least, a few sets of role players should perform in front of the class for about seven minutes.

Observers rate the role players on two dimensions, using a 1-to-5 scale from very poor to very good. One dimension is "effective use of human relations techniques." Focus on Maria's ability to effectively deal with sexual harassment. The second dimension is "acting ability." A few observers might voluntarily provide feedback to the role players in terms of sharing their ratings and observations. The course instructor might also provide feedback.

The Refrigerator Caper*

Two e-mail messages were sent at a technology company in Northern Virginia, covering the same topic:

From: Nestor, Jenna
Sent: Tuesday, August 7, 12:50 p.m.
To: All employees on 3rd, 4th, and 8th floors
Subject: Re: Refrigerator Etiquette
Importance: High

To the person who ate my lunch:

I would like to thank you for completely taking it upon yourself to deny me sustenance this afternoon. It is completely inappropriate to take things that are not yours. Are we in the 1st grade?

Please read Diana's e-mail that I have copied below. I would be happy to read it out loud and explain it to you if it is too hard to understand.

Jenna

A Very Angry Victim

P.S. In case you were wondering what that extra flavor was, each and every day I take the time to spit in my lunch. I hope you enjoyed it.

From: Sanders, Diana
Sent: Monday, July 30, 4:32 p.m.
To: All employees on 3rd, 4th, and 8th floors
Subject: Refrigerator Etiquette

Over the last month, a number of employees have been disappointed when they went to grab their lunch out of the refrigerator. Unfortunately, they found that someone had either taken part of their lunch out of their lunch bag and or the entire lunch was missing.

Please be respectful of others and do not eat anything from the fridge that is not your personal property. If you bring your lunch, please label with your name and date. Thank you for your immediate cooperation and consideration of coworkers.

Diana Sanders

Direction of Administration

Case Questions

1. What is the exact conflict in this situation? What is the source of the conflict?
2. What is your evaluation of Jenna Nestor's method of resolving the conflict over the stolen lunch?
3. How can professional adults really act in this manner?

*The company involved in this incident chose to remain anonymous.

Becoming an Effective Leader

Mary DiSalvo is the director of operations at a printing company that specializes in printing shrink-wrapped labels for food and consumer products, including bottled water, orange juice, and packaged meat. Company CEO Bruce Denton observed that over a six-year period, DiSalvo's group had the highest productivity and lowest employee turnover at the company. Denton had a hunch that DiSalvo's passion for people and her love of printing had something to do with her outstanding record. However, he wanted more insight into what made for the superb leadership at his company. So with Mary's permission, an outside human relations specialist interviewed several people about their experiences working in the company, and what they thought of Mary's leadership.

Cheryl, a shipping supervisor, described DiSalvo's leadership in these terms: "Mary is so gung ho about labels and production efficiency that her excitement rubs off on you. She makes us feel that we are on a crusade to produce the best labels in the business. At the same time, she really cares about everybody who works at the company. I remember when she personally went to help out a production worker whose house was severely damaged by a tree falling on it."

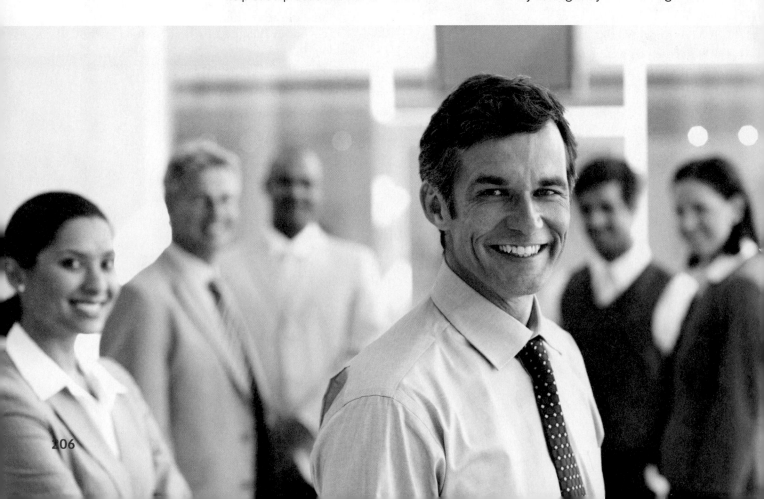

Objectives

After reading and studying this chapter and doing the exercises, you should be able to

1. Identify key leadership traits for personal development.
2. Develop several attitudes and behaviors that will help you appear charismatic.
3. Develop your team leadership skills.
4. Understand how you can develop your leadership potential.

Jeff, a quality technician, expressed these ideas to the human relations interviewer: "I don't have too much direct contact with Mary because she is two levels up the ladder from me. But I feel her impact almost everyday. Mary is committed to quality, and her e-mails to the company about quality make me feel that my work is very important. Mary is the hardest worker in the plant, so she sets a good example for us. She also has a great warm smile and a cheerful attitude that makes you want to do your best."[1]

As in the story just presented, effective leaders have a combination of admirable qualities, including expertise, a passion to succeed, high energy, and the ability to inspire others. In working toward improving your leadership ability, the following definition is a goal to strive for. **Leadership** is the ability to inspire support and confidence among the people who are needed to achieve company goals. A company president might have to inspire thousands of people, while a team leader is concerned with inspiring about six people. Both of these leaders nonetheless play an important role.

Leadership has also been defined in many other ways. An analysis of 221 definitions of leadership concluded that they basically all say the same thing—leadership is about one person getting one or more other people to do something.[2] The something usually refers to attaining a worthwhile company goal. In other words, the leader makes a difference.

Becoming a leader does not necessarily mean that the company has to put you in charge of others (or assign you a formal leadership position). Shortly after Sergio Marchionne became the CEO of the combined Fiat and Chrysler automotive company, he said that the company's chances for success depended in part on a culture "where everyone is expected to lead."[3] You can also rise to leadership when people come to respect your opinion and personal characteristics and are thus influenced by you. Leadership is thought by many to exist at all levels with people anywhere in the organization being able to influence others if they have the right skills or know the right work procedures.[4]

Your greatest opportunity for exerting leadership will come about from a combination of holding a formal position and exerting personal influence. An individual with appealing personal characteristics and expertise who is placed in a position of authority will find it relatively easy to exert leadership.

The purpose of this chapter is twofold. One is to make you aware of the basic concepts you need to become a leader. The other purpose is to point you toward developing skills necessary for leadership effectiveness.

KEY LEADERSHIP TRAITS TO DEVELOP

An important part of being an effective leader is to have the *right stuff*. This section and the following one about charisma describe personal attributes that help a person lead others in many situations. Recognize, however, that radically different situations require a different set of leadership characteristics. For example, a leader might have to be more assertive with group members performing distasteful work than with those whose work is enjoyable. Even if traits are but one facet of understanding leadership, they play an important role. Traits help explain individual differences in leadership.[5] For example, an assertive and self-confident leader will be able to take decisive actions.

Each of the ten leadership traits described next, and shown in Figure 10-1, can be developed. For such development to take place, you need to be aware of the importance

LEARNING OBJECTIVE 1

FIGURE 10-1 Ten Key Leadership Traits

People who possess the traits listed below are usually well suited to being an effective leader. However, many other traits and behaviors are also important contributors to effective leadership.

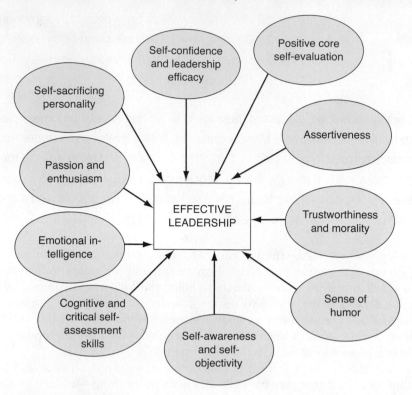

of the personal characteristic, and then monitor your own behavior to make progress. To assist you with such development, the description of each trait is accompanied by a suggestion for improvement.

Self-Confidence and Leadership Efficacy

In virtually every leadership setting, it is important for the leader to be realistically self-confident. A leader who is self-assured without being bombastic or overbearing instills confidence in group members. Self-confidence was among the first leadership traits researchers identified. Current research with leaders in many situations has continued to underscore the importance of this trait. A series of research studies have shown that increased self-confidence can bring about improvement in performance, including helping a group attain its goals.[6] In addition to being self-confident, the leader must project that self-confidence to the group.[7] Self-confidence is not only a personality trait. It also refers to the behavior a person exhibits in a number of situations. It is similar to being cool under pressure. We can conclude that a person is a self-confident leader when he or she retains composure during a crisis, such as when the company suffers flood damage during a busy season.

The inclusion of a feeling of efficacy in combination with self-confidence helps better pinpoint how confidence works. **Leadership efficacy** is a form of efficacy associated with confidence in the knowledge, skills, and abilities valuable for with leading others. In essence, the leader is confident that he or she has the tools necessary to lead a group. Another insight into leadership efficacy is that it helps the leader step up to meet his or her challenges.[8] The confidence therefore extends beyond attitudes about the self. A leader who had been a successful racquet sports director at one athletic club might have the leadership efficacy to carry out the many aspects of that role at another club.

You can appear more self-confident to the group by using definitive wording, maintaining good posture, and making appropriate gestures such as pointing an index finger outward. Developing self-confidence is a lifelong process of performing well in a variety of situations. You need a series of easy victories to establish self-confidence. Further development of your self-confidence requires performing well in challenging circumstances.

Taking risks, such as volunteering to work on an unfamiliar project, contributes to self-confidence when the risk proves to be worthwhile. As your self-confidence builds in several situations, you will also develop a strong sense of leadership efficacy.

Positive Core Self-Evaluation

The core self-evaluation was described in Chapter 2 as closely related to self-esteem. In more detail, the core self-evaluation captures a person's self-assessment. Its four components are self-esteem, locus of control, self-efficacy, and emotional stability (low neuroticism.)[9] Except for locus of control, these traits have already been defined in Chapter 2. In addition, we described how self-esteem in the form of self-confidence can be developed.

Locus of control deals with the way people look at causation in their lives. If you believe that you are controlled mostly by outside events beyond your control, you would have an external locus of control. A marketing specialist with an external control might say, "Our computer system is down today, so there is nothing constructive I can do. I'll just wait until the system is running again." With an internal locus of control, the marketing specialist might say, "The computer is down which will slow me down. However, I'll work on whatever I can do that does not require the company computer. I can do some research on markets in Africa with my smart phone."

An internal locus of control is better for leadership than an external locus of control. Leaders who believe that they can control events are more likely to inspire others and provide direction. High emotional stability is better for leadership than low emotional stability. Anyone who has ever worked for an unstable supervisor will attest to the importance of emotional stability as a leadership trait. Emotional stability is important for a leader because group members expect and need consistency in the way they are treated.

A useful tactic for developing an internal locus of control is to examine challenging situations, and search for what aspect of those situations might be in your control. The department leader might be informed that because of low profits, salaries will be frozen for the next year. The leader might say, "Okay, external events have created conditions for discontent in my department. However, I can still use recognition and interesting work assignments to boost morale." Emotional stability is difficult to develop, but people can learn to control many of their emotional outbursts. People who cannot control their emotions, yet still want to become leaders, should seek assistance from a mental health professional.

Assertiveness

A widely recognized leadership trait is **assertiveness,** being forthright in expressing demands, opinions, feelings, and attitudes. If you are self-confident, it is easier to be assertive with people. An assertive team leader might say, "I know that the ice storm put us out of business for 4 days, but we can make up the time by working smart and pulling together. Within 30 days, we will have met or surpassed our goals for the quarter." This statement reflects self-confidence in her leadership capabilities and assertiveness in expressing exactly what she thinks.

Assertiveness helps leaders perform many tasks and achieve goals. Among them are confronting group members about their mistakes, demanding higher performance, and setting high expectations. An assertive leader will also make legitimate demands on higher management, such as asking for equipment needed by the group. A recent experiment with students suggested that being assertive in the form of talking loudly and frequently is often perceived to be a leadership quality. The study indicated that individuals who have the tendency to behave in assertive and self-assured ways attain influence because such behavior makes them appear confident. However, being dominant is not sufficient for being perceived as a leader over time. You need to back up loud talk with constructive actions.[10]

To be assertive differs significantly from being aggressive or passive (or nonassertive). Aggressive people express their demands in an overly pushy, obnoxious, and abrasive manner. Passive people suppress their own ideas, attitudes, feelings, and thoughts as if they were likely to be perceived as controversial. Nonassertive people are also too accommodating. A series of three studies with a variety of workers indicated that leaders with moderate assertiveness were considered more effective than leaders low (passive) or high (aggressive) in this trait.[11]

Developing assertiveness is much like attempting to become less shy. You must force yourself to take the opportunity to express your feelings and demands. For example, if

assertiveness

Being forthright in expressing demands, opinions, feelings, and attitudes.

something a teammate does annoys you, make the statement, "I enjoy working with you in general, but what you are doing now annoys me." You can also practice expressing positive emotion, such as telling a coworker, "I'm happy that you and I are working on this project together, because I like your approach to work."

Expressing demands is easier for most people to practice than expressing feelings. People who do start expressing their demands are often surprised at the result. For example, if you are contemplating the purchase of an item that is beyond your budget, try this statement: "I like this product very much. Yet all I have to spend is $100 below your asking price. Can we do business?" For a reading on your own level of assertiveness, do Self-Assessment Quiz 10-1.

SELF-ASSESSMENT QUIZ 10-1

The Assertiveness Scale

Directions: Check whether each of the following statements is mostly true or mostly false as it applies to you. If in doubt about your reaction to a particular statement, think of how you would generally respond.

		Mostly true	Mostly false
1.	It is extremely difficult for me to turn down a sales representative if he or she is a nice person.	_____	_____
2.	I express criticism freely.	_____	_____
3.	If another person were being very unfair, I would bring it to his or her attention.	_____	_____
4.	Work is no place to let your feelings show.	_____	_____
5.	There's no use in asking for favors; people get what they deserve.	_____	_____
6.	Business is not the place for tact; say what you think.	_____	_____
7.	If a person looked as if he or she were in a hurry, I would let that person in front of me in a supermarket line.	_____	_____
8.	A weakness of mine is that I'm too nice a person.	_____	_____
9.	I usually give other people what they want rather than do what I think is best, just to avoid an argument.	_____	_____
10.	If I was trying to study in a library and the person next to me was talking loudly on her phone, I would bring my problem to his or her attention.	_____	_____
11.	People would describe me as too outspoken.	_____	_____
12.	I am quite willing to return merchandise that I find has even a minor blemish.	_____	_____
13.	I dread having to express anger toward a coworker.	_____	_____
14.	People often say that I'm too reserved and emotionally controlled.	_____	_____
15.	Nice guys and gals finish last in business.	_____	_____
16.	I fight for my rights down to the last detail.	_____	_____
17.	I have no misgivings about returning an overcoat to the store if it doesn't fit me right.	_____	_____
18.	After I have an argument with a person, I try to avoid him or her.	_____	_____
19.	I insist on my spouse (or roommate or partner) doing his or her fair share of undesirable chores.	_____	_____
20.	It is difficult for me to look directly at another person when the two of us are in disagreement.	_____	_____
21.	I have cried among friends more than once.	_____	_____
22.	If someone near me at a movie kept up a conversation with another person, I would ask him or her to stop.	_____	_____
23.	I am able to turn down social engagements with people I do not particularly care for.	_____	_____
24.	It is in poor taste to express what you really feel about another individual.	_____	_____
25.	I sometimes show my anger by swearing at or belittling another person.	_____	_____
26.	I am reluctant to speak up at a meeting.	_____	_____
27.	I find it relatively easy to ask friends for small favors, such as giving me a ride to work while my car is being repaired.	_____	_____

Trustworthiness and Morality

Group members consistently believe that leaders must display honesty, integrity, and credibility—and therefore be trustworthy. Right Management Consultants conducted a survey of 570 employees in which they found the white-collar workers value honesty and integrity in a manager more than any other trait. When asked, "What is the most important trait or attribute that the leader of your company should possess?" 24 percent of the survey participants cited honesty, and 16 percent named integrity/morals and ethics.[12] Leaders themselves believe that honesty makes a difference in their effectiveness.

It is almost an axiom in leadership studies that integrity is important for effective leadership. (Leaders who are trustworthy typically have high integrity.) Like most concepts in human relations, *integrity* has several connotations. Yet, the two key meanings of **integrity** are (a) consistency of words and deeds and (b) being true to oneself.[13] Being true to oneself refers to sticking with one's principles, such as a sales manager who preaches high ethics not giving kickbacks to customers for the purpose of closing a sale.

Being honest with team members helps build trust, which in turn leads to good cooperation and team spirit. In recent years, trust in business leaders has been damaged by financial scandals in well-known companies. Executives in those companies enriched themselves by selling company stock just before the time they correctly forecast that the stock price would tumble. At the same time, the executives encouraged employees not to sell their stock, or to purchase more. Also, records were falsified in order to enhance the value of stock purchases by executives.

To trust group members, the leader has to be willing to give up some control over them, such as letting group members make more decisions and not challenging their expense accounts. The following anecdote, told by Fred Smith, the founder of FedEx, illustrates what trust can mean in an organization:

A blizzard shut down a radio relay located on top of a mountain, cutting phone service to several FedEx offices. The phone company said it would take five days to repair the problem. On his own, a FedEx telecommunications expert named Hal chartered a helicopter to get to the site. The pilot was unable to land, but he got close enough to the ground for Hal to jump safely. Hal slogged through the deep snow and fixed the problem.

According to Smith, Hal went to such great lengths to keep the organization going because there was mutual trust between employer and employee. Hal knew he would not be reprimanded for going to such expense to fix the telephone problem.[14]

Being moral is closely linked to trustworthiness because a moral leader is more likely to be trusted. A leader with high morality would perceive that he or she had an ethical responsibility to group members, as well as outsiders.[15] The moral leader would therefore not give preferential treatment to workers with whom he had an outside-of-work friendship. At the same time, the moral leader would not try to fool customers or make up false excuses for not paying bills on time to suppliers.

A highly recommended way of communicating trustworthiness is through setting a good example. Alan Deutschman, a leadership consultant, argues that leaders are most effective when they rely on the power of their example. A classic example is that Ray Kroc, the founder of McDonald's, listed cleanliness as one of the chain's three key values (along with service and quality). An employee remembered Kroc personally picking up trash around the restaurant and scraping up gum with a putty knife.[16]

Chapter 15, about ethical behavior skills, provides details about honesty on the job. Being honest is an effective way of getting others to trust you. A starting point in developing a strong sense of honesty and morality is to follow a variation of the Golden Rule: Be as honest with others as you want them to be with you.

Sense of Humor

A sense of humor is on the borderline between being a trait or a behavior. However you classify it, the effective use of humor is considered an important part of a leader's role. Humor serves such functions in the workplace as relieving tension and boredom and defusing hostility. Because humor helps the leader dissolve tension and defuse conflict, it helps him or her exert power over the group. A study conducted in a large financial institution indicated that leaders who made frequent use of humor had higher performing units. (Another interpretation is that it's easier to laugh when the group is performing well!) Among the forms of humor used by the managers were "[using] humor to take the edge off during stressful periods" and "[making] us laugh at ourselves when we are too serious."[17]

Self-effacing humor is the choice of comedians and organizational leaders alike. When you are self-effacing, nobody else is insulted or slighted, yet a point can be made. A marketing executive at Gateway (now part of Acer Computer) said a few years ago to a subcontractor, "I want you people to design photo software so uncomplicated that even managers at my level could learn how to use it."

Creativity is required for humor. Just as creativity can be enhanced with practice, so can a sense of humor. To gather some experience in making humorous comments in the workplace, do Skill-Building Exercise 10-1.

SKILL-BUILDING EXERCISE 10-1

The Witty Leader

Students gather in problem-solving groups of about five to invent humorous comments a leader might make in the following scenarios. After the problem-solving groups have formulated their witty comments, the comments can be shared and compared. Groups also have the option of deciding that a particular scenario is too grim for humor.

Scenario 1: A store manager wants to communicate to employees that inventory slippage (merchandise stolen from the store by customers or store associates) has increased to an unacceptable level—twice the industry average.

Scenario 2: A leader has to communicate to the group that salaries have been frozen for another year due to limited business. The leader knows that group members have been eagerly awaiting news about the salary increase.

Scenario 3: Due to an unprecedented surge in orders, all salaried personnel will be required to work about 65 hours per week for the next 10 weeks. Furthermore, the office and factory must be staffed on Saturdays and Sundays.

Scenario 4: A consulting firm that specializes in helping companies downsize their workforce has seen the demand for its services decline substantially in recent months. The company must therefore downsize itself. The company founder has to announce the layoff decision to the company.

Observers might rate the attempts at humor on a 1 (low) to 10 (high) scale. Observe also if any of the role players made you laugh.

Self-Awareness and Self-Objectivity

Effective leaders are aware of their strengths and limitations. This awareness enables them to capitalize upon their strengths and overcome their weaknesses. A leader, for example, might realize that he or she is naturally distrustful of others. Awareness of this problem cautions the leader to not distrust people without good evidence. Another leader might realize that he or she is adept at counseling team members. This leader might then emphasize that activity in an effort to improve performance. Self-objectivity refers to being detached or nonsubjective about your perceived strengths and limitations.

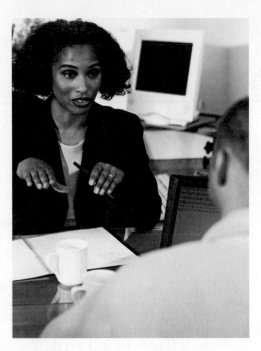

Another way in which self-awareness and self-objectivity contribute to leadership effectiveness is that these traits help a person become an authentic leader. Such a leader demonstrates passion for his or her purpose, practices values consistently, and leads with the heart as well as the head. Instead of being a phony, or acting out of character, the person is a genuine. Authenticity helps the leader be perceived as trustworthy.[18] "Being yourself" thus contributes to leadership effectiveness assuming that you have personal qualities, such as those presented in this chapter, that facilitate leadership. Mary, the leader described in the chapter opener, appears to be an authentic leader.

You can enhance your self-awareness and self-objectivity by regularly asking for feedback from others. You then compare the feedback to your self-perception of your standing on the same factor. You might, for example, think that you communicate in colorful, interesting terms. In speaking to others about your communication style, you might discover that others agree. You can then conclude that your self-awareness about your communication skills is accurate.

Another technique for improving self-awareness and self-objectivity is to take several self-examination exercises, such as those found in this text. Even if they do not describe you exactly, they stimulate you to reflect on your characteristics and behaviors.

Cognitive Skills Including Critical Assessments

Mental ability, as well as personality, is important for leadership success. To inspire people, bring about constructive changes, and solve problems creatively, leaders need to be mentally sharp. Problem-solving and intellectual skills are referred to collectively as **cognitive factors**. The term *cognition* refers to the mental process or faculty by which knowledge is gathered.

cognitive factors
The collective terms for problem-solving and intellectual skills.

Knowledge of the Business.   A major reason that cognitive skills have increased in importance for leadership is that they enable the leader to acquire knowledge. The processing of knowledge is now considered to be the *core competence* (key ability) of organizations. The leader's role is to both originate useful ideas and collect them from smart people throughout the organization.[19] Two cognitive skills were discussed in Chapter 2: cognitive ability and the personal factor of openness to experience. Another cognitive skill of major importance is *knowledge of the business,* or technical skill. An effective leader has to be technically or professionally competent in some discipline, particularly when leading a group of specialists. It is difficult for the leader to establish rapport with group members when he or she does not know what they are doing. A related damper on leadership effectiveness is when the group does not respect the leader's technical skill.

One of a large number of examples of how knowledge of the business is helpful for occupying a leadership position these days took place at the Cadillac division of General Motors Co. Vehicle designer Bryan Nesbitt was appointed to head the Cadillac brand. Typically, marketing and sales executives were chosen to head brands. Nesbitt had built a positive reputation when he designed the Chrysler PT Cruiser.[20] Such close knowledge of the business was thought necessary for the prosperity (or perhaps survival) of the Cadillac.

Critical Assessments.   Another major reason cognitive skills are so important for leadership is that they facilitate making critical assessments, or thinking critically, about challenges facing the group or entire organization. You will recall that critical thinking refers to making a judgment after analytically evaluating a problem. Almost any course you have ever taken is supposed to improve your critical thinking ability. Making a critical assessment often boils down to sizing up a situation, and analyzing how the group can profit from this situation. Muhtar Kent, the CEO of Coca-Cola, is effective at making critical assessments, as illustrated in his analysis of how the future is bright for Coca-Cola, as follows:

> Kent insists that the beverage industry is better positioned than many other businesses to weather economic difficulties. He says rapid urbanization and blossoming of the middle class in big emerging nations are juicing demand for on-the-go beverages. So many people are moving to urban centers that it's like "adding a city the size of New York to the world every three months."[21] (We might add to Kent's analysis that there are many more outlets for Coca-Cola brands in cities than rural areas.)

Independent Decision Making.   High intelligence is particularly important for leaders, when they have the opportunity to make decisions by themselves and provide direction (such as giving technical instructions) to group members.[22] Problem-solving ability is less important when the leader delegates most of his or her responsibilities to others (or empowers them). High intelligence is important for three major aspects of the leader's job. One aspect is dealing with tasks, such as developing ideas for cost cutting. A second aspect is working with and through other people, or the human relations focus. The third is judging oneself and adapting one's behavior accordingly as in self-awareness and self-objectivity.[23]

Increasing one's mental ability, or raw intelligence, may not be easy to accomplish. Yet, people can develop their cognitive skills by continuous study and by working on challenging problems. The mere act of keeping up with developments in your field can keep you mentally sharp. The comments about enhancing cognitive skills in Chapter 2 are also relevant here.

Emotional Intelligence

Emotional intelligence, as described in Chapter 2, refers to the ability to recognize your emotions and those of people around you. Emotional intelligence also refers to being able to work effectively with the emotions of others to resolve problems, including listening and empathizing. As such, emotional intelligence is a blend of psychological skills that enable the leader to relate effectively to people. Research conducted by Daniel Goleman in many different firms suggests that superb leaders all have one trait in common: superb emotional intelligence.[24] A specific example is that an effective manager or leader can often recognize the motives behind an employee's actions.

> *Visualize yourself as a team leader. Vanessa, one of the team members, says to you, "I'm worried about Rick. I think he needs help. He looks like he has a drinking problem." If you have good emotional intelligence, you might think to yourself, "I wonder why Vanessa is telling me this. Is she simply being helpful? Or is she out to backstab Rick?" Therefore, you would seek some tangible evidence about Rick's alleged problem before acting. You would also seek to spend more time with Vanessa so you can better understand her motives.*
>
> *With much less emotional intelligence, you would immediately get in touch with Rick, accuse him of having a drinking problem, and tell him to get help or get fired.*

Emotional intelligence is also reflected in a leader who incorporates the human touch into business activities, such as building personal relationships with employees and customers. Several years ago, Robert A. Eckert was recruited from Kraft Foods to become chair and CEO of toy maker Mattel. At that time Mattel was in deep financial trouble, and key managers were leaving the company. Eckert moved quickly to bring the famous toy manufacturer back to health. The first steps he took were to share meals with employees in the company cafeteria at every opportunity. During these lunches, he engaged in candid dialogue with employees chosen at random. He reassured employees that their personal growth and development was a major part of his plans for rebuilding Mattel.

Eckert notes, "In this case the emotional intelligence I'd developed over the years was even more important to my success than my traditional, analytical management skills were."[25]

Leaders with emotional intelligence are in tune with the thoughts and emotions of their own and those of other people. The emotionally intelligent leader recognizes that emotions are contagious, such as optimists making other workers optimistic, and pessimists making other workers pessimistic. At the same time, these leaders know that their own emotions are powerful drivers of their group member's moods, and ultimately performance[26]

Emotional intelligence can be developed through working on some of its components, as described in Chapter 2. It is also important to develop the habit of looking to understand the feelings and emotions of people around you. Ask yourself, "How do I feel about what's going on here?" When you have a hunch about people's motives, look for feedback in the future to see if you were right. For example, a little investigation might indicate that Vanessa and Rick are indeed rivals and have a personality clash.

Passion and Enthusiasm

A prominent characteristic of effective leaders is the passion and enthusiasm they have for their work, much like the same quality in creative people. The passion reflects itself in such ways as an intense liking for the business, the customers, and employees. Passion is also reflected in a relentless drive to get work accomplished, and an obsession for achieving company goals. Passion for their work is especially evident in entrepreneurial leaders and small-business owners who are preoccupied with growing their businesses. Many leaders use the term *love* to describe their passion for their work, business, and employees.

Passion and enthusiasm are particularly evident among entrepreneurial leaders. When business founders talk about their products or service, you can hear the excitement in their voices. A representative comment by an entrepreneur is "I love what I do, so it isn't work at all."[27]

To display passion and enthusiasm for your work, you must first find work that creates an inner spark. The work that you choose should be equally or more exciting than your favorite pastime. If not everything about your job excites you, search for its most satisfying or intrinsically motivating elements. For example, the Mattel executive described above is so excited about the interpersonal aspects of his work that his passion inspires employees.

Self-Sacrificing Personality

self-sacrificing personality

A tendency to be more concerned about the welfare and interests of others than those of oneself.

A final trait to be discussed here that contributes to leadership effectiveness is a **self-sacrificing personality**—a tendency to be more concerned about the welfare and interests of others than those of oneself. The self-sacrificing personality translates into a behavior while occupying a leadership role, because the leader acts in the best interest of group members. The self-sacrificing leader is sometimes referred to as a servant leader because his or her primary focus is to serve the group.

Leaders with a self-sacrificing personality are ethical and often forgo personal interests in order to focus on the mission and purpose of the group. Such a leader would be more concerned about the group having high morale and being productive than getting a large financial bonus. Self-sacrificing leaders often engage in personally risky behaviors to benefit the group. An example would be taking the risk of going over-budget to purchase appropriate furnishings for the employee lounge, thereby maintaining morale. A leader with a self-sacrificing personality is typically a good role model for the group in terms of focusing more on the needs of others than being self-centered.[28]

SUGGESTIONS FOR DEVELOPING CHARISMA

LEARNING OBJECTIVE 2

charisma

A special quality of leaders whose purposes, powers, and extraordinary determination differentiate them from others. (However, people besides leaders can be charismatic.)

The study of leadership in recent years has emphasized the importance of inspirational leaders who guide others toward great heights of achievement. Such leaders are said to possess **charisma**, a special quality of leaders whose purposes, powers, and extraordinary determination differentiate them from others.[29] Being charismatic can make a leader's job easier, because leaders have to energize group members.[30]

An important fact about charisma is that it reflects a subjective perception on the part of the person being influenced. Many people regard a leader such as Steve Jobs of Apple Corp. as being powerful and inspirational, and he is regarded as one of the key business leaders of the century. Yet he is also disliked by many people who consider him to be arrogant, prone to throwing tamper tantrums, and a control freak. He has also been involved in legally questionable ways of compensating himself and other members of his team by changing the dates on stock options, thereby guaranteeing a big payoff.

The term *charisma* is most frequently used in association with nationally and internationally known leaders. Yet first-level supervisors, team leaders, and minor sports coaches can also be charismatic. Possessing a naturally dynamic personality is a major contributor to charisma, but a person can engage in many tangible actions that also contribute to charisma. Following are a number of suggestions for behaving charismatically, all based on characteristics and behaviors often found among charismatic leaders. If you are not currently a leader, remember that being perceived as charismatic will help you become one.

1. **Communicate a vision.** A charismatic leader offers an exciting image of where the organization is headed and how to get there. A vision is more than a forecast because it describes an ideal version of the future of an entire organization or an organizational unit such as a department. Richard Branson, the colorful British entrepreneur, has inspired hundreds of employees with his vision of the Virgin brand being a leader in dozens of fields. Among his accomplishments to reach this vision are the Virgin Atlantic airline, Virgin Megastores, and Virgin Cinema. The supervisor of paralegal services might communicate a vision such as "Our paralegal group will become known as the most professional and helpful paralegal group in Arizona." A visionary leader should also have the courage to communicate the vision to others, and to help implement the vision.[31] For the paralegal supervisor, part of implementing the vision might be teaching new technology skills to the paralegals.

   An important part of communicating a vision for good effect is to be clear about what needs to be done to build a better future, even if the future is next week. Based on his study of some of the world's most successful business leaders, Marcus Buckingham concludes that the leader should define the future in vivid terms so that people can see where they are headed.[32]

   Skill-Building Exercise 10-2 will give you a chance to develop visioning skills (a buzzword in business).

2. **Make frequent use of metaphors and analogies.** To inspire people, the charismatic leader uses colorful language and exciting metaphors and analogies. Develop metaphors to inspire people around you. A metaphor commonly used after a group has suffered a setback is, "Like the phoenix, we will rise from the

SKILL-BUILDING EXERCISE 10-2

Creating a Vision

The class organizes into small problem-solving groups. Each group constructs a vision for a unit of an organization or for a total organization of its choosing. Students can choose a well-known business firm, government agency, or an organization with which they are familiar. The vision should be approximately 25 words long and depict a glorious future. A vision is not simply a straight-forward goal, such as "In 2013 our firm will gross $10 million in sales." Remember, the vision statement you draw should inspire people throughout the organization.

If class time permits, volunteers can share their visions with other class members who will provide feedback on the clarity and inspirational qualities of the visions presented.

ashes of defeat." To pick up the spirits of her maintenance group, a maintenance supervisor told the group, "We're a lot like the heating and cooling system in a house. A lot of people don't give us much thought, but without us their lives would be very uncomfortable."

3. **Inspire trust and confidence.** Make your deeds consistent with your promises. As mentioned earlier in this chapter, being trustworthy is a key leadership trait. Get people to believe in your competence by making your accomplishments known in a polite, tactful way. The *socialized charismatic* is likely to inspire trust and confidence because such a leader is ethical and wants to accomplish activities that help others rather than pursuing personal ends such as glory and power.[33]

4. **Be highly energetic and goal oriented.** Impress others with your energy and resourcefulness. To increase your energy supply, exercise frequently, eat well, and get ample rest. Closely related to being goal oriented is being optimistic about what you and the group can accomplish. People also associate optimism with energy. Being grumpy is often associated with being low on energy. You can add to an image of energy by raising and lowering your voice frequently, and avoiding a slow pace.

5. **Be emotionally expressive and warm.** A key characteristic of charismatic leaders is the ability to express feelings openly. Assertiveness is therefore an important component of charisma. In dealing with team members, refer to your feelings at the time, such as "I'm excited because I know we are going to hit our year-end target by mid-October." A study with firefighters showed that leaders who were perceived to be charismatic contributed to the happiness of the group particularly when the leader expressed positive emotion and had a positive outlook.[34]

   Nonverbal emotional expressiveness, such as warm gestures and occasional touching (nonsexual) of group members, also exhibits charisma. Remember, however, that many people resent being touched when at work. Frequent smiling is another way of being emotionally expressive. Also, a warm smile seems to indicate a confident, caring person, which contributes to a perception of charisma.

6. **Make ample use of true stories.** An excellent way of building rapport is to tell stories that deliver a message. People like to hear stories about how a department or company went through hard times when it started, such as how Dell Computer began in a dormitory room at the University of Texas. Telling positive stories has become a widely accepted technique for building relationships with employees. Storytelling adds a touch of warmth to the teller and helps build connections among people who become familiar with the same story.

7. **Be candid and direct.** Practice being direct in saying what you want, rather than being indirect and evasive. If you want someone to help you, don't ask, "Are you busy?" Instead, ask, "Can you help me with a problem I'm having right now?"

8. **Make everybody you meet feel that he or she is important.** For example, at a company social gathering, shake the hand of every person you meet. Also, thank people frequently both orally and by written notes.

9. **Multiply the effectiveness of your handshake.** Shake firmly without creating pain, and make enough eye contact to notice the color of the other person's eyes. When you take that much trouble, you project care and concern.[35]

10. **Stand up straight and use other nonverbal signals of self-confidence.** Practice good posture. Minimize fidgeting, scratching, foot tapping, and speaking in a monotone. Walk at a rapid pace without appearing to be panicked. Dress fashionably without going to the extreme that people notice your clothes more than they notice you.

11. **Be willing to take personal risks.** Charismatic leaders are typically risk takers, and risk taking adds to their charisma. Risks you might take would include extending additional credit to a start-up business, suggesting a bright but costly idea, and recommending that a former felon be given a chance in your firm.

12. **Be self-promotional.** Charismatic leaders are not shy. Instead, they toot their own horns and allow others to know how important they are. Without appearing self-absorbed, you, too, might let others know of your tangible accomplishments. Explain to others the key role that you played on your team or how you achieved a few tough goals.

Despite the importance of developing charisma, being excessively and flamboyantly charismatic can backfire because others may perceive you as self-serving. Therefore, the idea is to sprinkle your charisma with humility, such as admitting when you make a mistake. Also, in recent years top-level management at some companies have replaced high charismatic, rock-star-like leaders with those who concentrate more on running the business instead of gathering publicity for themselves.

DEVELOPING TEAM LEADERSHIP SKILLS

As organizations rely heavily on teams, some of the best opportunities for practicing leadership occur as a team leader. A team leader typically reports to a higher level manager. The team leader is not a boss in the old-fashioned sense, but a facilitator or coach who shares decision making with team members. (A facilitator is a person who helps make things happen without taking control.) A team leader practices **participative leadership,** or sharing authority with the group. Being a participative leader does not mean that the leader just stays out of the way and provides no guidance or encouragement to team members. Research conducted with Norwegian companies supports the belief that danger lurks in the hands of leaders who turn over all responsibility to the group. Employees who received almost no direction from their boss suffered from role ambiguity—confusion about what needs to be done. As a result, these employees suffered from stress, and often found themselves in conflict with each other, including bullying.[37] (The conflict and bullying may have stemmed from workers in dispute over who should do what.)

Self-Assessment Quiz 10-2 gives you an opportunity to gauge your attitudes toward being a participative leader. We will next discuss 10 techniques that would contribute to your effectiveness as a team leader, as outlined in Figure 10-2.

Engage in Shared Leadership

A major initiative for building teamwork is for the team leader to share, or distribute, leadership responsibilities among group members, depending on the task facing the group. So-called *collective leadership* is a reality of the modern workplace. Few leaders have enough skills to provide effective leadership in all situations.[38] The team leader might ask Ruby, who is skilled getting budget approvals, to take leadership of the budget project. Another time the team leader might ask Eric to take leadership on a project for recapturing lost customers because he is effective at damage control.

Research conducted by Craig L. Pearce and his associates at the Graduate School of Management at the University of California suggests that teams that perform poorly are often dominated by the team leader. In contrast, high-performing teams have a shared leadership structure. Part of the team's success can be attributed to the team spirit stemming from the shared leadership. If the organizational or national culture does not favor shared leadership, the good results might not be forthcoming.[39]

participative leadership

Sharing authority with the group.

> " The biggest leadership lesson I learned, and I learned it in the Army, is the importance of small gestures. Little things like saying 'please' and 'thank you'—just the basic respect that people are due, or sending personal notes. I spend a lot of time sending personal notes. "
>
> —Gary E, McCullough, president and chief executive of the Career Education Forum.[36]

FIGURE 10-2 Developing Teamwork

What Style of Leader Are You or Would You Be?

Directions: Check whether each of the following questions is mostly true or mostly false, keeping in mind what you have done, or think you would do, in the scenarios and attitudes described.

	Mostly true	Mostly false
1. I am more likely to take care of a high-impact assignment myself than turn it over to a group member.	_____	_____
2. I would prefer the analytical aspects of a manager's job rather than working directly with group members.	_____	_____
3. An important part of my approach to managing a group is to keep the members informed almost daily of any information that could affect their work.	_____	_____
4. It's a good idea to give two people in the group the same problem, and then choose what appears to be the best solution.	_____	_____
5. It makes good sense for the leader or manager to stay somewhat aloof from the group, so he or she can make a tough decision when necessary.	_____	_____
6. I look for opportunities to obtain group input before making a decision, even on straightforward issues.	_____	_____
7. I would reverse a decision if several of the group members presented evidence that I was wrong.	_____	_____
8. Differences of opinion in the work group are healthy.	_____	_____
9. I think that activities to build team spirit, like the team fixing up a low-income family's house on a Saturday, are an excellent investment of time.	_____	_____
10. If my group were hiring a new member, I would like the person to be interviewed by the entire group.	_____	

(Continued)

Build a Mission Statement

An early point in developing teamwork is to specify the team's mission. The mission should contain a specific goal and purpose, and it should be optimistic and uplifting. Here is an example from a service team at a Volvo dealership:

> To plan and implement a level of automobile service and repair of the highest quality, at a competitive price, that will delight customers and retain their loyalty.

The leader can help develop the mission statement when the team is first formed or at any other time. Developing a mission statement for a longstanding team breathes new life into its activities. Being committed to a mission improves teamwork, as does the process of formulating a mission statement. Skill-Building Exercise 10-3 gives you practice in developing a mission statement for a team.

Show Your Team Members That They Are Trusted

An effective leader is perceived as honest and trustworthy, and he or she trusts team members. The leader should recognize and reward ethical behavior, particularly when there is

Developing a Team Mission Statement

The class organizes into teams of about six people and appoints a team leader. Each team plays the role of a specific team within a company, government agency, or hospital. An example would be the customer service team at a utility company. The task is to develop a mission statement approximating the type described in the text. The team leader might also take notes for the group.

Remember that a mission statement contains a goal and a purpose, and it is uplifting and optimistic. Allow about 15 minutes for preparing the mission statements. The groups then compare mission statements. One representative from each group presents the mission statements to the rest of the class.

a temptation to be dishonest—such as not reporting a quality defect to a customer or cheating on tax returns. Raise expectations of honesty by telling group members you are confident that they will act in ways that bring credit to the organization.[40]

A practical way of demonstrating trust in group members is to avoid closely monitoring their work, and second-guessing their decisions about minor matters such as the best type of border for a report. A **micromanager** is one who closely monitors most aspects of group members' activities, sometimes to the point of being a control freak. As a result, the group members do not feel that the leader or manager trusts them to make even the smallest decisions. One manager checked travel Web sites himself for the best deal after a team member booked plans for a business trip. As a result, team members felt that they were not trusted to care about the financial welfare of the company.

Keep in mind that some micromanagers are successful even if micromanagement can hamper teamwork. Mickey Drexler, the former CEO of Gap, and now CEO of J. Crew, admits to being a control freak, happiest when he is involved in the smallest details of J. Crew's merchandise.[41]

> **micromanager**
>
> One who closely monitors most aspects of group members' activities, sometimes to the point of being a control freak.

Establish a Sense of Urgency and High Performance Standards

To build teamwork, members need to believe that the team has urgent, constructive purposes. A demanding performance challenge helps create and sustain the team. Team members also want to know exactly what is expected of them. The more urgent and relevant the rationale, the more likely it is that the team will perform well.[42] Based on this information, as a team leader you might project a sense of urgency and encourage setting high goals.

Hold Question-and-Answer Sessions with the Team

An effective way of demonstrating participative or team leadership is to hold question-and-answer sessions with team members. Both leader and members ask and answer questions, such as "How can we make an even bigger contribution to the company?" The Quality Department at Delta Dental Plan of California used question-and-answer sessions with success. The process not only boosted morale and made managers more accessible to employees, but also yielded more than 1,000 employee suggestions in the first year. The department head said, "This program totally revolutionized the company. Now employees from other divisions are eager to work in our department."[43]

Encourage Team Members to Recognize Each Other's Accomplishments

Members of a high-spirited team look for ways to encourage and praise each other, including the traditional "high five" signifying an important contribution to the team. Encouragement and praise from the team leader is important, but team members also play an important role in giving positive reinforcement to each other. Team spirit develops as members receive frequent positive feedback from each other.

Recognizing Team Accomplishments

The class organizes into teams of about six, ideally into teams or groups that already worked with each other during the course. If you have not worked with each other, you will have to rely on any impressions you have made of the other members of the team during the course. Team members will be equipped with about six 3 × 5 index cards. However, any other small-size piece of paper will work. Each member of the team thinks carefully about what other members of the team have accomplished during the course, including contribution to team problem-solving, class participation, or perhaps some accomplishment outside of class.

Assume that you have six members on the team. Prepare a card for each member by jotting down whatever accomplishments you have observed of the other team members. Each person therefore prepares five cards that will be handed to the person name on the card, and then given to that person. Each team member will receive five "accomplishment cards," one from the other five members. Each member studies his or her accomplishment cards,

consisting of statements of accomplishments, and perhaps a couple of words of praise. Here are two examples:

> *"I like the way you showed up on time for our study group, and were prepared for action. Nice job, Ben."*
> *"A few times you came up with great ideas in our problem-solving groups. Shauna, you are a really nice team player."*

After all cards have been read carefully, discuss your feelings about their cards and their potential contribution to teamwork. Cover observations, such as the following:

- How much closer to the group do you feel now?
- How much have your efforts in being a team player paid off?
- How useful a technique would this technique of accomplishment recognition be for a workplace team?
- What potential disadvantages do you see to the technique?

Encourage Honest Criticism

A superficial type of camaraderie develops when team members avoid honestly criticizing each other for the sake of group harmony. Avoiding criticism can result in groupthink. As a team leader, you should therefore explain that being a good team player includes offering honest feedback on mistakes and flawed ideas. The team benefits from mutual criticism. A stronger team spirit will develop because team members realize that they are helping each other through honest feedback. An example of honest criticism took place in the shipping department of a manufacturer of small kitchen appliances:

> *One member of a customer service team had designed a satisfaction survey to mail to customers. The purpose of the survey was to investigate whether the packing materials were of satisfactory quality. Another member said, "Are you sure you want to do this? Would we just annoy our customers by asking about packing ingredients? Why waste more paper? We've never had a complaint about packing materials."*

The person whose idea was challenged was miffed at first, but then expressed appreciation. She said, "I guess I went a little overboard on trying to measure customer satisfaction. Maybe we should save our survey dollars for a more important issue."

Use Team Symbols

Teamwork on the athletic field is enhanced by team symbols, such as uniforms and nicknames. The term "Lady Vols," for example, deserves some credit for contributing to the mystique of the University of Tennessee women's basketball team. Symbols can also be an effective team builder in business. Trademarks, logos, mottoes, and other indicators of products both advertise the company and signify a joint effort. Company jackets, caps, T-shirts, mugs, ballpoint pens, and business cards can be modified to symbolize a work unit. As a team leader, you might therefore invest part of your team's budget in an appropriate symbol. Use the opportunity to practice participative leadership. Conduct a group problem-solving session to develop a team logo to place on a T-shirt or cap.

Use Peer Evaluations

In the traditional performance-evaluation system, the manager evaluates group members at regular intervals. With peer-evaluation systems, the team members contribute to the evaluation by submitting evaluations of each other. The evaluations might consist of filling out rating forms about each other's performance. Sometimes brief essays are written about each other and then synthesized by the team leader.

Peer evaluations contribute to teamwork because team members realize that helping each other becomes as important as helping the boss. Similarly, team members recognize that pleasing each other counts as much as pleasing the boss. A potential disadvantage of peer evaluations, however, is that the group members will agree to give each other outstanding evaluations, or to get even with coworkers they do not like.

As a team leader, you might not have the authority to initiate a peer-evaluation system without first checking with your manager. Making a recommendation for peer input into evaluations might demonstrate that you are committed to participative leadership.

Help Team Members See the Big Picture

The team is likely to work together more smoothly when members have a clear understanding of how their work contributes to the company. Communicating the mission as described earlier is a good starting point. Showing the team its specific contribution to the overall organization is equally important. As the team leader you might create a flowchart that tracks an order from the time it is taken to when it is delivered. Show the team its role at each step. The team members may be aware how they contribute to the team, but not how the team contributes to the success of the organization.[44] The team leader of a shipping department at a distribution center explains to his team regularly, "Let's keep this clearly in mind. A big factor in determining whether a customer stays with us is whether the goods arrive on time and in good shape."

Minimize Formation of In-Groups and Out-Groups

An established leadership theory, the **leader-exchange model,** provides useful information for the aspiring team leader. According to this theory, leaders establish unique working relationships with group members. By so doing, they create in-groups and out-groups. The in-groups become part of a smoothly functioning team headed by the leader. Out-group members are less likely to experience good teamwork.[45] Figure 10-3 depicts the major concept of the leader-exchange model.

The in-group may come about because the leader prefers certain group members and therefore is motivated to form good working relationships with them. Conversely, the leader may neglect to form good relationships with people with whom he or she has limited rapport. First impressions count heavily when the leader decides on who is "in" and who is "out." Team leaders should therefore guard against the formation of out groups

leader-exchange model

A theory explaining that group leaders establish unique working relationships with group members, thereby creating in-groups and out-groups.

FIGURE 10-3 The Leader-Member Exchange Model

just because they are not fond of a few team members, or because a given team member gives a poor first impression.

The leader-exchange model does not mean that the team leader should avoid forming unique relationships with team members. What should be avoided is forming an out-group. A study investigated the relationships a group of female sales managers established with both men and women members of their sales groups. Treating members differently based on their needs contributed to leadership effectiveness, such as producing good results.[46] An example of a unique relationship would be to give more recognition to a sales representative who craved recognition.

A useful perspective in understanding the importance of developing teamwork is that leaders should be judged in terms of the performance of the teams or organizations they are responsible for.[47] Good teamwork helps bring about good team performance.

DEVELOPING YOUR LEADERSHIP POTENTIAL

LEARNING OBJECTIVE 4

Much of this book deals directly and indirectly with information that could improve your leadership effectiveness. Chapter 4, on communications, is a case in point. Improving your communications effectiveness would be one way to enhance your ability to lead people. Formal education and leadership development programs also contribute to enhancing leadership potential. (Many such programs include some of the activities found in this chapter.) Here we describe six strategies for developing your leadership potential, in addition to studying and participating in formal programs.

Our approach to developing leadership potential is based on the assumption that leaders are both born and made.[48] You need some basic cognitive and personality characteristics to have the potential to be a leader, yet you need to develop these characteristics through experience and practice. A person who has good problem-solving ability, and is charismatic, still needs to assume leadership responsibility and engage in certain actions to become an effective leader. Among these dozens of activities would be recognizing the accomplishments of others.

Skill-Building Exercise 10-5 about maintaining a personal leadership journal provides a start in practicing and refining leadership skills.

First-level supervisory jobs are an invaluable starting point for developing your leadership potential. It takes considerable skill to manage a rapid-service (fast-food) restaurant or direct a public playground during the summer. First-level supervisors frequently face situations in which group members are poorly trained, poorly paid, and not well motivated to achieve company objectives. Motivating and inspiring entry-level workers is one of the major challenges facing organizations. One of the lessons from the U.S. Marines is that if you want to fire up the front line, you must use discipline to develop pride. The point is that entry-level workers often take pride in being able to abide by tough rules.[49]

1. **Acquire broad experience.** Because leadership varies somewhat with the situation, a sound approach to improving leadership effectiveness is to attempt to gain supervisory experience in different settings. A person who wants to become an executive is well advised to gain supervisory experience in at least two different organizational functions, such as marketing and operations.

Procter & Gamble, long noted for its development of leaders and managers, emphasizes broad experience. If a promising young brand assistant wants to become an executive, the company tries to give him or her as broad an experience as possible. The person might be appointed as assistant manager of Cascade detergent. Later, he or she will run laundry products in Canada, before eventually overseeing all of Northeast Asia.[50]

2. **Model effective leaders.** Another strategy for leadership development is to observe capable leaders in action and then model some of their approaches. You may not want to copy a particular leader entirely, but you can incorporate a few of the behavior patterns into your own leadership style. For instance, most inexperienced leaders have difficulty confronting others. Observe how a skilled confronter handles the situation, and try that person's approach the next time you have unfavorable news to communicate to another person.

My Personal Leadership Journal

A potentially important assist in your development as a leader is to maintain a journal or diary of your leadership experiences. Make a journal entry within 24 hours after you carried out a leadership action of any kind, or failed to do so when the opportunity arose. You will therefore have entries dealing with leadership opportunities both capitalized upon and missed. An example, "A few of my neighbors were complaining about trash flying around the neighborhood on trash pick-up days, particularly when the wind was strong. I took the initiative to send e-mails and flyers to neighborhood residents discussing what could be done about the problem. I suggested that people pack their recycling boxes more tightly. I also suggested ever-so-politely that people should pick up their own flying trash. Soon the problem just about disappeared."

Also include in your journal such entries as feedback you receive on your leadership ability, leadership traits that you appear to be developing, and leadership ideas you learn about. Also, keep a list of leadership articles and books you intend to read. You might also want to record observations about significant acts of leadership or leadership blunders that you have observed in others, either firsthand or through the media.

Review your journal monthly, and make note of any progress you think you have made in developing your leadership skills. Also consider preparing a graph of your progress in developing leadership skills. The vertical axis can represent skill level on a 1-to-100 scale, and the horizontal axis might be divided into time intervals, such as calendar quarters.

3. Self-develop leadership traits and behaviors. Study the leadership traits and behaviors described earlier in this chapter. As a starting point, identify several attributes you think you could strengthen within yourself, given some determination and perhaps combined with the right training program. For example, you might decide that with some effort you could improve your sense of humor. You might also believe that you could remember to encourage honest criticism within the team. It is also helpful to obtain feedback from valid sources (such as a trusted manager) about which traits and behaviors you particularly need to develop.

4. Become an integrated human being. A philosophical approach to leadership suggests that the model leader is first and foremost a fully functioning person. According to William D. Hitt, mastering the art of leadership comes with self-mastery. Leadership development is the process of self-development. As a result, the process of becoming a leader is similar to the process of becoming an integrated human being. For example, you need to develop values that guide your behavior before you can adequately guide the behavior of others.

The model (or ideal) leader, according to Hitt, must possess six character traits: identity (know thyself), independence, authenticity, responsibility, courage, and integrity.[51] A more recent analysis of leadership development suggests that self-understanding is a major vehicle for improvement. After attaining self-insight, you can move forward with leadership development.[52] Suppose you discover that you feel intimidated by people who are older and more experienced than you. Armed with this self-insight you can gradually overcome the problem and feel more comfortable leading workers who are older and more experienced than you. All of the traits Hitt mentions have everyday meanings, but they can also have personal meanings. Part of becoming an integrated person is to answer such questions as "What do I mean when I say I have integrity?"

5. Practice a little leadership. An effective way to develop your leadership skills is to look for opportunities to exert a small amount of helpful leadership in contrast to waiting for opportunities to accomplish extraordinary deeds. The "little leadership" might involve such behaviors as mentoring a struggling team member, coaching somebody about how to use a new high-tech device, or making a suggestion about improving a product. In the words of Michael E. McGill and John W. Slocum, Jr., "For those who want to stand atop the dugout, dance with the elephants, fly with the buffaloes, soar with eagles, or perform other mystical and heroic acts of large leadership, our little leadership may seem all too managerial, too modest, and too mundane."[53]

6. Help your leader lead. According to Michael Useem, leaders need your assistance so that they can do a good job. "If people are afraid to help their leaders lead, their leaders will fail."[54] A group member is often closer to the market and closer to how the product is used. Therefore, he or she can provide useful information to the person in the formal leadership position. When you help the people above you avoid a mistake or capitalize upon an opportunity, you help the entire company. At the same time, you are developing your ability to take the initiative and lead.

SELF-ASSESSMENT QUIZZES IN OVERVIEW

Self-Assessment Quiz 10-1, The Assertiveness Scale, gave you an opportunity to measure your degree of assertiveness, a key personality trait that is important for leadership as well as many other interpersonal activities such as resolving conflict, volunteering for assignments, getting noticed by your manager, and finding companionship. Self-Assessment Quiz 10-2, What Style of Leader Are You or Would You Be?, takes you more specifically into the basics of leadership. For many situations, it will be helpful to emphasize participative or team leadership because organizations have become more democratic. For example, imagine yourself as the supervisor of a credit and collection group. It would probably be to your advantage to ask the credit specialists in your group what they think would be a few good ways to collect more payments on time. Yet in crisis situations, it may be more helpful to be more directive and tell people what to do without emphasizing group participation. For example, the company might ask you as the supervisor of credit and collections to bring in some money fast to help fend off bankruptcy.

Concept Review and Reinforcement

Key Terms

assertiveness 209
cognitive factors 213
self-sacrificing personality 215

charisma 216
participative leadership 218
micromanager 221

leader-exchange model 223

Summary

Effective leadership depends on having the right personal characteristics and taking the appropriate actions. Leadership is the ability to inspire support and confidence among the people who are needed to achieve company goals. People can exercise leadership whether or not they occupy a formal leadership position.

Certain traits contribute heavily to leadership effectiveness. Among them are self-confidence and leadership self-efficacy, positive core self-evaluation, assertiveness, trustworthiness and morality, sense of humor, self-awareness and self-objectivity, cognitive skills including critical assessments, emotional intelligence, passion and enthusiasm, and self-sacrificing personality.

Although charisma depends heavily on personal characteristics, people can work toward being charismatic. Suggestions for behaving charismatically include the following:

1. Communicate a vision
2. Make frequent use of metaphors and analogies
3. Inspire trust and confidence
4. Be highly energetic and action goal oriented
5. Be emotionally expressive and warm
6. Make ample use of true stories
7. Be candid and direct
8. Make everyone you meet feel that he or she is important
9. Multiply the effectiveness of your handshake
10. Stand up straight and use other nonverbal signals of self-confidence

11. Be willing to take personal risks
12. Be self-promotional.

A team leader acts as a facilitator or coach who shares decision making with team members, thus practicing participative leadership. The following are some techniques for effective team leadership:

1. Engage in shared leadership
2. Build a mission statement
3. Show your team members that they are trusted
4. Establish a sense of urgency and high performance standards
5. Hold question-and-answer sessions with the team
6. Encourage team members to recognize each other's accomplishments
7. Encourage honest criticism
8. Use team symbols
9. Use peer evaluations
10. Help team members see the big picture
11. Minimize formation of in-groups and out-groups.

In addition to participating in formal leadership development programs, six strategies for developing leadership potential are to (1) acquire broad experience, (2) model effective leaders, (3) self-develop leadership traits and behaviors, (4) become an integrated human being (a fully functioning person), (5) practice small leadership acts, and (6) help your leader lead.

Questions for Discussion and Review

1. Informal observation suggests that people who were voted "most likely to succeed" in high school are frequently found in leadership positions later in life. What explanation can you offer for these predictions about success so often being true?

2. In business organizations, leaders are usually paid way more than people in specialized positions, such as a chemist or auditor. Why should leaders be so highly paid?

3. What does it mean to say that a person has the "right stuff" for being a leader?

4. How can a person demonstrate to others in the company that he or she is trustworthy enough to be considered for a leadership position?

5. Why does a leader need good emotional intelligence? Shouldn't a leader be a take-charge person focused on obtaining results like making money or winning ball games?

6. What can you do this week to increase your charisma?

7. What might be the reason that small gestures such as saying "thank you" and writing notes of appreciation contribute to a leader's effectiveness?

8. In what ways do the concepts of charismatic leadership and participative leadership differ substantially from each other?

9. How might a person is in a highly specialized field, such as information technology or accounting, achieve broad experience in order to qualify for a leadership position?

10. Assume that a student obtains a part-time job as an assistant store manager. What can this person do to capitalize on this position for leadership experience?

The Web Corner

http://www.ccl.org
(Center for Creative Leadership)

http://www.core-edge.com
(Attaining power and charisma; includes a video)

http://www.buzzle.com
(Developing critical thinking skills)

Internet Skill Builder: Developing Your Charisma

One approach to developing charisma for leadership is to read brief clips about charismatic people and look for any practical suggestions from these stories. For example, you might read that a successful charismatic leader invests time in writing hand-written notes of appreciation to his or her subordinates. Search the Web for at least three brief stories about charismatic leaders. After studying these stories, arrive at least three practical suggestions for developing your charisma. Attempt to implement these suggestions during the next 12-month period and see if people react positively to your charismatic initiatives.

Developing Your Human Relations Skills

Interpersonal Relations Case 10.1

Chancellor Rhee Shakes up D.C.

Michelle Rhee took over the responsibility for the 144 schools in Washington D.C. in June 2007, when Mayor Adrian Fenty appointed her Chancellor, District of Columbia Public Schools. Her appointment stunned people connected with the D.C. school system. Rhee, aged 37 at that time, had no experience running a school. The challenge seemed overwhelming with 45,000 students who collectively ranked last in math among 11 urban school systems. With two years of being appointed chancellor, Rhee had developed the reputation of being hated by teachers and feared by principals.

When invited to interview for the position, Rhee was running a nonprofit organization called the New Teacher Project, which helps schools recruit good teachers. Another question mark was that Rhee is from Ohio rather than Washington D.C., and she is Korean American in a majority African-American city. She now says, "I was the worst pick on the face of the earth." However, Rhee was once an elementary teacher in Baltimore, and the experience taught her that good teachers could alter the lives of children.

Two years after Rhee's appointment, test scores released by the U.S. Department of Education showed that Washington's fourth graders made the largest gains in math among big city school systems during a two-year period. Rhee has replaced who she perceived to be ineffective principals, laid off teachers based on "quality, not by seniority," and shuttered failing schools.

Some of Rhee's thinking about her role as chancellor is revealed in her comments in relation to several aspects of her work, as described next.

How to Lead: I often get in trouble for saying this, but I actually think it's true that collaboration and consensus-building and all those things are quite frankly overrated. No CEOs run their company by committees. So why should we run a school district by committee? The bottom line is that in order to run an effective organization, you need one leader who has a very clear vision for what needs to happen and the authority to make that happen.

Firing Employees: We had to conduct a reduction in force of about 500 employees in the district. And that included about 250 or so teachers. We made the decision that we were going to conduct the layoffs by quality, not by seniority. It caused this firestorm. From a managerial standpoint, it would make no sense to do a layoff by seniority only. In a school district that is struggling as hard as ours is, we have to be able to look at the quality and value that different employees are adding.

Rhee recognizes that she has been often criticized, but she suggests that some ruthlessness is required. "Have I rubbed people the wrong way? Definitely. If I changed my style, I might make people a little more comfortable," she says. "But I think there's real danger in acting in a way that makes adults feel better. Because where does that stop?"

Money for Nothing: We spend more money per child in this city than almost any other urban jurisdiction in the country, and our results are at the absolute bottom. So it goes against the idea that you have to put more money into education, and that's how you are going to fix it.

It comes down to two basic things about why we spend so much money and the results aren't as good. First is a complete and utter lack of accountability in this system. And the second is a lack of political courage on the part of most people who are running cities and school districts.

We have a system in which you can have been teaching for 25 to 30 years. Every year, you could actually take your children backward—not just to improve their learning as much as you should, but your kids can move backward in your classroom every year—and you will continue to have a job. You will continue to get your step raise. You will continue to get your negotiated union increases. Where else can that happen, except in public education? So that lack of public accountability is a significant problem.

And then on the courage part, I think that when you're talking about making the difficult decision that are necessary in this climate—closing schools, firing teachers, removing principals, and so on—those are the thing that make most politicians run for the hills because it makes your phone ring off the hook and people are saying, "Oh, don't close this school," "Don't fire this person."

Michelle Rhee resigned in October 2010, a decision that the teacher's union immediately endorsed.

Case Questions

1. Identify three leadership traits in which Michelle Rhee score high or low, and cite your evidence.
2. What recommendations can you offer Rhee to help her become an even more effective leader?
3. What risks do you see of Rhee becoming a victim of workplace violence?
4. What evidence is found in this case that Michelle Rhee engages is good at making critical assessments?

5. Assume that Rhee held a leadership position in your field of interest, explain whether you would enjoy working for her.

Source: The opening facts in the story are from Amanda Ripley, "Can She Save Our Schools?" *Time*, December 8, 2008, p. 36. The quote about ruthlessness is from p. 40 of the same article. "Who's Got Michelle Rhee's Back? *The Wall Street Journal* (editorial), December 14, 2009, p. A24. The interview comments are from Michelle Rhee, "An Educated Work Force," *The Wall Street Journal*, November 23, 2009, p. R3.

Interpersonal Relations Case 10.2

So Is this How You Learn Leadership

Len Olsen, aged 23, was proud to be selected as part of the leader's program at a national chain of family restaurants. Workers selected for the leadership program are considered to be in line for running individual restaurants, and also as potential candidates in the long run for leadership positions in corporate headquarters. Before entering the key phase of the leadership program, all candidates must first work a minimum of one year as a server or bartender at one of the company stores (restaurants).

Len worked one year as a server in a downtown Chicago restaurant, and then was assigned to another Chicago restaurant to begin his formal leadership training as an assistant manager. His assignments as an assistant manager included scheduling the wait staff, conducting preliminary screen interviews of job applicants, and resolving problems with customers. After three months on the job, Len was asked by a member of the corporate human resources staff how his leadership training program was going; he replied, "I'm a little bit skeptical. I don't think I'm learning much about leadership."

When asked why he didn't think he was learning much about leadership, Len listed what he considered three recent examples of the type of responsibilities he faced regularly:

- At 11 yesterday morning, I received a phone call from Annie, one of the servers. She told me she wouldn't be able to work that afternoon because her Labrador retriever had become quite ill and she had

to take the Lab to the vet. I told Annie that we desperately needed her that afternoon because of a large luncheon party. Annie told me her dog was more important to her than the job.

- Two weeks ago, Gus, one of our salad chefs, showed up to work absolutely drunk. I told him that working while drunk was absolutely against the company rules. He got a little belligerent, but I did get him to take a taxi home at the company expense.

- Two days ago, a customer in the restaurant spilled a cup of hot coffee on herself while answering a call on her cell phone. She told me that the coffee was too hot and that she was going to sue the restaurant. I explained to her tactfully that unless she was truly burned, she had no claim. I offered to have the restaurant pay for her dry cleaning, and then she calmed down.

Olsen then said to the human resources manager, "What has stuff like this got to do with leadership? I mean, I'm not creating great visions or inspiring hordes of people. In what way am I becoming a leader?"

Case Questions

1. What is your opinion of the contribution of Olsen's representative experiences to his development as a leader?
2. What else can the restaurant chain do to help Olsen and others in the leadership program develop as leaders?

CHAPTER 11

Motivating Others

Steven A. Burd, the CEO of Safeway, Inc., and founder of the Coalition to Advance Healthcare Reform, wrote the following:

> At Safeway we believe that well-designed health care reform, utilizing market-based solution, can ultimately reduce our nation's health care bill by 40%. The key to achieving these savings is health care plans that reward healthy behavior. As a self-insured

After reading and studying this chapter and doing the exercises, you should be able to

1. Motivate people by responding to their self-interests.
2. Make effective use of positive reinforcement to motivate people in many situations.
3. Make effective use of recognition to motivate others.
4. Apply expectancy theory as a comprehensive way of motivating others.
5. Diagnose situations to analyze the strength of motivation present.
6. Identify effective techniques for self-motivation.

employer, Safeway designed just such a plan four years ago and has made continuous improvements each year. The results have been remarkable. During this four-year period, we have kept our per capita health care costs flat (that includes both the employer and employee portion), while most American companies' costs have increased 38% over the same four years.

Safeway's plan capitalizes on two key insights gained in 2005. The first is that 70% of all health care costs are the direct result of behavior. The second insight, which is well understood by providers of health care, is that 74% of all costs are confined to four chronic conditions (cardiovascular disease, cancer, diabetes, and obesity). Furthermore, 80% of cardiovascular disease and diabetes is preventable, 60% of cancers are preventable, and more than 90% of obesity is preventable.

The big difference between Safeway and most employers is that we have pronounced differences in premiums that reflect each covered member's behaviors. Currently we are focused on tobacco usage, healthy weight, blood pressure and cholesterol levels.

Safeway's Healthy Measures program is completely voluntary and currently covers 74% of the insured nonunion workforce. Employees are tested for the four measures cited above and receive premium discounts off a "base level" premium for each test they pass. Data is [are] collected by outside parties and not shared with company management. If they pass all four tests, annual premiums are reduced $780 for individuals and $1,560 for families. Should they fail any or all tests, they can be tested again in 12 months. If they pass or have made appropriate progress on something like obesity, the company provides a refund equal to the premium differences established at the beginning of the plan year.

At Safeway we are building a culture of heath and fitness. The numbers speak for themselves. Our obesity and smoking rates are roughly 70% of the national average and our health care costs for four years have held constant. When surveyed, 78% of our employees rated out plan good, very good, or excellent. In addition, 76% asked for more financial incentives to reward healthy behaviors. We have heard from dozens of employees who lost weight, lowered their blood pressure and cholesterol levels, and are enjoying better health because of this program. Many discovered for the first time that they have high blood pressure, and others have been told by their doctor that they have added years to their life.[1]

motivation

An internal state that leads to effort expended toward objectives; an activity performed by one person to get another to accomplish work.

The Safeway experience demonstrates that by rewarding workers for desirable behavior, they will often increase such behavior. You may not be in a position to offer health insurance premium discounts to a coworker who does what you want, but the principle of being systematic about motivating others remains the same. **Motivation** has two meanings: (1) an internal state that leads to effort expended toward objectives, and (2) an activity performed by one person to get another to accomplish work. We often think of a manager or leader as the one attempting to motivate group members. Yet, many people in the workplace have a need to motivate others. To accomplish their work, people must motivate individuals who report to them, coworkers, supervisors, or customers. Developing motivational skills will therefore help you accomplish more work than you would if you relied strictly on the good nature and team spirit of others.

This chapter describes how to develop motivational skills based on four related explanations of motivation. We progress from the simplest to the most complex explanation. We also describe techniques for motivating yourself. As a starting point in thinking through how to motivate others, do Self-Assessment Quiz 11-1.

SELF-ASSESSMENT QUIZ 11-1

My Approach to Motivating Others

Directions: Describe how often you act or think in the way indicated by the following statements when you are attempting to motivate another person. Circle the appropriate number for each statement using the following scale: Very infrequently (VI); Infrequently (I); Sometimes (S); Frequently (F); Very frequently (VF).

		VI	I	S	F	VF
1.	I ask the other person what he or she is hoping to achieve in the situation.	1	2	3	4	5
2.	I attempt to figure out whether the person has the ability to do what I need done.	1	2	3	4	5
3.	When another person is heel-dragging, it usually means he or she is lazy.	5	4	3	2	1
4.	I explain exactly what I want to the person I'm trying to motivate.	1	2	3	4	5
5.	I like to give the other person a reward up front so that he or she will be motivated.	5	4	3	2	1
6.	I give lots of feedback when another person is performing a task for me.	1	2	3	4	5
7.	I like to belittle another person enough so that he or she will be intimidated into doing what I need done.	5	4	3	2	1
8.	I make sure that the other person feels treated fairly.	1	2	3	4	5
9.	I figure that if I smile nicely I can get the other person to work as hard as I need.	5	4	3	2	1
10.	I attempt to get what I need done by instilling fear in the other person.	5	4	3	2	1
11.	I specify exactly what needs to be accomplished.	1	2	3	4	5
12.	I generously praise people who help me get my work accomplished.	1	2	3	4	5
13.	A job well done is its own reward. I therefore keep praise to a minimum.	5	4	3	2	1
14.	I make sure that I let people know how well they have done in meeting my expectations on a task.	1	2	3	4	5
15.	To be fair, I attempt to reward people similarly no matter how well they have performed.	5	4	3	2	1
16.	When somebody doing work for me performs well, I recognize his or her accomplishments promptly.	1	2	3	4	5
17.	Before giving somebody a reward, I attempt to find out what would appeal to that person.	1	2	3	4	5
18.	I make it a policy not to thank somebody for doing a job he or she is paid to do.	5	4	3	2	1

MOTIVATION SKILL BASED ON THE PRINCIPLE OF "WHAT'S IN IT FOR ME?"

LEARNING OBJECTIVE 1

The most fundamental principle of human motivation is that people are motivated by self-interest. This principle is referred to as "What's in it for me?" or WIIFM (pronounced wiff'em). Reflect on your own experience. Before working hard to accomplish a task, you probably want to know how you will benefit. If your manager asks you to work extra hours to take care of an emergency, you will most likely oblige. Yet underneath you might be thinking, "If I work these extra hours, my boss will think highly of me. As a result, I will probably receive a good performance evaluation and maybe a better-than-average salary increase."

If your instructor asks you to prepare a lengthy research paper, you might be motivated to work to the best of your ability. But before getting down to the task, it is likely that questions have raced through your mind, such as "Will this paper elevate my grade?" or "Will I pick up information that will help me in my career?"

Why Help Others?   A perplexing issue is how the WIIFM principle explains why people are motivated to help others. Why would a company CEO donate gift baskets of food to homeless people? Why hire a virtually unemployable person for a nonproductive job in the mailroom? People who perform acts of social good receive the reward of feeling better about themselves. In psychological terms, they satisfy their needs to nurture (take care of) others. More cynically, helping those less fortunate leads to recognition for being a Good Samaritan.

The widespread willingness of people to contribute to Web sites that provide useful information to others gives additional insights into what satisfaction many people obtain from working for free. According to Prabhakar Raghavan, chief of Yahoo!, approximately 4 to 6 percent of Yahoo's users contribute their energies for free in such matters as reviewing films or handling questions at Yahoo! Answers. The motivation is often pride. At other times, Net volunteers combine their motivation to help others with the motivation to build their online presence, or *personal brand*. ThisNext is a social network where participants exchange shopping leads, and many volunteers help run the site. Gordon Gould, the operator of ThisNext, says that volunteer workers prosper because "They can build their brands."[2] The takeaway here is that even when people do not get paid for working, they are usually obtaining an important personal benefit.

Appling the WIIFM Principle.   To use the WIIFM principle in motivating others, you have to be aware of the intensity of the person's desire.[3] A person can be highly motivated, mildly motivated, or only slightly motivated, depending on the intensity of his or her WIIFM principle. A company might offer outstanding performers the opportunity to work at home one day per week. Employees who are intensely motivated to work at home will work virtually up to the capacity to achieve a rating of outstanding performer.

To use the WIIFM principle in motivating others, you must find out what needs, desires, or motives a person is attempting to satisfy. A need acts as an internal energy force. You find out what these needs are by asking people what they want or by observing what interests them. For instance, the way a manager might motivate a recognition-hungry group member is to tell that person, "If you perform 10 percent above quota for six consecutive months, we will get you a plaque signifying your achievement to hang on the wall."

The Importance of Needs. One of the reasons needs are so important in understanding motivation is that needs lead to behavior, or what people actually do. A person might be extraverted because of a need to affiliate with others so that person might be motivated by the opportunity to work closely with others. Another person might be conscientious partly because of a need for achievement. This individual might be motivated by the opportunity to accomplish useful work.[4]

Employee needs have been classified in many ways, yet most of these lists overlap. According to a representative classification, 99 percent of employees are motivated by one or more of the following seven needs:

1. **The need for achievement.** Employees with strong achievement needs seek the satisfaction of completing projects successfully. They want to apply their talents to attain success, and they find joy in accomplishment for its own sake.

2. **The need for power.** Employees with a strong power need derive satisfaction from influencing and controlling others, and they aspire to become executives. These employees like to lead and persuade and be in charge of resources such as budgets.

3. **The need for affiliation.** Employees with a strong need for affiliation derive satisfaction from interacting with others, being part of a work group, and forming friendships. The same employees are motivated to avoid working alone for long periods of time.

4. **The need for autonomy.** Employees with a strong need for autonomy seek freedom and independence, such as having almost complete responsibility for a project. The same employees are motivated to avoid working in a team effort for long periods of time. Many industrial sales representatives (those who sell to companies) have a strong need for autonomy.

5. **The need for esteem.** Employees with a strong need for esteem want to feel good about themselves, and they judge their worth to a large extent based on how much recognition and praise they receive.

6. **The need for safety and security.** Employees with strong needs for safety and security seek job security, steady income, ample medical and dental insurance, and a hazard-free work environment.

7. **The need for equity.** Employees with a strong need for equity seek fair treatment. They often compare working hours, job responsibilities, salary, and privileges to those of coworkers, and they will become discouraged if coworkers are receiving better treatment.[5]

Recognizing such needs, as well as other needs and interests, helps you apply the WIIFM principle. Skill-Building Exercise 11-1 gives you the opportunity to do the preliminary work needed for applying the WIIFM principle.

behavior modification

An attempt to change behavior by manipulating rewards and punishments.

law of effect

Behavior that leads to a positive consequence for the individual tends to be repeated, whereas behavior that leads to a negative consequence tends not to be repeated.

USING POSITIVE REINFORCEMENT TO MOTIVATE OTHERS

A widely used formal method of motivating people in the workplace is **behavior modification,** an attempt to change behavior by manipulating rewards and punishments. Behavior modification is based on a fundamental principle of human behavior: the law of effect. According to the **law of effect,** behavior that leads to a positive consequence for the individual tends to be repeated, whereas behavior that leads to a negative consequence tends not to be repeated.

The focus of behavior modification on the job is to reward employees for behaving in ways that support what the organization is attempting to accomplish, such as improved productivity. Our approach to skill development in behavior modification is to emphasize positive reinforcement because this is the modification strategy most widely used in the workplace. **Positive reinforcement** means increasing the probability that behavior will be repeated by rewarding people for making the desired response. The phrase *increasing the probability* means that positive reinforcement improves learning and motivation but is not 100 percent effective. The phrase *making the desired response* is also noteworthy. To use positive reinforcement properly, a reward must be contingent upon doing something right. Simply paying somebody a compliment or giving the person something of value is not positive reinforcement. Behavior modification involves linking consequences to what the person has or has not accomplished.

positive reinforcement

Increasing the probability that behavior will be repeated by rewarding people for making the desired response.

Positive reinforcement is easy to visualize with well-structured jobs, such as data entry or producing parts. Yet positive reinforcement is also used to encourage desired behavior in highly paid, complex jobs. An accountant who developed a new method of the company getting paid faster might be rewarded with two extra days of vacation.

Negative reinforcement (or avoidance motivation) means rewarding people by taking away an uncomfortable consequence of their behavior. Negative reinforcement is a reward because a disliked consequence is avoided or withdrawn. You are subject to negative reinforcement when you are told, "Your insurance rate will go down if you receive no traffic violations for 12 months." The uncomfortable consequence removed is a high insurance premium. Removing the undesirable consequence is contingent upon your making the right response—driving within the law.

negative reinforcement (avoidance motivation)

Rewarding people by taking away an uncomfortable consequence of their behavior.

Be careful not to make the common mistake of confusing negative reinforcement with punishment. Negative reinforcement is the opposite of punishment. It involves rewarding someone by removing a punishment or uncomfortable situation.

To use positive reinforcement effectively, certain rules and procedures must be followed, as outlined in Figure 11-1. Although using rewards to motivate people seems straightforward, behavior modification requires a systematic approach. The rules are specified from the standpoint of the person trying to motivate another individual, such as a team member, coworker, supervisor, or customer.

Rule 1: State Clearly What Behavior Will Lead to a Reward. The nature of good performance, or the goals, must be agreed upon by the manager and group member. Clarification might take this form: "We need to decrease by 40 percent the number of new credit card customers who have delinquent accounts of 60 days or more."

Rule 2: Choose an Appropriate Reward. An appropriate reward is effective in motivating a given person and feasible from the standpoint of the individual or the company.

FIGURE 11-1 Rules and Procedures for Positive Reinforcement

1. State clearly what behavior will lead to a reward.
2. Choose an appropriate reward.
3. Supply ample feedback.
4. Schedule rewards intermittently.
5. Make the reward follow the observed behavior closely in time.
6. Make the reward fit the behavior.
7. Make the reward visible.
8. Change the reward periodically.
9. Reward the group or team also.

If one reward does not motivate the person, try another. The importance of choosing the right reward underscores the fact that not all rewards are reinforcers. A reward is something of perceived value by the person giving the reward. (A supervisor might think that giving a gift certificate to a particular fast-food restaurant is a reward, but if the employee dislikes that restaurant it is not a true reward.) If the reward does not lead to strengthening a desired response (such as wearing safety goggles), it is not a true reinforcer.[6]

Figure 11-2 provides a list of factors by employees as to what would satisfy them on the job. At the same time, these factors can be translated into potential rewards for employees. For example, if employees value bonuses, a high-performing employee

FIGURE 11-2 What Workers Want from Their Jobs and Their Employers

1. Competitive salary
2. 100 percent of health care coverage paid by employers
3. Company-matched 401(k) investments
4. Bonus programs
5. Flexible schedules
6. Compressed workweek
7. Good relationship with the boss
8. Being treated with respect
9. Making a contribution to the company and perhaps society.

Note: Although only factors 1, 2, and 3 are in rank order, factors 4 through 9 are also considered important for job satisfaction.

Source: Table prepared from survey of 1,051 workers presented in "Listen up Employers; Employees Know What They Want This Labor Day," *www.kronos.com*, August 2, 2006, p. 1. The survey was conducted by Harris Interactive and sponsored by Kronos Incorporated. Factor 9 is from Timothy R. Clark, "Engaging the Disengaged," *HR Magazine*, April 2008, p. 112.

might be given some assurance of receiving a bonus for above-average employment. Because all of these factors are ranked as *important* job factors by employees, all of them are potentially appropriate rewards.

Rule 3: Supply Ample Feedback. Positive reinforcement cannot work without frequent feedback to individuals. Feedback can take the form of simply telling people they have done something right or wrong. Brief e-mail messages or handwritten notes are other forms of feedback. Many effective motivators, including Jack Welch, the legendary former CEO of General Electric, made extensive use of handwritten thank-you notes. Negative feedback by e-mail should be written tactfully to avoid resentment.

Rule 4: Schedule Rewards Intermittently. Rewards should not be given on every occasion of good performance. **Intermittent rewards** sustain desired behaviors longer and also slow down the process of behaviors fading away when they are not rewarded. If each correct performance results in a reward, the behavior will stop shortly after a performance in which the reward is not received. Another problem is that a reward given continuously may lose its impact. Also, automatic rewards for doing the right thing become perceived as entitlements. As the reward becomes almost guaranteed, the employee feels entitled to it, and the reward loses its motivational effectiveness much like a weekly paycheck. A practical value of intermittent reinforcement is that it saves time. Few managers or team leaders have enough time to dispense rewards for every correct action by group members.

Rule 5: Make the Reward Follow the Observed Behavior Closely in Time. For maximum effectiveness, people should be rewarded soon after doing something right. A built-in, or intrinsic, feedback system, such as software working or not working, capitalizes on this principle. If you are administering rewards and punishments, strive to administer them the same day they are earned. Suppose a coworker feeds you exactly the information you need to make a PowerPoint presentation for the group. Send your coworker an e-mail or text message of appreciation right that day. Or, be old fashioned, and thank him or her in person.

Rule 6: Make the Reward Fit the Behavior. People who are inexperienced in applying positive reinforcement often overdo the intensity of spoken rewards. When an employee does something of an ordinary nature correctly, simple praise such as "Good job" is preferable to "Fantastic performance." A related idea is that the magnitude of the reward should vary with the magnitude of the accomplishment.

Recent research about leadership confirms the importance of making rewards contingent upon both doing the right thing, as well as the magnitude of the behavior or performance. A study in six banks indicated that when leaders made rewards based on true performance, workers perceived a higher degree of fairness in their work climate (or atmosphere).[7]

Rule 7: Make the Reward Visible. Another important characteristic of an effective reward is the extent to which it is visible, or noticeable, to other employees. When other workers notice the reward, its impact multiplies because other people observe what kind of behavior is rewarded.[8] Assume that you are being informed about a coworker having received an exciting assignment because of high performance. You might strive to accomplish the same level of performance. Rewards should also be visible, or noticeable, to the employee. A reward of 10 dollars per week for 30 weeks added to a person's paycheck might be hardly noticeable, after payroll deductions. However, a bonus check for $300 might be very noticeable.

Rule 8: Change the Reward Periodically. Rewards do not retain their effectiveness indefinitely. Employees and customers lose interest in striving for a reward they have received many times in the past. This is particularly true of a repetitive statement, such as "Nice job" or "Congratulations." It is helpful for the person giving out the rewards to study the list of potential rewards and try different ones from time to time. A general approach relating to the previous rules is to look for creative ways to apply behavior modification. The creativity might be in the selection

" The real opportunity for growth comes in utilizing your strengths. Great managers catch people doing the right things. "
—Curt Coffman of the Gallup Organization

intermittent reward
A reward that is given for good performance occasionally, but not always.

Positive Reinforcement

In both of the following scenarios, one student plays the role of the person attempting to give positive reinforcement, and therefore motivate the other individual. Another student plays the role of the person who is the recipient of these attempts at motivation.

Scenario 1: Rewarding a Customer Service Representative. The customer service manager carefully reviews customer service reports to discover that one service rep has resolved the most complaints for four consecutive weeks. Since this rep has been on the job only for six months, the manager wants to make sure that the rep feels amply rewarded and appreciated. The manager calls the rep into the office to discuss this outstanding performance and give an appropriate reward.

Scenario 2: Rewarding Your Boss. The group member has just received a wonderful assignment from the boss, offering the opportunity to spend a few days with key customers who are located out of town. This is the group member's first really exciting extra assignment. As a consequence, the worker wants to encourage the boss to keep him or her in mind for future assignments of this nature. The boss was not expecting to be rewarded for making an assignment that fit the company's needs.

For both scenarios, observers rate the role players on two dimensions, using a 1-to-5 scale from very poor to very good. One dimension is "effective use of positive reinforcement techniques." The second dimension is "acting ability." A few observers might voluntarily provide feedback to the role players in terms of sharing their ratings and observations. The course instructor might also provide feedback.

of the reward, or how the reward is administered. Several illustrative ideas include:

- **Applause:** Choose an especially effective employee, and at the end of the week or month have coworkers gather and clap for the person.
- **Giraffe award:** Give a certificate saying, "Thanks for sticking your neck out." The name of the reward and the certificate reward risk taking.
- **Safety jackpot:** Managers give five "lotto" cards to employees who follow safety practices. Workers scratch off the cards to learn how many points they have won. Points are then redeemed via a gift catalog or Web site.[9]

Rule 9: Reward the Group or Team Also. Positive reinforcement applies to groups as well as individuals in the sense that individuals within the group can be rewarded collectively. An obvious rule is that the group should receive a reward commensurate with its accomplishment. However, several of the other eight rules also apply. An example of a team reward is to implement a "Team of the Month" program.[10]

Perform Skill-Building Exercise 11-2 to practice several of these rules for using positive reinforcement.

BACK TO THE OPENING CASE

Safeway CEO Steven A. Burd is on the right track in terms of making effective use of positive reinforcement to both help employees improve their health, and at the same time reduce one of the major costs of operating a business—paying for health care costs. As the cost of health care insurance premiums has continued to rise, even with the new federal government health care program, the rewards in the form of insurance premium reductions have gained in potency.

USING RECOGNITION TO MOTIVATE OTHERS

LEARNING OBJECTIVE 3

Motivating others by giving them recognition and praise can be considered a direct application of positive reinforcement. Nevertheless, recognition is such a potentially powerful motivator that it merits separate attention. Also, recognition programs to reward and motivate employees are standard practice in business and nonprofit firms. Examples would be rewarding high-performing employees with a crystal vase (company logo inscribed) or designating them "employee of the month." Outstanding sales representatives ("beauty consultants") receive recognition, and at Mary Kay rewards in the form of pink cell phones, pink Buicks, and pink Cadillacs—in the United States, as well as in China and other countries.[11] The pink, however, is just a tinge of pink to give it a modern look. In keeping with the theme of this book, the emphasis is on individual, rather than organizational, use of recognition to motivate.

Why Recognition Is an Effective Motivator

Recognition is a strong motivator because it is a normal human need to crave recognition. At the same time, recognition is effective because most workers feel they do not receive enough notice. Several studies conducted over a 50-year time span have indicated that employees welcome praise for a job well done as much as a regular paycheck. Furthermore, according to one estimate, 79 percent of employees who quit their job point to lack of appreciation as a key factor for leaving. This finding should not be interpreted to mean that praise is an adequate substitute for salary. Employees tend to regard compensation as an entitlement, whereas recognition is perceived as a gift.[12] Workers, including your coworkers, want to know that their output is useful to somebody.

Recognition is also important as a motivator because it is often tied in with other motivators. Receiving a pay increase based on performance is a form of positive reinforcement. At the same time, the pay raise provides recognition for having performed well. An extensive study of call centers in the U.S. financial and retail industries over a seven-year period provides evidence of how recognition is tied in with promotions. Call center employees were more interested in promotion than in pay increases exclusively. Promotion, as they perceived it, brought them formal recognition as well as changes in status and responsibilities.[13]

Approaches to Giving Recognition

To appeal to the recognition need of others, identify a meritorious behavior and then recognize that behavior with an oral, written, or material reward. E-mail, instant messaging, and text messaging are useful vehicles for providing quick recognition when in-person appreciation is not feasible. Also, sometimes people like to print a copy of the recognition they receive. The rules for the use of positive reinforcement are directly applicable. An additional suggestion relates closely to making rewards visible: Time your praise for when it will do the most good. Praise delivered during a staff meeting, for example, can be a potent form of recognition.[14] The recognition award should help the employee feel appreciated for having made a contribution. The economic value of the award, such as engraved metal bowl, is much less important.

Some specific examples of using recognition to sustain desired behavior (a key aspect of motivation) are as follows:

- A coworker shows you how to more effectively perform an important task on the Internet. Three days later, you send her an e-mail message with a copy to the boss: "Hi, Jessica. Your suggestion about using Twitter to gain some visibility for our newest product was dynamite. I've used it five times with success since you showed me what to do." (You are reinforcing Jessica's helpful and cooperative behavior.)

- As the team leader, you receive a glowing letter from a customer about how Kent, one of your team members, solved his or her problem. You have the letter laminated and present it as a gift to Kent. (The behavior you are reinforcing is good customer service.)

- One member of your department, Jason, is a mechanical engineer. While at a department lunch taking place during National Engineers Week, you stand up and say, "I want to toast Jason in celebration of National Engineers Week. I certainly wouldn't want to be sitting in this office building today if a mechanical engineer hadn't assisted in its construction." (Here the only behavior you are reinforcing is the goodwill of Jason, so your motivational approach is general rather than specific.)

As you might have inferred from the examples presented, statements of recognition tend to be more effective when they are expressed in specific, rather than general terms. "You're doing a great job" is an example of a general recognition statement. Here are a few more specific recognition statements:

"You really made a difference by . . ."
"You're right on the mark with . . ."
"We couldn't have done it without your . . ."[15]

A high-powered approach to recognizing the achievements of others is for the manager, supervisor, or team leader to hold personal celebrations of outstanding accomplishment. The celebration takes place in person in contrast to disseminating an electronic message, thereby making the celebration more personal. Such types of public recognition might be part of an employee recognition and celebration program. Personal celebrations include having a meal in a restaurant or in the workplace in honor of an outstanding accomplishment such as a major cost-saving suggestion, a major sale, or receiving a patent. Intense group recognition of this type will often boost the self-esteem of the employee who is celebrated.

A worker might conduct a personal celebration of accomplishment by honoring a coworker during a luncheon or beverage break. A warm touch would be to have a T-shirt custom-lettered to describe the accomplishment, such as "Dragon Slayer" or "Anti-Virus Queen."

Fine Points about Using Recognition to Motivate Others

An outstanding advantage of recognition, including praise, as a motivator is that it is no cost or low cost, yet powerful. Recognition thus provides an enormous return on investment in comparison to a cash bonus. Nevertheless, a challenge in using recognition effectively is that not everyone responds well to the same form of recognition. A good example is that highly technical people tend not to like general praise such as "Great job" or "Awesome." Instead, they prefer a laid-back, factual statement of how their output made a contribution. Furthermore, women are slightly more responsive to praise than are men, as revealed in a study of working adults.[16]

Giving recognition to others as a motivational tactic is more likely to be effective if a culture of recognition exists within the company. This is true because the person giving the recognition will feel that what he or she is doing fits what top management thinks is appropriate behavior. At the same time, the recipient of the recognition is likely to take it seriously.

The rules for positive reinforcement described above also apply to giving recognition. For example, a recognition reward given too frequently either becomes stale or regarded as an entitlement. In one business firm, the CEO traditionally bought lunch for all employees every Friday to recognize their contributions. Soon, employees were asking him to be reimbursed for lunch if they ate outside of the company on a Friday.[17]

USING EXPECTANCY THEORY TO MOTIVATE OTHERS

So far we have described motivating others through applying the principle of WIIFM and behavior modification, including recognition. We now shift to expectancy theory, a more comprehensive explanation of motivation that includes elements of the two other approaches. Expectancy theory is given special attention here for these reasons. First, expectancy theory can help you diagnose motivational problems. Second, it gives the person is comprehensive because it incorporates many different aspects of motivating others. Third, it gives the person attempting to motivate others many guidelines for triggering and sustaining constructive effort from group members.

expectancy theory

A motivation theory based on the premise that the effort people expend depends on the reward they expect to receive in return.

Capsule Overview of Expectancy Theory

The **expectancy theory** of motivation is based on the premise that how much effort people expend depends on the reward they expect to receive in return. (Notice the similarity to WIIFM?) Expectancy theory assumes that people are rational and logical, and the

242   CHAPTER 11

process resembles rational gambling. In any given situation, they want to maximize gain and minimize loss. The theory assumes that people choose among alternatives by selecting the one they think they have the best chance of attaining. Furthermore, they choose the alternative that appears to have the biggest personal payoff. How intensely they want that alternative is also an important consideration. Given a choice, people select an assignment they think they can handle and that will benefit them the most.

An example will help clarify the central thesis of expectancy theory. Hector, a 27-year-old credit analyst at a machine tool company, recognizes that he needs to increase his income by about $500 per month to cover his expenses. After carefully reviewing his options, Hector narrows his alternatives to the following three choices:

1. Work as a dining-room server one night a week and on most weekends, with a variable income of somewhere between $600 and $850 per month.
2. Work for an income tax preparation service about four months per year for 20 hours per week, yielding an annual income of about $7,000.
3. Work extra hard at his regular job, including taking a course in corporate finance, to improve his chances of receiving a promotion and a salary increase of $700 per month.

Hector rejects the first choice. Although he knows he can do the work, he anticipates several negative outcomes. He would much prefer to engage in extra work related to his field of expertise. The unpredictable income associated with being a dining-room server is also a concern. Hector sees merit in the second alternative because income tax preparation work relates to his accounting background. Furthermore, the outcome (amount of pay) is relatively certain. But Hector also has some concerns that working so many extra hours for four months a year could hurt his performance on his day job.

Hector decides to take a chance with the third alternative of going all out to position himself for promotion. He is confident that he can elevate his performance, but he is much less certain that hard work will lead to promotion. Yet Hector attaches such high value to being promoted and upgrading his professional credentials that he is willing to gamble.

Basic Components of Expectancy Theory

All versions of expectancy theory have the following three major components: effort-to-performance expectancy, performance-to-outcome expectancy, and valence.[18] Figure 11-3 presents a glimpse of expectancy theory.

Effort-to-Performance Expectancy is the probability assigned by the individual that effort will lead to performing the task correctly. An important question rational people ask themselves before putting forth effort to accomplish a task is this: "If I put in all this work, will I really get the job done properly?" Each behavior is associated in the individual's mind with a certain expectancy, or subjective hunch of the probability of success.

Expectancies range from 0 to 1.0. The expectancy would be 0 if the person thought that there was no chance of performing the task correctly. An expectancy of 1.0 would signify absolute faith in being able to perform the task properly. Expectancies thus influence whether you will even strive to earn a reward. Self-confident people have higher expectancies than do those with low self-confidence. Being well trained will also increase your subjective hunch that you can perform the task.

effort-to-performance expectancy

The probability assigned by the individual that effort will lead to performing the task correctly.

FIGURE 11-3   A Basic Version of Expectancy Theory

Person will be motivated under these conditions {
A. Effort-to-performance expectancy is high: Person believes he or she can perform the task.
B. Performance-to-outcome expectancy is high: Person believes that performance will lead to certain outcomes.
C. Valence is high: Person highly values the outcomes.
}

self-efficacy

The confidence in your ability to carry out a specific task.

performance-to-outcome expectancy

The probability assigned by the individual that performance will lead to outcomes or rewards.

valence

The value, worth, or attractiveness of an outcome.

The importance of having high expectancies for motivation meshes well with a thrust in work motivation that emphasizes the contribution of **self-efficacy,** the confidence in your ability to carry out a specific task. If you have high self-efficacy about the task, your motivation will be high. Low self-efficacy leads to low motivation.[19] Some people are poorly motivated to skydive because they doubt they will be able to pull the ripcord while free falling at 120 mph.

Performance-to-Outcome Expectancy is the probability assigned by the individual that performance will lead to certain outcomes or rewards. When people engage in a particular behavior, they do so with the intention of achieving a desired outcome or reward. Performance-to-outcome expectancies also range from 0 to 1.0. If you believe there is no chance of receiving the desired reward, the assigned probability is 0. If you believe the reward is certain to follow from performing correctly, the assigned probability is 1.0, for example, "I know for sure that if I show up for work every day this month, I will receive my paycheck."

Valence is the value, worth, or attractiveness of an outcome. It signifies how intensely you want something (as described in WIIFM). In each work situation, there are multiple outcomes, each with a valence of its own. Remember Hector, the credit analyst? The potential outcomes of working part time as an income tax preparer would include extra income, new experience, and interference with his day job.

In the version of expectancy theory presented here, valences range from −100 to +100. A valence of +100 means that you desire an outcome strongly. A valence of −100 means that you are strongly motivated to avoid an outcome, such as being fired. A valence of 0 means that you are indifferent toward an outcome, and it is therefore no use as a motivator. An outcome with a probable valence of 0 would be as follows: To gain the cooperation of coworkers, you promise them gold stars as a reward (or outcome).

Skill-Building Exercise 11-3 will help sensitize you to the importance of estimating valences when attempting to motivate others. A major problem faced by managers and others who attempt to motivate others is that they have limited knowledge about the valences of their motivators (or rewards).

How Moods Influence Expectancy Theory

LEARNING OBJECTIVE 5 Expectancy theory emphasizes the rational side of people, yet emotions still play a key role in determining the impact of expectancies, instrumentalities, and valences. Moods are relatively long-lasting emotional states that do not appear to be tied to a clear source of the emotion. For example, a person might be in a good mood despite experiencing a negative situation such as an automobile breaking down. Also, people may feel glum despite good news such as having won a prize.

Several studies have shown that moods shape people's perceptions of expectancies and valence in expectancy theory. A positive mood increases the perceived connection between effort and performance (E→P expectancy), between performance and desired outcome (P→O expectancy) and in the valence attached to those outcomes. When we are in a good mood, we are more likely to believe that we can accomplish a task, so we have more of a "can do" attitude. We are also more optimistic about the outcomes (rewards) of our effort, and the outcomes look even better to us.[20] The opposite might also be true—when we are in a bad mood, we feel less capable of task accomplishment; we are more pessimistic about getting the reward; and the reward appears less enticing.

Diagnosing Motivation with Expectancy Theory

An important potential contribution of expectancy theory to interpersonal relations is that it helps a person diagnose whether

Estimating Valences for Applying Expectancy Theory

Directions: Listed here are rewards and punishments (outcomes) stemming from job scenarios. Also included is a space for rating the reward or punishment on a scale of −100 to +100. Work with about six teammates, with each person rating all the rewards and punishments. Compute the mean (average) rating for each reward and punishment.

Potential Outcome   *Rating (−100 to + 100)*

1. A 20 percent salary increase _____
2. Profit-sharing plan in successful company _____
3. Stock ownership in company _____
4. Fully paid three-day leave _____
5. A $8,000 performance bonus _____
6. A $400 gift certificate _____
7. Outstanding performance review _____
8. Above-average performance review _____
9. One-step promotion _____
10. Two-step promotion _____
11. Flexible working hours _____
12. Chance to work at home one day per week _____
13. Chance to do more of preferred task _____
14. Take over for supervisor when the supervisor is away _____
15. Fancy job title without change in pay _____
16. Bigger cubicle _____
17. Private office _____
18. Company-paid smart phone _____
19. Wall plaque indicating accomplishment _____
20. Employee-of-the-month designation _____
21. Warm smile and word of appreciation _____
22. Compliment in front of others _____
23. Threat of being suspended for a month _____
24. One-month suspension without pay _____
25. Demotion to undesirable job _____
26. Being fired _____
27. Being fired combined with promise of negative references _____
28. Being placed on probation _____
29. Being ridiculed in front of others _____
30. A 30 percent pay reduction _____

After completing the ratings, discuss the following topics:

1. Which outcomes received the most variable ratings?
2. Which outcomes received the most similar ratings?
3. Which are the three most desirable rewards?
4. Which are the three most undesirable punishments?

Another analytical approach would be to compute the class mean for all 30 outcomes. Each student could then compare his or her rating with the class average.

To apply this technique to the job, modify the preceding outcomes to fit the outcomes available in your work situation. Explain to team members that you are attempting to do a better job of rewarding and disciplining and that you need their input. The ratings made by team members will give strong clues to which rewards and punishments would be the most effective in motivating them.

motivation is present and the intensity of the motivation. In performing your diagnosis, seek answers to the following questions:

1. Does the person I am attempting to motivate have the skills and self-efficacy to do the job? If the person feels ill-equipped to perform, he or she will be discouraged and show very little motivation.

2. What assurance does the person have that if he or she performs the work, the promised reward will be forthcoming? Does the company have a decent reputation for following through on promises? What about me? Have I established my credibility as a person who follows through on promises? (If you or the company is not trusted, motivation could be reduced to zero.)

3. How badly does the person want the reward being offered in the situation? Am I offering a reward that will make it worthwhile for the person to do what I need done? If the sum of the valences of the outcomes in the situation is close to 0 (some positive, some negative), motivation will be absent.

4. Are there any zeroes in response to the first three questions? If there are, motivation will be absent, because the expectancy theory equation is Motivation = (effort-to-performance expectancies) × (performance-to-outcome expectancies) × (the sum of the valences for all the outcomes). Remember what happens when you multiply by 0 in an equation.

5. Is the person in a reasonably good mood? Perhaps the person is poorly motivated today because of being in a bad mood.

Guidelines for Applying Expectancy Theory

The information about expectancy theory presented so far provides ideas for motivating others. Here we discuss several additional specific guidelines to improve your skill in motivating others.

1. **Train and encourage people.** If you are a manager, you should give employees the necessary training and encouragement to be confident that they can perform the required tasks. Some employees who appear to be poorly motivated simply lack the right skills and self-efficacy.

2. **Make explicit the link between rewards and performance.** Employees should be reassured that if they perform the job up to standard, they will receive the promised reward. It is sometimes helpful for employees to speak to coworkers about whether they received promised rewards.

3. **Make sure that the rewards are large enough.** Some rewards fail to motivate people because, although they are the right kind, they are not in the right amount. The promise of a large salary increase might be motivational, but a 1 percent increase will probably have little motivational thrust for most workers. An extreme approach is to give outstanding performers something luxurious or self-indulgent that they would rarely purchase for themselves even if they could afford it. For example, at the small firm PharmaLogics Recruiting, every six months the highest performing sales representative receives an all-expenses-paid week's vacation at a luxury villa in Costa Rica. The sales rep scramble to win the award.[21]

4. **Understand individual differences in valences.** To motivate others in the workplace effectively, you must discover individual differences in preferences for rewards. An attempt should be made to offer a worker rewards to which he or she attaches a high valence. For instance, one employee might value a high-adventure assignment; another might attach a high valence to a routine, tranquil assignment. Also keep individual differences in mind when attempting to motivate customers. One customer might attach a high valence to a volume discount, while another might favor follow-up service.

5. **Use the Pygmalion effect to increase effort-to-performance expectancies.** The **Pygmalion effect** refers to the phenomenon that people will rise (or fall) to the expectations another person has of them. Even if these expectations are not communicated explicitly, the other person will catch on to the nonverbal language. As the levels of expectation increase, so will performance. The high expectations thus become a self-fulfilling prophecy.

Pygmalion effect

The phenomenon that people will rise (or fall) to the expectations that another person has of them.

It is difficult to keep all the points made about expectancy theory in your head at the same time. Nevertheless, with practice and by referring to this book and your notes, you can apply many of the ideas. Skill-Building Exercise 11-4 will help you get started applying expectancy theory.

SKILL-BUILDING EXERCISE 11-4

Applying Expectancy Theory

One student plays the role of the manager of a telemarketing firm (selling over the telephone). Another student plays the role of Terry, a telemarketing specialist who has been with the company for three months. Terry is 40 percent below target in selling magazine renewals. The manager calls Terry into the office for a discussion of the problem.

Terry goes on at length to explain how confusing the job has become. Terry makes comments, such as "I don't even know if I have the right kind of voice for this job. People I reach on the phone think I'm just a kid." Terry also wonders what kind of money he can make in this job and whether it is a dead-end job. (The student who plays the role of Terry can improvise about more of these kinds of problems.)

The manager will apply expectancy theory to motivate Terry to achieve satisfactory performance. Other class members should jot down statements the manager makes that indicate the use of expectancy theory. Also, observe whether it appears that Terry is being helped.

TECHNIQUES FOR SELF-MOTIVATION

Many people never achieve satisfying careers and never realize their potential because of low motivation. They believe that they could perform better but admit that "I'm simply not a high-initiative type" or "I'm simply not that motivated." Here we describe seven techniques for self-motivation.

LEARNING OBJECTIVE 6

1. Set goals for yourself. Goal setting is one of the most important techniques for self-motivation. If you set long-range goals and support them with a series of smaller goals set for shorter time spans, your motivation will increase.

2. Find intrinsically motivating work. A major factor in self-motivation is to find work that is fun or its own reward. Intrinsic motivation refers to the natural tendency to seek out novelty and challenges, to extend and use one's capacities, to explore, and to learn.[22] The intrinsically motivated person is involved in the task at hand, such as a technology enthusiast surfing the Web for hours at a time. Finding a job that offers you motivators in ample supply will help enhance your intrinsic motivation. For example, you might have good evidence from your past experience that the opportunity for close contact with people is a personal motivator. Find a job that involves working in a small, friendly department or team.

Intrinsically motivating work often takes the form of *meaningful work*, or work that has personal meaning to you based on your values and interests. One person might think that working as a store manager for the Salvation Army is meaningful. Another person might think that working as an electronics technician at a missile defense systems company is meaningful.

Based on circumstances, you may have to take whatever job you can find, or you may not be in a position to change jobs. In such a situation, try to arrange your work so that you have more opportunity to experience the reward(s) that you are seeking. Assume that solving difficult problems excites you but that your job is 85 percent routine. Develop better work habits so that you can take care of the routine aspects of your job more quickly. This will give you more time to enjoy the creative aspects of your job.

3. Get feedback on your performance. Few people can sustain a high level of motivation without receiving information about how well they are doing. Even if you find your work challenging and exciting, you will need feedback. One reason positive feedback is valuable is that it acts as a reward. If you learn that your efforts achieved a worthwhile purpose, you will feel encouraged. For example, if a graphics display you designed was well received by company officials, you would probably want to prepare another graphics display.

A study conducted with management students demonstrated that participants adjusted their goals upward after receiving positive feedback and downward after negative feedback. It was also found that when the students were more emotional about the feedback, the positive and negative results were more pronounced.[23] The link here to self-motivation is that when goals are higher, motivation will be higher.

4. Apply behavior modification to yourself. Many people have used behavior modification to change their own behavior. Specific purposes include overcoming eating disorders, tobacco addiction, Internet abuse, nail biting, and procrastination. To boost your own motivation through behavior modification, you would have to first decide what specific motivated actions you want to increase (such as working 30 minutes longer each day). Second, you would have to decide on a suitable set of rewards and punishments. You may choose to use rewards only because rewards are generally better motivators than punishments.

5. Improve your skills relevant to your goals. According to expectancy theory, people hold back effort when they are not confident that their efforts will lead to accomplishments. You should, therefore, seek adequate training to ensure that you have the right abilities and skills to perform your work. The training might be provided by the employer or on your own through a course or self-study. Appropriate training gives you more confidence that you can perform the work. The training also increases your feelings of self-efficacy.[24] By recognizing your ability to mobilize your own resources to succeed,

Working on My Own Motivators

The focus of this chapter has been the skill of motivating others. Yet, if you neglect motivating yourself, you (a) might not gain a formal position in which you can motivate others, and (b) you will not be able to motivate others by leading through example. Apply some of the concepts in this chapter to help work through this exercise.

What Motivates Me?

Think back on what situations, and factors within a situation, have prompted you to put forth your best effort and work the hardest—on the job, at community work, at school, in sports, or in other recreational activities such as being a band member. Which needs were you attempting to satisfy? Which tangible or intangible rewards were you pursuing? Here is a portion of a sample answer:

"I was lucky enough to be entered in Domino's national speed contest for making a store-usable pizza. I jumped into the situation like somebody obsessed. Here I was at 20 years old with a chance to win a national contest and be lifted up over the head of my buddies. I would have been King Pizza for a day. I didn't win, but I came close."

"Now I know that competition and recognition get my adrenalin flowing. I think that's why I will be successful in industrial sales. I need that big carrot dangling out in front of me."

What Can I Do to Capitalize on My Motivators?

It is helpful to know what motivates you, but it is even more helpful to follow up by placing yourself in situations in which you will be highly motivated. The Pizza King aspirant provides us a good example. Attempt to manage your career by placing yourself in highly motivational situations. For example, if the opportunity to work alone without supervision and the opportunity to schedule your own time motivate you, strive to work at home in the near future.

Now write down the type of situations that will most likely enable you to work at your motivated best.

---

your self-confidence for the task will be elevated. Another motivational advantage of self-efficacy is that you are likely to commit more resources, such as time and money, to attaining a goal when you feel confident that you can perform the task.[25] For example, if you had confidence in your skills to develop an eBay business, you might be willing to spend a lot of time in designing the business, and money in buying products to sell on the site.

> "Remind yourself that you have personal power, and that you can make things happen. Erase those negative mental tapes that say "No, I can't.""
>
> —E. Carol Webster, clinical psychologist, quoted in *Black Enterprise Magazine*, September 2005, p. 157.

6. Raise your level of self-expectation. Another strategy for increasing your level of motivation is to simply expect more of yourself. If you raise your level of self-expectation, you are likely to achieve more. Because you expect to succeed, you do succeed. The net effect is the same as if you had increased your level of motivation. The technical term for improving your performance through raising your own expectations is the **Galatea effect.** High self-expectations and a positive mental attitude take a long time to develop. However, they are critically important for becoming a well-motivated person in a variety of situations.

7. Develop a strong work ethic. A highly effective strategy for self-motivation is to develop a strong work ethic. If you are committed to the idea that most work is valuable and that it is joyful to work hard, you will automatically become strongly motivated. A person with a weak work ethic cannot readily develop a strong one because the change requires a profound value shift. Yet if a person gives a lot of serious thought to the importance of work and follows the right role models, a work ethic can be strengthened. The shift to a strong work ethic is much like a person who has a casual attitude toward doing fine work becoming more prideful.

Skill-Building Exercise 11-5 provides a practical approach to self-motivation.

SELF-ASSESSMENT QUIZ IN OVERVIEW

Self-Assessment Quiz 11-1 is different than the other quizzes presented in this text because it emphasizes cognitive knowledge about the subject (in this case motivation). Nevertheless, your attitudes toward people often become translated into knowledge about motivation. For example, if you are warm and supportive toward people, you would likely respond "very frequently" to statement 8, "I make sure that the other person feels treated fairly." And, if you are essentially hostile toward people, you would respond "very frequently" to statement 3, "When another person is heel-dragging, it usually means he or she is lazy."

Concept Review
and Reinforcement

Key Terms

motivation 234
behavior modification 236
law of effect 236
positive reinforcement 237
negative reinforcement (avoidance
    motivation) 237

intermittent reward 239
expectancy theory 242
effort-to-performance expectancy 243
self-efficacy 244
performance-to-outcome
    expectancy 244

valence 244
pygmalion effect 246

Summary

Motivation refers to an internal state that leads to effort expended toward objectives and to an activity performed by one person to get another person to work. Managers, as well as people working individually, often need to motivate others.

The most fundamental principle of human motivation is that people are motivated by self-interest, referred to as "What's in it for me?" (WIIFM). Even those who help others are simultaneously helping themselves by feeling good. In using the WIIFM principle, be aware of the intensity of a person's desire for a reward. Key employee needs that might require satisfaction include achievement, power affiliation, autonomy, esteem, safety and security, and equity.

Behavior modification is an attempt to change behavior by manipulating rewards and punishments. Its key principle is the law of effect—behavior that leads to a positive effect tends to be repeated, while the opposite is also true. Negative reinforcement, or avoidance motivation, can be used to supplement positive reinforcement. Rules for the effective use of positive reinforcement include the following:

1. State clearly what behavior will lead to a reward.
2. Choose an appropriate reward.
3. Supply ample feedback.
4. Schedule rewards intermittently.
5. Make the reward follow the observed behavior closely in time.
6. Make the reward fit the behavior.
7. Make the reward visible.
8. Change the reward periodically.
9. Reward the group or team also.

A general approach to applying the above rules is to look for creative ways to apply positive reinforcement.

Motivating others by giving them recognition and praise is a direct application of positive reinforcement. Recognition is a strong motivator because it is a normal human need to crave recognition, and most workers feel they do not get enough recognition. Also, recognition is often tied in with other motivators, such as a promotion providing recognition to the person. To appeal to the recognition need of others, identify a meritorious behavior and then recognize that behavior with an oral, written, or material reward. Choosing when to deliver recognition can be important.

Recognition and praise are low-cost, powerful motivators. Statements of recognition tend to be more effective when they are specific. High technical people tend not to like general praise, but instead prefer a laid-back factual statement of how their output made a contribution. Recognition is more likely to be an effective motivator in a culture of recognition.

The expectancy theory of motivation assumes that people are decision makers who choose among alternatives by selecting the one that appears to have the biggest personal payoff at the time. Expectancy theory has three major components: expectancies about being able to perform, expectancies about performance leading to certain outcomes, and valence (the value attached to the reward). A positive mood state can enhance the components of expectancy theory.

Expectancy theory is useful in diagnosing whether motivation is present by examining the strength of the expectancies and the valences of the rewards. If any element is 0, motivation will not be present. Expectancy theory provides important ideas for motivating others, including the following:

1. Train and encourage people.
2. Show the link between rewards and performance.
3. Make the rewards large enough.
4. Observe individual differences.
5. Use the Pygmalion effect to increase effort-to-performance expectancies.

Techniques for self-motivation described here are as follows:

1. Set goals for yourself.
2. Find intrinsically motivating work.
3. Get feedback on your performance.
4. Apply behavior modification to yourself.
5. Improve your skills relevant to your goals.
6. Raise your level of self-expectation.
7. Develop a strong work ethic.

Questions for Discussion and Review

1. If people are already paid by their employer to carry out a job, why should it still be important for somebody to motivate them?
2. Suppose a worker is much more interested in personal and family life than performing well or getting promoted. What approach might the worker's supervisor use to motivate him or her toward high performance?
3. For what purpose would someone need to motivate his or her supervisor?
4. If people really live by the WIIFM principle, how can a leader still achieve teamwork?
5. What evidence can you suggest that some people prefer exciting and interesting work over exceptional financial rewards?

6. Identify several factors in Figure 11-1 that you think would be particularly effective in motivating managers and professional-level workers. Explain your reasoning.
7. Answer question 6 for entry-level service workers, such as supermarket cashiers.
8. How do individual differences show themselves in attempting to motivate others?
9. What evidence do you see that some students taking the course for which you are studying this textbook are better motivated than others?
10. How might cultural differences affect the valence ratings in Skill-Building Exercise 11-3?

The Web Corner

http://www.awards.com
(One-stop super-site for rewards and recognition.)

http://www.ZeroMillion.com
(Search for Positive Reinforcement in the Workplace.)

http://www.About.com: Human Resources
(Search for The Pygmalion Effect for Employee Motivation.)

Internet Skill Builder: Motivating Other People

Visit www.nelson-motivation.com to watch a five-minute video clip of one of Bob Nelson's talks. After watching the video, answer the following questions: (1) What have I learned that I could translate into a skill motivating other people as well as employees? (2) Which theory, or approach, to motivation does Nelson emphasize in his presentation?

Developing Your Human Relations Skills

Interpersonal Relations Case Problem 11.1

On Time at Prime Time

Prime Time Furniture is a manufacturer and distributor of inexpensive, ready-to-assemble furniture for the home and small business, including home-based businesses. Among its products are bookcases, television stands, computer workstations, and kitchen tables. Some of the higher-end products are manufactured at the Wisconsin factory and distribution center. The vast majority of products, however, are imported from Malaysia and then placed in the distribution center until sold.

Demand for ready-to-assemble furniture has increased steadily as more people are looking for ways to reduce household expenses. To meet the increased demand, more companies have entered the field, making the business more competitive and therefore reducing prices.

Eton Westin, the distribution center manager, searches continuously for ways to make the center more efficient. During a two-hour productivity meeting with supervisors, Westin learned that employee lateness is costing Prime Time a lot of money. Ashley Novak explained the problem in these terms:

"We are short-handed as it is. When an employee is late it makes it more difficult to ship on time. We have learned the hard way that when we do not ship on time, we lose some business. A big part of our business now comes from online sales through Amazon and other resellers. These outfits promise rapid delivery, and when we don't ship on time, we get heat from both the resellers and the end customers." (The resellers inform the end customer that Prime Time Furniture is the source of the furniture.)

Jimmy Gerber, the director of administration and human resources, said he had an idea for improving punctuality that has worked in other companies. The program is set up by a company specializing in performance improvement. Gerber then outlined the basics of the program.

"We run a punctuality race with each department being represented by a horse, assigned a name by the department. The consulting company sets up the race with their own software, and we visit our race Web site any time we want. The setup looks like a video game. You can see graphically the relative positions of the horses as they run the 'punctuality race.'"

"Every time a worker arrives on time, that fact is entered into the database, and the department's horse gets two points. Every time a worker is late the department's horse is penalized two points. Coming back from breaks on time earns one point, and coming back late is a one-point penalty. Leaving work, or leaving early, also follows the same one-point value."

"At the end of each month, the points are totaled. The team with the winning horse can then convert the points into gifts from a catalog or gift certificates to a few selected restaurants."

Westin asked the group for their opinion on the horse race to improve punctuality. "I'm a little concerned," he said. "Isn't this too childlike? I mean, running a horse race for coming to work on time. Let's get real."

"In all respect, Eton," said Liz Lopez, the shipping supervisor. "Adults are motivated by games and small prizes. We are all children at heart, even Prime Time employees."

Case Questions

1. What do you predict will be the outcome of the horse-race motivation program if implemented?
2. Which approach, or approaches, to motivating people does this horse-race program represent?
3. What other program for improving punctuality might you recommend?

The Home-Retention Consultant Blues

Alicia works in real estate as a home-retention consultant. Among the services offered by her employer, Magnum Properties, is to help people who are facing foreclosure stay in their homes. She works with clients to help them figure out a way to work with their mortgage holder to renegotiate loans, and often to prevent being evicted. Alicia also works with mortgage holders to guide them through short sales or selling homes for less than the balance on the mortgage when the property owners are way behind on their payments.

Back in 2010, the foreclosure rate in the United States was still relatively high with 1 of 13 homeowners either behind 60 days behind in their mortgage payments or facing foreclosure. Alicia was earning a high income because Magnum Properties' niche in the real estate market was prospering. When asked by an old friend who located her on Facebook how she was doing in her career, Alicia responded:

> It's a mixed bag for me. I see a lot of positives in my work. I make a lot of money, and I drive a sharp car. I'm very modern because I deal with foreclosures and short sales. I am helping a lot of people because I enable some of them to keep a roof over their heads.

> My big problem is that the negatives in my work on dragging me down. Some days I can hardly muster up enough energy to follow up on leads of people in trouble to help. In some ways I feel like I'm dealing with the underbelly of humanity. A lot of people I'm trying to help have dug their own graves. They have plenty of money for beer and wine, and to run up huge bills for cell phone and online video rentals. But they don't have the money to pay their mortgages.

> I need to stay pumped to keep earning a good living, but some days I just don't know how to stay motivated. Any suggestions, my friend?

Case Questions

1. What recommendations do you have for Alicia to help her increase her level of self-motivation?
2. To what extent do you think it might be advisable for Alicia to simply switch fields, such as going into traditional real estate selling, so she can stay better self-motivated?
3. What suggestions might you offer Alicia's manager at Magnum Properties to help her stay motivated?

Helping Others Develop and Grow

Mark Mollenkopf is the president of Cutting Edge Laser Technologies, Inc., in New York State. The company was founded in 2002 with a very simple mission: To help medical professionals integrate technology into their practice to improve the performance of their business, patient care, and client satisfaction. Mollenbkopf said:

> We started by securing an exclusive distribution agreement for surgical lasers for the North American veterinary medicine market. We got the business started by hiring two people in the office and five as outside sales representatives in large markets across the country. Our focus was on helping veterinarians practice better medicine by using lasers instead of scalpels for their surgeries. We were fortunate to have success early, and to be able to grow the business internally.

After reading and studying this chapter and doing the exercises, you should be able to

1. Understand how being a nurturing, positive person can influence the development of coworkers.
2. Specify the behaviors and skills helpful for being a mentor and role model.
3. Acquire beginning skills in coaching and training.
4. Deal with difficult people on the job.

The best part of my job is being able to see our strategic plans for growth go from the whiteboard to implementation. Over the past eight years, I have been very fortunate to be able to watch many of our employees grow along with the growth of the company. Historically, we have had very little turnover within the company. It has been rewarding to see employees develop and grow to support the business.

The hardest part of my job is ensuring that we have the right people in the right positions with the necessary resources to support our key initiatives. It is people that are behind every successful business, and I have found that continuing to find and develop the human capital within the business is one of the most critical areas for success.[1]

The comment of the executive whose company provides technology that helps the welfare of animal patients emphasizes how important the growth and development of human workers is for business success. However, the growth and development of workers is not the sole responsibility of managers or training specialists. Companies are placing increasing emphasis on workers training and developing each other. The Great Recession of 2008–2009 gave impetus to this movement as training budgets were slashed.[2]

This chapter describes the major ways in which employees help each other, and lays the groundwork for skill development in these vital activities. Learning to take the initiative to help others is particularly important because there is a natural tendency for people to be embarrassed or fearful of asking for help. The concern is that the person asking for help will be seen as deficient in some important way. Despite these concerns, a company is at an advantage when workers help each other.[3]

Among the key helping roles are nurturing others, mentoring, coaching and training, and helping difficult people become more cooperative. A study of how new employees are developed, involving 378 recent graduates, underscores the importance of workers helping each other. Among the findings relevant in the study were that (1) buddying with a coworker was the most helpful developmental method, and (2) the company did not provide enough mentoring despite its importance.[4]

Do Self-Assessment Quiz 12-1 to gain preliminary insight into your attitudes toward helping others in the workplace.

BEING A NURTURING, POSITIVE PERSON

LEARNING OBJECTIVE 1

A major strategy for helping others grow and develop is to be a nourishing, positive person. A **nurturing person** promotes the growth of others. Nurturing people are positive and supportive and typically look for the good qualities in others. A **toxic person** stands in contrast to a nourishing person, because he or she dwells on the negative. Visualize the following scenario to appreciate the difference between a nurturing person and a toxic one.

nurturing person

One who promotes the growth of others.

toxic person

One who negatively affects others.

Attitudes Toward Helping Others

Directions: Describe how well you agree with the following statements by circling the appropriate letter after each statement: disagree (D), neutral (N), or agree (A).

1. If I see a coworker make a mistake, I do not inform him or her of the mistake.   D   N   A
2. It should be part of everybody's job to share skills and ideas with coworkers.   D   N   A
3. The manager should have exclusive responsibility for coaching people within the work unit.   D   N   A
4. I can think of many instances in my life when somebody thanked me for showing him or her how to do something.   D   N   A
5. I have very little patience with coworkers who do not give me their full cooperation.   D   N   A
6. To save time, I will do a task for another person rather than invest the time needed to show him or her how to do it.   D   N   A
7. I would take the initiative to put an inexperienced worker under my wing.   D   N   A
8. As a child, I often took the time to show younger children how to do things.   D   N   A
9. Rather than ask a coworker for help, I will wait until the manager is available to help me.   D   N   A
10. It is best not to share key information with a coworker, because that person could then perform as well as or better than me.   D   N   A
11. "Give a person a fish and he or she will have one meal. Teach that person to fish, and he or she will eat for life."   D   N   A

Total Score _____

Scoring and Interpretation: Use the following score key to obtain your score for each answer, and then calculate your total score.

1. D = 3, N = 2, A = 1	5. D = 3, N = 2, A = 1	9. D = 3, N = 2, A = 1
2. D = 1, N = 2, A = 3	6. D = 3, N = 2, A = 1	10. D = 3, N = 2, A = 1
3. D = 3, N = 2, A = 1	7. D = 1, N = 2, A = 3	11. D = 1, N = 2, A = 3
4. D = 1, N = 2, A =3	8. D = 1, N = 2, A = 3	

28–33 You have very positive attitudes toward helping, developing, and training others in the workplace. Such attitudes reflect strong teamwork and a compassion for the growth needs of others.

19–27 You have mixed positive and negative attitudes toward helping, developing, and training others in the workplace. You may need to develop more sensitivity to the growth needs of others to be considered a strong team player.

13–18 You have negative attitudes toward helping, developing, and training others in the workplace. Guard against being so self-centered that it will be held against you. Being a nurturing, positive person is a lifelong process rather than a tactic that can be used at will. Nevertheless, making a conscious attempt to be nurturing and positive can help you develop the right mindset. For example, today you might encourage a coworker or friend who is facing a work or personal problem. Skill-Building Exercise 12-1 provides an opportunity to practice being a positive person.

The Nurturing, Positive Person

One student plays the role of Pat, a worker who is experiencing difficulty on the job and in personal life. Pat approaches a coworker during lunch in the company cafeteria and says, "What a day. I just received a rotten performance review. If my work doesn't improve within a month, the company may let me go. To add to my woes, my fiancé has threatened to break off the engagement if I don't get a big raise or a promotion. My hard drive went down, taking with it my collection of music, videos, and photos. I feel like my whole world is collapsing." The other person plays the role of Leslie, who attempts to be nurturing and positive in order to help get Pat out of the doldrums. Run the role-play for about 10 minutes.

The rest of the class provides feedback on Leslie's skill in being nurturing and helpful. Jot down specific behaviors you think are nurturing and helpful. Also be on the alert for any toxic behaviors.

Randy, a purchasing specialist, enters the office where two coworkers are talking. One person is nurturing, the other is toxic. With a look of panic, Randy says, "I'm sorry to barge in like this, but can anybody help me? I've been working for three hours preparing a spreadsheet on the computer, and it seems to have vanished. Maybe one of you can help me retrieve it."

Margot, the nourishing person, says, "I'm no computer expert, but since I'm not the one who lost the document, I can be calm enough to help. Let's go right now." Ralph, the toxic person, whispers to Margot: "Tell Randy to use the help function. If you help him now, you'll only find him on your doorstep every time he needs help."

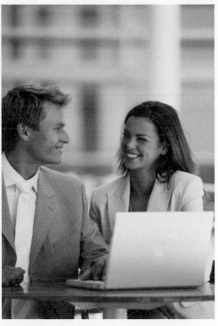

If you listen to toxic people long enough, you are likely to feel listless, depressed, and drained. Toxic people have been described as energy vampires because they suck all the positive energy out of you.[5] Nurturing people, in contrast, are positive, enthusiastic, and supportive. The guideline for skill development here is to engage in thoughts and actions every day that will be interpreted by others as nourishing. Three actions and attitudes that support being a nourishing person are as follows:

1. **Recognize that most people have growth needs.** Almost everybody has a need for self-fulfillment, although people vary widely in the extent of this need. If you recognize this need, it may propel you toward helping people satisfy the need. You might engage in interactions with coworkers, such as sharing new skills with them, forwarding relevant news articles from the Internet, or telling them about an important new Web site you have discovered. You might also tell them about an exciting course you have taken that has enhanced your self-confidence.

2. **Team up with a coworker inside or outside your department so that the two of you can form a buddy system.** The buddy system is used during war combat and with children in a swimming program. You and a friend can use the same system to keep each other informed of decisions and events that could affect your careers. You might nurture your buddy by telling about growth opportunities in the company he or she might not have heard about. Your buddy would reciprocate. One person told her buddy about expanding opportunities for company employees who were fluent in both English and Spanish. The two buddies, who already knew some Spanish, worked together to become fluent.

3. **Be a role model for others.** An indirect way of being a nurturing, positive person is to conduct yourself in such a way that others will model your behavior. By serving as a role model, you help another person develop. How to become a role model for coworkers is as comprehensive a topic as learning to be successful. Among the many factors that make you role model material are a strong work ethic, job expertise, personal warmth, good speaking ability, a professional appearance, and great ethics. Do you qualify yet, or do you need some more work?

> " Help others get ahead. You will always stand taller with someone else on your shoulders. "
> —Bob Moawad, chair and CEO of Edge Learning Institute

BEING A MENTOR TO COWORKERS

In Homer's tale the *Odyssey,* Mentor was a wise and trusted friend as well as a counselor and adviser. The term *mentor* has become a buzzword in the workplace, as well as in the community. A **mentor** is an individual with advanced experience and knowledge who is committed to giving support and career advice to a less experienced person. The less experienced person is the **protégé** (from the French word for "protected"). Here we look at various characteristics of mentoring, followed by behaviors that will be useful to you in mentoring others.

mentor

An individual with advanced experience and knowledge who is committed to giving support and career advice to a less experienced person.

protégé

The less experienced person in a mentoring relationship who is helped by the mentor.

Characteristics and Types of Mentoring

The term *mentoring* is used so widely and in so many contexts that it can refer to almost any type of helping relationship. From a more technically precise perspective, mentoring is characterized as:

- A unique relationship between two people
- A learning partnership that involves emotional and task-related career support
- A reciprocal helping relationship
- A frequently changing relationship between the mentor and the mentored[6]

A mentor usually outranks the protégé and is often older. For the present purpose, however, be aware that one coworker can be a mentor to another. As long as you are more experienced and wiser than a coworker in some important aspect of the job, you can be a mentor. A person who is not a manager can also be a mentor in another important way. He or she can select an entry-level person in the firm and serve as the inexperienced person's coach and adviser. Even when a person has a high-ranking person as a mentor, you can also be his or her mentor. The reason is that having more than one mentor improves a person's chances for developing job and career skills.[7]

Mentoring is more important than ever because it supports the modern, team-based organization. Also, after years of downsizing, many organizations have fewer managers available to mentor employees. Coworkers often have to fill this void. More people work together as equals, and they are expected to train and develop each other. Mentoring facilitates such learning and also supports the current emphasis on continuous learning.

Mentoring often takes the form of the mentor and protégé communicating by e-mail, referred to as *virtual* (or *online*) *mentoring*. Many companies have established electronic matching programs that enable employees to receive mentoring from workers who are geographically distant from them. The virtual mentoring can include Web sites for matching mentors and protégés, following the model of online dating sites.[8]

As the time of corporate professionals and managers has become more scarce, virtual mentoring increases in practicality. Also, online mentoring gives the protégé an opportunity to be mentored by a geographically distant mentor, overseas as well. The person being mentored might send a quick e-mail, instant message, or text message to the mentor explaining that he just received an outstanding performance review. The mentor might reply back with an encouraging message. When asked about a problem facing the protégé, the mentor might reply with advice quickly. Answers by the mentor within 48 hours are recommended to communicate an attitude of concern.[9]

Mentoring coworkers can take place in one of two ways. With informal mentoring, the mentor and protégé come together naturally, in the same way that friendships develop. The formal approach is for the company to assign you somebody to mentor. Several studies have shown that mentoring is likely to be more effective when both the mentor and protégé have some input into the matching.[10] Measures of mentoring effectiveness include rate of promotions, salary increases, and job satisfaction. Being mentored is also a career-advancement tactic, and will be discussed in Chapter 17.

Serving as a mentor is an excellent way of helping others on the job. Mentoring is also widely practiced off the job. Many communities have developed programs whereby working adults volunteer to serve as mentors to youths. Mentoring in these programs is designed to help the adolescents and teenagers succeed at school and avoid a life of crime and substance abuse.

Specific Mentoring Behaviors

To be a mentor, a person engages in a wide range of helping behaviors, all related to being a trusted friend, coach, and teacher. To prepare you for mentoring a less experienced person, a list of specific mentoring behaviors follows:[11]

- **Sponsoring.** A mentor actively nominates somebody else for promotions and desirable positions. In some situations, one person is asked to nominate a coworker for a promotion to supervisor or team leader or for a special assignment.

- **Coaching.** A mentor gives on-the-spot advice to the protégé to help him or her improve skills. Coaching is such an important part of helping others that it receives separate mention in this chapter.

- **Protecting.** A mentor might shield a junior person from potentially harmful situations or from the boss. For example, the mentor might tell her protégé, "In your meeting today with the boss, make sure you are well prepared and have all your facts at hand. He is in an ugly mood and will attack any weakness."

- **Sharing challenging assignments.** One member of the team does not ordinarily give assignments to another, yet in some situations you can request that your protégé help you with a difficult task. You would then offer feedback on your protégé's performance. The purpose of these high demands is to help the protégé develop more quickly than if he or she were brought along too slowly.

- **Acting as a referral agent.** The mentor sometimes refers the protégé to resources inside and outside the company to help with a particular problem. For example, the protégé might want to know how one goes about getting the employee benefits package modified.

- **Role modeling.** An important part of being a mentor is to give the protégé a pattern of values and behaviors to emulate. Several of the specific behaviors included under being a role model were described earlier in connection with being a positive, nurturing person.

- **Giving support and encouragement.** A mentor can be helpful just by giving support and encouragement. In turn, the protégé is supposed to support the mentor by offering compliments and defending the mentor's ideas. In a team meeting, for example, the protégé might make a statement, such as "I think John's ideas will work wonders. We should give them a try."

- **Counseling.** A mentor listens to the protégé's problems and offers advice. Given that counseling plays such a central role in helping others, it also receives separate mention in this chapter.

- **Providing friendship.** A mentor is, above all, a trusted friend, and the friendship extends two ways. "Trusted" means that the mentor will not pass on confidential information or stab you in the back. (It is also possible to mentor someone who is not a friend, providing that person is interested primarily in learning business or technical skills from you.)

- **Encouraging problem solving.** Mentors help their protégés solve problems by themselves and make their own discoveries. A comment frequently made to mentors is "I'm glad you made me think through the problem. You triggered my thinking."

- **Explaining the ropes.** A general-purpose function of the mentor is to help the protégé learn the ropes, which translates into explaining the values and do's and don'ts of the organization.

- **Teaching the right skills.** The original role of the mentor in teaching skills (such as a master teaching an apprentice) is highly relevant today. Among the many skills a mentor can help the protégé develop are those dealing with communication technology, customer service, corporate finance, achieving high quality, and thinking strategically.

- **Encouraging of continuous learning.** A major role for the modern mentor is to encourage the protégé to keep learning. Part of encouraging lifelong learning is to emphasize that formal education and an occasional workshop are not sufficient for maintaining expertise in today's fast-changing workplace. The individual has to stay abreast of new developments through courses and self-study. A specific way in which the mentor can encourage continuous learning is to ask the protégé questions about new developments in the field.

As implied by the preceding list, mentoring is a complex activity that involves a variety of helping behaviors. To develop mentoring skills, you need to offer help to several people for at least six months. Skill-Building Exercise 12-1 is a good starting point in mentoring. In preparation for more advanced mentoring, it is helpful to think of the type of person you would prefer to have as a protégé. Skill-Building Exercise 12-2 is designed to help you think through this issue. Be prepared for a potential protégé seeking you out because many people serious about advancing their careers search for potential mentors with whom they have rapport. Similarly, if you are looking for a mentor, take the initiative to establish contact with someone you like and whom you think could help you.

Mentoring is designed to help another individual grow and develop; yet, mentoring can also help your employer at the same time. A key way in which the company benefits from coworker mentoring is that the mentor passes along, or transfers, valuable knowledge to the protégé.[12] For example, the mentor might share with the protégé a few good tricks for collecting money from a delinquent debtor. Workers who receive mentoring are likely to feel more satisfied about their jobs and stay with the organization longer. A study of more than 1,300 U.S. Army officers showed that officers who were mentored felt more emotionally committed to the Army than did their nonmentored counterparts. Furthermore, mentored officers felt more likely to stay in the Army, and were less likely to leave the military voluntarily.[13]

As business has become highly internationalized, mentoring people from different cultures has become more frequent. In general, to engage in cross-cultural mentoring effectively, you need to follow the principles described in Chapter 8 about cross-cultural relations.

COACHING AND TRAINING OTHERS

LEARNING OBJECTIVE 3

Two direct approaches to helping others in the workplace are coaching and training. In the traditional organization, managers have most of the responsibility for coaching and training, with some assistance from the human resources department. In the new workplace, team members share responsibility for coaching and training. High-tech companies, such as Google and Microsoft, heavily emphasize workers sharing knowledge with each other. Open workspaces, including the presence of whiteboards, are used to facilitate workers exchanging ideas and passing along information. Although coaching and training are described separately in the following subsections, recognize that the two processes are closely related.

Coaching Skills and Techniques

Most readers probably have some experience in coaching whether or not the activity was given a formal label. If you have helped somebody improve his or her performance on the job, on the athletic field, in a musical band, or on the dance floor, you have some coaching experience. In the workplace, **coaching** is a method of helping workers grow and improve their job competence by providing suggestions and encouragement. The suggestions for coaching are generally easier to implement if you have formal authority over the person being coached. Nevertheless, with a positive, helpful attitude on your part, coworkers are likely to accept coaching from you.

Ideal Characteristics of Peer Coaching. Considerable workplace coaching is performed by professional coaches who specialize in helping managers improve their interpersonal skills.[14] Our focus here is coaching by workers themselves rather than by paid professionals. **Peer coaching** is a type of helping relationship based on qualities, such as high acceptance of the other person, authenticity, mutual trust, and mutual learning. According to researchers Polly Parker, Douglas T. Hall, and Kathy E. Kram, peer coaching has five critical qualities, to be described next. These qualities, however, tend toward being an ideal state and we cannot realistically expect all peer coaching to attain this high status.

1. **Equal status of peers.** The equal status of peers eliminates the power relationships found in many other relationships, such as superior-subordinate relationship. Peers are able to plan and initiate their learning opportunities and work toward a shared goal of mutual learning.

2. **Personal and professional development of both peers.** Peers strive to obtain an in-depth understanding of the subjective experiences, including the worldview of the other peer. Each person attempts to make sense of the other person's worldview. Each participant chooses issues of personal interest to express and explore.

3. **Integration of reflection and practice.** Effective peer coaching requires personal reflection on one's own actions and behaviors. Through reflection, the peer coach builds awareness of cognitive, emotional, and spiritual dimensions of himself or herself.

4. **Importance of attention to process.** Peer coaching provides a medium for peers to learn a process for how to do a better job of attending to other people. The focus is on understanding the self and other people rather than acquiring content or facts.

5. **Accelerating career learning.** Peer counseling helps people learn rapidly and continually, which helps them succeed in the modern world.[15]

We emphasize again that these characteristics of a peer coach are ideals to strive for. You can still be an effective peer coach by learning the coaching skills and techniques described next without attaining all the five characteristics described above.

Suggestions for Coaching. Coaching other employees requires skill. One way of acquiring this skill is to study basic principles and then practice them on the job. Another way is to coach under simulated conditions, such as role-playing and modeling an effective coach. Here are 11 suggestions for effective coaching, as outlined in Figure 12-1. For the best results, combine them with the suggestions for effective listening presented in Chapter 4.

1. **Build relationships.** A starting point in being an effective coach is to build relationships with coworkers before coaching them. Having established rapport with coworkers or subordinates facilitates entering into coaching relationships with them. The

FIGURE 12-1   Coaching Skills and Techniques

1. Build relationships.
2. Provide specific feedback.
3. Make criticism pain-free and positive.
4. Encourage the person you are coaching to talk.
5. Ask powerful questions.
6. Give emotional support.
7. Give some constructive advice.
8. Coach with "could," not "should."
9. Interpret what is happening.
10. Allow for modeling of the desired performance and behaviors.
11. Applaud good results.

suggestions below about giving encouragement and support are part of relationship building. Another vital aspect of relationship building is to be trusted by the people you coach.[16] For example, the person being coached has to believe that the coach is trying to help rather than undermine him or her.

2. Provide specific feedback. Instead of making generalities about an improvement area for another person, pinpoint areas of concern. A generality might be, "You just don't seem as if you're interested in this job." A specific on the same problem might be, "You neglect to call in on days that you are going to be out ill. In this way, you are letting down the team." Sometimes it can be effective to make a generalization (such as not being "interested in the job") after you first produce several concrete examples. Closely related to minimizing generalizations is to avoid exaggerating, for example, by saying such things as, "You are always letting down the team." Specific feedback is sometimes referred to as **behavioral feedback** because it pinpoints behavior rather than personal characteristics or attitudes. "Neglecting to call in" pinpoints behavior, whereas "not into the job" focuses more on an attitude.

behavioral feedback

Information given to another person that pinpoints behavior rather than personal characteristics or attitudes.

3. Make criticism pain-free and positive. To be an effective coach, you will inevitably have to point out something negative the person you coach has done, or is planning to do. It is helpful to come right to the point about your criticism, such as "In our department meeting this morning, you acted so angry and hostile that you alienated the rest of the group. I know that you are generally a positive person, so I was surprised. My recommendation is that you keep your bad days to yourself when in a meeting." The positive aspect is important because you want to maintain good communications with the person you coach, whether you are the person's supervisor or coworker.[17]

4. Encourage the person you are coaching to talk. Part of being a good listener is encouraging the person being coached to talk. Ask the person you are coaching open-ended questions. Closed questions do not provide the same opportunity for self-expression, and they often elicit short, uninformative answers. Assume that you are coaching a coworker on how to use the intranet system properly. An effective open-ended question might be, "Where are you having the biggest problems using our intranet." A closed question covering the same topic might be, "Do you understand how to use the intranet?" The latter question would not provide good clues to specific problem areas faced by your coworker. A useful technique is to begin each coaching session with a question to spark the other person's thinking.[18] An example is to ask, "What new ideas do you have for decreasing turnover among our teenage cashiers?"

5. Ask powerful questions. A major role for the coach is to ask *powerful* or *tough* questions that help the protégé think through the strengths and weaknesses of what he or she is doing or thinking. The powerful question is confrontational in a helpful way. The person being coached might be thinking of selling management on a program of distributing free ginkgo baloba (a food supplement believed to stimulate mental energy) to every employee to enhance productive thinking. Your powerful question might be, "What kind of figures are you going to use to support your expensive idea?"

6. Give emotional support. By being helpful and constructive, you provide much-needed emotional support to the person who needs help in improving job performance. A coaching session should not be an interrogation. An effective way of providing emotional support is to use positive rather than negative motivators. For example, as a team leader you might say to a team member, "If you learn how to analyze manufacturing costs, you will be eligible for an outstanding performance review." A negative motivator on the same topic might be, "If you don't learn how to analyze manufacturing costs, you're going to get zapped on your performance review."

Workers who are performing well can also profit from praise and encouragement, often so they can perform even better. Also, even the best performers have flaws that might be preventing them from elevating their performance.[19] As a team leader or coworker, you can therefore make a contribution by giving emotional support to a star performer.

7. Give some constructive advice. Too much advice-giving interferes with two-way communication, yet some advice can lead to improved performance. Assist the person being coached to answer the question, "What can I do about the problem?" Advice in the form of a question or suppositional statement is often effective. One example is, "Could the root of your problem be that you have not studied the user manual?"

8. Coach with "could," not "should." When instructing somebody else to improve, tell the person he or she *could* do something rather than he or she *should* do it. *Should* implies the person is doing something morally wrong, such as "You should recycle the empty laser cartridges." *Could* leaves the person with a choice to make: to accept or reject your input and weigh the consequences.[20]

9. Interpret what is happening. An interpretation given by the person doing the coaching is an explanation of why the person being coached is acting in a particular manner. The interpretation is designed to give the person being coached insight into the nature of the problem. For instance, a food service manager might be listening to the problems of a cafeteria manager with regard to cafeteria cleanliness. After a while the food service manager might say, "You're angry and upset with your employees because they don't keep a careful eye on cleanliness. So you avoid dealing with them, and it only makes problems worse." If the manager's diagnosis is correct, an interpretation can be extremely helpful.

10. Allow for modeling of the desired performance and behaviors. An effective coaching technique is to show the person being coached an example of what constitutes the desired behavior. A customer service representative was harsh with customers when facing heavy pressure. One way the supervisor coached the service representative was by taking over the manager's desk during a busy period. The representative then watched the supervisor deal tactfully with demanding customers.

11. Applaud good results. Effective coaches on the playing field and in the workplace are cheerleaders. They give positive reinforcement by applauding desired results. Some effective coaches shout in joy when the person coached achieves outstanding results; others give high-fives or clap their hands in applause. [21]

Many people are concerned that if they offer too much coaching and feedback to others, they will be perceived as interfering with their work, or being a *micromanager*. In reality, the majority of workers believe that they do not receive enough coaching and guidance on the job. RainmakerThinking Inc. has conducted long-term research suggesting that the undermanaged worker struggles because his or her supervisor is not sufficiently engaged to provide the needed direction and support.[22]

One implication of the coaching suggestions just presented is that some people are more adept at coaching than others. Self-Assessment Quiz 12-2 provides insight into the

Characteristics of an Effective Coach

Directions: Following is a list of traits, attitudes, and behaviors of effective coaches. Indicate under each trait, attitude, or behavior whether you need to improve on it (e.g., "Yes, patience toward people"). Then in the right column, prepare an action plan for improving each trait, attitude, or behavior that you need to develop. Sample action plans are provided.

Trait, attitude, or behavior	*Action plan for improvement*
Empathy	*Sample:* Will listen until I understand the person's point of view.
	Your own:
Listening skill	*Sample:* Will concentrate extra hard to listen.
	Your own:
Ability to size up people	*Sample:* Will jot down observations about people upon first meeting, then verify in the future.
	Your own:
Diplomacy and tact	*Sample:* Will study a book of etiquette.
	Your own:
Patience toward people	*Sample:* Will practice staying calm when someone makes a mistake.
	Your own:
Concern for welfare	*Sample:* When interacting with another person, will ask self, of others, "How can this person's interests best be served?"
	Your own:
Self-confidence	*Sample:* Will attempt to have at least one personal success each week.
	Your own:
Noncompetitiveness	*Sample:* Will keep reminding myself that all boats with team members rise with the same tide.
	Your own:
Enthusiasm for people	*Sample:* Will search for the good in each person.
	Your own:
Work on my personal development thereby leading by example	*Sample:* Overcome projecting the attitude that people who disagree with me are really stupid.
	Your own:
Develops trust and respect[23]	*Sample:* Consistently tells the truth to people.
	Your own:

right stuff for being an effective coach. After doing that exercise and reading the suggestions, you will be prepared for Skill-Building Exercise 12-4 about coaching.

Training Others

A direct way of helping others in the workplace is to train them. **Training** is the process of helping others acquire a job-related skill. The emphasis on continuous learning by employees to keep up with changes in technology and work methods has helped elevate the importance of on-the-job training.[24] Another training opportunity for some workers is to assist in the remedial learning of lesser-skilled employees. According to a Conference Board report, nearly half of 217 employers surveyed indicated that they provide remedial training to strengthen employees' writing, math, and problem-solving deficiencies.[25] Even

Coaching a Mediocre Performer Role-Play

Visualize a busy sports medicine clinic, and you are the chief administrator. You recognize that many of your patients urgently need the medical help your clinic offers because they have been injured substantially while participating in sports. Yet, a good proportion of your patients are visiting the clinic for rehabilitation exercises that they can do on their own or learn from downloaded videos. As a consequence, being pleasant and hospitable is a requirement for all staff members, physicians, physical therapists, and support personnel alike. You want to keep your practice thriving through the rehabilitation patients.

One of your intake specialists, Tanya, goes about her work in a bland, mechanical manner. She makes relatively few errors in processing patient information, but she expresses very little warmth and appreciation toward patients. You have frequently observed patients appearing perplexed and displeased when Tanya deals with them. You have decided to get started coaching Tanya this afternoon toward becoming a warmer, more cheerful intake specialist.

One student plays the role of the chief administrator, and one student plays the role of Tanya who has not clue as to why you want to coach her. To your knowledge, you are a thoroughly professional sports medicine intake specialist.

For both scenarios, observers rate the role players on two dimensions, using a 1-to-5 scale from very poor to very good. One dimension is "effective use of coaching techniques" (for the chief administrator). The second dimension is "acting ability." A few observers might voluntarily provide feedback to the role players in terms of sharing their ratings and observations. The course instructor might also provide feedback.

---

if employees lacking basic skills do receive classroom instruction, they may still need the assistance from workers at a higher skill level.

Supervisors and trainers are responsible for much of the training in organizations. Yet as mentioned at the outset of the chapter, to save money more responsibility to training has shifted to workers themselves. Also, as organizations operate with fewer managers, coworkers have more responsibility to train each other.

While training others, keep in mind certain time-tested principles that facilitate learning—and therefore training. Applying these principles consistently will increase the chances that the people you are training will acquire new skills. A considerable amount of training has shifted to e-learning (also referred to as distance learning and online learning), especially for acquiring cognitive knowledge and skills.[26] Traditional training principles apply to e-learning, and you will still have opportunities to help the trainee. Many e-learners still need to ask a coworker a question, such as "I've been studying the metric system, and I can figure out how to convert Celsius to Fahrenheit, but I'm still having trouble going in the opposite direction. I'm doing something wrong. Can you help?" Then training principles are as follows:

1. **Encourage concentration.** Not much learning takes place unless the trainee concentrates carefully on what is being learned. Concentration improves the ability to do both mental and physical tasks. In short, encourage the person you are training to concentrate.

2. **Use motivated interest.** People learn best when they are interested in the problem facing them. Explain to the trainee how the skill being taught will enhance his or her value as an employee, or relate the skill to the person's professional goals. Trainees can be encouraged to look for some relationship between the information at hand and their personal welfare. With this relationship in mind, the person will have a stronger intention to learn.

3. **Remind learners to intend to remember.** We often fail to remember something because we do not intend to commit it to memory. Many executives are particularly effective at remembering the names of employees and customers. When one executive was asked how she could commit so many names to memory, she replied, "I look at the person, listen to the name, and try hard to remember." An example of reminding a protégé to remember would be to advise him or her to memorize the company mission statement.

4. **Ensure the meaningfulness of material.** The material to be learned should be organized in a meaningful manner. Each successive experience should build on the other. In training another person how to process a customer order, you might teach the skill in terms of the flow of activities from customer inquiry to product delivery.

HELPING OTHERS DEVELOP AND GROW   265

5. **Give feedback on progress.** As a person's training progresses, motivation may be maintained and enhanced by providing knowledge on his or her progress. To measure progress, it may be necessary to ask the trainee questions or ask for a job sample. For example, you might ask the person being trained on invoices to prepare a sample invoice.

6. **Ask the trainee to reflect on what he or she has learned.** Research indicates that if you think carefully about what you have learned, your retention of the information increases. The idea is to step back from the experience to ponder carefully and persistently its meaning to you.[27] After participating in a team development exercise involving white-water rafting, a person might reflect, "What did I really learn about being a better team player? How was I perceived by my teammates in the rubber raft? Did they even notice my contribution? Or did they think I was an important part of the team success?"

7. **Deal with trainee defensiveness.** Training is sometimes retarded because the person being trained is defensive about information or skills that clash with his or her beliefs and practices. The person might have so much emotional energy invested in the status quo that he or she resists the training. For example, a sales representative might resist learning how to use e-commerce because she believes that her warm smile and interpersonal skills have made her an excellent communicator. She is concerned that if she communicates with customers exclusively through e-mail or a company Web site, her human touch will be lost. Sensing this defensiveness, the trainer is advised to talk about e-commerce as being a supplement to, but not a substitute for, in-person communication. (However, the sales rep might also be worried that her position will be eliminated.)

8. **Take into account learning style.** Another key factor that influences training is **learning style,** the way in which a person best learns new information. An example of a learning style is passive learning. People who learn best through passive learning quickly acquire information by studying texts, manuals, magazine articles, and Web sites. They can juggle images in their mind as they read about abstract concepts such as supply and demand, cultural diversity, or customer service. Others learn best by doing rather than studying—for example, learning about customer service by dealing with customers in many situations.

learning style

The way in which a person best learns new information.

Another key dimension of learning styles is whether a person learns best by working alone or cooperatively in a study group. Learning by oneself may allow for more intense concentration, and one can proceed at one's own pace. Learning in groups through classroom discussion allows people to exchange viewpoints and perspectives.

Because of differences in learning styles, you may decide to design training to fit these differences. For example, if your trainees prefer cooperative learning you could combine learning from reading books, articles, and online information with discussions in a conference room.

To start applying these principles of learning to a training situation, do Skill-Building Exercise 12-5.

SKILL-BUILDING EXERCISE 12-5

Designing a Training Program

The class organizes into training design teams of approximately six people. Each team sketches the design of a training program to teach an interpersonal skill to employees, such as being polite to customers or interviewing job candidates. The teams are not responsible for selecting the exact content of the training program they choose. Instead, they are responsible for designing a training program based on the principles of learning. Two examples here would be (a) how to encourage the trainees to concentrate and (b) developing a mechanism to provide feedback to the trainee.

The activity should take about 15 minutes and can therefore be done inside or outside the class. After the teams have designed their programs, they can compare the various versions.

HELPING DIFFICULT PEOPLE

A challenge we all face from time to time is dealing constructively with workers who appear intent on creating problems. For a variety of reasons, these difficult or counterproductive people perform poorly themselves or interfere with the job performance of others. A **difficult person** is an individual who creates problems for others, yet has the skill and mental ability to do otherwise. The difficult person may meet or exceed attendance and performance standards, yet has a toxic personality.[28] Here we will discuss briefly various types of difficult people, and then emphasize methods for helping them behave more productively. To pretest your skill in dealing with and helping difficult people, do Self-Assessment Quiz 12-3.

difficult person

An individual who creates problems for others, even though he or she has the skill and mental ability to do otherwise.

SELF-ASSESSMENT QUIZ 12-3

Helping Difficult People

Directions: For each of the following scenarios, circle the letter of what you think is the most effective way to handle the situation. There may be more than one correct method listed.

1. A coworker in the cubicle next to you is talking loudly on the phone about the fabulous weekend she and a few friends enjoyed. You are attempting to deal with a challenging work problem. To deal with this situation, you

   a. get up from your chair, stand close to her, and say loudly, "Shut up, you jerk! I'm trying to do my work."
   b. slip her a handwritten note that says, "I'm happy that you had a great weekend, but I have problems concentrating on my work when you are talking so loudly. Thanks for your help."
   c. get the boss on the phone and ask that she please do something about the problem.
   d. wait until lunch and then say to her, "I'm happy that you had a great weekend, but I have problems concentrating on my work when you are talking so loudly. Thanks for your help."

2. One of your coworkers, Olaf, rarely carries his fair load of the work. He forever has a good reason for not having the time to do an assignment. This morning he has approached you to load some new software onto his personal computer. You deal with this situation by

   a. carefully explaining that you will help him, providing he will take over a certain specified task for you.
   b. telling him that you absolutely refuse to help a person as lazy as he is.
   c. counseling him about fair play and reciprocity.
   d. reviewing with him a list of five times when he has asked other people to help him. You then ask if he thinks this is a good way to treat coworkers.

3. In your role as supervisor, you have noticed that Diane, one of the group members, spends far too much work time laughing and joking. You schedule a meeting with her. As the meeting opens, you

   a. joke and laugh with her to establish rapport.
   b. explain to Diane that you have called this meeting to discuss her too-frequent laughing and joking.
   c. talk for a few moments about the good things Diane has done for the department, then confront the real issue.
   d. explain to Diane that she is on the verge of losing her job if she doesn't act more maturely.

4. As a team member, you have become increasingly annoyed with Jerry's ethnic, racist, and sexist jokes. One day during a team meeting, he tells a joke you believe is particularly offensive. To deal with the situation, you

   a. meet privately with the team leader to discuss Jerry's offensive behavior.
   b. catch up with Jerry later when he is alone, and tell him how uncomfortable his joke made you feel.
   c. confront Jerry on the spot and say, "Hold on Jerry. I find your joke offensive."
   d. tell the group an even more offensive joke to illustrate how Jerry's behavior can get out of hand.

5. You have been placed on a task force to look for ways to save the company money, including making recommendations for eliminating jobs. You interview a supervisor about the efficiency of her department. She suddenly becomes rude and defensive. In response, you

   a. politely point out how her behavior is coming across to you.
   b. get your revenge by recommending that three jobs be eliminated from her department.

(Continued)

Types of Difficult People

Dozens of types of difficult people have been identified, with considerable overlap among the types. For example, one method of classifying difficult people might identify the dictator, while another method might identify the bully. A major challenge in classifying types of difficult people is that some of the types are manifestations of a severe underlying problem referred to as a **personality disorder.** (Such a disorder is defined as a pervasive, persistent, inflexible, maladaptive pattern of behavior that deviates from expected cultural norms.) One of these 10 different disorders is the narcissistic personality whose behavior includes being grandiose, needing admiration, and lacking empathy. As a difficult person, the narcissistic personality might be labeled a "high-maintenance person," "a me-first," or a "know-it-all expert."

Another important consideration about classifying difficult people is that most of them are a mixture and blend of various types, rather than being a pure type.[29] For example, a bully might be really a blend of a bully, a know-it-all, and an exploder. (Watch out for that guy or gal!)

For our purposes, I will list a sampling of the many types of difficult people found in the workplace and as customers. As you read the following list, look for familiar types.[30]

- *Know-it-alls* believe that they are experts on everything. They have opinions on every issue, yet when they are wrong they pass the buck or become defensive.
- *Blamers* are workers who never solve their own problems. When faced with a challenge or a hitch, they think the problem belongs to the supervisor or a group member.
- *Gossips* spread negative rumors about others and attempt to set people against each other.
- *Bullies* cajole and intimidate others. They are blunt to the point of being insulting, and will sometimes use harsh, vulgar language to attain their goals. Bullies constantly make demands on workmates.
- *Exploders* readily lose self-control when something important or trivial does not go their way such as having their creative suggestion rejected by the group or being informed that their cubicle will be reduced in size. The loss of self-control frequently takes the form of a temper tantrum.
- *Repulsives* are people whose poor personal hygiene, eating habits, appearance, or foul language disrupts the tranquility of others.
- *Yes-people* agree to any commitment, promise any deadline, but rarely deliver. Although sorry about being late, they cannot be trusted to deliver as promised.
- *No-people* are negative and pessimistic and quick to point out why something will not work. They are also inflexible, resist change, and complain frequently.
- *Jekyll and Hydes* have a split personality. When dealing with supervisors, customers, or clients, they are pleasant, engaging people; yet, when carrying out the role of supervisors, they become tyrannical.

personality disorder

A pervasive, persistent, inflexible, maladaptive pattern of behavior that deviates from expected cultural norms.

- *Whiners* gripe about people, processes, and company regulations. They complain about being overworked and underpaid, or not receiving assignments up to their true capabilities.
- *Backstabbers* pretend to befriend you and encourage you to talk freely about problems or personality clashes you face. Later, the backstabber reports the information—often in exaggerated form—to the person you mentioned in a negative light. Or, the backstabber simply says negative things about you behind your back to discredit you to others.
- *High-maintenance types* require considerable attention from others in such forms as demanding much of the supervisor's time, making unusual requests to the human resources department, and taking the maximum number of sick days and personal days allowable. High-maintenance types are often a combination of several of the previous types described above.
- *Clods* are master procrastinators who can find plenty of excuses as to why a project has not been started. When the clod finally gets started on a project, the work proceeds so slowly that other people who need the clod's input fall behind schedule and become stressed.
- *Minimalists* are apathetic and low-performing, and do just enough work to avoid being fired. They do the bare minimum, are thrive on being mediocre.
- *Office cheats* take claim for the ideas of other people, and benefit from these ideas, leaving the originator of the idea without receiving deserved credit, and feeling frustrated because of the stolen ideas.

Tactics for Dealing with Difficult People

How one deals most effectively with a difficult person depends to some extent on the person's type. For example, you might need more time to get through to a passive person than to a bully. Figure 12-2 presents specific ideas for dealing with a bully. (You will recall that bullying was described in Chapter 9 as a source of workplace conflict.) The following techniques have wide applicability for helping difficult people change to a more constructive behavior pattern. This general approach should prove more helpful than being concerned with specific tactics for each type of difficult person you encounter. A principle to keep in mind in dealing with difficult people is that they vary in their amount of personality disturbance. Workers classified as difficult people whose behavior is propelled by a personality disorder will be the least amenable to change.

FIGURE 12-2 How to Be a Bully Buster

Christine Pearson, a management professor at the University of North Carolina at Chapel Hill, says that employees can take steps to keep uncivil behavior out of the workplace.[25]

- The first step is to admit to yourself that you are being bullied and that the bullying is unfair and unjustified.
- If the bully is affecting you physically, see your doctor.
- Stand up for yourself and be confident.
- Check out your body language. If you stoop, hang your head, or hunch over, you may be giving off victim signals.
- Try not to show that the bully has upset you; the bully may get bored and leave you alone.
- Don't suffer in silence; tell someone you trust.
- Find out about your rights, consider using any complaints procedure available in your company, and if necessary, consult a lawyer.

The problems difficult people (sometimes referred to collectively as *office jerks*) create have received considerable attention in recent years from managers. The precise definition of an office jerk is someone who consistently leaves people feeling demeaned, belittled, and de-energized. In addition, the office jerk typically targets people of lesser power than he or she possesses.[31] (Despite the frequent use of the term, labeling people as *jerks* tends to exclude constructive thinking about dealing with the problem, and is not good human relations practice.)

Such companies as Google and Southwest Airlines have taken many of the steps described next to minimize the negative impact difficult people have on productivity and job satisfaction. Another problem is some positive contributors will quit when forced to work permanently with a difficult person. Many difficult people are also being fired instead of counseled because of the problems they create.[32]

Stay Calm. A good starting point in dealing with many types of difficult people is to stay calm so that you can confront the other person in a professional manner. Staying calm also helps you think of a useful approach on the spot. Imagine that an exploder is upset because the new chair she was assigned has a broken height adjustment. You might calmly say to her, "I can imagine that having a chair that does not adjust is inconvenient, but what would you like me to do?" When you are calm, the difficult person's anger will often simmer down, and the problem that triggered the person can be solved.

Give Ample Feedback. The primary technique for dealing with counterproductive behavior is to feed back to the difficult person how his or her behavior affects you. As in other forms of feedback, be clear about what you want. Focus on the person's behavior rather than on characteristics or values. If a *repulsive type* is annoying you by constantly eating when you are working together, say something to this effect: "I have difficulty concentrating on the work when you are eating." Such a statement will engender less resentment than saying, "I find you repulsive, and it annoys me." As in coaching, it is better to avoid *should* statements because they often create defensiveness instead of triggering positive behavior. Instead of saying "You shouldn't be eating when you are working," you might try, "Could you find another place to eat when we are working together?"

Feedback will sometimes take the form of confrontation, and it is important not to lose emotional control during the confrontation. If the difficult person has criticized you unjustly in your eyes, attempt not to be defensive. Ask the difficult person exactly what he or she is upset about rather than argue. In this way, the burden of responsibility is now back on the antagonist. For example, if a bully was swearing at you during a meeting, later ask for the reason behind the outburst. Following the technique of disarming the opposition described in Chapter 9, you might agree with at least one of the bully's points. This will help establish rapport.[33] An example here would be, "Yes, I should have consulted you before making the final report. I apologize for the oversight."

Criticize Constructively. Feedback sets the stage for criticism. It is best to criticize in private and to begin with mild criticism. Base your criticism on objective facts rather than subjective impressions. Point out, for example, that the yes-person's lack of follow-through resulted in $10,000 in lost sales. Express your criticism in terms of a common goal. For example, "We can get the report done quickly if you'll firm up the statistical data while I edit the text." When you criticize a coworker, avoid acting as if you have formal authority over the person.

Help the Difficult Person Feel More Confident. Many counterproductive employees are simply low in self-confidence and self-efficacy. They use stalling and evasive tactics because they are afraid to fail. Working with your manager or team leader, you might be able to arrange a project or task in which you know the difficult person will succeed. With a small dose of self-confidence and self-efficacy, the person may begin to complain less. With additional successes, the person may soon become less difficult.[34] Self-confidence building takes time. However, self-efficacy can build more quickly as the person learns a new skill.

Use Tact and Diplomacy. Tactful actions on your part can sometimes take care of annoying behavior by coworkers without having to confront the problem. Close your door, for example, if noisy coworkers are gathered outside. When subtlety does not work, it may be necessary to proceed to a confronting type of feedback.

Tact and diplomacy can still be incorporated into confrontation. In addition to confronting the person, you might also point out one of the individual's strengths. In dealing with a know-it-all, you might say, "I realize you are creative and filled with good ideas. However, I wish you would give me an opportunity to express my opinion."

Use Nonhostile Humor.   Nonhostile humor can often be used to help a difficult person understand how his or her behavior is blocking others. Also, the humor will help you defuse the conflict between you and that person. The humor should point to the person's unacceptable behavior, yet not belittle him or her. Assume that you and a coworker are working jointly on a report. For each idea that you submit, your coworker gets into the know-it-all mode and informs you of important facts you neglected. An example of nonhostile humor that might jolt the coworker into realizing that his or her approach is annoying is as follows:

> *If there is ever a contest to choose the human being with a brain that can compete against a Zip file, I will nominate you. But even though my brain is limited to human capacity, I still think I can supply a few facts for our report.*

Your humor may help the other person recognize that he or she is attempting to overwhelm you with facts at his or her disposal. You are being self-effacing and thereby drawing criticism away from your coworker. Self effacement is a proven humor tactic.

Work Out a Deal.   A direct approach to dealing with problems created by a difficult person is to work out a deal or a negotiated solution. Workers who do not carry their load are successful in getting others to do their work. The next time such a worker wants you to carry out a task, agree to it if he or she will reciprocate by performing a task that will benefit you. For working out a deal to be effective, you must be specific about the terms of the deal. The worker may at first complain about your demands for reciprocity, so it is important to be firm.

Reinforce Civil Behavior and Good Moods.   In the spirit of positive reinforcement, when a generally difficult person is behaving acceptably, recognize the behavior in some way. Reinforcing statements would include "It's fun working with you today" and "I appreciate your professional attitude."

SKILL-BUILDING EXERCISE 12-6

Dealing with Difficult People

In both of the following scenarios, one person plays the role of a group member whose work and morale suffer because of a difficult person. The other person plays the role of the difficult person who may lack insight into what he or she is doing wrong. It is important for the suffering person to put emotion into the role.

Scenario 1: A Bully. A bully is present at a meeting called to plan a company morale-boosting event. Several students play the roles of the group members. One student plays the role of a group member who suggests that the event center on doing a social good, such as refurbishing a low-income family's house or conducting a neighborhood cleanup. Another student plays the role of a bully who doesn't like the idea. The group member being intimidated decides to deal effectively with the bully (or dictator).

Scenario 2: A No-Person. One student plays the role of a worker with a lot of creative energy whose manager is a no-person. The energetic worker has what he or she thinks is a wonderful way for the company to generate additional revenue—conduct a garage sale of surplus equipment and furnishings. The worker presents

this idea to the no-person manager, played by another student. If the manager acts true to form, the worker will attempt to overcome his or her objections.

Scenario 3: A Repulsive. Your team is so busy that you are having a working lunch today in a company conference room. This is the first time the team has had lunch with the newest member of the team. She talks loudly while eating, slurps her beverage in a loud manner, and interrupts the flow of conversation twice with vile descriptions of airplane lavatories being overloaded. As the team leader, you know that criticizing workers in public is poor human relations, but you have to do something to salvage the meeting that the repulsive member is interrupting.

For the three scenarios, observers rate the role players on two dimensions, using a 1-to-5 scale from very poor to very good. One dimension is "effective use of human relations techniques." The second dimension is "acting ability." A few observers might voluntarily provide feedback to the role players in terms of sharing their ratings and observations. The course instructor might also provide feedback.

Ask the Difficult Person to THINK Before Speaking. Human relations specialist John Maxwell suggests that you ask the difficult person to THINK before he or she speaks, with "THINK" referring to the acronym:[35]

T   Is it true?

H   Is it helpful?

I   Is it inspiring?

N   Is it necessary?

K   Is it kind?

Although Maxwell's suggestion is aimed at difficult people, is would be a helpful rule of thumb for building relationships with people in many situations.

Have a Job Description That Disallows Difficult Behavior. When difficult behavior is prohibited by the job description, the difficult person can be reminded that his or her behavior is out-of-bounds. A legalistic approach like this must be executed tactfully. Employment law specialist David Wimmer encourages employers to add like similar to the following to job descriptions:

> *Employee must be able to relate to other people beyond giving and receiving instructions: (a) can get along with coworkers without exhibiting behavior extremes; (b) perform work activities requiring negotiating, instruction, supervising, persuading, or speaking with others; and (c) respond appropriately to criticisms from a superior.*[36]

Using this legalistic approach, you might say to a coworker who keeps swearing at teammates, and telling them to shut up when he or she disagrees with them, "You are getting your work done, and that pleases me. Yet, I think your behavior is not in line with the complete job description that we all have to work by."

The tactics for dealing with the difficult people just described require practice to be effective. When you next encounter a difficult person, try one of the tactics that seems to fit the occasion. Role-plays, such as those presented in Skill-Building Exercise 12-5, are a good starting point for implementing tactics in dealing with difficult people.

SELF-ASSESSMENT QUIZZES IN OVERVIEW

Self-Assessment Quiz 12-1, Attitudes toward Helping Others, deals with perhaps the most humanistic topic in the book. If you truly believe in helping others you will be a better coworker, team leader, supervisor, manager, coach, or mentor. If your attitudes toward helping others are not so positive, perhaps this might be an area for improvement so you can be more effective in the various roles just mentioned. Self-Assessment Quiz 12-2, Characteristics of an Effective Coach, takes you one step further into self-reflection in relation to helping others. You will notice that the characteristics of an effective coach are similar to good interpersonal skills in general, such as using diplomacy and tact and being enthusiastic. Self-Assessment Quiz 12-3, Helping Difficult People, prompts to think about the most demanding interpersonal skills of all—dealing effectively with work associates who are uncooperative and often unpleasant.

Concept Review and Reinforcement

Key Terms

nurturing person 255
toxic person 255
mentor 257
protégé 257

coaching 261
peer coaching 261
behavioral feedback 262
training 264

learning style 266
difficult person 267
personality disorder 268

Summary

Workers have a responsibility to help each other learn, grow, and develop. A major strategy for helping others grow and develop is to be a nurturing, positive person. A toxic person stands in contrast to a nurturing person because he or she dwells on the negative. Nurturing people are positive, enthusiastic, and supportive. Three actions and attitudes that support being a nurturing person are to (1) recognize growth needs in others, (2) use the buddy system, and (3) be a role model.

Being a mentor is another way to help others. As long as you are experienced and wiser than a coworker in some important aspect of the job, you can be a mentor. Virtual, or online, mentoring is possible. Mentors can be selected by the company or chosen informally. To be a mentor, a person engages in a wide range of helping behaviors. Among them are sponsoring, coaching, protecting, sharing challenging assignments, and being a referral agent. Mentors also help protégés solve problems and learn the ropes of an organization. Mentoring can sometimes help the organization by helping workers become more committed to the firm.

Coaching and training are direct helping roles. Coaching is a method of helping workers grow and develop by providing suggestions and encouragement. The five ideal characteristics of peer coaching are (1) equal status of peers, (2) personal and professional development of both peers, (3) integration of reflection and practice, (4) importance of attention to process, and (5) accelerating career learning. Suggestions for effective coaching include the following:

1. Build relationships.
2. Provide specific feedback.
3. Make criticism pain-free and positive.
4. Encourage the person you are coaching to talk.
5. Ask powerful questions.
6. Give emotional support.
7. Give some constructive advice.
8. Coach with "could," not "should."
9. Interpret what is happening.
10. Allow for modeling of the desired performance and behaviors.
11. Applaud good results.

Training involves helping people acquire job skills. To facilitate training, apply principles of learning such as the following: (1) encourage concentration, (2) use motivated interest, (3) remind learners to intend to remember, (4) ensure the meaningfulness of material, (5) give feedback on progress, (6) ask the trainee to reflect on what he or she has learned, (7) deal with trainee defensiveness, and (8) take into account learning style.

Dealing with difficult people is a major challenge in helping others. Some difficult people have a personality disorder. The many types of difficult people include know-it-alls, blamers, gossips, bullies, exploders, repulsives, yes-people, no-people, Jekyll and Hydes, whiners, backstabbers, high-maintenance types, and office cheats. Companies are concerned about the damage difficult people create, and sometimes fire them.

Workers classified as difficult people whose behavior is propelled by a personality disorder will be the least amenable to change. Tactics for dealing with difficult people include (1) giving ample feedback including confrontation, (2) criticizing constructively, (3) helping the difficult person feel more confident, (4) using tact and diplomacy, (5) using humor, (6) working out a deal, (7) reinforcing civil behavior and good moods, (8) asking the person to THINK before speaking, and (9) having a job description that disallows difficult behavior.

Questions for Discussion and Review

1. What is your opinion on whether workers have a responsibility to help each other grow and develop?
2. What is your opinion of the potential effectiveness of the buddy system in your career?
3. Visualize yourself in a full-time professional job working for a company that believed strongly in mentoring. Explain whether you would prefer to find a mentor for yourself, or be assigned a mentor by the company.
4. In what way does a coach in the workplace function much like an athletic coach?
5. Describe any constructive advice you have received from anybody who has coached you. What was the impact of this advice?
6. Many career-minded workers today hire their own coach, much like a personal trainer for solving job problems and advancing. Explain whether you would be willing to invest money to hire a "business coach" for yourself.
7. What might be a problem in relying heavily on "FAQs (frequently asked questions)" to help in training employees?
8. How might one employee coach or train another employee by use of Twitter and text messaging?
9. Many human resource professionals believe that training employees is the best method of enhancing organizational productivity. Why do you think this might be true?
10. How might humor help you deal with the repulsive type of difficult person? Supply an example of a witty comment you might use.

The Web Corner

http://www.jobshadow.org/
(Job shadowing as a form of mentoring)

http://www.BlueSuitMom.com/career/management/difficultpeople.html
(Strategies for dealing with difficult people)

http://www.mygroup.com/coaching.html
(Coaching for various stages in a person's career)

Internet Skill Builder: Mentoring Online

As mentioned in the chapter, many mentors stay in touch with the people they mentor primarily through e-mail and Web sites, including company and social networking Web sites. Such virtual networking has advantages and disadvantages. Search the Internet for three useful ideas about how to mentor effectively online. Try the search terms "virtual mentoring" and "online mentoring" as well as other terms you think might work. Think through which of these ideas you would use as an online mentor.

Developing Your
Human Relations Skills

Interpersonal Relations Case 12.1

The Reality Coach

Kara was excited about her new position as Internet sales manager at a food supplement company. The company's dozens of products included pills and liquids for improving skin health, lowering blood pressure, improving digestion, and improving vision. Many of the company's sales were in bulk to supermarkets, pharmacies, and health food stores. In addition, many orders came in over the Internet and by toll-free numbers. Kara's responsibilities included revitalizing the company Web site periodically, and finding ways to direct more Internet traffic to the site.

During Kara's first week on the job, she was assigned a coach and mentor, Malcolm, the manager of order fulfillment. Malcolm was to act in the dual role of coaching and mentoring Kara, in addition to assisting in her *onboarding* (getting oriented into the company). During their first meeting, Malcolm was friendly and constructive, saying that his role was to help Kara in any feasible way.

The second meeting between Kara and Malcolm was quite brief, with Malcolm asking Kara if she were yet having any problems he could provide assistance with. Kara replied that all was going well so far.

One week later, Malcolm dropped by Kara's cubicle, and said to her, "I've noticed that Internet sales have been flat since you came on board. What is it that you are doing that is adding value to the company?" Kara replied that enhancing Internet sales takes considerable time.

Ten days later, Malcolm sent Kara an e-mail asking that she meet with him in his cubicle at 4 p.m. Malcolm asked Kara how she was doing, and then said he had some advice for her as her coach and mentor. "Quite frankly, I think you could make a more professional appearance. Your hair is too long, and you wear too much dangling

jewelry. I think that you need to tone down your appearance a little to be successful as an Internet sales manager."

Kara replied, "Nobody else has complained. Besides, most of my important interactions are over the Internet, and not with customers face to face. So long hair and dangling jewelry should not be a problem."

Kara was beginning to wonder if Malcolm was really a help or just an irritant. She then devoted most of her energies the next couple of weeks in revamping and modernizing the company Web site. Her boss, as well as several coworkers, made approving comments about the new Web site. Malcolm, however, had his own opinion of the revamped Web site. He said to Kara in person, "I have heard that a few people like the changes you made to the Web site. But Kara, I am disappointed. You just tweaked the site instead of making radical changes that would increase sales substantially. I know that you can do better."

Kara replied, "Malcolm, isn't there anything I can do to please you? Are you my coach and mentor, or just my heckler?"

Malcolm retorted, "Do you think you might be too thin-skinned to succeed in business? As your coach and mentor I have to be frank. Otherwise I can't help you."

Case Questions

1. How effective do you think Malcolm is in his role as Kara's coach and mentor?
2. What suggestions can you offer Malcolm to be more effective in his role?
3. What suggestions might you offer Kara so that she can benefit more from the coaching and mentoring the company is providing her?

Interpersonal Relations Case 12.2

What to Do about Brian?

Brian is one of 10 home mortgage refinance specialists working in his department of Cypress Finance, a substantial size financial services firm. Most of the customer contact

work of the mortgage refinance department is conducted over the telephone (using a toll-free number), even when potential customers initiate their inquiry through the company Web site. Each refinance specialist does considerable individual work, including interacting with customers and potential customers and evaluating the mortgage applicant's credit worthiness. Credit checks are made with computerized databases, but occasionally clarifying information is sought.

Refinance specialists have to cooperate with each other on complex cases. The cooperation often takes the form of asking a teammate's opinion on the creditworthiness of the risk. A member of management, however, gives final approval to all but the most routine refinance applications.

At times, the supervisor of the group, Nina, makes assignments to balance the workload among the specialists. However, the work piles up so quickly that the specialists are supposed to look for ways to spread the work out evenly among themselves to prevent delays in processing refinance applications.

Nina perceives Brian to be a superior performer. His most recent performance evaluation stated that he was an outstanding refinance specialist with potential for promotion to a supervisory position in the future. Nina also rated Brian's sales performance to be outstanding. A "sale" means that an inquiry over the telephone or Web site is converted into an application to refinance that becomes approved. Despite his outstanding performance, Nina did mention that Brian could strengthen his teamwork skills. She specifically mentioned that Brian was sometimes so busy with his individual cases that he neglected to help out other team members.

During a recent team meeting, Nina told the group, "Once again I am pleased to announce that Brian has been the outstanding producer in the department. I know that we work together as a team yet still have our individual goals. Brian is great at closing applicants with good credit risks, and he still contributes his share as a team player."

Kenny, one of the other refinance specialists, gave a gentle nudge with his elbow to Cindy, a specialist seated to his right. Kenny murmured, "What a kiss-up this guy is. Nina should know what an annoyance Brian is in the office."

After the meeting, Kenny, Cindy, and Lindsay, a third specialist, were standing together near the elevator. Lindsay said while giggling, "Did you see the look on Brian's face? All smiles, like he was voted the MVP of the Super Bowl. Brian sometimes forgets that we help him with his trickiest applications, and then he grabs the glory. But ask Brian for a little help, and he will say something to the effect that he is too busy closing a major deal. You would think he was refinancing the Empire State Building." Kenny, Cindy, and Lindsay giggled simultaneously.

The next workday at Cypress was one of the busiest ever. Newspaper and television reports throughout the country announced that mortgage rates were expected to climb by one and one-half percent the following month. The number of applicants for refinancing doubled as many home owners were eager to lock in the present low rates for refinancing. The refinance specialists were asked to put in 60-hour weeks until the workload drifted back to normal.

During the lunch break on one of the peak-load days, Brian approached the three other specialists taking the break at the same time as he with this proposition, "As everyone in this office knows, I am really talented at closing deals. And the more deals we close as a group, the bigger will be the group bonus at the end of the year. So I'm suggesting that when I have a couple of big deals on the hook, I send my minnows over to you. [Minnows refer to small deals.] Also, I would like your cooperation in doing some of the detail work, such as a lengthy credit inquiry for a major deal. My time is better invested in reeling in the big deals."

One of the specialists said, "Sounds good to me." Cindy took an opposite approach, as she told Brian, "Happy fishing, but you're not my boss. Why should I volunteer to help you when you never volunteer to help me?"

Brian retorted, "Cindy, you may be a nice person, but I think you're a rotten team player. We have to divide up responsibilities for the good of the team."

Later that day, Cindy chatted with Kenny and Lindsay about the incident during the lunch break. She said, "We've got to do something about Brian, but I don't know what. It's tough when you have to do battle with the boss's pet."

Questions

1. Is Brian a *difficult person*? Explain.
2. What steps should the refinance specialists take who object to Brian's work style?
3. How might a system of peer evaluation (workers contributing to the evaluation of each other) help Nina in her supervision of the department?
4. Do you think Cindy is being a rotten team player?

Positive Political Skills

Todd Averett is director, global supply chain design, and sourcing at Payless ShoeSource, the largest family footwear dealer in the Western Hemisphere. The official name of the company is now Collective Brands, Inc. Averett wrote the following about the importance of organizational citizenship behavior at his company:

> Most organizational leaders, when asked, would say they prefer to staff their organizations with individuals who are good "organizational citizens"—individuals who go above and beyond the call of duty. In recent years Payless ShoeSource has strived to develop a culture that focuses on principles and values related to organizational citizenship. At Payless, this focus began with the realization at the executive level that

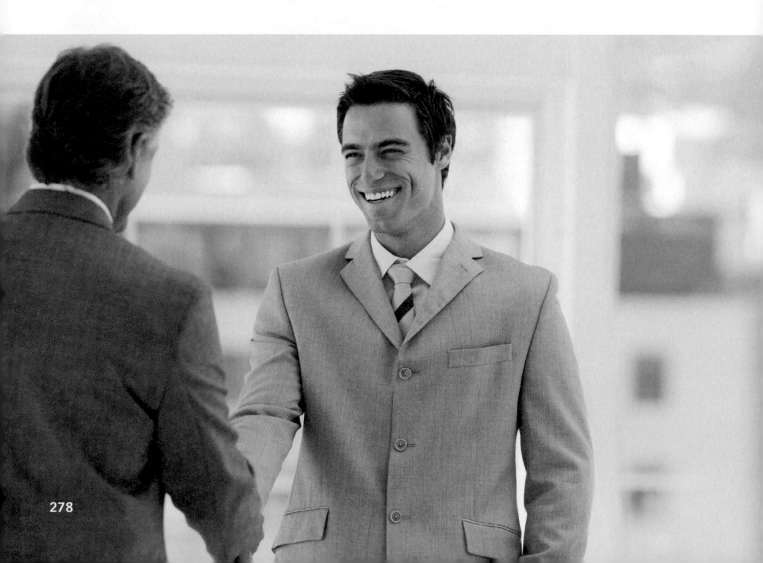

After reading and studying this chapter and doing the exercises, you should be able to

1. Explain the importance of political skill and social intelligence for becoming skilled at using positive political tactics.

2. Manage effectively the impression you give, including developing an awareness of the rules of business etiquette.

3. Implement political techniques for building relationships with managers and other key people.

4. Implement political techniques for building relationships with coworkers and other worker associates.

5. Avoid committing political blunders.

to reach our full potential as an organization, the hearts and minds of our Associates had to be fully engaged in achieving common goals. For Payless, a retailer in a competitive market, this meant moving from a culture of "results at all costs" to a culture driven by "Guiding Values." These Guiding Values are: personal accountability, risk taking and innovation, teamwork, change, and open communication. To change the culture, Payless had to convince employees to let go of longstanding norms and accept, on faith, that living the Guiding Values would bring greater success for both the company and themselves.

Similar to Payless' Guiding Values, the essence of organizational citizenship is employee behavior that goes above and beyond the call of duty. Perhaps more importantly these behaviors represent, or are the manifestations of, beliefs that individuals have about their roles at work.[1]

The comments by the learning and development director at Payless Shoes emphasize one of the themes of this chapter: Organizational citizenship behavior helps the company, and is also good organizational politics because such behavior helps you develop a solid relationship with your manager and coworkers. The proper use of positive political tactics helps build good interpersonal relationships. In turn, these good relationships can facilitate achieving career goals. Recognize, however, that being competent in your job is still the most effective method of achieving career success. After skill come hard work and luck as important success factors.

A fourth ingredient is also important for success—positive political skills. Few people can achieve success for themselves or their group without having some awareness of the political forces around them and how to use them to advantage. It may be necessary for the career-minded person to take the offensive in using positive and ethical political tactics. As used here, **organizational politics** refers to gaining power through any means other than merit or luck. (Luck, of course, is what happens when preparation meets opportunity.) Politics are played to achieve power, either directly or indirectly. **Power** refers to the ability or potential to control anything of value and to influence decisions. The results of such power may take diverse forms like being promoted, being transferred, receiving a salary increase, or avoiding an uncomfortable assignment.

Organizational politics can also be regarded from the standpoint of interpersonal relationships and sizing up the environment. As described by author and speaker Donna Cardillo, office politics refers to understanding the unwritten rules of the workplace that involve getting along with others, getting recognized for one's efforts, and following the protocol of how things get accomplished.[2]

organizational politics

Gaining power through any means other than merit or luck.

power

The ability or potential to control anything of value and to influence decisions.

FIGURE 13-1 **Relationship among Politics, Power, and Influence. Political tactics, such as developing contacts with key people, lead to power, which enables one to control and influence others.**

As you study this chapter, it will become evident that communication skills and team player skills are necessary for being skilled at politics. Figure 13-1 depicts the relationship among politics, power, and control and influence. Political tactics, such as developing contacts with key people, lead to power, which enables one to control and influence others.

In this chapter, we approach skill development in organizational (or office) politics from several standpoints. Information is presented about such topics as managing your impression, using political tactics to improve interpersonal relationships, and avoiding hazardous political mistakes. To measure your current tendencies toward playing politics, do Self-Assessment Quiz 13-1.

SELF-ASSESSMENT QUIZ 13-1

Organizational Politics Questionnaire

Directions: For each of the following statements, check whether you mostly agree or mostly disagree, even if it is difficult for you to decide which alternative best describes your opinion.

	Mostly agree	*Mostly disagree*
1. The boss or the team leader is always right.	_____	_____
2. It is wise to flatter important people.	_____	_____
3. If you do somebody a favor, remember to cash in on it.	_____	_____
4. Given the opportunity, I would go out of my way to develop friendships with powerful people.	_____	_____
5. I would be willing to say nice things about a rival in order to get that person transferred from my department.	_____	_____
6. If it would help me get ahead, I would take credit for someone else's work.	_____	_____
7. Given the chance, I would offer to help my boss fix something in his or her home.	_____	_____
8. I laugh heartily at my boss's humor, even if I do not think it is funny.	_____	_____
9. Dressing to create a favorable appearance is foolish. At the office, wear clothing that you find to be the most comfortable.	_____	_____
10. Never waste lunchtime by eating with somebody who can't help you solve a problem or gain advantage.	_____	_____
11. I think using e-mail to zap somebody for his or her mistake, and sending copies to key people, is a good idea.	_____	_____
12. If somebody higher up in the organization offends you, look for ways to get even with him or her.	_____	_____
13. Being candid is the best policy even if it means insulting somebody.	_____	_____
14. Obtaining power for its own sake would make me feel wonderful.	_____	_____
15. If I had a legitimate gripe against my employer, I would express my views publicly (such as distributing my comments on a blog or social networking site).	_____	_____

16. I would invite my boss or team leader to a party at my home even if I didn't like him or her.   _____   _____

17. An effective way to impress people is to tell them what they want to hear.   _____   _____

18. Having a school, college, or skyscraper named after me would be an incredible thrill.   _____   _____

19. Hard work and good performance are usually sufficient for career success.   _____   _____

20. Even if I made only a minor contribution to a project, I would get my name listed as being associated with it.   _____   _____

21. I would never publicly correct mistakes made by my supervisor or team leader.   _____   _____

22. I would never use my personal contacts to gain a promotion.   _____   _____

23. If you happen to dislike a person who receives a big promotion in your firm, don't bother sending that person a congratulatory note.   _____   _____

24. I would never openly criticize a powerful executive in my organization.   _____   _____

25. I would stay late in the office just to impress my supervisor or team leader.   _____   _____

Total Score _____   _____

Scoring and Interpretation: Give yourself a +1 for each answer you gave in agreement with the keyed answer. Note that I did not use the term *correct answer*. Whether or not an answer is correct is a question of personal values and ethics. Each question that receives a score of +1 shows a tendency toward playing organizational politics. The scoring key is as follows:

1. Mostly agree	10. Mostly agree	19. Mostly disagree
2. Mostly agree	11. Mostly agree	20. Mostly agree
3. Mostly agree	12. Mostly disagree	21. Mostly agree
4. Mostly agree	13. Mostly disagree	22. Mostly disagree
5. Mostly agree	14. Mostly agree	23. Mostly disagree
6. Mostly agree	15. Mostly disagree	24. Mostly agree
7. Mostly agree	16. Mostly agree	25. Mostly agree
8. Mostly agree	17. Mostly agree	
9. Mostly disagree	18. Mostly agree	

In an earlier version of this test, based on a sample of 750 men and women managers, professionals, administrators, sales representatives, and business owners, the mean score is 10. Scores of 1 through 7 suggest a below-average tendency to play politics. Scores between 8 and 12 suggest an average tendency to play office politics. Scores of 13 and above suggest an above-average tendency to play office politics and a strong need for power.

Sources: Andrew J. DuBrin, "Career Maturity, Organizational Rank, and Political Behavior Tendencies: A Correlational Analysis of Organizational Politics and Career Experience," *Psychological Reports,* vol. 63, 1988, pp. 531–537; DuBrin, "Sex Differences in Endorsement of Influence Tactics and Political Behavior Tendencies," *Journal of Business and Psychology,* Fall 1989, pp. 3–14.

POLITICAL SKILL AND OTHER HUMAN RELATIONS SKILLS

Political skill does not stand alone, separated from other human relations skills. Here we look at how political skill relates to awareness of one's surroundings, emotional intelligence and social intelligence, relationship building with the leader, and coping with an unjust environment.

LEARNING OBJECTIVE 1

Sensitivity to Your Surroundings

For starters, being sensitive to your surroundings and to other people helps make you politically aware. Cultural sensitivity, as described in Chapter 8 about cross-cultural relations and diversity, is a specific type of sensitivity to one's surroundings that deals with sizing up the cultural environment.

Imagine that you are applying for a position at Google doing exactly the kind of work you want. You have seen photos of Google employees, and you have visited its headquarters before your interview just to see what the company looks like. No Goggle worker including the founders is ever seen in a business suit, yet this fact escapes you. You show up for your interview wearing a business suit and leather shoes as if you were applying for a position as an investment banker trainee at a Wall Street firm. Zap, you are done. The Google employees wearing jeans, casual shirts and blouses, and running shoes think you would be a poor cultural fit despite your intelligence and talent. You were not sensitive enough to the environment to choose the appropriate attire for you interview.

Emotional Intelligence and Social Intelligence

Political skill relates to emotional intelligence because you need to be able to read the emotions of others to establish rapport with them. For example, a person with good emotional intelligence would ask for a raise when the boss appeared to be in a good mood. Also, the person would avoid asking for a raise when the boss was upset, preoccupied, and in an ugly mood.

Political skill is also directly related to **social intelligence,** an understanding of how relationships with bosses and colleagues, family, and friends shape our brains and affect our bodies. Social intelligence is a book-length subject, yet we can take away a couple of basic lessons that are linked to positive political skill.[3] Social intelligence tells us that good relationships act like vitamins, energizing us to perform well. In contrast, bad relationships are like poison that undermines our cognitive efficiency and creativity. The person with good social intelligence would work at having positive relationships with others on the job, so as to being able to concentrate on the task and perform well.

Another aspect of having social intelligence would be to recognize that being arrogant or derisive toward others can cause emotional distress that impairs the brain's ability to learn and think clearly. So a good team player or a manager would relate more positively toward others in order to help attain a productive workplace.

CEO Steve Bennett of Intuit exemplifies a manager who deliberately practices social intelligence. For instance, he gives constructive criticism but avoid angry attacks. During one meeting, he criticized a senior manager who was dominating a meeting even though the subject was not his field of expertise. Bennett attempted to criticize him in a joking way rather than being hostile.[4]

Relationship Building with the Leader

A major purpose of organizational politics including political skill is to develop good relationships with your superior, as described later in this chapter. More specifically, strong political skills can help you develop a higher quality leader-member exchange (LMX). A new study suggests that having good political skills can help a person develop a positive LMX even when the two parties are demographically different. Previous research had shown that LMXs tend to be more positive when the leader and group member are demographically similar, such as being the same sex or race, or similar in age.

The study in question involved 189 participants in a retail service organization. Seventy-six percent of the sample was white (Caucasian), and 56 percent was women. The average age of participants was 30. Participants all took the political skill inventory presented in Self-Assessment Quiz 13-2, and that has been used in many other studies. Political skill was shown to improve relationships with racially dissimilar leaders and

social intelligence

An understanding of how relationships with bosses and colleagues, family, and friends shape our brains and affect our bodies.

Political Skill Inventory

Instructions: Using the following 7-point scale, write in each box the number that best describes how much you agree with the statement. 1 = strongly disagree; 2 = disagree; 3 = slightly agree; 4 = neutral; 5 = slightly agree; 6 = agree; 7 = strongly agree.

1. I spend a lot of time and effort networking with others. ❑
2. I am able to make most people feel comfortable and at ease around me. ❑
3. I am able to communicate easily and effectively with others. ❑
4. It is easy for me to develop good rapport with most people. ❑
5. I understand people very well. ❑
6. I am good at building relationships with influential people at work (or at school). ❑
7. I am particularly good at sensing the motivations and hidden agendas of others. ❑
8. When communicating with others, I try to be genuine in what I say and do. ❑
9. I have developed a large network of colleagues and associates at work (or school) who I can call on for support when I really need to get things done. ❑
10. At work (or at school), I know a lot of important people and I am well connected. ❑
11. I spend a lot of time at work (or at school) developing connections with others. ❑
12. I am good at getting people to like me. ❑
13. It is important that people believe I am sincere in what I do and say. ❑
14. I try to show a genuine interest in other people. ❑
15. I am good at using my connections and network to make things happen at work (or at school). ❑
16. I have good intuition and savvy about how to present myself to others. ❑
17. I always seem to instinctively know the right things to say or do to influence others. ❑
18. I pay close attention to people's facial expressions. ❑

Total = ❑   Total ÷ 18 = ❑

Scoring and interpretation: Compute your overall score by adding together your response scores on all the questions and dividing the total by 18. You will have an overall political score between 1 and 7. Larger scores identify people who have higher political skill, and smaller scores identify people who have lower political skill.

Source: Adapted from Gerald R. Ferris et al., "Development and Validation of the Political Skill Inventory," *Journal of Management,* vol. 31, 2005, pp. 126–152.

group member (better LMX scores). It was also found that the quality of the LMX was not due to gender or age. The researchers concluded that political skill enables subordinates who are racially dissimilar to their subordinates to get around the potential relationship problems based on these differences.[5]

Overcoming the Effects of Injustice

To illustrate further the positive impact of political skill, some evidence suggests that having political skill can help overcome the effects of unfairness in the organization. The study in question was a government agency, and two types of justices were measured by questionnaires—procedural and distributive. Procedural justice is the perceived fairness of the policies and procedures used to make decisions. Distributive justice is how fairly outcomes or rewards are distributed based on these procedures, such as receiving a deserved salary increase. Political skill was measured by the political skill inventory mentioned above, and job performance was measured by supervisory ratings of performance.

The study found that under conditions of injustice, political skill was associated with high performance. Highly politically skilled workers were rated similarly regardless of the level of distributive justice. In other words, having good political skill helped overcome the effects of low justice. Another finding was that under conditions of injustice, low political skill is harmful to performance ratings.[6] You need political skills to help combat an unfair system.

IMPRESSION MANAGEMENT AND ETIQUETTE

LEARNING OBJECTIVE 2

impression management

A set of behaviors directed at enhancing one's image by drawing attention to oneself.

Being an effective, responsible contributor is not always sufficient to gain the attention you deserve. It may also be necessary to make others aware of your capability. **Impression management** is a set of behaviors directed at enhancing one's image by drawing attention to oneself. Often the attention is directed toward superficial aspects of the self, such as clothing and appearance. Yet, impression management also includes doing a good job, telling people about your accomplishments and appearing self-confident. The next subsections list specific tactics of impression management and discuss business etiquette. We discuss etiquette here because how you behave in certain situations shapes your image.

Tactics of Impression Management

Managing the impression you create encompasses hundred of specific tactics, limited only by your imagination of what will impress others. Impression management is also regarded as the process by which people control the impression others form of them. Part of your power in the organization stems from your formal position, as well as how you are perceived by others. Creating the right image is the practice of impression management.[7]

Although impression management can be used in a variety of relationships, it is most commonly found in the attempt of a worker to please the manager. For example, impression management is frequently used during performance evaluation in order to impress the manager with the worker's accomplishments. Six positive tactics of impression management are described next.

Display Organizational Citizenship Behavior. We mention organizational citizenship behavior in several places in our study of human relations because of its contribution to effective interpersonal relationships. A highly effective and meritorious way of creating a good impression is to step outside your job description to help coworkers and the company. You become admired for going beyond the call of duty.[8] Organizational citizenship behavior is generally aimed at helping others, yet it is possible that the motive underlying citizenship behavior is to foster a good impression. A prime example is that volunteering for special assignments helping others may provide workers with an opportunity to show off their talents and knowledge, leading to an enhanced image.

Impression management theorists argue that a primary human motive is to be viewed positively by others, and to avoid being viewed negatively. Engaging in organizational citizenship behavior is an effective means of being viewed positively in the sense of having positive motives for engaging in constructive behavior such as collecting relief funds for a coworker whose apartment burned down.

Whether or not organizational citizenship behavior has an element of trying to look good, the balance of evidence is that citizenship behavior helps both individuals and the organization. Based on 168 studies involving more than 50,000 workers, it was found that organizational citizenship behavior helped individuals receive better performance ratings and salary increases. Organizations benefited in such ways higher productivity, lowered costs, and better customer service.[9]

BACK TO THE OPENING CASE

Todd Averett and other managers at Payless ShoeSource have continued to emphasize the importance of organizational citizenship behavior as a corporate value. One of many positive consequences is that the employees build good relationships with managers, and are satisfied with their good working conditions. Employee turnover is low by industry standards, and profits are high.

Build Trust and Confidence.   A key strategy for creating a positive impression with your immediate superior and higher ranking managers is to build trust and confidence. Project the authentic impression of a person who can be trusted to carry out responsibilities faithfully and ethically. Rather than take action without permission (e.g., spending beyond budget), know the bounds of your authority and work within those bounds. Be aware that your boss has other responsibilities, so do not take more than your fair share of his or her time. You will generate an impression of confidence if you suggest alternative solutions to the problems you bring to your manager.[10]

Be Visible and Create a Strong Presence.   An essential part of impression management is to be perceived as a valuable contributor on the job. Visibility is attained in many ways such as regular attendance at meetings and company social events, being assigned to important projects, and doing volunteer work in the community. Helping in the launch of a new product or redesigning work methods are other ways of attaining visibility and creating a strong presence. Face-to-face visibility is perhaps the best, but electronic visibility can also be effective. This includes making intelligent contributions to company intranets and blogs, and sending e-mail messages of substance to the right people. Saying nice things about your company on social networking sites is valuable also. Terry Bragg observes that many employees are shocked to learn that they lost their jobs during a downsizing because upper management did not know that they were valuable contributors.[11]

Admit Mistakes.   Many people believe that to create a good impression, it is best to deny or cover up mistakes. In this way, you will not appear vulnerable. A higher level of political skill is to admit mistakes, thereby appearing more forthright and trustworthy. The simple statement "I goofed" will often gain you sympathy and support, whereas an attempted cover up will decrease your social capital. For purposes of impression management, the bottom line of being wrong is to (a) admit the error, (b) request guidance, (c) step up repair, and (d) learn from it.[12] Requesting guidance is important because it conveys the impression that you have humility and that you trust the advice and counsel of others. Here is an example of this tactic in action:

> Cindy, a call center operator, is listening on the phone to a woman rant and rave about a $5.87 charge on her credit card that seems unwarranted. Thinking that she has the telephone receiver covered, Cindy says in a sigh of exasperation to a coworker, "I'm about to scream. I'm talking to the biggest jerk of year right now." Unfortunately "the biggest jerk of the year" heard the comment and reported it to Cindy's supervisor.
>
> During a review of the incident with her supervisor, Cindy said, "Yes indeed I made the comment," and then asked how to deal with the pressures of such an overreacting customer. Cindy offered to send a written apology to the customer. So far, Cindy has learned from her error and not repeated the incident.

Minimize Being a Yes-Person.   A conventional view of organizational politics suggests that being a yes-person is an excellent way of developing a good relationship with higher-ups, and generating the impression of a loyal and supportive subordinate. The yes-person operates by the principle, "the boss is always right." Often the boss cultivates yes-person behavior among subordinates by being intimidating, and unapproachable.[13] When working for an emotionally secure and competent manager, you are likely to create a better impression by not agreeing with all the boss's ideas and plans. Instead, express constructive disagreement by explaining how the boss's plan might be enhanced, or an error be avoided.

> Assume that you work in the marketing department of Jitterbug, a simplified cell phone that focuses on the senior market. Your boss suggests an advertising theme suggesting that even people with arthritis and who are technically challenged can easily operate a Jitterbug. Your intuition tells you this theme would be a humiliating insult to seniors. So, you respond to your boss, "I know that Jitterbug targets seniors, but I suggest that we tone down the terms "arthritis"

and "technically challenged." What not be positive and state that the keys are easy to manipulate, and that the Jitterbug is as easy to operate as a land-line phone?"

Create a Healthy Image. A superficial yet important part of impression management is to project a healthy, physically fit appearance. Appearing physically fit in the workplace has gained in importance as many business firms offer workers rewards for being physically fit and avoiding smoking and obesity. Among the rewards offered by employers are electronic gadgets, discounted health insurance, and cash bonuses. At IBM Corp. employees get as much as $300 annually for exercising regularly, quitting smoking, or logging on to the company's preventive-care Web site.[14] Microsoft has a wellness program directed specifically at combating obesity with such features as a personal trainer, custom nutritional plan, and health spa facilities.[15] From an impression management perspective, being obese at health-conscious companies would be a negative.

Projecting an image of emotional fitness also contributes to a healthy image. *Emotional fitness* would include such behaviors as appearing relaxed, appropriate laughing and smiling, and a minimum of nervous mannerisms and gestures. Being physically fit helps project emotional fitness. When managing the impression you create, be mindful of the advice offered by William L. Gardner III. He urges that you be yourself. When selecting an image, do not attempt to be somebody you are not because people will see through this facade. Gardner concludes, "Make every effort to put your best foot forward—but never at the cost of your identity or integrity!"[16] Impression management is geared toward looking good, but not creating a false impression.

You need good political skills to be effective at impression management. A study of 204 employees working on environmental issues indicated that when employees with good political skill use impression management tactics, they are likely to receive higher job performance ratings from their supervisor. In contrast, individuals low in political skill who engage in impression management tend to be seen less positively by their supervisors.[17] In other words, you need a little finesse and sensitivity to people to be good at office politics.

Another essential part of impression management is to avoid creating a negative impression through such behaviors as being absent or late frequently, speaking poorly, or talking in a meeting while the presenter is speaking. The discussion of etiquette helps guide a person away from behaviors that would bring him or her negative attention.

Skill-Building Exercise 13-1 gives you an opportunity to try out a highly practical application of impression management.

SKILL-BUILDING EXERCISE 13-1

The Elevator 30-Second Speech

A long-standing suggestion in career development and impressing higher-ups is to make a 30-second impromptu presentation when you have a chance encounter with a key person in your organization. If you work in an office tower, the chance encounter is likely to take place in an elevator—and it is generally frowned upon to have long conversations in an elevator. So the term *elevator speech* developed to describe a brief opportunity to impress a key person. Imagine that you have a chance encounter with a high-ranking executive in your area on the elevator, escalator, parking lot, or during a company picnic, or some other location. You then give that person a 30-second pitch geared to make a positive impression. Because you must boil your pitch down to 30 seconds, you will need to prepare for a long time. (Credit President Abraham Lincoln with that insight.)

About six different pairs (impresser and person to be impressed) will carry out this role-play in front of the class. The evaluators will put themselves in the role of the key person who was the target

of the 30-second evaluation. Consider using the following scale, and answering the two questions:

_____ Wow, I was impressed. (5 points)

_____ I was kind of impressed with the person I ran into. (4 points)

_____ He or she left me with at least an average impression. (3 points)

_____ I found the person to be somewhat annoying. (2 points)

_____ That person I met left with a terrible impression. (1 point)

1. What I liked about person's 30-second pitch?

2. What I saw as possible areas for improvement?

Find a mechanism to feed back some of your observations to the role players. Volunteer to present the findings in class, give the person your comments on note paper, or send him or her an e-mail or text message.

Business Etiquette

A major component of managing your impression is practicing good etiquette. **Business etiquette** is a special code of behavior required in work situations. The term *manners* has an equivalent meaning. Both *manners* and *etiquette* generally refer to behaving in a refined and acceptable manner. Jim Rucker and Jean Anna Sellers explain that business etiquette is much more than knowing how to use the correct utensil or how to dress in a given situation. Businesspeople today must know how to be at ease with strangers and with groups, be able to offer congratulations smoothly, know how to make introductions, and know how to conduct themselves at company social functions.[18]

business etiquette

A special code of behavior required in work situations.

Studying etiquette is important because knowing and using proper business etiquette contributes to individual and business success. People who are considerate of the feelings of others, and companies that are courteous toward customers, are more likely to succeed than their rude counterparts. Another perspective on etiquette is that it is a way of presenting yourself with the kind of polish that shows you can be taken seriously. So many people are rude and uncivil today that practicing good etiquette will often give you a competitive advantage.[19]

Business etiquette includes many aspects of interpersonal relations in organizations, as described in the following discussion.[20] We have already discussed in Chapter 5 several aspects of etiquette in relation to the digital workplace. What is considered proper etiquette and manners in the workplace changes over time and may vary with the situation. At one time, addressing one's superior by his or her first name was considered brash. Today it is commonplace behavior. A sampling of etiquette guidelines is nevertheless helpful. A general principle of being considerate of the feelings of work associates is more important than any one act of etiquette or courtesy. Keep in mind, also, that you will find a few contradictory statements in writings about etiquette.

Etiquette for Work Behavior and Clothing. Work behavior etiquette includes all aspects of performing in the work environment, such as completing work on time, punctuality, being a good team player, listening to others, and following through. For instance, having the courtesy to complete a project when it is due demonstrates good manners and respect for the work of others.

Clothing might be considered part of general work behavior. The casual standards in the information technology field, along with dress-down days, have created confusion about proper office attire. A general rule is that *casual* should not be interpreted as sloppy, such as torn jeans or a stained sweatshirt. Many companies have moved back toward emphasizing traditional business attire, such as suits for men and women. In many work situations, dressing more formally may constitute proper etiquette.

Introductions. The basic rule for introductions is to present the lower ranking person to the higher ranking person regardless of age or sex. "Ms. Barker (the CEO), I would like you to meet my new coworker, Reggie Taylor." (Observe that the higher ranking person's name is mentioned first.) If the two people being introduced are of equal rank, mention the older one first. Providing a little information about the person being introduced is considered good manners. When introducing one person to the group, present the group to the individual. "Sid Foster, this is our accounts receivable team." When being introduced to a person, concentrate on the name and repeat it soon, thus enhancing learning. A fundamental display of good manners is to remember people's names and to pronounce them correctly. When dealing with people senior to you or of higher rank, call them by their last name and title until told otherwise. (Maybe Ms. Barker, above, will tell you, "Please call me Kathy.")

It is good manners and good etiquette to remember the names of work associates to whom you are introduced, even if you see them only occasionally. If you forget the name of a person, it is better to admit this than to guess and come up with the wrong name. Just say, "I apologize, but I have forgotten your name. Tell me once more, and I will not forget your name again."

Both men and women are expected to extend their right hand when being introduced. Give a firm, but not overpowering, handshake, and establish eye contact with the person you are greeting. However, some people are concerned about handshakes being unhygienic, so be willing to use the modern fist-to-fist light touch often used in social life. If the other person extends the fist, you do the same.

Relationships between Men and Women and between People of Different Ages. Social etiquette is based on chivalry and the gender of the person, whereas business etiquette is based on generally equal treatment for all. Women should no longer be treated differently when approaching a door, riding in an elevator, or walking in the street. According to the new rules, the person in the lead (no matter the gender or age) should proceed first and hold the door for the others following. However, a man should still follow a woman when using an escalator. When using stairs, a man usually follows a woman going up and precedes her going down. Men no longer have to walk next to the street when walking with one or two women. Elders should still be respected, but not in such ways as holding doors open for them, helping them off with their overcoats, or getting coffee for them.

Unless you are good friends who typically hug when meeting, it is best to avoid touching others of the same or opposite sex except for a handshake. Some people believe that nonsexual touching is part of being charming and warm, yet many workers are offended when touched by another worker. The subject is controversial because public figures often drape their arms around others, and physical touching is part of the ritual of offering congratulations in sports. Of note, many athletic coaches have switched to fist-to-fist touching to say hello or offer congratulations to teenagers and young children to avoid being charged with sexually suggestive contact.

Dining. Etiquette surrounding meals involves planning for the meeting, making seating arrangements, bill paying, tipping, using proper table manners, and appropriate drinking of alcoholic beverages. We all know not to slurp spaghetti one strand at a time, pour ketchup over sauce, or leave a 50 cent tip. The key point is not to draw negative attention to you. Less obvious are the following guidelines:

- Arrange seating for meal meetings in advance.
- Establish with the server who will be paying the check.
- Place your napkin on your lap immediately after being seated.
- Bread should not be used to push food onto a fork or spoon.
- Attempt to pace your eating to those of others at the table.
- The wait staff, not the diners, should be responsible for moving plates around the table.
- Circulate rolls and bread to the right, not the left.
- Order an alcoholic beverage only when invited to do so by the person sponsoring the meal, and then only if he or she does. Do not get drunk or even high.

Working in a Cubicle. Workplace cubicles were invented by fine arts professor Bob Probst in the 1960s, and they have been praised and condemned ever since. The praise generally relates to saving the company money on office space and having more open communication. The condemnation usually relates to lack of privacy, and therefore ties in directly with workplace etiquette.

Cubicles represent a major etiquette challenge because a variety of coworkers and superiors can observe your everyday work behavior.[21] Among the many etiquette challenges for the cubicle dweller are: (a) speaking low enough into a wired phone so as not to annoy others or reveal confidential information, (b) not allowing a personal cell phone ring during the workday, (c) not displaying material on the computer that others might find offensive, unless the subject is business related, (d) not wearing a sports cap indoors unless an acceptable part of the company culture, and (e) not taking care of personal hygiene such as dental flossing, hair spraying, or nail clipping.

Cubicle sizes have been shrunk recently to save on company real estate. As a result, people work even closer to each other physically. The etiquette challenges just mentioned have thereby intensified, particularly with respect to invading the privacy of others.[22]

Cross-Cultural Relations. What constitutes proper etiquette may differ from culture to culture. Be alert to differences in etiquette in areas such as gift giving, dining, drinking alcoholic beverages, and when and where to discuss business. A culture must be studied carefully, including asking questions, to understand what constitutes proper etiquette.

Many of these differences in customs were described in Chapter 8. Violating these customs is poor etiquette. For example, using the index finger to point is considered rude in most Asian and Middle Eastern countries. Also, people in Middle Eastern countries tend to stand as close as two or three inches from the person with whom they are talking. To back away is interpreted as an insult. An American visitor to China nearly lost a major sale because after receiving a business card from the Chinese company representative, he stuffed it in his pocket without first carefully reading the card. Proper etiquette in China is to carefully read the giver's business card, and perhaps holding it with both hands out of respect. We emphasize again that stereotypes such as those just mentioned refer to typical behavior and are accurate perhaps only about 70 percent of the time.

Suppose you are in doubt about the proper etiquette for any situation, and you do not have a handbook of etiquette readily available. As a substitute, observe how your host or a successful person in the group behaves.

Interaction with People with Physical Disabilities. Many able-bodied people are puzzled by what is proper etiquette in working with people with disabilities. Be as natural and open as you can. In addition, consider these guidelines for displaying good manners when dealing with a physical disability:

- Speak directly to a person with a disability, not to the person's companion.
- Don't assume that a person with a disability needs help. If someone is struggling, ask for permission to assist.
- When talking to a person in a wheelchair, place yourself at that person's eye level.
- When speaking to a person with impaired vision, identify yourself and anyone who may be with you. Do not shout when speaking to a blind person.
- To get the attention of a deaf person, tap the person's shoulder or wave your hand.
- Treat a person with a disability as you would anyone else except for the differences noted in this list.[23]

As shown in Figure 13-2, impression management combined with managing relationships and avoiding political blunders contributed to being a more polished and successful professional worker.

Skill-Building Exercise 13-2 gives you an opportunity to practice appropriate etiquette in several situations.

FIGURE 13-2 Relationship between Positive Political Behaviors and Individual Success

Impression management, building relationships with influential people, and avoiding political blunders all contribute to being a more polished and successful professional worker

Tactics of Impression Management and Good Business Etiquette

Building Relationships with Managers and Other Key People

Building Relationships with Coworkers

Avoiding Political Blunders

More Polished and Successful Professional Worker

Business Etiquette

An effective way of improving business etiquette is by using your best manners in real-life situations. Role-playing etiquette scenarios can also contribute to helping you develop the right mental set for using good etiquette.

Scenario 1: Dining Etiquette. A small group of students plan to conduct a high-etiquette meal at a local family restaurant during nonpeak hours. Pretend the stainless steel utensils are fine silver and that the glasses are crystal. Each class member uses his or her best etiquette. At the same time, each group member carefully observes the etiquette displayed by the other members.

At the conclusion of the meal, critique each other's etiquette. If you were courteous enough to invite your instructor to your high-etiquette meal, get his or her feedback.

Scenario 2: Telephone Etiquette. Two people using cell phones are separated by about six feet. Several pairs of students might conduct phone conversations covering such matters as discussing customer complaints, inquiring about a job, or asking about product availability. (*Note:* The students merely *pretend* they are using the phone, rather than waste phone minutes. However, should phone minutes not be an issue a real phone call will add to the authenticity of the exercise.) Students not making the calls will carefully observe the callers. Look for examples of good and poor telephone etiquette. Feedback will be provided after the phone conversations are completed.

BUILDING RELATIONSHIPS WITH MANAGERS AND OTHER KEY PEOPLE

LEARNING OBJECTIVE 3

The political purpose of building good relationships with managers is to gain power through such means as being recommended for promotion and key assignments. A good relationship with the boss is also important for the basic purpose of receiving a good performance evaluation. Building these good relationships is also important because it helps create a positive, supportive work environment for you. Good relationships can also be established with managers for the nonpolitical purpose of trying to get the job accomplished. The strategies and tactics described next are outlined in Figure 13-3.

Network with Influential People

networking

Developing contacts with influential people, including gaining their trust and confidence. Also, contacting friends and acquaintances and building systematically on these relationships to create a still wider set of contacts that might lead to employment.

A basic success strategy is developing contacts, or **networking**, with influential people. In addition to making contacts, networking involves gaining the trust and confidence of the influential people. (Networking for job finding is described in Chapter 17.) Before you can network with influential people, you must identify who those power players are.[24] You might make observations of your own, such as listening for whose names are mentioned frequently by people in the company. Asking the opinions of others about which people influence decision making can be illuminating. Sometimes a person without a fancy job title might be a highly influential person. An example is that an administrative assistant might exert heavily influence the decisions of his or her boss.

FIGURE 13-3 Strategies and Tactics for Building Relationships with Managers and Other Key People

1. Network with influential people.
2. Help your manager succeed.
3. Understanding unwritten boundaries.
4. Volunteer for assignments.
5. Flatter influential people sensibly.
6. Use information power.
7. Appear cool under pressure.
8. Laugh at your manager's humor.
9. Express constructive disagreement.
10. Present a clear picture of your accomplishments.

Networking also takes place with people inside and outside the organization who are not your managers. Developing contacts with influential people is likely to pay big career dividends. A standard procedure is to create a card or computer file of the people in your network and update it frequently. To keep your network effective, it is necessary to contact people on your list periodically. Developing a network of influential people requires alertness and planning. You have to identify influential people and then think of a sensible reason to contact them. Here are a few possibilities:

- Send an e-mail message to a high-ranking manager, offering a money-saving or revenue-producing suggestion. A related tactic is to inform the person of something of significance you did that might lie directly in his or her area of interest. Social networking sites such as Facebook, Linkedin, and Twitter can be used for networking with influential people. An influential person who joins such a site is usually open to making new contacts. (You may find, however, that many influential people are not willing to become your "friend." However, you will often be able to at least send them a message.)

- Do a standout job as a member of a task force or committee that includes a high-ranking official.

- Discuss your career plans with a neighbor who has an outstanding position.

- Take the initiative to develop a friendship with an influential person who is a member of your athletic club, YMCA, YWCA, or place of worship.

Networking is so often used—and abused—that suggestions and guidelines for networking etiquette have emerged. A starting point is to be clear, concise, and specific when making requests of networking contacts. Explain, for example, that you want to become an industry specialist and would like to acquire specific information. Be frank about the amount of time you would want from the network member, such as 15 minutes per month of e-mail and telephone contact.

After making contact with a potential network member, explain the benefit this person is likely to derive from his or her association with you. Provide a *benefit statement* for interacting with you and helping you with you career.[25] Indicate specifically how this person might benefit from you being in his or her network. (If a person is in your network, you are also in that person's network.) If the potential network member is more powerful than you, it is still possible to think of what benefit you might be able to provide. Two examples follow:

- I would like to contact you a few times a year about career concerns. In return, I would be happy to help you identify some groups on Twitter that might be worthwhile for our company to contact.

- In return for my receiving career advice from you from time to time, I would be happy to collect information for you about how people in my area perceive one of your products. I have lots of useful contacts in my community.

Avoid being a pest. Many influential people are bombarded with requests to be part of someone's network, so ask for a modest amount of time and assistance. Good networking etiquette is to request a collaborative relationship in which you give as much as you get. The benefit statement just mentioned will place you in a collaborative relationship with the influential person.

Help Your Manager Succeed

The primary reason you are hired is to help your manager achieve the results necessary to succeed. Avoid an adversarial relationship with your manager. Also figure out both obvious and subtle ways of ensuring the manager's success. One subtle way of increasing your manager's chances for success is to help out that person when he or she is under attack from another department. One example would be to supply information to support your manager's position on a controversial issue. Also keep in mind the cornerstone tactic of performing your job superbly. Your manager will then share in your success.

A specific relationship-building advantage of helping your manager succeed is that he or she is likely to develop loyalty toward you in such matters as recommending you for a bigger salary increase, and giving you a better performance evaluation. And during a downsizing, you are less likely to be tapped for job loss.

Understand Unwritten Boundaries

A person skilled at positive organizational politics is able to read unwritten rules about who has the authority to do what. According to psychologist Judith Sills, there exist **unwritten boundaries,** or dividing lines of behavior appropriate to different roles. Many workers struggle with office problems that are boundary issues in disguise. Sills observes that boundaries for office interactions are like the rope lanes in a swimming pool. The purpose of the ropes is to enhance safety, but they can be budged or even removed depending on need, skill, and circumstance.

Unwritten boundaries deal with such issues as when it is appropriate to correct your boss, how much anger to display, which influential people you can invite to a social engagement, and whose speech or appearance you can criticize. A person with an exaggerated sense of his or her worth may have trouble that a boundary exists at all, such as one woman who felt free to protest angrily when her boss changed something in her report.[26] Two other examples of unacceptable boundary crossing are (a) a man who told a vice president that his hairpiece looked phony, and (b) a woman who told her boss that she needed to upgrade her information technology skills to be a credible leader.

An example of successful boundary crossing took place when an accounts receivable specialist sent an unsolicited e-mail to the director of marketing. The young worker said that he grew up in Mexico and would be happy to provide input for the company's plans to penetrate the Mexican market. Although the accounts receivable worker was from outside of the marketing department, he was invited to participate in a focus group about expanding into the Mexican market.

Look for indicators as to whether boundaries can be crossed in your company. First, count the layers in your company's organization structure. The more layers (or more hierarchical) the company, the less welcome boundary crossing is likely to be. Look for established border crossings. Observe where people of different rank in the company mix. Among the possibilities are the fitness center, the cafeteria, and after-hours drinks. Make your first attempts at border crossing at those places.[27]

Volunteer for Assignments

An easily implemented method of winning the approval of superiors is to become a "hand raiser." By volunteering to take on assignments that do not fit neatly into your job description, you display the kind of initiative valued by employers. At the same time, you are practicing organizational citizenship behavior. Among the many possible activities to volunteer for are fundraising campaigns assigned to your company, project membership, and working overtime when most people prefer not to (e.g., on a Saturday in July). Task force and committee assignments are also useful for being noticed by key people in the organization. Offer to help coordinate a charity campaign such as the United Way. As a team member, volunteer to assume any leadership responsibility you think you can handle. If your team offers rotating leadership assignments, express an interest in taking your turn.

Flatter Influential People Sensibly

One of the most effective relationship builders is to flatter people sensibly and credibly. Despite the risk of being called obsequious or a cheap office politician, the flatterer wins. A study on how to advance in big business pointed out that a company's top employees tend to be equal in performance. Advancing was based on image (30%) and contact time with the manager (50%). Flattery can play a big role in both.[28] Another study indicated that even at the highest positions in business, flattery helps a person get ahead. Specifically, ingratiating yourself to the CEO, including flattery, was a major factor in receiving an appointment as a board of director at major companies. Not carefully monitoring (carefully scrutinizing) the CEO's activities also worked in a person's favor for obtaining a board appointment.[29] You might interpret not finding fault with a CEO to be a subtle form of flattery.

Flattery is likely to be effective because most people want to receive accolades, even if they are not completely warranted. People who pay us compliments are likely to be treated kindly in turn.[30] Remember, however, the discussion about recognition in Chapter 11 suggesting that less technically oriented people are often the most receptive to praise and flattery. Flattery geared toward the more technically oriented person might have to be more concrete and tied to specific accomplishments. Recent evidence supports the idea that constructive compliments are not overblown. Descriptions of what went right are more effective than evaluative phrases, such as "magnificent" or "extraordinary." An effective, general-purpose piece of flattery is to tell another person that you are impressed by something he or she accomplished. Rather than telling an influential person that he or she is a genius, you might say to a manager after a meeting:[31] "Everyone in the meeting was listening so attentively when you gave your report. And the industry statistics you found really drove home the point."

Another way of flattering somebody is to listen attentively. If you actively listen to the other person, he or she will feel flattered. The person might think, "What I have to say is valuable. This person really cares about what I have to offer." Flattery can also take the form of quoting another person, or referring to something he or she said to you earlier.

During the next two weeks, try flattering an influential person. In the interim, do Skill-Building Exercise 13-3.

Use Information Power

Power accrues to those who control vital information. At the same time, being a source of useful information will help you build constructive working relationships with managers. You will be relied on as an important contributor. Controlling vital information includes knowing how to gain access to useful information that others do not know how to retrieve. Many workers are aware of the mechanics of using the Internet, but fewer have the skills to use the Internet to retrieve commercially useful information. During a tight labor market, for example, human resource specialists can acquire power if they know how to use the Internet to find talented people who might want to join the company. These specialists have knowledge beyond using commercially available Internet recruiting services.

Information power is closely related to *expert power*, which refers to having valuable expertise. If your expertise or skill is in high demand at the moment, power will flow in your direction. Currently, an important type of expert power is being able to use social

SKILL-BUILDING EXERCISE 13-3

Flattering an Influential Person

A perceptive, intelligent reader like you has probably already guessed the nature of this role-play. One student plays the role of a newcomer to the organization who is seeking to advance, or at least to secure, his or her position in the organization. Another person plays the role of a vice president of marketing who is visiting the newcomer's department. The company holds this vice president in high esteem because he or she recently spearheaded the introduction of a highly successful product, a *smart mattress*. The mattress adjusts to the temperature requirements and firmness of its user. In some models, the two sides of the mattress can have different settings to adapt to the heat and firmness preferences of two users sharing the same mattress.

The newcomer is asked to escort the vice president to another part of the building. The walk should take about five minutes, giving the newcomer an opportunity to work in some flattery. Fortunately, the newcomer has read the sales literature about the smart mattress, and has even tried out one in the factory showroom. Although the vice president is not naive, he or she is proud of his or her accomplishments. The two role players conduct the five-minute walk, perhaps circling the classroom.

Observers rate the role players on two dimensions, using a 1-to-5 scale from very poor to very good. One dimension is "effective use of flattery." The second dimension is "acting ability." A few observers might voluntarily provide feedback to the role players in terms of sharing their ratings and observations. The course instructor might also provide feedback.

networking sites to gain publicity for products (including creating a buzz for the product), and to recruit employees.

Appear Cool under Pressure

Showing signs of panic generally hurts your reputation with influential people. In contrast, appearing to be in emotional control when things around you are falling apart helps convey the impression that you are worthy of additional responsibility. Being cool under pressure is part of emotional stability, and it is a key leadership characteristic. Coolness under pressure is often displayed during a crisis such as a flood, hurricane, or fire. The manager who can get the operation, including store, factory, hospital, or call center, back and running within a week is perceived to work extraordinarily well under pressure. Many managers at McDonald's and Wal-Mart enhanced their relationship with corporate executives because they responded so quickly and positively, to the ravages of Hurricane Katrina. Locating and aiding displaced employees were part of the heroic efforts of these managers.

Laugh at Your Manager's Humor

When you indicate by your laughter that you appreciate your manager's sense of humor, it helps establish rapport between the two of you. An indicator of good two-way communication between people is that the two parties comprehend each other's subtle points. Most humor in the workplace deals with subtle meanings about work-related topics. To implement the tactic of laughing at your manager's jokes, do not worry excessively about having heard the joke before.

Express Constructive Disagreement

At one time the office politician thought an effective way of pleasing the boss was to be a "yes-person," as mentioned earlier. A more intelligent tactic in the modern business world is to be ready to disagree in a constructive manner when you sincerely believe that the boss is wrong. In the long run, you will probably earn more respect than if you agree with the boss just to please him or her. Constructive disagreement is based on a careful analysis of the situation and is also tactful.

The right way to disagree means not putting your manager in a corner or embarrassing your manager by confronting him or her loudly or in public. If you disagree with your boss, use carefully worded, inoffensive statements. In this way, you minimize the chances of a confrontation or hostile reaction. Remember the smart mattress mentioned in Skill-Building Exercise 13-3? Suppose the marketing vice president claims that the mattress is geared exclusively toward the senior citizen market, and you disagree. You might say, "I think that marketing our smart mattress to seniors is a breakthrough. Yet, I also see some other possibilities. There are loads of cold-sensitive young people who wanted a heated mattress. Also, a lot of young people with athletic injuries or orthopedic problems would welcome an adjustable mattress. Does my thinking make any sense?"

The reason constructive disagreement helps you build a good relationship with most managers is that the boss comes to respect your job knowledge and your integrity. However, if you are working with a very insecure boss, he or she may be taken aback by disagreement. In that case, you have to be extra tactful in expressing disagreement.

Present a Clear Picture of Your Accomplishments

"What have you done for me lately?" is a question on the minds of many managers. To the extent that you can clearly document what you have accomplished recently, as well as in the past, you are therefore likely to enhance your relationship with your manager. You can help your manager better understand your contributions by explaining exactly what work you are doing, problems you are solving, and the successes you are attaining. Document legitimately what you have accomplished, and communicate it in a factual, matter-of-fact manner. The occasional FYI e-mail provides useful documentation, providing you do not appear to be bragging.[32] A collection agent might report to her boss, "In March, I collected an average of $310 from my block of delinquent accounts. So far, I have collected at least something from 25 out of the 31 accounts I am currently assigned. We should be getting something from three more of these delinquent accounts."

BUILDING RELATIONSHIPS WITH COWORKERS AND OTHER WORK ASSOCIATES

LEARNING OBJECTIVE 4

Another strategy for increasing your power is to form alliances with coworkers and other work associates. You need the support of these people to get your work accomplished. Also, when you are being considered for promotion, coworkers and other work associates may be asked their opinion of you. Under a peer-evaluation system, the opinion of coworkers about your performance counts heavily. Long-term research conducted by Tom Rath of the Gallup Organization with many thousands of employees emphasizes the contribution of friendships and alliances in the workplace. Rath concludes that employees who have a best friend in the office are more productive and more likely to have positive interactions with customers, share ideas, and stay longer on the job. Also, many workers succeed or fail based on the support and involvement of best friends.[33] (The term *best* appears to imply that the contact is not simply an acquaintance or someone on your contact list on a social networking Web site.)

Another perspective on the importance of cooperation in the workplace is that cooperation enhances happiness and satisfaction. Long-term research by the University of Haifa psychology professor Richard Schuster says that it is natural for humans, as well as other animals, to want to cooperate. Schuster posits that evolution has prodded us toward enjoying the company of other people, and toward cooperation. He adds that social behavior is its own reward.[34]

Figure 13-4 lists eight strategies and techniques for developing good interpersonal relationships at or below your level. The information about developing teamwork skills presented in Chapter 6 is also relevant here.

> " If you want to be happier and more engaged at work, considering developing a few strong friendships at the office, maybe even one with your boss. "
>
> —Tom Rath, head of the Gallup Organization's Workplace Research and Leadership Consulting, and author of *Vital Friends*[35]

Maintain Honest and Open Relationships

Although being honest may appear to contradict organizational politics, it is representative of the nature of positive politics. Openness and honesty also helps build trust among coworkers. Giving coworkers frank but tactful answers to their requests for your opinion is one useful way of developing open relationships. Assume that a coworker asks your opinion of an e-mail he intends to send to his supervisor. As you read it, you find it somewhat incoherent and filled with spelling and grammatical errors. An honest response to this message might be: "I think your idea is a good one. But I think your e-mail needs more work before that idea comes across clearly."

Accurately expressing your feelings, whether positive or negative, also leads to constructive relationships. If you have been singled out for good performance, let other team

FIGURE 13-4 Strategies and Tactics for Developing Relationships with Coworkers and Other Work Associates

1. Maintain honest and open relationships.
2. Make others feel important.
3. Be diplomatic.
4. Exchange favors.
5. Ask for advice.
6. Share constructive gossip.
7. Minimize microinequities.
8. Follow group norms.

members know that you are happy and proud. If you arrive at work upset over a personal problem and appearing obviously fatigued, you can expect some reaction. A coworker might say, "What seems to be the problem? Is everything all right?" A dishonest reply would be "Everything is fine." In addition to making an obviously untrue statement, you would also be perceived as rejecting the person who asked the question. If you prefer not to discuss your problem, an honest response would be, "Thanks for your interest. I am facing some problems today. But I think things will work out."

Another advantage of honest and open relationships is that they foster collaboration, which improves teamwork and organizational performance. When John Thain was the chairman and chief of Merrill Lynch & Co., he said, "Fostering teamwork, collaboration, and cross-selling enable us to generate innovations and ideas to give us the best competitive advantage."[36]

One of the swiftest ways of breaking down honest and open relationships with coworkers is to **backstab**—an attempt to discredit by underhanded means, such as innuendo, accusation, or the like. The backstabber will pretend to be your friend, but will say something negative behind your back in an attempt to discredit you. For example, your rival might say to the manager, "I'm worried about the health of _____. She seems so preoccupied that it's difficult to get her attention to talk about any work problems." During times of less job security, including downsizings due to mergers, workers are more likely to say negative things about coworkers to gain advantage. Also, when a promotion is at stake, coworkers are more likely to say negative things about each other to a common boss.[37]

Make Others Feel Important

A fundamental principle of fostering good relationships with coworkers and others is to make them feel important. Visualize that everyone in the workplace is wearing a small sign around the neck that says, "Please make me feel important."[38] Although the leader has the primary responsibility for satisfying this recognition need, coworkers also play a key role. One approach to making a coworker feel important would be to bring a notable accomplishment of his or hers to the attention of the group. Investing a small amount of time in recognizing a coworker can pay large dividends in terms of cultivating an ally. Expressing an interest in the work of others helps them feel important. A basic way to accomplish this end is to ask other employees questions that express an interest in their work, such as the following:

- How is your work going?
- How does the company use output from your department?
- How did you establish all the contacts you did to be so successful in sales?
- How did you develop the skills to do your job?

Expressing an interest in the work of others is also an effective tactic because so many people are self-centered. They are eager to talk about their own work, but rarely pause to express a genuine interest in others. Expressing an interest in the work of others is also effective because it is a form of recognition.

Self-Assessment Quiz 13-3 gives you an opportunity to think about your tendencies toward making others feel important.

Be Diplomatic

Despite all that has been said about the importance of openness and honesty in building relationships, most people fail to be convinced. Their egos are too tender to accept the raw truth when faced with disapproval of their thoughts or actions. Diplomacy is still an essential part of governmental and office politics. Translated into action, diplomacy often means finding the right phrase to convey disapproval, disagreement, or discontent. Here is an example of a delicate situation and the diplomatic phrase used to handle it.

During a staff meeting, a coworker suggests that the entire group schedule a weekend retreat to formulate a strategic plan for the department. The boss looks around the room to gauge the reactions of others to the proposal. You want to

backstab

An attempt to discredit by underhanded means, such as innuendo, accusation, or the like.

say: "*What a stupid idea. Who needs to ruin an entire weekend to do something we could easily accomplish on a workday afternoon?*" The diplomatic response is: "*I've heard that retreats sometimes work. But would spending that much time on the strategic plan be cost effective? Maybe we could work on the plan during one long meeting. If we don't get the planning accomplished in that time frame, we could then consider the offsite.*"

Exchange Favors

An important part of human interaction on and off the job is to reciprocate with others. Exchanging favors with others can make it easier for people to accomplish their work because they are able to call on assistance when needed. The adept political player performs a favor for another employee without asking a favor in return. The favor is then cashed in when a favor is needed. Several examples of workday exchanges are as follows:

- A paralegal agrees to help another overburdened paralegal in the same law office, knowing that the other paralegal will reciprocate if needed in the future.
- A credit manager agrees to expedite a credit application for a sales representative. In reciprocation, the sales rep agrees not to commit the company to a delivery date on the next sale until the customer's credit has been evaluated.
- An assistant restaurant manager agrees to substitute for another assistant manager on New Year's Eve. A month later the first person asks the second to take over her shift so that she can get away for the weekend.

Linda Noeth, Training and Development Manager for Unisys Inside Sales and Marketing, Describes Cooperative Work Relationships

Linda Noeth, the training and development manager for Unisys inside sales and marketing, reflects back on some of her job experiences in these words:

I remember my surprise when I realized that the birthday celebrations at my new company involved more than someone just bringing in cake. This meant everyone on the birthday person's team brought something. I soon learned that this exuberance was just the top of the facility's "food paradigm," a tradition that underlay fundamental rules critical to the success of the business.

For example, not only did we celebrate birthdays frequently, we also celebrated teamwork and goal accomplishment. I learned that managers and employees were encouraged to recognize not only exceptional performance but steady dependable performance, and reward it appropriately. Whether it was a formal monetary award, a pat on the back or a giant cookie, there was an expectation that good work would be appreciated.

The generosity of the birthday celebrations carried over to the extraordinary amount of charitable giving and volunteerism the employees at my new company donated. Again, there were no formal guidelines. No one said you must give, but there was an intangible attitude that said we would reach out and help others, not just around the holidays, but year-round.

While observing the management in my new organization, I recognized the upbeat feeling of our unit could, in some part be attributed to the fact that most of our supervisors and managers were able to relax and enjoy our reasons to celebrate as well. Not only were they approachable, but I found they were comfortable enough in their roles to be good sports. They dressed up for Halloween, they washed employees' cars to raise money for the holiday party, and they allowed themselves to be spoofed during the annual kickoff meetings.

Again, there were no formal procedures to follow for this type of management behavior, but I knew it was part of the group's paradigm and it had a huge impact on the work environment.

Questions

1. In what way does this case history illustrate positive office politics?
2. What would be at least two interpersonal skills you would need to succeed in the work group described in this case?
3. How could the office birthday celebrations and the charitable giving contribute to the success of the business? Aren't the activities described in the case just a frivolous waste of time?

Source: Linda Noeth, "All Those Unwritten Rules of the Office Also Guide Policy," *Democrat and Chronicle*, Rochester, New York, February 8, 2009, p. 2E.

Exchanging favors is yet another form of cooperation in the workplace. The accompanying Job-Oriented Interpersonal Skills in Action provides additional insight into the advances of cooperation among workers.

Ask for Advice

Asking advice on technical and professional topics is a good way of building relationships with other employees. Asking for advice from another person—someone whose job does not require giving it—will usually be perceived as a compliment. Asking advice transmits the message, "I trust your judgment enough to ask your opinion on something important to me." You are also saying, "I trust you enough to think that the advice you give me will be in my best interest." Asking advice is also a subtle form of flattery because it shows that you value the person's judgment.

To avoid hard feelings, inform the person whose advice you are seeking that his or her opinion will not necessarily be binding. A request for advice might be prefaced with a comment, such as "I would like your opinion on a problem facing me. But I can't guarantee that I'll be in a position to act on it." As with any other political tactic, asking for advice must be done in moderation. Too much advice asking can make you appear to be indecisive or a pest.

Share Constructive Gossip

An effective way of building workplace relationships is to share constructive gossip with others. Gossip has been defined in many ways, but as used here refers to talk about other people, usually assumed to be based on fact.[39] Gossip serves as a socializing force because it is a mode of intimate relationships for many employees. Workers get close to each other through the vehicle of gossip. It also serves as the lifeblood of personal relationships on the job. If you are the person supplying the gossip, people will develop positive attitudes toward you. **Constructive gossip** is unofficial information that supports others, is based

constructive gossip

Unofficial information that supports others, is based on truth, and excepts confidential information.

on truth, and respects confidential information. Given these restrictions, here are two examples of positive gossip:

- "I heard that business is really picking up. If this week is any example, the company's profits for the quarter will far exceed expectations."
- "I heard yesterday that the director of public relations just got engaged to a cool guy she met on a cruise."

Minimize Microinequities

A potent way of alienating coworkers is to snub them, or put them down, in a small way without being aware of your behavior. A **microinequity** is a small, semiconscious message we send with a powerful impact on the receiver. A microinequity might also be considered a subtle slight. The inequity might take the form of ignoring another person, a snub, or a sarcastic comment. Understanding microinequities can lead to changes in one-on-one relationships that may profoundly irritate others.[40]

microinequity
A small, semiconscious message we send with a powerful impact on the receiver.

Imagine that you are in line in the company cafeteria with three coworkers. You turn around and notice an old friend from school who is visiting the company. Next, you introduce your old friend to two of the coworkers with you, but not the third. That coworker is likely to feel crushed and irritated, and it will take you awhile to patch your relationship. Looking at a microinequity from the standpoint of the receiver, a work associate might say to you, "Some computer illiterate sent me an e-mail this morning without the attachment he said was there." You respond, "Excuse me, but that *computer illiterate* was me."

To overcome giving microinequities, it is important to think through the consequences of what you are doing and saying before taking action. In the cafeteria situation above, you might say to yourself, "Here comes time for an introduction, and this is not easy for me. I will remember to introduce everybody to my old friend."

Follow Group Norms

A summary principle to follow in getting along with coworkers is to heed **group norms**, the unwritten set of expectations for group members. Group norms also take the form of social cues about how to act, and therefore contribute to the organizational culture. Representative group norms include the following: (1) help coworkers with problems if you have the right expertise, (2) do not wear formal business attire on casual dress days, (3) have lunch with your coworkers at least once a week, (4) do not complain to the boss about a coworker unless his or her negative behavior is outrageously bad, (5) do not take a sick day unless you are really sick, (6) take your turn in bringing snacks to a meeting at least once a month, and (7) side with your coworkers rather than management when there is a dispute between the two groups.

group norms
The unwritten set of expectations for group members.

If you do not deviate too far from these norms, the group will accept much of your behavior. If you do deviate too far, you will be subject to much rejection and therefore lose some of your power base. Yet if you conform too closely to group norms, higher level management may perceive you as unable to identify with management. Employees are sometimes blocked from moving up the ladder because they are regarded as "one of the gang."

Some of the relationship building described in the above eight strategies and tactics is now being done on company social networking sites. These sites are being used to connect employees who have limited opportunity to meet face-to-face, or who simply prefer the Internet for most of their social interactions. Often the company social networking sites are supplemented with Web sites such as Facebook and Twitter because so many employees from the same firm might be members. For many workers, social networks provide a desirable way of communicating because they include photos, videos, and personal information like hobbies and music preferences all of which are good for relationship building.

Skill-Building Exercise 13-4 provides an opportunity to practice several of the techniques for building interpersonal relationships with coworkers and other work associates.

Getting Along with Coworkers Role Play

An inventory auditor in a department store chain decides to take action aimed at getting along better with coworkers. In each of the following two scenarios, one person plays the role of the inventory auditor. Another person plays the role of an employee whom the auditor is attempting to cultivate.

Scenario 1: Exchanging Favors. The auditor decides to strike a bargain with a store associate. (The role player decides what this exchange of favors should be.) Unknown to the auditor, the store associate is concerned about an inventory audit because he or she is worried about being accused of stealing merchandise.

Scenario 2: Expressing an Interest in Their Work. The auditor decides to express an interest in a tech fixer because he or she can be a valuable ally when conducting an inventory audit. The

inventory audit is computerized, and the appropriate software is confusing and crashes frequently. The tech fixer has a heavy workload and is not prone toward small talk, but he or she does get excited talking about information technology.

For both scenarios, observers rate the role players on two dimensions, using a 1-to-5 scale from very poor to very good. One dimension is "effective use of human relations techniques." The second dimension is "acting ability." A few observers might voluntarily provide feedback to the role players in terms of sharing their ratings and observations. The course instructor might also provide feedback.

After these scenarios have been completed, the class might discuss favors they have exchanged on the job that helped build relationships. Strive for at least five students to present examples of exchanges that enhanced their working relationships.

AVOIDING POLITICAL BLUNDERS

LEARNING OBJECTIVE 5

A strategy for not losing whatever power you have accumulated is to refrain from making power-eroding blunders. Committing these politically insensitive acts can also prevent you from attaining power. Self-Assessment Quiz 13-4 will get you started thinking about blunders. Several leading blunders are described in the quiz.

1. **Criticizing your manager in a public forum.** The oldest saw in human relations is to "praise in public and criticize in private." Yet in the passion of the moment, you may still surrender to the irresistible impulse to criticize your manager publicly.

SELF-ASSESSMENT QUIZ 13-4

The Blunder Quiz

Directions: Check whether you agree or disagree with the following statements.

	Agree	Disagree
1. It's fine to criticize your manager in a meeting as long as the criticism is valid.	_____	_____
2. If I objected to a decision made by top management, I would send a company-wide e-mail explaining my objection.	_____	_____
3. I am willing to insult any coworker if the insult is deserved.	_____	_____
4. I see no problem in using competitors' products or services and letting my superiors know about it.	_____	_____
5. If I thought the CEO of my company were way overpaid, I would send him or her an e-mail making my opinion known.	_____	_____
6. Never bother with company-sponsored social events, such as holiday parties, unless you are really interested.	_____	_____
7. I would not attend a company social function if I had the chance to attend another social activity of more interest to me.	_____	_____
8. I am very open about passing along confidential information.	_____	_____
9. I openly criticize most new ventures my company or department is contemplating.	_____	_____
10. I avoid any deliberate attempt to please or impress coworkers or superiors.	_____	_____

Scoring and Interpretation: The greater the number of statements you agree with, the more prone you are to political blunders that can damage your interpersonal relationships and your career. You need to raise your awareness level of blunders on the job.

As a result, the manager will harbor resentment toward you and perhaps block your chances for advancement.

2. **Bypassing the manager.** Many people believe that because most organizations are more democratic today, it is not important to respect the layers of authority (the chain of command). In reality, following etiquette is highly valued in most firms. Going around the manager to resolve a problem is therefore hazardous. You might be able to accomplish the bypass, but your career could be damaged and your recourses limited. It is much better to work out differences with your manager using standard methods of resolving conflict.

3. **Displaying disloyalty.** Being disloyal to your organization is a basic political blunder. Making it known that you are looking for a position elsewhere is the best-known form of disloyalty. Criticizing your company in public settings, praising the high quality of competitors' products, and writing angry internal e-mail messages about your company are others. You may not get fired, but overt signs of disloyalty may place you in permanent disfavor.

4. **Being a pest.** Common wisdom suggests that diligently pressing for one's demands is the path to success. This may be true up to a point, but when assertiveness is used too often it becomes annoying to many people. The overpersistent person comes to be perceived as a pest, and this constitutes a serious political blunder. An example of being a pest would be asking your manager every month when you are going to receive the raise you deserve.

5. **Being (or being perceived as) a poor team player.** An employee is expected to be a good team player in almost all organizations because cooperation makes collective effort possible. If you are a poor team player, or are perceived as such, your chances for promotion will diminish because you will be recognized as having poor interpersonal skills. Among the ways to be perceived as a poor team player are to engage in social loafing, miss many department meetings, take too much credit for group accomplishments, and minimize your interactions with coworkers. In short, if you ignore all the advice about team play presented in Chapter 6, you will be committing a political blunder.

6. **Burning your bridges.** A potent political blunder is to create ill will among former employers or people who have helped you in the past. The most common form of bridge burning occurs when a person departs from an organization. A person who leaves involuntarily is especially apt to express anger toward those responsible for the dismissal. Venting your anger may give a temporary boost to your emotional well-being, but it can be detrimental in the long run.

7. **Indiscreet behavior in private life.** Employees are representatives of the company, so their behavior off the job is considered to contribute to their performance—particularly for managers, supervisors, and professionals with visible jobs. Embarrassing the company will often lead to dismissal, combined with a negative reputation that will be difficult to shake for purposes of future employment. Indiscreet behavior in private life that can lead to dismissal includes being caught shoplifting, a citation for drunk driving, being arrested for a drug offense, charges of sexual harassment or rape, and assault and battery.

8. **Making derogatory comments about your employer on the Internet.** Large numbers of employees in recent years have been reprimanded or fired because they wrote nasty comments about their company on a blog or social networking site. (One such comment on Twitter: "Our CEO should hire a bodyguard. He rakes in millions yet fires thousands.") As we all know, a rant about your company or boss on a social networking site becomes a permanent record, and will almost inevitably be referred to a company executive. Even if you are not fired or severely reprimanded for your public display of hostility, you will have lost considerable political capital—even if your rant is merited.

If you want to overcome having committed a blunder, avoid defensiveness. Demonstrate that you are more interested in recovering from the blunder than in trying to share the blame for what happened. Focus on solutions to the problem rather than faultfinding. Suppose you have been too critical of your team leader in a recent team meeting. Explain that your attempts to be constructively critical backfired and that you will choose your words more carefully in the future.

Another way to patch up a blunder is to stay poised. Admit that you made the mistake and apologize, but don't act or feel inferior. Mistakes are inevitable in a competitive work environment. Avoid looking sad and distraught. Instead, maintain eye contact with people when you describe your blunder.

SELF-ASSESSMENT QUIZZES IN OVERVIEW

Four self-assessment quizzes were presented in this chapter. Collectively they should heighten your awareness of the importance of positive politics, and also point you toward developing political skills. Self-Assessment Quiz 13-1 measured your tendency toward engaging in political behavior on the job, whereas Self-Assessment Quiz 13-2 is designed to measure political skill or ability. Self-Assessment Quiz 13-3 measured your tendency toward a key aspect of relationship building—making others feel important. Self-Assessment 13-4 measured your tendency to suffer from "foot-in-the-mouth disease," or committing political blunders.

Concept Review and Reinforcement

Key Terms

organizational politics 279
power 279
social intelligence 282
impression management 284

business etiquette 287
networking 290
backstab 296
constructive gossip 298

microinequity 299
group norms 299

Summary

Positive political tactics help build good interpersonal relationships. Organizational politics refers to gaining power through any means other than merit or luck. Power refers to the ability or potential to control anything of value and influence decisions. Organizational politics can also be regarded from the standpoint of interpersonal relationships and sizing up the environment. Political skill is related to awareness of one's surroundings, emotional and social intelligence, relationship building with the leader, and coping with an unjust environment.

Impression management is one aspect of organizational politics. Managing the impression you create encompasses a wide range of behaviors designed to create a positive influence on work associates, including display organizational citizenship behavior, build trust and confidence, be visible and create a strong presence, minimize being a yes-person, and create a healthy image. Also, attempt to be authentic, be aware that political skill is needed to manage one's impression, and avoid creating a negative impression.

A major component of managing the impression you create is business etiquette. The general principle of etiquette is to be considerate of the feelings of work associates. Areas of business etiquette include the following: work behavior and clothing, introductions, relationships between men and women and between people of different ages, working in a cubicle, cross-cultural relations, and interaction with people with disabilities. (Etiquette related to the digital world was covered in Chapter 5.)

Political strategies and tactics for building relationships with managers and other key people include networking with influential people, helping your manager succeed, understanding unwritten boundaries, volunteering for assignments, flattering influential people sensibly, using information power, admitting mistakes, appearing cool under pressure, laughing at your manager's humor, expressing constructive disagreement, and presenting a clear picture of your accomplishments.

Political strategies and tactics for developing relationships with coworkers and other work associates include maintaining honest and open relationships, making others feel important, being diplomatic, exchanging favors, asking for advice, sharing constructive gossip, minimizing microinequities, and following group norms.

A strategy for not losing whatever power you have accumulated is to refrain from making political blunders. Political blunders can also prevent you from attaining power. Representative blunders include criticizing your manager publicly, bypassing your manager, displaying disloyalty, being a pest, being a poor team player and burning your bridges, indiscreet behavior in private life, and making derogatory comments about your employer on the Internet. If you want to make up for a blunder, avoid defensiveness and stay poised.

Questions for Discussion and Review

1. To what extent are office politics skills important for a person who is technically competent and hardworking?

2. In what way might organizational citizenship behavior be part of playing office politics?

3. Identify three jobs in which you think practicing good business etiquette would be extremely important.

4. A physically able man encounters his vice president, a frail woman, as they are both entering an airport. From an etiquette perspective, should the man ask to carry the woman's bags to the check-in counter? (The man does not have a suitcase with him.)

5. It has been observed that corporate employees who work mostly from their homes put more effort into building their networks than people who work in a traditional office. Why might this be true?

6. It has been said that although most businesspeople can see through flattery, the technique still works. How would you explain this observation?

7. Okay animal lovers among our readers, it's your turn now. What evidence can you present to support the contention that nonhuman animals cooperate?

8. Give an example of a *microinequity* that you have been subjected to, or that you observed happen to another person. Explain why the incident is a microinequity.

9. In what way might being politically incorrect be a political blunder?

10. Why might the study of organizational politics seem more relevant to people with at least several years of work experience than to career beginners?

The Web Corner

http://money.cnn.com/quizzes/
(Quiz about knowledge of office politics.)

http://lovequizzes.netfirms.com/boss.html
(Quiz about your relationship with your boss.)

http://www.ExecutivePlanet.com
(Guide to international business culture and etiquette in more than 35 countries.)

Internet Skill Builder: Sharpening Your Compliments

An important part of being a skilled office politician, as well as a government one, is to compliment people effectively.

The information about flattery contained in the chapter gave you some ideas about how to use compliments effectively. Search the Internet for a few more useful suggestions for giving compliments to others. A good starting point for this assignment is www.KissMeGoodnight.com because it provides intelligent suggestions about giving compliments. Try out this week the best idea you find in this skill-building assignment. Observe the results of your compliment so that you can refine your technique.

Developing Your Human Relations Skills

Interpersonal Relations Case 13.1

Passed Over Pete

Pete Gupta was enjoying his career as a real estate agent at Barclay Properties, a real estate development company. The business model adopted by the founders of Barclay is to purchase and then rehabilitate distressed office buildings. Many of the older buildings the company rehabilitated were then converted into mixed used, such as office space, retail space, and loft condominium apartments. Part of the plan was to restore majestic older buildings, thereby fitting into the environmental trend of preserving what exists rather than consume enormous amounts of energy and material in the construction of new office towers.

As Barclay Properties continued to expand, seven agents were working full-time all of whom reported to Katie Logan, the company cofounder. Gupta's major responsibility was to find tenants as well as condominium buyers for the rehabilitated buildings. His passion for the business, combined with his knowledge of the business and sales skills, enabled him to become the leading agent in terms of sales volume.

Katie Logan specialized in supervising rehabilitation of the older buildings. Her role required that she spend considerable time with architects, construction firms, and local zoning boards. Ralph Parsons, the other cofounder, concentrated his efforts more in finding properties and working with financial institutions to fund the projects. Logan and Parsons agreed that Barclay had expanded enough to warrant hiring a manager to provide leadership to the sales group. Katie Logan enjoyed working with the real estate agents, but she was too occupied with other activities to provide much assistance or direction to the agents.

Logan and Parson agreed jointly that it would be a plus for the firm to offer the promotion to sales director to one of the seven agents. The new director of sales would continue to contribute as a sales agent, but would also function as the manager of the group. After considerable discussion, the director of sales position was offered to Sara Morales who readily accepted the offer. For the previous year, Morales was the third highest producer in terms of dollar volume.

After learning of Morales' appointment, Pete Gupta demanded an explanation from Logan and Parsons. He said angrily, "I am the number one agent here, and you didn't even discuss the promotion with me. What's going on?"

Logan responded, "Ralph and I are well aware that you are a star performer, and we expect that you will make Barclay a long-term career. But we needed more of a team player for the sales director position. We see you as an individual star who doesn't get too involved with the rest of the sales group. The buzz we obtained from your colleagues is that you are great with clients, but that you are a lone wolf. You don't appear to have too much interest in working as a team member. You never share your expertise with the guys and gals in the group."

Gupta replied, "I thought the name of this game is bring in the big bucks. Spending time with colleagues seems less important."

Parsons said in response, "Sales volume is obviously very important. But we needed a little more of an internal person for this position."

Case Questions

1. In what way does this case study relate to lateral relations?
2. What do you think of the logic behind the decision of Logan and Parsons to pass over Pete Gupta?
3. What tactics should Gupta use if he wants to reverse his image as a lone wolf?
4. How ethical was it for the cofounders to listen to "buzz" about Gupta to help them reach their decision?
5. What should Logan and Parsons do to increase the chances that Gupta will not quit because he was passed over for promotion?

Lunch 2.0 for Free

A few months after Google, Inc., fired Mark Jen for blogging about work, he slipped into one of the company's cafeterias to score a free lunch with friends. He had no idea that he was also helping to launch a nationwide phenomenon. "We thought this was a great way to check out different companies and also get a free lunch," said Jen, now a programming manager at Tagged, Inc., a San Francisco-based online social network.

That lunch went so well, and the group decided to make it a regular event: They began meeting at corporate cafeterias around the Bay Area in an effort to rub elbows with employees at other technology companies—and share some of the free food that many tech companies provide. They posted their lunch schedule on a blog, and opened the meetings to anyone interested. "We are in Silicon Valley, which has a lot of tech companies," says Jen. But he says that employees "don't really branch out and meet other people from other companies."

The concept—dubbed Lunch 2.0 by its founders—has grown into a social networking phenomenon that now draws hundreds of engineers, venture capitalists, and even summer interns to various companies for free meals and conversations. It used to be that the group, which initially consisted of fewer than 10 people, practically had to sneak through company doors. Some attendees would get in with friends who were employees, while others sneaked by security. (Google, where it all started, allows employees to bring guests to the company cafeteria. Jen got in with a friend who worked there.)

But now, as the lunches have begun to draw larger crowds, companies are inviting in the Lunch 2.0-goers as a way to woo potential hires and push their products to influence bloggers who attend. Employers ranging from social networking company Facebook, Inc., to Microsoft Corp. have hosted Lunch 2.0 events.

And the idea is spreading. Similar lunch groups have already sprouted in Seattle and Germany, followed by chapters in Bangalore and Los Angeles. The Lunch 2.0 founders have received inquiries from employees who want to start chapters in New York, Atlanta, and Singapore.

"Lunch 2.0 builds positive brand associations both for those who attend and those who hear about it later in conversation, posted photos, and blog entries," says Paul C. Jeffries, a consultant to start-ups in Silicon Valley. Although the events are now hosted by companies, they still have a "guerrilla feel, like the tech community is crashing the gate and taking over the company."

Other than name tags, the events are unstructured—and hardly swanky. For one thing, everyone shows up in jeans, typical of the Bay Area culture. One time, about 300 people showed up at a Plaxo lunch in Mountain View, California, to eat Popeye's chicken. "We went for the comfort food," says John McCrea, the vice president of marketing, adding that a couple of employees decided to deejay the event.

Lunch 2.0 attendees aren't necessarily looking for a job. Some show up just to talk shop. Others simply crave a free meal outside their own cafeterias. "It's a perfect applicant pool because they are gainfully employed people who are geared toward passively looking for a job," says Tey Scott, recruiting manager at Time Warner Inc.'s AOL. A recent lunch at AOL drew about 200 people into the company's Mountain View office for pizza. The company had set up a table with information for prospective hires.

Attendees say the casual atmosphere makes it easy to interact with higher-ups at a company while getting a glimpse of the networking environment. For instance, Mike Miller, a former senior staff engineer at Sun Microsystems, Inc., met both a senior recruiter and Linkedin Chief Executive Dan Nye at the company's Lunch 2.0 event.

"I though it was really cool," says Miller, who says he enjoyed playing Wii, and took home a ball for his kids. "It was a high energy atmosphere." After the lunch, the recruiter contacted him for an interview. Miller was hired as a principal software engineer in July.

Recently representatives of employee recruiting firms have started to attend Lunch 2.0 lunches. Also, vendors of recruiting services have also been noticed at the events.

Case Questions

1. How might you use Lunch 2.0 events to assist your career? (Note that these lunches have expanded to other occupations as well as information technology workers.)
2. What do you think of the ethics of people who attend a Lunch 2.0 gathering just to get a free lunch?

3. If you were your company's organizer of Lunch 2.0, what steps would you take to keep recruiting firms and recruiting vendors off the premises?

Source: Anjali Athavaley, "The Power Lunch, Cafeteria-Style," *The Wall Street Journal*, August 29, 2007, pp. D1, D8. Permission obtained through the Copyright Clearance Center. www. Seattlelunch20.com, accessed January 4, 2010.

Customer Satisfaction Skills

ConServe, a company that specializes in collecting student loans, said it expects to add at least 150 jobs over the next two years because of a contract it has won with the U.S. Department of Education. The company was added to the Education Department's elite student loan collection contract in the unrestricted business size category. Previously, ConServe held a small business contract with the department, but advanced to the unrestricted business size category after ranking first in the country in resolution rate among the Education Department's small business vendors.

Mark Davitt, who started ConServe in 1985, said that third-party debt collectors are often entering emotionally charged situations, and attributed the company's success to a staff filled with "good listeners and problem solvers." "We're looking for a good sense of empathy," said Davitt. "Rather than float like a cork in the ocean, our opportunity is to empower people to take control of their situation."

Davitt said the Education Department contract could result in a 40 percent increase in revenue for ConServe, or an increase as much as $18 million annually.[1]

Whether or not you admire student loan collection agents, the anecdote just presented illustrates a couple of important points about dealing with customers. Among the skills required are empathy, listening, problem solving, and accepting empowerment to deal with customers. Dealing with people who owe the company money makes these customer-relationship skills all the more important. This chapter presents information and exercises that can enhance your ability to satisfy both external and internal customers at a high level.

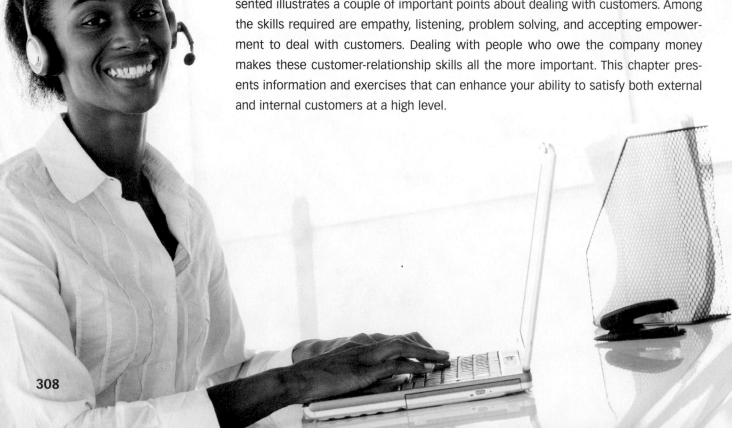

After reading and studying this chapter and doing the exercises, you should be able to

1. Explain the three components of customer experience (or service).
2. Enhance your ability to satisfy customers by using general principles of customer satisfaction.
3. Create bonds with present or future customers.
4. Have a plan for dealing effectively with customer dissatisfaction.

External customers fit the traditional definition and include clients, guests, and patients. External customers can be classified as retail or industrial. The latter represents one company buying from another, such as purchasing steel or a gross of printer cartridges. *Internal customers* are the people you serve within the organization or those who use the output from your job. Also, everyone you depend upon is an internal customer. The emphasis in this chapter is on satisfying external customers. Much of the rest of the book deals with better serving internal customers, because improved interpersonal relationships enhance the satisfaction of work associates.

Customer satisfaction skills are necessary for all workers in contact with customers, including sales representatives, customer service representatives (those who back up sales and take care of customer problems), and store associates. Workers in a wide variety of jobs need good customer satisfaction skills. The founder of a technology consulting firm observes, "Ninety percent of the time when a client has an issue with a consultant, it's related to soft skills."[2] Another way of understanding the importance of customer satisfaction skills is to recognize that employees who can satisfy customers contribute heavily to profits. The chief executive of a firm that surveys approximately 20 million customers a year for retail and restaurant chains concludes "A good employee or a good sales associate might be worth five or 10 times an average one. We've seen that. It's unreal."[3]

Various aspects of developing customer satisfaction skills are divided into three parts in this chapter: following the general principles of customer satisfaction, bonding with customers, and dealing with customer dissatisfaction. As you work through this chapter, you will observe that to implement its suggestions you need many of the interpersonal skills you have been acquiring, such as communication, teamwork, motivation, and conflict resolution. To reflect on your attitudes toward satisfying customers, do Self-Assessment Quiz 14-1.

SELF-ASSESSMENT QUIZ 14-1

The Customer Service Orientation Quiz

Directions: Answer each of the following statements about dealing with customers as "mostly true" or "mostly false." The statements relate to your attitudes, even if you lack direct experience in dealing with customers. Your experiences as a customer will also be helpful in responding to the statements.

	Mostly True	Mostly False
1. All work in a company should be geared toward pleasing customers.	____	____
2. The real boss in any business is the customer.	____	____
3. Smiling at customers improves the chances of making a sale.	____	____
4. I would rather find a new customer than attempt to satisfy one who is difficult to please.	____	____
5. Dealing with customers is more (or as) rewarding than dealing with coworkers.	____	____

(Continued)

6. I enjoy (or would enjoy) helping a customer solve a problem related to the use of my product or service. _____ _____

7. The best way to get repeat business is to offer steep discounts. _____ _____

8. In business, your customer is your partner. _____ _____

9. Dealing directly with customers is (or would be) the most boring part of most jobs. _____ _____

10. If you have the brand and model the customer wants, being nice to the customer is not so important. _____ _____

11. A good customer is like a good friend. _____ _____

12. If you are too friendly with a customer, he or she will take advantage of you. _____ _____

13. Now that individual consumers and companies can shop online, the personal touch in business is losing importance. _____ _____

14. Addressing a customer by his or her name helps build a relationship with that customer. _____ _____

15. Satisfying a customer is fun whether or not it leads to a commission. _____ _____

Scoring and Interpretation: Give yourself a +1, for each of the following statements receiving a response of "mostly true": 1, 2, 3, 5, 6, 8, 11, 14, and 15. Give yourself a +1 for each of the following statements receiving a response of "mostly false": 4, 7, 9, 10, 12, and 13.

13–15 points: You have a strong orientation toward providing excellent customer service.

8–12 points: You have an average customer service orientation.

1–7 points: You have a below-average orientation toward providing excellent customer service.

THE THREE COMPONENTS OF CUSTOMER EXPERIENCE (SERVICE)

LEARNING OBJECTIVE 1

A useful starting point in becoming skilled at satisfying customers is to understand how customers form impressions of their experience. The term *experience* is often used as to replace *service* because customer service is often perceived as getting help from a call center or returning merchandise in a retail store. According to the research of marketing professors Leonard L. Berry, Eileen A. Wall, and Lewis P. Carbone, customers form three clues about the service experience based on their presence or absence. A clue is anything the customer can see, hear, taste, or smell. It is often small clues that influence a customer's overall perception of an experience, such as a customer service rep yawning while taking care of the person's problem.[4]

The key point is that customers form perceptions based on three components of the experience. First are functional clues derived from the technical performance of the service, such as the technician from the call center enabling you to get your new printer up and running. Second are mechanical clues stemming from the sensory presentation of the service, including sights, smells, sounds, tastes, and textures. At Target stores, the mechanical clues include the red-color scheme, the wide isles, and the numerous checkout counters. Third are the human interaction clues detected from the behavior and appearance of service providers. Such clues include the service provider's choice of words, tone of voice, enthusiasm, body language, and dress. Much of this chapter deals with the human-touch component of the customer experience.

Human interaction in the service experience offers the biggest opportunity to deepen customers' emotional connection to the company and the service provider. For example, many customers return to a given restaurant because the server is so polite, friendly, and helpful—assuming the food and décor are also satisfactory.

Figure 14-1 presents an overview of the three components of, or clues about, customer experience. Notice that only the functional clues are based mostly on rational perceptions of quality of service. If the call-center technician gets your printer working, you are not so concerned about his or her lack of warmth and enthusiasm. In contrast, the

FIGURE 14-1   Clue Influences on Customer Perceptions

Source: Adapted from Leonard L. Berry, Eileen A. Wall, and Lewis P. Carbone, "Service Clues and Customer Assessment of the Service Experience: Lessons from Marketing," *Academy of Management Perspectives*, May 2006, p. 46.

mechanical and human interaction clues are based mostly on emotional perceptions of the quality of service. For example, you might return to a hotel mostly because of the view of the bay and the soothing beige colors in the room. For the customer service to be truly outstanding, all three clues should be positive.

FOLLOWING THE GENERAL PRINCIPLES OF CUSTOMER SATISFACTION

LEARNING OBJECTIVE 2

Knowing how to satisfy customers is a subset of effective interpersonal relations in organizations. Nevertheless, there are certain general principles that will sharpen your ability to satisfy customers and thereby improve customer retention. This section presents eight key principles for satisfying customers. Remember, however, that satisfaction is considered a minimum expectation. If you do an outstanding job of satisfying customers, they will experience delight, as shown in Figure 14-2.

Customer satisfaction is important for several reasons. To begin with, without satisfying customers, a business would cease to exist. The slogan of Tops Markets, Inc., a super-market chain, is "Customer satisfaction is our only business." Satisfied customers are likely to tell friends and acquaintances about their satisfactory experiences, helping a firm grow its business. In contrast, dissatisfied customers—especially those with an unresolved problem—are likely to tell many people about their dissatisfaction, thus dissuading

FIGURE 14-2   Levels of Customer Satisfaction

a large number of people from becoming new customers. Studies indicate that an upset or angry customer tells an average of between 10 and 20 other people about an unhappy experience.[5] Customer satisfaction is also highly valued because it breeds customer loyalty, which in turn is very profitable. Repeat business is a success factor in both retail and industrial companies.

Another reason for satisfying customers is the humanitarian aspect. Satisfying people enhances their physical and mental health, whereas dissatisfaction creates negative stress. Have you ever been so angry at poor service that you experienced stress?

Be Satisfied So You Can Provide Better Customer Service

Employees who are happy with their jobs are the most likely to satisfy customers. As stated by Frank DeRiso, a local president of the United Food and Commercial Workers union, "The employees are your No. 1 asset. You don't have a customer base without employees."[6] Treating employees well puts them in a better frame of mind to treat their customers well and provide better service, especially in the human interaction aspect of service. According to consumer behavior specialist James Hazen, good service comes down to creating a positive and memorable customer experience. For example, Starbucks can command a premium price for its coffee beverages not simply because of the quality of its beans and its stylish cardboard cups, but because of the overall experience. And the employees—particularly the baristas—are part of that experience.[7] Although Starbucks has reduced many prices in recent years, its customers still have the option of purchasing lower price coffee at fast-food chains and convenience stores.

Acting alone, you cannot improve company conditions that contribute to job satisfaction. What you can control to some extent, however, is your own attitudes that are related to job satisfaction. A checklist of attitudes and beliefs related to job satisfaction, and over which you can exert some control, follows:

- **Interest in the work itself.** Job satisfaction stems directly from being interested in what you are doing. People who love their work experience high job satisfaction and are therefore in the right frame of mind to satisfy customers.

- **A feeling of self-esteem.** If you have high self-esteem, you are more likely to experience high job satisfaction. High-status occupations contribute more to self-esteem than do those of low status. Feelings of self-esteem also stem from doing work the individual sees as worthwhile. This perception is less influenced by external standards than it is the status associated with a particular job or occupation.

- **Optimism and flexibility.** An optimistic and flexible person is predisposed to be a satisfied employee. A pessimistic and rigid person will most likely be a dissatisfied employee. Every company has its share of "pills" who always find something to complain about. Some evidence suggests that a tendency toward optimism versus pessimism is inherited.[8] If you have a predisposition toward pessimism, you can still become more optimistic with self-discipline. For example, you can look for the positive aspects of a generally unpleasant situation.

- **Positive self-image.** People possessing a positive self-image are generally more satisfied with their jobs than are those possessing a negative self-image. One explanation is that the people who view themselves negatively tend to view most things negatively. You have to like yourself before you can like your job.

- **Positive expectations about the job.** People with positive expectations about their jobs are frequently more satisfied than are those with low expectations. These expectations illustrate a self-fulfilling prophecy. If you expect to like your job, you will behave in such a way that those expectations will be met. Similarly, if you expect your job not to satisfy your needs, you will do things to make your expectations come true. Assume that a worker expects to earn low commissions in a sales job. The person's negativism may come through to customers and prospective customers, thereby ensuring low customer satisfaction and low commissions.

- **Effective handling of abuse from customers.** Customer service workers are often verbally abused by customers over such matters as products not working, merchandise returns not being acceptable, and the customer having been charged a late fee. Automated telephone-answering systems often force callers to hack through a thicket of prompts before reaching a human being. By the time a live person is reached, the customer is angry and ready to lash out at the customer service representative.[9] To prevent these oral tirades from damaging one's job satisfaction, it is essential to use effective techniques of dealing with criticism and resolving conflict as described in Chapter 9. The section of dealing with dissatisfied customers presented later in this chapter is also important. Combating sexual harassment by customers is also important for retaining emotional equilibrium.

High job satisfaction contributes to good customer service in another important way. Employees who are satisfied with their jobs are more likely to engage in service-oriented organizational citizenship behavior. As you will recall, *organizational citizenship behavior* relates to going beyond your ordinary job description to help other workers and the company. A customer service worker with high organizational citizenship behavior will go beyond ordinary expectations to find ways to solve a customer problem.[10] A member of the tech support staff in a consumer electronics store volunteered to drop by a customer's house to help him install a video recorder even though such home visits were not required. As a result of the technician's kindness, the man purchased a $6,000 plasma screen TV receiver from the store.

Receive Emotional Support from Coworkers and Management to Give Better Customer Service

Closely related to the idea that satisfied workers can better satisfy customers is the finding that the emotional support of coworkers often leads to providing better customer service. According to a study, the support of coworkers is even more important than supervisory support. The participants in the study were 354 customer service workers employed in service-based facilities. Customer satisfaction surveys were collected from 269 customers. The major finding was that employees who perceived their coworkers to be supportive had a higher level of commitment to their customers.

The researchers concluded that it is important to have a supportive group of coworkers by your side to help you perform service-related duties. In this study, supervisory support was less important than coworker support in terms of bringing about a strong customer orientation. (A *customer service orientation* includes a desire to help customers, and a willingness to act in ways that would satisfy a customer.) Another important conclusion drawn from the study was that customer satisfaction was positively associated with the strength of the service worker's customer orientation.[11]

Research also supports the idea that the type of leadership sales representatives receive influences the type of relationships the reps build with customers. The study in question involved 300 pairs of sales managers and 1,400 sales people reporting directly to them. Sales managers who were charismatic and good at setting visions strongly affected the use of customer-oriented selling behaviors, such as building good relationships. Other key factors related to building good relationships with customers were the level of support the sales workers received from the organization, and how much cohesiveness (closeness) they felt with coworkers.[12]

A similar study conducted in Taiwan with 450 hair stylists and 112 store managers found that charismatic and visionary leaders enhanced employee service. In turn, better service was associated with customers coming back to the salon.[13] You probably already knew that if your hair stylist gives good service, you will return—but now there is a quantitative study to support your belief.

The major point here is that the organization plays an important role in how well your ability or willingness to build relationships with customers. A thought to take away is that if you perceive your manager to be charismatic, you are more likely to provide better customer service.

Understand Customer Needs and Put Them First

The most basic principle of selling is to identify and satisfy customer needs. One challenge is that many customers may not be able to express their needs clearly. To help identify customer needs, you may have to probe for information. For example, the associate in a camera and video store might ask, "What uses do you have in mind for a video camera?" Knowing such information will help the associate identify which camcorder will satisfy the customer's needs.

The concept of adding value for customers is widely accepted as a measure of satisfying customer needs. If you satisfy customer needs, you are adding value for them. A person might be willing to pay $20 more per ticket to watch an athletic event if the extra $20 brought a better view and a chair instead of a backless bench. (The better view and more comfortable back add value for the spectator.) After customer needs have been identified, the focus must be on satisfying those needs rather than the needs of oneself or the company. Assume that the customer says, "The only convenient time for me to receive delivery this week would be Thursday or Friday afternoon." The sales associate should not respond, "On Thursday and Friday our truckers prefer to make morning deliveries." Instead, the associate should respond, "I'll do whatever is possible to accommodate your request."

A major contributor to identifying customer needs is to listen actively to customers. Listening can take place during conversations with customers, and "listening" can also mean absorbing information sent by e-mail and written letters. Many improvements in customer service today stem from suggestions and complaints made in blogs or on Twitter. For example, several dollar stores have moved into upscale shopping centers because it was suggested on blogs that so many people today "shop down" to save money.

Focus on Solving Problems, Not Just Taking Orders

Effective selling uses sales representatives to solve problems rather than merely have them taking orders. An example is the approach taken by sales representatives for Xerox Corporation. Instead of focusing on the sale of photocopiers, printers, and related equipment, the sales reps look to help customers solve their information flow problems. The solution could involve selling machines, but it might also involve selling consulting services.

customer-centric sales process

A sales process emphasizing a low-pressure environment in which the sales staff acts as consultants, offering information and explaining how the product or service can help solve a customer's problem.

Consultative selling is also referred to as customer-centric. A **customer-centric sales process** emphasizes a low-pressure environment in which the sales staff acts as consultants, offering information and explaining how the product or service can help solve a customer's problem. The customer-centric approach is evident both at an Apple Store or a Container Store. At an Apple Store, customers can obtain free assistance from the Genius Bar. At a Container Store, sales associates are extensively trained to offer a light, informative touch.[14] Among the many problems discussed might be how to store clothing in a basement to avoid the risk of mold.

The focus on problem solving enables sales reps to become partners in the success of their customers' businesses. By helping the customer solve problems, the sales rep enhances the value of the supplier–customer relationship to the customer. The customer is receiving consulting services in addition to the merchandise or service being offered. In some situations, a store associate can capitalize on the same principle. If the customer appears unsure about a purchase, ask him or her which problem that the product should solve. The following scenario in a computer store illustrates this point:

Customer: I think I would like to buy this computer. I'm pretty sure it's the one I want. But I don't know too much about computers other than how to use them for word processing, e-mail, forwarding articles from Web sites, and basic search.

Store Associate: I am happy you would like to purchase a computer. But could you tell me what problems you are facing that you want a computer to help you solve?

Customer: Right now I feel I'm not capitalizing on the Internet revolution. I want to do more online, and get into digital photography so that I can send cool photos to friends all over. Friends and family members also want me to have a webcam. I also want to purchase music online, so I can walk around with an MP3 player like my friends do.

Store Associate: To solve your problem, you will need a more powerful computer than the one you are looking at. I would like you to consider another model that is about the same price as the one you have chosen. The difference is that it has the memory you need to e-mail photos and download music from a subscription service.

Respond Positively to Moments of Truth

An effective customer contact person performs well during situations in which a customer comes in contact with the company and forms an impression of its service. Such situations are referred to as **moments of truth.** If the customer experiences satisfaction or delight during a moment of truth, the customer is likely to return when the need for service arises again. A person who is frustrated or angered during a moment of truth will often not be a repeat customer. A moment of truth is an important part of customer service because what really matters in a service encounter is the customer's perception of what occurred.[15] Visualize a couple who has just dined at an expensive restaurant as part of celebrating their anniversary. The food, wine, and music might have been magnificent, but the couple perceives the service as poor because one of them slipped on ice in the restaurant parking lot.

You can probably visualize many moments of truth in your experiences with service. Reflect on how a store associate treated you when you asked for assistance, the instructions you received when an airplane flight was canceled, or how you were treated when you inquired about financial aid. Each business transaction has its own moment of truth, yet they all follow the same theme of a key interaction between a customer and a company employee. At Publix Super Markets, Inc., a successful supermarket chain of more than 1,000 stores, one of the moments of truth is considered to be having a bagger at the checkout lane. When the president of Publix was visiting a store in St. Augustine Florida, he spotted a checkout lane without a bagger. He responded by helping out a customer before a store employee interceded.[16]

One way you can track moments of truth is to prepare a cycle-of-service chart, as shown in Figure 14-3. The **cycle-of-service chart** summarizes the moments of truth encountered by a customer during the delivery of a service.[17] To gain insight into these charts, do Skill-Building Exercise 14-1.

moments of truth

Situations in which a customer comes in contact with a company and forms an impression of its service.

cycle-of-service chart

A method of tracking the moments of truth with respect to customer service.

FIGURE 14-3   A Cycle-of-Service Chart for Obtaining a Car Loan at a Bank

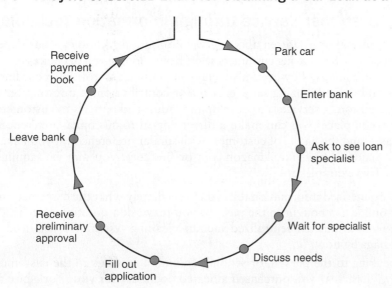

Moments of Truth

The class organizes into small groups to discuss what can go right versus what can go wrong during customer moments of truth. First refer to the cycle-of-service chart shown in Figure 14-3. Discuss what can go right or wrong at each moment of truth. Second, have the team develop its own cycle-of-service chart for another service, using its own experiences and imagination. After making the two analyses, discuss the usefulness of a cycle-of-service chart for improving customer satisfaction.

For additional practice in identifying the three components of customer of service, label each moment of truth into one of three perceptions: functional, mechanic, or human interaction. For example, you might have observed that the retail store had a nice scent (a perception of mechanics).

Be Ready to Accept Empowerment

empowerment

The process of managers transferring, or sharing, power with lower ranking employees.

A major strategy for improving customer service is to empower customer contact employees to resolve problems. **Empowerment** refers to managers transferring, or sharing, power with lower ranking employees. In terms of customer relations, it means pushing decision making and complaint resolution downward to employees who are in direct contact with customers. The traditional method of dealing with all but the most routine customer problems is for the customer contact worker to refer them to the manager. Many manufacturing firms and service firms now authorize customer contact workers to take care of customer problems within limits. For example, Ritz-Carlton, the luxury brand of Marriott International Inc., authorizes front-desk workers to credit dissatisfied customers up to $2,000 without supervisory approval.[18]

Empowerment is not giving away the store, especially because limits are established to the customer contact worker's authority. Empowerment does involve taking a reasonable risk based on company principles to provide meaningful customer service. For empowerment to work, the company must grant decision-making latitude to employees. The employees, in turn, must be willing to accept empowerment (or decision-making authority). Imagine yourself in a customer contact position. For empowerment to work effectively, you should be able to answer affirmatively to the following statements:

- I am willing to arrive at a quick decision as to whether the company or the customer is right.
- I would be willing to admit to a customer that the company has made a mistake.
- I would be willing to take the risk that at times I will lose money for the company on a given transaction.
- I would be comfortable making an out-of-the-ordinary decision about a customer problem without consulting a manager.

Enhance Customer Service through Information Technology

Much has been said and written about how information technology has depersonalized customer service, such as having customers select from a long menu of choices on a telephone. Information technology, however, also plays an important role in recording customer preferences and individualizing service. A major contribution of information technology to enhancing customer service is to develop individualized appeals to customers. With the right software in place, you can make a direct appeal to customer preferences based on past purchases, and the habits of customers with similar preferences. If you have purchased online at a major e-tailer like Amazon.com or Buy.com, you may be familiar with this technology. Two examples follow:

1. Computerized information tells you immediately what the customer on the phone or online has bought in the past, so you may ask a question such as, "Two years ago you installed a centralized vacuum cleaning system. Do you need another set of bags by now?"
2. Speaking to the person, or sending an e-mail message to the customer, you may say, "Last year you purchased a heated doghouse for your Yorkshire terrier. Our

information suggests that people who own a heated doghouse are also interested in dog sweaters. Please take a moment to look at our new line of dog sweaters for the canines who appreciate warmth."

Developing individualized appeals to customers is likely to be included in customer relationship management (CRM) software. The complex software is used to implement a strategy of interacting with your customers to bring them more value, and more profits to your firm. One of its basic purposes is to make the company easier for customers to do business with, including facilitating placing orders over the Internet.[19] As such, the individual customer service worker would not have the authority to install such a system. Yet the individual worker can always look for ways to apply the CRM system (such as that provided by Salesforce.com, or SAP) in a way that best serves the customer.

A major challenge in providing good customer service when using information technology is to preserve the human touch. Here are some hints for adding a personal touch to your electronic communications to help build customer loyalty.

Using voicemail

1. Vary your voice tone and inflection when leaving messages and in your greeting to avoid sounding bored or uninterested in your job and the company.

2. Smile while leaving your message—somehow a smile gets transmitted over the telephone wires or optic fibers!

3. Use voice mail to minimize "telephone tag" rather than to increase it. If your greeting specifies when you will return, callers can choose to call again or to leave a message. When you leave a message, suggest a good time to return your call. Another way to minimize telephone tag is to assure the person you are calling that you will keep trying.

4. Place an informative and friendly greeting (outgoing message) on your voice mail. Used effectively, a voicemail greeting will minimize the number of people irritated by not talking to a person.

5. When you respond to a voicemail outgoing message, leave specific, relevant information. As in the suggestions for minimizing telephone tag, be specific about why you are calling and what you want from the person called. The probability of receiving a return call increases when you leave honest and useful information. If you are selling something or asking for a favor, be honest about your intent.

6. When leaving your message, avoid the most common voicemail error by stating your name and telephone number clearly enough to be understood. Most recipients of a message dislike intensely listening to it several times to pick up identifying information.

7. The company using computerized calls (or "robocalls") should determine if these calls are perceived as helpful or so annoying that they harm business.[20] One of the many uses of an automated calling service is to remind patients of upcoming medical and dental appointments. Some patients appreciate the reminder, whereas others slam down the phone in disgust because they expect more a more personal touch from a dental or medical office.

Using e-mail

1. Use the customer's name. Begin the greeting, "Hello, Lisa King." Many companies now greet customers by their first name only, but a minority customers consider this practice to be rude. However, few people are likely to be offended when you use both their first and last names.

2. Choose a human e-mail address. Marysmith@kaset.com feels more personal than an odd sequence of numbers, letters, and dashes. To enhance your credibility and professional stature, avoid cool electronic addresses, such as Steelabs@aol.com or Angellady42@gmail.com.

3. Be conversational. Mention events you have shared, such as "I enjoyed seeing you at the company meeting."

4. Sign your name. Don't neglect your signature. "Best regards, Jim Woods."[21]

Avoid Rudeness and Hostility toward Customers

I have reserved the most frequently violated principle of good customer service for last: Avoid being rude or hostile to customers. Although rudeness to customers is obviously a poor business practice, the problem is widespread. Rudeness by customer contact personnel is a major problem from the employer's standpoint. A widely practiced form of rudeness is for two store associates to converse with each other about nonwork matters while a customer waits for attention. Or, how about a store associate making a personal phone call while waiting on you?

Rude treatment creates more lost business than does poor product quality or high prices. Several years ago McDonald's franchises were facing a downturn in sales. Surveys indicated that one of the problems facing McDonald's Corporation was the indifferent and rude behavior by many frontline workers. McDonald's then increased the training of store employees and upgraded the menu, to achieve a substantial rebound in sales.

Rudeness is sometimes a form of hostility because rudeness, such as grimacing at a customer, stems from anger. Being outright hostile toward customers can be a bigger problem than rudeness, which is more subtle. The impact of service provider hostility on customer satisfaction was explored by studying 142 naturally occurring service interactions at a telephone service center of a bank. A typical interaction would be a customer phoning the bank to inquire about an account balance. (Today, such calls would only be in reference to what appeared to be inaccuracies in the online statement, or the one retrieved through the automated phone service.) Service interactions usually lasted about two minutes. Customers were later contacted to complete a quality survey about their transaction. Hostility was measured through raters' judgment of the tone of the service providers' voices.

A major finding of the study was that when the technical performance (e.g., providing the information needed) was low, hostility by the service provider lowered customer satisfaction considerably. When the technical performance of the service provider was good, hostility had a less negative impact on service quality.[22] When you get the information you need from a service provider, you are willing to put up with a few angry tones! The overall message supports a human relations perspective: Being hostile toward customers lowers their perception of the quality of service.

To elevate your awareness level about rudeness among customer contact personnel, do Self-Assessment Quiz 14-2.

SELF-ASSESSMENT QUIZ 14-2

Am I Being Rude?

Directions: Following is a list of behaviors that would be interpreted as rude by many customers. Check "Yes" if you have engaged in such behavior in your dealings with customers or if you would be *likely* to do so if your job involved customer contact, and "No" if you would not engage in such behavior.

	Yes	No
1. I talk to a coworker while serving a customer.	_____	_____
2. I conduct a phone conversation with someone else while serving a customer.	_____	_____
3. I address customers by their first names without having their permission.	_____	_____
4. I address customers as "You guys."	_____	_____
5. I chew gum or eat candy while dealing with a customer.	_____	_____
6. I laugh when customers describe an agonizing problem they are having with one of our company's products or services.	_____	_____
7. I minimize eye contact with customers.	_____	_____
8. I say the same thing to every customer, such as "Have a nice day," in a monotone.	_____	_____

9. I accuse customers of attempting to cheat the company before carefully investigating the situation. ___ ___

10. I hurry customers when my breaktime approaches. ___ ___

11. I comment on an attractive customer's appearance in a flirtatious, sexually oriented way. ___ ___

12. I sometimes complain about or make fun of other customers when I am serving a customer. ___ ___

13. I sometimes look and act impatient if a customer fumbles around trying to locate his or her credit card, debit card, or cash. ___ ___

Interpretation: The more of these behaviors you have engaged in, the ruder you are and the more likely it is that you are losing potential business for your company. If you have not engaged in any of these behaviors, even when faced with a rude customer, you are an asset to your employer. You are also tolerant.

CREATING A BOND WITH YOUR CUSTOMER

LEARNING OBJECTIVE 3

Another key perspective on achieving customer satisfaction and delight is to create a bond—or emotional relationship—with customers. The rationale is that if you form warm, constructive relationships with your customers, they will keep buying. Staying focused on the importance of customers will help provide the motivation for forming such a bond. The willingness to form a bond with the customer is part of having a **strong customer orientation**, defined as "a set of basic individual predispositions and an inclination to provide service, to be courteous and helpful in dealing with customers and associates."[23] You may recall Self-Assessment Quiz 14-1 about customer orientation at the outset of the chapter. Service-oriented organizational citizenship behavior relates to the same idea of focusing on customer needs.

strong customer orientation
A set of individual predispositions and an inclination to provide service, to be courteous and helpful in dealing with customers and associates.

Creating a bond is aimed at increasing sales, but it also enhances service. If the customer relies on and trusts the sales representative, the customer will perceive the service to be of high quality. Similarly, people perceive medical and legal services to be of high quality if they trust the physician or lawyer. Virtually all of the principles and techniques presented in this chapter will help form a bond with customers. However, six key principles are as follows:

1. Create a welcoming attitude, including a smile.
2. Provide exceptional service.
3. Show care and concern.
4. Make the buyer feel good.
5. Build a personal relationship.
6. Invite the customer back.

Create a Welcoming Attitude, Including a Smile

An effective starting point in creating a customer bond is to use enthusiastic expressions, including a smile, when greeting customers. Attempt to show a sincere, positive attitude that conveys to customers and prospects, "I'm here to make you happy."[24] In addition to being an effective greeting, smiling is also a natural relationship builder and can help you bond with your customer. Smile several times at each customer meeting, even if your customer is angry at your product or service. A camcorder is a useful device for getting feedback on the quality of your smile. Practicing your smile in a mirror might feel a little less natural, but it is still helpful. Smiling at customers has a potential disadvantage, despite its general effectiveness. If your smile is too friendly and inviting, the customer might think that you want to get to know him or her outside the business relationship.

Smiling is such a key part of bonding with customers that the smiles of customer service workers have been the subject of scientific study. Twenty pairs of first-year college students who were trained as coders for the experiment observed 220 employee-consumer encounters in food/coffee services. Customers were later asked to report their mood, appraisal of service quality, and encounter satisfaction. Several of the findings were as follows: Even in brief encounters, substantial smiling by employees made customers smile in return. Smiling employees were perceived as providing quality service, and the customers felt overall satisfaction with their encounters. Smiling somehow did not affect customer mood after the encounter. One interpretation of the study is that service employees should keep smiling, but not the point that they lack authenticity.[25] Phony smiles backfire in work and personal life.

Provide Exceptional Service (or Customer Experience)

The best-accepted axiom about keeping customers is to provide exceptional service or experience. Many successful companies contend that their competitive advantage is good service. An important part of the comeback of Burger King in the mid-2000s was a subtle way of providing top service to the company's most profitable demographic group, males between the ages of 18 and 34 who visit the stores three to four times a week. These "Super Fans" want indulgent, fat-laden, high-caloric, tasty food. So Burger King served up the Enormous Omelet Sandwich. Greg Brenneman, who was CEO at the time, said he gives his customers what they want, not what others (such as nutritionists and physicians) think they should have.[26]

Exceptional service includes dozens of customer transactions, including prompt delivery, a fair-returns policy, accurate billing, and prompt attention to a customer's presence. Exceptional service also includes giving customers good advice about using the product or service. As shown in Figure 14-2, providing exceptional service leads to customer delight.

Another way of understanding the importance of exceptional customer service is to study what happens when service declines. Part of the demise of the once popular Circuit City was attributed to a decline in customer service. The CEO at the time, Phillip Schoonover, decided to reduce costs by dismissing many veteran workers and replace them with inexperienced (and lower paid) workers.[27] With fewer knowledgeable associates in the Circuit City stores, many customers chose to make consumer electronic purchases at competitors.

Show Care and Concern

During contacts with the customer, the sales representative should show concern for the customer's welfare. The rep should ask questions such as: "How have you enjoyed the optical scanner you bought awhile back?" "How much time and money have you saved since you installed the new system?" After asking the questions, the sales rep should project a genuine interest in the answer. Microsoft is one of many companies that asks about the quality of its service, and the inquiries are pointed and specific rather than canned. For example, a small business owner responded to an inquiry about service Microsoft provided, and he complimented "Jocelyn" for pointing him in the right direction. A team manager at Microsoft wrote back: "Thank you for taking the time to commend Jocelyn on a Job Well Done. Our primary goal at Microsoft is that our customers are very satisfied with the support they receive. I am pleased to read that we have met that goal in your case."

Make the Buyer Feel Good

A fundamental way of keeping a relationship going is to make the buyer feel good about himself or herself. In addition, the customer should be made to feel good because of having bought from the representative. Offer compliments about the customer's appearance or about a report that specified vendor requirements clearly. In retail, an effective feel-good line is to point out how well the product fits the customer, such as "It looks like Toro made that riding mower just for you." An effective feel-good line is: "I enjoy doing business with you."

Sometimes giving the customer or potential customer a small treat will make that person feel good enough to take decisive action. Microsoft enterprise sales manager, LaShonda Anderson-Williams reports, "I once had a purchase order that needed to be signed by the end of our fiscal year. We called the CFO's assistant, and she said it was sitting on his desk. So I sent her a basket of cookies. The next day she got him to sign. To get my $1.2 million deal done, I spent $40."[28] We caution that you need good sensitivity to the situation to avoid giving a small treat that could backfire. An example might be sending Warren Buffet (usually ranked as one of the richest people in the world) a $25 gift certificate to Macy's in order to sell to his company.

Making the buyer feel good about having made the purchase can be particularly important when selling luxury items to consumers. This helps minimize feelings of guilt for having been so extravagant. Sales consultant Jean-Marie Brücker trains store associates sell luxury products such as using the *macaroon* technique that refers to the *macaron*, a sandwich-like pastry. The technique proceeds in this manner: "Madame, this timepiece (or diamond or handbag) comes from our finest workshop and has a value of $10,000. If you buy it, your children are sure to enjoy it for generations to come." The high price is sandwiched between the product's more romantic benefits. The idea is to sell the emotion of luxury. To further enhance the purchaser's emotions, Brücker insists that sales associates flatter customers by such means as complimenting the customer's own watch, even it is made by a competitor.[29]

Build a Personal Relationship through Interaction with Customers

Interacting with customers in a personal way often enhances the customer experience, leading to repeat business. Interaction with pleasant staff members gives customers a temporary feeling of friendship that many of them value. Executives at Staybridge Suites recognize how human interaction contributes to profitability, and use this principle as a guide for making investments in customer service. Staybridge, similar to other extended-stay hotels, provides limited services and is sparsely staffed to reduce costs. Rooms are fully cleaned only once a week, and the front desk is usually staffed by only one or two people.

Instead of providing loads of amenities, Staybridge concentrates its customer service on staff members interacting with guests. "A lot of our guests really want that personal interaction—the thing they get from home that they'd like to get from a hotel," says Rob Radomski, the vice president for brand management for Staybridge Suites. "There are conversations between guests and staff about projects they're working on, and their family back home, and the kid, the dog." Staybridge also offers "Sundowner receptions" on Tuesday, Wednesday, and Thursday evening in the lobby. General managers are required to attend the receptions in which guests are given a free meal and an opportunity to socialize. Radomski believes the meals are cost-effective in terms of developing customer loyalty.[30]

Another way of building relationships with large numbers of customers is to interact with them through company blogs or the social media. The company representative is authorized to chat with hundreds of customers and potential customers by placing informal comments on the authorized company blog. The worker lets out tidbits of information to customers without betraying company confidences or making defamatory statements about the company. However, the blog entries are not usually as positive as advertisements, which help form bonds with the customers. Many customers post replies and swap ideas with the company rep.

Company-approved blogs are widely used as customers demand information presented in a more unvarnished way. A major advantage of blogs is that they humanize large organizations, such as the company representative mentioning a favorite recipe as well as chatting about a new product.

Invite the Customer Back

The southern U.S. expression "Y'all come back, now!" is well suited for bonding with customers. Specific invitations to return may help increase repeat business. The more focused

Bonding with Customers

Role players in this exercise will demonstrate two related techniques for bonding with customers: show care and concern and make the buyer feel good.

Scenario 1: Show Care and Concern. A sales representative meets with two company representatives to talk about installing a new information system for employee benefits. One of the company reps is from the human resources department and the other is from the information systems department. The sales rep will attempt to show care and concern for both company representatives during the same meeting.

Scenario 2: Make the Buyer Feel Good. A couple, played by two role players, enter a new car showroom to examine a model they

have seen advertised on television. Although they are not in urgent need of a new car, they are strongly interested. The sales representative is behind quota for the month and would like to close a sale today. The rep decides to use the tactic "make the buyer feel good" to help form a bond.

For both scenarios, observers rate the role players on two dimensions, using a 1-to-5 scale from very poor to very good. One dimension is "effective use of human relations techniques." The second dimension is "acting ability." A few observers might voluntarily provide feedback to the role players in terms of sharing their ratings and observations. The course instructor might also provide feedback.

and individualized the invitation, the more likely it will have an impact on customer behavior. ("Y'all come back, now!" is sometimes used too indiscriminately to be effective.) Pointing out why you enjoyed doing business with the customer, and what future problems you could help with, is an effective technique. An industrial cleaning company supervisor might say, "Our crew enjoyed cleaning such a fancy office. Keep us in mind when you would like your windows to sparkle."

Skill-Building Exercise 14-2 gives you an opportunity to practice techniques for bonding with customers.

Despite the importance of forming a bond with your customer, getting too personal can backfire. Most customers want a business relationship with the company, and are not looking for a personal relationship with a company representative. As Daniel Askt observes, "Most customers want value and service without contending that a salesman who insists that he wants to be like family to you. Chances are you've already got a family, and for most of us, one is enough."[31]

DEALING WITH CUSTOMER DISSATISFACTION

LEARNING OBJECTIVE 4

Most companies put honest effort into preventing customer dissatisfaction. In addition to employing many of the principles and techniques already cited, many companies routinely survey customers to detect problem areas that could lead to dissatisfaction. A representative survey used by a successful company in its field is shown in Figure 14-4. Despite all these efforts to achieve total customer satisfaction, some customer dissatisfaction is inevitable. One reason is that mistakes in serving customers are almost inevitable; for example, a piece of equipment may have a faulty component unknown to the seller. A second reason is that some customers have a predisposition to complain. They will find something to complain about with respect to any product or service. Visualize the billions of transactions that take place every year between Wal-Mart service personnel and customers. Inevitably, some customer, somewhere is going to rant and rave about poor service no matter how hard Wal-Mart managers and store associates try to please.

An important point to remember in dealing with dissatisfied customers is that the negative personality traits of customers can bring down your level of customer service. For example, a study conducted in two major fast-food chains in Singapore found that customers who scored high on the trait of agreeableness tended to bring out positive emotion by the service personnel. In contrast, customers who scored high on negative affectivity (being disagreeable) brought out negative emotion among customer service personnel.[32] A service worker cannot change the personality traits of customers, yet a

FIGURE 14-4   A Chain Restaurant Customer Satisfaction Survey

We would like to hear about your visit and how we can improve. Thank you!

Date: Time: AM/PM   Which location did you visit? _____

Name: _____

Address: _____

Email: _____

Phone: _____

Check Number: _____

Please rate us:

	Poor	Fair	Good	Very Good	Excellent
Host/Hostess Hospitality	1	2	3	4	5
Server's Hospitality	1	2	3	4	5
Server's Attentiveness	1	2	3	4	5
Bartender's Hospitality	1	2	3	4	5
Bartender's Attentiveness	1	2	3	4	5
Quality of Food	1	2	3	4	5
Value of Meal	1	2	3	4	5
Cleanliness	1	2	3	4	5
Likely to Return	1	2	3	4	5
Manager Visit Table?	Yes	No			

Host/Hostess' Name: _____   Hair color: _____

Server's Name: _____   Hair color: _____

Bartender's Name: _____   Hair color: _____

What did you order today or tonight?
_____

Was this your first visit?   Would you like to be a Secret Shopper?

☐ Yes   ☐ No   ☐ Yes   ☐ No

Comments on your visit: _____
_____
_____

The information provided will be used to help us better serve you and will not be shared.

little self-management of emotion is in order. The service worker might reflect, "I won't let this nasty customer get me down. I will do my best to do my job without overreacting." Be careful not to fake your emotion too frequently because it can create stress. Instead be assertive with a comment like, "I want to help you, but might you tell me what you want in a more positive way?"

The next subsections describe three approaches to handling customer dissatisfaction: dealing with complaints and anger, involving the customer in working out a problem, and handling an unreasonable request.

Deal Constructively with Customer Complaints and Anger

In an era when customer satisfaction is so highly valued, both retail and industrial customers are likely to be vocal in their demands. When faced with an angry customer, use one or more of the following techniques recommended by customer satisfaction specialists.[33]

1. **Acknowledge the customer's point of view.** Make statements such as "I understand," "I agree," and "I'm sorry." Assume, for example, a customer says, "The accounts receivable department made a $1,000 overcharge on my account last month. I want this fixed right away." You might respond, "I understand how annoying this must be for you. I'll work on the problem right away." At AirTran Airways, flight attendants are trained to listen to make sure that they understand the customer's concern, such as why they have to pay a fee for premium bottled water.[34]

2. **Avoid placing blame on the customer.** Suggesting that the customer is responsible for the problem intensifies the conflict. With the customer who claims to have been overcharged, refrain from saying: "Customers who keep careful account of their orders never have this problem."

3. **Use six magic words to defuse anger.** The magic words are *I understand* (that this is a problem), *I agree* (that it needs to be solved), and *I'm sorry* (that this happened to you). The six magic words help communicate your empathy, which is considered vital to dealing with customer problems. For example, technical support agents at Comcast are taught that they must show empathy on every call even if they have heard the same problem for 15 consecutive calls.[35]

4. **Apologize for the problems created by you or by your company.** To recover from a breakdown in customer service, it is best to acknowledge an error immediately. Apologies are most effective when stated in the first person (such as "I created the problem" or "I'm very sorry for what happened."). The corporate "we're sorry" sounds less sincere than when one specific person accepts responsibility for what went wrong. Professional workers at the Kaiser Permanente HMO receive training in how to apologize to patients for medical errors. Sincere apologies can significantly reduce the cost of settling lawsuits, and may even convince unhappy patients not to sue at all. A sincere apology includes a statement of what the apologizer is going to do to fix the problem.[36]

5. **Take responsibility, act fast, and be thorough.** This technique is a simplified framework for managing customer dissatisfaction. As illustrated by Mark Delp, the manager of a fleet maintenance service, "Suppose a customer calls about an oil leak after Fleet Response services a car. I have the car immediately picked up from his office and clean any oil spots that may have been left on the driveway. I make sure there are no further leaks. Furthermore, I apologize and accept full responsibility, even if the problem is not our fault, such as when a part fails."[37] Part of taking responsibility is to ask, "What can I do to make this right?"

6. **Tell the difficult customers how much you value them.** Quite often customers with problems feel unappreciated. Just before resolving the problem of a difficult customer, explain how important he or she is to your firm. You might say, "We value your business, so I want to correct this for you quickly."[38] (Of course, you would value the customer even more after he or she becomes less difficult.)

7. **Follow up on the problem resolution.** Following up to see whether the resolution to the problem is satisfactory brings closure to the incident. The follow-up also helps the service deliverer know that he or she can rebound from an episode of customer dissatisfaction. One useful form of follow-up is to telephone or send an e-mail to the customer whose problem was solved. For example, a representative from the service department of an automobile dealership might telephone a customer whose new car required substantial warranty repairs. "Hello, this is Jill Gordon from Oak Automotive. We replaced your original transmission last month. How is the new transmission working?" The Microsoft example presented earlier in the chapter illustrates the use of e-mail for follow-up on problem resolution.

8. **Do your best to make sure the problem does not happen again.** The preceding steps are all valuable in resolving the complaints of angry customers. In addition, the customer needs some assurance that the problem will not happen again. Without such assurance, repeat business is at risk. The *recovery paradox* refers to the fact that customers will sometimes be more delighted by a skillful resolution of a problem than they are by service that was failure-free to begin with. For example, a customer might be delighted that a false roaming charge of $145 was removed from a phone bill—when the customer had never visited the country in which the charge occurred.

A less personal, and usually less effective, form of follow-up is to send a customer satisfaction questionnaire to the person with the problem. The questionnaire will often be interpreted as a company procedure that does not reflect specific concern about the individual's problem.

Involve the Customer in Working Out the Problem

Mistakes and problems in serving customers are inevitable regardless of how hard service workers strive for perfection. To minimize the perception of poor service, the customer must be involved in deciding what should be done about the problem. By being involved in the solution to the problem, the customer is more likely to accept a deviation from the service promised originally. The ideal condition is for the customer service representative and dissatisfied customer to work as partners in resolving the problem. The following case history illustrates the technique of customer involvement and partnering.

> *Seth Bradbury is a sales promotion specialist at an advertising agency. A furniture store hired the agency to prepare and mail 3,000 postcards advertising a new line of furniture. One side of the postcard contained a photograph of the furniture, and the other side contained product details and space for addressing and stamping the card. After the cards were mailed, Seth received an urgent call from the client. "The photograph of the furniture is printed vertically. It looks horrible. We agreed on a horizontal shot. This means 3,000 cards have been mailed with a mistake."*
>
> *After allowing the client to finish his complaint, Seth responded, "You're right, it is a vertical shot. Perhaps we misinterpreted your directions. However, I think your furniture still looks beautiful. The extra white space the vertical shot provides creates an interesting effect. It's unfortunate that the cards have already been mailed. What would you like us to do? It's important that you are satisfied."*
>
> *The client responded, "I guess there is nothing we can do to change the photograph. Would you be willing to give us a discount off the price we agreed on?"*

A survey conducted with more than 75,000 customers supports the importance of dealing directly with customer dissatisfaction. The customers in the study were people dealing directly with contact-center representatives or using self-service channels. It was found that generous approaches to satisfying customers such as giving them a refund, a free product, or a free service such as expedited shipping did not have much impact on customer loyalty. What customers really want is a simple, rapid resolution to their problem.[39] For example, if a customer is not receiving the satellite television channels he or she subscribed to, all the customer wants is to receive the channels. A discount coupon will most likely not recapture his or her loyalty.

Anticipate How to Handle an Unreasonable Request

No matter how hard the customer contact worker attempts to provide outstanding customer service, at some point a customer comes along with an unreasonable request—or the customer may raise an unfair objection. Speak to any experienced store associate to obtain a case history of a "customer from Hell." For example, a small-business owner demanded that a store associate grant him exchange credit for six inkjet cartridges. The cartridges were purchased four years previously and were now obsolete.

Recognize that the customer who makes an unreasonable demand is usually aware of the unreasonableness. The customer may not expect to be fully granted the request. Instead, the customer is bargaining by beginning with an unreasonable demand. The small-business owner who brought in the cartridges was probably looking to salvage whatever he could.

Sales representatives and other customer contact workers who stand their ground with dignity and courtesy generally will not lose customers with unreasonable requests. These suggestions will help you deal with unreasonable demands while retaining the customer's business.[40]

- Let your customers retain their dignity by stating your position politely and reasonably.
- Avoid arguing with an upset customer. As the adage says, "You never win an argument with a customer."
- Appeal to your customer's sense of fair play and integrity. Explain that your intention is to do what is right and fair.
- Be firm by repeating the facts of the situation, but keep your temper under control.
- Accept responsibility for your decision rather than blaming company policy or your manager. Making somebody else the villain may intensify the problem.
- Be willing to say "no" to a customer when it is justifiable. Saying "yes" to an outrageous demand opens the door for a series of outrageous demands.

Maintain a Realistic Customer Retention Attitude

Some customers are too unreasonable, and therefore may not be worth keeping. A realistic goal is to retain as many profitable customers as possible. At times it may be possible to retain a customer by modifying the service. For example, customers who do not pay their bills on time or at all might be changed to a prepaid service such as done by phone companies and some Internet service providers.[41] In this way, the customers who have difficulty paying bills can still receive service.

An extreme example of a customer not worth keeping is the airline passenger who engages in *air rage*. Symptoms of air rage include (1) insisting on being served more alcoholic beverages than permissible by airline regulations, (2) sexually harassing or physically attacking flight attendants or other passengers, (3) refusing to fasten their seat belts, (4) using electronic gear such as cell phones and laptop computers when not allowed by regulations, (5) smoking in the lavatory, and (6) using the aisles for a lavatory.

It is best to set limits for unruly customers and see if their behavior changes. If the customer insists on creating disturbances, it is best to suggest the customer never return. Another problem is that some customers require so much service, or demand such high discounts, that they are unprofitable to retain. Good service to these customers means there is less time available to respond to the needs of profitable customers.

Customers can be unreasonable and unruly also because they are late paying their bills or do not pay them. Such customers divert resources away from more loyal and profitable customers and clients. Kishau Rogers, the owner of Websmith Group LLC, is a case in point. She finally had to drop or avoid clients who are high-maintenance or habitually late paying their bills. Her clients are mostly retail stores or entrepreneurs. They often asked for discounts because of their tight budgets or an expanded level of service beyond

Dealing with Difficult Customers

The following scenarios require one person to play the role of the customer contact worker and another person to play the difficult customer. As usual, the role players project their feelings into the role-play by imagining how they would behave in the situation.

Scenario 1: One person is a store associate in a high-fashion women's clothing store. A woman who bought a $2,000 gown the previous week brings back the gown today. She claims that she is returning the gown because it doesn't fit comfortably. The store associate strongly suspects the woman bought the gown originally with the intent of wearing it for a special occasion and then returning it.

Scenario 2: One person plays the role of a customer service representative in a consumer electronics store. Another person plays the role of a customer who purchased a $3,500 giant-screen television receiver three months ago. He comes up to the service rep's counter ranting about the store's ineptitude. The customer claims that the TV has broken down three times. After the first repair, the TV worked for two weeks and then broke down again. The second repair lasted two weeks, only for the TV to break down during a Super Bowl party at his house. The customer is red in the face and shouting loudly. The service rep wants to resolve the customer's problem and prevent him from bad-mouthing the store.

the agreed-upon contract. Rogers said that terminating 5 percent of her clientele, ". . . was the best decision I've made, because it really reduced the level of frustration I was experiencing. It freed me up to the clients that are loyal and pay on time."[42] In this way, the service she offered to other clients improved.

Dealing diplomatically and effectively with difficult customers requires an awareness of the types of tactics described in the previous several pages. Practice on the firing line is indispensable. The type of experience provided by Skill-Building Exercise 14-3 is helpful.

SELF-ASSESSMENT QUIZZES IN OVERVIEW

Two self-assessment quizzes were presented in this chapter and the two quizzes support each other. Self-Assessment Quiz 14-1 is designed to measure your orientation toward serving customers well. A high service orientation is obviously a plus for dealing with customers. Self-Assessment Quiz 14-2 measured tendencies toward being rude toward customers. A low rudeness score is certainly a plus, and it contributes to having a strong service orientation.

Concept Review and Reinforcement

Key Terms

Summary

Many companies today emphasize total customer satisfaction because it leads to goodwill, repeat business, and referrals. Customer satisfaction skills are necessary for all workers in contact with customers. Internal customers must also be taken into consideration.

Customers form three clues about the service experience. Functional clues are derived from the technical performance of the service. Mechanical clues stem from the sensory presentation of the service, including sights, smells, sounds, tastes, and textures. Human interaction clues are detected from the behavior and appearance of the service provider.

Eight key principles for satisfying and delighting customers are as follows:

1. Be satisfied so that you can provide better customer service. (Some of your own attitudes, such as optimism and flexibility, influence your job satisfaction.)
2. Receive emotional support from coworkers and management so that you can give better customer service.
3. Understand customer needs and put them first.
4. Focus on solving problems, not just taking orders.
5. Respond positively to moments of truth (points at which the customer forms an impression of company service).
6. Be ready to accept empowerment. (Being empowered enables you to solve customer problems.)
7. Enhance customer service through information technology.
8. Avoid rudeness and hostility toward customers. (Rude and hostile treatment of customers creates lost business.)

Another key perspective on achieving customer satisfaction and delight is to create a bond—or emotional relationship—with customers. Almost any act of good customer service helps create a bond, but six principles are highlighted here:

1. Create a welcoming attitude, including a smile.
2. Provide exceptional service (or customer experience).
3. Show care and concern.
4. Make the buyer feel good.
5. Build a personal relationship through interaction with customers.
6. Invite the customer back.

Despite the best efforts on the company's part, some customer dissatisfaction is inevitable. Also, some customers have a predisposition to complain. One approach to dealing with customer dissatisfaction is to deal constructively with customer complaints and anger. Tactics for achieving this end include the following:

1. Acknowledge the customer's point of view.
2. Avoid placing blame on the customer.
3. Use six magic words to defuse anger. (These words help communicate empathy.)
4. Apologize for the problem created by you or by your company.
5. Take responsibility, act fast, and be thorough.
6. Tell the difficult customers how much you value them.
7. Follow up on the problem resolution.
8. Do your best to make sure the problem does not happen again.

Another approach to dealing with customer dissatisfaction is to involve the customer in working out the problem. The customer contact worker must sometimes deal with an unreasonable request. Remember that the customer probably recognizes that he or she is being unreasonable. Do not argue with an unreasonable customer, but at times you must say "no." Maintain a realistic customer retention attitude, meaning that as hard as you try to please, some customers are not worth keeping. Customers who are late paying bills or who do not pay divert resources away from more loyal and profitable customers.

Questions for Discussion and Review

1. For what reason do you think it is important for loan collection agents to display empathy toward the customers who owe the money?

2. Assume that you find it necessary to telephone a call center to help you with a technical problem with your cell phone or computer. Identify the functional, mechanic, and human-interaction clues that you are likely to encounter in the resolution of your problem.

3. For what reason is a satisfied employee more likely to provide better customer service?

4. A couple walks into an automobile showroom and say they want a big safe vehicle for them and their three children, yet they are unsure about what vehicle they should purchase. Describe how you might identify customer needs in this situation.

5. Describe several customer moments of truth you have experienced this week. What made you classify them as moments of truth?

6. Visualize yourself as an executive at Target. Develop a policy to empower customer service desk associates to resolve customer problems, including the limits to their empowerment.

7. What is your opinion of the impact of information technology on customer service? Offer at least two specifics in your answer.

8. Can you identify any ways in which a customer contact worker made you feel good? If so, provide the details.

9. Imagine yourself as a marketing and sales executive at a company that sold to other business firms. What would a large customer have to do before you took the initiative to end your relationship with that customer?

10. How effective is the principle "the customer is always right" when dealing with dissatisfied customers?

The Web Corner

http://www.csmassociation.org/
(Customer Satisfaction Measurement Association)

http://www.customersatisfaction.com
(Improving customer satisfaction and retention)

http://www.customer-service.com
(Improving your customer service)

Internet Skill Builder: Building Customer Relationships

An axiom of business is that customer relationships are essential. Direct your Internet search for this assignment toward finding customer-relationship building suggestions that can be converted into specific interpersonal skills, such as making a phone call to see how things are going. An example of a Web site that offers concrete suggestions for building customer relationships related to interpersonal skills is www.sideroad.com. Walk away from this exercise with a couple of ideas you might put into practice in dealing with customers.

Developing Your Human Relations Skills

Interpersonal Relations Case 14.1

The Rumpled Claims Forms

Rob is the supervisor of scanning operations at Insurance Resource, a firm that specializes in digitizing handwritten insurance claims. The client companies mail in their insurance claims in batches to Insurance Resource for processing into a digital format. In addition to scanning the handwritten documents, Insurance Resource also creates computer files for clients, and forwards the claims to the appropriate insurance company for reimbursement.

With profit margins being small in insurance claims processing, the document scanning technicians must work rapidly as well as processing a large volume of claims. One day when Rob asked Wendy to improve her speed, he received a response that he had heard many times in the past.

"How can I work fast when so many of these claims are rumpled, crumpled, and incomplete? We get some forms with missing names and addresses. The other scanning technicians say the same thing. We even have to stop to remove staples from the forms. If we are not careful, the staples get caught in scanners, and then we have to call tech support to de-jam the machine."

"My speed problem is that some of our clients are just stupid. The speed problem is theirs, not ours. I know that we can send the documents with missing information to our research department. But that takes time from my scanning."

Rob replied, "Wendy, you have a point. Some of our clients make work difficult for us, but they are still valued customers. If we put too much pressure on them to give us claims forms that are easier to scan, they might look for another outsourcing firm."

"I'm going to get with Kim (the vice president of operations), and see if we can get a task force set up to work on this problem of difficult-to-scan documents right away."

Case Questions

1. In what way does this case deal with a customer service problem?
2. What steps do you recommend that Insurance Resource take to get clients to send the company documents that are easier to manage?
3. What suggestions can you offer Wendy and the other scanning technicians to process their work more effectively for now?

Source: Case researched by Stefanie Donaldson, Rochester, New York, January 2010.

Interpersonal Relations Case 14.2

Indigo Takes on Shady Shoppers

Sandra Petrie is the owner and operator of Indigo, a boutique shop in Estes Park, Colorado. Two bloggers wrote the following about Indigo:

Linda E. 5 Indigo (The 5 refers to a rating of 5 out of 5)

There were three of us who shopped at Indigo in August of 2008 and we all three loved this store. It has all sizes and the clothes were unique rather than what you can get anywhere. The owner was fabulous—super friendly, super helpful and told you the honest truth about stuff—things like, if you're not sure about this, then you're probably better off not buying it. How many store owners take that approach? We're heading back to Estes again in August of 2009 and I can't wait to shop at Indigo again!

Posted 04/05/09

Anonymous 5 Indigo (The 5 refers to a rating of 5 out of 5)

Indigo is a little gem of a store in the Courtyard Shops in Estes Park. They carry all sorts of wonderful and unique clothes for regular and plus size women, and their handbags and jewelry are awesome! The owner was very friendly and helpful, and I really enjoyed myself while I was there. Be sure to check them out if you visit Estes Park!

Posted 06/06/07

Petrie is now addressing friendly fraud tactics by so-called "serial return artists." These customers patronize her clothing store, wear and wash the merchandise, and then haggle for a cash return. "People want to make a return four months later," says Petrie.

Petrie began implementing stricter return policies at her shop last year. She now only allows returns to be exchanged for store credit within two weeks of purchase, with tags still attached. At the time she said, "I hope the new policy won't negatively affect business, but I'm not naive and I anticipate that people will rethink before purchasing," she said.

She also added that during the first two weeks of the new policy, most of the customers seemed comfortable with the new rules, with the exception of "those who just come in and grab a bunch of things they intend to return later."

Case Questions

1. What do you think will be the impact of Indigo's new return policy on sales?
2. What alternatives might Petrie have for dealing with customers who fraudulently attempt to return merchandise?
3. How justified is Petrie in implementing her new return policy?

Source: Emily Maltby, "Shady Shoppers Beware: Merchants Find New Ways to Fight Customer Fraud," *The Wall Street Journal*, November 24, 2009, p. B6. Blogs from www.insiderpages.com/b/15240009701.

15

Enhancing Ethical Behavior

Touring the grounds of Electronic Recylers International in Fresno, California, is unnerving, like an unarmed walk through a prison yard. Tattooed, muscular men tear apart computers with hammers and electric grills. A guy with a gang insignia etched on his neck hoists a monitor over his head. Another rips the face off an old television with his bare hands. Machines chomp and grind gadgets and cell phones, spitting out shards of metal, plastic, and glass. Sharp edges and ex-cons are everywhere you look.

But ERI Chief Executive John S. Shegerian strolls comfortably through the place, dressed in a three-piece suit, green tie, cufflinks, and Rolex. Like a lot of like-minded businessmen these days, he espouses the importance of doing good while making a profit. "I believe you can recycle everything," he says, "including lives."

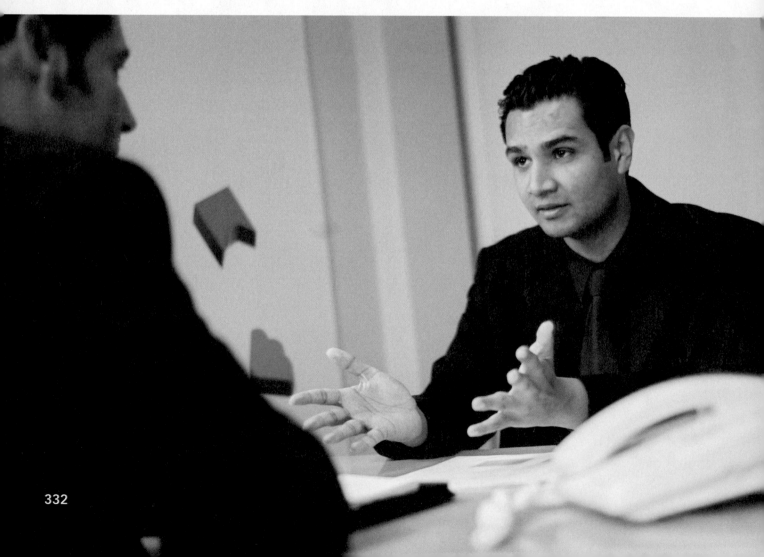

After reading and studying this chapter and doing the exercises, you should be able to

1. Recognize the importance of ethical behavior for establishing good interpersonal relationships in organizations.
2. Describe why the character trait of virtuousness contributes to being ethical in the workplace.
3. Identify job situations that often present ethical dilemmas.
4. Use a systematic method for making ethical decisions and behaving ethically.

Shegerian aims to be the biggest among the 700 or so electronic recyclers in the United States. He's already a leader in California, which in 2006 banned all electronics from its landfills. Electronics can contain toxins such as cadmium, mercury, and chromium. "..."

"Electronics are the fastest-growing solid waste stream in the world," he says. "..."

At a big enough scale, Shegerian hopes to stanch the flow of electronic waste exported to poor countries overseas. Over the next three years, Americans will throw out maybe 110 million computers, 80 million television sets, and 350 million cell phones. The majority of electronics recyclers don't even bother recycling this waste. They just ship it to India, Southeast Asia, China, and Africa. Organizations such as Basel Action Network and Greenpeace say the workers in those countries are often children making pennies a day. They troll mounds of garbage in search of computers and TVs. Lacking proper tools to tear open computer shells, they burn the plastic to get to the valuable stuff inside, breathing noxious fumes. They dip circuit boards in acid and melt lead in the same pans they use to cook their meager meals. They toss any remains back on the pile, where toxins seep into water supplies. "..."

Shegerian wants to open his next few recycling centers in rusty, neglected neighborhoods. It's all very much in keeping with his drive to rehabilitate whatever he comes in contact with: people, places, things. One-third of ERI's 200 full- and part-time employees are in its "second chance" program, which includes ex-cons and former addicts. It so happens these workers have a 17% turnover rate, half that of other employees.[1] "..."

Character trait

An enduring characteristic of a person that is related to moral and ethical behavior.

The scenario just described illustrates that some business people make it their mission in life to engage in activities that will help the environment as well as downtrodden people. As such they are being highly ethical on the job, as well as being socially responsible. (We are making the value judgment here, that preserving the environment and helping to rehabilitate ex-cons are ethical acts. Some people might disagree.)

People performing all types of work need a good sense of ethics (and etiquette) to be successful. Also, you often need to have an ethical reputation to get the job you want. *Ethics* refers to moral choices, or what is good and bad, right and wrong, just and unjust, and what people should do. Ethics is the vehicle for turning values into action. If you value fair play, you will do such things as giving honest performance evaluations to members of your group.

We study ethics here because a person's ethical code has a significant impact on his or her interpersonal relationships. This chapter's approach will emphasize the importance of ethics, common ethical problems, and guidelines for behaving ethically. Self-Assessment Quiz 15-1 gives you the opportunity to examine your ethical beliefs and attitudes.

The Ethical Reasoning Inventory

Directions: Describe how well you agree with each of the following statements, using the following scale: disagree strongly (DS); disagree (D); neutral (N); agree (A); agree strongly (AS). Circle the number in the appropriate column.

		DS	D	N	A	AS
1.	When applying for a job, I would cover up the fact that I had been fired from my most recent job.	5	4	3	2	1
2.	Cheating just a few dollars in one's favor on an expense account is okay if a person needs the money.	5	4	3	2	1
3.	Employees should report on each other for wrongdoing.	1	2	3	4	5
4.	It is acceptable to give approximate figures for expense account items when one does not have all the receipts.	5	4	3	2	1
5.	I see no problem with conducting a little personal business on company time.	5	4	3	2	1
6.	Just to make a sale, I would stretch the truth about a delivery date.	5	4	3	2	1
7.	I would fix up a purchasing agent with a date just to close a sale.	5	4	3	2	1
8.	I would flirt with my boss just to get a bigger salary increase.	5	4	3	2	1
9.	If I received $400 for doing some odd jobs, I would report it on my income tax return.	1	2	3	4	5
10.	I see no harm in taking home a few office supplies.	5	4	3	2	1
11.	It is acceptable to read the e-mail messages and faxes of coworkers, even when not invited to do so.	5	4	3	2	1
12.	It is unacceptable to call in sick to take a day off, even if only done once or twice a year.	1	2	3	4	5
13.	I would accept a permanent, full-time job even if I knew I wanted the job for only six months.	5	4	3	2	1
14.	I would first check company policy before accepting an expensive gift from a supplier.	1	2	3	4	5
15.	To be successful in business, a person usually has to ignore ethics.	5	4	3	2	1
16.	If I felt physically attracted toward a job candidate, I would hire that person over a more qualified candidate.	5	4	3	2	1
17.	On the job, I tell the truth all the time.	1	2	3	4	5
18.	If a student were very pressed for time, it would be acceptable to either have a friend write the paper or purchase one.	5	4	3	2	1
19.	I would be willing to put a hazardous chemical in a consume product if the product makes a good profit for the company.	5	4	3	2	1
20.	I would never accept credit for a coworker's ideas.	1	2	3	4	5

Total Score _____

Scoring and Interpretation: Add the numbers you have circled to obtain your total score.

90–100 You are a strongly ethical person who may take a little ribbing from coworkers for being too straitlaced.

60–89 You show an average degree of ethical awareness, and therefore should become more sensitive to ethical issues.

41–59 Your ethics are underdeveloped, but you at least have some awareness of ethical issues. You need to raise your level of awareness of ethical issues.

20–40 Your ethical values are far below contemporary standards in business. Begin a serious study of business ethics.

WHY BE CONCERNED ABOUT BUSINESS ETHICS?

LEARNING OBJECTIVE 1

When asked why ethics is important, most people would respond something to the effect that "Ethics is important because it's the right thing to do. You behave decently in the workplace because your family and religious values have taught you what is right and wrong." All this is true, but the justification for behaving ethically is more complex, as described next.[2]

A major justification for behaving ethically on the job is to recognize that people are motivated by both self-interest and moral commitments. Most people want to maximize gain for themselves (remember the expectancy theory of motivation?). At the same time, most people are motivated to do something morally right. As one of many examples, vast numbers of people donate money to charity, although keeping that amount of money for themselves would provide more personal gain.

Many business executives want employees to behave ethically because a good reputation can enhance business. A favorable corporate reputation may enable firms to charge premium prices and attract better job applicants. A favorable reputation also helps attract investors, such as mutual fund managers who purchase stock in companies. Certain mutual funds, for example, invest only in companies that are environmentally friendly. Managers want employees to behave ethically because unethical behavior—for example, employee theft, wasting time on the job, and lawsuits— is costly.

Behaving ethically is also important because many unethical acts are illegal as well, which can lead to financial loss and imprisonment. According to one estimate, the cost of unethical and fraudulent acts committed by U.S. employees totals $400 billion per year. A company that knowingly allows workers to engage in unsafe practices might be fined, and the executives may be held personally liable. Furthermore, unsafe practices can kill people. In recent years many people have perished in night club fires because there was only one door in operation, or unsafe pyrotechnics were on the premises. The financial scandals in recent years that resulted in major losses for millions of investors stemmed in part from financial managers making such risky investments that they were unethical. Securities were sold to the public that were based on loans to consumers with very poor credit ratings.

A subtle reason for behaving ethically is that high ethics increases the quality of work life. Ethics provides a set of guidelines that specify what makes for acceptable behavior. Being ethical will point you toward actions that make life more satisfying for work associates. A company code of ethics specifies what constitutes ethical versus unethical behavior. When employees follow this code, the quality of work life improves. Several sample clauses from ethical codes are as follows:

- Demonstrate courtesy, respect, honesty, and fairness.
- Do not use abusive language.
- Do not bring firearms or knives to work.
- Do not offer bribes.
- Maintain confidentiality of records.
- Do not harass (sexually, racially, ethnically, or physically) subordinates, superiors, coworkers, customers, or suppliers.

To the extent that all members of the organization abide by this ethical code, the quality of work life will improve. At the same time, interpersonal relations in organizations will be strengthened.

WHY WE HAVE SO MANY ETHICAL PROBLEMS

To become more skilled at behaving ethically, it is important to familiarize yourself with common ethical problems in organizations. Whether or not a given situation presents an ethical problem for a person depends to some extent on its **moral intensity**, or how deeply others might be affected.[3] A worker might face a strong ethical conflict about dumping mercury into a water supply but would be less concerned about dumping cleaning fluid. Yet both acts would be considered unethical and illegal. Here we first look at why being ethical is not as easy as it sounds. We then look at some data about the frequency of ethical problems and an analysis of predictable ethical temptations, and also examine the subtle ethical dilemma of choosing between rights.

LEARNING OBJECTIVE 2

moral intensity

In ethical decision making, how deeply others might be affected by the decision.

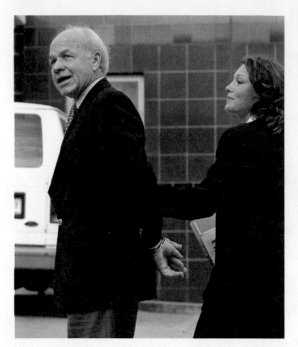

Why Being Ethical Isn't Easy

As analyzed by Linda Klebe Treviño and Michael E. Brown, behaving ethically in business is more complex than it seems on the surface for a variety of reasons.[4] To begin with, ethical decisions are complex. For example, someone might argue that hiring children for factory jobs in overseas countries is unethical. Yet if these children lose their jobs, many would starve or turn to crime to survive. Second, people do not always recognize the moral issues involved in a decision. The home-maintenance worker who finds a butcher knife under the bed might not think that he has a role to play in perhaps preventing murder. Sometimes language hides the moral issue involved, such as when the term "file sharing" music replaces "stealing" music.

Another complexity in making ethical decisions is that people have different levels of moral development. At one end of the scale, some people behave morally just to escape punishment. At the other end of the scale, some people are morally developed to the point that they are guided by principles of justice and want to help as many people as possible. The environment in which we work also influences whether we behave ethically. Suppose a restaurant owner encourages such practices as serving customers food that was accidentally dropped on the kitchen floor. An individual server is more likely to engage in such behavior to obey the demands of the owner—even though the server knows that dangerous bacteria may have attached to the food.

A fundamental reason that being unethical is not always easy is that some people have a predisposition to be unethical. The predisposition works almost like a personality trait, compelling certain people to be devious. A person with a **utilitarian predisposition** believes that the value of an act's outcomes should determine whether it is moral.[5] A server with this predisposition might be willing to serve food that dropped on the floor so long as no customer became sick or sued the restaurant. A small business owner with a utilitarian predisposition might be willing to sell fake luxury goods on the Internet so long as nobody complained and he or she was not caught. When asked about why he sold imitation watches, one vendor said, "What's the difference? My watches look like the real thing, and they tell time."

Another major contributor to ethical problems is the same factor that motivates people to do many things—acting out of self-interest. John Bogle, the founder and former chief executive of the Vanguard Groups of Mutual Funds, believes that self-interest contributed to the financial scandals of recent years. "But self-interest got out of hand. It created a bottom-line society in which success is measured in monetary terms. Dollars became the coin of the new realm. Unchecked market forces overwhelmed traditional standards of professional conduct, developed over centuries."[6] Another take on self-interest is that employee fraud intensifies during difficult financial times where workers are experiencing financial pressures in their personal lives. Among these frauds are check-forgery schemes, petty-cash thefts, and taking money from fabricated customer returns.[7] All of these schemes are illegal as well as unethical.

A Survey of the Extent of Ethical Problems

The ethical misdeeds of executives have received substantial publicity in recent years. However, ethical violations by rank-and-file employees are widespread, with stealing and sexual harassment making the list. Figure 15-1 presents data about unethical behavior noticed by employees. As found in other surveys, lying is another widespread ethical problem in the workplace. Lying to either employees or outsiders was observed by 31 percent of employees. These findings might suggest that workers are observant of ethical problems, and willing to note them on a survey.

Frequent Ethical Dilemmas

Certain ethical mistakes, including illegal actions, recur in the workplace. Familiarizing oneself can be helpful in monitoring one's own behavior. The next subsections describe a

FIGURE 15-1   Questionable Workplace Behavior as Reported by Employees

Despite a heightened emphasis on business ethics following scandals earlier
this decade, a significant number of employees say they still witness questionable workplace behavior. Here is the percentage of employees who say
they observed certain behaviors in the previous year, according to a survey
of 2,852 workers by the Ethics Resource Center.

Lying to employees	19%
Engaging in conflicts of interest	16%
Lying to outside stakeholders	12%
Engaging in health and safety violations	11%
Producing poor product quality	9%
Stealing	9%
Sexual harassment	7%

Source: National Business Ethics Survey, Ethics Resource Center, Arlington, VA, 2009 survey. (www.ethics.org).

number of common ethical problems faced by business executives as well as by workers
at lower job levels.[8] Figure 15-2 outlines these problems.

Illegally Copying Software.   A rampant ethical problem is whether or not to illegally copy
computer software. According to the Business Software Alliance, approximately 35 percent
of applications used in business are illegal.[9] Figure 15-3 offers details about and insight
into this widespread ethical dilemma.

Treating People Unfairly.   Being fair to people means equity, reciprocity, and impartiality. Fairness revolves around the issue of giving people equal rewards for accomplishing equal amounts of work. The goal of human resource legislation is to make
decisions about people based on their qualifications and performance—not on the basis

FIGURE 15-2   Frequent Ethical Dilemmas

Many ethical temptations face the individual on the job, forcing him or her to think through
ethical issues practically every workday.

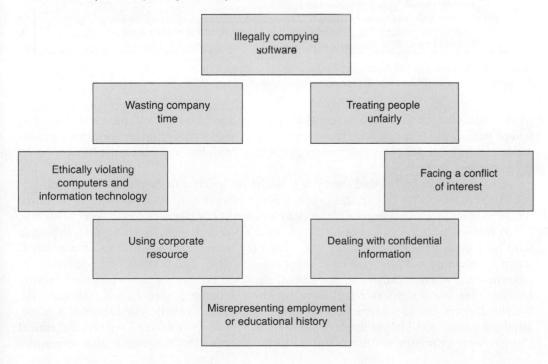

FIGURE 15-3 The Top Ten Reasons for Illegally Copying Software (and Why None of Them Are Good Enough)

A flagrant unethical and **illegal** job behavior is unauthorized copying of software. When confronted with software pirating, people are quick to rationalize their actions. Here are the top ten defenses of software pirates. (None of them are likely to hold up if you are caught.)

1. **I'm allowed to make a backup disk in case something happens to the original, so it must be okay to use it on another machine.** A backup is strictly a backup to be used on the same computer. The original should be safely locked away, and the copy should be stored away only as a backup.
2. **I didn't copy it—a friend gave it to me.** Technically you are right. You would not be guilty of illegally copying software in this case, although your friend would. However, since illegally copied software is regarded as stolen property, you are just as guilty as you would be for stealing it in the first place.
3. **My boss (or department head, or instructor) told me to. It's that person's problem.** The defense "I was just following orders" is a weak one. Complying with your boss's demands to commit an illegal act does not get you off the hook. You could be fired for obeying an order to commit a crime.
4. **I bought the software; shouldn't I be able to do what I want with it?** Software is seldom ever sold to individuals. What is sold is a license to use the software, not full rights to do what you want. When you break open the package, the law assumes that you have agreed to abide by those terms.
5. **It's not like I'm robbing somebody.** Software is intellectual property just like a song, a book, an article, or a trademark. You are taking bread from the table of software engineers when you copy their work.
6. **It's OK if you're using the software for educational purposes.** If education were a justification for theft, driving instructors would be able to steal cars with impunity. There is a doctrine of **fair use** that allows some limited use of written materials in classrooms without permission from the copyright holder.
7. **I needed it, but the price was unreasonably high. If I had to actually pay for it, there is no way I could ever afford it.** Software prices are high for the same reason the price of houses is high: both require a lot of highly skilled labor to create. You cannot steal a DVD player just because you cannot afford one.
8. **I didn't know it was illegal.** Unauthorized duplication of software is a felony in many states and provinces. State and federal laws provide for civil and criminal penalties if you are convicted. It would be difficult to convince a judge or jury that you had no idea that unauthorized copying was illegal.
9. **It's only illegal if you get caught.** Criminal behavior is illegal whether or not you are caught. If you do get caught illegally copying software, you could face fines, imprisonment, and/or civil penalties. Some educational institutions take disciplinary action against software pirates, including suspension.
10. **Oh, come on, everyone is doing it.** This excuse has been used to justify everything from speeding to lynching. The popularity of a criminal act does not make it legal.

Source: The Top Ten Reasons for Illegally Copying Software (and Why None of Them Are Good Enough). Rochester Institute of Technology. Reprinted with permission.

of demographic factors such as gender, race, or age. A fair working environment is where performance is the only factor that counts (equity). Employer–employee expectations must be understood and met (reciprocity). Prejudice and bias must be eliminated (impartiality).

Treating people fairly—and therefore ethically—requires a de-emphasis on political factors, or favoritism. Yet this ethical doctrine is not always easy to implement. It is human nature to want to give bigger rewards (such as fatter raises or bigger orders) to people we like.

A major contributor to treating people unfairly is cronyism, or giving jobs to people who have done personal favors for you. Often the unqualified friend is given a position when competent, and qualified candidates are available. Cronyism is often practiced in government, where heads of government agencies are sometimes appointed mostly because they are a supporter and friend of the person in power. Earl E. Devaney, the Interior Department's inspector general said at a hearing, "Simply stated short of a crime, anything goes at the highest levels of the Department of the Interior." Among the ethical charges were cronyism and cover-ups of incompetence.[10] Cronyism is also sometimes found in business, with buddies, relatives, and lovers often being chosen over more qualified workers for a variety of positions.

Sexually Harassing Coworkers.   In Chapter 9, we looked at sexual harassment as a source of conflict and an illegal act. Sexual harassment is also an ethical issue because it is morally wrong and unfair. All acts of sexual harassment flunk an ethics test. Before sexually harassing another person, the potential harasser should ask, "Would I want a loved one to be treated this way?"

Facing a Conflict of Interest.   Part of being ethical is making business judgments only on the basis of the merits or facts in a situation. Imagine that you are a supervisor who is romantically involved with a worker within the group. When it comes time to assign raises, it will be difficult for you to be objective. A **conflict of interest** occurs when your judgment or objectivity is compromised. Conflicts of interest often take place in the sales end of business. If a company representative accepts a large gift from a sales representative, it may be difficult to make objective judgments about buying from the rep. Yet being taken to dinner by a vendor would not ordinarily cloud one's judgment. Another common example of a conflict of interest is making a hiring decision about a friend who badly needs a job, but is not well qualified for the position.

Blogging has created a new type of conflict of interest because many bloggers are paid for those kind, supposedly objective, comments they insert on the Internet about products and services. The Federal Trade Commission now requires bloggers to clearly disclose any payments or freebies they receive from companies for publishing reviews about their products or services. Penalties include a maximum fine of up to $11,000 per violation.[11]

Dealing with Confidential Information.   An ethical person can be trusted by others not to divulge confidential information unless the welfare of others is at stake. Suppose a coworker tells you in confidence that she is upset with the company and is therefore looking for another job. Behaving ethically, you do not pass along this information to your supervisor even though it would help your supervisor plan for a replacement. Now suppose the scenario changes slightly. Your coworker tells you she is looking for another job because she is upset. She tells you she is so upset that she plans to destroy company computer files on her last day. If your friend does find another job, you might warn the company about her contemplated activities.

The challenge of dealing with confidential information arises in many areas of business, many of which affect interpersonal relations. If you learned that a coworker was indicted for a crime, charged with sexual harassment, or facing bankruptcy, there would be a temptation to gossip about the person. A highly ethical person would not pass along information about the personal difficulties of another person.

Misrepresenting Employment or Education History.   Many people are tempted to distort in a positive direction information about their employment or education history on their job résumé, job application form, and during the interview. Distortion, or lying, of this type is considered to be unethical and can lead to immediate dismissal if discovered. Misrepresentation of credentials takes place at all job levels. Inflated credentials in the executive suite have been an embarrassment to many companies. A survey of 358 senior executives at 53 publicly traded companies has uncovered seven instances of inaccurate claims that an individual had received an academic degree. In recent years, misrepresentation of academic credentials has cost top corporate officials their positions at companies, including RadioShack Corp., vitamin maker Herbalife Ltd., and Usana Health Sciences, Inc.[12]

Using Corporate Resources.   A corporate resource is anything the company owns, including its name and reputation. If Jake Petro worked for Ford Motor Company, for example, it would be unethical for him to establish a body shop and put on his letterhead and Web site, "Jake Petro, Manufacturing Technician, Ford Motor Company." (The card and Web site would imply that the Ford Motor Co. supports this venture.) Other uses of corporate resources fall more into the gray area. It might be quite ethical to borrow a

conflict of interest

A situation that occurs when a person's judgment or objectivity is compromised.

FIGURE 15-4   Eleven Commandments for Computer Ethics

1. Do not use a computer to harm other people. Avoid all obscene, defamatory, threatening, or otherwise harassing messages. Take precautions against others developing repetitive motion disorders.
2. Do not interfere with other people's computer work. (This includes intentionally spreading computer viruses.)
3. Do not snoop around in other people's files.
4. Do not use a computer to steal.
5. Do not use a computer to bear false witness.
6. Do not use or copy software for which you have not paid (see Figure 15-1).
7. Do not use other people's resources without authorization.
8. Do not appropriate other people's intellectual output.
9. Do not use the employer's computer for the personal promotion of commercial goods or services, unless granted permission by the employer.
10. Do think about the social consequences of the program you write.
11. Do use a computer in ways that show consideration and respect.

Source: Adapted and updated from Arlene H. Rinaldi and Florida Atlantic University, rinaldi@acc.fau.edu; "Code of Conduct for Computer and Network Use," *http://www.rit.edu/computerconduct.*

laptop computer for the weekend from your employer to conduct work at home. But it would be less ethical to borrow the laptop computer to prepare income taxes. In the latter case, you might be accused of using corporate resources for personal purposes. Loading personal software on company computers so that you can access your bank account and so forth also can be considered an ethical violation.

Ethically Violating Computers and Information Technology.   As computers dominate the workplace, many ethical issues have arisen in addition to pirating software. One ethical dilemma that surfaces frequently is the fairness of tracking the Web sites a person visits and those he or she buys from. Should this information be sold, like a mailing list? The scams that appear on e-mail every day are another prime example of the unethical use of information technology. Another issue is the fairness of having an employee work at a keyboard for 60 hours in one week when such behavior frequently leads to repetitive motion disorder, vision problems, and back pain. Figure 15-4 lists some major ethical issues involved in computer use.

Wasting Company Time.   Many workers waste company time in the pursuit of personal interests. Among these time wasters are making personal phone calls, shopping by phone or the Internet, visiting sports and pornography sites, talking about personal matters with coworkers, daydreaming, and spending long periods of time smoking outside the building. The problem has become so severe with cell phone calls and text messaging that many employers forbid the use of cell phones while working. The section in Chapter 16 about personal productivity presents data about time wasting on the job.

You may have observed that these common ethical problems are not always clear-cut. Aside from obvious matters such as prohibitions against stealing, lying, cheating, and intimidating, subjectivity enters into ethical decision making. Skill-Building Exercise 15-1 provides an opportunity to try out your ethical reasoning.

Choosing between Two Rights: Dealing with Defining Moments

Ethical decision making usually involves choosing between two options: one we perceive to be right and one we perceive to be wrong. A challenging twist to ethical decision making is to sort through your values when you have to choose between two rights, or two morally sound choices. Joseph L. Badaracco, Jr., uses the term **defining moment** to describe choosing between two or more ideals in which we deeply believe.[13] If you can

defining moment

Choosing between two or more ideals in which one deeply believes.

The Ethics Game

Many companies teach ethics by asking small teams of employees to confront difficult scenarios such as those that follow. Discuss these ethical problems in teams. As you discuss the scenarios, identify the ethical issues involved.

Scenario 1: One of your assignments is to find a contractor to conduct building maintenance for your company headquarters. You invite bids for the job. High-Performance Cleaners, a firm staffed largely by teenagers from troubled families who have criminal records, bids on the job.

Many of these teenagers also have severe learning disabilities and cannot readily find employment. High-Performance Cleaners proves to be the second highest bidder. You:

A. advise High-Performance Cleaners that its bid is too high for consideration and that your company is not a social agency.

B. award the bid to High-Performance Cleaners and justify your actions with a letter to top management talking about social responsibility.

C. falsify the other bids in your report to management, making High-Performance Cleaners the low bidder—and thus the contract winner.

D. explain to High-Performance Cleaners that it lost the bid, but you will award the company a piece of the contract because of its sterling work with teenagers in need.

Scenario 2: You live in Texas, and your company sends you on a three day trip to New York City. Your business dealings in the Big Apple will keep you there Wednesday, Thursday, and Friday morning. You have several friends and relatives in New York, so you decide to stay there until Sunday afternoon. Besides, you want to engage in tourist activities such as taking a boat tour around Manhattan and visiting Radio City Music Hall. When preparing your expense report for your trip, you request payment for all your business-related costs up through Friday afternoon, plus

A. your return trip on Sunday.

B. the return trip and the room cost for Friday and Saturday nights.

C. the return trip, one-half of your weekend food expenses, and two extra nights in the hotel.

D. the return trip and your food costs for the weekend (which you justify because you ate at fast-food restaurants on Wednesday, Thursday, and Friday).

Scenario 3: You are the leader of a self-managing work team in a financial services company. The work of your team has expanded to the point where you are authorized to hire another team member. The team busily interviews a number of candidates from inside and outside the company. The other team members agree that one of the candidates (Pat) has truly outstanding credentials. You agree that Pat is a strong candidate, yet you don't want Pat on the team because the two of you were emotionally involved for about a year. You think that working with Pat would disrupt your concentration and bring back hurtful memories. You decide to

A. tell the group that you have some negative information about Pat's past that would disqualify Pat for the job.

B. telephone Pat and beg that Pat find employment elsewhere.

C. tell the group that you agree Pat is qualified, but explain your concerns about the disruption in concentration and emotional hurt.

D. tell the group that you agree Pat is right for the position, and mention nothing about the past relationship.

Scoring and Observation: Scenario 1, about High-Performance Cleaners, raises dozens of ethical questions, including whether humanitarian considerations can outweigh profit concerns. Teams that chose "a" receive 0 points; "b", 20 points; "c", −10 points; "d", 10 points. (Answer "d" is best here because it would not be fair to give the bid to the second-highest bidder. However, you are still finding a way to reward the High-Performance Cleaners for its meritorious work in the community. Answer "c" is the worst because you would be outright lying.)

Scenario 2 raises ethical issues about using company resources. Teams that chose "a" receive 20 points; "b", 10 points; "c", −15 points; "d", 0 points. (Answer "a" is fairest because the company would expect to reimburse you for your roundtrip plus the expenses up through Friday afternoon. Answer "c" is the worst because it would be unjustified for you to be reimbursed for your vacation in New York.)

Scenario 3 raises issues about fairness in making selection decisions. Teams that chose "a" receive −20 points; "b", −10 points; "c", 15 points; "d", 0 points. (Answer "c" is the most ethical because you are being honest with the group about the reason you do not wish to hire Pat. Answer "a" is the most unethical because you are telling lies about Pat. Furthermore, you might be committing the illegal act of libel.)

learn to work through defining moments, your ethical skills will be enhanced. Let's first take a nonwork example to illustrate a defining moment.

> *Imagine yourself as a basketball referee in a league for boys 10 years old and younger. Luis, the smallest boy on the team, has a self-confidence problem in general, and he has not scored a basket yet this season. This is the final game of the season. The other team is ahead by 10 points with one minute to go. Luis lets fly with a shot that goes into the basket, but his right heel is on the line. If the goal is allowed, Luis will experience one of the happiest moments in his life, and his self-confidence might increase. You strongly believe in helping people grow and develop. Yet you also strongly believe in following the rules of sports. What should you do?*

You may have recognized that a defining moment is a role conflict in which you have to choose between competing values. A CEO might deeply believe that she has an obligation

Dealing with Defining Moments

The toughest ethical choices for many people occur when they have to choose between two rights. The result is a defining moment, because we are challenged to think in a deeper way by choosing between two or more ideals. Working individually or in teams, deal with the two following defining moments. Explain why these scenarios could require choosing between two rights, and explain the reasoning behind your decisions.

Scenario 1: You are the manager of a department in a business firm that assigns each department a fixed amount of money for salary increases each year. An average-performing member of the department asks you in advance for an above-average increase. He explains that his mother has developed multiple sclerosis and requires the services of a paid helper from time to time. You are concerned that if you give this man an above-average increase,

somebody else in the department will have to receive a below-average increase.

Scenario 2: You are the team leader of an e-tailing (retail selling over the Internet) group. In recent months each team member has been working about 60 hours per week, with little prospect of the workload decreasing in the future. Since the e-tailing project is still losing money, higher management insists that one person be dropped from the team. One member of the team, Mildred, is willing to work only 45 hours per week because she spends considerable time volunteering with autistic children. Mildred's work is satisfactory, but her output is the lowest in the group because of her shorter number of working hours. You must make a decision about whether to recommend that Mildred be dismissed.

to the stockholders to make a profit, and also believe in being generous and fair toward employees. However, to make a profit this year she will be forced to lay off several good employees with long seniority. The CEO now faces a moment of truth. Badaracco suggests that the individual can work through a defining moment by discovering "Who am I?" You discover who you are by soul searching answers to three questions:

1. What feelings and intuitions are coming into conflict in this situation?
2. Which of the values that are in conflict are the most deeply rooted in my life?
3. What combinations of expediency and shrewdness, coupled with imagination and boldness, will help me implement my personal understanding of what is right?

Skill-Building Exercise 15-2 gives you an opportunity to deal with defining moments. The three questions just asked could help you find answers, but do not be constrained by these questions.

GUIDELINES FOR BEHAVING ETHICALLY

LEARNING OBJECTIVE 3

Following guidelines for ethical behavior is the heart of being ethical. Although many people behave ethically without studying ethical guidelines, they are usually following guidelines programmed into their minds early in life. The Golden Rule exemplifies a guideline taught by parents, grandparents, and kindergarten teachers. In this section, we approach ethical guidelines from five perspectives: (1) developing virtuousness, (2) following a guide to ethical decision making, (3) developing strong relationships with work associates, (4) using corporate ethics programs, and (5) following an applicable professional code of conduct.

Developing Virtuousness

A deep-rooted approach to behaving ethically is to have strong moral and ethical principles, or to be virtuous. A person of high virtue has good character, and genuine motivation and intentions. A major problem in becoming virtuous is to agree on what values constitute virtuousness. Management professor Edwin A. Locke has prepared a modern analysis of what values constitute virtue in a business environment.[14] Here we highlight his findings because they are representative of what constitutes virtuousness. Other observers might have a different list of virtuous values.

1. Rationality is a principle that leads to being virtuousness. Being rational includes taking reality (facts) seriously, thinking hard, thinking long range, and thinking of the consequences of one's actions. A rational parachute technician would not ship a defective parachute just because it was close to quitting time, and he did not want to work late. And we hope that the manager is rational (and therefore ethical) when writing performance evaluations.

2. Honesty, the refusal to fake reality, is a value that contributes directly to ethical behavior. Being dishonest can also be illegal, such as when a company lies to the Internal Revenue Service about expenses it incurred or hides revenue when preparing a tax report. Dishonesty in terms of making false statements about the financial health of an enterprise has been one of the most frequent business frauds. Being caught lying can lead to dismissal at many employers. An example of such a lie would be blaming someone else for a mistake of your own. *Integrity* means loyalty to one's rational convictions, or sticking with one's principles. If you believe that favoritism is immoral, then you would not recommend that the company hire a friend of yours who you know to be unqualified.

3. Independence refers to the responsibility of using your own rational judgment rather than relying too heavily on the thinking of others. In personal life, being independent means not relying too heavily on others for permanent support. A worker with a strong value of independence would not readily go along with the thinking of the group if he or she had a better idea.

4. Productivity means creating, or obtaining through trade, the materials values your life requires. You are therefore virtuous if are productive on the job and contribute enough to be worth of your compensation. *Justice* refers to looking at the facts of the character and achievements of others and judging them objectively. To be just is to be fair, such as willing to pay somebody what they are worth, or pay a fair price for merchandise. When a big company executive "squeezes" a supplier to the point that the supplier can barely make a profit, the executive is not practicing justice.

5. Forgiveness is a virtue providing the breach of morality was not too severe, such as forging an employee who at a sandwich without paying when eating food without paying was not authorized. *Pride* in the context of virtues refers to working to perfect one's moral character. You would thus be proud because you are virtuous.

The above values that contribute to being virtuousness are useful in the study of human relations because they all translate into interpersonal skills, such as knowing how to be productive and treat people justly.

Following a Guide to Ethical Decision Making

A powerful strategy for behaving ethically is to follow a guide for ethical decision making. Such a guide for making contemplated decisions includes testing ethics. **Ethical screening** refers to running a contemplated decision or action through an ethics test. Such screening makes the most sense when the contemplated action or decision is not clearly ethical or unethical. If a sales representative were to take a favorite customer to Pizza Hut for lunch, an ethical screen would not be necessary. Nobody would interpret a pizza, salad, and a beer or soft drink to be a serious bribe. Assume, instead, that the sales rep offered to give the customer an under-the-table gift of $1000 for placing a large offer with the rep's firm. The sales representative's behavior would be so blatantly unethical that conducting an ethical screen would be unnecessary.

Several useful ethical screens, or guides to ethical decision making, have been developed. A guide developed by Treviño and Nelson is presented here because it incorporates the basic ideas in other ethical tests.[15] After studying this guide, you will be asked to ethically screen three different scenarios. The eight steps to sound ethical decision making follow.

1. Gather the facts. When making an important decision in business, it is necessary to gather relevant facts. Ask yourself the following questions: "Are there any legal issues involved here?" "Is there precedent in our firm with respect to this type of decision?" "Do I have the authority to make this decision?" "Are there company rules and regulations governing such a decision?"

The manager of a child care center needed to hire an additional child care specialist. One of the applicants was a 55-year-old male with experience as a father and grandfather. The manager judged him to be qualified, yet she knew that many parents would

LEARNING OBJECTIVE 4

ethical screening

Running a contemplated decision or action through an ethics test.

not want their preschool children to be cared for by a middle-aged male. Many people perceive that a younger woman is better qualified for child care than an older man. The manager therefore had to gather considerable facts about the situation, including facts about job discrimination and precedents in hiring males as child care specialists.

Gathering facts is influenced by emotion, with the result that ethical decision making is not an entirely rational process.[16] We tend to interpret facts based upon our biases and preconceived notions. For example, if the child care center manager has heard negative information about middle-aged men who want to engage in child care, the manager might look hard for indicators that this candidate should be disqualified.

2. Define the ethical issues. The ethical issues in a given decision are often more complicated than a first glance suggests. When faced with a complex decision, it may be helpful to talk over the ethical issues with another person. The ethical issues might involve character traits such as being kind and caring and treating others with respect. Or the ethical issues might relate to some of the common ethical problems described earlier in the chapter. Among them are facing conflict of interest, dealing with confidential information, and using corporate resources.

The manager of the child care center is facing such ethical issues as fairness, job discrimination, and meeting the demands of customers at the expense of job applicants. The manager is also facing a diversity issue: Should the workforce in a child care center be culturally diverse, or do we hire only young women?

3. Identify the affected parties. When faced with a complex ethical decision, it is important to identify all the affected parties. Major corporate decisions can affect thousands of people. If a company decides to shut down a plant and outsource the manufacturing to a low-wage country, thousands of individuals and many different parties are affected. Workers lose their jobs, suppliers lose their customers, the local government loses out on tax revenues, and local merchants lose many of their customers. You may need to brainstorm with a few others to think of all the parties affected by a given decision.

The parties affected by the decision about hiring or not hiring the 55-year-old male include the applicant himself, the children, the parents, and the board of directors of the child care center. The government might also be involved if the man were rejected and filed charges of age and sex discrimination.

4. Identify the consequences. After you have identified the parties affected by a decision, the next step is to predict the consequences for each party. It may not be necessary to identify every consequence, yet it is important to identify the consequences with the highest probability of occurring and those with the most negative outcomes. The problem is that many people can be harmed by an unethical decision, such as not fully describing the possible side effects of a diet program.

Both short-term and long-term consequences should be specified. A company closing a plant might create considerable short-term turmoil, but in the long term the company might be healthier. People participating in a diet program might achieve their short-term objective of losing weight. Yet in the long term, their health might be adversely affected because the diet is not nutritionally balanced.

The *symbolic* consequences of an action are important. Every action and decision sends a message (the decision is a symbol of something). If a company moves manufacturing out of a community to save on labor costs, it means that the short-term welfare of domestic employees is less important than profit or perhaps the company surviving.

We return to the child care manager and the job applicant. If the applicant does not get the job, his welfare will be adversely affected. He has been laid off by a large employer and cannot find work in his regular field. His family will also suffer because he will not be able to make a financial contribution to the family. Yet if the man is hired, the child care center may suffer. Many traditionally minded parents will say, "Absolutely not. I do not want my child cared for by a middle-aged man. He could be a child molester." (It may be unethical for people to have vicious stereotypes, yet they still exist.) If the child care center does hire the man, the act will symbolize the fact that the owners of the center value diversity.

5. Identify the obligations. Identify the obligations and the reasons for each obligation when making a complex decision. The manufacturer of automotive brakes has an obligation to produce and sell only brakes that meet high safety standards. The obligation is to the auto manufacturer who purchases the brakes and, more important, to the ultimate consumer whose safety depends on effective brakes. The reason for the obligation to make safe brakes is that lives are at stake. The child care center owner has an obligation to provide for the safety and health of the children at the center. She must also provide for the peace of mind of the parents and be a good citizen of the community in which the center is located. The decision about hiring the candidate in question must be balanced against all these obligations.

6. Consider your character and integrity. A core consideration when faced with an ethical dilemma is how relevant people would judge your character and integrity. What would your family, friends, significant others, teachers, and coworkers think of your actions? To refine this thinking even further, how would you feel if your actions were publicly disclosed in the local newspaper or over e-mail? Would you want the world to know that you gave an under-the-table kickback or that you sexually harassed a frightened teenager working for you? If you would be proud for others to know what decision you made when you faced an ethical dilemma, you are probably making the right decision.

The child care center manager might ponder how she would feel if the following information were released in the local newspaper or on the Internet:

> The manager of Good Times Child Care recently rejected the application of a 55-year-old man for a child care specialist position. She said that although Mr. _____ was well qualified from an experience and personality standpoint, she couldn't hire him. She said that Good Times would lose too much business because many parents would fear that Mr. _____ was a child molester or pedophile.

7. Think creatively about potential actions. When faced with an ethical dilemma, put yourself in a creative-thinking mode. Stretch your imagination to invent several options rather than thinking you have only two choices—to do or not do something. Creative thinking may point toward a third, and even fourth, alternative. Imagine this ethical dilemma: A purchasing agent is told that if her firm awards a contract to the sales representative's firm, she will find a leather jacket of her choice delivered to her door. The purchasing agent says to herself, "I think we should award the contract to the firm, but I cannot accept the gift. Yet if I turn down the gift, I will be forfeiting a valuable possession that the company simply regards as a cost of doing business."

The purchasing agent can search for another alternative. She may say to the sales rep, "We will give the contract to your firm because your products fit our requirements. I thank you for the offer of the leather jacket, but instead I would like you to give the jacket to the Salvation Army."

A creative alternative for the child care manager might be to offer the applicant the next position that opened for an office manager or maintenance person in the center. In this way, she would be offering a qualified applicant a job, but placing him in a position more acceptable to parents. Or, do you feel this is a cop-out?

8. Check your intuition. So far we have emphasized the rational side of ethical decision making. Another effective way of conducting an ethical screen is to rely on your intuition. How does the contemplated decision feel? Would you be proud of yourself, or would you hate yourself if you made the decision? Imagine how you would feel if you took money from the handbag of a woman sleeping in the park. Would you feel the same way if you took a kickback, sold somebody a defective product, or sold an 80-year-old man an insurance policy he didn't need? How will the manager of the child care center feel if she turns down the man for the child care specialist position? In general, experienced workers rely more heavily on intuition when making ethical choices. The reason is that intuition is based largely on experience.[17] Rules for ethical behavior are important, yet often we have to follow our hunches. Experience and rules are not wasted because intuition includes both experienced and having studied rules in the past.

You are encouraged to use the guide for ethical decision making when you next face an ethical dilemma of consequence. Skill-Building Exercise 15-3 gives you an opportunity to practice using the eight steps for ethical decision making.

Ethical Decision Making

Working in small groups, take one or more of the following ethical dilemmas through the eight steps for screening contemplated decisions. If more than one group chooses the same scenario, compare your answers for the various steps.

Scenario 1: To Recycle or Not. Your group is the top management team at a large insurance company. Despite the movement toward digitizing all records, your firm still generates tons of paper each month. Customer payments alone account for truckloads of envelopes each year. The paper recyclers in your area claim that they can hardly find a market any longer for used paper, so they will be charging you just to accept your paper for recycling. Your group is wondering whether to recycle.

Scenario 2: The Hole in the Résumé. Emily has been working for the family business as an office manager for five years. Because the family business is being sold, Emily has started a job hunt. She also welcomes the opportunity to work in a larger company so that she could learn more about how a big company operates. As she begins preparing her job résumé, she ponders how to classify the year of unemployment prior to working at the family business. During that year, she worked a total of 10 weeks in entry-level jobs at three fast-food restaurants. Otherwise she filled her time

with such activities as walking in the park, watching daytime television shows, surfing the Internet, playing video games, and pursuing her hobby of visiting graveyards. Emily finally decides to tack that year onto the five years in the family business. She indicates on her résumé that she has been working six years at the family business. As Emily says, "It's a tight job market for office managers, and I don't want to raise any red flags." Evaluate the ethics of Emily's decision to fill in the year off from work, and perhaps offer her some advice.

Scenario 3: The High-Profit Toys. You are a toy company executive starting to plan your holiday season line. You anticipate that the season's hottest item will be Robo-Woman, a battery-operated crime fighter and superheroine. Robo-Woman should wholesale for $25 and retail for $45. Your company figures to earn $15 per unit. You receive a sales call from a manufacturing broker who says he can produce any toy you want for one-third of your present manufacturing cost. He admits that the manufacturer he represents uses prison labor in China, but insists that his business arrangement violates no law. You estimate you can earn $20 per unit if you do business with the manufacturing broker. Your decision is whether to do business with him.

Developing Strong Relationships with Work Associates

A provocative explanation of the causes of unethical behavior emphasizes the strength of relationships among people.[18] Assume that two people have close professional ties to each other, such as having worked together for a long time or knowing each other both on and off the job. As a consequence, they are likely to behave ethically toward one another on the job. In contrast, if a weak professional relationship exists between two individuals, either party is more likely to engage in an unethical relationship. The owner of an auto service center is more likely to behave unethically toward a stranger passing through town than toward a long-time customer. (The section in Chapter 13 about building relationships with coworkers and work associates provides suggestions for developing strong relationships.) The opportunity for unethical behavior between strangers is often minimized because individuals typically do not trust strangers with sensitive information or valuables.

The ethical skill-building consequence of information about personal relationships is that building stronger relationships with people is likely to enhance ethical behavior. If you build strong relationships with work associates, you are likely to behave more ethically toward them. Similarly, your work associates are likely to behave more ethically toward you. The work associates I refer to are all your contacts, both internal and external customers.

Self-Assessment Quiz 15-2 provides an opportunity to think of the ethical aspects of your relationships with coworkers.

Using Corporate Ethics Programs

Many organizations have various programs and procedures for promoting ethical behavior. Among them are committees that monitor ethical behavior, training programs in ethics, and vehicles for reporting ethical violations. The presence of these programs is designed to create an atmosphere in which unethical behavior is discouraged and reporting on unethical behavior is encouraged.

Ethics hotlines are one of the best established programs to help individuals avoid unethical behavior. Should a person be faced with an ethical dilemma, the person calls a toll-free line to speak to a counselor about the dilemma. Sometimes employees ask questions to help interpret a policy, such as "Is it okay to ask my boss for a date?" or "Are

The Ethical Workplace Relationships Inventory

Directions: Describe how well you agree with each of the following statements, using the following scale: disagree strongly (DS); disagree (D); neutral (N); agree (A), agree strongly (AS). Circle the number in the appropriate column.

		DS	D	N	A	AS
1.	I would give a sexually suggestive hug to a team member who I thought was physically attractive.	5	4	3	2	1
2.	If I were asked to purchase pizza and soft drinks for the group, I would be willing to ask for more in reimbursement than I actually paid.	5	4	3	2	1
3.	If I were the manager of my group, I would be willing to put pressure on group members to purchase direct sales items from me, such as beauty and health products.	5	4	3	2	1
4.	I would be willing to recommend for promotion to supervisor a worker from a different racial group than my own.	1	2	3	4	5
5.	If I didn't get along with my manager or team leader, I would be willing to start a rumor that he or she was undergoing bankruptcy.	5	4	3	2	1
6.	To damage the reputation of a coworker I didn't like, I would be willing to write a negative blog about the company and sign his or her name.	5	4	3	2	1
7.	I like the idea of encouraging a coworker to complain about a mutual boss, and then report those negative comments back to the boss.	5	4	3	2	1
8.	If I were the team member who made a serious error on a project, I would quickly inform our team leader before the blame was placed on another team member.	1	2	3	4	5
9.	If I heard that a company executive was arrested in a domestic violence incident, I would immediately inform other employees.	5	4	3	2	1
10.	Stealing an idea from a coworker, and then taking credit for that idea is totally unacceptable under any circumstance.	1	2	3	4	5

Total Score _____

Scoring and Interpretation: Add the numbers you have circled to obtain your total score.

45–50 You are strongly ethical in your relationships with coworkers.

30–44 You show an average degree of ethical behavior in your workplace relationships and should therefore become more sensitive to ethical issues.

10–29 Your ethical values could lead you to develop a negative relationship with work associates, assuming that your unethical behavior is caught. Begin a serious study of business ethics.

we supposed to give senior citizen discounts to customers who qualify but do not ask for one?" At other times, a more pressing ethical issue might be addressed, such as "Is it ethical to lay off a worker just five months short of his qualifying for a full pension?"

Human resource professionals contend that no amount of training will ensure that employees will act ethically in every situation, particularly because ethics deals with subtle matters rather than strictly right or wrong. Deborah Haliczer, director of employee relations at Northern Illinois University, explains, however, that training is valuable in starting a useful dialogue about right and wrong behavior that employees could remember in murky situations.[19]

Wells Fargo & Co., a mammoth bank, emphasizes both a code of conduct and ethics training. Its Code of Ethics and Business Conduct specifies policies and standards for employees, covering a variety of topics from maintaining accurate records to participating in civic activities. Each year, employees also participate in ethics training. Any Wells Fargo employee may ask questions or report ethical breaches anonymously using an ethics hotline or dedicated e-mail address. The company will fire violators, dismissing

FIGURE 15-5 Representative Suggestions for Helping a Company Contribute to a Sustainable Environment

1. Conserve energy by adjusting thermostats to keep working areas cooler during cold months, and warmer during warm months.

2. Do what you can to encourage your company and coworkers to send to recycling centers no-longer-in-use electronic devices, such as desktop computers, laptop computers, cell phones, and personal digital assistants.

3. Spread the word about the environmental good that be accomplished from making new products from recycled goods, such as paving stones and park benches made from recycled bottles and tires. The entire re-manufacturing industry relies on the re-use of manufactured materials.

4. Do what you can to create a buzz about the possibilities of photovoltaic technology that is used to convert sunlight into clean energy. Alert influential people to energy-saving and money-saving solar heating systems, such as solar buildings that provide solar hot water and solar heating.

5. Place a lawn on the roof that can reduce its surface temperature by 70° F and internal temperatures by 15° F.

6. Carpool to work with at least three coworkers, and provide preferred parking spaces for carpoolers and hybrid or electric cars.

7. Campaign for a 4-day, 40-hour work week, which can save enormous amounts of energy by less commuting along with less heating and cooling of the workplace. (However, if the employees drive considerably on their day off and use more heating and cooling at home, much of the energy savings will be lost.)

8. Encourage employee use of mass transportation, and provide company shuttle busses from locations convenient to where employees live.

9. Offer employees at least $2,000 toward the purchase of a hybrid vehicle or electric car.

10. Turn off electronic machines when not in use unless starting and stopping them frequently uses more energy than leaving the machines turned on during working hours. Encourage the replacement of incandescent bulbs with fluorescent ones (providing the replacement bulb provides enough light for the purpose).

11. Recycle as many packages as possible and purchase products, such as office furniture and driveways, made from recycled products including vehicle tires. When possible, use old newspapers for packing material instead of new paper and plastic.

12. Use mugs instead of Styrofoam and set up bins to recycle aluminum cans and plastic bottles.

13. When constructing a new building, seek Leadership in Energy and Environmental Design (LEED) certification from the U.S. Green Building Council.

14. Provide bicycle racks and shows that enable employees to bike to work. Biking to work will save considerable energy as well as decrease carbon dioxide emissions.

15. Construct a system that captures rainwater to be reused for irrigation.

16. Grow as much vegetation on company premises as feasible, including celebrating special events by planting another tree. Use plants that are native to the region because native vegetation does not require as much maintenance, fertilizer, chemical sprays, or water.

17. Drink as much tap water as possible to minimize the use of bottled water, or filter tap water to one's specifications.

18. Combat litter and clutter in your work area and on company premises to help attain a pleasant, environmentally friendly atmosphere. Take such actions as alerting the company to exposed, rusted pipes, broken concrete in the parking lot, peeling paint, and broken fences.

19. Encourage people in your network not to drive at high speeds or sit in an idling vehicle while making phone calls or sending text messages. Encourage safe driving in general because vehicular accidents consume enormous amounts of energy, including tow trucks, salvage operations, and life-sustaining hospital stays. Also encourage them to walk to errands instead of driving, whenever feasible.

20. A general guideline is to use less stuff and less energy.

21. My suggestions. _____

Sources: Several of the ideas are from Ben Elgin and Brian Grow, "The Dirty Secret of Recycling Electronics," *Business* Week, October 27, 2008, pp. 040–044; Letita M. Aaron, "The Big Payback," *Black Enterprise*, May 2009, pp. 64–66; Michael Barbaro, "At Wal-Mart, Lessons in Self-Help," *The New York Times* (*nytimes.com*), April 5, 2007; Bryan Walsh, "Thank God It's Thursday," Time, September 7, 2009, p. 58; Melanie Warner, "Plastic Potion No. 9," *Fast* Company, September 2008, p. 88; Charles Lockwood, "Building the Green Way," *Harvard Business Review*, June 2006, pp. 129–137; David Roberts, "Another Inconvenient Truth," *Fast Company*, March 2008, p. 70; Tom Szaky, *Revolution in a Bottle* (New York: Portfolio, 2009).

about 100 people a year for misconduct ranging from conflicts of interest to cheating on incentive plans. Patricia Callahan, executive vice president and director of human resources at the bank, says, "I'm the biggest soft touch in the world. But when someone lies or cheats, you can't have people like that representing us to our customers, whose trust is all we have."[20]

The link between the programs just described and individual ethical skills is that these programs assist a worker's skill development. For example, if you become comfortable in asking about ethical issues, or turning in ethical violators, you have become more ethically skilled.

Being Environmentally Conscious

Another ethical skill is to be *green* or to do your job in helping sustain the physical environment. (*Green* derives from the idea that green vegetations such as trees and forests are a plus for the environment.) The reasoning behind this statement is that it is morally responsible to protect the environment. Do not be concerned with taking sides on the issue of global warming. Whether or not humans and the carbon dioxide emissions they create have contributed to global warming, the physical environment needs your help.

The skill of being environmentally conscious has two major components. First is to take as many steps as you can individually to help preserve the environment even in such small steps as carrying a reusable cloth bag to the grocery store, and not throwing a plastic bottle on a lawn. Second is to be an advocate for the environment by mentioning its importance at work. You might, for example, present data to management about how solar heating can save the company money in the long run, and how benches and walkways made from recycled tires and plastics are attractive and economical. Figure 15-5 gives you a starting point for contributing to a sustainable environment. You might want to add to this list with suggestions of your own, or those you find in the media and scientific articles.

You may need to use your communication persuasion skills to make an impact on the environment. And you will also need to use your positive political skills so that you will not be perceived as an environmental, tree-hugging, pest.

You are invited to do Skill-Building Exercise 15-4 to get started right away in improving the physical environment.

BACK TO THE OPENING CASE

John S. Sherigan, the CEO of Electronic Recyclers International, has chosen a path that most people would consider to be highly ethical. His company removes toxic waste from the environment, and he assists in the rehabilitation of former convicts. At the same time, the company, ERI, continues to prosper and grow. Sherigan is another example of "doing well by doing good."

Following an Applicable Professional Code of Conduct

Professional codes of conduct are prescribed for many occupational groups, including physicians, nurses, lawyers, paralegals, purchasing managers and agents, and real estate salespeople. A useful ethical guide for members of these groups is to follow the code of conduct for their profession. If the profession or trade is licensed by the state or province, a worker can be punished for deviating from the code of conduct specified by the state. The code of conduct developed by the profession or trade is separate from the legal code, but usually supports the same principles and practices. Some of these codes of conduct developed by the professional associations are 50 and 60 pages long; yet, all are guided by the kind of ethical principles implied in the ethical decision-making guide described earlier. Figure 15-6 presents a sampling of provisions from these codes of conduct.

Be Ready to Exert Upward Ethical Leadership

upward ethical leadership

The leadership displayed by individuals who take action to maintain ethical standards, although higher-ups engage in questionable moral behaviors.

A politically delicate situation can arise when a worker wants to behave ethically, yet he or she works for an unethical manager. He or she might worry that being ethical will lead to being reprimanded or job loss. The ethical person working for an unethical boss might feel that his or her values are being compromised, such as a virtuous credit card specialist being told to approve credit cards for people who will probably wind up paying many late fees. **Upward ethical leadership** is leadership displayed by individuals who take action to maintain ethical standards, although higher-ups engage in questionable moral behaviors.[21]

FIGURE 15-6   Excerpts from Professional Codes of Conduct

Professional Organization	Sample of Ethical Guidelines and Regulations
Institute of Management Accountants	1. Maintain an appropriate level of professional competence by ongoing development of their knowledge and skills. 2. Refrain from disclosing confidential information acquired in the course of their work and monitor their activities to assure the maintenance of that confidentiality. 3. Actual or apparent conflicts of interest and advise all appropriate parties of any potential conflict.
National Association of Legal Assistants	1. A legal assistant (paralegal) must not perform any of the duties that attorneys only may perform nor take any actions that attorneys may not take. 2. A legal assistant may perform any task which is properly delegated and supervised by an attorney, as long as the attorney is ultimately responsible to the client, maintains a direct relationship with the client, and assumes professional responsibility for the work product. 3. A legal assistant must protect the confidences of a client and must not violate any rule or statute now in effect or hereafter enacted controlling the doctrine of privileged communications between a client and an attorney.
National Association of Purchasing Management	1. Avoid the intent and appearance of unethical or compromising practice in relationships, actions, and communications. 2. Refrain from any private business or professional activity that would create a conflict between personal interests and the interest of the employer. 3. Refrain from soliciting or accepting money, loans, credits, or prejudicial discounts, and the acceptance of gifts, entertainment, favors, or services from present or potential suppliers which might influence, or appear to influence purchasing decisions.

Sources: Institute of Management Accountants Code of Ethics; National Association of Legal Assistants Professional Standards; National Association of Purchasing Management Principles and Standards of Purchasing Practice.

Confronting the Unethical Boss

One student plays the role of Fred, a manager who makes frequent business trips by airplanes. Fred also likes to fly frequently on vacation, and appreciates accumulating frequent-flyer miles. Company policy allows employees to keep the frequent-flyer miles they accumulate for work. So Fred will often take indirect trips to a destination to accumulate more air miles. For example, to fly to San Francisco, he will flew from Boston to Atlanta, and then to San Francisco. In this instance, he could have made a shorter trip by flying directly from Boston to San Francisco, or from Boston to Chicago to San Francisco. In general, the longer, indirect flights are more expensive.

Another person plays the role of Kelly, the office administrative assistant who sometimes helps Fred prepare his travel vouchers. Kelly, who has good knowledge of geography, notices this strange pattern of Fred taking indirect flights. She is also aware of company policy that permits employees to accumulate frequent flyer miles that are earned on business trips. Kelley is disturbed about what she perceives to be an inappropriate use of company resources—and therefore an ethical violation.

Kelly decides to discuss with Fred this most likely ethical violation. The role-play takes place in Fred's cubicle, and you can imagine how defensive Fred is going to be.

Run the role-play for about five minutes. For both scenarios, observers rate the role players on two dimensions, using a 1-to-5 scale from very poor to very good. One dimension is "effective use of human relations techniques." Observers look to see if Kelly can preserve her sense of ethics while not doing too much damage to her relationship with her boss, Fred. The second dimension is "acting ability." A few observers might voluntarily provide feedback to the role players in terms of sharing their ratings and observations. The course instructor might also provide feedback.

At the extreme, an employee might blow the whistle on the boss, and report the unethical behavior to top management or a government agency. An example would be telling the Consumer Protection Agency that your company was selling cribs that could trap a baby's head after your boss refused to accept your complaint.

The upward leadership approach would be to attempt to resolve the problem before going to the extreme of whistle blowing. The employee who spots the immoral or unethical behavior would use problem-solving and communication skills, along with conflict resolution skills. For example, the employee who spotted the potential head-trap problem might say to the boss, "I have a problem and I would like to discuss it with you." The employee would therefore be engaging the boss in helping solve the problem. Recognizing that you have less power than your boss, you would have to be diplomatic and nonaccusatory. It would be important to point to the problem (the possibility of an infant getting his or her head stuck) rather than accusing the boss of being unethical or immoral.

Skill-Building Exercise 15-5 gives you an opportunity to practice upward leadership skills for correcting unethical behavior.

SELF-ASSESSMENT QUIZZES IN OVERVIEW

Self-Assessment Quiz 15-1, The Ethical Reasoning Inventory, can be used as an alert to keep your ethical values in mind whenever faced with an ethical dilemma. Although you may study ethics and learn to use a guide to ethical decision making, your values will continue to exert a strong influence on your behavior. For example, if a person values the environment, he or she will not empty a car ashtray of cigarette butts on a parking lot pavement. If you know that your ethical values are in the low range, you will have to work extra hard to be ethical in work and personal life. Self-Assessment Quiz 15-2, The Ethical Workplace Relationships Inventory, is also about ethical reasoning but focuses on interpersonal relationships in the workplace. How ethically you relate to others is a major factor in building your ethical reputation.

Concept Review and Reinforcement

Key Terms

character trait 333
moral intensity 335

conflict of interest 339
defining moment 340

ethical screening 343
upward ethical leadership 350

Summary

Ethics refers to moral choices, or what is good and bad, right and wrong, just and unjust, and what people should do. Ethics turn values into action. A person's ethical code has a significant impact on his or her interpersonal relationships.

Understanding ethics is important for a variety of reasons. First, people are motivated by self-interest and a desire to be morally right. Second, good ethics can enhance business and avoid illegal acts. Third, having high ethics improves the quality of work life.

Being ethical isn't always easy for several reasons, including the complexity of ethical decisions, lack of recognition of the moral issues, poor moral development, and pressures from the work environment. Ethical violations in the form of lying are widespread in the workplace. Another problem is that some people have a utilitarian predisposition that tends toward unethical behavior. Self-interest drives many people toward unethical behavior.

Commonly faced ethical dilemmas include illegally copying software, treating people unfairly including cronyism, sexually harassing coworkers, facing a conflict of interest, dealing with confidential information, misrepresenting employment and educational history, using corporate resources, ethically violating computers and information technology, and wasting company time.

A challenging twist to ethical decision making is to sort through your values when you have to choose between two morally sound choices. A defining moment is when you have to choose between two or more ideals in which you deeply believe.

One strategy for behaving ethically is to develop virtuousness that includes rationality, honesty, independence, productivity, and forgiveness. A key strategy for behaving ethically is to follow the eight steps in making a contemplated decision:

1. Gather the facts.
2. Define the ethical issues.
3. Identify the affected parties.
4. Identify the consequences.
5. Identify the obligations (such as to customers and society).
6. Consider your character and integrity.
7. Think creatively about potential actions.
8. Check your intuition.

Another way to raise the level of ethical behavior is to form strong professional relationships with work associates. This is true because people tend to behave more ethically toward people who are close to them. At times using a corporate program such as an ethics hotline can help a person resolve ethical dilemmas. Being environmentally conscious contributes to ethical behavior. Following an applicable code of professional conduct, such as that for accountants, paralegals, and purchasing specialists, is another guide to behaving ethically. Upward leadership behavior can help you deal with the situation of maintaining ethical standards when the boss engages in questionable moral behavior.

Questions for Discussion and Review

1. To what extent does the owner of the electronics recycling business described in the chapter opener have an ethical obligation to tell customers that many of his employees have a prison record?

2. How can behaving ethically improve a person's interpersonal relationships on the job?

3. What would most likely be some of the specific behaviors of a manager who scored 20 points on the ethical reasoning inventory?

4. What is your opinion of the ethics of using the wi-fi access of other people, including business firms when you are not a customer, without asking permission?

5. What evidence can you present that coworkers or fellow students really care if you behave ethically?

6. Provide an example of an action in business that might be unethical but not illegal.

7. Virtually all accountants have studied ethics as part of their education, yet many business scandals involve accountants. What's their problem?

8. Based on your knowledge of human behavior, why do professional codes of conduct—such as those for doctors, paralegals, and realtors—not prevent all unethical behavior on the part of members?

9. Check out the Web site of a couple of major business corporations. What conclusion do you reach about whether an environmentally conscious (or green) person would fit in those companies?

10. What decision of ethical consequence have you made in the last year that you would not mind having publicly disclosed?

The Web Corner

http://www.ethics.org
(Ethics Resource Center)

http://www.ita.doc
(Information about sustainability and being green presented by the International Trade Administration of the U.S. Department of Commerce)

http://globalethicsuniversity.com
(An examination of many phases of business ethics)

Internet Skill-Builder: Learning from Ethical Role Models

One of the many ways of learning ethical skills is to get good ideas from ethical role models. For example, you might observe a professor who takes the initiative to change a grade upward because she later discovered a calculation error. This Internet skill-builder is more abstract than some others, so you might find it a little frustrating. Search for a few specific ways in which you can learn from an ethical role model. To illustrate, you might learn from a business executive, sports figure, or public servant you admire.

Developing Your
Human Relations Skills

Interpersonal Relations Case 15.1

Is This Company Going Really "Going Out of Business"?

When Cyrus Hassankola moved to Dallas, Texas, a couple of years ago after successfully going out of business in several locales, he decided to settle down and go out of business permanently. "The response was good from day one," the carpet salesman says. Customers rooting through the stacks of oriental rugs in the store he opened on a busy road in North Dallas would sometimes say how sorry they were that he was going out of business. "We're not," Hassankola told them. "It's just the name of the store."

A business literally called "Going Out of Business" didn't sit well in some quarters, one of them the Texas Attorney General's office. So Hassankola—for a limited time only—has stopped going out of business. Now he's running "total liquidations" that "beat every going-out-of-business price." In his vocation, this is established practice. But the arrival of hard times has thrown the survival of the going-out-of-business model into doubt. Everybody else is slashing prices as if there's no tomorrow. Old-line going-out-of-businesses are lost in the crowd.

In 2000 Hassankola flew to the United States, found a green card sponsor and hit the road. He recounts steering rug stores out of business in Maryland, Tennessee, South Carolina, North Carolina, and Georgia. Tired of traveling, Hassankola move to Dallas and in late 2007 opened his extended-stay rug store. When he registered its name as "Going Out of Business," he doesn't recall any tax clerk or bank officer blinking. But when David Beasley caught sight of the sign, his eyes popped.

Beasly, 26, works for the Better Business Bureau. One morning he was cruising around Dallas in his Chevy Cavalier on a preposterous-sales hunt. The banner on an apartment complex read, "Free Rent." On a bedding showroom: "Nobody beats our prices." On a furniture outlet: "Bankruptcy liquidation."

"I understand the desire to stay in business," Beasley said as he drove along. "But you can't do it by going out of business."

Hassankola doubts Texas would have bugged him if Beasley hadn't gotten a TV station to show his "Going Out of Business" sign on local news. When the attorney general's office phoned to scold him, he dropped his "just-the-name-of-the-store" routine without a peep and regrouped.

He replaced the sign with "Cyrus Rug Gallery," and then let fly with a flier: "Due to the impending demolition and redevelopment of our premises, we are forced to sell at auction. *Let our loss be your gain.*" The demolition crisis went on for months. The wreckers didn't arrive. Lately, Hassankola has been hanging a "Liquidation Sale" banner out front.

Case Questions

1. What is your evaluation of the ethics of Cyrus Hassankola labeling his rug store, "Going Out of Business"?
2. What kind of ethical behavior can you really expect from somebody in the retail rug business?
3. What would you advise Hassankola to do to become more ethical and more profitable at the same time?

Source: Barry Newman, "In Texas, There's No Business Like 'Going Out of Business'," *The Wall Street Journal*, June 24, 2009, pp. A1, A2.

Interpersonal Relations Case 15.2

Am I Paid to Be My Manager's TV Repair Technician?

Karen worked for a division of a pharmaceutical company as a member of the technical support team. Among her many responsibilities were keeping the division's desktop computers, laptop computers, printers, and smart phones in working order. Gus, her manager, who had been with the company for about 10 years, had a general understanding of what the tech support staff was doing, but he was more of an administrator than a specialist in communication technology.

Several times in recent weeks, Gus complained to Karen and a few other team members about a problem he was having with a digital television set connected to an internal (rabbit ears) antenna. During a lunch break, he explained to Karen, "I'm going a little crazy. I have four television sets at home. The two big ones are satellite connected and they work just fine. I have a small set in the family room in the basement connected to rabbit ears, and the reception is reasonably good. I am picking up the digital signals with a few halts here and there, but I am getting the reception I need."

"The problem I have is with a relatively new set connected in our upstairs bedroom. I did the channel scan about one year ago, and I was getting the network channels I needed. A few weeks ago I stopped receiving the channels I needed. All that was left was HSN (Home Shopping Network). I must have done a channel scan twenty times to try to fix the problem. Plus, I rotated the antenna a few times. I called tech support at the manufacturer of my set, and the rep couldn't help. He told me to telephone the FCC (Federal Communication Commission). I did that, followed the rep's instructions, and still no signal."

Karen agreed that Gus was facing a frustrating problem, but that many people using antennas on their TV sets have lost reception since the conversion from analog to digital in 2009.

A week later, Gus spoke to Karen again about his TV reception woes. He then asked Karen, "How about you coming over after work some night to help straighten out my TV problem? My wife and I would really appreciate your help. You're a great tech fixer."

Karen pondered for a moment, thinking that Gus was making an unreasonable demand. She replied, "Gus, let me think about your request. I really don't know a lot about TV reception. Also, I am pretty much tied up after work for a couple of weeks."

With a frown on his face, Gus said, "Karen, I know you can help. Please don't let me down."

Case Questions

1. What do you see as any potential ethical issues in Gus' request that Karen attempt to fix his TV set reception problem?
2. What advice might you offer Karen for dealing with this problem?
3. How do Gus' demands fit into the category of expecting Karen to exhibit strong organizational citizenship behavior?

Interpersonal Skills Role-Play

Dealing with an Unusual Request from the Boss

The case about the manager's request for tech support for this television set provides the background information for this role-play. The scenario is another meeting between Gus and Karen. One student plays the role of Gus who is now increasingly frustrated that he cannot get the reception he wants. Just last week he telephoned a television repair service, and was told politely that he should simply hook up the set to cable or satellite TV. But Gus and his wife do not want any more wires running through their house. So this time, Gus is more insistent that Karen come over to his house to fix the problem.

Another person plays the role of Karen who has thought through Gus's request some more, and she feels that his demand is both inappropriate and unethical. However, Karen still wants to maintain a good professional relationship with Gus.

Run the role-play for about five minutes. For both scenarios, observers rate the role players on two dimensions, using a 1-to-5 scale from very poor to very good. One dimension is "effective use of human relations techniques." The second dimension is "acting ability." A few observers might voluntarily provide feedback to the role players in terms of sharing their ratings and observations. The course instructor might also provide feedback.

16

Stress Management and Personal Productivity

Lynaia Lutes is taking time to focus. An account supervisor at a small Texas advertising and public relations agency, Lutes not long ago was a master of executing the details of work, without always focusing on strategy and long-term vision. Glued to her personal digital assistant, she shot off e-mails night and day, yet felt overwhelmed and sometimes did work that didn't pass muster with her bosses.

"A couple of times, I basically completed an assignment but didn't approach it strategically," admits Lutes. Now, taking the time to think and focus deeply has become one of Lutes' performance goals. And, she and the 14 other employees at the Blanchard Schaefer agency in Arlington are expected to make appointments with themselves just to contemplate, even daydream, for an hour. New on the premises, a "womb room," spartan and unwired, allows employees to retreat to let ideas flow without interruption.

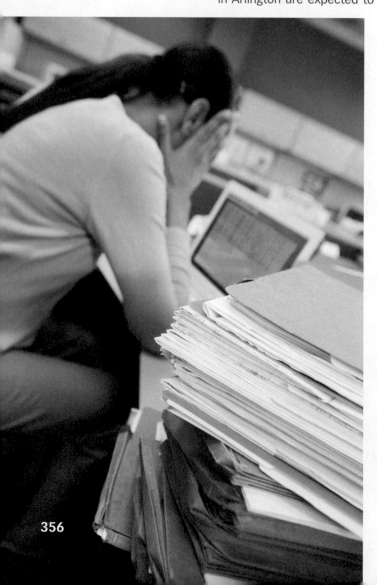

"Our society has gotten to a place where we reward those who micromanage: Did I respond immediately on my BlackBerry; was I online at 11 p.m.", asserts agency president Ken Schaefer. "Having time to think is absolutely critical to creating good strategy. We view it as a competitive advantage."[1]

The account supervisor just described is attempting to become more productive by spending time thinking instead of responding to small messages of the moment. At the same time, she is attempting to get over the stressor of feeling overwhelmed. Although this book is primarily about interpersonal skills, information about managing stress and enhancing personal productivity is relevant. Having your work under control and not being stressed out enables you to focus better on interpersonal relationships.

The first half of this chapter deals with the nature of stress and how it can be managed, whereas the second half describes various approaches to improving personal productivity. The two topics are as closely related as nutrition and health. When you effectively manage stress, you can be more productive. And when your work is under control, you avoid the heavy stress of feeling overwhelmed. A useful thought to keep in mind is that many readers of this book will become

After reading and studying this chapter and doing the exercises, you should be able to

1. Explain many of the symptoms and consequences of stress, including burnout.
2. Describe personality factors and job factors that contribute to stress.
3. Manage your own stress effectively.
4. Reduce any tendencies you might have toward procrastination.
5. Identify attitudes and values that will enhance your productivity.
6. Identify work habits and skills that will enhance your productivity.
7. Pinpoint potential time wasters that drain your productivity.

or are already **corporate athletes**, workers who engage in high-level performance for sustained periods.[2] To be a corporate athlete, you have to manage your energy and stress well, in addition to having good work habits and time management.

corporate athletes

Workers who engage in high-level performance for sustained periods.

UNDERSTANDING AND MANAGING STRESS

A major challenge facing any worker who wants to stay healthy and have good interpersonal relationships is to manage stress effectively. Although *stress* is an everyday term, a scientific definition helps clarify its meaning. **Stress** is an adaptive response that is the consequence of any action, situation, or event that places special demands on a person. Note that stress, as used here, refers to a reaction to the situation, not the situation or force itself. A **stressor** is the external or internal force that brings about the stress.

Individual differences in the perception of an event play a key role in determining what events are stressful. Giving a presentation to management, for example, is stressful for some people but not for others. Some people perceive a presentation as a threatening and uncomfortable experience, while others might perceive the same event to be an invigorating challenge.

The term *special demands* is also critical because minor adjustments, such as an ink cartridge that runs dry, are usually not perceived as stressful. Yet piling on of minor adjustments, such as having 10 small things go wrong in one day, is stressful. This is true because stress is additive: A series of small doses of stress can create a major stress problem.

This textbook's approach to understanding stress centers on its symptoms and consequences, personality and job factors that contribute to stress, and methods and techniques for stress management. Managing stress receives more emphasis because the same techniques can be used to combat a variety of stressors.

Symptoms and Consequences of Stress

The physiological changes that take place within the body in response to stress are responsible for most stress symptoms. These physiological changes are almost identical for both positive and negative stressors. Ski racing, romantic attraction, and being downsized can make you feel about the same physically. The experience of stress helps activate hormones that prepare the body to run or fight when faced with a challenge. This battle against the stressor is referred to as the **fight-or-flight response**. It helps you deal with emergencies.

The brain is the organ that decides whether a situation is stressful and produces the behavioral and physiological responses. Yet, the brain's response is based on personal experience and culture. Eating seal meat would rarely be stressful for an Eskimo, yet might be for a Floridian. The brain senses stress as damage to well-being and therefore sends out a signal to the body to cope. The brain is thus a self-regulating system that helps us cope with stressors.

LEARNING OBJECTIVE 1

fight-or-flight response

The body's physiological and chemical battle against a stressor in which the person tries to cope with the adversity head-on or tries to flee from the scene.

Physiological Reactions. The activation of hormones when the body has to cope with a stressor produces a short-term physiological reaction. Among the most familiar reactions is an increase in heart rate, blood pressure, blood glucose, and blood clotting. The stress hormone cortisol and other chemical responses to a stress can increase the cardiovascular function and the immune system in the short term. To help you recognize these symptoms, try to recall your internal bodily sensations the last time you were almost in an automobile accident or heard some wonderful news. Less familiar changes are a redirection of the blood flow toward the brain and large muscle groups and a release of stored fluids from places throughout the body into the bloodstream.

If stress is continuous and accompanied by these short-term physiological changes, annoying and life-threatening conditions can occur. Damage occurs when stress levels rarely subside. Eventually the immune system is suppressed, and memory is impaired. When the immune system is impaired, the severity of many diseases and disorders increases. For example, people whose stress level is high recover more slowly from colds and injuries, and they are more susceptible to sexually transmitted diseases.

A stressful life event usually leads to a high cholesterol level (of the unhealthy type) and high blood pressure. Other conditions associated with stress are cardiac disease, migraine headaches, ulcers, allergies, skin disorders, irritable bowel syndrome, and cancer. People under continuous negative stress, such as having severe family problems or having a life out of control, also age more quickly partially because of cell damage.[3] (Have you ever observed that stressed out friends of yours appear older looking than their chronological age?) A study of 812 Swedish workers conducted over a 25-year period found that work stress doubles the risk of dying from a heart attack. Seventy-three of the workers died from cardiac disease during the study. The major type of stress studied was having high work demands with little control over the work, combined with being underpaid.[4]

Stress symptoms vary considerably from one person to another. A general behavioral symptom of intense stress is for people to exaggerate their weakest tendencies. For instance, a person with a strong temper who usually keeps cool under pressure may throw a tantrum under intense pressure. Some common stress symptoms are listed in Figure 16-1.

Job Performance Consequences. Stress has both negative and positive consequences. **Hindrance stressors** are those stressful events and thoughts that have a negative effect on motivation and performance. Many of these have already been mentioned. In contrast, **challenge stressors** have a positive direct effect on motivation and performance.[5] A study with 215 employees across 61 offices of a state agency showed that when faced with challenge stressors, employees performed better on their regular tasks, citizenship behavior, and customer service. In contrast, performance on the three dimensions decreased when

hindrance stressors

Those stressful events that have a negative effect on motivation and performance.

challenge stressors

Stressful events that have a positive direct effect on motivation and performance.

FIGURE 16-1   A Variety of Stress Symptoms

Mostly Physical and Physiological	
Shaking or trembling	Mouth dryness
Dizziness	Upper and lower back pain
Heart palpitations	Frequent headaches
Difficulty breathing	Low energy and stamina
Chronic fatigue	Stomach problems
Unexplained chest pains	Constant craving for sweets
Frequent teeth grinding	Increased alcohol or cigarette consumption
Frequent nausea	Frequent need to eliminate
Mostly Emotional and Behavioral	
Difficulty concentrating	Anxiety or depression
Nervousness	Forgetfulness
Crying	Restlessness
Anorexia	Frequent arguments with others
Declining interest in sex	Feeling high strung much of the time
Frequent nail biting or hair tugging	Decrease in daily happiness

Note: Anxiety is a general sense of dread, fear, or worry not linked to a specific event, such as being anxious about your future.

FIGURE 16-2   Relationship between Stress and Job Performance

employees experienced hindrance stressors. An example of a challenge stressor was having high responsibility; having to deal with a lot of red tape to get the job done was an example of a hindrance stressor.[6]

The right amount of stress prepares us for meeting difficult challenges and spurs us on to peak intellectual and physical performance. An optimum level of stress exists for most people and most tasks. In general, performance tends to be best under moderate amounts of stress. If the stress is too great, people become temporarily ineffective; they may freeze or choke. Under too little stress, people may become lethargic and inattentive. Figure 16-2 depicts the relationship between stress and job performance. An exception to this relationship is that certain negative forms of stress are likely to lower performance even if the stress is moderate. For example, the stress created by an intimidating supervisor or worrying about radiation poisoning—even in moderate amounts—will not improve performance.

Job stress can also lower job performance indirectly because distressed workers are more likely to be absent from the job, thereby not accomplishing as much work. A study of 323 health service workers in the United Kingdom found that job-related psychological distress, particularly depression, was associated with more days absent, and a greater number of times absent.[7]

The optimum amount of stress is a positive force that is the equivalent of finding excitement and challenge. Your ability to solve problems and deal with challenge is enhanced when the right amount of adrenaline flows in your blood to guide you toward peak performance. In fact, highly productive people are sometimes said to be hooked on adrenaline.

Burnout and Stress.   One of the major problems of prolonged stress is that it may lead to **burnout**, a condition of emotional, mental, and physical exhaustion in response to long-term stressors. Burnout is also referred to as work exhaustion because fatigue is usually involved. Burned-out people are often cynical. Two other examples of burnout symptoms are irritability and impatience.

Burnout is a complex phenomenon with its causes centering on five factors. First is a feeling of limited autonomy or control in the workplace. Not being able to decide how to accomplish a task is significant, as well as having little say in choosing what tasks to do. Second is receiving insufficient recognition for accomplishments. Third is not having advancement opportunities and feeling stifled on the job. Fourth is having poor relationships with coworkers, including not getting much respect. Fifth is working in an organizational culture that is incompatible with your belief system, such as a vegetarian working for a poultry producer.[8] A recent study with Dutch workers suggests that having a charismatic leader can help reduce some of the problems that lead to burnout.[9] For example, a charismatic leader is likely to give ample recognition.

burnout

A condition of emotional, mental, and physical exhaustion in response to long-term stressors.

FIGURE 16-3 Cause of Stress among the General Population

Source of Stress	People Affected
Work	67%
Money	78%
The economy	75%
Relationships (spouse, kids, girl/boyfriend)	59%
Family responsibilities	58%
Personal health concerns	58%
Health problems affecting my family	61%
Housing costs (e.g., mortgage or rent)	59%
Job stability	58%
Personal safety	42%

Source: APA (American Psychological Association) Stress in America Survey, published in Michael Price, "The Recession is Stressing Men More than Women," *Monitor on Psychology*, July/August 2009, p. 10.

The key symptom of burnout is the distancing that occurs in response to work over-load. Burnout sufferers shift into a mode of doing the minimum as a way of protecting themselves. They start leaving work early and dehumanizing their clients, patients, or customers. People experiencing burnout may do their jobs, but their heart is not in it anymore.[10]

A synthesis of dozens of studies shows that burnout often damages the physical health of workers. Partly because burnout is a consequence of stress, burnout increases the risk for cardiovascular disease as much as well-known risk factors such as smoking, an elevated body mass index, and too much bad cholesterol. Other potential links between burnout and health problems include poor health behaviors and sleep disorder.[11]

Personality and Job Factors Contributing to Stress

LEARNING OBJECTIVE 2

Workers experience stress for many different reasons, including personal predisposi-tions, factors stemming from the job, or the combined influence of both. If a person with an extreme negative predisposition has to deal with irate customers, he or she is most likely to experience substantial stress. Here we describe a sampling of important individ-ual and organizational factors that contribute to job stress. Keep in mind, however, that a large number of potential stressors exist and that many of them overlap. For example, financial problems are a major source of stress, and they might contribute to relation-ship and health problems. Fighting about money harms relationships, and worrying about money can create health problems. Figure 16-3 lists some stressors facing the gen-eral population, and these sources of stress duplicate some of the stressors described in the following pages.

Personality Factors Predisposing People toward Stress.   Individuals vary considerably in their susceptibility to job stress based on their personality traits and characteristics. Four such factors are described next.

Low Perceived Control   A key factor in determining whether workers experience stress is how much they believe they can control a given adverse circumstance. **Perceived control** is the belief that an individual has at his or her disposal a response that can control the negative aspects of an event. A survey of over 100 studies indicated that people with a high level of perceived control had low levels of physical and psychological symptoms of stress. Conversely, people with low perceived control are more likely to experience work stress.[12]

Low Self-Efficacy   Self-efficacy, like perceived control, is another personal factor that influences susceptibility to stress. (Note that because self-efficacy is tied to a specific situation

perceived control

The belief that an individual has at his or her disposal a response that can control the negative aspects of an event.

it is not strictly a personality trait.) When workers have both low perceived control and low self-efficacy, the stress consequences may be much worse. However, having high self-efficacy softens the stress consequences of demanding jobs.[13] If you believe that you can successfully resolve a difficult problem, such as troubleshooting the reason for packages being sent to incorrect addresses, you will be less stressed.

Type A Behavior and Hostility   A person with **Type A behavior** is demanding, impatient, and overstriving and is therefore prone to negative stress. Type A behavior has two main components. One is the tendency to try to accomplish too many things in too little time. This leads the Type A individual to be impatient and demanding. The other component is free-floating hostility. Because of this sense of urgency and hostility, trivial things irritate these people. People with Type A behavior are aggressive and hardworking.

Type A personalities frequently have cardiac diseases, such as heart attacks and strokes, at an early age, but only certain features of the Type A personality pattern may be related to coronary heart disease. The heart attack triggers are hostility, anger, cynicism, and suspiciousness, as contrasted to impatience, ambition, and being work driven. In fact, hostility is more strongly associated with coronary heart disease in men than smoking, drinking, overeating, or high levels of bad (LDL) cholesterol.[14] A review of studies confirms that there is no significant association between Type A personalities and heart disease. However, there is a strong association between hostility and coronary heart disease. Hostility of the sort seen in habitual angry driving is also a heart disease risk factor.[15] Note that the heart attack triggers also make for strained interpersonal relationships.

Negative Affectivity   A major contributor to being stress prone is **negative affectivity**, a tendency to experience aversive emotional states. In more detail, negative affectivity is a pervasive disposition to experience emotional stress that includes feelings of nervousness, tension, and worry. The same disposition also includes such emotional states as anger, scorn, revulsion, guilt, self-dissatisfaction, and sadness.[16] Such negative personalities seem to search for important discrepancies between what they would like and what exists. Poor interpersonal relationships often result from the frequent complaining of people with negative affectivity.

Job Sources of Stress.   Almost any job situation can act as a stressor for some employees, but not necessarily for others. As just described, certain personality factors make it more likely that a person will experience job stress. Furthermore, other personal life stressors may spill over into the workplace, making it more likely that a person will experience job stress. In the words of human resource writer Pamela Babcock, "Employees' job-related anxieties such as deadline pressures and demanding bosses are compounded by recession-induced financial worries and domestic tensions that many workers find at home."[17] Six frequently encountered job stressors are outlined in Figure 16-4 and described below.

Role Overload Including Extreme Jobs   Having too much work to do, **role overload**, can create negative stress in two ways. First, the person may become fatigued and thus be less able to tolerate annoyances and irritations. Second, a person subject to unreasonable work demands may feel perpetually behind schedule, a situation that is itself a powerful stressor. Downsizing often creates overload because fewer people are left to handle the same workload as before. (If work is carefully streamlined, role overload is minimized.)

Work overload often takes the form of an **extreme job** in which the incumbent works at least 60 hours per week in a position that usually requires tight deadlines and heavy travel. Many of these jobs with long hours are found in information technology and financial services fields; yet, many business owners work comparable hours. The availability of work associates across the globe in different time zones facilitates extreme jobs. One financial analyst who immigrated to the United States from India reportedly works 120 hours per week, leaving only 48 hours for nonwork activities including sleep. Although many extreme job holders experience considerable job stress, many are exalted by the excitement and the high income.[18]

In extreme form, role overload can kill. For example, death from too much work is so common in Japan that the word *karoshi* has been coined to label the situation. In a celebrated case, a Toyota chief engineer worked up to 114 hours of overtime a month in

Type A behavior

A behavior pattern in which the individuals is demanding, impatient, and overstriving, and therefore prone to negative stress.

negative affectivity

A tendency to experience aversive emotional states.

role overload

Having too much work to do.

extreme job

Job in which the incumbent works at least 60 hours per week in a position that usually requires tight deadlines and heavy travel.

FIGURE 16-4 Six Significant Sources of Job Stress

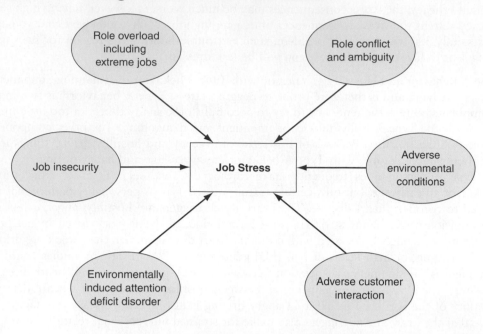

the six months before he died of heart failure. For decades, the Japanese government has been attempting without much success to set limits on hours of work, The consequences of role overload show up in claims for death and disability from overwork, and also in suicides attributed to work fatigue. Among 2,207 work-related suicides in Japanese companies in one year, the most frequent reason (672 suicides) was overwork.[19]

Role Conflict and Role Ambiguity Role conflict, described in Chapter 9 as an important workplace conflict, is also a major workplace stressor. People experience stress when they have to choose between two sets of expectations. Suppose an accountant is asked by her manager to state company earnings in a way that conflicts with the professional norms of accountants. If she complies with her manager, she will feel that she is betraying her profession. If she does not comply with her manager, she will enter into dispute with the manager. The woman is likely to experience job stress.

Role ambiguity is a condition in which the jobholder receives confusing or poorly defined expectations. Workers in many organizations are placed in situations in which they are unsure of their true responsibilities. Some workers who are placed on a work team experience role ambiguity because they are asked to solve many problems by themselves. It is less ambiguous to have the manager tell you what to do. Many people experience stress symptoms when faced with role ambiguity.

role ambiguity

A condition in which the job holder receives confusing or poorly defined expectations.

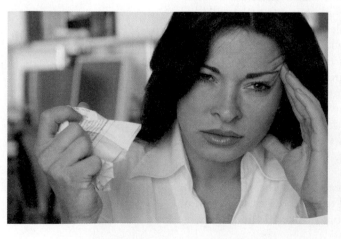

Adverse Environmental Conditions A variety of adverse organizational conditions are stressors, as identified by the National Institute for Occupational Safety and Health (NIOSH). Among these adverse organizational conditions are unpleasant or dangerous physical conditions, such as crowding, noise, air pollutions, or ergonomic problems. Enough polluted air within an office building can create a sick building in which a diverse range of airborne particles, vapors, molds, and gases pollute the indoor environment. The result can be headaches, nausea, and respiratory infections as well as the stress created by being physically ill.[20]

Ergonomic problems refer to a poor fit between the physical and human requirements of a job. The demands of the modern workplace contribute to the development of musculoskeletal disorders. Working at a computer monitor for prolonged periods of time can lead to adverse physical and psychological reactions. The symptoms include headaches and fatigue, along with eye problems. According to the Vision Syndrome Information Center, about 90 percent of people working on computers more than three hours a day have vision problems, with some 10 million a year seeking treatment. Common visual problems are dry eyes and blurred or double vision. Another vision-related problem is that people lean forward to scan the monitor, leading to physical problems such as back strain.

The repetitive-motion disorder most frequently associated with keyboarding and the use of optical scanners is **carpal tunnel syndrome**. The syndrome occurs when repetitive flexing and extension of the wrist causes the tendons to swell, thus trapping and pinching the median nerve. Carpal tunnel syndrome creates stress because of the pain and misery. About one in five computer users will suffer from carpal tunnel syndrome at some point.[21] A less publicized problem is a sore thumb (overuse syndrome) related to continuous use of the space bar and mouse. The "BlackBerry thumb" stems from using the thumb to type on the very small keyboard.

The thoughts of having to permanently leave a job requiring keyboarding is another potential stressor. If ergonomic principles, such as erect posture, are incorporated into computer usage, these stress symptoms diminish. Office chairs developed in recent years allow for more flexibility of movement as workers shift rapidly between tasks such as moving toward the computer screen, placing feet on the desk, and then turning for a face-to-face conversation.[22]

Commuting to and from work is a major stressor for many people that could be classified as an adverse environmental condition. We emphasize *for many people* because individual differences again come into play. Some people enjoy driving, or being on a train or bus, for such reasons as the opportunity to listen to the radio or read. A study with New Jersey–New York commuters found that train rides of over one hour are particularly stressful for commuters. Longer commutes were associated with elevated cortisol (a stress hormone) poorer performance on a proofreading task given the study participants, and high levels of perceived commuting stress. The researcher also observed that for many workers commuting is the most stressful aspect of work.[23]

To avoid the stress of commuting in rush hour traffic, some workers leave home several hours before work, and then use the early arrival time to have breakfast, read the newspaper, or visit an athletic club near the work site.[24] Furthermore, a major reason many people work from home is to avoid the stresses associated with commuting.

Adverse Interaction with Customers and Clients and Emotional Labor   Interactions with customers can be a major stressor. Part of the problem is that the sales associate often feels helpless when placed in conflict with a customer. The sales associate is told that "the customer is always right." Furthermore, the store manager usually sides with the customer in a dispute with the sales associate. Unreasonable demands by clients and customers can also be stressful, such as customers who offer to buy a product or service below cost. During the Great Recession, many potential customers would frustrate car dealer sales reps by making offers 50 percent below sticker price, with an attitude of "take it or leave it." Being subjected to sexual harassment by clients and customers is another stressor widely experienced by store sales associates, especially young women.

Related to adverse customer interaction is the stressor of having to control the expression of emotion to please or to avoid displeasing a customer. Imagine having to smile at a customer who belittles you or your employer. Alicia A. Grandey, associate professor of psychology at Penn State University, defines **emotional labor** as the process of regulating both feelings and expressions to meet organizational goals.[25] The process involves both surface acting and deep acting. Surface acting means faking expressions, such as smiling, whereas deep acting involves controlling feelings, such as suppressing anger toward a customer you perceive to be annoying.

A study with 285 pairs of employees and customers suggests that deep acting, rather than maintaining an artificial smile, leads to better customer service.[26] As a result of the better customer service, it is possible that the customer will treat the associate better resulting in less stress for the latter.

Sales workers and customer service representatives often experience emotional labor because so often they have to fake facial expressions and feelings so as to please customers. Nevertheless, according to one study, the top five occupations in terms of emotional labor demands are (1) police and sheriff's patrol officers, (2) social workers, (3) psychiatrists, (4) supervisors of police and detectives, and (5) registered nurses. Bill and account collectors ranked 15![27]

Engaging in emotional labor for prolonged periods of time can lead to job dissatisfaction, stress, and burnout. Surface acting creates more dissatisfaction. A contributing cause is that faking expressions and emotions takes a physiological toll, such as the intestines churning. Workers who engage in emotional labor may also develop cardiovascular problems and weakened immune systems. The good news is that being extraverted helps reduce some of the stress associated with both surface acting and deep acting.[28] (Perhaps if you like people, you can better tolerate their unruly behavior.)

Environmentally Induced Attention Deficit Disorder   According to psychiatrist Edward Hallowell, many people suffer from an attention deficit disorder brought on by technology and activity overload. (The condition is similar to communication or information overload.) This problem appears to be a combination of the environment and the individual who chooses to overuse information technology devices. The symptoms of environmentally induced attention deficit disorder include frequently feeling rushed and impatient, being easily distracted, forgetfulness, and having little time for creative thought. In short, the person feels frazzled. A major cause of this type of attention deficit disorder is attempting to do more in less time.[29] Many of the suggestions about work habits and time management described later are useful in coping with environmentally induced attention deficit disorder.

Job Insecurity and Job Loss   Worrying about losing your job is a major stressor. Even when jobs are plentiful, having to search for another job and facing the prospect of geographic relocation are stressors for many people. Downsizing and corporate mergers (which usually result in downsizing) have contributed to job insecurity. The anticipation of layoffs among employees can increase negative stress and lower job performance. In addition, the survivors of a downsizing often experience pressure from the fear of future cuts, loss of friends, and worry about a sudden increase in workload.

Job loss is usually a more intense stressor than worrying about losing one's job. Losing a job often leads to the stressors of financial problems and relationship conflict. Some people who lose their job become so stressed and depressed that they commit suicide. An unfortunate example is that between 2006 and 2008, France Télécom laid off approximately 22,000 workers. Twenty-four laid off workers committed suicide, with the labor union blaming the layoffs for most of the suicides.[30] We hypothesize here that workers with good resources, such as supportive friends and family, good professional contacts, and effective job search skills are the least likely to commit suicide after job loss.

So which of the job stressors described have the most adverse effect on job performance? An analysis of 69 groups, comprising 35,265 employees indicated that role ambiguity and situational constraints are the most negatively related to job performance. A *situational constraint* refers to a situation in which conditions in an employee's job setting inhibit or constrain performance, such as improper machinery or inadequate supplies.[31] The job stressor, adverse environmental conditions, includes a few situational constraints.

Methods and Techniques for Stress Management

LEARNING OBJECTIVE 3

Unless stress is managed properly, it may lead to harmful long-term consequences, including disabling physical illness and career retardation. Managing stress refers to controlling stress by making it a constructive force in your life. Managing thus refers to both preventing and reducing stress. However, the distinction between methods of preventing and reducing stress is not clear-cut. For example, physical exercise not only reduces stress, it also contributes to a relaxed lifestyle that helps you prevent stress.

A key principle about managing stress is that you are less likely to experience distress from stressors if you have the right resources. Having the right personality characteristics such as high perceived control, high self-efficacy, and not being hostile helps ward off stress. External resources to help ward off negative stress include having a network of friends who provide support, an encouraging manager, and programs for helping distressed employees.[32] Assume, for example, that a worker is heavily stressed by a long rush hour commute. If the company provides flexible working hours that help decrease commuting during rush hour, the worker experience less of a hindrance stressor.

Coping with, or managing, stress includes hundreds of activities, with substantial individual differences in which technique is effective. Running is a case in point. For many people, running or jogging is an excellent method of stress reduction. Others find that running creates new stressors, such as aching knees, shin splints, dizziness from breathing in vehicle exhausts, and worrying about being hit by vehicles. In general, coping efforts involve cognitions and behaviors aimed at managing the stressor and its associated emotions. For example, you might have to decrease the troublesome elements in your job (such as role overload) and also deal with the tension generated by overwork. The following subsections describe eight methods for managing stress, including a list of everyday stress busters.

Eliminate or Modify the Stressor.   The most potent method of managing stress is to eliminate or modify the stressor giving you trouble. One value of relaxation techniques and tranquilizing medication is that they calm a person enough so that he or she can deal constructively with the stressor. A helpful way to attack the cause of stress is to follow the steps in problem solving and decision making. You clarify the problem, identify the alternatives, weigh the alternatives, and select one alternative. One difficulty, however, is that your evaluation of the real problem may be inaccurate. There is always a limit to self-analysis. For example, a person might think that work overload is the stressor when the true stressor is low self-efficacy.

A major strategy for modifying a stressor is to rethink your belief about a challenging situation. According to the **cognitive behavioral approach to stress management**, people learn to recognize how pessimistic and distorted thoughts of gloom and doom create stress. After recognition of the problem, the person learns to replace the overly pessimistic thinking with more realistic or optimistic thinking. Assume that Mandy is stressed about the prospects of losing her job. Using a cognitive-behavioral approach to stress management, she begins to think, "Would losing this job really be that bad? If this job folds, I could move to Denver where I've always wanted to live, and restart my career." Mandy is right on target because a synthesis of many studies found that cognitive-behavioral approaches are the most effective method of combating workplace stress.[33]

Get Appropriate Physical Exercise.   A moderate amount of physical exercise is a cornerstone of managing stress and achieving wellness. To manage stress, it is important to select an exercise program that is physically challenging but does not lead to overexertion and muscle and bone injury. Competitive sports, if taken too seriously, can actually increase stress. Aerobic exercises are most beneficial because they make you breathe faster and raise your heart rate. Walking is highly recommended as a stress reducer because it is inherently relaxing, and offers many of the benefits of other forms of exercise with a minimum risk of physical danger. Doing housework, yard work, and washing and waxing a vehicle are examples of everyday forms of gentle exercise that offer the side benefits of getting tasks accomplished. A major mental and emotional benefit of physical exercise stems from endorphins produced in the thalamus portion of the brain. The endorphins are associated with a state of euphoria referred to as "runner's high." Endorphins also work like pain killers, adding to their stress-reduction value.

Physical exercise directly reduces stress, and also reduces the risk of disorders that are both debilitating themselves, and as a result become intense stressors. As researched by the American College of Sports Medicine, among the benefits of exercise are (a) a 50 percent reduction in the incidence of diabetes, (b) a 40 percent reduction in the incidence of high blood pressure, (c) a 40 percent reduction in the risk of developing Alzheimer's disease, and (d) a decrease in depression as effective as Prozac or behavioral therapy.[34]

Millions of people seek to reduce and prevent stress through yoga, which is both physical exercise and a way of developing mental attitudes that calm the body and mind. One of yoga's many worthwhile goals is to solder a union between the mind and body, thereby achieving harmony and tranquility. Another benefit of yoga is that it helps people place aside negative thoughts that act as stressors. A caution about Yoga is that too much bending too soon can lead to injured hamstring muscles and torn blood vessels.

Rest Sufficiently. Rest offers benefits similar to those of exercise, such as stress reduction, improved concentration, improved energy, and better tolerance for frustration. Achieving proper rest is closely linked to getting proper exercise. The current interest in adult napping reflects the awareness that proper rest makes a person less stress prone and enhances productivity. A study was conducted of 23,681 healthy Greek adults over a six-year period, many of whom napped for about 30 minutes three times a week. Study participants who napped had 37 percent lower risk of dying from a heart attack than the people who did not. A criticism offered of this study is that the people who napped may also take better care of their bodies and mind in general.[35] The connection of this study to stress management is that many heart attacks are stress induced.

A growing number of firms have napping facilities for workers, and many workers nap at their desks or in their parked vehicles during lunch breaks. Naps of about 15 minutes duration taken during the workday are used both as energizers and as stress reducers. Napping can help a worker become less stressed as well as more productive. A rested brain is a more effective brain. To keep the effectiveness of workday napping in perspective, workers who achieve sufficient rest during normal sleeping hours have less need for a nap during working hours.[36]

Maintain a Healthy Diet. Another practical method of stress reduction and prevention is to maintain a well-balanced, and therefore healthy, diet. Nutritious food is valuable for physical and mental health, making it easier to cope with frustrations that are potential stressors. Some non-nutritious foods, such as those laden with caffeine or sugar, tend to enhance a person's level of stress. According to the Dietary Guidelines of the United States Department of Agriculture, a healthy diet is one that

- Emphasizes fruits, vegetables, whole grains, and fat-free or low-fat milk and milk products
- Includes lean meats, poultry, fish, beans, eggs, and nuts
- Is low in saturated fats, *trans* fats, cholesterol, salt (sodium), and added sugars.

These recommendations are for the general public over two years of age. Using MyPyramid, the government personalizes a recommended diet, taking into account our age, sex, and amount of physical exercise. Consult *http://www.mypyramid.gov*, as shown in Figure 16-5. Also, nutritionists highly recommend fibers found in whole-grain breads, rolls and cereals, and brown rice.

FIGURE 16-5 Dietary Guidelines for Americans, developed by the U.S. Department of Agriculture

The Food Groups

Grains

Vegetables

Fruits

Milk

Meat & Beans

Oils

Source: U.S. Department of Agriculture, *http://www.mypyramid.gov.*

Visualization for Stress Reduction

A standard, easy-to-use method for reducing stress symptoms is to visualize a pleasant and calm experience. You need to concentrate carefully on your object or scene, otherwise stress reduction is unlikely to take place. If you are experiencing stress right now, try the technique. Otherwise, wait until the next time you perceive your body to be experiencing stress. In this context, visualization means to picture yourself doing something that you would like to do. Whatever fantasy suits your fancy will work, according to the advocates of this relaxation technique. Visualizations that work for some people include smiling at a loved one, floating on a cloud, caressing a baby, petting a kitten or puppy, and walking in the woods. Notice that all of these scenes are relaxing rather than exciting. What visualization would work for you?

To implement the technique, close your eyes and bring the pleasant image into focus in your mind. Think of nothing else at the moment (as in meditation). Imagine that a DVD of the pleasant experience is playing on the television screen in your brain. Breathe softly and savor the experience. Slowly return to reality, refreshed, relaxed, and ready to tackle the challenges of the day.

Build a Support Network. A **support network** is a group of people who can listen to your problems and provide emotional support. These people, or even one person, can help you through your difficult episodes. Members of your network can provide you with a sense of closeness, warmth, and acceptance that will reduce your stress. Also, the simple expedient of putting your feelings into words can be a healing experience. The way to develop this support network is to become a good listener so that the other person will reciprocate. A support network is therefore a method of stress management based squarely on effective interpersonal skills.

Practice Visualization and Meditation. Perhaps the most effortless and enjoyable relaxation technique for managing stress is to visualize a pleasant experience, as explained in Skill-Building Exercise 16-1. Visualization, like so many stress-reduction techniques, including meditation, requires concentration. Concentrating helps slow down basic physiological processes, such as the heartbeat and dissipates stress. Visualization, meditation, prayer, and chanting all appear to offer such advantages as lowering heart rate, blood pressure, and oxygen consumption. These techniques also alleviate symptoms associated with such conditions as hypertension, insomnia, depression, and anxiety.[37] Forcing yourself to concentrate is also valuable because a key stress symptom is difficulty in concentrating.

Meditation is a relaxation technique used to quiet the mind, as well as to relieve stress, and is more complicated than simple visualization. (The well-known relaxation response is essentially a form of meditation.) A typical meditation technique proceeds as follows: Hold your back straight, and relax the body. Take three gentle breaths, breathing in and out through the nostrils. Let the respiration follow its natural flow. Your body breathes as if it was fast asleep, yet you remain vigilant. If you become distracted, simply let go of the thought, and return to the breath. It is helpful to count each inhale up to 21. Each time your mind wanders, return back to one. Practice meditating about 20 minutes a day, and meditate on the spot after a stressful event or thought.[38] The breathing part of meditation is so important that it is an everyday method of stress reduction itself.

Practice Everyday Methods of Stress Reduction. The simple expedient of learning how to relax is an important method of reducing the tension and anxiety brought about by both challenge and hindrance stressors. Visualization of a pleasant experience is one such method. A sample of everyday suggestions for relaxation and other methods of stress reduction are presented in Figure 16-6. If you can accomplish these, you are less likely to need tranquilizing medication to keep you calm and in control. Your stress symptoms will ordinarily return, however, if you do not eliminate and modify the stressor. If the stress is an emotional conflict you do not see or understand, assistance from a mental health professional is recommended.

Now that you have studied various method of managing stress, reinforce your thinking by doing Skill-Building Exercise 16-2.

support network

A group of people who can listen to your problems and provide emotional support.

FIGURE 16-6   Stress Busters

- Take a deep breath and exhale slowly. Inhale and your heart beats faster. Exhale and your heart beats more slowly, and slow down the cardiac muscle.[31]
- Place your thumbs behind your ears and spread your fingers on the top of your head. Move your scalp back and forth gently by rotating your fingers for 15-20 seconds.
- Give in to your emotions. If you are angry, disgusted, or confused, admit your feelings. Suppressing your emotions adds to stress.
- Take a brief break from the stressful situation and do something small and constructive, such as washing your car, emptying a wastebasket, or getting a haircut.
- Get a massage, because it can loosen tight muscles, improve your blood circulation, and calm you down.
- Get help with your stressful task from a coworker, supervisor, or friend.
- Concentrate intensely on reading, surfing the Internet, a sport, or a hobby. Contrary to common sense, concentration is at the heart of stress reduction.
- Have a quiet place at home and have a brief idle period there every day.
- Take a leisurely day off from your routine.
- Finish something you have started, however small. Accomplishing almost anything reduces some stress.
- Stop to smell the flowers, make friends with a young child or elderly person, or play with a kitten or puppy.
- Strive to do a good job, but not a perfect job.
- Work with your hands, doing a pleasant task.
- Find somebody or something that makes you laugh, and have a good laugh.
- Minimize drinking caffeinated or alcoholic beverages, and drink fruit juice or water instead. Grab a piece of fruit rather than a can of beer.
- Help somebody less fortunate than you. The flood of good feelings will act like endorphins.

SKILL-BUILDING EXERCISE 16-2

Personal Stress Management Action Plan

Most people face a few powerful stressors in their work and personal life, but few people take the time to clearly identify these stressors or develop an action plan for remedial action. The purpose of this exercise is to make you an exception. Here is an opportunity to develop an inventory of your stressors, think through the problems they may be causing you, and develop action plans you might take to remedy the situation. Use the form below or create one with a word processing table or a spreadsheet.

Work or School Stressor	Symptoms This Stressor Is Creating for Me	My Action Plan to Manage This Stressor
1.		
2.		
3.		
Personal Life Stressor	Symptoms This Stressor Is Creating for Me	My Action Plan to Manage This Stressor
1.		
2.		
3.		

Seven days after preparing this work sheet, observe if any of your stress symptoms have diminished. Also, identify those stressors for which only a long-term solution is possible. One student reported that a major work stressor he faced is that he wanted to work in international business, and emphasize doing business with Italian fashion companies. Yet he was experiencing stress because he had almost zero knowledge of the Italian language or culture. (By the way, can you offer this man any suggestions?)

IMPROVING PERSONAL PRODUCTIVITY

Achieving personal productivity is more in vogue than ever. Companies strive to operate with smaller staffs than in the past by pushing workers to achieve higher productivity. Particularly during a recession, workers pressure themselves to produce more per hour of work because many of them fear for their jobs. At the same time, there is a movement toward simplifying personal life by reducing clutter and cutting back on tasks that do not add much to the quality of life. **Personal productivity** refers to the amount of resources, including time, you consume to achieve a certain level of output. We approach productivity improvement from four perspectives: (1) dealing with procrastination, (2) attitudes and values that enhance personal productivity, (3) work habits and skills that enhance personal productivity, and (4) overcoming time wasters.

personal productivity
The amount of resources, including time, you consume to achieve a certain level of output.

Dealing with Procrastination

The person who **procrastinates** delays action for no good reason on tasks that need to be done. Procrastination results in a gap between intention and action. A major reason why people procrastinate is that they want to feel good at the moment rather than reap future rewards. As such, procrastination is a form of impulsivity.[39] Why bother getting in touch with my boss to discuss my prospects for promotion when I can send a Tweet to 500 people right now?

LEARNING OBJECTIVE 4

procrastination
Delaying action on tasks that need to be done for no good reason.

Procrastination lowers productivity because it wastes time and many important tasks never get done. Another serious problem is that undone tasks rumble around in the back of your consciousness, thereby decreasing your concentration. Chronic procrastination can even lead to debt, divorce, and job loss. Even productive people sometimes procrastinate. If these people did not procrastinate, they would be even more productive.

Many people regard procrastination as a laughable weakness, particularly because procrastinators themselves joke about the problem. Yet procrastination has been evaluated as a profound, debilitating problem, with between 20 and 25 percent of working adults identifying themselves as chronic procrastinators.[40] Approximately 90 percent of college students report problems with overdue papers and delayed studying. About 25 percent are chronic procrastinators, and many of them drop out of school.[41] The enormity of the procrastination problem makes it worthwhile to examine methods for bringing it under control. Do Self-Assessment Quiz 16-1 to think through your own tendencies toward procrastination—and don't wait until tomorrow.

Choose from among the following suggestions for controlling procrastination, based on those that appear to best fit your type of procrastination. A combination of techniques is likely to be the most effective.

1. **Commit to what you want in life.** If you are not committed to something you want in life, you are likely to be chronic procrastinator. The reason is that it is difficult to prioritize and take action. (See the later discussion about a personal mission and work habits.)[42] Your commitment to what you want in life will often translate into forgoing short-term pleasure, such as stopping by a café, in order to finish a project due today.

2. **Calculate the cost of procrastination.** You can reduce procrastination by calculating its cost. You might lose out on obtaining a high-paying job you really want by not having your résumé and cover letter ready on time. Your cost of procrastination would include the difference in compensation between the job you do find and the one you really wanted. Another cost would be the loss of potential job satisfaction.

Procrastination Tendencies

Directions: Circle yes or no for each item:

1.	I usually do my best work under the pressure of deadlines.	Yes	No
2.	Before starting a project, I go through such rituals as sharpening every pencil, straightening up my desk more than once, and reading and responding to all possible e-mail.	Yes	No
3.	I crave the excitement of the "last-minute rush," such as researching and writing a paper right before the deadline.	Yes	No
4.	I often think that if I delay something, it will go away, or the person who asked for it will forget about it.	Yes	No
5.	I extensively research something before taking action, such as obtaining three different estimates before getting the brakes repaired on my car.	Yes	No
6.	I have a great deal of difficulty getting started on most projects, even those I enjoy.	Yes	No
7.	I keep waiting for the right time to do something, such as getting started on an important report.	Yes	No
8.	I often underestimate the time needed to do a project, and say to myself, "I can do this quickly, so I'll wait until next week."	Yes	No
9.	It is difficult for me to finish most projects or activities.	Yes	No
10.	I have several favorite diversions or distractions that I use to keep me from doing something unpleasant, such as a difficult homework assignment.	Yes	No

Total Yes Responses _____

Scoring and Interpretation: The greater the number of "yes" responses, the more likely it is that you have a serious procrastination problem. A score of 8, 9, or 10 strongly suggests that your procrastination is lowering your productivity.

3. **Follow the WIFO principle, which stands for "worst in, first out."**[43] If you tackle the worst task on your list first, doing the other tasks may function like a small reward. You get to do what you dislike the least by doing first what you dislike the most. WIFO is particularly effective when faced with a number of tasks simultaneously.

4. **Break the task into manageable chunks.** To reduce procrastination, cut down a task that seems overwhelming into smaller projects that seem less formidable. If your job calls for preparing an enormous database, begin by assembling some readily available information. Then take the next step by assembling another small segment of the database—perhaps all customers whose last names begin with Z. Think of your task as pulling together a series of small databases that will fit into a master database.

5. **Make a commitment to other people.** Try to make it imperative that you get something done on time by making it a commitment to one or more other people. You might announce to coworkers that you are going to get something accomplished by a certain date. If you fail to meet this date, you are likely to feel embarrassed.

6. **Remove some clutter from your mind.** Procrastination escalates when people have many unfinished projects in the back of their mind, draining their concentration. Having too much to do can freeze us into inaction. Just eliminating a few trivial items from your to-do list can give you enough mental energy to overcome procrastination on a few major tasks. This approach to overcoming procrastination requires that you apply enough self-discipline to take the first step. Notice the unfortunate cycle: Procrastination leads to poor concentration (as described above), and procrastination hampers concentration.

7. **Satisfy your stimulation quota in constructive ways.** If you procrastinate because you enjoy the rush of scrambling to make deadlines, find a more constructive way of using busyness to keep you humming. If you need a high level of stimulation,

enrich your life with extra projects and learning new skills. The fullness of your schedule will provide you the stimulation you had been receiving from squeezing yourself to make deadlines and reach appointments on time.[44]

8. **Eliminate tangible rewards you are giving yourself for procrastinating.** If you are procrastinating through socializing with coworkers, taking a walk to obtain a beverage, surfing the Internet, or any other pleasant experience—stop rewarding yourself. Just sit alone in your work area doing nothing while procrastinating. If you remove the pleasant activities from your stalling routine, you may be able to reduce procrastination.

Enhancing Personal Productivity through Attitudes and Values

LEARNING OBJECTIVE 5

Developing good work habits and time management practices is often a matter of developing the right attitudes toward your work and toward time. If, for example, you think that your schoolwork or job is important and that time is a precious resource, you will be on your way toward developing good work habits. In this section, we describe a group of attitudes, values, and beliefs that can help a person become more productive through better use of time and improved work habits.

Begin with a Mission and Goals. A mission, or general purpose, propels you toward being productive. Assume that a person says, "My mission is to be an outstanding professional in my field and a loving, constructive spouse and parent." The mission serves as a compass to direct your activities, such as being well organized in order to accomplish more work and be highly valued by your employer. Goals are more specific than mission statements; they support the mission statement, but the effect is the same. Being committed to a goal also propels you toward good use of time. If you know that you can obtain the position in international business that you really want by mastering a second language, you are likely to work diligently on learning that language. Consultant Dean Fuhrman supports our point with this advice:

> If you really want to manage your time and get stuff done, have a burning life and work purpose that is a beacon for what you do. While they are useful, the lists, the shortcuts—all that stuff—pales in comparison to purpose for time management.[45]

Skill-Building Exercise 16-3 gives you the opportunity to establish a mission statement and supporting goals.

SKILL-BUILDING EXERCISE 16-3

Using a Mission Statement and Goals to Power Work Habits

People with a well-defined mission statement and supporting goals tend to have better work habits and time management than those who do not. The following exercise is designed to help you establish a mission statement and goals so that you will be energized to be more productive.

A. *Mission Statement:* To help develop your mission statement, or general purpose in life, ask yourself, "What are my five biggest wishes in life?" These wishes give you a hint to your purpose because they point toward an ideal purpose in life. Feel free to think big, because mission statements tend toward being idealistic.

B. *Long-Range Goals to Support Mission Statement:* Now write down what long-range goals would support your mission statement. Suppose your mission statement related to "creating a better life for people who are disadvantaged." Your long-range goals might include establishing a foundation that would fund your efforts. You would also need to be successful enough in your career to get the foundation started.

C. *Intermediate-Range Goals to Support Long-Range Goals:* Write down the intermediate-range goals needed to support the long-range goals. You will probably need to complete your education, obtain broad experience, and identify a lucrative form of self-employment.

D. *Weekly Goals to Support Intermediate-Range Goals:* Write down what you have to do this week to help you complete your education, such as researching and writing a paper for a particular course, registering for courses for next term, and inquiring about career opportunities in your field.

E. *Today's Goals to Support Weekly Goals (My To-Do List):* Here's where your lofty purpose in life gets translated into reality. What do you have to do today to get that paper written? Do you need to get your car battery replaced, so you can get to the library, so you can write your paper, so you can graduate, so you can become rich, so you can ultimately help all those people who are disadvantaged? Get going.

Work Smarter, Not Harder.   People caught up in trying to accomplish a job often wind up working hard, but not in an imaginative way that leads to good results. Much time and energy are therefore wasted. A working-smart approach also requires that you spend a few minutes carefully planning how to implement your task. An example of working smarter, not harder, is to invest a few minutes of critical thinking before conducting a telemarketing campaign for home replacement windows. Develop a list of homeowners of houses of at least 15 years old. People with relatively new homes are poor prospects for replacing their windows.

A new perspective on working smarter, not harder, is to keep perfecting your skills through **deliberate practice**—strong effort to improve target performance over time. Practice alone does not lead to nearly as much improvement as thinking through what you have done to look for areas for improvement.[46] Feedback from others is also helpful. Assume that a loan officer at a bank signs off on loans to small business owners. She engages in deliberate practice by following the history of these loans to evaluate which business owners proved to be good risks, and those that proved to be poor risks. She frequently asks herself, "What did I miss here? "What did I do right here?" In this way, the loan officer is working smarter by honing her risk-evaluation skills.

deliberate practice

Strong effort to improve target performance over time.

Value Orderliness and Cleanliness.   An orderly desk, work area, briefcase, hard drive, or storage drive does not inevitably indicate an orderly mind. Yet, it does help most people become more productive because they can better focus their mind. Being surrounded by a collection of small, unfinished tasks interferes with your ability to focus on major tasks. Also, less time is wasted and less energy is expended if you do not have to hunt for information that you thought you had on hand. The central message of the best-seller *Getting Things Done* by David Allen is that to achieve maximum efficiency and relaxation is to clear clutter both outside and inside your mind.[47] One way of clearing clutter from your mind is to write down your tasks on to-do lists. If you are orderly, you clear clutter.

Knowing where information is and what information you have available is a way of being in control of your job. When your job gets out of control, you are probably working at less than peak efficiency. Valuing cleanliness improves productivity in several ways. According to the Japanese system, cleanliness is the bedrock of quality. Also, after you have thoroughly cleaned your work area, you will usually attain a fresh outlook.

As with any suggestions about human behavior, individual differences exist with respect to the impact of clutter on productivity. Internet guru Esther Dyson has a work area so cluttered that she gives the impression of being an exaggerated case of a person needing help from a personal productivity consultant. It has also been argued that focusing too much on tidiness might detract from creative thinking, and that many messy people, such as Albert Einstein, believe that a messy work area facilitates their creative thinking. To quote the great man, "If a cluttered desk is a sign of a cluttered mind, of what the, is an empty desk?"[48]

Value Good Attendance and Punctuality.   Good attendance and punctuality are expected of both experienced and inexperienced employees. You cannot be productive unless you are physically present in your work area. The same principle applies whether you work on company premises or at home. One exception is that some people can work through solutions to job problems while engaged in recreation. Keep in mind, too, that being late for or absent from meetings sends the silent message that you do not regard the meeting as being important. Also, being late for a meeting, whether face-to-face or virtual, is regarded quite negatively by many managers. Some managers even lock the door to the meeting room after the meeting has begun. Whether the person is late or absent for work, or just for a meeting, the behavior is interpreted by many as demonstrating irresponsibility.

Attain a Balance in Life and Avoid Being a Workaholic.   A productive attitude to maintain is that overwork can lead to negative stress and burnout. Proper physical rest and relaxation can contribute to mental alertness and an improved ability to cope with frustration. Many people do not achieve enough rest and relaxation as inferred from the avoidance of vacations. A recent survey by Right Management showed that 66 percent of 667 surveyed workers had not used all their vacation time in the year studied.[49] During a recession, the tendency increases to not take all the vacation time allotted to the employee.

The environmentally induced attention deficit disorder and extreme jobs described above represent a life out of balance. A strategy for preventing overwork is to strive for a balance in which you derive satisfaction from various spheres of life. Major spheres in addition to work include family life, romance, sports, the arts and music, faith, and intellectual growth.

A strongly recommended technique for attaining balance between work and other spheres of life is to learn how to say no diplomatically to your boss and family members.[50] For example, your boss might ask you to take on a project when you are already overloaded. It would be necessary to *occasionally* explain that you are so overloaded that you could not do a good job with the new assignment. And, you might have to *occasionally* turn down your family's or friend's request to take a weekend vacation when you face heavy work demands.

Neglecting the normal need for rest and relaxation can lead to **workaholism**, an addiction to work in which not working is an uncomfortable experience. Some types of workaholics are perfectionists who are never satisfied with their work and therefore find it difficult to leave work behind, and have no real hobbies outside of the office. In addition, the perfectionist-type workaholic may become heavily focused on control of people and information, leading to rigid behavior and strained interpersonal relationships. Many workaholics take laptops to bed, and leave their cell phones on during the night to catch any potential calls from distant time zones. However, some people who work long and hard are classified as achievement-oriented workaholics who thrive on hard work and are usually highly productive.[51] For example, a person with strong family values might nevertheless work 65 hours per week for one year while establishing a new business. In contrast, giving up on the income and status you are striving for to avoid working long hours may not be a good idea.

workaholism

An addiction to work in which not working is an uncomfortable experience.

Increase Your Energy. According to Tony Schwartz, the founder of the Energy Project in New York City, increasing your energy is the best way to get more done faster and better. Becoming more energetic leads to more productivity gains than merely working longer hours. Schwartz believes that energy has four wellsprings—the body, emotions, mind, and spirit. Rituals can be established to build energy in the four areas, highlighted as follows:

1. **Body.** Increasing bodily energy closely follows some of the guidelines for stress management described above. Proper nutrition, moderate physical exercise, adequate rest, and taking brief breaks form work all enhance a person's energy level.

2. **Emotions.** Positive emotions bring us much more energy than do negative ones. Being in the fight-or-flight mode too frequently lowers emotional energy. Deep abdominal breathing can help ward off negative emotion. A powerful ritual that helps generate positive emotion is to express appreciation to others, following the suggestions for giving recognition presented in Chapter 11. Overcoming the idea that you are a victim can also bring about positive energy.

3. **Mind.** To enhance mental energy, it is particularly important to minimize distractions that lead to constant multitasking. Switching to another task increases the amount of time required to complete the primary tasks by up to 25 percent, a phenomenon know as *switching time.*

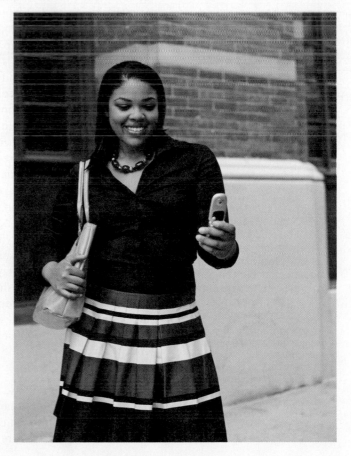

We recognize, however, that you still have to live in a modern world. If you are preparing a report, and your boss sends you an urgent IM, or your sick parent or child sends you a text message, it is natural to be distracted away from your primary task. The sensible strategy is to minimize distractions, not eliminate them completely.

4. Spirit. Participating in activities that give you a sense of meaning and purpose, such coaching and mentoring others, boosts the energy of the spirit. Being attentive to your deeper needs, such as being concerned about human or animal welfare, can boost your effectiveness and satisfaction on the job.[52]

You may have observed that this energy program for business executives is quite similar to what you have been studying in relation to developing interpersonal skills.

Enhancing Personal Productivity through Work Habits and Skills

LEARNING OBJECTIVE 6

Overcoming procrastination and developing the right attitudes contribute to personal productivity. Effective work habits and skills are also essential for high productivity. Six key work habits and skills are described next. They represent a mixture of traditional productivity boosters and those geared toward information technology.

Prepare a To-Do List and Set Priorities.   At the heart of every time management system is list making, whether the list is placed on an index card, in a leather-bound planner, or in a personal digital assistant, or smart phone. The to-do list is the basic tool for achieving your daily goals, which in turn helps you achieve bigger goals and your mission. Almost every successful person in any field composes a list of important and less important tasks that need to be done. Many business executives stick a to-do list in their jacket pocket each morning. Before you compose a useful list, you need to set aside a few minutes of quiet time every day to sort out the tasks at hand. This is the most basic aspect of planning.

The "Getting Things Done" system of time management guru David Allen is built on a base of a to-do list. First, you transfer all the tasks floating around in your head onto paper or into software, and sort them into a system of prioritized lists. Second, you take the items on the to-do lists (such as "sanitize the bakery") into "next actions," or necessary steps to accomplish the goal.[53] For the task in question, you might send an e-mail to a commercial cleaning company in your area.

As is well known, it is helpful to set priorities for items on the to-do list. A typical system is to use A to signify critical or essential items, B to signify important items, and C for the least important ones. Although an item might be regarded as a C (e.g., emptying the wood shavings from the electronic pencil sharpener), it still makes a contribution to your management of time and sense of well-being. Accomplishing anything reduces some stress. Also, many people obtain satisfaction from crossing off an item on their list, however trivial. If you are at all conscientious, small, unaccomplished items will come back to interfere with your concentration.

To-do lists contribute enormously to productivity, yet a to-do list may have to be revamped to meet the changing demands of the day. Marissa Mayer, vice president, Search Products and User Experience, at Google, explains that she keeps a task list in a text file. She uses the list as high-priority things to focus on. "But at Google things can change pretty fast. This morning I had my list of what I thought I was going to do today, but now I'm doing entirely different things," says Mayer.[54] As a result, she quickly prepares a new to-do list.

Preparing to-do lists should not become an end in itself, with so much time devoted to list making that accomplishing some of the tasks are neglected. The compulsive list maker sometimes neglects seeing the big picture of what needs to get done. Another danger is filling the to-do list with items you would have to accomplish anyway, such as "check e-mail" or "handle customer inquiry." The to-do list can become so long that it becomes an overwhelming task.

Streamline Your Work and Emphasize Important Tasks.   As companies continue to operate with fewer workers than in the past despite prosperity, more unproductive work must be eliminated. Getting rid of unproductive work is part of *business process improvement* in which work processes are radically redesigned and simplified. Every employee is expected

> " Time is your most precious commodity. You students live as if you had infinite time. You can always make more money later. But you can't make more time. Time, like money, must be explicitly managed. "
>
> —Paraphrased from comments made to his students by Randy Pausch, Professor of computer science at Carnegies Mellon University, and co-author of the best-seller, *The Last Lecture* (New York: Hyperion, 2008).[55] Before and after his death at age 47, Pausch attained a cult following.

to get rid of work that does not contribute to productivity or help customers. In general, to streamline your work, look for duplication of effort and waste. An example of duplication of effort would be to routinely send people e-mail and voicemail messages covering the same topic. An example of waste would be to call a meeting for disseminating information that could easily be communicated by e-mail.

Emphasizing important tasks means that you make sure to take care of A items on your to-do list. It also implies that you search to accomplish a few work activities that, if done well, would make a big difference in your job performance. Although important tasks may take less time to accomplish than many routine tasks, they can represent the difference between success and failure. Five minutes of telephone conversation with a major customer might do more good for your company than three hours of arranging obsolete inventory in the warehouse.

Concentrate on One Important Task at a Time Instead of Multitasking.   While working on important tasks, concentrate on what you are doing. Effective executives and professionals have a well-developed capacity to concentrate on the problem or person facing them, however surrounded they are with other obligations. Intense concentration leads to crisper judgment and analysis and also minimizes major errors. Another useful by-product of concentration is that it helps reduce absentmindedness. If you really concentrate on what you are doing, the chances diminish that you will forget what you intended to do.

While concentrating on an important task, such as performing analytical work or writing a report, avoid multitasking, or performing more than one activity simultaneously. Common forms of multitasking include surfing the Internet or reading e-mail while engaged in a phone conversation with a coworker or customer. Both experimental evidence and opinion have accumulated that multitasking while performing important tasks leads to problems in concentration, along with significant errors—for most people. The information about mental energy described above applies here. Multitasking on routine tasks has less negative consequences, and can sometimes be a legitimate time saver. For example, waiting in line at the airport during business travel provides a good opportunity to review company documents or catch up on work-related news.

David E. Meyer, the director of the Brain, Cognition and Action Laboratory at the University of Michigan, notes that when people attempt to perform two or more related tasks at the same time or alternating rapidly—instead of doing them sequentially—two negative consequences occur. Errors increase substantially, and the amount of time to perform the task may double.[56] Also, according to recent research about the brain, few people can concentrate on more than four tasks at once.[57]

Multitasking has enormous potential negative consequences when the lives of others are at stake, such as when driving a car, truck, or flying an airplane. In a celebrated case, two Northwest airline pilots lost their job because they used their personal laptops while in flight. As a result, they lost track of their responsibilities, and neglected frantic messages from air-traffic controllers, and flew past their destination airport in Minneapolis. The two pilots failed to establish radio contact with controllers for 78 minutes, and overshot their destination by more than 100 miles.[58]

Place the potential dangers of multitasking on a personal level. Would you want a cardiac surgeon to operate on a loved one while she was receiving personal calls on her cell phone? Would you want your commercial airline pilot to be sending text messages to "friends" on a social network while he was flaying through a storm? (Using personal laptops while in flight is not reassuring either.)

BACK TO THE OPENING CASE

Lynai Lutes and her coworkers at the advertising agency in Arlington, Texas, are prospering. One of the reasons for their success is that they do not subscribe to the idea that workers at a small firm are too busy to spend time thinking, and instead must chase after details continuously. Instead, the group invests enough time in quiet reflection to find creative solutions for their clients. Also, the time devoted to concentrating on one major task helps reduce stress.

Stay in Control of Paperwork and Electronic Work.   Although it is fashionable to complain about paperwork in responsible jobs, the effective career person does not neglect paperwork. (Paperwork includes electronic work, such as electronic mail and voicemail.) Paperwork involves taking care of administrative details such as correspondence, invoices, human resource reports, expense reports, and inventory forms. A considerable amount of electronic work results in paperwork because many e-mail messages and attachments wind up being printed. Unless paperwork and electronic work are attended to, a person's job may get out of control. A small amount of time should be invested in paperwork every day. Nonprime time (when you are at less than your peak of efficiency but not overfatigued) is the best time to take care of paperwork.

An effective technique is to respond quickly to high-priority e-mail messages, and permanently delete those you will most likely not need to refer to again. Print and file only those e-mail messages of high importance to avoid being overwhelmed with piles of old messages. For many types of work, it is important to be able to access old e-mails. However, some workers complain (brag?) of having 6,000 e-mails in their inbox. In addition to clogging the servers, this large accumulation of e-mails is distracting, thereby lowering productivity. Old e-mails should be archived, and others moved to appropriate folders.[59]

Communicating by e-mail or telephone with coworkers in distant time zones creates special challenges in terms of staying in control of electronic work. Assume that Pedro working in Washington DC has clients in London who want to have telephone conferences at 9 a.m. their time. Pedro has to be on the phone at 3 a.m. his time, so it is best to make all his 3 a.m. calls one morning per week rather than having a life out of control because he has to be on the phone many mornings at 3 a.m.

Work Productively from Your Home Office or Virtual Office.   A growing segment of the workforce works either full or part time from home or from a **virtual office**. Estimates vary considerably, but it appears that about 4 percent of corporate employees work primarily from the home. Such an office is a place of work without a fixed physical location from where the worker or workers communicate their output electronically. A virtual office might be in a car, train, airplane, or hotel room; on a park bench; or wherever the worker happens to be at the time. Many people adapt well to working at home and from virtual offices because they are self-starters and self-disciplined. Many other workers lack the self-discipline and effective work habits necessary to be productive outside of a traditional office. Following is a list of representative suggestions for being productive while working independently.[60]

- Act as if you work in a traditional office. Set specific working hours, get dressed, go outside the house for a few minutes, then return and get to work. Also, close your office at home or virtual office at some regular time. Otherwise, you are open for business all the time. If you work at home, establish a clear workspace and let your family and friends know when you cannot be disturbed.
- Stay in touch with teammates to enhance your team player skills and not lose out on important information that could lower your effectiveness (such as missing an appointment at the traditional office). Stay in touch with other workers also, such as visiting an office supply store or attending networking meetings. In this way, you will feel less isolated from the workforce—assuming feeling isolated is a problem for you.
- Minimize conducting your personal life at the same time as working (e.g., working while watching television, talking to neighbors, or shopping over the Internet).
- Schedule regular times for meals and snacks; otherwise, you will lose many minutes and gain many pounds taking food and beverage breaks.

The practice of working at home or from virtual offices is increasing rapidly, so these suggestions merit careful consideration. Several of the productivity ideas also fit the conventional office. Best Buy is attempting to foster the virtual office movement with its results-only work environment (ROWE). The idea is that workers are free to do whatever they want, wherever they want, so long as the work gets done.[61] Of course, sales associates

virtual office

A place of work without a fixed physical location, where the output is communicated electronically.

Productivity Boosting through Work Habits

The chapter has already given you ideas about using work habits to increase productivity. Here is a chance to make some personal applications of your own. Gather into small teams or work individually to identify 10 ways in which good work habits, as well as using the Internet, can increase personal productivity either on the job or at home. To supplement your own thinking, you might search the Internet for ideas on how the Internet is supposed to boost productivity.

do not fit this system because a worker cannot demonstrate HDTVs to customers while at an Internet café. Also, if part of your job is to help other workers in person, or answer their spontaneous questions, a virtual office is not an effective option.

Enhance Your Internet Search Skills. An important job skill is searching the Internet for a variety of information. It follows that if you develop your Internet search skills, you will be more productive by obtaining the results you need within a reasonable time. First, it is helpful to rely on several search engines to seek needed information. Several meta-search engines claim to be so comprehensive that no other engine is required. Such claims are exaggerated, because the same search word entered into several different comprehensive engines will reveal a different list of sources. Millions of people believe that conducting an Internet search means only that you google your search term.

Second, give careful thought to the search word or phrase you use. The more specific you are, the better it is. Assume that you wanted to find software to enhance your productivity, and that you enter the word "software" into a search engine. You will probably receive a message indicating that approximately one billion entries have been located in response to your personal inquiry. You are better advised to use the search phrase "Software for increasing personal productivity."

Third, for many searches, framing the query as a phrase by enclosing it in quotation marks refines the number of hits (or sites) returned. Place quotation marks before and after the search word, such as "software for improving work habits." Fourth, if you don't find what you want in your initial search, reframe your question in another way or change the terms. How about "software for time management" or "computer programs for increasing personal efficiency"? Skill-Building Exercise 16-4 will help you make better use of the Internet to enhance your personal productivity.

Overcoming Time Wasters

Another basic thrust to improve personal productivity is to minimize wasting time. The average U.S. worker wastes 28 percent of the day with interruptions, such as checking e-mail, responding to an instant message, clicking on YouTube, or posting a personal message on Twitter or Facebook. The wasted time includes doing the task and recovery time, with the combination resulting in an estimated productivity drain of $650 billion per year.[62] Recognize, however, that answer the phone or responding to an e-mail with a legitimate work purpose is not an interruption—it is part of your job.

Many of the techniques already described in this chapter help save time, such as eliminating nonessential work. Whether or not an activity is a time waster depends on the purpose of the activity. Suppose you play computer solitaire for 10 minutes to reduce stress and then return to work refreshed and more productive. In contrast, another worker who spends 10 minutes playing solitaire just for fun is wasting time.

Figure 16-7 presents a list of common time wasters. Being aware of time wasters will help sensitize you to the importance of minimizing them. Even if you saved just 10 minutes per workday, the productivity gain over a year could be enormous.

To analyze whether you might be wasting time, do Skill-Building Exercise 16-5 Self-Assessment Quiz 16-2 gives you an opportunity to think through your tendencies toward a subtle type of time wasting.

LEARNING OBJECTIVE 7

FIGURE 16-7   Ways to Prevent and Overcome Time Wasting

1.   Get your desk, as well as your work space (usually a cubicle or office) in order for good because sorting through disorder wastes so much time. Also, keep track of important names, places, and things to avoid wasting time searching for them.

2.   Use a time log for two weeks to track time wasters. (See Skill-Building Exercise 16-5.)

3.   Avoid the computer as a diversion from work, such as sending jokes back and forth to work members, playing video games, and checking out recreational Web sites during working hours.

4.   Cluster together tasks such as returning phone calls or responding to e-mail messages. For example, in most jobs it is possible to be polite and productive by reserving two or three 15-minute periods per day for taking care of e-mail correspondence.

5.   Socialize on the job just enough to build your network. Chatting with coworkers is a major productivity drain.

6.   Be prepared for meetings by, for example, having a clear agenda and sorting through the documents you will be referring to. Make sure electronic equipment is in working order before attempting to use it during the meeting.

7.   Set a time limit for tasks after you have done them once or twice.

8.   Prepare a computer template for letters and computer documents that you send frequently. (The template is essentially a form letter, especially with respect to the salutation and return address.)

9.   When you arrive at work, be ready to get started working immediately. Greet people quickly, avoid checking your personal e-mail, and shut off your cell phone.

10. Take care of as much e-mail correspondence as you can after you have finished your other work, unless a key part of your job is dealing with e-mail. It consumes substantial time.

11. Avoid perfectionism, which leads you to keep redoing a project. Let go and move on to another project.

12. Make use of bits of time—for instance, five minutes between appointments. Invest those five minutes in sending a work-related e-mail message or revising your to-do list.

13. Minimize procrastination, the number one time waster for most people.

14. Avoid spreading yourself too thin by doing too many things at once, such as having one project too many to handle. When you are overloaded, time can be wasted because of too many errors.

15. Manage interruptions by letting coworkers know when you are available for consultation, and when you need to work independently—except for emergencies. Respond to instant messages only if your job requires responding immediately. Batch your instant messages just as you would other e-mails.

Sources: Suggestion 1 is from Toddi Gutner, "Beat the Clock," *Business Week,* February/March 2008, p. 58; Suggestions 6, 7, and 7 are based on Stephen R. Covey with Hyrum Smith, "What If You Could Chop an Hour from Your Day for Things That Matter Most?" *USA Weekend,* January 22–24, 1999, pp. 4–5; suggestion 10 is from Anita Bruzzese, "Tips to Avoid Wasting Time," Gannet News Service, August 9, 2004. Support for suggestion 13 is found in Vince Thompson, "Make the Most of Your White Space," *jobs@UpLadder.com,* October 3, 2007. Data about the productivity drain of interruptions are analyzed in Quintus R. Jett and Jennifer M. George, "Work Interrupted: A Closer Look at the Role of Interruptions in Organizational Life," *Academy of Management Review,* July 2003, pp. 494–507.

SKILL-BUILDING EXERCISE 16-5

Maintaining a Time Log

An effective starting point to avoid wasting time is to identify how you spend the 168 hours you have each week (24 hours × 7 days). For two weeks, catalog all the time you spend, down to as much detail as you can tolerate. Include the large obvious items, as well as the small items that are easy to forget. Keep track of any activity that requires at least five minutes. Major items would include working, attending class, studying, reading, watching television, sleeping, eating, going places, and time with loved ones and friends (hanging out). Small items would include visiting the coffee shop or vending machine, purchasing gum, and clipping your nails.

If you multitask, such as walking and listening to music, do not double-count the time.

When your time logs have been completed, search for complete wastes of time, or activities that could be shortened. You might find, for example, that you spend about 45 minutes per day in the pursuit and consumption of coffee. If you reduced that time to 30 minutes, you would have an additional 15 minutes per day that you could invest in your career. However, if coffee time includes forming alliances with people or maintaining relationships, maybe the 45-minute-per-day investment is worthwhile.

Tendencies toward Perfectionism

Directions: Many perfectionists hold some of the behaviors and attitudes described below. To help understand your tendencies toward perfectionism, rate how strongly you agree with each of the statements below on a scale of 0 to 4 by circling the appropriate number. 0 means disagree, 4 means agree.

1.	Many people have told me that I am a perfectionist.	0	1	2	3	4
2.	I often correct the speech of others.	0	1	2	3	4
3.	It takes me a long time to write an e-mail because I keep checking and rechecking my writing.	0	1	2	3	4
4.	I often criticize the color combinations my friends are wearing.	0	1	2	3	4
5.	When I purchase food at a supermarket, I usually look at the expiration date so that I can purchase the freshest.	0	1	2	3	4
6.	I can't stand when people use the term "remote" instead of "remote control" or "cell" instead of "cell phone."	0	1	2	3	4
7.	If a company representative asked me "What is your *social*," I would reply something like, "Do you mean my *social security number?*"	0	1	2	3	4
8.	I hate to see dust on furniture.	0	1	2	3	4
9.	I like the Martha Stewart's idea of having every decoration in the home just right.	0	1	2	3	4
10.	I never put a map back in the glove compartment until it is folded just right.	0	1	2	3	4
11.	Once an eraser on a pencil of mine becomes hard and useless, I throw away the pencil.	0	1	2	3	4
12.	I adjust all my watches and clocks so that they show exactly the same time.	0	1	2	3	4
13.	It bothers me that clocks on personal computers are often wrong by a few minutes.	0	1	2	3	4
14.	I clean the keyboard on my computer at least every other day.	0	1	2	3	4
15.	I organize my e-mail messages and computer documents into many different, clearly labeled files.	0	1	2	3	4
16.	You won't find old coffee cups or soft drink containers on my desk.	0	1	2	3	4
17.	I rarely start a new project or assignment until I have completed my present project or assignment.	0	1	2	3	4
18.	It is very difficult for me to concentrate when my work area is disorganized.	0	1	2	3	4
19.	Cobwebs in chandeliers and other lighting fixtures bother me.	0	1	2	3	4
20.	It takes me a long time to make a purchase such as a digital camera because I keep studying the features on various models.	0	1	2	3	4
21.	When I balance my checkbook, it usually comes out right within a few dollars.	0	1	2	3	4
22.	I carry enough small coins and dollar bills with me so that when I shop I can pay the exact amount without requiring change.	0	1	2	3	4
23.	I throw out any underwear or T-shirts that have even the smallest holes or tears.	0	1	2	3	4
24.	I become upset with myself if I make a mistake.	0	1	2	3	4
25.	When a fingernail of mine is broken or chipped, I fix it as soon as possible.	0	1	2	3	4
26.	I am carefully groomed whenever I leave my home.	0	1	2	3	4
27.	When I notice packaged goods or cans on the floor in a supermarket, I will often place them back on the shelf.	0	1	2	3	4
28.	I think that carrying around antibacterial cleaner for the hands is an excellent idea.	0	1	2	3	4

(Continued)

29. If I am with a friend, and he or she has a loose hair on the shoulder,   0   1   2   3   4
I will remove it without asking.

30. I am a perfectionist.   0   1   2   3   4

Total Score _____

Scoring and Interpretation: Add the numbers you circled to obtain your total score.

91 or over You have strong perfectionist tendencies to the point that it could interfere with your taking quick action when necessary. Also, you may annoy many people with your perfectionism.

61–90 You have a moderate degree of perfectionism that could lead you to produce high-quality work and be a dependable person.

31–60 You have a mild degree of perfectionism. You might be a perfectionist in some situations quite important to you, but not in others.

0–30 You are not a perfectionist. You might be too casual about getting things done right, meeting deadlines, and being aware of details.

SELF-ASSESSMENT QUIZZES IN OVERVIEW

Self-Assessment Quiz 16-1 measures tendencies toward procrastination. Thinking about the extent of your procrastination, and overcoming excessive amounts, can help you develop career thrust. You might be able to get by procrastinating small tasks, but delaying the completion of large, complex tasks like preparing a budget or developing a report about customer service will eventually result in low performance. Self-Assessment Quiz 16-2 measures perfectionism which in large doses can lead to procrastination and not getting things done. However, like fat in the diet, a healthy dose of perfectionism is an asset because it can lead to high levels of performance. Oprah Winfrey and Donald Trump are both perfectionists without being obsessed over details.

Concept Review and Reinforcement

Key Terms

Summary

A major challenge facing any worker who wants to stay healthy and have good interpersonal relationships is to manage stress effectively. Individual differences play a big role in determining whether an event will lead to stress. The physiological changes that take place within the body in response to stress are responsible for most of the stress symptoms. The fight-or-flight response is the battle against the stressor.

The activation of hormones, such as cortisol, when the body has to cope with a stressor produces short-term physiological reactions, including an increase in heart rate and blood pressure. When stress levels rarely subside, the physiological changes create damage. People under continual negative stress age quickly. Hindrance stressors have a negative effect on motivation and performance. However, the right amount of stress (challenge stressors) prepares us for meeting difficult challenges and improves performance. An optimum level of stress exists for most people and most tasks. In general, performance tends to be best under moderate amounts of stress.

One of the major problems of prolonged stress is that it may lead to burnout, a condition of emotional, mental, and physical exhaustion in response to long-term stressors. Feelings of having limited control and not being recognized are major contributors to burnout. Burnout also creates cynicism and a distancing from tasks and people. Workers who perceive the cause of burnout to be external are more likely to become less committed to the firm and more cynical. Burnout also damages the physical health of workers.

Four personality factors predisposing people toward stress are low perceived control, low self-efficacy, Type A behavior and hostility, and negative affectivity. The heart attack triggers associated with Type A behavior are hostility, anger, cynicism, and suspiciousness, with hostility having the biggest impact. Frequently encountered job stressors are role overload including extreme jobs, role conflict and ambiguity, adverse environmental conditions including carpal tunnel syndrome and long commutes, environmentally induced attention deficit disorder, and job insecurity and job loss. Another frequent job stressor is adverse interactions with customers and clients and emotional labor.

Managing stress refers to controlling stress by making it become a constructive force in your life. Coping with, or managing, stress includes hundreds of activities, with substantial individual differences in which technique is effective. Seven representative stress management methods are to eliminate or modify the stressor, get appropriate physical exercise, rest sufficiently, maintain a healthy diet, build a support network, practice visualization and meditation, and practice everyday methods of stress reduction.

Achieving high personal productivity on the job is more in demand than ever. A starting point in improving productivity is to minimize procrastination, an enormous problem for many people that can be approached as follows: Commit to what you want in life; calculate the cost of procrastination; follow the worst in, first out (WIFO) principle; break the task into manageable chunks; make a commitment to other people; remove some clutter from your mind; satisfy your stimulation quota in constructive ways; and eliminate rewards for procrastinating.

Developing good work habits and time management practices is often a matter of developing the right attitudes toward your work and toward time, as follows: (1) Begin with a mission and goals; (2) work smarter, not harder including the use of deliberate practice (3) value orderliness and cleanliness; (4) value good attendance and punctuality; (5) attain a balance in life and avoid being a workaholic, and (6) increase your energy (body, emotions, mind, and spirit).

Effective work habits and skills are essential for high productivity, including the following: (1) Prepare a to-do list and set priorities, (2) streamline your work and emphasize important tasks, (3) concentrate on one important task at a time instead of multitasking, (4) stay in control of paperwork and electronic work, (5) work productively from your home office or virtual office, and (6) enhance your Internet search skills.

Another basic thrust to improved personal productivity is to minimize time wasting. Whether or not an activity is a time waster depends on its purpose. Being aware of time wasters such as those presented in Figure 16-6 will sensitize you to the importance of minimizing them.

Questions for Discussion and Review

1. Why might it be true that people who love their work live much longer than people who retire early because they dislike working?

2. Why might having your stress under control improve your interpersonal relationships?

3. Give an example of adverse interaction with a customer that you have personally experienced, or that you have witnessed. What could the worker have done to decrease some of the stress in the situation?

4. Interview a person in a high-pressure job in any field. Find out whether the person experiences significant stress and what method he or she uses to cope with it.

5. Provide an example from your own or somebody else's life of how having a major goal in life can help a person be better organized.

6. Executives at Toyota, among many other Japanese companies, emphasize that clean work areas in the factory enhance productivity. What might explain this relationship between cleanliness and productivity?

7. Describe any way in which you have used information technology to make you more productive.

8. Use information in this chapter to explain how a person might be well-organized yet still not get very far in his or her career.

9. For many young corporate professionals, a date often consists of the two people getting together in his or her place to spend three hours doing office work on their laptop computers, followed by a take-out meal. What is your evaluation of this approach to boosting personal productivity?

10. With millions of workers making regular use of personal digital assistants and smart phones throughout the world, why hasn't productivity in organizations taken a dramatic leap forward?

The Web Corner

http://www.stress.org
(Institute for Stress Management)

http://stress.about.com
(Considerable information about stress plus several self-quizzes)

http://ub-counseling.buffalo.edu/ stressprocrast.shtml
(Overcoming procrastination for students)

Internet Skill Builder: Getting Personal Help from Your Employer

Use your favorite search engines to learn about an Employee Assistance Programs (EAPs). After visiting several sights, answer these questions: (1) What type of help can an employee expect to receive from an EAP? (2) How does an EAP help with stress management? (3) Does the EAP counselor typically tell the company the nature of the problem facing the employee who sought assistance? (4) What benefits do companies expect from offering an EAP to employees? (5) What would I tell the company if I needed help with problems that are causing me severe stress?

Internet Skill Builder: What Are You Doing with Your Time?

Go to www.getmoredone.com/tabulator.html to find the Pace Productivity Tabulator. This interactive module enables you to enter the time you spend on 11 major activities (such as employment, eating, sleeping, and television watching) and compare your profile to others. You are also able to enter your ideal profile to see where you would like to be. You just follow the straightforward instructions. After arriving at your personal pie chart, ask yourself, "What have I learned that will enhance my personal productivity?"

Developing Your Human Relations Skills

Interpersonal Relations Case 16.1

Rachel Runs the Treadmill

Six thirty Tuesday morning, 38-year-old Rachel Mendez hops out of her bed while her husband Ben Mendez is still sleeping. Rachel's first stop is to wake up her nine-year-old daughter, and encourage her to start getting ready to meet the school bus on time. By 8 a.m. Rachel is in her car and on her way to her job as a business development specialist for a human resource outsourcing company. Her primary responsibility is to entice small- and medium-size companies to turn over most of their human resource functions to her firm.

Just as Rachel begins to manage her e-mail and plan her agenda for the day, she places her right hand about three inches to the right of her heart. Rachel can feel the tightness next to her heart, and in her left arm. She thinks to herself, "This feels like I'm going to have a heart attack, but it doesn't make sense for a woman my age to be a heart attack victim. But I'm happy that I have an appointment at the cardiology center on Thursday."

At the North Side Cardiology Center, Rachel is first interviewed by Nurse Practitioner Janet Trudeau before her interview with Dr. Harry Ching, the cardiologist. Trudeau first took a brief medical history, followed by an interview. Parts of the interview with Trudeau went as follows:

Trudeau: So tell me in more detail why you came to visit our cardiology center.

Mendez: I have these annoying chest pains next to my heart and in my left arm. The pains usually start when I am extremely aggravated and frustrated. I have the pains about once a day.

Trudeau: Do you ever faint or become light-headed during the pains?

Mendez: No, my problem is just the pains. I keep doing whatever I'm doing when the pain hits.

Trudeau: Tell me about the situations you find so aggravating and frustrating.

Mendez: I'm really stressing out. I have a ton of aggravations and worries. To begin my nine-year-old daughter Samantha has seizures. She is under treatment but the problem remains, and it's worrisome. I worry every day that Samantha will have a seizure and strike her head or get involved in an accident.

My work is also quite worrisome. I work mostly on commission selling human resource services. Our business has grown rapidly in the last few years, but we have kind of dried up the territory. I have to travel more to find new clients. My earnings are taking a turn downward despite the extra travel.

Trudeau: Are you the sole breadwinner in the family?

Mendez: No, my husband Alex is an assistant manager at a Ruby Tuesday restaurant, and he makes a modest living. But talking about aggravation, my husband is a decent guy but he gives me chest pains. I think he cares much more about professional sports, especially the NFL and the NHL than he does about Samantha and me. If he's watching a game, I can forget about talking about something serious.

And then, of course, Alex works the hours of a restaurant manager, which means that he is often working when I am not working, like on Saturdays and Sundays.

Trudeau: Any other major aggravations in your life?

Mendez: Yes, commuting on busy highways. I can feel my chest pains starting when I think of sitting still for 15 minutes during rush-hour traffic.

Trudeau: Thank you Rachel. I will be studying this information before your interview with Dr. Ching. Have a seat in the waiting room. He will be with you in about 10 minutes.

Later that day Mendez had an extensive cardiology exam, including an electrocardiogram. Dr. Ching informed her that despite the muscle tension she was experiencing, her heart was in excellent condition.

Case Questions

1. What sources of stress does Rachel Mendez appear to be facing?
2. What do you recommend Mendez do about the stressors she is facing?
3. Given that Mendez does not have a heart problem, should she be concerned about the stressors in her life? Explain your answer.
4. How might Mendez organize her work and her life better to feel that her life is less out of control?

Interpersonal Relations Case 16.2

Stress Busting at the Agriculture and Markets Group

The State Department of Agriculture and Markets was having a demanding year. The mission of the group is to inspect grocery stores for possible health violations, such as unsanitary conditions and the sale of tainted food and meats. The group had a record number of complaints to investigate partially because so many stores were purchasing packaged goods, products, and meats from bottom-price suppliers in order to trim costs. At the same time, the Department of Agriculture and Markets was on a mandated cutback in spending. As a result, a few of the inspectors who had quit could not be replaced. The remaining inspectors were therefore carrying a much heavier workload.

The reality of a heavier workload with fewer staff available to make on-site visits created a high-pressure work environment. Michelle and Trevor, two of the more junior inspectors, decided together that the group needed to find a good way of blowing off steam. Their plan was to organize a few "prankster nights." On the first such night, six inspectors from the office got together to have a few drinks after work. During the drinking session at a bar close to the office, Michelle and Trevor announced their plan to relieve stress in a big way by pulling off a major prank.

The prank was the "popcorning" often executed by professional basketball players. The group would purchase a massive amount of popcorn and stuff into the vehicle of their supervisor Alicia Gordon, who typically parked her car in a remote spot in the garage to the state building. The three group members will pull off the prank "popcorned" her sports car the next Monday during lunch hour.

Tuesday morning, every employee at the State Department of Agriculture and Markets received an e-mail explaining that a misdemeanor had been committed in the parking lot in the form of damaging Alicia's vehicle. The e-mail also stated that the cruel act had violated the rights of Alicia Gordon to a harassment-free work environment. Anyone who knew who could have committed the hostile act of damaging Gordon's vehicle was urged to reply immediately to the e-mail.

Michelle and Trevor quickly sent text messages to each other. Michelle wrote, "Can't Alicia take a joke? What's her problem?"

Trevor wrote back, "Maybe we did lower our stress. But I'm afraid our stress is going to bump up now."

Case Questions

1. What is your evaluation of the effectiveness of the stress-reduction techniques created by Michelle and Trevor?
2. What might have been a more effective method of the group from Markets and Agriculture to have used to decrease their stress?
3. What do you recommend Michelle, Trevor, and the rest of the group do with respect to taking responsibility for their prank?

GLOSSARY

acceptance of power and authority The degree to which members of a society expect, and should expect, power to be distributed unequally.

action plan A series of steps to achieve a goal.

active listener A person who listens intensely, with the goal of empathizing with the speaker.

assertiveness Being forthright in expressing demands, opinions, feelings, and attitudes. In relation to cultural values, the degree to which individuals are (and should be) assertive, confrontation, and aggressive in their relationships with one another.

backstab An attempt to discredit by underhanded means, such as innuendo, accusation, or the like.

behavioral feedback Information given to another person that pinpoints behavior rather than personal characteristics or attitudes.

behavior modification An attempt to change behavior by manipulating rewards and punishments.

blind spots Areas of unawareness about our attitudes, thinking, and behaviors that contribute to poor decisions.

brainstorming A group problem-solving technique that promotes creativity by encouraging idea generation through noncritical discussion.

brainwriting Brainstorming by individuals working alone.

bullies People who verbally, and sometimes physically, attack others frequently.

burnout A condition of emotional, mental, and physical exhaustion in response to long-term stressors.

business etiquette A special code of behavior required in work situations.

career path A sequence of positions necessary to achieve a goal.

carpal tunnel syndrome A condition that occurs when repetitive flexing and extension of the wrist causes the tendons to swell, thus trapping and pinching the median nerve.

casual time orientation A cultural characteristic in which people view time as an unlimited and unending resource and therefore tend to be patient.

challenge stressors stressful events that have a positive direct effect on motivation and performance.

character trait An enduring characteristic of a person that is related to moral and ethical behavior.

charisma A special quality of leaders whose purposes, powers, and extraordinary determination differentiate them from others. (However, people besides leaders can be charismatic.)

coaching A method of helping workers grow and develop and improve their job competence by providing suggestions and encouragement.

cognitive behavioral approach to stress management A method for people learning to recognize how pessimistic and distorted thoughts of gloom and doom create stress.

cognitive factors The collective term for problem-solving and intellectual skills.

cognitive fitness A state of optimized ability to remember, learn, plan, and adapt to changing circumstances.

cognitive restructuring Mentally converting negative aspects into positive ones by looking for the positive elements in a situation.

cognitive style Modes of problem solving.

collective efficacy A group's belief that it can handle certain tasks.

collectivism A feeling that the group and society should receive top priority, rather than the individual.

communication The sending, receiving, and understanding of messages.

compromise Settlement of differences by mutual concessions.

concern for others An emphasis on personal relationships and a concern for the welfare of others.

conflict A situation in which two or more goals, values, or events are incompatible or mutually exclusive.

conflict of interest A situation that occurs when a person's judgment or objectivity is compromised.

confrontation Taking a problem-solving approach to differences and identifying the under lying facts, logic, or emotions that account for them.

consensus General acceptance by the group of a decision.

constructive gossip Unofficial information that supports others, is based on truth, and respects confidential information.

corporate athletes Workers who engage in high-level performance for sustained periods.

cross-functional team A work group composed of workers from different specialties, and about the same organizational level, who come together to accomplish a task.

cultural fluency The ability to conduct business in a diverse, international environment.

cultural intelligence (CQ) An outsider's ability to interpret someone's unfamiliar and ambiguous behavior the same way that person's compatriots would.

cultural sensitivity An awareness of and willingness to investigate the reasons why people of another culture act as they do.

cultural training A set of learning experiences designed to help employees understand the customs, traditions, and beliefs of another culture.

customer-centric sales process An approach to sales that emphasizes a low-pressure environment in which the sales staff acts as consultants, offering information and explaining how the produce or service can help solve a customer's problem.

cycle-of-service chart A method of tracking the moments of truth with respect to customer service.

defensive communication The tendency to receive messages in such a way that our self-esteem is protected.

defining moment Choosing between two or more ideals in which one deeply believes.

denial The suppression of information we find uncomfortable.

developmental need A specific area in which a person needs to change or improve.

difficult person An individual who creates problems for others, even though he or she has the skill and mental ability to do otherwise.

diversity training Training that attempts to bring about workplace harmony by teaching people how to get along better with diverse work associates.

effort-to-performance expectancy The probability assigned by the individual that effort will lead to performing the task correctly.

electronic brainstorming Method of generating ideas with the aid of a computer. Group members simultaneously and anonymously enter their suggestions into a computer, and the ideas are distributed to monitors of other group members.

emotional intelligence Qualities such as understanding one's own feelings, empathy for others, and the regulation of emotion to enhance living.

emotional labor The process of regulating both feelings and expressions to meet organizational goals.

empathy In communication, imagining oneself in the receiver's role, and assuming the viewpoints and emotions of that individual.

employee network (or affinity) group A group composed of employees throughout the company who affiliate on the basis of group characteristics, such as race, ethnicity, gender, sexual orientation, or physical ability status.

empowerment The process of managers transferring, or sharing, power with lower ranking employees.

ethical screening Running a contemplated decision or action through an ethics test.

ethics The moral choices a person makes. Also, what is good and bad, right and wrong, just and unjust, and what people should do.

expectancy theory A motivation theory based on the premise that the effort people expend depends on the reward they expect to receive in return.

extreme job hunting An offbeat way of attracting an employer's attention, with a small probability of success.

feedback In communication, messages sent back from the receiver to the sender.

fight-or-flight response The body's physiological and chemical battle against a stressor in which the person tries to cope with the adversity head-on or tries to flee from the scene.

formality A cultural characteristic of attaching considerable importance to tradition, ceremony, social rules, and rank.

frame of reference The fact that people perceive words and concepts differently because their vantage points and perspectives differ. Also, a lens through which we view the world.

g (general) factor A factor in intelligence that contributes to the ability to perform well in many tasks.

Galeta effect A type of self-fulfilling prophecy in which high expectations lead to high performance.

gender egalitarianism The degree to which a culture minimizes, and should minimize, gender inequality.

group decision making The process of reaching a judgment based on feedback from more than one individual.

group norms The unwritten set of expectations for group members.

groupthink A deterioration of mental efficiency, reality testing, and moral judgment in the interest of group solidarity.

hindrance stressors Those stressful events that have a negative effect on motivation and performance.

humane orientation The degree to which a society encourages and rewards, and should encourage and reward, individuals for being fair, altruistic, caring, and kind to others.

impression management A set of behaviors directed at enhancing one's image by drawing attention to oneself.

incivility In human relations, employees' lack of regard for each other.

individual differences Variations in how people respond to the same situation based on personal characteristics.

informal learning The acquisition of knowledge and skills that take place naturally outside a structured learning environment.

informality A cultural characteristic of a casual attitude toward tradition, ceremony, social rules, and rank.

information overload A phenomenon that occurs when people are so overloaded with information that they cannot respond effectively to messages.

in-group collectivism The degree to which individuals express, and should express, pride, loyalty, and cohesiveness in their organizations and families.

integrity (a) consistency of words and deeds, and (b) being true to oneself.

intelligence The capacity to acquire and apply knowledge, including solving problems.

intermittent reward A reward that is given for good performance occasionally, but not always.

interpersonal skill training The teaching of skills in dealing with others so they can be put into practice.

intuition An experience-based way of knowing or reasoning in which the weighing and balancing of evidence are done automatically.

law of effect Behavior that leads to a positive consequence for the individual tends to be repeated, whereas behavior that leads to a negative consequence tends not to be repeated.

leader-exchange model A theory explaining that group leaders establish unique working relationships with group members, thereby creating in-groups and out-groups.

leadership The ability to inspire support and confidence among the people who are needed to achieve company goals.

leadership efficacy A form of efficacy associated with confidence in the knowledge, skills, and abilities associated with leading others.

learning style The way in which a person best learns new information.

locus of control The way people look at causation in their lives.

mentor An individual with advanced experience and knowledge who is committed to giving support and career advice to a less experienced person.

message A purpose or idea to be conveyed.

metacommunication To communicate about your communication to help overcome barriers or resolve a problem.

microinequity A small, semiconscious message we send with a powerful impact on the receiver.

micromanager One who closely monitors most aspects of group members' activities, sometimes to the point of being a control freak.

mirroring Subtly imitating someone.

moments of truth Situations in which a customer comes in contact with a company and forms an impression of its service.

moral intensity In ethical decision making, how deeply others might be affected by the decision.

motivation An internal state that leads to effort expended toward objectives; an activity performed by one person to get another to accomplish work.

motivational state Any active needs and interests operating at a given time.

multiple intelligences A theory of intelligence contending that people know and understand the world in distinctly different ways and learn in different ways.

multitasking (a) You have two or more projects that you are working on, but you do not work on these projects at the same time. (b) The person does two or more things simultaneously.

negative affectivity A tendency to experience aversive emotional states.

negative reinforcement (avoidance motivation) Rewarding people by taking away an uncomfortable consequence of their behavior.

negotiating Conferring with another person to resolve a problem.

networking Developing contacts with influential people, including gaining their trust and confidence. Also, contacting friends and acquaintances and building systematically on these relationships to create a still wider set of contacts that might lead to employment.

noise Anything that disrupts communication, including the attitudes and emotions of the receiver.

nominal group technique (NGT) A group problem-solving technique that calls people together in a structured meeting with limited interaction.

nonverbal communication The transmission of messages through means other than words.

nurturing person One who promotes the growth of others.

organization culture A system of shared values and beliefs that influence worker behavior.

organizational citizenship behavior The willingness to go beyond one's job description without a specific reward apparent.

organizational politics Gaining power through any means other than merit or luck.

paraphrase To repeat in your own words what the sender says, feels, and means.

participative leadership Sharing authority with the group.

peak performance Exceptional accomplishment in a given task.

peer coaching A type of helping relationship based on qualities, such as high acceptance of the other person, authenticity, mutual trust, and mutual learning.

perceived control The belief that an individual has at his or her disposal a response that can control the negative aspects of an event.

performance orientation The degree to which a society encourages, or should encourage, and reward group members for performance improvement and excellence.

performance-to-outcome expectancy The probability assigned by the individual that performance will lead to outcomes or rewards.

personal brand For career purposes, what makes you unique, thereby distinguishing you from the competition.

personality Persistent and enduring behavior patterns that tend to be expressed in a wide variety of situations.

personality clash An antagonistic relationship between two people based on differences in personal attributes, preferences, interests, values, and styles.

personality disorder A pervasive, persistent, inflexible, maladaptive pattern of behavior that deviates from expected cultural norms.

personal productivity The amount of resources, including time, you consume to achieve a certain level of output.

person–organization fit The compatibility of the individual and the organization.

person–role conflict The situation that occurs when the demands made by the organization clash with the basic values of the individual.

political correctness Being careful not to offend or slight anyone, and being extra civil and respectful.

political decision-making model The assumption about decision making that people bring preconceived notions and biases into the decision-making situation.

positive self-talk Saying positive things about yourself.

positive reinforcement Increasing the probability that behavior will be repeated by rewarding people for making the desired response.

positive visual imagery Picturing a positive outcome in your mind.

power The ability or potential to control anything of value and to influence decisions.

proactive personality A person who is relatively unconstrained by situational forces and who brings about environmental change.

procrastination Delaying action for no good reason on tasks that need to be done.

protégé The less experienced person in a mentoring relationship who is helped by the mentor.

Pygmalion effect The phenomenon that people will rise (or fall) to the expectations that another person has of them.

rational decision-making model The traditional, logical approach to decision making based on the scientific method.

role ambiguity A condition in which the job holder receives confusing or poorly defined expectations.

role conflict The situation that occurs when a person has to choose between two competing demands or expectations.

role overload Having too much work to do.

role-person conflict A situation that takes place when the role(s) your organization expects you to occupy is in conflict with your basic values.

s (special) factors Specific components of intelligence that contribute to problem-solving ability.

self-efficacy The confidence in your ability to carry out a specific task.

self-esteem The overall evaluation people make about themselves whether positive or negative.

self-sacrificing personality A tendency to be more concerned about the welfare and interests of others than of oneself.

sexual harassment Unwanted sexually oriented behavior in the workplace that results in discomfort and/or interference with the job.

social intelligence An understanding of how relationships with bosses and colleagues, family and friends, shape our brains and affect our bodies.

social loafing The psychological term for shirking individual responsibility in a group setting.

social support seeking The degree to which people seek out others to help them with difficult problems through such means as listening, offering sympathy, and giving advice.

stress An adaptive response that is the consequence of any action, situation, or event that places special demands on a person.

stressor The external or internal force that brings about stress.

strong customer orientation A set of individual predispositions and an inclination to provide service, to be courteous and helpful in dealing with customers and associates.

summarization The process of summarizing, pulling together, condensing, and thereby clarifying the main points communicated by another person.

support network A group of people who can listen to your problems and provide emotional support.

synergy A situation in which the group's total output exceeds the sum of each individual's contribution.

team A small number of people with complementary skills who are committed to a common purpose, set of performance goals, and approach for which they hold themselves mutually accountable.

time orientation The importance nations and individuals attach to time.

toxic person One who negatively affects others because he or she dwells on the negative.

training The process of helping others acquire a job-related skill.

triarchic theory of intelligence An explanation of mental ability holding that intelligence is composed of three different subtypes: analytical, creative, and practical.

Type A behavior A behavior pattern in which the individual is demanding, impatient, and overstriving, and therefore prone to negative stress.

universal training need An area for improvement common to most people.

unwritten boundaries Dividing lines of behavior appropriate to different roles.

upward ethical leadership The leadership displayed by individuals who take action to maintain ethical standards, although higher-ups engage in questionable moral behaviors.

urgent time orientation A cultural characteristic of perceiving time as a scarce resource and tending to be impatient.

utilitarian predisposition A belief that the value of an act's outcomes should determine whether it is moral.

valence The value, worth, or attractiveness of an outcome.

value The importance a person attaches to something.

virtual office A place of work without a fixed physical location, where the output is communicated electronically.

virtual team A small group of people who conduct almost all of their collaborative work by electronic communication rather than face-to-face meetings.

win–win The belief that after conflict has been resolved both sides should gain something of value.

workaholism An addiction to work in which not working is an uncomfortable experience.

work–family conflict A state that occurs when an individual's roles of worker and active participant in social and family life compete with each other.

work orientation The number of hours per week and weeks per year people expect to invest in work versus leisure, or other nonwork activities.

REFERENCES

CHAPTER 1

1. Kevin Helliker, "Even Laundries Tumble in This Economic Cycle," *The Wall Street Journal,* November 4, 2009, p. A 20.
2. *Dale Carnegie Training* brochure, Spring–Summer 2005, p. 12.
3. Joanne Lozar Glenn, "Lessons in Human Relations," *Business Education Forum,* October 2003, p. 10.
4. Cited in Donna Nebenzahl, "Turning the Page on Corporate Leadership," *www.thestar.com (The Toronto Star)* September 19, 2009, p. 2. Based on Susan Scott, *Fierce Conversations: Achieving Success at Work & In Life, One Conversation at a Time* (New York: Random House, 2009).
5. Research cited in Bob Wall, *Working Relationships: The Simple Truth About Getting Along with Friends and Foes at Work* (Palo Alto, CA: Davies-Black, 1999).
6. George B. Yancey, Chante P. Clarkson, Julie D. Baxa, and Rachel N. Clarkson, "Example of Good and Bad Interpersonal Skills at Work," *http://www.psichi.org/pubs/articles/article_368.asp,* p. 2, accessed February 2, 2004.
7. Edward Muzio, Deborah J. Fisher, Erv R. Thomas, and Valerie Peters, "Soft Skill Quantification (SSQ) for Project Manager Competencies," *Project Management Journal,* June 2007, pp. 30–31.
8. Marshall Goldsmith, "How Not to Lose the Top Job," *Harvard Business Review,* January 2009, p. 77.
9. The model presented here is an extension and modernization of the one presented in Thomas V. Bonoma and Gerald Zaltman, *Psychology for Management* (Boston: Kent, 1981), pp. 88–92.
10. Gary P. Latham, "The Motivational Benefits of Goal-Setting," *Academy of Management Executive,* November 2004, pp. 126–127.
11. Susan B. Wilson and Michael S. Dobson, *Goal Setting: How to Create an Action Plan and Achieve Your Goals,* 2nd edition (New York: American Management Association, 2008).
12. Roger B. Hill, "On-Line Instructional Resources—Lesson 3, Interpersonal Skills," *http://www.coe.uga.edu/~rhill/workethic/less3.htm,* p. 1, accessed March 17, 2005.
13. Nancy Day, "Informal Learning Gets Results," *Workforce,* June 1998, pp. 30–36; Marcia L. Conner, "Informal Learning," *Ageless Learner,* 1997–2005, *http://agelesslearner.com/intros/informal.html,* p. 2.
14. Andrew Paradise, "Informal Learning: Overlooked or Overhyped?" *www.astd.org/lc/2008/0708_paradise.html,* pp. 1–2. Accessed January 3, 2010.
15. Morgan W. McCall, Jr., *High Flyers: Developing the Next Generation of Leaders* (Boston: Harvard Business School Press, 1998).

CHAPTER 2

1. Tom Belden, "Winging It: Sullenberger Touts the Value of Training," *Philly.com,* October 5, 2009; "Security Tape Shows Plane's Hudson Landing," *The Associated Press,* January 23, 2009; Andy Pastor, "Hero Pilot 'Sully' Stars at Hearing," *The Wall Street Journal,* June 10, 2009, p. A2.
2. Marvin Zuckerman, "Are You a Risk Taker?" *Psychology Today,* November/December 2000, p. 53.
3. Remus Ilies and Timothy A. Judge, "On the Heritability of Job Satisfaction: The Mediating Role of Personality," *Journal of Applied Psychology,* August 2003, pp. 750–759.
4. Cited in Ranit Mishori, "Why Optimism Is Powerful Medicine," *Parade,* November 15, 2009, p. 27.
5. Robert R. McRae and Juri Allik, eds, *The Five-Factor Model of Personality Across Cultures* (New York: Kluwer, 2002).
6. Sarah E. Strang and Karl W. Kuhnert, "Personality and Leadership Development Levels as Predictors of Leader Performance," *The Leadership Quarterly,* June 2009, p. 423.
7. Daniel Nettle, "The Evolution of Personality Variation in Human and Other Animals," *American Psychologist,* September 2006, p. 622.
8. "Which Traits Predict Job Performance?" *APA Help Center, http://www.apahelpcenter.org/articles/article.php?id=33,* accessed March 22, 2005.
9. Nicole M. Dudley, Karin A. Orvis, Justin E. Lebiecki, and José M. Cortina, "A Meta-Analytic Investigation of Conscientiousness in the Prediction of Job Performance: Examining the Intercorrelations and the Incremental Validity of Narrow Traits," *Journal of Applied Psychology,* January 2006, p. 51.
10. Gregory M. Hurtz and John J. Donovan, "Personality and Job Performance: The Big Five Revisited," *Journal of Applied Psychology,* December 2000, pp. 869–879.
11. David V. Day, Deidra J. Schleicher, Amy L. Unckless, and Nathan J. Hiller, "Self-Monitoring Personality at Work: A Meta-Analytic Investigation of Construct Validity," *Journal of Applied Psychology,* April 2002, pp. 390–401.
12. Gerald L. Blakely, Martha C. Andrews, and Jack Fuller, "Are Chameleons Good Citizens? A Longitudinal Study of the Relationship Between Self-Monitoring and Organizational Citizenship Behavior," *Journal of Business and Psychology,* Winter 2003, pp. 131–144; Research synthesized in Ori Brafman and Rom Brafman, "To the Vulnerable Go the Spoils," *Bloomberg Business Week,* June 14–June 2, 2010, p. 72.
13. Nathan P. Podsakoff, Whiting, S.W., Podsakoff, P.M., and Blume, B.D, "Individual- and Organizational-Level Consequences of Organizational Behaviors: A Meta-Analysis, *Journal of Applied Psychology,* January 2009, pp. 122–141.
14. Jeff Joireman, Dishan Kamdar, Denise Daniels, and Blythe Duell, "Good Citizens to the End? It Depends: Empathy and Concern with Future Consequences Moderate the Impact of a Short-Term Time Horizon on Organizational Citizenship Behaviors," *Journal of Applied Psychology,* November 2006, p. 1315.
15. Ryan D. Zimmerman, "Understanding the Impact of Personality Traits on Individuals' Turnover Decisions: A Meta-Analytic Path Model," *Personnel Psychology,* Summer 2008, pp. 309–348.
16. Cited in David Stipp, "A Little Worry Is Good for Business," *Fortune,* November 24, 2003, p. 68.
17. L. A. Witt, Lisa A. Burke, Murray R. Barrick, and Michael K. Mount, "The Interactive Effects of Conscientiousness and

Agreeableness on Job Performance," *Journal of Applied Psychology,* February 2002, pp. 164–169.

18. Carl J. Thoresen, Jill C. Bradley, Paul D. Bliese, and Joseph D. Thoresen, "The Big Five Personality Traits and Individual Job Performance Growth Trajectories in Maintenance and Transitional Job Stages," *Journal of Applied Psychology,* October 2004, pp. 835–853.

19. Isabel Briggs Myers, *Introduction to Type,* 6th ed. (Mountain View, CA: CPP, Inc., 1996), p. 10. (Revised by Linda K. Kirby and Katharine D. Myers.)

20. John Patrick Golden, *Golden Personality Type Profiler Technical Manual* (San Antonio, TX: Pearson TalentLens, 2005).

21. Golden, *Golden Personality Type Profiler,* p. 27.

22. Golden, *Golden Personality Type Profiler,* p. 24.

23. Brian S. Young, Winfred Arthur, Jr., and John Finch, "Predictors of Managerial Performance: More than Cognitive Ability," *Journal of Business and Psychology,* Fall 2000, pp. 53–72.

24. Roderick Gilkey and Clint Kitts, "Cognitive Fitness," *Harvard Business Review,* November 2007, pp. 53–66.

25. Research reported in Shirley S. Wang, "Ginkgo Fails to Postpone Dementia," *The Wall Street Journal,* November 19, 2008, p. D3. Steven T. DeKosky et al., "Ginkgo Biloba for Prevention of Dementia: A Randomized Control Trial," *Journal of the American Medical Association,* vol., 19, 2008, pp. 2253–2262.

26. Robert J. Sternberg, *Beyond IQ: A Triarchic Theory of Human Intelligence* (New York: Cambridge University Press, 1985); Bridget Murray, "Sparking Interest in Psychology Class," *APA Monitor,* October 1995, p. 51.

27. Howard Gardner, *Intelligence Reframed: Multiple Intelligence in the 21st Century* (New York: Basic Books, 1999).

28. Malcolm Gladwell, *Outliers: The Story of Success* (Boston: Little, Brown, 2008). See also Geoff Colvin, "Why Talent is Over-Rated," *Fortune,* October 27, 2008, pp. 138–147.

29. Charles G. Morris and Albert A. Maisto, *Psychology: An Introduction,* 11th edition (Upper Saddle River, NJ: Prentice Hall, 2002), p. 11.

30. Sharon Begley, "Critical Thinking: Part Skill, Part Mindset and Totally up to You," *The Wall Street Journal,* October 20, 2006, p. B1.

31. John D. Mayer, Peter Salovey, and David R. Caruso, "Emotional Intelligence: New Ability or Eclectic Traits?" *American Psychologist,* September 2008, pp. 503–515.

32. Daniel Goleman, Richard Boyatzis, and Annie McKee, "Primal Leadership: The Hidden Driver of Great Performance," *Harvard Business Review,* December 2001, pp. 42–51.

33. David A. Morand, "The Emotional Intelligence of Managers: Assessing the Construct Validity of a Nonverbal Measure of 'People Skills,'" *Journal of Business and Psychology,* Fall 2001, pp. 21–33.

34. Research cited in Mayer, Salovey, and Caruso, "Emotional Intelligence," p. 512.

35. Shalom H. Schwartz, "Universals in the Content and Structure of Values: Theoretical Advances and Empirical Tests in 20 Countries." In Mark P. Zanna, ed., *Advances in Experimental and Social Psychology* (New York: Academic Press, vol. 25, 1992), pp. 1–65.

36. 2008 Annual Report of the APA Policy and Planning Board, "How Technology Changes Everything (and Nothing) in Psychology, *American Psychologist,* July–August 2009, p. 454.

37. Jeff Payne, "Generation Jones, Still Striving," *HR Magazine,* December 2008, p. 15. (From Readers section.)

38. David C. McClelland, "How Motives, Skills, and Values Determine What People Do," *American Psychologist,* July 1985, p. 815.

39. Jeffrey R. Edwards and Daniel M. Cable, "The Value of Value Congruence," *Journal of Applied Psychology,* May 2009, pp. 654–677.

40. Jean M. Twenge, *Generation Me* (New York: The Free Press, 2006).

41. "Get Ready for 'Millennials' at Work," *Manager's Edge,* January 2006, p. 1.

CHAPTER 3

1. Dawn Fallik, "A Finance Executive Walks Away to Work His Way up from Waiter," *The Wall Street Journal,* September 22, 2009, p. D7.

2. Michelle K. Duffy, Jason D. Shaw, Kristin L. Scott, and Bennett J. Tepper, "The Moderating Roles of Self-Esteem and Neuroticism in the Relationships Between Group and Individual Undermining Behavior," *Journal of Applied Psychology,* September 2006, p. 1067.

3. April O'Connell, Vincent O'Connell, and Lois-Ann Kuntz, *Choice and Change: The Psychology of Personal Growth and Interpersonal Relationships,* 7th edition (Upper Saddle River, NJ: Pearson/Prentice Hall, 2005), p. 3.

4. "Better Self-Esteem," www.utexas.edu/student/cmhc/booklets/selfesteem/selfest.html, 1999, p. 2.

5. Ibid.

6. Cited in Randall Edwards, "Is Self-Esteem Really All that Important?" *The APA Monitor,* May 1995, p. 43.

7. Research reported in Jeffrey Zaslow, "The Most-Praised Generation Goes to Work," *The Wall Street Journal,* April 20, 2007, p. W7.

8. David De Cremer et al., "Rewarding Leadership and Fair Procedures as Determinants of Self-Esteem," *Journal of Applied Psychology,* January 2005, pp. 3–12.

9. Eugene Raudsepp, "Strong Self-Esteem Can Help you Advance," *CareerJournal.com (The Wall Street Journal),* August 10, 2004.

10. Timothy A. Judge, Charlice Hurst, and Lauren S. Simon, "Does It Pay to Be Smart, Attractive, or Confident (or All Three)? Relationships Among General Mental Ability, Physical Attractiveness, Core Self-Evaluation, and Income," *Journal of Applied Psychology,* May 2009, pp. 742–755. The definition of core self-evaluation is from Christian J. Resick, et al., "The Bright-Side and the Dark-Side of CEO Personality: Examining Core Self-Evaluations, Narcissism, Transformational Leadership, and Strategic Influence," *Journal of Applied Psychology,* November 2009, p. 1367.

11. Research reported in Melissa Dittman, "Study Links Jealousy with Aggression, Low Self-Esteem," *Psychology Today,* February 2005, p. 13.

12. Jon L. Pierce, Donald G. Gardner, Larry L. Cummings, and Randall B. Dunman, "Organization-Based Self-Esteem: Construct Definition, Measurement, and Validation," *Academy of Management Journal,* September 1989, p. 623.

13. Nathaniel Branden, *Self-Esteem at Work: How Confident People Make Powerful Companies* (San Francisco: Jossey-Bass, 1998); Timothy A. Judge and Joyce E. Bono, "Relationship of Core Self-Evaluations Traits—Self-Esteem, Generalized Self-Efficacy, Locus of Control, and Emotional Stability—With Job Satisfaction and Job Performance: A Meta-Analysis," *Journal of Applied Psychology,* February 2001, pp. 80–92.

14. Duffy et al., "The Moderating Role of Self-Esteem and Neuroticism," 2006, p. 1069.

15. Quoted in Carlin Flora, "The Measuring Game: Why You Think You'll Never Stack Up," *Psychology Today,* September/October 2005, p. 44.

16. "Building Self-Esteem: A Self-Help Guide," *Health* (athealth.com/Consumer/disorder/self-esteem.html), p.1.

17. Research mentioned in book review by E. R. Snyder in *Contemporary Psychology,* July 1998, p. 482.

18. "Better Self-Esteem," pp. 3–4.

19. Ibid, pp. 4–5.
20. Cited in "Self-Esteem: You'll Need It to Succeed," *Executive Strategies*, September 1993, p. 12.
21. Raudsepp, "Strong Self-Esteem Can Help You Advance."
22. "Building Self-esteem: A Self-Help Guide," *http:// mentalhealth. samhsa.gov/*, p. 2, accessed September 7, 2007.
23. Marilyn E. Gist and Terence R. Mitchell, "Self-Efficacy: A Theoretical Analysis of Its Determinants and Malleability," *Academy of Management Review*, April 1992, pp. 183–211.
24. George P. Hollenbeck and Douglas T. Hall, "Self-confidence and Leader Performance," *Organizational Dynamics*, Issue 3, 2004, pp. 261–264.
25. Jay T. Knippen and Thad B. Green, "Building Self-Confidence," *Supervisory Management*, August 1989, pp. 22–27.
26. Quoted in "Entrepreneurs Need Attitude: Power of Being Positive Can Help You to Succeed In Spite of Setbacks," *Knight Ridder*, September 16, 2002.
27. John Derbyshire, *We Are Doomed* (New York: Crown Forum, 2009).
28. D. Brian McNatt and Timothy A. Judge, "Boundary Conditions of the Galatea Effect: A Field Experiment and Constructive Replication," *Academy of Management Journal*, August 2004, pp. 550–565.
29. Price Pritchett, *HardOptimism: Developing Deep Strengths for Managing Uncertainty, Opportunity, Adversity, and Change* (Dallas, TX: Pritchett, 2004), p. 16.
30. Frances Thornton, Gayle Privette, and Charles M. Bundrick, "Peak Performance of Business Leaders: An Experience Parallel to Self-Actualization Theory," *Journal of Business and Psychology*, Winter 1999, pp. 253–264.
31. Joshua D. Margolis and Paul G. Stoltz, "How to Bounce Back from Adversity," *Harvard Business Review*, January–February 2010. pp. 91–92.

CHAPTER 4

1. Jim Blasingame, "There Are No Handshakes 'In the Clouds,'" *The Wall Street Journal* (Special Advertising Feature), October 13, 2009, B5.
2. Ritch Sorenson, Grace DeBord, and Ida Ramirez, *Business and Management Communication: A Guide Book*, 4th edition (Upper Saddle River, NJ: Prentice Hall, 2001), pp. 6–10.
3. Steven Pinker, *The Stuff of Thought* (New York: Viking, a Member of Penguin Group (USA), Inc., 2007).
4. Linda Talley, "Body Language: Read It or Weep," *HR Magazine*, July 2010, p. 64.
5. Talley, "Body Language," p. 65.
6. Jeffrey Jacobi, *The Vocal Advantage* (Upper Saddle River, NJ: Prentice Hall, 1996).
7. Quoted in Joyce M. Rosenberg, "Don't Take Voice Message for Granted," Associated Press, February 21, 2006.
8. Eric Kress, "The Unintended Word," *HR Magazine* August 2006, p. 51.
9. Research presented in "We Can Measure the Power of Charisma," *Harvard Business Review*, January–February 2010, p. 34.
10. Benice Atufunwa, "The Art of Effective Communi-cation," *Black Enterprise*, November 2009, p. 47.
11. An of empathy in both humans and other animals is Frans de Waal, *The Age of Empathy* (New York: Harmony, 2009).
12. Robert Lee Hotz, "How Your Brain Allows You to Walk in Another's Shoes," *The Wall Street Journal*, August 17, 2007, p. B1.
13. Jared Sandberg, "'It Says Press Any Key. Where's the Any Key?'" *The Wall Street Journal*, February 20, 2007, p. B1.
14. Paul Hemp, "Death by Information Overload," *Harvard Business Review*, September 2009, p. 83.
15. Mark Henricks, "Can We Talk? Speaking Up about the Value of Dialogue," *Entrepreneur*, January 1998, p. 82.
16. Sharon Lund O'Neil, "An Empowered Attitude Can Enhance Communication Skills," *Business Education Forum*, April 1998, pp. 28–30.
17. Frank Luntz, "Words That Pack Power," *Business Week*, November 3, 2008, p. 106; Roberta H. Karapelsl and Vanessa D. Arnold, "Speaker's Credibility in Persuasive Work Situations," *Business Education Forum*, December 1997, pp. 24–26; Interview by Alyssa Danigelis, "Like, Um, You Know," *Fast Company*, May 2006, p. 99.
18. Jean Mausehund and R. Neil Dortch, "Communications—Presentation Skills in the Digital Age," *Business Education Forum*, April 1999, pp. 30–32.
19. "Avoid Words That Mar Your Image," *Administrative Professional Today*, January 2009, pp. 1–2.
20. For more details, see Brian Fugere, Chelsea Hardaway, and Jon Warshawsky, *Why Business People Speak Like Idiots* (New York: Free Press, 2005).
21. Joann Baney, *Guide to Interpersonal Communication* (Upper Saddle River, NJ: Pearson/Prentice Hall, 2004), p. 7.
22. Quoted in Jessica Shambora, "Stop Talking and Start Listening," *Fortune*, November 9, 2009, p. 24.
23. Daniel Araoz, "Right Brain Management (RBM): Part 2," *Human Resources Forum*, September 1989, p. 4.
24. Cited in Matthew S. Scott "Five Keys to Effective Listening," *Black Enterprise*, March 2005, p. 113.
25. Ideas from Marshall Goldsmith cited in "Eliminate Bad Words," *Manager's Edge*, special issue, 2008, p. 5.
26. Quoted in Mimi Whitefield, "Listen Up—Your Job Could Depend on It," *Miami Herald* (www.miamiherald.com), April 20, 2009.
27. The information in this section is from Holly Weeks, "Taking the Stress Out of Stressful Conversations," *Harvard Business Review*, July–August 2001, pp. 112–119. The quote is from p. 117.
28. Deborah Tannen, *Talking from 9 to 5* (New York: William Morrow, 1994); Tannen, "The Power of Talk: Who Gets Heard and Why," *Harvard Business Review*, September–October 1995, pp. 138–148; Daniel J. Canary and Kathryn Dindia, *Sex Differences and Similarities in Communication* (Mahwah, NJ: Erlbaum, 1998), p. 318; John Gray, *Men Are from Mars, Women Are from Venus* (New York: HarperCollins, 1992).

CHAPTER 5

1. Several of the facts in this case are from Jessica Marquez, "Corporations Footing the Bill for Co-Working," *Workforce Management*, August 11, 2008, pp. 10–11.
2. Many of the ideas in this list are based on the following sources: Louise Lee, "Cell? Well . . . Use Your Phone for Good, Not Evil," *Business Week Small Biz*, February/March 2009, p. 22; Cathrine Hatcher, "11 Rules For Good Cell Phone Etiquette," *http:// cbs1tv. com*, Accessed December 30, 2007; Amy Novotney, "Dangerous Distractions," *Monitor on Psychology*, February 2009, pp. 32–36.
3. The sources in endnote 2 also apply to endnote 3. In addition are the following: Christine Rosen, "Our Cell Phones, Ourselves," *The New Atlantis*, Summer 2004, p. 31; Alex Williams, "Mind Your BlackBerry or Mind Your Manners," *The New York Times* (*www. nytimes.com*); "Cell Phone Etiquette at the Office, *Articlesbase*, April 27, 2009; Lynette Spicer, "Civility in the Workplace," *Iowa State University Extension*, (www.extension.iastate/edu/mt/civility), May 4, 2009.
4. Quoted in Rosen, "Our Cell Phones, Ourselves," *The New Atlantis*, p. 31.
5. Research cited in Novotney, "Dangerous Distractions," p. 32.
6. Quoted in Barbara Kiviat, "Résumé? Check. Nice Suit? Check. Webcam?" *Time Magazine*, November 9, 2009, p. 50.
7. Several of the suggestions for what to do and what not to do during a webcam interview are from Kiviat, "Résumé? Check. Nice Suit? Check. Webcam?" *Time Magazine*, November 9, 2009, p. 50.
8. Abby Ellin, "Auditioning in a Video Résumé," *The New York Times (nytimes.com)*, April 21, 2007, p. 3.

9. Quoted in Heather Huhman, "Use Youth to Your Advantage," *www.examiner.com,* accessed April 21, 2009.

10. Paul Hemp, "Death by Information Overload," *Harvard Business Review,* September 2009, p. 85.

11. "Goes Without Saying, but Say It Anyway: No Porn at Work," *HR Specialist: New York Employment Law,* June 2008, p. 1.

12. For a useful perspective on how social networking is changing society, see Steven Johnson, "How Twitter Will Change the Way We Live." *Time,* June 15, 2009, pp. 32–37.

13. Bridget Carey, "Bosses Should Set Social Networking Rules," *The Miami Herald* (www.miamiherald.com), August 11, 2009.

14. Alex Taylor III, "Fixing Up Ford," *Fortune,* May 25, 2009, p. 49.

15. "Go 'Topless'," *Manager's Edge,* August 2008, p. 6.

16. Alex Williams, "Mind Your BlackBerry or Mind Your Manners," *The New York Times* (www.nytimes.com), June 22, 2009.

17. Ibid.

18. Joann S. Lublin, "Some Dos and Don'ts To Help You Hone Videoconference Skills," *The Wall Street Journal,* February 7, 2006, p. B1.

19. "Work à la Modem," *Business Week,* October 4, 1999, p. 176.

20. "Bridge Gaps with Remote Workers," *Manager's Edge,* July 2008, p. 1.

21. Michelle Conlin, "Telecommuting: Out of Sight, Yes. Out of Mind, No," *Business Week,* February 18, 2008, p. 060.

22. "Telecommuting Tips," *Manager's Edge,* December 2007, p. 1.

23. Stephen Behnke, "Ethics in the Age of the Internet," *Monitor on Psychology,* July/August 2008, pp. 74–75.

24. Anita Hamilton, "Outsmart Your Haters," *Time,* October 6, 2008, pp. 67–68.

25. Bridget Carey and Niala Boodhoo, "How to Deal with What Feels Like Online Identity Theft," *The Miami Herald (miamiherald.com),* April 14, 2009.

CHAPTER 6

1. Carol Hymowitz, "H-P's Ann Livermore Keeps Eye on 'Team'," *The Wall Street Journal,* June 2, 2008, p. B.

2. Conference Board report cited in "CEO Leadership Skips Teamwork, Article Says," Rochester, New York, *Democrat and Chronicle,* February 17, 2002, p. 1E.

3. Jon R. Katzenbach and Douglas K. Smith, "The Discipline of Teams," *Harvard Business Review,* March–April 1993, p. 112.

4. Claus W. Langfred, "Too Much Trust a Good Thing? Negative Effects of High Trust and Individual Autonomy in Self-Managing Teams," *Academy of Management Journal,* June 2004, pp. 385–399.

5. "Shepherding Communications When the Flock Is Scattered," *Flexible Workplace Management,* sample issue, 2001.

6. "Bridge Gaps with Remote Workers," *Manager's Edge,* July 2008, p. 1.

7. Arvind Malhotra, Ann Majchrzak, and Benson Rosen, "Leading Virtual Teams," *Academy of Management Perspectives,* February 2007, p. 62.

8. Cited in Adam Bryant, "Ensemble Acting, in Business," *The New York Times* (www.nytimes.com), June 7, 2009.

9. Matt Bolch, "Rewarding the Team," *HR Magazine,* February 2007, pp. 91–93; www.wikiinvest.com, December 4, 2009.

10. "When Committees Spell Trouble: Don't Let Individuals Hide Within a Group," *WorkingSMART,* August 1998, p. 1; Ross Kerber, "For Abigail Johnson, a Leadership Test," *The Boston Globe (boston.com),* August 21, 2007, p. 1.

11. Irving L. Janus, *Victims of Groupthink: A Psychological Study of Foreign Policy Decisions and Fiascos* (Boston: Houghton Mifflin, 1972); Glen Whyte, "Groupthink Reconsidered," *Academy of Management Review,* January 1989, pp. 40–56.

12. Martha A. Peak, "Treating Trauma in Teamland," *Management Review,* September 1997, p. 1.

13. "R. Meredith Belbin," in *Business: The Ultimate Resource* (Cambridge, MA: Perseus, 2002), pp. 966–967; Belbin, *Management Teams* (London: Elsevier Butterworth-Heinemann, 2003); Belbin® Team-Roles, *http://www.belbin.com/belbin-teamroles.htm.*

14. From a review of Meredith Belbin, *Management Teams,* by Colin Thomson appearing in *http://www.accountingweb.co.uk.,* accessed April 14, 2004.

15. Jeffrey m. O'Brien, "Team Building in Paradise," *Fortune,* May 26, 2008, pp. 112–122.

16. Romanus Wolter, "Get Team-Focused," *Entrepreneur,* February 2009, p. 124.

17. Cited in "Gather Round, People!" *Entrepreneur,* September 2009, p. 21.

18. "Fly in Formation: Easy Ways to Build Team Spirit," *WorkingSMART,* March 2000, p. 6.

19. "Score a Perfect '10' on Teamwork," *Manager's Edge,* May 2006, p. 1.

20. Pamela Lovell, "Healthy Teams Display Strong Vital Signs," *Teamwork,* sample issue, the Dartnell Corporation, 1997.

21. Glenn M. Parker, *Cross-Functional Teams: Working with Allies, Enemies, & Other Strangers* (San Francisco: Jossey-Bass, 1994), p. 170.

22. Jessica R. Mesmer-Magnus and Leslie A. DeChurch, "Information Sharing and Team Performance: A Meta-Analysis," *Journal of Applied Psychology,* March 2009, pp. 535–546.

23. Mary J. Waller et al., "The Effect of Individual Perceptions of Deadlines on Team Performance," *Academy of Management Review,* October 2001, p. 597.

24. Mark G. Ehrhant and Stefanie E. Naumann, "Organizational Citizenship Behavior in Work Groups: A Group Norms Approach," *Journal of Applied Psychology,* December 2004, pp. 960–974.

25. Daniel G. Bachrach, Benjamin C. Powell, Elliot Bendoly, and R. Glenn Richey, "Organizational Citizenship Behavior and Performance Evaluations: Exploring the Impact of Task Interdependence," *Journal of Applied Psychology,* January 2006, pp. 193–201.

26. Jeffrey A. LePine et al., "A Meta-Analysis of Teamwork Processes: Tests of a Multidimensional Model and Relationships with Team Effectiveness Criteria," *Personnel Psychology,* Summer 2008, pp. 273–307.

CHAPTER 7

1. "Spacecraft Will Examine Mars in Greater Detail than Ever Before," *http://mars.jpl.nasa.gov/mro/spotlight/2004706.html,* accessed July 6, 2004.

2. Dan Ariely, "The End of Rational Economics," *Harvard Business Review,* July–August 2009, pp. 78–84.

3. Cited in Marcia A. Reed-Woodard, "What Were You Thinking?" *Black Enterprise,* January 2009, p. 87.

4. Thomas H. Davenport, "Make Better Decisions," *Harvard Business Review,* November 2009, p. 117.

5. Felix C. Brodbeck et al., "Group Decision Making under Conditions of Distributed Knowledge: The Information Asymmetries Model," *Academy of Management Review,* April 2007, pp. 459–460.

6. Andrew E. Schwartz and Joy Levin, "Better Group Decision Making," *Supervisory Management,* June 1990, p. 4.

7. Debra Wheatman, "Problem Solving in the Workplace," *San Francisco Examiner* (www.examiner.com), June 28, 2009.

8. Michael Mercer, *Absolutely Fabulous Organizational Change* (Lake Zurich, IL:Castlegate, 2000); Duncan Maxwell Anderson, "Hidden Forces," *Success,* April 1995, p. 1.

9. Alexander D. Stajkovic, Dongseop Lee, and Anthony J. Nyberg, "Collective Efficacy, Group Potency, and Group Performance: Meta-Analysis of their Relationships, and Test of a Mediation Model," *Journal of Applied Psychology,* May 2009, p. 815.

10. Cited in Jason Zweig, "How Group Decisions End Up Wrong-Footed," *The Wall Street Journal,* April 25–26, 2009, p. B1.

11. Kay Lovelace, Debra L. Shapiro, and Laurie R. Weingart, "Minimizing Cross-Functional New Product Teams' Innovativeness and Constraint Adherence: A Conflict Communications Perspective," *Academy of Management Journal,* August 2001, pp. 779–793.

12. Stuart D. Sidle, "Do Teams Who Agree to Disagree Make Better Decisions?" *Academy of Management Perspectives,* May 2007, pp. 74–75. The Sidle article is a review of S. Schultz-Hardt et al., "Group Decision Making in Hidden Profile Situations: Dissent as a Facilitator for Decision Quality," *Journal of Personality and Social Psychology,* No. 6, 2006, pp. 1080–1093.

13. David A. Garvin and Michael A. Roberto, "What You Don't Know about Making Decisions," *Harvard Business Review,* September 2001, pp. 110–111.

14. Leigh Thompson, "Improving the Creativity of Work Groups," *Academy of Management Executive,* February 2003, p. 99.

15. "Better Brainstorming," *Manager's Edge,* September 2009, p. 4.

16. "Future Edisons of America: Turn Your Employees into Inventors," *WorkingSMART,* June 2000, p. 2.

17. Robert C. Litchfield, "Brainstorming Reconsidered: A Goal-Based View," *Academy of Management Review,* July 2008, pp. 649–668.

18. Owen Thomas, "The Three-Minute Huddle," *Business 2.0,* April 2006, p. 94.

19. "How Google Got Is New Look," *Bloomberg Businessweek,* May 10–May 16, 2010, p. 60.

20. Allen C. Bluedorn, Daniel B. Turban, and Mary Sue Love, "The Effects of Stand-Up and Sit-Down Meeting Formats on Meeting Outcomes," *Journal of Applied Psychology,* April 1999, pp. 277–285.

21. Howard Baker, "Promoting Interaction and Teamwork with Electronic Mail," *Business Education Forum,* October 1994, pp. 30–31.

22. "Introduction to Groupware," *http://www.usabilityfirst.com/groupware/intro.html.* Accessed October 1, 2007.

23. Quoted in Lee Gimpel, "Cloaked Room," *Entrepreneur,* January 2008, p. 22.

24. "Nail Down Decision Making," *Manager's Edge,* July 2009, p. 1.

25. Erika Packard, "Meetings Frustrate Task-Oriented Employees, Study Finds," *Monitor on Psychology,* June 2006, p. 10; Steven G. Rogelberg, Desmond J. Leach, Peter B. Warr, and Jennfer L. Burnfield, "'Not Another Meeting!' Are Meeting Time Demands Related to Employee Well-Being?" *Journal of Applied Psychology,* January 2006, pp. 83–96.

26. Several of the suggestions are based on Rachel Zupek, "Horrible, Terrible Meeting Mistakes," *www.CNN.com,* August 29, 2007, pp. 1–3.

27. Research described in Craig L. Pearce, "Follow the Leaders," *The Wall Street Journal,* July 7, 2008, p. R12.

Solutions to the problems in Skill-Building Exercise 7-2

The solution to Seven Tennis Balls in a Tube is to simply fill the pipe with water and the balls will float to the top. For the *Too-Low Truck,* carefully deflate the four tires about 2 inches, and then drive through the tunnel under the bridge. Harley management solved the Aging Members of HOG quite nicely by developing a motor tricycle that has become popular. However, Harley has also made other modifications of their models to make them easier for older people to control, such as being more comfortable and less powerful.

CHAPTER 8

1. "Walgreens 15th Distribution Center Opens in Connecticut and Creates Jobs for People with Disabilities," *Walgreens News Room* (http://walgreens.com), April 15, 2009; "Walgreens Recruits Employees with Disabilities through New, Highly Accessible Web Site," *Medical News Today* (www.medicalnewstoday.com), July 8, 2006, pp. 1–2; Mika Brzezinski, "Program Puts the 'Able' in Disabled," msnbc.com, July 2, 2007, pp. 1–2.

2. Quoted in Diane Cadrain, "Accommodating Sex Transformations," *HR Magazine,* October 2009, p. 59.

3. Angela Ka-yee Leung, William W. Maddox, Adam D. Galinsky, and Chi-yue Chu, "Multicultural Experience Enhances Creativity," *American Psychologist,* April 2008, pp. 169–181.

4. Michael Bowker, "Corporate Diversity Driving Profits," *Hispanic Business,* September 2008, pp. 12, 14.

5. Patrick F. McKay, Derek R. Avery, and Mark A. Morris, "A Tale of Two Climates: Diversity Climate from Subordinates' and Managers' Perspectives and Their Role in Store Unit Sales Performance," *Personnel Psychology,* Winter 2009, pp. 767–791.

6. Eric Kearney, Diether Gebert, and Sven C. Voelpel, "When and How Diversity Benefits Teams: The Importance of Team Members' Need for Cognition," *Academy of Management Journal,* June 2009, pp. 581–598.

7. Apnara Joshi and Hyuyntak Roh, "The Role of Context in Work Team Diversity Research: A Meta-Analytic Review," *Academy of Management Journal,* June 2009, pp. 599–627.

8. Arvind V. Phatak, *International Dimensions of Management* (Boston: Kent, 1983), p. 167.

9. Robin J. Ely, Debra Meyerson, and Martin N. Davidson, "Rethinking Political Correctness," *Harvard Business Review,* September 2006, p. 80.

10. Quoted in "Leveraging Diversity at Work," *Hispanic Business,* November 2006, p. 70.

11. P. Christopher Earley and Elaine Mosakowski, "Cultural Intelligence," *Harvard Business Review,* October 2004, p. 140. The example is from the same source, same page.

12. P. C. Earley and E. Mosakowski, "Toward Culture Intelligence: Turning Cultural Differences into a Workplace Advantage," *Academy of Management Executive,* August 2004, pp. 154–155.

13. Ann Pomeroy, "She's Still Lovin' It," *HR Magazine* December 2006, p. 60.

14. Scott B. Button, "Organizational Efforts to Affirm Sexual Diversity: A Cross-Level Examination," *Journal of Applied Psychology,* February 2001, pp. 17–28.

15. Charlene Marmer Solomon, "Global Operations Demand That HR Rethink Diversity," *Personnel Journal,* July 1994, p. 50.

16. Mansour Javidan, Peter W. Dorfman, May Sully de Luque, and Robert J. House, "In the Eye of the Beholder: Cross Cultural Lessons in Leadership from Project GLOBE," *Academy of Management Perspectives,* February 2006, pp. 69–70. Similar were dimensions were described in Geert Hofstede, *Culture's Consequences: International Differences in Work Related Values* (Beverly Hills, CA: Sage, 1980); updated and expanded in "A Conversation with Geert Hofstede," *Organizational Dynamics,* Spring 1993, pp. 53–61; Hofstede, "Who Is the Fairest of Them All? Galit Ailon's Mirror," *Academy of Management Review,* July 2009, pp. 570–571. Dimension 8 is not included in the above research. Paul J. Taylor, Wen-Dong Li, Kan Shi, and Walter C. Borman, "The Transportability of Job Information Across Countries," *Personnel Psychology,* Spring 2008, pp. 72–76.

17. Study reported in Bradley S. Klapper, "Report: U.S. Workers Are the Most Productive," Associated Press, September 2, 2007.

18. Heejung S. Kim, David K. Sherman, and Shelley E. Taylor, "Culture and Social Support," *American Psychologist,* September 2008, pp. 518–526.

19. Lee Gardenswartz and Anita Rowe, "Cross-Cultural Awareness," *HR Magazine,* March 2001, p. 139.

20. Ellyn Ferguson, "Many Firms Seek Bilingual Workers," Gannett News Service, May 13, 2007.

21. Daren Fonda, "Selling in Tongues," *Time,* November 26, 2001, pp. B12–B13.

22. Paraphrasing of citation in Ferguson, "Many Firms Seek Bilingual Workers."

23. Carolena Lyons Lawrence, "Teaching Students How Gestures Communicate Across Cultures," *Business Education Forum,* February 2003, p. 39.

24. Jeffrey Sanchez-Burks, Caroline A. Bartel, and Sally Blount, "Performance in Intercultural Interactions at Work: Cross-Cultural Differences in Response to Behavioral Mirroring," *Journal of Applied Psychology,* January 2009, pp. 216–233.

25. Roger E. Axtell, *Gestures: The Do's and Taboos of Body Language Around the World* (New York: Wiley, 1990).

26. Siri Carpenter, "Why Do 'They All Look Alike'?" *Monitor on Psychology,* December 2000, p. 44.

27. Kathleen Begley, "Managing Across Cultures at Home," *HR Magazine,* September 2009, p. 115.

28. Mei Fong, "Chinese Charm School," *The Wall Street Journal,* January 13, 2004, p. B1.

29. P. Christopher Earley and Randall S. Peterson, "The Elusive Cultural Chameleon: Cultural Intelligence as a New Approach to Intercultural Training for the Global Manager," *Academy of Management Learning and Education,* March 2004, p. 106.

30. Kathryn Tyle, "I Say Potato, You Say *Patata,*" *HR Magazine,* January 2004, p. 85.

31. Rohini Anahand and Mary-Frances Winters, "A Retrospective View of Corporate Diversity Training from 1964 to the Present," *Academy of Management Learning & Education,* September 2008, p. 356.

32. Gillian Flynn, "The Harsh Reality of Diversity Programs," *Workforce,* December 1998, p. 29.

33. Kathryn Tyler, "Cross-Cultural Connections: Mentoring Programs Can Bridge Gaps between Disparate Groups," *HR Magazine,* October 2007, pp. 77–83.

CHAPTER 9

1. Quoted in Rebecca Dana, "What's Next for Newsmagazines?" *The Wall Street Journal,* April 4, 2008, p. B2.

2. Michael T. Ford, Beth A. Heinen, and Krista L. Langkamer, "Work and Family Satisfaction and Conflict: A Meta-Analysis of Cross-Domain Relations," *Journal of Applied Psychology,* January 2007, pp. 57–80.

3. Timothy A. Judge, Remus Ilies, and Brent A. Scott, "Work-Family Conflict and Emotions: Effects at Work and at Home," *Personnel Psychology,* Winter 2006, pp. 779–814.

4. Quoted in Naomi Schaefer Riley, "Work and Life—and Blogging the Balance," *The Wall Street Journal,* July 17, 2009, p. W11.

5. Jenny M. Hoobler, Sandy J. Wayne, and Grace Lemmon, "Bosses' Perceptions of Family-Work Conflict and Women's Promotability: Glass Ceiling Effects," *Academy of Management Journal,* October 2009, pp. 939–957.

6. Joyce M. Rosenberg, "Equitable Time-Off Policies Avert Staff Conflicts," *Associated Press,* September 3, 2007.

7. Kathryn Tyler, "Beat the Clock," *HR Magazine,* November 2003, p. 103.

8. Jennifer Schramm, "Work/Life Hold?" *HR Magazine,* October 2008, p. 120.

9. Judith Sills, "When Personalities Clash," *Psychology Today,* November/December 2006, p. 61.

10. Peter Svensson, "CFO's Court Case Reveals Ugly Infighting at Motorola," *The Miami Herald* (www.miamiherald.com), May 19, 2009.

11. Vincent J. Roscigno, Steven H. Lopez, and Randy Hodson, "Supervisory Bullying, Status Inequalities, and Organizational Context," *Social Forces,* July 2009, pp. 1561–1589.

12. Gary Namie, "(Still) Bullying with Impunity: Labor Day Survey," *Workplace Bullying* Institute, September 2009; Namie, "U.S. Workplace Bullying Survey," *Workplace Bullying Institute and Zogby International,* September 2007.

13. Quoted in Mickey Meece, "Backlash: Women Bullying Women at Work," *The New York Times* (www.nytimes.com), May 9, 2009.

14. Study reported in Deborah Smith, "I/O Conference Examines Army Special Forces, Workplace Incivility," *Monitor on Psychology,* June 2003, p. 11.

15. Lilia M. Cortina and Vicki J. Magley, "Patterns and Profiles of Responses to Incivility in the Workplace," *Journal of Occupational Health Psychology,* July 2009, pp. 272–288.

16. Comment made by John Derbyshire in a review of Lynne Truss, *Talk to the Hand* (New York: Gotham, 2005), *The Wall Street Journal,* November 5–6, 2005, p. P8; Loretta Chao, "As Workloads Increase, So Does Office Rudeness," *WSJ.com College Journal, (The Wall Street Journal Online),* January 23, 2006, p. 1.

17. Chris Pentila, "Talking about My Generation," *Entrepreneur,* March 2009, p. 55; "The Multigenerational Workforce: Opportunity for Competitive Success," *SHRM Research Quarterly,* First Quarter-2009, pp. 1–2.

18. "Workplace Violence," *www.osha.gov,* p. 1, updated July 20, 2007.

19. Cited in Susan M. Heathfield, "Workplace Violence: Violence Can Happen; Recognizing the Potential for Workplace Violence," *About.com Human Resources,* 2009.

20. Kenneth Thomas, "Conflict and Conflict Management," in Marvin D. Dunnette, ed., *Handbook of Industrial and Organizational Psychology* (Chicago: Rand McNally College Publishing, 1976), pp. 900–902. Some of the information about when to use each style is from Dean Tjosvold, *The Conflict Positive Organization* (Reading, MA: Addison-Wesley, 1991).

21. Simon, cited in Mark Liu, "You Can Learn to Be Less Accommodating—If You Want To," Rochester, New York, *Democrat and Chronicle,* April 25, 1999, p. 1C.

22. "7 Steps to Conflict Resolution," *Executive Leadership,* June 2007, p. 7. As adapted from The Common Sense Guy Blog, by Bud Bilanich, *www.commonsenseguy.com.*

23. The first three suggestions are from Connirae Andreas and Steve Andreas, *Heart of the Mind* (Moab, UT: Real People Press, 1991). Suggestion four is from Deb Koen, "How to Handle Criticism at Work," Rochester, New York, *Democrat and Chronicle,* June 20, 2004.

24. "Conquer Conflict with this Technique," *Manager's Edge,* September 2007, p. 5. As adapted from Maria Broomhower, "Dissolving Conflict through Reframing," *www.conflict911.com.*

25. Jared Curhan, Hilary Anger Elfenbein, and Heng Xu "What Do People Value When They Negotiate? Mapping the Domain of Subjective Value in Negotiation," *Journal of Personality and Social Psychology,* vol. 3, 2006, pp. 493–512.

26. Deepak Malhotra and Max H. Bazerman, "Investigative Negotiation," *Harvard Business Review,* September 2007, pp. 72–78.

27. William Ury, *The Power of a Positive No* (New York: Random House, 2007).

28. Mark Diener, "Mad Skills," *Entrepreneur,* April 2003, p. 79.

29. Steve Alper, Dean Tjosvold, and Kenneth S. Law, "Conflict Management, Efficacy, and Performance in Organizational Teams," *Personnel Psychology,* Autumn 2000, pp. 625–642.

30. Maria Rotundo, Dung-Hanh Nguyen, and Paul R. Sackett, "A Meta-Analytic Review of Gender Differences in Perceptions of Sexual Harassment," *Journal of Applied Psychology,* October 2001, pp. 914–922.

31. Jennifer L. Berdhahl and Karl Aquino, "Sexual Behavior at Work: Fun or Folly" *Journal of Applied Psychology,* January 2009, pp. 34–47.

32. Remus Ilies, Nancy Hauserman, Susan Schwochau, and John Stibal, "Reported Incidence Rates of Work-Related Sexual Harassment in the United States: Using Meta-Analysis to Explain Rate Disparities," *Personnel Psychology,* Autumn 2003, pp. 607–631.

33. Hilary J. Gettman and Michele J. Gelfand, "When the Customer Shouldn't Be King: Antecedents and Consequences of Sexual Harassment by Clients and Customers," *Journal of Applied Psychology,* May 2007, pp. 757–770.

34. Jennifer L. Berdahl. "The Sexual Harassment of Uppity Women," *Journal of Applied Psychology,* March 2007, pp. 425–437.

35. Jennifer L. Berdahl and Celia Moore, "Workplace Harassment: Double Jeopardy for Minority Women," *Journal of Applied Psychology,* March 2006, pp. 426–436.

36. Quoted in Steve Stecklow, "Sexual-Harassment Cases Plague U.N.," *The Wall Street Journal,* May 21, 2009, p. A1.

37. Chelsea R. Willness, Piers Steel, and Kibeom Lee, "A Meta-Analysis of the Antecedents and Consequences of Workplace Sexual Harassment," *Personnel Psychology,* Spring 2007, p. 141.

38. Kathleen Neville, *Corporate Attractions: An Inside Account of Sexual Harassment with the New Sexual Roles for Men and Women on the Job* (Reston, VA: Acropolis Books, 1992); Joanne Cole, "Sexual Harassment: New Rules, New Behavior," *HRfocus,* March 1999, pp. 1, 14–15.

39. Jathan W. Janove, "Sexual Harassment and the Three Big Surprises," *HR Magazine,* November 2001, p. 123.

40. Robert McGarvey, "Hands Off! How Do the Latest Supreme Court Decisions on Sexual Harassment Affect You?" *Entrepreneur,* September 1998, p. 86; Cole, "Sexual Harassment: New Rules," p. 14.

CHAPTER 10

1. Case history collected in Rochester, New York, January 2008.

2. E. D. Kort, "What, after All, Is Leadership? 'Leadership' and Plural Action," *Leadership Quarterly,* August 2008, p. 409.

3. Quoted in Peter Gumbel, "The Turnaround Artista," *Time,* June 29, 2009, p. 42.

4. Joseph A. Raelin, *Creating Leaderful Organizations: How to Bring Out Leadership in Everyone* (San Francisco: Berrett-Koehler, 2003).

5. Timothy A. Judge, Ronald F. Piccolo, and Tomek Kosalka, "The Bright and Dark Sides of Leader Traits: A review and Theoretical Extension of the Leader Trait Paradigm," *Leadership Quarterly,* December 2009, p. 871.

6. George P. Hollenbeck and Douglas T. Hall, "Self Confidence and Leader Performance," *Organizational Dynamics,* no. 3, 2004, pp. 254–269.

7. Shelley A. Kirkpatrick and Edwin A. Locke, "Leadership: Do Traits Matter?" *Academy of Management Executive,* May 1991, pp. 26–27.

8. Sean T. Hannah, Bruce J. Avolio, Fred Luthans, and P. D. Harms, "Leadership Efficacy: Review and Future Directions," *Leadership Quarterly,* December 2008, pp. 669–692.

9. Judge, Piccolo, and Kosalka, "The Bright and Dark Sides of Leader Traits," p. 866.

10. Cameron Anderson and Gavin Kilduf, "Why Do Dominant Personalities Attain Influence in Face-to-Face Groups? The Competence-Signaling Effects of Trait Dominance," *Journal of Personality and Social Psychology,* February 2009, pp. 491–503.

11. Daniel R. Ames and Francis J. Flynn, "What Breaks a Leader: The Curvilinear Relation between Assertiveness and Leadership," *Journal of Personality and Social Psychology,* vol. 92, 2007, pp. 307–324.

12. Survey cited in "What Are the Most Important Traits for Bosses?" *Employee Recruitment & Retention,* Sample Issue, 2006.

13. Michael E. Palanski and Francis J. Yammarino, "Integrity and Leadership: A Multi-Level Conceptual Framework," *Leadership Quarterly,* June 2009, p. 406.

14. Reported in "Developing Trust Pays Off," *Manager's Edge,* April 1999, p. 9.

15. Douglas R. May, Adrian Y. L. Chan, Timothy D. Hodges, and Bruce J. Avolio, "Developing the Moral Component of Authentic Leadership," *Organizational Dynamics,* no. 3, 2003, pp. 247–260.

16. Alan Deutschman, *Walk the Walk* (New York: Portfolio, 2009).

17. Bruce J. Avolio, Jane M. Howell, and John J. Sosik, "A Funny Thing Happened on the Way to the Bottom Line: Humor as a Moderator of Leadership Style Effects," *Academy of Management Journal,* April 1999, pp. 219–227.

18. Bill George, Peter Sims, Andrew N. McLean, and Diana Mayer, "Discovering Your Authentic Leadership," *Harvard Business Review,* February 2007, p. 129.

19. Dale E. Zand, *The Leadership Triad: Knowledge, Trust, and Power* (New York: Oxford, University Press, 1997), p. 8.

20. John D. Stoll, "Fix-It Experts Appointed at GM," *The Wall Street Journal,* July 24, 2009, p. B2.

21. Betsy McKay, "Can New CEO Put Fizz Back in Coke?" *The Wall Street Journal,* June 30, 2008, p. B1.

22. Studies on this topic are reviewed in Timothy A. Judge, Amy Colbert, and Remus Ilies, "Intelligence and Leadership: A Quantitative Review and Test of Theoretical Propositions," *Journal of Applied Psychology,* June 2004, p. 548.

23. John Menkes, *Executive Intelligence: What All Great Leaders Have* (New York: Collins, 2006).

24. Daniel Goleman, "What Makes a Leader?" *Harvard Business Review,* November–December 1998, p. 92; Goleman, "Never Stop Learning," *Harvard Business Review,* January 2004, pp. 28–28.

25. Robert A. Eckert, "Where Leadership Starts," *Harvard Business Review,* November 2001, pp. 53–61. The quote is from page 54.

26. Richard Boyatzis and Annie McKee, *Resonant Leadership* (Boston: Harvard Business School Press, 2005).

27. Nancy Dahlberg, "One Trait Links All Successful Entrepreneurs: Passion," *The Miami Herald,* (www.miamiherald.com), November 9, 2009, pp. 1–2.

28. David De Cremer, David M. Mayer, Marius van Dijke, Barbara S. Schouten, and Mary Bardes, "When Does Self-Sacrificial Leadership Motivate Prosocial Behavior? It Depends on Followers' Prevention Focus," *Journal of Applied Psychology,* July 2009, pp. 887–899.

29. Jay A. Conger, *The Charismatic Leader: Behind the Mystique of Exceptional Leadership* (San Francisco: Jossey-Bass, 1989).

30. Jack and Suzy Welch, "It's Not about Empty Suits," *Business Week,* October 16, 2006, p. 132.

31. Luisa Beltran, "Standout Performer," *Hispanic Business,* April 2007, p. 26.

32. Bill Breen, "The Clear Leader," *Fast Company,* March 2005, pp. 65–67.

33. Michael E. Brown and Linda K. Treviño, "Socialized Charismatic Leadership, Values, Congruence, and Deviance in Work Groups," *Journal of Applied Psychology,* July 2006, p. 955.

34. Amir Erez, Vilmos F. Misangi, Diane E. Johnson, Marcie A. LePine, and Kent C. Halverson, "Stirring the Hearts of Followers: Charismatic Leadership as the Transferal of Affect," *Journal of Applied Psychology,* May 2008, pp. 602–616.

35. Suggestions 7, 9, and 10 are from Roger Dawson, *Secrets of Power Persuasion* (Upper Saddle River, NJ: Prentice Hall, 1992), pp. 181–183.

36. Quote paraphrased from Interview with Gary E. McCullough, "The Lesson of the 38 Candy Bars," *The New York Times (nytimes.com),* August 9, 2009, p. 1.

37. A. Skogtad et al., "The Destructiveness of Laissez-Faire Leadership Behavior," *Journal of Occupational Health Psychology,* January 2007, pp. 80–92.

38. Tamara L. Friedrich et al., "A Framework for Understanding Collective Leadership: The Selective Utilization of Leader and Team Expertise within Networks," *Leadership Quarterly,* December 2009, pp. 933–958.

39. Craig L. Pearce, Charles C. Manz, and Henry P. Sims, Jr., "Where Do We Go from Here? Is Shared Leadership the Key to Success?" *Organizational Dynamics,* July–September 2009, pp. 234–238.

40. "Bring Out the Leader in Everyone," *Managing People at Work,* sample issue, 2000, p. 4.

41. John Brodie, "King of Cool," Fortune, September 1, 2008, p. 52.

42. Jon R. Katzenbach and Douglas K. Smith, "The Discipline of Teams," *Harvard Business Review,* March–April 1993, p. 118.

43. "Pump Up Your Leadership Style," *Manager's Edge,* March 2007, p. 3. Adapted from Patricia Fripp, "Leadership Lesson 2: 'I'm Glad You Asked'" *www.fripp.com.*

44. "What It Takes to Be an Effective Team Leader," *Manager's Edge,* March 2000, p. 6.

45. Terri A. Scandura and Chester A. Schriesheim, "Leader-Member Exchange and Supervisor Career Mentoring as Complementary Constructs in Leadership Research," *Academy of Management Journal,* December 1994, pp. 1588–1602; George Graen and J. F. Cashman, "A Role Making Model of Leadership in Formal Organizations: A Developmental Approach," in J. G. Hunt and L. L. Larson, eds., *Leadership Frontiers* (Kent, OH: Kent State University Press, 1975), pp. 143–165.

46. Francis J. Yammarino, Alan J. Dubinsky, Lucette B. Comer, and Marvin A. Jolson, "Women and Transformational and Contingent Reward Leadership: A Multiple-Levels-of-Analysis Perspective," *Academy of Management Journal,* February 1997, pp. 205–222.

47. Robert B. Kaiser, Robert Hogan, and S. Bartholomew Craig, "Leadership and the Fate of Organizations," *American Psychologist,* February–March 2008, pp. 96–110.

48. This issue is treated at length in Bruce J. Avolio, *Leadership in Balance: Made/Born* (Mahwah, NJ: Earlbaum, 2005).

49. Jon R. Katzenbach and Jason A. Santamaria, "Firing Up the Front Line," *Harvard Business Review,* May–June 1999, pp. 116–117.

50. Mina Kimes, "P & G's Leadership Machine," *Fortune,* April 13, 2008, p. 22.

51. William D. Hitt, *The Model Leader: A Fully Functioning Person* (Columbus, OH: Battelle Press, 1993).

52. Manuel London, *Leadership Development: Paths to Self-Insight and Professional Growth* (Mahwah, NJ: Erlbaum, 2002).

53. Michael E. McGill and John W. Slocum, Jr., "A *Little* Leadership Please?" *Organizational Dynamics,* Winter 1998, p. 48.

54. Bill Breen, "Trickle-Up Leadership," *Fast Company,* November 2001, pp. 70–72.

CHAPTER 11

1. Excerpted from Steven A. Burd, "How Safeway Is Cutting Health-Care Costs," *The Wall Street Journal,* June 12, 2009, p. A15.

2. Quoted in Stephen Baker, "Will Work for Praise," *Business Week,* February 16, 2009, pp. 046–049.

3. Gerald Kushel, *Reaching the Peak Performance Zone: How to Motivate Yourself and Others to Excel* (New York: AMACOM, 1994), p. 66.

4. Piers Steel and Cornelius J. König, "Integrating Theories of Motivation," *Academy of Management Review,* October 2006, pp. 895–896.

5. Research summarized in "One of These Seven Things Will Motivate Any Employee in the Company," *Motivational Manager,* sample issue, 1998 (Lawrence Ragan Communications, Inc.).

6. Fred Luthans and Alexander D. Stajkovic, "Reinforce for Performance: The Need to Go Beyond Pay and Even Rewards," *Academy of Management Executive,* May 1999, p. 52.

7. Fred O. Walumbwa, Cindy Wu, and Bani Orwa, "Contingent Reward Transactional Leadership, Work Attitudes, and Organizational Citizenship Behavior: The Role of Procedural Justice Climate Perceptions and Strength," *The Leadership Quarterly,* June 2008, pp. 251, 261.

8. Steven Kerr, *Ultimate Rewards: What Really Motivates People to Achieve* (Boston: Harvard Business School Publishing, 1997).

9. "Simple Rewards Are Powerful Motivators," *HRfocus,* August 2001, p. 10.

10. "5 Ways to Create Team Motivation," *Manager's Edge,* November 2007, p. 4.

11. Martin Booe, "Sales Force at Mary Kay China Embraces the American Way," *Workforce Management,* April 2005, pp. 24–25.

12. Jennifer Laabs, "Satisfy Them with More Than Money," *Workforce,* November 1998, p. 43; Charlotte Garvey, "Meaningful Tokens of Appreciation," *HR Magazine,* August 2004, pp. 101–106; Adrian Gostick and Chester Elton, *The Carrot Principle* (New York: The Free Press, 2007).

13. Philip Moss, Harold Salzman, and Chris Tilly, "Under Construction: The Continuing Evolution of Job Structures in Call Centers, *Industrial Relations,* Vol. 47, 2008, pp. 173–208.

14. "Time Your Praise to Make It Last," *WorkingSMART,* June 2000, p. 2.

15. "Ten Sentences That Will Help You Retain Your Best Employees," *Employee Recruitment & Retention,* Lawrence Ragan Communications, Inc., sample issue, 2004.

16. Andrew J. DuBrin, "Self-Perceived Technical Orientation and Attitudes Toward Being Flattered," *Psychological Reports,* vol. 96, 2005, pp. 852–854.

17. Susan M. Heathfield, "Five Tips for Effective Employee Recognition," *About.com Human Resources* (www.humanresources.about.com), August 6, 2009.

18. The original version of expectancy theory applied to work motivation is Victor Vroom, *Work and Motivation* (New York: Wiley, 1964). A scholarly update of the theory is presented in Steel and König, "Integrating Theories of Motivation," pp. 893–895.

19. Alexander D. Stajkovic and Fred Luthans, "Social Cognitive Theory and Self-Efficacy: Going Beyond Traditional Motivational and Behavioral Approaches," *Organizational Dynamics,* Spring 1998, p. 66.

20. Steve McShane, "Getting Emotional about Employee Motivation," *Currents* (published by New York: McGraw-Hill), September 2004, p. 1; Amir Erez and Alice M. Isen, "The Influence of Positive Affect on the Components of Expectancy Motivation," *Journal of Applied Psychology,* December 2002, pp. 1055–1067.

21. Mark Henricks, "Start their Engines," *Entrepreneur,* January 2008, p. 85.

22. Richard M. Ryan and Edward L. Deci, "Self-Determination Theory and the Facilitation of Intrinsic Motivation, Social Development, and Well-Being," *American Psychologist,* January 2000, p. 70; Mark Henricks, "Thrill and Fulfilled," *Entrepreneur,* June 2008, pp. 78–80.

23. Remus Ilies and Timothy A. Judge, "Goal Regulation across Time: The Effects of Feedback and Affect," *Journal of Applied Psychology,* May 2005, pp. 453–467.

24. P. Christopher Earley and Terri R. Lituchy, "Delineating Goals and Efficacy: A Test of Three Models," *Journal of Applied Psychology,* February 1992, p. 96.

25. Jeffrey B. Vancouver, Kristen M. More, and Ryan J. Yoder, "Self-Efficacy and Resource Allocation: Support for a Nonmonotonic, Discontinuous Model," *Journal of Applied Psychology,* January 2008, pp. 35–47.

CHAPTER 12

1. Excerpted with permission from Jim Stinson, "Firm Markets Lasers to Veterinarians, Therapists," *Democrat and Chronicle* (Rochester, New York). November 16, 2009, pp. 5B, 6B.

2. Kathryn Tyler, "15 Ways to Train on the Job," *HR Magazine,* p. 105.

3. Alina Tugend, "Why Is Asking for Help So Difficult?" *The New York Times* (nytimes.com), July 7, 2007, p. 1.

4. Elwood F. Holton III, "New Employee Development Tactics: Perceived Availability, Helpfulness, and Relationship with Job Attitudes," *Journal of Business and Psychology,* Fall 2001, pp. 73–85.

5. Jeffrey Keller, "Associate with Positive People," a supplement to the *Pryor Report,* 1994.

6. Tammy Ellen and Lillian Eby, eds., *The Blackwell Handbook of Mentoring: A Multiple Perspectives Approach* (Malden, MA: Blackwell Publishing, 2007).

7. Monica C. Higgins and Kathy E. Kram, "Reconceptualizing Mentoring at Work: A Developmental Network Perspective," *Academy of Management Review*, April 2001, pp. 264–288.

8. Donna M. Owens, "Virtual Mentoring," *HR Magazine*, March 2006, pp. 105–107.

9. Anne Field, "No Time to Mentor? Do It Online," *BusinessWeek*, March 3, 2003, p. 126; Stephenie Overman, "Mentors without Borders," *HR Magazine*, March 2004, pp. 83–85.

10. Tammy D. Allen, Lillian T. Eby, and Elizabeth Lentz, "Mentoring Behaviors and Mentorship Quality Associated with Formal Mentoring Programs: Closing the Gap between Research and Practice," *Journal of Applied Psychology*, May 2006, pp. 567–578.

11. Based mostly on Kathy E. Kram, *Mentoring at Work: Developmental Relationships in Organizational Life* (Glenview, IL: Scott Foresman, 1985), pp. 22–39; Erik J. Van Slyke and Bud Van Slyke, "Mentoring: A Results-Oriented Approach," *HRfocus*, February 1998, p. 14.

12. Steve Trautman, *Teach What You Know: A Practical Leader's Guide to Knowledge Transfer Using Peer Mentoring* (Upper Saddle River, NJ: Prentice Hall, 2007).

13. Stephanie C. Payne and Ann H. Huffman, "A Longitudinal Examination of the Influence of Mentoring on Organizational Commitment and Turnover," *Academy of Management Journal*, February 2005, pp. 158–168.

14. Diane Coutu and Carol Kauffman, "What Can Coaches Do for You?" *Harvard Business School*, January 2009, pp. 91–97.

15. Polly Parker, Douglas T. Hall, and Kathy E. Kram, "Peer Coaching: A Relational Process for Accelerating Career Learning," *Academy of Management Learning & Education*, December 2008, p. 490.

16. "Coaching—One Solution to a Tight Training Budget," *HRfocus*, August 2002, p. 7; Sharon Ting and Peter Scisco, eds., *The CCL Handbook of Coaching: A Guide for the Leader Coach* (San Francisco: Jossey-Bass, 2006).

17. Editors of *Managers Edge, The Successful Manager's Guide to Giving and Receiving Feedback* (Alexander, VA: Briefings Publishing Group, 2004), p. 14.

18. Anne Fisher, "Turn Star Employees into Superstars," *Fortune*, December 13, 2004, p. 70.

19. "Coach Your Employees to Success with This Plan," *Manager's Edge*, May 2000, p. 1.

20. "Coach with 'Could,' Not 'Should,'" *Executive Strategies*, April 1998, p. 1.

21. Andrew J. DuBrin, *Leadership: Research Findings, Practice, and Skills*, sixth edition (Boston: Houghton Mifflin, 2010), p. 305.

22. Bruce Tulgan, "The Under-Management Epidemic," *HR Magazine*, October 2004, p. 119.

23. This one item is from John M. Ivancevich and Thomas N. Duening, *Management: Skills, Application, Practice, and Development* (Cincinnati, OH: Atomic Dog Publishing, 2006), p. 282.

24. Pamela Babcock, "Always More to Learn," *HR Magazine*, September 2009, pp. 51–54.

25. Survey cited in Mark Schoeff, Jr., "A U.S. Training Upgrade," *Workforce Management*, September 14, 2009, p. 32.

26. Bill Roberts, "Hard Facts about Soft-Skills E-Learning," *HR Magazine*, January 2008, pp. 76–78.

27. Kent W. Seibert, "Reflection in Action: Tools for Cultivating On-the-Job Learning Conditions," *Organizational Dynamics*, Winter 1999, p. 55.

28. Jathan Janover, "Jerks at Work," *HR Magazine*, May 2007, p. 111.

29. Laurence Miller, *From Difficult to Disturbed: Understanding and Managing Dysfunctional Employees* (New York: AMACOM, 2008).

30. Career Track seminar, *How to Deal with Difficult People*, 1995; Fred Pryor Seminar, *How to Deal with Unacceptable* Behavior,

2007; Kenneth Kaye, *Workplace Wars and How to End Them: Turning Personal Conflicts into Productive Teamwork* (New York: AMACOM, 1994); Jared Sandberg, "Staff 'Handfuls' and the Bosses Who Coddle Them," *The Wall Street Journal*, October 8, 2003, p. B1; Darnell Morris-Compton, "How to Unmask Workers who Cheat," *Indianapolis Star* syndicated story, March 13, 2005.

31. Leigh Buchanam, "The Bully Rulebook," *Inc. Magazine (Inc.com)*, February 2007; Patrick White, "Sometimes Office Jerks Finish First," *Detroit News (detnews.com)*, July 23, 2007.

32. Quoted in Jessica Guynn, "Bullying Behavior Affects Morale as Well as the Bottom Line," Knight Ridder syndicated story, November 2, 1998.

33. Nando Pelusi, "Dealing with Difficult People," *Psychology Today, (psychologytoday.com)*, 2006.

34. "How to Deal with 'Problem' Workers," *Positive Leadership*, sample issue, distributed 2001; Martien Eerhart, "Top 7 Ideas for Dealing with Difficult Employees," *http://top7business.com/archives/personnel/050499.html*.

35. John C. Maxwell, *Winning with People: Discover the People Principles That Work for You Every Time* (Nashville, TN: Nelson Books, 2004), pp. 1428–1429.

36. Janover, "Jerks at Work," p. 117.

CHAPTER 13

1. Todd Averett, Executive Commentary in response to Mark C. Bolino and William H. Turnley, "Going the Extra Mile: Cultivating and Managing Employee Citizenship Behavior," *Academy of Management Executive*, August 2003, pp. 72–73. Updated January 2010 through personal communication with Everett.

2. Cited in Linda Noeth, "All those Unwritten Rules of the Office Also Guide Policy," *Democrat and Chronicle*, February 8, 2009, p. 2F.

3. Daniel Goleman, *Social Intelligence: The New Science of Human Relationships* (New York: Bantam, 2006); Carol Hymowitz, "Business is Personal, So Managers Need to Harness Emotions," *The Wall Street Journal*, November 13, 2006, p. B1.

4. Hymowitz, "Business is Personal," p. B1.

5. Robyn L. Brouer, Allison Duke, Darren C. Treadway, and Gerald R. Ferris, "The Moderating Effect of Political Skill on the Demographic Dissimilarity–Leader-Member Exchange Quality Relationship," *Leadership Quarterly*, April 2009, pp. 61–69.

6. Martha C. Andrews, K. Michele Kacmar, and Kenneth J. Harris, "Got Political Skill? The Impact of Justice on the Importance of Political Skill for Job Performance," *Journal of Applied Psychology*, November 2009, pp. 1427–1437.

7. Amos Drory and Nurit Zaidman, "The Politics of Impression Management in Organizations: Contextual Effects," in Eran Vigoda-Gadot and Amos Drory eds., *Handbook of Organizational Politics* (Northampton, MA: Edward Elgar, 2006), p. 75.

8. Andrew J. DuBrin, *Impression Management in the Workplace: Research, Theory, and Practice* (New York: Routledge, 2011), p. 73.

9. Nathan P. Podsakoff, Steven W. Whiting, Philip M. Podaskoff, and Brian D. Blume, "Individual- and Organizational-Level Consequences of Organizational Citizenship Behaviors: A Meta-Analysis," *Journal of Applied Psychology*, January 2009, pp. 122–141.

10. "Career Article 103: Getting Along with Your Boss," *www.seekingsuccess.com*, 2002–2006, p. 2.

11. Terry Bragg, "Nine Strategies for Successfully Playing Office Politics," *www.tbragg.addr.com*, July 15, 2005, p. 1.

12. Tamara E. Holmes, "Admitting When You're Wrong," *Black Enterprise*, May 2007, p. 124.

13. "Get Rid of 'Yes Men,'" *Manager's Edge*, Special Bulletin, Spring 2006, p. 2.

14. Daniel Yi, "For Many Employees, Fitness Has Its Prize," *The Los Angeles Times (latimes)*, March 12, 2007.

15. "Nu-Living Weight Management-Microsoft Program," *www.nu-living.com/microsoft*, May 24, 2007.

16. William L. Gardner III, "Lessons in Organizational Dramaturgy: The Art of Impression Management," *Organizational Dynamics*, Summer 1992, p. 45.

17. Kenneth J. Harris, K. Michele Kacmar, Suzanne Zivnuska, and Jason D. Shaw, "The Impact of Political Skill on Impression Management Effectiveness," *Journal of Applied Psychology*, January 2007, pp. 278–285.

18. Jim Rucker and Jean Anna Sellers, "Changes in Business Etiquette," *Business Education Forum*, February 1998, p. 43.

19. Paula Gamonal, "Business Etiquette: More that Just Eating with the Right Fork," *Ravenwerks Business Etiquette Blog, www.ravenwerks.com*, accessed October 24, 2007.

20. This section of the chapter is based on "Business Etiquette: Teaching Students the Unwritten Rules," *Keying In*, January 1996, pp. 1–8; Rucker and Sellers, "Changes in Business Etiquette," pp. 43–45; Letitia Baldrige, *The Executive Advantage* (Washington, DC: Georgetown Publishing House, 1999); "Culture Shock?" *Entrepreneur*, May 1998, p. 46; Ann Perry, "Finer Points of the Meet and Eat," *Toronto Star (http://www.thestar.com)*, January 2, 2004; Blanca Torres, "Good Dining Manners Can Help Bet a Bigger Slice of the Job Pie," *Baltimore Sun* story, April 5, 2005; Erin White, "The Jungle: Focus on Recruitment, Pay and Getting Ahead," *The Wall Street Journal*, November 2, 2004, p. B8. The quotes are from the same sources.

21. James F. Thompson, *The Cubicle Survival Guide* (New York: Villard, 2007).

22. Sarah E. Needleman, "Office Space Is Crowded Out," *The Wall Street Journal*, December 7, 2009, p. B7.

23. "Disability Etiquette," *Human Resources Forum* (a supplement to *Management Review*), June 1997, p. 3; "Helping Today's Blind Children Become the Winners of Tomorrow," American Blind Children's Council (flyer), 2002.

24. Jared Sandberg, "How Office Tyrants in Critical Positions Get Others to Grovel," *The Wall Street Journal*, August 21, 2007, p. B1.

25. Brian Hilliard and James Palmer, *Networking Like a Pro* (Atlanta, GA: Agito Consulting, 2003,), p. 52.

26. Judith Sills, "How to Be a Rising Star," *Psychology Today*, March/April 2006, pp. 38–39.

27. Ibid, p. 39.

28. *Monster Career Centre, Monster.com.* "Managing Your Boss— How to Play Your Cards Right, vol. 4, 2002, p. 2.

29. James D. Westphal and Ithai Stern, "Flattery Will Get You Everywhere (Especially If You Are a Male Caucasian): How Ingratiation, Boardroom Behavior, and Demographic Minority Status Affect Additional Board Appointments at U.S. Companies," *Academy of Management Journal*, April 2007, pp. 267–288.

30. Marshall Goldsmith, "All of Us Are Stuck on Suck-Ups," *Fast Company*, December 2003, p. 117.

31. Research reported in Jeffrey Zaslow, "The Most-Praised Generation Goes to Work," *The Wall Street Journal*, April 20, 2007, p. W7.

32. Judith Sills, "How to Improve Your Credit Rating," *Psychology Today*, March/April 2008, p. 67.

33. Tom Rather, *Vital Friends: The People You Can't Afford to Live Without* (New York: Gallup Press, 2006).

34. Cited in Lea Winerman, "You Rub My Fin, I'll Rub Yours," *Psychology Today*, January 2009, pp. 56–59.

35. Quoted in Anita Bruzzese, "On-the-Job Friends Improve Workplace," *Gannett News Service*, August 21, 2006.

36. Susanne Craig, "Merrill CEO Presents New Leadership Team," *The Wall Street Journal*, April 30, 2008, p. C3.

37. Andrew J. DuBrin, *Political Behavior in Organizations* (Thousands Oak, CA: Sage, 2009), p. 234.

38. Shelia Murray Bethel, *Making a Difference* (New York: Putnam's Sons, 1989).

39. Lea Winerman, "Have Your Heard the Latest?" *Monitor on Psychology*, April 2006, p. 57.

40. Gary M. Stern, "Small Slights Bring Big Problems," *Workforce*, August 2002, p. 17; Joann S. Lublin, "How to Stop the Snubs That Demoralize You and Your Colleagues," *The Wall Street Journal*, December 7, 2004, p. B1.

CHAPTER 14

1. Sean Dobbin, "Perinton Debt Collecting Company Adding 150 Jobs," *Democrat and Chronicle*, Rochester, New York, May 7, 2009, p. 5B.

2. Quoted in Mark Hendricks, "Paying in Kind: How Can You Ensure Employees Give Service with a Smile?" *Entrepreneur*, February 2006, p. 82.

3. Quoted in Ryan Chittum, "Price Points: Good Customer Service Costs Money. Some Expenses are Worth It—and Some Aren't," *The Wall Street Journal*, October 30, 2006, p. R7.

4. Leonard L. Berry, Eileen A. Wall, and Lewis P. Carbone, "Service Clues and Customer Assessment of the Service Experience: Lessons from Marketing," *Academy of Management Perspectives*, May 2006, pp. 43–57.

5. Paul R. Timm, *Customer Service: Career Success Through Customer Satisfaction*, 2nd ed. (Prentice Hall, 2001), p. 8.

6. Quoted in Deborah Alexander, "Keep Tops Intact, Workers Urge," Rochester, New York, *Democrat and Chronicle*, December 1, 2006, p. 9D.

7. Quoted in Lin Grensing-Pophal, "Building Service with a Smile," *HR Magazine*, November 2006, p. 86.

8. Barry M. Stow and Jerry Ross, "Stability in the Midst of Change: A Dispositional Approach to Job Attitudes," *Journal of Applied Psychology*, August 1985, p. 471.

9. Sue Shellenbarger, "Domino Effect: The Unintended Results of Telling Off Customer-Service Staff," *The Wall Street Journal*, February 5, 2004, p. D1.

10. Lance A. Bettencourt, Kevin P. Gwinner, and Matthew L. Meuter, "A Comparison of Attitude, Personality, and Knowledge Predictors of Service-Oriented Organizational Citizenship Behavior," *Journal of Applied Psychology*, February 2001, pp. 29–41.

11. Alex M. Susskind, K. Michele Kacmar, and Carl P. Borchgrevink, "Customer Service Providers' Attitudes Relating to Customer Service and Customer Satisfaction in the Customer-Server Exchange," *Journal of Applied Psychology*, February 2003, pp. 179–187.

12. Craig A. Martin and Alan J. Bush, "Psychological Climate, Empowerment, and Customer-Oriented Selling: An Analysis of the Sales Manager-Salesperson Dyad," *Journal of the Academy of Marketing Science*, No. 3, 2006, pp. 419–438.

13. Hui Lao and Aichia Chuang, "Transforming Service Employees and Climate: A Multilevel, Multisource Examination of Transformational Leadership in Building Long-Term Service Relationships," *Journal of Applied Psychology*, July 2007, pp. 1006–1019.

14. Jeremy Quittner, "The Art of the Soft Sell," *Business Week Small Biz*, October/November 2009, p. 50.

15. Richard B. Chase and Sriram Dasu, "Want to Perfect Your Company's Service? Use Behavioral Science," *Harvard Business Review*, June 2001, pp. 78–84.

16. Timothy W. Martin, "May I Help You?" *The Wall Street Journal*, April 23, 2009, p. R4.

17. Karl Abrecht, *The Only Thing That Matters* (New York: HarperCollins, 1992).

18. Stefan Michel, David Bowen, and Robert Johnson, "Making the Most of Customer Complaints," *The Wall Street Journal*, September 22, 2008, p. R11.

19. Amanda C. Kooser, "Crowd Control," *Entrepreneur,* August 2003, pp. 33–34.

20. Ken Belson, "For Half a Cent, a Call That Informs, and Annoys," *The New York Times* (nytimes.com), July 16, 2008, pp. 1–3.

21. Adapted from "For Extraordinary Service," *The Customer Service Professional,* October 1997, p. 3.

22. Lorna Ducet, "Service Provider Hostility and Service Quality," *Academy of Management Journal,* October 2004, pp. 761–771.

23. D. J. Cran, "Towards the Validation of the Service Orientation Construct," *The Service Industries Journal,* vol. 14, 1994, p. 36.

24. Dot Yandle, "Helping Your Employees Give Customers What They Want," *Success Workshop* (a supplement to *Manager's Edge*), November 1998, p. 1.

25. Patricia B. Barger and Alicia A. Grandey, "Service with a Smile and Encounter Satisfaction: Emotional Contagion and Appraisal Mechanisms," *Academy of Management Journal,* December 2006, pp. 1229–1238.

26. Steven Gray, "Flipping Burger King," *The Wall Street Journal,* April 26, 2005, B1.

27. Miguel Bustillo and Ann Zimmerman, "Circuit City's Chief Executive Is Ousted," *The Wall Street Journal,* September 23, 2008, p. B1.

28. Quoted in Jia Lunn Yang, "How to Sell in a Lousy Economy," *Fortune,* September 29, 2008, p. 102.

29. Christina Binkley, "How to Sell a $35,000 Watch in a Recession," *The Wall Street Journal,* July 23, 2009. p. D6.

30. Ryan Chittum, "Price Points: Good Customer Service Costs Money," p. R7.

31. Daniel Akst, book review of *Hug Your Customers* by Jack Mitchell (Hyperion, 2003), appearing in *The Wall Street Journal,* November 14, 2003, p. W9.

32. Hwee Hoon Tan, Maw Der Foo, and Min Hui Kwek, "The Effects of Customer Personality Traits on the Display of Positive Emotions," *Academy of Management Journal,* April 2004, pp. 287–296.

33. Chip R. Bell and Ron Zemke, "Service Breakdown—The Road to Recovery," in *Service Wisdom: Creating and Maintaining the Customer Service Edge* (Minneapolis, MN: Lakewood Books, 1992), Michel, Bowen, and Johnson, "Making the Most of Customer Complaints," pp. R4, R11; Louise Lee, "Oops," *Business Week Small Biz,* August/September 2009, p. 22.

34. Kelly Yamanouchi, "AirTran Exec: 'We Want to Make Sure that Good Judgment Prevails,'" *The Atlanta-Journal Constitution* (www.ajc.com/business), December 12, 2009, p. 2.

35. Jon Yates, "Tuning In to Comcast's Customer Service." *Chicago Tribune,* November 15, 2009, Section 2, p. 1.

36. Patrick J. Kiger, "The Art of the Apology," *Workforce Management,* October 2004, p. 62.

37. Jan Norman, "Caring about Clients Helps Companies Handle Crises," *Knight Ridder* story, December 3, 2000.

38. Hal Hardy, "Five Steps to Pleasing difficult, Demanding Customers," *First-Rate Customer Service,* No. 1, 2005, p. 1.

39. "Customer Problem Clinics," in Making . . . Serving . . . Keeping Customers, published by Dartnell, 4660 Ravenswood Avenue, Chicago, IL 60640.

40. Matthew Dixon, Karen Freeman, and Nicholas Toman, "Stop Trying to Delight Your Customers," *Harvard Business Review,* July–August 2010, pp. 116–122.

41. Vikas Mittal, Matthew Sarkees, and Feisal Murshed, "The Right Way to Manage Unprofitable Customers," *Harvard Business Review,* April 2008, p. 102.

42. Raymond Flandez, "It Just Isn't Working? Some File for Customer Divorce," *The Wall Street Journal,* November 10, 2009, p. B7.

CHAPTER 15

1. Erika Brown, "Rehab, Reuse, Recycle," *Forbes,* April 21, 2008, pp. 70, 72; "Electronic Recyclers International CEO John S. Shegarian Named Ernst & Young Entrepreneur of the Year 2008 Award Recipient in Northern California," www.businesswire.com, June 25, 2008.

2. Linda K. Treviño and Katherine A. Nelson, *Managing Business Ethics: Straight Talk about How to Do It Right* (New York: Wiley, 1995), pp. 24–35; O. C. Ferrell, John Fraedrich, and Linda Ferrell, *Business Ethics: Ethical Decision Making and Cases,* 4th ed. (Boston: Houghton Mifflin, 2000), pp. 13–16; Anita Bruzzese, "Tools Take Ethics to the Real World," Gannett News Service, May 16, 2005; Roger Parloff, "Wall Street: It's Payback Time," *Fortune,* January 19, 2009, pp. 56–69.

3. Thomas M. Jones, "Ethical Decision Making by Individuals in Organizations: An Issue Contingent Model," *Academy of Management Review,* April 1991, p. 391.

4. Linda Kelbe Treviño and Michael E. Brown, "Managing to Be Ethical: Debunking Five Business Ethics Myths," *Academy of Management Executive,* May 2004, pp. 69–72.

5. Scott J. Reynolds, "Moral Awareness and Ethical Predispositions: Investigating the Role of Individual Differences in the Recognition of Moral Issues," *Journal of Applied Psychology,* January 2006, p. 234.

6. John C. Bogle, "A Crisis of Ethic Proportions," *The Wall Street Journal,* April 21, 2009, p. A19.

7. Simona Covel, "Small Businesses Face More Fraud in Downturn," *The Wall Street Journal,* February 19, 2009, p. B5.

8. The basic outline for this section is from Treviño and Nelson, *Managing Business Ethics,* pp. 47–64.

9. Data reported in "McAfee Anti Piracy Information," *http://www.networkassociates.com/us/antipircacy_policy.htm,* accessed January 6, 2010.

10. Edmund L. Andrews, "Interior Official Assails Agency for Ethics Slides," *The New York Times* (nytimes.com), September 14, 2006.

11. "FTC: Bloggers Must Disclose Payments for Reviews," Associated Press, October 5, 2009.

12. Keith J. Winstein, "Inflated Credentials Surface in Executive Suite," *The Wall Street Journal,* November 13, 2008, p. B1.

13. Joseph L. Badaracco, Jr., "The Discipline of Building Character," *Harvard Business Review,* March April 1998, pp. 114–124.

14. Edwin A. Locke, "Business Ethics: A Way Out of the Morass," *Academy of Management Learning & Education,* September 2006, pp. 328–330.

15. Treviño and Nelson, *Managing Business Ethics,* pp. 71–75.

16. Scott Sonenshein, "The Role of Construction, Intuition, and Justification in Responding to Ethical Issues at Work: The Sensemaking-Intuition Model," *Academy of Management Review,* October 2007, p. 1030.

17. Sonenshein, "The Role of Construction, Intuition," p. 1033.

18. Daniel J. Brass, Kenneth D. Butterfield, and Bruce C. Skaggs, "Relationships and Unethical Behavior: A Social Network Perspective," *Academy of Management Review,* January 1998, pp. 14–31.

19. Cited in Jean Thilmany, "Supporting Ethical Employees," *HR Magazine,* September 2007, p. 106.

20. "The Optima Awards: They've Got Game," *Workforce Management,* March 2005, p. 44.

21. Mary Uhl-Bien and Melissa K. Carsten, "Being Ethical When the Boss Is Not," *Organizational Dynamics,"* Issue 2, 2007, p. 197.

CHAPTER 16

1. Maggie Jackson, "Quelling Distraction: Help Employees Overcome 'Information Overload.'" *HR Magazine,* August 2008, p. 43.

2. Cait Murphy, "The CEO Workout," *Fortune,* July 10, 2006, pp. 43–44.

3. Research reported in Christine Gorman, "6 Lessons for Handling Stress," *Time,* January 29, 2007, p. 82.

4. *British Medical Journal* study reported in "Trop de Stress au Travail Double le Risque de Mourir d'une Crise de Coeur," *Journal de Montréal,* 18 October, 2002, p. 7. (Too much work stress doubles the risk of dying from a heart attack.)

5. Jeffery A. Lapine, Nathan P. Podsakoff, and Marcie A. Lepine, "A Meta-Analytic Test of the Challenge-Stressor-Hindrance-Stressor Framework: An Explanation for Inconsistent Relationships among Stressors and Performance," *Academy of Management Journal,* October 2005, pp. 764–775.

6. J. Craig Wallace et al., "Work Stressors, Role-Based performance, and the Moderating Influence of Organizational Support," *Journal of Applied Psychology,* January 2009, pp. 254–262.

7. Gillian E. Hardy, David Woods, and Toby D. Wall, "The Impact of Psychological Distress on Absence from Work," *Journal of Applied Psychology,* April 2003, pp. 306–314.

8. Christina Maslach and Michael Leiter, *The Truth about Burnout* (San Francisco: Jossey-Bass, 1997). Research updated in interview, Emily Waters, "Burnout on the Rise: Recognizing the Unconventional Telltale Signs," *NY Workplace Examiner* (www.examiner.com), June 18, 2009.

9. Annebel H. B. De Hoog and Deanne N. Den Hartog, "Neuroticism and Locus of Control as Moderators of the Relationships of Charismatic and Autocratic Leadership with Burnout," *Journal of Applied Psychology,* July 2009, pp. 1058–1067.

10. Maslach and Leiter, *The Truth About Burnout.*

11. Research reported in Deborah. Smith Bailey, "Burnout Harms Workers' Physical Health through Many Pathways," *Monitor on Psychology,* June 2006, p. 11.

12. M. Afalur Rahim, "Relationships of Stress, Locus of Control, and Social Support to Psychiatric Symptoms and Propensity to Leave a Job: A Field Study with Managers," *Journal of Business and Psychology,* Winter 1997, p. 159.

13. Steve M. Jex, Paul O. Bliese, Sheri Buzell, and Jessica Primeau, "The Impact of Self-Efficacy on Stressor-Strain Relations: Coping Style as an Explanatory Mechanism," *Journal of Applied Psychology,* June 2001, pp. 401–409.

14. Jeffrey R. Edwards and A. J. Baglioni, Jr., "Relationships between Type A Behavior Pattern and Mental and Physical Symptoms: A Comparison of Global and Component Measures," *Journal of Applied Psychology,* April 1991, p. 276; related research reported in Etienne Benson, "Hostility Is among Best Predictors of Heart Disease in Men," *Monitor on Psychology,* January 2003, p. 15.

15. Research reviewed in Nadja Geipert, "Don't Be Mad: More Research Links Hostility to Coronary Risk," *Monitor on Psychology,* January 2007, pp. 50–51.

16. Peter Y. Chen and Paul E. Spector, "Negative Affectivity as the Underlying Cause of Correlations between Stressors and Strains," *Journal of Applied Psychology,* June 1991, p. 398.

17. Pamela Babcock, "Workplace Stress? Deal with It!" *HR Magazine,* May 2009, p. 68.

18. Sylvia Ann Hewlett and Carolyn Buck Luce, "Extreme Jobs: The Dangerous Allure of the 70-Hour Work Week," *Harvard Business Review,* December 2006, pp. 49–59.

19. Blaine Harden, "Japan's Overtime Proves to Be Killer," *Washington Post* syndicated story, July 16, 2008.

20. William Atkinson, "Causes of Workplace Stress," *HR Magazine,* December 2000, p. 107; Michele Conlin, "Is Your Office Killing You?" Business Week, June 5, 2000, pp. 114–128; "Sick Building Syndrome," *www.doctorfungus.org,* accessed January 22, 2007, p. 1.

21. The data on vision and carpal tunnel syndrome are from the Computer Vision Syndrome Center reported in Anita Bruzzese, "Computer Users often Strain Eyes," Gannett News Service, September 13, 2004; Christine A. Sprigg et al., "Work Characteristics, Musculoskeletal Disorders, and the Mediating Role of Psychological Strain: A Study of Call Center Employees," *Journal of Applied Psychology,* September 2007, pp. 1456–1466.

22. Christina Binkley, "Sitting Pretty When You're Hard at Work," *The Wall Street Journal,* June 11, 2009. pp. D1, D7.

23. Study reported in Deborah Smith Bailey, "Longer Train Commutes Are More Stressful, Study Finds," *Monitor on Psychology,* September 2006, p. 12.

24. Larry Copeland, "Drivers Rising Earlier to Beat the Traffic," *USA Today* syndicated story, September 16, 2007.

25. Alicia A. Grandey, "Emotion Regulation in the Workplace: A New Way to Conceptualize Emotional Labor," *Journal of Occupational Health Psychology,* 5; 1, 2000, pp. 95–110; Grandey, "When the 'Show Must Go On:' Surface Acting and Deep Acting as Determinants of Emotional Exhaustion and Peer-Related Service Delivery," *Academy of Management Journal,* February 2003, pp. 86–96.

26. Markus Groth, Thornsen Henning-Thurau, and Gianfranco Walsh, "Customer Reactions to Emotional labor: The Roles of Employee Acting Strategies and Customer Detection Accuracy," *Academy of Management Journal,* October 2009, pp. 958–974.

27. Theresa M. Glomb, John D. Kammeyer-Mueller, and Maria Rotundo, "Emotional Labor Demands and Compensating Wage Differentials," *Journal of Applied Psychology,* August 2004, p. 707.

28. Timothy A. Judge, Erin Fluegge Woolf, and Charlice Hurst, "Is Emotional Labor More Difficult for Some than Others? A Multilevel, Experience-Sampling Study," *Personnel Psychology,* Spring 2009, pp. 57–88.

29. Edward Hallowell, *CrazyBusy: Overstretched, Overbooked, and about to Snap—Strategies for Coping in a World Gone ADD* (New York: Ballantine Books, 2006); "Zen and the Art of Thinking Straight," *Business Week,* April 3, 2006, p. 116; Maggie Jackson, "Quelling Distraction: Help Employees Overcome 'Information Overload,'" *HR Magazine,* August 8, 2008, pp. 42–46.

30. "Executive Quits after Suicides at France Télécom," The Associated Press, October 6, 2009.

31. Simona Gilboa, Arie Shirom, Yitzhak Fried, and Cary Cooper, "A Meta-Analysis of Work Demand Stressors and Job Performance: Examining Main and Moderating Effects," *Personnel Psychology,* Summer 2008, pp. 227–271.

32. Jan de Jonge and Christian Dormann, "Stressors, Resources, and Strain at Work: A Longitudinal Test of the Triple-Match Principle," *Journal of Applied Psychology,* November 2006, pp. 1359–1374.

33. Katherine M. Richardson and Hannah R. Rothstein, "Effects of Occupational Stress Management Intervention Programs: A Meta-Analysis," *Journal of Occupational Health Psychology,* January 2008, pp. 69–93.

34. Data reported in Laura Landro, "The Hidden Benefits of Exercise," *The Wall Street Journal,* January 5, 2010, p. D1.

35. Lisa Belkin, "Some Respect, Please, for the Afternoon Nap," *The New York Times (nytimes.com),* February 25, 2007. p. 1.

36. Lea Winerman, "Sleep Deprivation Threatens Public Health, Says Research Award Winner," July/August 2004, p. 61.

37. Research reported in Sara Martin, "The Power of the Relaxation Response," *Monitor on Psychology,* October 2008, p. 33.

38. Katherine Ellison, "Mastering Your Own Mind," *Psychology Today,* October 2006, p. 75.

39. Stephen Kotler, "Escape Artists," *Psychology Today,* September/October 2009, pp. 73–75.

40. Data reported in Kotler, "Escape Artists," p. 75.

41. Maia Szalavitz, "Stand & Deliver," *Psychology Today,* July/August 2003, p. 50.

42. Cited in Kotler, "Escape Artists," p. 76.

43. Shale Paul, as cited in "Tips to Keep Procrastination Under Control," Gannet News Service, November 9, 1998.

44. Dru Scott, *How to Put More Time in Your Life* (New York: New American Library, 1980), p 1.

45. Quoted in Jana McGregor (Editor), "Making Every Hour Count," *Business Week,* September 1, 2008, p. 68.

46. Christopher Percy Collier, "The Expert on Experts," *Fast Company,* November 2006, p. 116.

47. David Allen, *Getting Things Done* (New York: Penguin, 2001, 2007).

48. Quoted in Adrian Wooldridge, "Why Clean Up Your Desk? Delight in Disorder Instead," *The Wall Street Journal,* January 2, 2007, p. D7. Book review of Eric Abrahamson and David Freedman, *A Perfect Mess* (New York: Little, Brown & Co., 2007).

49. João-Pierre Ruth, "Report: Employees Not Taking All Vacation Time," *NJBIZ* (www.njbiz.com), January 4, 2010.

50. Anne Fisher, "The Rebalancing Act," *Fortune,* October 6, 2003, p. 110; Andrea Kay, "Avoid 'Traps' to Gain the Free Time You Need," Gannet News Service, January 10, 2005.

51. Brenda Goodman, "A Field Guide To the Workaholic," *Psychology Today,* May/June 2006, p. 41.

52. Tony Schwartz, "Manage Your Energy, Not Your Time," *Harvard Business Review,* October 2007, pp. 63–74.

53. Jana McGregor, "Getting Serious about Getting Things Done," *Business Week,* September 1, 2008, p. 069.

54. "Secrets of Greatness: Marissa Mayer," *Fortune,* March 20, 2006, p. 68.

55. Quoted paraphrased from information in "You Can't Make More Time: Randy Pausch's Heart-Felt Views on Using Time to the Fullest," *Business Week,* August 25/September 1, 2008, p. 071.

56. The scientific information about multitasking is reviewed in Claudia Wallis, "The Multitasking Generation," *Time,* March 27, 2006, pp. 48–55. See also Joshua S. Rubinstein, David E. Meyer, and Jeffrey E. Evans, "Executive Control of Cognitive Processes in Task Switching," *Journal of Experimental Psychology—Human Perception and Performance,* vol. 26, January 2000, No. 4, pp. 763–769.

57. Research from the University of Oregon reported in "The Problem with Extreme Multitasking," *The Wall Street Journal,* February 12, 2008, p. B4.

58. Andy Pasztor, "Laptops Drive Pilots to Distraction," *The Wall Street Journal,* October 27, 2009, p. A3.

59. Ellen Joan Pollock, "How I Got a Grip on My Workweek," *Business Week,* April 6, 2009, p. 086.

60. Michelle Conlin, "Out of Sight, Yes. Out of Mind, No," *Business Week,* February 18, 2008, p. 060; Sue Shellenbarger, "When Working at Home Doesn't Work: How Companies Comfort Telecommuters," *The Wall Street Journal,* August 24, 2006, p. D1; E. Jeffrey Hill, Brent C. Miller, Sara P. Weiner, and Joe Colihan, "Influences of the Virtual Office on Aspects of Work/Life Balance," *Personnel Psychology,* Autumn 1998, pp. 667–683.

61. Cali Ressler and Jody Thomson, "Make Results Matter," *HR Magazine,* April 2009, pp. 77–79.

62. Survey cited in Maggie Jackson, "May We Have Your Attention Please?" *Business Week,* June 23, 2008, p. 055.

CHAPTER 17

1. David Whelan, "Work Reinvented," *Forbes,* June 8, 2009, pp. 93–94.

2. Donna Rawady, "Market Yourself Across Multiple Tracks," *Democrat and Chronicle* (Rochester, New York), October 18, 2009, p. 2E.

3. Joann S. Lublin, "Lessons of Extreme Job Hunting," *The Wall Street Journal,* September 1, 2009, pp. D1, D4.

4. "Kat & Dale Talk Jobs," King Features Syndicate, April 14, 2002.

5. "Checking Credit of Job Candidates Drives Concerns about Civil Rights," *Christian Science Monitor,* January 19, 2007.

6. Chris Pentila, "Risky Business," *Entrepreneur,* September 2003, pp. 78–79.

7. Joann S. Lublin, "Silence Is Golden Rule for Résumés of People Who Have Broken It," *The Wall Street Journal,* October 2, 2007, p. B1.

8. Geoffrey A. Fowler, "In Search for a Hot Job Title, Enter the Ninja," *The Wall Street Journal,* April 7, 2010, pp. A1, A12.

9. "A Word on Résumés," *Philly.com,* July 13, 2009.

10. Sarah E. Needleman, "Creating a Résumé that Sells," *The Wall Street Journal,* November 24, 2009, p. D2.

11. Sarah E. Needleman, "Special Résumé Looks Can Do Quite a Job at Getting You Noticed," *The Wall Street Journal,* August 21, 2007, p. B6.

12. Data presented in "Fake It and You're Busted," *TimesJobs.com,* January 23, 2009, p. 1.

13. Greg Faherty, "Cover Letter Secrets," *NY Resume Writing Examiner* (www.sanfranciscoexaminer.com), December 10, 2009.

14. Sarah E. Needleman, "Speed Interviewing Grows as Skills Shortage Looms," *The Wall Street Journal,* November 6, 2007, p. B15.

15. The suggestion about desperation is from Deb Koen, "Be Calm, Centered, in Your Interview," *Democrat and Chronicle* (Rochester, New York), September 6, 2009.

16. Quoted in Eileen Alt Powell, "Research, Practice Can Lead to a Stronger Job Interview," The Associated Press, April 6, 2007.

17. Anne Field, "Coach, Help Me Out with This Interview," *Business Week,* October 22, 2001, p. 134.

18. Joann S. Lublin, "The New Job Is in the Details," *The Wall Street Journal,* January 5, 2010, p. D5.

19. Cited in Dawn Klingensmith, "Power Accessories for Your Interview Wardrobe," *Philly.com,* December 21, 2009.

20. Dawn Klingensmith, "5 Most Annoying Interview Phrases," *www.philly.com,* January 22, 2010.

21. Laura Fitzpatrick, "We're Getting off the Ladder," *Time,* May 25, 2009; Diane Brady, "Yes, Winning Is Still the Only Thing," *Business Week,* August 21/28, 2007, p. 52.

22. Jonnelle Marte, "Boom Time for Young Workers," *The Wall Street Journal,* April 20, 2010, p. D4.

23. Marcus Buckingham, *Go Put Your Strengths to Work* (New York: Free Press, 2007).

24. Judy Martin, "Aligning Your Passion with Your Personal Brand," *San Francisco Examiner* (www.examiner.com), March 7, 2009.

25. Sukhinder Singh Cassidy, "The Best Advice I Ever Got," *Fortune,* July 6, 2009, p. 47.

26. Richard Boyatzis, Annie McKee, and Daniel Goleman, "Reawakening Your Passion for Work," *Harvard Business Review,* April 2002, pp. 86–94.

27. Janet Banks and Diane Coutu, "How to Protect Your Job in a Recession," *Harvard Business Review,* September 2008, p. 114.

28. Scott E. Seibert, Maria L. Kraimer, and J. Michael Crant, "What Do Proactive People Do? A Longitudinal Model Linking Proactive Personality and Career Success," *Personnel Psychology,* Winter 2001, pp. 845–874; Scott E. Seibert, J. Michael Crant, and Maria L. Kraimer, "Proactive Personality and Career Success," *Journal of Applied Psychology,* June 1999, pp. 416–427.

29. Douglas J. Brown et al., "Proactive Personality and the Successful Job Search: A Field Investigation with College Graduates," *Journal of Applied Psychology,* May 2006, pp. 717–726.

30. Michelle Conlin, "How to Shine in Dark Times," *Business Week,* November 3, 2008, p. 053.

31. Pamela Babcock, "Always More to Learn," *HR Magazine,* September 2009, p. 51.

32. Cited in Cheryl Dahle, "Showing Your Worth Without Showing Off," *nytimes.com,* September 19, 2004; *http://www.bragbetter.com.*

33. Quoted in Michelle Conlin, "Are People in Your Office Acting Oddly?" *Business Week,* April 13, 2009, p. 054.

34. Carlin Flora, "Personal Packaging," *Psychology Today,* July/August 2009, p. 61.

35. Philip L. Hunsaker, "Projecting the Appropriate Image," *Supervisory Management,* May 1989, p. 26.

36. Matthew Daneman, "Web Title's Breadth Fuels Growth Despite Recession," *Democrat and Chronicle* (Rochester, New York), November 23, 2009, pp. 5B, 6B.

37. Quoted in Louise Dobson, "Skirting the Line: In the Office, Wardrobe Mistakes Can Be Disastrous," *Psychology Today,* July/August 2006, p. 13; Flora, "Personal Packaging," p. 61.

38. Quoted in "Taking Charge in a Temp World," *Fortune,* October 21, 1998, pp. 247–248.

39. Donna M. Owens, "Success Factors: The Right Experiences Can Increase Your Leadership Potential," *HR Magazine,* p. 88.

40. Harriet Barovick, "The Return of the Calling Card," *Time,* August 11, 2008, p. 57.

41. Hans-Georg Wolff and Klaus Moser, "Effects of Networking on Career Success: A Longitudinal Study," *Journal of Applied Psychology,* January 2009, pp. 196–206.

42. Dawn E. Chandler, Douglas T. Hall, and Kathy E. Kram, "How to Be a Smart Protégé," *The Wall Street Journal,* August 17, 2009, p. R5.

43. Erin White, "The First Job Blues: How to Adjust, When to Move On," *The Wall Street Journal,* July 25, 2006, p. B7.

44. Amy L. Kristof-Brown, Ryan D. Zimmerman, and Erin C. Johnson, "Consequences of Individuals' Fit at Work: A Meta-Analysis of Person-Job, Person-Organization, Person-Group, and Person-Supervisor Fit," *Personnel Psychology,* Summer 2005, pp. 281–342.

45. Quoted in Robyn D. Clarke, "Rewards of Risk Taking: How to Move Out of Your Comfort Zone," *Black Enterprise,* March 2006, p. 105.

46. Victoria Barret, "Pockets of Prosperity," *Forbes,* October 27, 2008, pp. 36–37.

47. Quoted in Heather Huhman, "CEOs Under 25: Collin Wheeler," *www.sanfranciscoexaminer.com,* April 30, 2009. See also www. 123JUNK.com.

48. David Wessel, "The Future of Jobs: New Ones Arise, Wage Gap Widens, "*The Wall Street Journal,*" April 2, 2004; Peter Svensson, "Hands-On Jobs May Be the Safest," Associated Press, July 9, 2004.

49. Jack and Suzy Welch, "The Importance of Being There," *Business Week,* April 16, 2007, p. 92.

INDEX